ICSA

STUDY TEXT

Professional Paper 14

Administration of Corporate Affairs

New in this September 2000 edition

- Developments in electronic commerce
- Updated material on computer security
- Changes in state pension provision
- Stakeholder pensions

FOR 2001 EXAMS

BPP Publishing
September 2000

First edition 1994
Sixth edition September 2000

ISBN 0 7517 5138 3 (Previous edition 0 7517 5028 X)

British Library Cataloguing-in-Publication Data
A catalogue record for this book
is available from the British Library

First published by

BPP Publishing Limited
Aldine House, Aldine Place
London W12 8AW

Reprinted in the UK under licence from BPP Publishing Limited by

ICSA Publishing Limited
16 Park Crescent
London W1B 1AH

Printed in Great Britain by The Basingstoke Press Limited

We are grateful to the Institute of Chartered Secretaries and Administrators for permission to reproduce in this text the syllabus of which the Institute holds the copyright.

We are grateful to the Institute of Chartered Secretaries and Administrators, the Association of Accounting Technicians, and the Chartered Institute of Management Accountants for permission to reproduce past examination questions. The suggested answers have been prepared by BPP Publishing Limited.

HOW TO USE THIS STUDY TEXT

Aims of this Study Text

To provide you with the knowledge and understanding, skills and application techniques that you need if you are to be successful in your exams

This Study Text has been carefully written around the official ICSA **Administration of Corporate Affairs** syllabus.

- It is **comprehensive**. We do not omit sections of the syllabus: the examiner may examine any part of the syllabus from any angle- and you do not want to be left high and dry.
- It keeps you **up-to-date** with developments in administration of corporate affairs, the way in which the examiner is designing questions and relevant legislation etc.
- It is **on-target**. We do not include any material which is not examinable. You can therefore rely on the BPP Study Text as the stand-alone source of all your information for the exam, without worrying that any of the material is irrelevant.

To allow you to study in the way that best suits your learning style and the time you have available, by following your personal Study Plan

You may be studying at home on your own until the date of the exam, or you may be attending a full-time course. You may like to read every word, or you may prefer to skim-read and devote the remainder of your time to question practice. Whatever your approach, you will find the BPP Study Text meets your needs in designing and following your personal Study Plan.

To tie in with the rest of the BPP Effective Study Package to ensure you have the best possible chance of passing the exam

The BPP Effective Study Package

Recommended period of use	Elements of the BPP Effective Study Package
3-12 months before exam	**Study Text** Use the Study Text to acquire knowledge, understanding, skills and the ability to use application techniques.

↓

1-3 months before exam	**Practice & Revision Kit** Attempt the tutorial questions and read the helpful checklists which are provided for each topic area in the Kit. Then try the numerous examination questions, for which there are realistic suggested answers.

Settling down to study

By this stage in your career you are probably very experienced at learning and taking exams. But have you ever thought about *how* you learn? Let's have a quick look at the key elements required for effective learning.

Key element of learning	Using the BPP Study Text
Motivation	You can rely on the comprehensiveness and technical quality of BPP material. You've chosen the right Study Text - so you're in pole position to pass your exam!
Clear objectives and standards	Do you want to be a prizewinner or simply achieve a pass? Only you can decide.
Feedback	Work through the examples in this text and do the Exercises and Test your knowledge quizzes. Evaluate your efforts critically - how are you doing?
Study Plan	You need to be honest with yourself about your progress - don't be over-confident, but don't be negative either. Make your Study Plan (see below) and try to stick to it. Focus on the short-term objectives - completing two chapters a week, say - but beware of losing sight of your study objectives.
Practice	Use the Test your knowledge quizzes and Chapter roundups to refresh your memory after you have completed your initial study of each chapter.

These introductory pages let you see exactly what you are up against. But however you study, there are two things you should do.

- **Read through the syllabus and syllabus commentary:** these will help you to identify areas you have already covered, perhaps at a lower level of detail, and areas that are totally new to you.
- **Study the examination paper section,** where we show you the format of the exam and analyse the recent papers **including the one set in June 2000.**

Developing your personal Study Plan

Preparing a Study Plan (and sticking closely to it) is one of the key elements in learning success. First you need to be aware of your style of learning. There are four typical learning styles. Consider yourself in the light of the following descriptions and work out which you fit most closely. You can then plan to follow the key study steps in the sequence suggested.

Learning styles	Characteristics
Theorist	Seeks to understand principles before applying them in practice
Reflector	Seeks to observe phenomena, thinks about them and then chooses to act
Activist	Prefers to deal with practical, active problems; does not have much patience with theory
Pragmatist	Prefers to study only if a direct link to practical problems can be seen; not interested in theory for its own sake

Key study steps

We have broken the learning process down into a series of key steps, which you can apply to each chapter in turn. We list them here in the order which seems to work best for **theorists** and **reflectors**. If you are an **activist** or a **pragmatist** you may prefer to use a different sequence. The various options are summarised after the table of steps. Tackle the chapters in the order you find them in the Study Text. Taking into account your individual learning style, follow these key study steps for each chapter.

Key study steps	Activity
Step 1 *Chapter topic list*	Study the list. Each numbered topic is a numbered section in the chapter.
Step 2 *Introduction*	Read through it. It is designed to show you *why* the topics in the chapter need to be studied - how they lead on from previous topics, and how they lead into subsequent ones.
Step 3 *Explanations*	Proceed methodically through the chapter, reading each section thoroughly and making sure you understand. Where a topic has been examined, we state the month and year of examination against the appropriate heading. You should pay particular attention to these topics.
Step 4 *Note taking*	Take brief notes if you wish, avoiding the temptation to copy out too much.
Step 5 *Examples*	Follow each through to its solution very carefully.
Step 6 *Case examples*	Study each one, and try to add flesh to them from your own experience - they are designed to show how the topics you are studying come alive (and often come unstuck) in the real world.
Step 7 *Exercises*	Make a very good attempt at each one in the chapter. These are designed to put your knowledge into practice.
Step 8 *Solutions*	Check yours against ours, and make sure you understand the reasons why they may differ.
Step 9 *Chapter roundup*	Work through it very carefully, to make sure you have grasped the major points it is highlighting.
Step 10 *Test your knowledge quiz*	When you are happy that you have covered the chapter, use the Test your knowledge quiz to check how much you have remembered of the topics covered. The answers are in the paragraphs in the chapter that we refer you to.
Step 11 *Illustrative questions*	Either at this point, or later when you are thinking about revising, make a full attempt at the question(s) suggested at the very end of the chapter. You can find these at the end of the Study Text, along with the answers so you can see how you did.

Learning style approaches

Learning style	Sequence of key study steps in the BPP Study Text
Theorist	1, 2, 3, 5, 6, 7, 8, 9, 10, 11, (4 continuous)
Reflector	
Activist	1, 2, 7/8 (read through), 5, 6, 9, 3, 7/8 (full attempt), 10, 11 (4 continuous)
Pragmatist	7/8 (read through), 2, 5, 6, 9, 1, 3, 7/8 (full attempt), 10, 11 (4 continuous)

Planning your studies

Next you should complete the following checklist.

Am I motivated? (a) ☐

Do I have an objective and a standard that I want to achieve? (b) ☐

Am I a theorist, a reflector, an activist or a pragmatist? (c) ☐

How much time do I have available per week, given: (d) ☐

- The standard I have set myself
- The time I need to set aside later for work on the Practice and Revision Kit
- The other exam(s) I am sitting, and (of course)
- Practical matters such as work, travel, exercise, sleep and social life?

Now:

- Take the time you have available per week for this Study Text (d), and multiply it by the number of weeks available to give (e). (e) ☐
- Divide (e) by the number of chapters to give (f) (f) ☐
- Set about studying each chapter in the time represented by (f), following the key study steps in the order suggested by your particular learning style.

This is your personal Study Plan.

Moving on...

However you study, when you are ready to embark on the practice and revision phase of the BPP Effective Study Package, you should still refer back to this Study Text, both as a source of reference (you should find the index particularly helpful for this) and as a refresher (the Chapter roundups and Test your knowledge quizzes help you here).

And remember to keep careful hold of this Study Text - you will find it invaluable in your work.

SYLLABUS

Objective

To develop an understanding of the need for effective administration of corporate affairs including physical, human and intangible corporate resources, and knowledge of the legal environment.

Decision making forums and meetings

Decision making forums

Forms of collective decision making and deliberation, authority and accountability. Delegation of authority and responsibility, executive discretion. The structure and management of committees and meetings within organisations. The impact of Corporate Governance principles on decision making. Strategic, tactical and operational decision-making and its place in the organisation.

Meetings

The conduct and management of meetings

The powers and duties of a Chairman

The role of the Secretary before, during and after a meeting

Constitutional and procedural issues relating to standing orders, rules of debate, committee composition and co-option, quorum, notice, agenda and papers, motions, amendments and voting

The preparation of agendas, minutes, reports, and the dissemination of information and decisions

Corporate information needs

Information, data and technology as corporate resources

Technological change and its impact on organisation and management information

Security and integrity of information and data, including the control of access

Legislation requirement imposed on the protection of data

The impact of legislative requirements on the protection of data as it affects organisations

Pensions, insurance and risk

Insurance and risk

General insurance issues

Classes of insurance and liability

The insurance markets (brokers and intermediaries)

The control and management of business risks

The requirement for disaster planning in organisations

Pensions

Types of schemes and their relevance

The proper control of pension schemes including scheme management alternatives and the duties of trustees in law

Best practice principles; current pensions issues including legislative requirements

The impact of legislative requirements on the management of pension schemes

Management of corporate assets

Tangible and intangible assets, and their contribution to corporate efficiency, including the need for protection

The role and functions of Facilities Management in contemporary organisation

The principles of security management and their application

The management of physical assets by the organisation

The impact of Health & Safety and environmental legislation

SYLLABUS EXPANSION

Note that the following points are made in the ICSA's syllabus booklet.

'All modules are based on English and EU derived law and practice, except where national alternatives are shown.'

'Students are expected to keep abreast of changes in the law affecting the modules which they are studying. However, a detailed knowledge of new legislation will not be examined within six months of the passing of the relevant Act.

The ICSA provides the following syllabus expansion notes in its Qualifying Pack.

Decision-making forums and meetings

Decision-making forums:	This section requires detailed knowledge of the following: how different types of organisations in the public and private sector make collective decisions, the levels of authority and responsibility within organisations, the theory of decision-making including published commentaries. Candidates also need to understand in depth how committees and meetings are structured and managed in organisations and how the principles of corporate governance have impacted on the decision-making process.
Meetings:	This section requires knowledge of: the principles of the law and practice of meetings including relevant case law (but not in relation to company meetings), the separate but connected roles of chairman and secretary, all constitutional and procedural issues relating to the management of meetings and a specific understanding of best practice in relation to the preparation of minutes and report writing.
Weighting:	*Full* Forms of collective decision-making, authority and accountability. The conduct and management of meetings. The preparation of reports and minutes. *Broad* Delegation of authority and responsibility, the structure and management of committees. The role of a secretary before, during and after a meeting. Strategic tactical and operational aspects of decision-making. *Intermediate* The impact of corporate governance principles on decision-making. Published theories on decision-making.

Corporate information needs

This section requires knowledge of the following: the use of information, data and technology as corporate resources in the contemporary organisation, the way in which technological change has impacted on organisations' methods of working and disseminating information, the benefits and risks associated with the introduction of information technology in organisations, the requirement for protection and security of hardware and software in organisations, different types of management information systems such as executive information systems and decision support systems, the development of the 'virtual organisation' and the development of electronic commerce systems. Candidates will be expected also to have a detailed knowledge of data protection legislation, the Computer Misuse Act, EU legislation affecting information technology and also to be familiar with recent case law affecting electronic mail usage in organisations.

Weighting: *Full*
The requirement for organisations to manage their corporate information resources efficiently and in a cost-effective manner, developments in information technology, security of information technology systems, legislative requirements for the protection of data, the benefits and risks associated with information technology.

Broad
Management information systems, general security systems in use in organisations, contractual implications of electronic commerce, the way in which corporate information needs affect the general role of the Chartered Secretary in organisations, the impact of forward planning for computer systems.

Intermediate
Systems and procedures relating to information technology best practice, the control of unauthorised access to computer systems, the development of the 'virtual' office environment.

Pensions, insurance and risk

Pensions: The different types of pension scheme available in organisations and to employees, the role of the chairman, secretary and trustees of pension schemes, the provisions and implications of the Pensions Act 1995 and best practice principles relating to pension scheme administration in organisations.

Insurance and risk: General business insurance issues including the various classes of insurances, the key components of a business insurance portfolio, the way in which brokers and intermediaries function, insurance issues relevant to acquisition and disposal of companies, the minimum legal requirements for insurance policies, disaster planning in organisations, risk management principles and best practice in organisations. Candidates also need to be aware of the benefits and risks of outsourcing insurance administration and the legal implications that remain with the organisation.

Weighting: *Full*
Pensions scheme administration, the role of the secretary and trustees of pension schemes, insurance policies and cover requirements of commercial organisations, the control and management of business risks by the contemporary organisation.

Broad
The impact of recent pension scheme legislation, the requirement for contingency and disaster planning in organisations, the purpose and benefits of appropriate insurance cover in organisations, business continuity and disaster planning.

Intermediate
Recent case law affecting pension scheme and insurance administration, the use of captive insurance companies, risk retention and transfer outside the organisation, the role of brokers and the functions of the insurance market.

Management of corporate assets

A broad knowledge of the requirement for effective and efficient management of corporate assets in organisations is required for this section of the module. (Corporate assets include tangible and intangible assets such as patents, trademarks, goodwill and know-how.) The principles of security management and their application in the workplace are important in this section, as is the role and functions of facilities management in the contemporary organisation. The benefits and risks associated with outsourcing management functions are also important in this section. Candidates will need to be aware of the practical issues connected with the requirement for effective purchasing systems and procedures and the range of administrative services required in contemporary organisations.

Weighting:

Full
The practice and principles of effective security systems, facilities management best practice in organisations, the management of physical assets by organisations. Recent developments in the office environment and in information technology.

Broad
The benefits and risks of outsourcing the management of corporate assets, the impact of information technology on the management of corporate assets.

Intermediate
The impact of health and safety at work and environmental legislation on the management of corporate assets, systems and procedures used by organisations for effective management of assets, purchasing procedures and systems.

Grades

The 'grades' are Full, Broad and Intermediate, and are explained more fully below.

Full

This grade refers to sections of syllabuses where you must be familiar with the whole area. Questions can be expected on topics in this category in each examination diet.

Broad

A general overview of topics within this area is expected. While you are not expected to answer full questions on topics indicated as 'broad', you will be expected to make reference to 'broad' types within answers to questions categorised under the 'full' designations.

Intermediate

This category corresponds to topics which, while not pivotal to a full understanding of the module, may assist in interpretation of a topic categorised as 'full' or 'broad'.

THE EXAMINATION PAPER

Paper requirements and format

Section A: 1 compulsory situational question. Relates to 'Decision Making Forums and Meetings'. Caries 35 marks.

Section B: 1 question from a choice of 2. Each question carries 20 marks. Relates to 'Corporate Information Needs'.

Section C: 1 question from a choice of 2. Each question carries 30 marks. Relates to 'Pensions, Insurance and Risk.

Section D: 1 question from a choice of 2. Each question carries 15 marks. Relates to 'Management of Corporate Assets.

4 questions in total to be answered

Note. Prior to December 1996 candidates had a choice of 1 from *3* questions in Section B.

Key features of students' abilities to be demonstrated

- Awareness of legal requirements
- Awareness of individual and organisational obligations and needs
- Identifying the issues, opportunities and threats surrounding given problems
- Providing solutions to problems
- Effective means of minimising the risk of non completion of tasks or dealing with consequences of inappropriate actions

Methods/characteristics of assessment

Situational questions

Essay questions

Analysis of past papers

June 2000

Section A (Compulsory – 35 marks)
1 Committee structure

Section B (Answer one question – 20 marks each)
2 Integration of information systems
3 New internal and external communications systems

Section C (Answer one question – 30 marks each)
4 Duties, responsibilities and liabilities of pension scheme trustees
5 Risk management

Section D (Answer one question – 15 marks each)
6 Trademarks
7 Oursourcing

December 1999

Section A (Compulsory – 35 marks)

1 Meeting procedures

Section B (Answer one question – 20 marks each)

2 New software

3 Investment in technology

Section C (Answer one question – 30 marks each)

4 Captive insurance company

5 Insurance and risk issues in acquisitions

Section D (Answer one question – 15 marks each)

6 E commerce

7 Health and safety in acquisitions

June 1999

Section A (Compulsory - 35 marks)

1 Organisation, management and minuting of meetings

Section B (Answer one question - 20 marks each)

2 Year 2000 compliance

3 Data protection legislation

Section C (Answer one question - 30 marks each)

4 Types of pension scheme

5 Disaster planning

Section D (Answer one question - 15 marks each)

6 Reduction in paperwork

7 Purchase or leasing of equipment and vehicles

December 1998

Section A (Compulsory - 35 marks)

1 Committee system

Section B (Answer one question - 20 marks each)

2 Data protection legislation and computer security

3 E mail code of practice

Section C (Answer one question - 30 marks each)

4 Pensions manager

5 Insurance arrangements by acquired and divested companies

Section D (Answer one question - 15 marks each)

6 Outsourcing

7 Lease negotiation

June 1998

Section A (Compulsory - 35 marks)
1 Proceedings at meetings of district hospital

Section B (Answer one question - 20 marks each)
2 Choice and implementation of multi-site information system
3 Risks arising from electronic means of commerce

Section C (Answer one question - 30 marks each)
4 Duties of pension scheme trustees; role of regulatory authorities
5 Risks facing chemical manufacturer

Section D (Answer one question - 15 marks each)
6 Role of facilities manager
7 Audit of resources

December 1997

Section A (Compulsory - 35 marks)
1 Board committees and non-executive directors

Section B (Answer one question - 20 marks each)
2 Developments in communication with remote workers
3 Legal requirements affecting computer data storage

Section C (Answer one question - 30 marks each)
4 Communication with pension scheme members
5 Insurance brokers

Section D (Answer one question - 15 marks each)
6 Property register
7 Computer protection

June 1997

Section A (Compulsory - 35 marks)
1 Best practice for minuting meetings

Section B (Answer one question - 20 marks each)
2 The benefits and risks of networks and intranets
3 The Year 2000 problem

Section C (Answer one question - 30 marks each)
4 Money purchase v final salary schemes
5 Outline disaster management plan

Section D (Answer one question - 15 marks each)
6 Leasing or purchasing office space
7 Information security

December 1996

Section A (Compulsory - 35 marks)

1 Good practice for directors of a NHS Trust

Section B (Answer one question - 20 marks each)

2 Software for maintaining statutory records

3 Technological developments and information sourcing

Section C (Answer one question - 30 marks each)

4 Legislation and administration of pension scheme

5 Insurance: IT aspects

Section D (Answer one question - 15 marks each))

7 The paperless office

8 Office facilities: environmental and safety considerations

June 1996

Section A (Compulsory - 35 marks)

1 Mini-case: annual public meeting of a company limited by guarantee. Prepare a report on procedural rules, agenda items, press rights, motions, resolutions, conduct, voting and points of order

Section B (Answer one question - 20 marks each)

2 Technology and the flow of information from field sales staff to head office

3 Establishing, maintaining and controlling a database

4 Technological developments and meetings and training

Section C (Answer one question - 30 marks each)

5 Pensions: funds collection, communication with members, trustee duties

6 Risk management and risk reduction

Section D (Answer one question - 15 marks each))

7 Open plan offices

8 Buying equipment and vehicles versus leasing. Buying second hand

Part A

Decision-making forums and meetings

Chapter 1

DECISIONS AND DECISION-MAKING

This chapter covers the following topics.

1 Decisions

2 Authority, responsibility and accountability

3 Approaches to decision making

4 Decision-making forums

5 Corporate governance and decision-making

Introduction

The bulk of this first part of the Study Text is concerned with the procedures for collective decision making in meetings of various kinds. Before getting into detail however we need to think about what sort of decisions have to be made and how they can be made, since this will determine what sort of decision making forum is appropriate.

1 DECISIONS **6/95, 12/95, 12/96**

1.1 Organisations face a changing environment which they cannot always control, but to which they must **respond** and **adapt**. Decisions will be necessary because it may adapt in a number of different ways.

1.2 Similarly, as the organisation is a complex social system, on a day to day basis the conflicting demands of the various departments must be **harmonised** in some way and priorities must be established. There may be a number of options or choices available.

1.3 Decisions must therefore be taken in response to choices and options regarding how the organisation **responds** to the **environment**, and how its **internal activities** are to be run.

Planning and control

1.4 All managers, and many employees, make both **planning** and **control decisions**. A factory foreman, for example, might speak to an employee about the quality or speed of his work, and also tell him which job will be allocated to him next. A marketing manager disappointed with the sales of a particular product might revise his estimates for the future marketability of the product, whilst at the same time making an attempt to boost current sales (perhaps by arranging a re-allocation of sales promotion effort). Koontz wrote that 'planning and control are so closely interconnected as to be singularly inseparable' and Anthony noted that different companies refer to the same activity as 'production planning' in some cases and 'production control' in others.

1.5 Anthony in fact identifies *three* areas of decision-making.

- **Strategic** planning
- **Management** control or tactical decisions
- **Operational** control

1.6 Strategic planning, management control and operational control may be seen as a hierarchy of decisions. Management control is always in the middle of the range.

(a) Top level management make **strategic plans**, and low level managers make **operational control** decisions.

(b) **Strategic** planning tends to cover a **longer time** period than management control, whereas **operational** control is exercised **day-to-day**.

(c) The **most important** decisions are usually **strategic**, and the **least important** are **operational**.

Strategic planning decisions

1.7 Strategic planning is a process of deciding on **objectives** of the organisation, on changes in these objectives, on the **resources** used to attain these objectives and on the **policies** that are to govern the acquisition, use and disposition of these resources.

1.8 Strategic planning involves choosing objectives and planning how to achieve those objectives. Although much strategic planning is done with a view to the **long-term** future, its consequences and results might also be short term.

1.9 Strategic planning is largely a process of formulating **plans**, but it also includes an important element of **control**. A board of directors might set as a policy objective diversification of the business, so that a decision might be taken to purchase for shares a company which manufactures umbrellas (say) with a view to acquiring a 50% share of the market for umbrella sales and obtaining a financial return on investment of 20%. Strategic decision-making has a number of elements.

- Long term
- High levels of uncertainty and risk (the future is unpredictable)
- Situations that do not necessarily recur
- Complex issues

Management control decisions (tactical decisions)

1.10 Anthony defined management control as ensuring that resources are obtained and used **effectively** and **efficiently** in the accomplishment of the organisation's objectives. Management control decisions are taken within the framework of strategic plans and objectives which have previously been made, or set.

(a) **Efficiency** means that resources input to a process produce the optimum (maximum) amount of outputs.

(b) **Effectiveness** means that the resources are used to achieve the desired ends.

1.11 This type of decision can encompass planning activities. A decision about how to price a new product, given that a lower price offers a lower unit profit but prospects of higher sales volumes, would be 'management control' planning.

Operational control

1.12 Operational control decisions ensure that specific **tasks** are carried out **effectively** and **efficiently**. It focuses on individual tasks, and is carried out within the strictly defined guidelines issued by strategic planning and management control decisions.

1.13 Many **operational control decisions** can be **automated** or **programmed**. 'Programmed control' exists where the relationship between inputs and outputs is clearly defined, so that an optimal relationship can be specified for every activity. Mathematical models can be designed to provide optimal solutions to problems.

Choices

1.14 Anthony's classification focuses on where in the organisational hierarchy the decision is made. It is also possible to look at decisions from the point of view of the nature of the choice to be made. From this perspective there are basically two types of decision.

(a) **Accept or reject decisions**. A decision must be taken on the merits of a particular opportunity under review 'without having to compare it with other available projects'. An 'accept' decision (a decision to go ahead with a particular course of action) will place no restrictions on the organisation's ability to do anything else as well. Therefore the organisation would be free to take up any other opportunities that might also become available.

(b) **Ranking decisions**. A choice must be made between two or more competing opportunities:

  (i) Either there is a **scarcity of resources** so that there are not enough to go round all the opportunities which might otherwise be pursued

  (ii) Or the opportunities involve **different means** to the same or similar ends, in a decision whether a new regional office of a company should be located in Nottingham or in Birmingham, for example, both opportunities are different means towards the same end of choosing a location for the new office.

Frequency and impact

1.15 Yet another type of classification considers decisions in terms of how often they have to be made and how significant they are.

(a) **Routine planning decisions**, for example, budgeting. **Budgeting** decisions commonly analyse fixed and variable costs, together with revenues, over a one year period. They are also often concerned with how to make the best use of scarce resources.

(b) **Short-run problem decisions**, typically, unforeseen 'one-off' special decisions of a non-recurring nature, where the costs and benefits are all obtained within a relatively short period. For example, should a contract be accepted or rejected? What price should be quoted in the tender for a contract?

(c) **Investment or disinvestment decisions**, for example should an item of equipment be purchased? Should a department be shut down? Decisions of this nature often have long-term consequences.

(d) **Longer-range decisions**, meaning decisions made once and reviewed infrequently, but which are intended to provide a continuing solution to a continuing or recurring problem. They include decisions about selling and distribution policies, such as whether goods should be sold through middlemen or direct to customers or whether a new product or service should be launched.

(e) **Control decisions**, these are sometimes made on a regular basis (for example when reviewing a monthly budget) and sometimes on a one-off basis, in response to a particular event. Should disappointing performance be investigated, given that the benefits expected must exceed the costs from investigation and control? How should performance be measured?

1.16 **Pricing decisions** are sometimes put into a category of their own, but pricing decisions span most of the range of decision categories above. Routine pricing decisions are made at periodic price reviews. 'One-off' short-run pricing decisions might be made for specific jobs or contracts or to dispose of surplus stocks. Long-range decisions about price must be made for services, products or product ranges and some control decisions might have to be made about prices (are excessive discounts being allowed?).

2 AUTHORITY, RESPONSIBILITY AND ACCOUNTABILITY 6/95, 12/95, 12/96

2.1 Decisions are made in different ways in different situations.

(a) In some organisations decisions are arrived at **collectively** through negotiation or voting. A referendum is a means of taking such a decision. In many cases, the right or **authority** to make decisions is delegated to specific groups or individuals. In most limited companies, the owners will appoint directors to act on their behalf, and to manage the organisation's activities.

(b) Within an organisation, different types of decision are taken at different **levels**. Senior management will be involved in strategic decision making, for example. In short, decision making is often a function of management, and some decisions will be **delegated** to middle management.

(c) Certain kinds of decision are **routine**, in that the same remedy will be applied to a situation which recurs regularly, or which is relatively simple. For example, an organisation might decide to have a policy of sending out reminder notes if its customers have not paid their bills after 30 days. If customer Y is late in payment, the conditions specifying the organisation's response have been determined in advance. Future decisions are **programmed** decisions. (This does not necessarily refer to computer programs. A set of clerical procedures laid down in a manual would be just the same.) Programmed decisions have a number of features.

(i) They respond to simple problems (where only a few factors are relevant).

(ii) They have few possible solutions (for example whether to send or not to send reminder notes).

(iii) They are easy to make, as the relationship between the problem and the decision is easy to determine.

Authority

2.2 **Authority** is the right to do something. In an organisation, it refers to the scope and amount of discretion given to a person to make decisions, by virtue of the position he or she holds in the organisation: it is conferred 'from the top down' because each manager can pass on some of his or her authority to subordinates in assigning tasks to them. However, authority is **not only bestowed** by the **organisation** (that is, by more senior people in it). Authority can be **bestowed** 'from the **bottom up**', when it is conferred on a leader figure by people at **lower levels** in the hierarchy for example by election: trade union officials have this kind of authority.

Responsibility and accountability

2.3 **Responsibility** is the liability of a person to be called to account for exercising his authority, actions and results. It is therefore a formal obligation to do something. **Accountability** is the duty of an individual to report to his superior how he has fulfilled his responsibilities.

2.4 It is important to realise that a manager's personal accountability cannot be 'delegated' or passed on to a subordinate. A manager may **delegate authority** and **responsibility** to a subordinate (if that authority is within his **own power** to delegate) - but he remains **accountable** to his own boss for explaining how the work has been done, albeit by the subordinate rather than by himself personally.

Exercise 1

Make sure you understand this point by considering your own situation. What authority do you have, what are you responsible for and who are you accountable to? How do others (your boss, your staff) stand in relation to you?

Devolving authority

2.5 **Delegation** thus refers to the process whereby a superior gives a subordinate the authority and responsibility to carry out a given aspect of the superior's own task. Delegation shapes the **hierarchical structure** of the formal organisation, where authority and responsibility are passed down the 'chain of command' and accountability passes back up.

2.6 There should be a careful **balance** between delegated authority and responsibility in the organisation.

(a) A manager who is not held responsible for any area of his authority is free to exercise it in a capricious way: he is not bound to do otherwise.

(b) A manager who is held responsible for aspects of performance, but has not been given authority to control them, is in an impossible position. Sufficient authority must be given to enable the individual to do what is expected of him.

2.7 The **boundaries** of each manager's authority should be clear, to avoid ambiguity and overlap. 'Unity of command', that each individual should report to only one superior, has advantages. It can avoid conflicts and doubts created by dual command. Dual command systems have, however, proved workable in practice, for example where there is project/product management: either clarified boundaries of authority or consensus management is required.

Consultative management and the exercise of authority

2.8 Jaques (the 'Glacier investigations') found that even a well-defined role in the organisation posed problems for the person expected to fill it with regard to the exercise of authority. In particular, he found that in an organisation committed to consultative management, a superior may become more and more reluctant to exercise his authority. Mechanisms for avoiding responsibility and authority included:

(a) The exercise of a **purely consultative relationship** with others while ignoring roles involving line authority

(b) **Misuse** of formal **joint consultation** processes - using contact between higher management and workers' representatives as an excuse to ignore responsibility for immediate subordinates. Consultation must not by-pass intervening roles in the chain of command

(c) **Pseudo-democracy** - for example a superior, senior member on a committee asserting 'I'm just an ordinary member'

One of the most important conclusions of the Glacier studies was that there is a distinctive leadership role in groups, and that members (in their roles as participants) **expect** it to be properly filled.

Exercise 2

We will not make much of this point here, but it is important that you pause to consider it. The suggestion is that organisations can get addicted to meetings and consultation and that rather than being a convenient vehicle for the efficient administration of the decision making process meetings can be a way of *avoiding* decisions.

How may ways can you think of to delay a collective decision?

Delegation

2.9 It is generally recognised that in any large complex organisation, management must delegate some authority and responsibility.

(a) There are physical and mental **limitations** to the work load of any individual or group in authority.

(b) Routine or less important **decisions** can be **passed 'down the line'** to subordinates, freeing the superior to concentrate on the more important aspects of the work, like planning, and allowing the organisation to respond more quickly to the demands made on it.

(c) The increasing size and complexity of organisations calls for **specialisation**, both managerial and technical.

(d) Employees in today's organisations have **high expectations** with regard to job satisfaction - including discretion and participation in decision-making.

(e) The managerial succession plan depends on junior managers gaining same experience of management processes in order to be '**groomed**' for promotion.

2.10 In practice many managers are reluctant to delegate and attempt to do many routine matters themselves in addition to their more important duties. These are various common reasons for this reluctance.

(a) **Low confidence** and **trust** in the abilities of the subordinates: the suspicion that 'if you want it done well, you have to do it yourself'

(b) The **burden** of **responsibility** and **accountability** for the mistakes of subordinates

(c) A desire to '**stay in touch**' with the department or team - both in terms of workload and staff - particularly if the manager does not feel 'at home' in a management role, and/or misses aspects of the subordinate job or the camaraderie

(d) An **unwillingness** to **admit** that subordinates have developed to the extent that they could perform some of the manager's duties. The manager may feel threatened by this sense of 'redundancy'

(e) **Poor control and communication systems** in the organisation, so that the manager feels he has to do everything himself, if he is to retain real control and responsibility for a task, and if he wants to know what is going on

(f) An **organisational culture** that has failed to reward or recognise effective delegation by superiors, so that the manager may not realise that delegation is regarded positively (rather than as 'shirking responsibility')

(g) **Lack of understanding** of what delegation involves - that is, realising that it does *not* mean giving the subordinates total control, making the manager himself redundant

(h) A desire to continue to operate within their **personal** '**comfort zone**', doing things that are familiar to them and then claiming that they are too busy to tackle the jobs they really should be doing, which are risky because they involve thought, forward planning, performance improvement and the initiation of change

2.11 Handy writes of a 'trust-control dilemma' in a superior-subordinate relationship, in which the sum of trust + control is a constant amount.

$$T + C = Y$$

T = The trust the superior has in the subordinate, and the trust which the subordinate feels the superior has in him

C = The degree of control exercised by the superior over the subordinate

Y = A constant, unchanging value

Any increase in C leads to an equal decrease in T: if the superior retains more 'control' or authority, the subordinate will immediately recognise that he is being trusted less. If the superior wishes to show more trust in the subordinate, he can only do so by reducing C, in other words by delegating more authority.

2.12 To overcome the reluctance of managers to delegate, it is necessary to undertake the following.

(a) Provide a system of **selecting subordinates** who will be capable of handling delegated authority in a responsible way. If subordinates are of the right 'quality', superiors will be prepared to trust them more.

(b) Install a system of **open communications,** in which the different levels in the hierarchy freely interchange ideas and information. If the subordinate is given all the information he needs to do his job, and if the superior is aware of what the subordinate is doing:

(i) The subordinate will make better-informed decisions.
(ii) The superior will not 'panic' because he does not know what is going on.

Although open lines of communication are important, they should not be used by the superior to command the subordinate in a matter where authority has been delegated to the subordinate; in other words, communication links must not be used by superiors as a means of reclaiming authority.

(c) Ensure that a **system of control** is established. Superiors are reluctant to delegate authority because they retain absolute responsibility for the performance of their subordinates. If an efficient control system is in operation, responsibility and accountability will be **monitored** at all levels of the management hierarchy, and the 'dangers' of relinquishing authority and control to subordinates are significantly lessened.

(d) **Reward effective delegation** by superiors and the efficient assumption of authority by subordinates. Rewards may be given in terms of pay, promotion, status, or official approval.

(e) **Set the example** from the very top of the organisation. An MD who has a hands-on approach to every aspect of the organisation's activities is unlikely to be able to encourage his managerial team to let go.

3 APPROACHES TO DECISION MAKING

3.1 It is possible to identify certain features that are common to all decisions, or, more precisely, that are common to the decision-making process.

(a) Decisions are taken in response to a **problem.** Identification of the problem is the first stage. In confusing situations, the problem may need to be clearly defined.

(b) A problem must be **analysed** and **structured** in such a way as to define alternative courses of action.

(c) The decision is taken from among the **available alternatives**.

(d) The decision has to be **communicated** to those who implement it.

(e) The decision maker might wish to **review** the effect of the decision made to see if it has been implemented properly and whether, once implemented, it has had the anticipated effect.

Simon's approach

3.2 One of the first theorists to analyse the decision-making process was Herbert Simon, who also developed much of current thinking on artificial intelligence. He identified three distinct stages in the process.

(a) The **intelligence** stage, during which the decision makers collect data on the nature of the problem and attempt to define its scope

(b) The **design** stage, where alternative courses of action are identified and the likely effect of each is assessed

(c) The **choice** stage, where a decision is reached on the basis of the decision makers' analysis of the relative merits of each alternative

3.3 From this intelligence-design-choice concept of decision-making has developed the science of decision analysis. Decision analysis is based on three rules.

- A choice must be made from a number of **identifiable alternatives.**
- The **consequence** of the decision depends upon the alternative selected.
- **Outcomes** can be **ranked** in order of preference by the decision makers.

3.4 To recap, the stages in making a decision are as follows.

- Problem recognition
- Problem definition and structuring
- Identifying alternative courses of action
- Making and communicating the decision
- Implementation of the decision
- Monitoring the effects of the decision

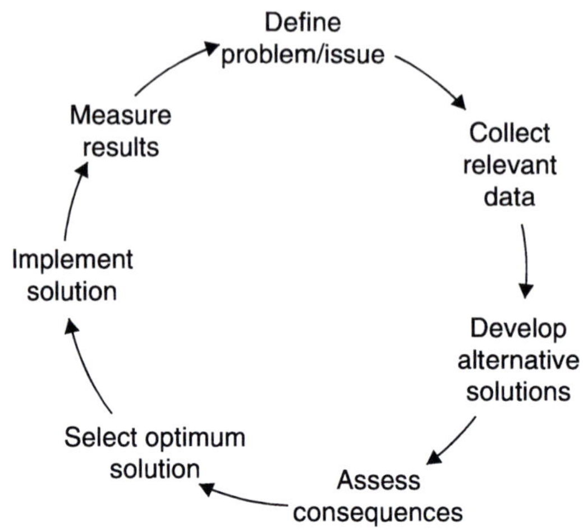

Exercise 3

Which of the stages of the decision making process would take place in a meeting?

Solution

Potentially all of them, or none of them, depending on the type of decision. For a typical decision, involving a number of interested parties, meetings might be needed to:

(a) Define the problem
(b) *Share* information once collected
(c) Generate and share ideas for solutions
(d) Assess the consequences of different courses of action
(e) Select the optimum solution
(f) *Consider* the results.

Activities taking place outside the meeting would be the collection of information, the implementation of the decision and the collection of results data.

Problem recognition

3.5 The decision makers need to be informed of a problem in the first place or reminded of it if it is a recurring problem. This is sometimes referred to as the **decision trigger**. Normally further information is required and may be collected initially outside the decision making forum.

Problem definition and structuring

3.6 The **problem** must be **defined**. Consider, for example, a company with falling sales: the fall in revenue would be the trigger. Further information would be needed to identify where the revenue deficiencies were occurring. The problem can therefore be defined. If our company discovers that sales of product X in area Y are falling, the problem could be defined as 'decline of sales of product X in area Y due to new competitor: how can the decline be reversed?' An alternative formulation of the problem might lead to a completely different set of solutions: 'Given that sales of product X in area Y are falling what new product can we offer this market?'

3.7 One of the purposes of defining the problem is to **identify** the **relationships** between the various factors in it, especially if the problem is complex. New definitions may suggest previously unthought of relationships. Definitions should be as clear and specific as possible to encourage focused discussion.

4 DECISION-MAKING FORUMS 12/95, 6/00

4.1 The variety of decision-making forums in contemporary organisations is potentially very wide.

Company meetings

4.2 Company meetings may be the following types.

- Annual General Meeting (AGM)
- Extraordinary General Meeting (EGM)
- Class meeting (meeting of holders of a class of shares in the company)
- Board of Directors meeting
- Board committee meeting
- Meeting of the contributors or of creditors in liquidation

These meetings are covered in detail in the BPP Study Text *Company Secretarial Practice*.

Committees

4.3 Detailed problem solving of the type we have been discussing in this chapter would generally be remitted to a body of 'experts', possibly called a '**committee**'. There are various types of committee.

- Executive committees
- Standing committees
- Special or 'ad hoc' committees
- Sub-committees
- Joint committees

These are described in Chapter 8, together with conferences.

Informal meetings

4.4 Many matters in organisations are decided on a much less formal basis through one-to-one meetings (for example a staff appraisal agreeing new performance targets) or meetings of groups (for example quality circles). Such meetings are very relevant to the administration of corporate affairs. However they are more appropriately dealt with in the context of management skills (*Management Principles* at Pre-Professional level and *Management Practice* at Professional level are the relevant modules).

The value of decision making in forums

4.5 Anthony Jay has argued that 'even the most apparently futile of meetings serves some wider corporate purpose as well as preserving the mental health of those who attend'. In other words the role of group discussions is a wide-ranging one. Not all meetings are about 'getting things done', and 'getting things done' is only one of the purposes of setting up a decision-making forum.

4.6 The wider corporate purposes of meetings include the following.

(a) **Ritual**. If, as Mintzberg suggests, a manager has a ceremonial role, it is quite possible that this is acted out in meeting. Often, meetings (between the managing directors of supplier and customer) might merely be the ritual ending of a months of negotiation.

(b) **Communication and personal contact**. A meeting helps people to get to know one another. Establishing good personal relationships is important in organisational life.

(c) Meetings also enable colleagues to 'let off steam'. Arguably, there is sometimes a good purpose in having an argumentative session in which most **grievances become aired**. Disagreement might be seen as a useful way of generating new ideas.

(d) Even though meetings do not do anything, they may **legitimise** other managerial decisions. For example, the formal organisation structure may not be effective. Instead, a strong informal organisation may exist. A committee meeting may give authority to power.

(e) The fact, or at least the illusion, of participation in decisions may improve individual **motivation**.

(f) Meetings enable the various **different interests** in a decision to be represented as 'equals'.

(g) Meetings can be used to **delay decisions**. There are certain instances when this can be of benefit to the organisation or to managers.

(h) Meetings can also be used to **put individuals on the spot**. They can enforce commitment, or at least indicate where battle lines are drawn.

(i) Some meetings can be **inspirational**, if they are used to persuade, cajole or encourage a sense of values.

(j) Finally, bringing people together underlines the fact that they belong to the **same organisation**, and in theory should be working to the same purpose. Perhaps this is a function of the ritual aspect outlined above.

Exercise 5

Decision by consensus is a method of problem solving and decision making in groups in which all the parties involved actively discuss the issues surrounding the decision. The group thus pools the knowledge and experience of all its members. Any final decision must be supported by each member of the group. The ideas and feelings of all the members are integrated into a group decision, thus allowing several people to work together on a common problem, rather than producing a 'we-they' stand-off.

As you might imagine, decision by consensus is usually difficult to attain and will consume more time than other methods of deciding an issue. As the energies of the group become focused on the problem at hand (rather than on defending individual points of view), the quality of the decision tends to be enhanced. Research indicates, in fact, that this approach to problem-solving and decision making results in a significantly higher-quality decision than other methods such as the use of majority power (voting), minority power (persuasion), and compromise.

In the decision-by-consensus process, each group member is asked to:

1 Prepare his/her own position as well as possible prior to meeting with the group (but to realize that the task is incomplete and that the missing pieces are to be supplied by the other members of the group).

2 Recognize an obligation to express his/her own opinion and explain it fully, so that the rest of the group has the benefit of all members' thinking.

3 Recognize an obligation to listen to the opinions and feelings of all other group members and be ready to modify his/her own position on the basis of logic and understanding.

4 Avoid conflict-reducing techniques such as voting, compromising, or giving in to keep the peace and to realize that differences of opinion are helpful; in exploring differences, the best course of action will make itself apparent.

(Source: Mullins, *Management and Organisational Behaviour,* 1993)

(a) Why do you think decision by consensus is usually difficult to attain?
(b) How can a company secretary assist in achieving decision by consensus?

---

5 CORPORATE GOVERNANCE AND DECISION-MAKING 12/96

5.1 Corporate governance can be defined as 'the system by which companies are **directed** and **controlled**'. Corporate governance is therefore closely related to decision-making, and it has an impact on the conduct and management of meetings. You will meet corporate governance issues in various places in your studies, particularly *Company Secretarial Practice,* so we will summarise the main points and developments here. The section finishes with some comments on the direct impact of corporate governance on decision making.

Why corporate governance has become an issue

5.2 In general terms, corporate governance becomes more and more difficult as the size of an organisation increases. Small companies, which are frequently owner-managed, have only one or two shareholders to report to (or sometimes a few in family companies) and relatively few major creditors (the bank and perhaps one or two major trade creditors).

5.3 Larger organisations have a large number of capital providers: shareholders, debentureholders, loan creditors, banks, trade creditors and so on, ie '**stakeholders**'. For large companies, control is delegated to the directors by this large constituency of stakeholders, because each stakeholder cannot exercise that control themselves.

5.4 Here is the principal problem of corporate governance: how can be stakeholders ensure that the directors act in the stakeholders' interests and not in their own?

5.5 The laws relating to company reporting and auditing have developed in order to answer this problem by delineating the relationships between the directors, the auditors and the shareholders. This started with the concept of the '**stewardship**' of the directors over the assets of the company which they managed on behalf of the shareholders and accounting for that stewardship to the shareholders in the annual report.

5.6 There are three main developments in corporate governance which we will summarise here.

- The Cadbury report
- The Greenbury report
- The Hampel report

The Cadbury report

5.7 The Cadbury committee was set up in May 1991 because of the lack of confidence which was perceived in financial reporting and in the ability of auditors to provide the assurances required by the users of financial statements.

Corporate governance

5.8 The committee focused on corporate governance, defined above as the system by which companies are directed and controlled.'

5.9 The roles of those concerned with the financial statements are described in the report.

(a) The **directors** are responsible for the corporate governance of the company.

(b) The **shareholders** are linked to the directors via the financial reporting system.

(c) The **auditors** provide the shareholders with an external objective check on the directors' financial statements.

(d) Other concerned **users,** particularly employees (to whom the directors owe some responsibility) are indirectly addressed by the financial statements.

The committee aimed to set out the responsibilities of each group involved in the reporting process.

Code of best practice

5.10 This was aimed at the directors of all UK plcs, but the directors of all companies are encouraged to use the code for guidance. The code is reproduced as an appendix to this chapter.

5.11 The major provisions of the Cadbury report were as follows.

Board of directors

5.12 The report stressed the importance of the board of **directors meeting** on a regular basis, retaining **full control** over the company and **monitoring** executive management. Certain matters such as major acquisitions or disposals of assets should be referred automatically to the board. There should be a **clear division of responsibilities** with no one person having complete power.

Non-executive directors

5.13 The report saw non-executive directors as important figures because of the **independent judgement** they brought to bear on important issues.

Executive directors

5.14 The report contained provisions about the length of **service contracts** and disclosure of **remuneration** which were developed further in the Greenbury and Hampel reports (see below).

The audit committee

5.15 The audit committee was seen by the Cadbury committee as a key board committee. The audit committee should **liase** with internal and external auditors, and provide a **forum** for both to express their concerns. The committee should also review half yearly and annual statements.

Accounts

5.16 The Cadbury committee stressed the importance of the board presenting a **balanced** and **understandable assessment** of the company's position. The directors should explain their responsibilities for preparing accounts. Statements should also be made about the company's ability to continue as a going concern, and the effectiveness of its internal controls.

The Greenbury report

5.17 In July 1995 the Greenbury committee's report on **directors' remuneration** was published. The report developed a number of recommendations of the Cadbury committee. Greenbury stressed the importance of the role of the remuneration committee, which the report recommended should consist entirely of non-executive directors.

5.18 The recommendations about directors' remuneration are grouped under four main headings, most of the details of which are beyond the scope of this syllabus.

- A remuneration committee of non-executive directors (see Chapter 8)
- Disclosures of directors' remuneration
- Remuneration policy
- Service contracts and compensation

1/3 of any BoD as NEDs.

The Hampel report

5.19 The Hampel committee was set up in 1996 to carry out the following tasks:

(a) Conduct a **review** of the Cadbury code and its implementation to ensure that the original purpose is being achieved, proposing amendments to and deletions from the code as necessary.

(b) Keep under review the **role of directors**, executive and non-executive, recognising the need for board cohesion and the common legal responsibility of all directors.

(c) Be prepared to pursue any relevant matters arising from the **Greenbury** report.

(d) Address as necessary the **role of shareholders** and auditors in corporate governance issues.

(e) Deal with any other relevant matters.

5.20 The Hampel committee produced a final report in January 1998. The committee followed up matters raised in the Cadbury and Greenbury reports, aiming to restrict the regulatory burden on companies and substituting **principles** for detail whenever possible. The introduction to the report also states that whilst the Cadbury and Greenbury reports concentrated on the prevention of abuses, Hampel was equally concerned with the positive contribution good corporate governance can make.

5.21 The introduction to the report pointed out that the primary duty of directors was to shareholders, to **enhance** the value of **shareholders' investment** over time. Relationships with other stakeholders were important, but making the directors responsible to other stakeholders would mean there was no clear yardstick for judging directors' performance.

5.22 The Hampel committee was also against treating the corporate governance codes as sets of prescriptive rules, and judging companies by whether they have complied. The report stated that there may be guidelines which would normally be appropriate, but the differing circumstances of companies mean that sometimes there were valid reasons for exceptions.

5.23 The major recommendations of the report were as follows.

Directors

5.24 The committee stressed that executive and non-executive directors should continue to have the **same duties** under the law. The committee stated that the roles of chairman and chief executive should generally be separate, but whether or not the roles of chairman and chief executive are combined, a senior non-executive director should be identified. The report also stressed the importance of **monitoring director performance** with all directors submitting themselves for re-election at least once every three years, and boards assessing the performance of individual directors and collective board performance.

Directors' remuneration

5.25 In common with the Cadbury and Greenbury reports, the Hampel committee saw the remuneration committee as the key mechanism for setting the pay of executive directors. Remuneration committees should develop **policy** on remuneration and devise **reasonable remuneration packages** for individual executive directors. The committee believed that boards should try and reduce directors' contract periods to one year or less. The accounts should include a general statement on remuneration policy, but the committee saw no need for this statement to be the subject of an AGM vote.

Shareholders and the AGM

5.26 The major recommendations of the committee were that shareholders should be able to **vote separately** on each substantially separate issue; and that the practice of 'bundling' unrelated proposals in a single resolution should cease. Companies should propose a resolution at the AGM relating to the report and accounts. Notice of the AGM and related papers should be sent to shareholders at least 20 working days before the meeting.

Accountability and audit

5.27 The Hampel committee stressed, as the Cadbury committee had, the importance of the audit committee. However, whilst the report stated that directors should report on internal control, the committee did not believe that the directors should be required to report on the effectiveness of controls. Auditors should report privately on internal controls to directors. Directors should maintain and review controls relating to all relevant control objectives, and not merely financial controls.

Comments on the Hampel report

5.28 Reaction to the Hampel report has been mixed. Some commentators have welcomed the emphasis on common-sense guidance and the primary need to generate returns for shareholders.

5.29 However other commentators have criticised the Hampel report for stating that the **debate** on **accountability** has obscured the first responsibility of a board, to enhance the **prosperity** of a company over time. Critics have argued that accountability and prosperity should be seen as compatible. Hampel's emphasis on principles rather than detailed guidelines has also come in for adverse comment. Some critics have commented that the principles set out in the Hampel report are so broad that they are of little use as a guide to best corporate governance practice

5.30 In addition Hampel has been criticised for

(a) Dropping the Cadbury requirement for the board to report publicly on the effectiveness of internal controls

(b) Dropping the requirement for the auditors to report publicly on the statement made by the board

(c) For paying insufficient attention to the needs of stakeholders other than shareholders

Stock Exchange requirements

5.31 In June 1998 a combined corporate governance code, which was derived from the recommendations of the Cadbury, Greenbury and Hampel reports, was issued. The Stock Exchange Listing Rules were amended to take account of the recommendations of the combined code.

5.32 The Stock Exchange requires listed companies to include in their accounts:

(a) A **narrative statement** of how they applied the **principles** set out in the combined code, providing explanations which enable their shareholders to assess how the principles have been applied

(b) A statement as to whether or not they **complied** throughout the accounting period with the provisions set out in the Combined Code and give details of any non-compliance

5.33 Listed companies are also required to include a statement on **directors' remuneration**, which must contain a statement of the company's policy on the remuneration of executive directors, the amount of each element in the remuneration package for the period under review (including salary, benefits in kind, bonuses and compensation for loss of office and other information about share options, pensions and service contracts.)

5.34 In September 1999 an ICAEW working party published further guidance on internal controls *Internal Control Guidance for Directors on the Combined Code (the Turnbull report).*

5.35 The working party suggested that the system of internal control should be embedded in the operations of the company, be appropriate for the company, include procedures for reporting any major control weaknesses, and remain relevant in the changing business environment.

5.36 The guidance points out that the control system can only provide reasonable assurance against a company failing to meet its business objectives or all material losses, frauds or breaches of laws and regulations.

5.37 The report recommends that when assessing the effectiveness of internal control, boards should consider the following:

(a) The **nature** and **extent** of the **risks** which face the company and which it regards as **acceptable** for the company to bear within its particular business

(b) The **threat** of such **risks becoming** a **reality**

(c) If that happened, the company's ability to **reduce** the **incidence** and **impact** on the business

(d) The **costs and benefits** related to operating relevant controls

5.38 In order to be able to carry out an effective review, boards should regularly receive and review reports on internal control, concentrating.

(a) What the **risks** are and how they have been **identified, evaluated** and **managed**

(b) The **effectiveness** of the internal control system in the management of risk

(c) Whether **actions** are being taken to **reduce** the risks found

(d) Whether the results indicate that **internal control** should be **monitored more extensively**

5.39 The board should disclose as a minimum in the accounts, the existence of a **process** for **managing risks,** how the board had **reviewed** the **effectiveness** of the process and that the **process accords** with the **ICAEW's guidance**. The board should also disclose:

(a) An **acknowledgement** that they are responsible for the company's system of internal financial control and reviewing its effectiveness

(b) An **explanation** that such a system is designed to **manage** rather than eliminate the risk of **failure** to **achieve business objectives,** and can only provide **reasonable** and not absolute **assurance** against material misstatement or **loss**

(c) A **summary** of the process that the **directors** (or a board committee) have **used to review the effectiveness** of the system of internal financial control and consider the need for an internal audit function if the company does not have one. There should also be disclosure of the process the board has used to deal with **material internal control aspects** of **any significant problems** disclosed in the annual accounts

(d) **Information** about those **weaknesses** in internal financial control that have resulted in material losses, contingencies or uncertainties which require disclosure in the financial statements or the auditor's report on the financial statements.

5.40 The statement should be based on an annual assessment of internal control which should confirm that the board has considered **all significant aspects** of internal control. In particular the assessment should cover:

(a) The **changes** since the last **assessment** in **risks** faced, and the company's **ability** to **respond** to **changes** in its business environment

(b) The **scope** and **quality** of management's monitoring of risk and internal control, and of the work of internal audit, or consideration of the need for an internal audit function if the company does not have one

(c) The **extent** and **frequency** of reports to the board

(d) **Significant controls, failings** and **weaknesses** which have or might have material impacts upon the accounts

(e) The **effectiveness** of the **public reporting** processes

5.41 An article by Robin Johnson in August 1999's *Chartered Secretary* highlighted how the Turnbull committee's recommendations might affect the work of a company secretary.

5.42 The article emphasises that companies will need to carry out an internal risk audit, focusing on contractual relationships and how risk is managed in relation to customers, suppliers, regulators, employees or consumers. The audit should consider how risk is **managed** and **controlled**, and whether the risks that are being run are **acceptable** (how probable it is that they will crystallise, what would happen if a major risk occurred and the cost of controlling and minimising the risk). Audits should be conducted by appropriately senior staff, who have access to non-executive directors and the audit committee.

5.43 Once the audit team has reported, a programme of **risk minimisation** and **control** must be implemented; this will involve systems training, communication and constant identification of opportunities and risks.

5.44 The article warns that failure by directors to consider risk management may lead to negligence claims and strict criminal liability.

5.45 We shall consider risk management further when we discuss insurance in Part C of this Text.

Corporate governance and decision making

5.46 You should realise from the above that corporate governance principles can have a significant impact on decision making.

5.47 Firstly, certain decisions have been formalised and delegated to specific non-executive committees by the reports and codes discussed above.

(a) The **remuneration committee** takes decisions related to all aspects of directors' pay and perks.

(b) The **audit committee** deals with most audit matters, both internal and external.

5.48 Secondly, the way the board of directors operates is specified, particularly in the separation of the posts of chairman and chief executive. The matters to be decided by the directors should also be formalised, according to the Cadbury report.

5.49 The impact of corporate governance on meetings is also important, and this has an impact on the next few chapters. In particular, note the Hampel committee's comments on the AGM.

5.50 You should watch out for further developments in corporate governance, including publication of alternative views on the subject by organisations such as PIRC Ltd.

Chapter roundup

- One of the key uses of information is in **decision making**. Decisions must be taken in response to choices and options regarding how an organisation responds to its environment and runs its internal activities.
- Decisions may be categorised into a **three-level hierarchy**.
  - **Strategic planning** is concerned with the long-term goals of the organisation.
  - **Management control** involves ensuring that resources are used effectively and efficiently to achieve those goals.
  - **Operational control** ensures that specific tasks are carried out effectively and efficiently.
- Decisions may also be classified as 'accept or reject' decisions or ranking decisions, or as routine, short-run, investment, longer-range or control decisions.
- In organisations, **authority** refers to the right to make decisions. To be **responsible** is to be liable to be called to account for exercising authority. **Accountability** is the duty of an individual to report to his superior how he has fulfilled his responsibilities.
- **Corporate governance** is an important and topical issue and it has an impact on decision making.
- The **Cadbury Report** made recommendations on the following subjects.
  - The board
  - Non-executive directors
  - Executive directors
  - Audit committees
  - Internal controls
  - Interim reports, auditors' fees, rotation of audit partners, reporting to regulatory authorities
- The **Greenbury Report** focused on directors' remuneration, which should be determined by a remuneration committee. Disclosures in the accounts should include details of each director's remuneration package and the company's overall remuneration policy.
- The **Hampel Report** made recommendations on the following subjects.
  - Directors
  - Directors' remuneration
  - Shareholders
  - Accountability and audit

Test your knowledge

1 What part of the organisational hierarchy will make a decision about the use of resources? (see para 1.10)

2 What is authority? (2.2)

3 Why might management delegate some of its work? (2.9)

4 What is involved in the process of decision making? (3.4)

5 Why is it important to define problems? (3.6, 3.7)

6 Is the purpose of a decision-making forum to make decisions? (4.5, 4.6)

7 What is meant by 'corporate governance'? (5.1)

8 What are the main provisions of the Cadbury Code in relation to the board of directors? (5.12)

9 How according to the Hampel Report can companies improve the usefulness of AGMs? (5.26)

Now try illustrative question 1 at the end of the Study Text

Chapter 2

MEETINGS: PRINCIPLES AND TYPES

This chapter covers the following topics.

1 General principles of meetings

2 Types of meeting

3 What is a public meeting?

4 Regulating the conduct of public meetings

5 Public Order Act 1986

6 Public Order Act 1936

7 Disorder on private premises

8 Admission of the press to meetings

Introduction

In this chapter we look at the general principles of law and practice relating to meetings including the distinction between public and private meetings, rights and restrictions regarding the holding of meetings, admission and preservation of order.

1 GENERAL PRINCIPLES OF MEETINGS

1.1 Meetings can be distinguished by **character** or **purpose**. The syllabus specifically includes 'the distinction between private and public meetings'. Meetings might also be classified according to the type of body or organisation holding them, the type of business to be conducted, the formality of the proceedings, the power given to the participants to make decisions and initiate action and so on.

1.2 As an illustration of the range of contrasts embraced in the general term 'meeting', take the cases of:

(a) A public meeting called in the town square to protest at some proposed development which causes much concern to local residents

(b) The essentially private meetings of a board of directors, held at regular intervals, attended by a small group of people, and concerned with reviewing the progress of and taking policy decisions on the continuing commercial enterprise of the company

1.3 What such meetings have in common is mainly that in each case a group of individuals gather to **exchange views** and to **seek agreement** on some matter of common concern. We might take this as a first broad definition of a meeting: 'two or more individuals coming together for the furtherance of common interests'.

1.4 In the case of *Sharp v Dawes 1876* a meeting was defined as:

> 'an assembly of people for a lawful purpose.'

From that brief description, we may draw some conclusions about the nature of a meeting.

Assembly of people

1.5 An '**assembly**' implies the presence of **more than one person** to constitute a meeting. There are some exceptions in the context of company meetings, where a single person may be treated as a 'meeting', but generally there must be at least two (which was the point in *Sharp v Dawes*).

1.6 'Assembly' also implies that the persons who constitute a meeting must be **present** in the **same place** at the **same time**. It is, however, arguable that if two or more persons in different places are in communication, for instance by telephone, there may be a meeting. Modern teleconferencing facilities enable several parties in different locations to have audio and visual contact with each other via video screens. Such methods have been sanctioned as a way of linking a meeting of large numbers of people seated in several different rooms in *Byng v London Life Association 1989* (discussed in a later chapter).

Purpose of meeting

1.7 The other key phrase in the definition quoted above is *purpose*. To constitute a meeting the assembly must have a common purpose. In the case of a meeting, however, there are various purposes for each person present.

(a) **Communicate** with (or at least to listen to) others who are also present with the same purpose

(b) **Reach a collective decision**

(c) **Express** a shared **opinion** on some matter with which they are all dealing

1.8 Finally, our definition requires the purpose of the meeting to be '**lawful**'. The implication is that persons who assemble for an unlawful purpose may often be committing a criminal offence by doing so. As an additional sanction to ensure that the law is observed, the proceedings of the gathering will be denied recognition or legal effect if the common purpose is not lawful.

Organisation and procedure

1.9 To achieve their purpose, those who attend a meeting must generally conform or respond to a measure of **organisation** and **procedure**.

(a) There is usually a **chairman**, or at least an organiser, who guides the proceedings of the meeting and aims to maintain order. A meeting can hardly function efficiently if it is or is allowed to become a Tower of Babel in which everybody talks at once.

(b) There is often a **sequence of business**, or at least of speeches, to express points of view or reach decisions on the common purpose of the meeting. It is not essential to formalise this point with an agenda, but private meetings usually do have one.

(c) The purpose of the meeting is achieved by **reaching some decision** or **expressing an opinion** at the end of the discussion. In some circumstances this may lead to taking a vote to determine what is the majority view.

2 TYPES OF MEETING

2.1 The main types of meeting considered in this Study Text are as follows.

(a) **Public meetings**. These are in some respects the oldest traditional type of meeting, from which private meetings derive some of their features in different form. Public meetings present a number of characteristic problems, to which further consideration is given in the remainder of this chapter.

(b) **Meetings of members of unincorporated bodies,** such as social clubs, sporting associations and other common interest societies or groups. These bodies usually have a constitution which includes rules for holding meetings, but they are unlikely to be elaborate.

In addition, meetings of the elected members of **local authorities** are of various types, from parish councils to county or metropolitan councils.

2.2 Much of the information in this Study Text is also relevant to meetings of registered companies such as general meetings and board meetings. However, these are included in the module *Company Secretarial Practice* and are covered in the BPP Study Text of that title.

Public and private meetings

2.3 The most fundamental distinction to be made is between **public meetings** and **private meetings** (such as those in categories (b) and (c) above).

2.4 A '**public' meeting** is not always held in a 'public' place. Admission may be controlled or limited in some way if the meeting is held in private premises. But generally speaking, a public meeting has the characteristics that:

(a) Admission is **not limited** by **membership** or other specific criteria; essentially it is open to any members of the public who may wish to attend.

(b) It is **not subject** to the **regulations** of a constituted body: there is no set procedure and common law rules apply.

2.5 In contrast to a public meeting, a '**private' meeting** is always held in a '**private' place**, with **admission restricted** to certain categories of people, such as members, and others to whom permission to attend is granted by the organisers of the meeting. The procedure, especially for company and local authority meetings, is regulated by articles of association, standing orders, bye-laws etc, and so there is a greater formality.

2.6 However, public and private meetings do share certain common features, such as the liabilities which may be incurred by anyone who is disorderly, or who makes defamatory statements.

3 WHAT IS A PUBLIC MEETING?

3.1 The Public Order Act 1986 does not contain a definition of a public meeting, so the most useful statutory definition is that contained in s 9 of the Public Order Act 1936: a public meeting is:

> 'any meeting in a public place and any meeting which the public or any section thereof are permitted to attend, either on payment or otherwise.'

Meeting

3.2 We must look at this definition a little more closely. A 'meeting' is an assembly for the purpose of:

- **Discussing matters** of public interest
- **Expressing views** on such matters

The definition may then apply to any number of persons meeting for a particular purpose - two persons could constitute a meeting.

Public place

3.3 A public meeting must be held in 'a public place'. Under s 16 Public Order Act 1986 this means any highway and any place to which the public or any section of the public has access, on payment or otherwise, as of right or by virtue of express or implied permission. Thus a public place may include:

- Highways and private roads
- Public transport, parks, gardens and footpaths
- Public offices, such as town halls
- Pubs, restaurants, hotels and shops
- Private clubs, dance-halls, cinemas etc where entry is by payment of a fee
- Private premises and land where presence is not an act of trespass

---

Exercise 1

By way of contrast, consider the annual general meeting of a club. Why is this not a public meeting?

Solution

(a) Only members (and perhaps others, such as press representatives, who have been duly invited) are able to attend.

(b) The meeting is likely to be on private premises, to allow the exclusion of other persons.

(c) The matters for discussion are the affairs of the club - which are not of general public interest.

Use of the highway

3.4 There is no satisfactory statutory definition of what constitutes a highway; at common law a highway can be said to be any way over which there is a **public right of passage**. If there is a right to close off a particular piece of land, then it may be prevented from being a highway; this is the case, for example, as regards the Piccadilly Circus underground station subways.

3.5 However, a merely temporary closing off may not be enough to prevent a way from being a highway; police restrictions imposed under the Metropolitan Police Act 1839 s 52 on a road during the Wapping industrial dispute were not enough to have this effect in *R v Dubbins 1986*, for instance, since the closing off had no great degree of finality, nor was it made (for example) under a court order.

3.6 The significance of whether a particular place is a highway lies in the fact that it is an offence to obstruct the free passage of the highway. S 137 Highways Act 1980 provides that 'if a person without lawful authority or excuse, in any way wilfully obstructs the free passage along a highway he shall be guilty of an offence.'

3.7 Since there is no specific right to hold a public meeting in a public place, s 137 is often invoked in situations involving picketing or other public demonstrations. The offence has three elements, concerning which there is now quite a body of relevant case law.

(a) **Without lawful authority or excuse**

Ordinary people may have difficulty in showing that they had 'lawful authority or excuse'. In particular, peaceful picketing does not provide a defence of lawful authority or excuse: *Broome v DPP 1974.* Police officers, by contrast, may (for example) set up road blocks or control traffic if the circumstances justify it: *Johnson v Phillips 1975.*

(b) **Wilfully**

This means simply 'by an exercise of his or her free will' (*Arrowsmith v Jenkins 1963*), in other words intentionally, not merely accidentally. The driver of a car, for instance, does not act 'wilfully' in accidentally knocking over a cyclist: *Eaton v Cobb 1950.*

(c) **Obstructs**

Whether a particular use of the highway can be said to be an obstruction is a moot point. The crux of the matter is whether this particular use of the highway is unreasonable having regard to all the circumstances, and whether it causes an actual (as opposed to a potential) obstruction: *Nagy v Weston 1966.*

3.8 In *Cooper v Metropolitan Police Commissioner 1986*, a club tout was convicted of the offence, having approached four separate groups of pedestrians in a thirteen minute period to engage them in conversation for 'a minute or so'. The result was that some members of the public had to step out into the roadway to pass by. In *Waite v Taylor 1985* a juggler using lit firebrands was convicted of the offence having juggled in the street.

3.9 In the *Waite* case the court described the test as follows: 'Where stopping on the highway cannot properly be said to be ancillary to or part and parcel of the exercise of one's right to pass and repass along the highway, then the obstruction becomes unreasonable and there is an obstruction contrary to the provisions of the subsection'.

3.10 This was a stricter test than was applied in Cooper's case, where the court held that the correct approach was firstly to decide (as a matter of common sense) whether there had been an obstruction at all (taking into account such factors as the duration of the alleged obstruction, its place, its purpose and whether it was an actual as opposed to potential obstruction in deciding whether or not it was reasonable). Then, having established *prima facie* obstruction, the court should consider whether the defendant was merely exercising his right to pass and re-pass along the highway.

> *Hirst and Another v Chief Constable of West Yorkshire Police 1986*
> *The facts:* Members of a group of animal rights campaigners exhibited banners bearing slogans and offered leaflets to passers-by in a large pedestrian precinct outside a furriers.
>
> *Decision:* The original conviction of the pickets was quashed on the grounds that the question of whether or not there had been lawful authority or excuse had not been considered. However the case is more important for its approval of the test laid down in Cooper's case, and its disapproval of the *Waite v Taylor* test as being too harsh. The test of reasonableness in *Nagy v Weston* was emphasised in the judgement, and the court also stated that the right to protest and demonstrate on matters of public concern is a right that is in the public interest that individuals should possess and exercise without impediment so long as no wrongful act is done and there is no impediment to traffic.

Particular public places

3.11 Despite the basic principle that an individual has a right to be in a public place, there are certain restrictions on an individual's presence in particular public places at particular times, in addition to the general principle that rights of passage on the highway take precedence over any other use of it. The following are examples.

(a) Many local authorities have **statutory delegated powers** to regulate the use of public places within their areas. It is common, for example, to publish notices at the entrance to gardens or parks to the effect that they are closed (to the public) between sunset and sunrise. There may also be regulations prohibiting any meeting on common land.

(b) The **Department of the Environment** has power to grant or refuse permission for holding meetings in Trafalgar Square.

(c) There is no right to hold a meeting in Hyde Park - prior permission must be obtained from the **relevant authority**.

3.12 In this context you may also note that local authorities frequently **let out rooms** in town halls etc, which are private places, for use in holding public meetings. In making these lettings the local authority, like any other owner of premises, may **impose conditions** as to the use to be made of them under the letting. This practice is, of course, different in its nature from regulating the use of public places; it is part of the general right of a landowner to treat as a trespasser anyone who comes on to his land without his permission.

Recent legislation

3.13 The Criminal Justice and Public Order Act 1994 contains provisions relating to trespass to land, powers in relation to rave parties, powers to deal with disruptive trespass, trespasser assemblies and squatters and powers to remove unauthorised campers.

4 REGULATING THE CONDUCT OF PUBLIC MEETINGS 12/99

4.1 A distinction has again to be made between public meetings which are held in public places, and those which are held in private premises.

(a) In a **public place** each person who is present at the meeting is exercising his **individual right** to be there at the time. The organisers of the meeting may have the initiative in steering proceedings through to the end but, unless a person commits a criminal offence, they cannot order him to withdraw from the meeting.

(b) If a public meeting is held on **private premises**, whether indoors or out of doors, the organisers should **conform** to whatever conditions the owner has laid down. Since there is no general right to be present, the organisers may also impose their own conditions, for example by granting admission only to those who have bought tickets. Provided that the sale of tickets is not narrowly restricted, it will still be a public meeting.

Just as permission is required for entry at the outset, the right of any person to remain until the end of the meeting ends if permission is later withdrawn. On that basis the chairman may order **any person** to **leave** the premises on which the meeting is held, though if the person has paid an admission charge, the organisers' right to remove him is often limited to specific circumstances.

Disorder at public meetings

4.2 It is an offence for any person to act in a **disorderly manner** at a lawful public meeting, or to incite others to do so, if the purpose of such action is to prevent the transaction of the business for which the meeting was called: Public Meetings Act 1908 s 1. Refusal to give name and address to a constable who, on the chairman's request, has required it to be given following suspicion of s 1 offences, is also an offence. The same prohibition as that in s 1 extends specifically to conduct at public meetings held in the course of election of a member of Parliament: Representation of the People Act 1983 s 97. Mere heckling or interruption of speakers will not generally suffice to bring these sanctions into play. Threats of violence might do so.

4.3 If trouble is anticipated, **stewards** may well be present to enforce the chairman's orders for expulsion, by reasonable force. This practice is recognised by the Public Order Act 1936 (s 2) which provides that it is lawful to appoint stewards 'to assist in the preservation of order at any public meeting held on private premises'. The same principle applies to a private meeting. However stewards have no greater protection under the law than anyone else if they use more force than is considered 'reasonable' in the expulsion of a trespasser. In addition stewards should not either wear a uniform denoting political affiliation or usurp the function of the police and armed forces.

4.4 The main responsibility for maintaining order at a meeting lies with the following persons.

(a) **The police**. The police have the duty and power to prevent a breach of the peace, anticipated or actual, in public places and, with some restrictions, in private premises. This is discussed further below.

(b) **The chairman of the meeting**. The chairman may be able to keep order by his own personal authority and tact. Should trouble be anticipated, he may have the support of appointed stewards, and may call in the police at need. Seating arrangements (such as separating antagonistic parties) directed by the chairman or stewards may also be helpful.

(c) **The organisers or promoters**. The organisers will be responsible for appointing stewards and arranging a police presence if necessary. They will also have considered whether the meeting is to be held on public or private premises, how large the meeting is to be, whether an admission fee is to be charged: the relevance of these factors to keeping order will be considered below. Particular attention should be paid to the terms stipulated by the lessor of premises, including fire and safety arrangements.

The role of the police

4.5 It is not the policy of the police to intervene at meetings on their own initiative, unless **breaches of the peace** (acts of violence, as distinct from mere interruptions) have occurred or seem likely to occur: *Thomas v Sawkins 1935*.

4.6 However, the chairman of a public meeting may request a police constable (who is already present or has been summoned for the purpose) to **take the name** and address of a person who is causing a disturbance of any kind. If the constable has reasonable grounds for suspecting that an offence has been or is being committed or attempted, and

(a) A summons for arrest is impracticable because he cannot ascertain the person's name.

(b) He doubts the name given to him.

(c) The address given cannot be ascertained and may be false.

(d) The person must be prevented from causing or suffering physical injury or causing loss or damage to property, then he may arrest without warrant: s 25 Police and Criminal Evidence Act 1984.

This is probably the main deterrent to disruptive behaviour at a meeting.

4.7 Those who have been excluded from a meeting may try to **force an entry.** To discourage this the law makes it an offence to use or threaten violence against any person or property (without lawful authority such as police or bailiffs may have) in order to gain entry to premises against the will of another person on those premises. It is also illegal to trespass while carrying a 'weapon of offence'. In these cases also the police may arrest without warrant: Criminal Law Act 1977 s 6.

4.8 The Public Order Act 1986 s 39 permits the police in certain specified circumstances to **direct trespassers** to leave land which they have entered as trespassers. Insofar as this relates to meetings, the specified circumstances are where:

- Two or more persons have entered the land as trespassers.
- They have the common purpose of residing there for any purpose.
- They cause damage or use threatening, abusive or insulting words or behaviour.

4.9 If 'disorder' at a meeting erupts into violence, such as fighting between incensed individuals or rival factions, there is said to be a breach of the peace. It is then the duty of the police to intervene and probably to make arrests.

5 PUBLIC ORDER ACT 1986

5.1 When does a meeting cease to be a meeting and become an outbreak of public disorder? It is to this question that the Public Order Act 1986 addresses itself.

5.2 The former common law offences of unlawful assembly, riot, rout and affray are abolished, and five new offences are created by the Act:

- Riot
- Violent disorder
- Affray
- Causing fear or provoking violence
- Causing harassment, alarm and distress

5.3 Where a whole meeting becomes so inflamed that there is or is likely to be violence or breach of the peace, these sanctions may be used as penalties against the collective action of the meeting. For example, a meeting of workers on strike may resolve to force an entry to their place of work in order to occupy it or to damage property.

Riot (s 1)

5.4 Statutory riot occurs when **twelve** or more persons present together in a public or private place use or threaten to use **unlawful violence** for a **common purpose** such as would cause a person of reasonable firmness present at the scene to **fear** for his **personal safety**. The prosecution need not show that such a person was actually present and so affected, and they actually use violence for the common purpose.

5.5 The requirements as to there being 'persons present together' and a 'common purpose' mean that both their presence and their activity should be proximate in time and place. The essential ingredient of riot is the aggravated seriousness of violent behaviour where committed collectively by a crowd of like-minded persons whatever the role of the individual participants may be.

5.6 The common purpose which is an essential part of riot may be inferred from the conduct of the offenders. It need not be shown that the conduct on which the charge is based was simultaneous on the part of the 12 or more persons present: a sequence of individual acts may be taken into account.

5.7 'Violence' includes violent conduct towards persons or property: s 8. It includes actions which actively cause or which are intended to cause injury or damage, and other forms of violent conduct, such as throwing stones, which may cause injury or damage. Firing a gun at someone or brandishing a knife is threatened violence, as are shouted threats, but mere 'abuse, swearing and shouting' in order to intimidate is not threatened violence: *News Group Newspapers Ltd v SOGAT (1982) 1986*.

5.8 Unless he has used violence, a person who takes part in a riot may not be prosecuted on that account, though he may be guilty of lesser offences.

Violent disorder (s 2)

5.9 This differs from riot in three main respects.

(a) It need only be shown that **three** or more persons were present, in circumstances which would otherwise be riot (by twelve). As emphasised in *R v Worton 1989*, this means that if one of three defendants is found not guilty, then the other two must also be acquitted.

(b) **Common purpose** need **not** be shown.

(c) The mere **threat** of sufficient violence can be an offence as can, of course, its use.

5.10 The offence of violent disorder is intended to replace the old common law offence of unlawful assembly. It is intended to be used as the normal charge in serious outbreaks of public disorder, where riot is too heavy a charge.

Affray (s 3)

5.11 Even **one person** may be guilty of affray if he uses or threatens violence so as to cause a person of reasonable firmness to fear for his personal safety. However if only threats are alleged as the charge, there must have been more than mere use of threatening words.

5.12 Affray has often been used as a charge where there has been a fight, for instance outside a pub. It is a means of obtaining a criminal conviction where the individual roles of the participants have been difficult to identify.

Causing fear or provoking violence (s 4)

5.13 This is a new offence whose title explains itself. However, it is not an offence if the person at fault and the persons exposed to his conduct were all within a dwelling; it is not an offence within a domestic context, although it can take place in a private place.

5.14 The offender must use **threatening, abusive** or **insulting words** or behaviour towards another person, intending that other person to believe that immediate unlawful violence will ensue or intending to provoke such violence. The offence extends to writing, signs or other visible representations which are threatening, abusive or insulting.

Disorderly conduct (s 5)

5.15 This is the lowest-level public order offence, penalising **threatening, abusive or insulting words or behaviour**, or disorderly words or behaviour within the hearing or sight of a person likely to be caused harassment, alarm or distress. The offender need not intend these effects, and harassment etc should only be likely, not proven.

5.16 Like s 4, conduct entirely within a dwelling is excluded from the offence, though it may occur in a private place which is not a 'dwelling'. There are certain statutory defences, such as that the defendant's conduct was 'reasonable'.

Mental elements

5.17 Except for s 5, the prosecution must show that the defendant **intended** or was aware that his conduct would have the effect which constitutes the offence: s 6.

Processions and assemblies (ss 11-16)

5.18 Police powers, previously conferred by s 3 of the Public Order Act 1936, are redefined in more precise terms. The following innovations should be noted.

(a) **Six days' notice** must be given to the police of intention to hold a procession (s 11). No advance notice is required of an assembly.

(b) A senior police officer (the Chief Constable or Metropolitan Police Commissioner, or the most senior police officer at the scene) may impose **conditions** on a procession if he believes that the procession may otherwise result in serious public disorder, in serious damage to property, in serious disruption to the life of the community or that the organiser's purpose is the intimidation of others: s 12.

(c) If the s 12 powers are deemed insufficient to prevent serious public disorder, the chief police officer must **ban** the procession: s 13.

(d) A senior police officer has power to **impose conditions** in relation to a **public assembly**: s 14.

(e) A public assembly is an assembly of **twenty or more persons** in a public place which is wholly or partly open to the air: s 16.

Racial hatred (ss 17-19)

5.19 There are new provisions to replace part of the Race Relations Act 1976 (incorporated in the Public Order Act 1936 as s 5A).

(a) It is an offence to use words or behaviour or to display material intended or likely to stir up **racial hatred.**

(b) '**Display**' includes the performance of a play, showing an oral or visual recording, and making a broadcast.

(c) It is an offence to be in **possession** of such material, and there are powers to seize or forfeit it: s 30.

5.20 These provisions apply to both public and private places, except dwellings.

Disorder at football matches

5.21 In appropriate cases, the court may make orders to exclude persons convicted of relevant offences from attending matches at designated grounds.

6 PUBLIC ORDER ACT 1936

6.1 The Public Order Act 1936 bans quasi-military organisations, the carrying and display of offensive weapons, and the wearing of uniforms by political bodies. The following practices, however, are still lawful:

(a) The employment of **stewards,** wearing badges for identification, to assist in maintaining order at meetings on private premises

(b) The wearing of uniforms by **private bodies,** such as the Salvation Army, if they have no political purpose

7 DISORDER ON PRIVATE PREMISES 6/98

7.1 The main responsibility for maintaining order at a meeting which is held on private premises, (whether it is a public or a private meeting) rests on the **organiser(s)** of the meeting. As no one has a general right, as a member of the public, to enter private premises, anyone who enters **without leave**, or persists in remaining after the original leave to be present has been withdrawn, is a trespasser, who may be ejected from the premises by **reasonable force.**

7.2 If an individual has entered the premises with permission to do so, and the organiser later wishes to withdraw his permission for the individual to remain there, an important distinction will have to be made.

(a) If leave was granted **without** payment of an **entrance fee**, the leave may be withdrawn without any reason being given. In terms of contract law, there is no 'consideration' and hence no binding obligation to continue the leave which was previously given.

Lucas v Mason 1875
The facts: A public meeting held on private premises was becoming disorderly. The chairman instructed the stewards to remove those who were causing the disturbance. Lucas, who was not in fact a party to the disorder, was forcibly removed. He sued the chairman for assault and battery.

Decision: L's claim against the chairman must be dismissed as the chairman had not instructed that L in particular be removed. L might have sued the stewards - for assault - but he could not have maintained a claim that he was entitled in any event to remain on the premises.

Marshall v Tinnelly 1937
The facts: A chairman presiding at a meeting of a local authority had a member removed because he was being disorderly and refused to withdraw. M sued the chairman for assault.

Decision: The order for M's removal was within the chairman's powers.

(b) If payment has been made for admission the person who makes it is entitled to remain, so that leave to be present cannot be withdrawn until the purpose for which the leave was granted has been fulfilled. The case below does not relate to admission to a meeting, but does illustrate the point about leave granted in return for a **payment**.

Hurst v Picture Theatres Ltd 1915
The facts: Hurst paid for admission to a cinema but before the film show was over he was asked to leave, on the ground that he had not paid for his seat (as it was thought).

Decision: This was breach of a binding agreement that H should remain until the show was over. He recovered damages of £150. In this instance there was no allegation of forcible removal.

7.3 Hurst's case does not mean that once a person has been admitted on payment, he has an unqualified right to remain.

(a) He must **conform** to the **conditions** of admission by behaving in an orderly manner.

(b) If he **deceives** those responsible into allowing him entry, for instance by lying about his age in a nightclub, they may require him to leave since no binding obligation arises from having accepted his entrance money in those circumstances.

↳ contract becomes a nullity.

Police intervention on private premises

7.4 When the organiser of a meeting (or other function) on private premises invites the police to enter, or when the police themselves insist on entering to maintain or restore order, various aspects of the situation will have to be taken into account.

(a) The police may **decline** to assist in ejecting a trespasser. Unless there is a breach of the peace, which is a criminal offence, the police are not concerned with the purely civil rights of an occupier against a trespasser (but remember criminal trespass: s 39 1986 Act).

(b) If, however, there has been a **breach of the peace**, a police officer may arrest without warrant, and without having witnessed the incident himself, provided that he reasonably expects that it may continue or be repeated. This is so even if no member of the public is present: *McConnell v Chief Constable of Greater Manchester Police 1989*.

(c) The police have **no general right** to **enter private premises** against the wishes of the occupier. But if the police reasonably expect that a breach of the peace may occur, it is their right and duty to enter and remain, despite the opposition of the occupier. *Thomas v Sawkins 1935.*

Breach of the peace

7.5 The police must exercise their judgement as to what is or is likely to become a 'breach of the peace', as this is not a defined term. What is known as the 'Queen's Peace' is reckoned to be the normal state of tranquillity of a civilised community. A brawl, and still more acts of violence or assault, are clearly breaches of that state. In a less obvious case, if the police judge that a situation is likely to get out of hand and result in actual violence, they are entitled to order those involved to stop. If the antagonists refuse to do so, they are obstructing the police in the course of their duty: *Duncan v Jones 1936*. It is worth noting, however, that mere interruption and heckling of speakers at a meeting is not a breach of the peace: *Wooding v Oxley 1839*.

8 ADMISSION OF THE PRESS TO MEETINGS **6/96, 6/98, 12/99**

8.1 'The Press' includes representatives of all news and broadcasting media: TV, radio, newsagency, newspapers and journals etc.

8.2 Meetings of local authorities are in a special category, but in other circumstances the press has exactly the same right to attend meetings as any other member of the public.

(a) If a public meeting is held in a public place, anyone (including a representative of the press) may exercise his **right** to be there, as long as his behaviour is within the law.

(b) If a meeting, public or private, is held on private premises, the organisers may:

(i) **Decide whom to admit** (which may or may not include press representatives);

(ii) **Require the press**, in the same circumstances as anyone else, to **leave** before the end of the meeting

---

Exercise 2

You may have attended what you thought was a public meeting. Did it fulfil the definition of a public meeting given in this chapter?

Chapter roundup

- **Meetings** as such are not defined by statute law, but case law has called a meeting 'an assembly of people for a lawful purpose'.
- There are four main **types** of meeting.
  - A public meeting
  - A meeting of an unincorporated body
  - A meeting of a registered body (such as a company)
  - A meeting of elected members of local authorities

  The distinction between public and private meetings is particularly important.
- It is also important to understand the nature and significance of a **public meeting**, particularly regarding public meetings in a public place as opposed to on private premises. The responsibility for disorder as such meetings is that of the organiser, the chairman and (to some extent) the police.
- **Public disorder** - riot, violent disorder, affray, causing fear and causing harassment, alarm and distress - constitutes offences even when there is no meeting or when it is not public.
- The police have certain **powers** in relation to processions and assemblies which you should note.
- Action in respect of **disorder on private premises** can hinge on whether or not an entrance fee was paid; the role of the police is different in these cases.

Test your knowledge

1. What is a meeting? (see paras 1.4, 3.2)
2. Give examples of the different kinds of meeting. (2.1)
3. Define a public meeting. (3.1)
4. What factors affect the right to hold a public meeting on the highway? (3.4 - 3.10)
5. How may the organisers of a public meeting seek to regulate its conduct? (4.1)
6. What are the basic legal sanctions against disorder at a public meeting? (4.2 - 4.4)
7. What are the ways in which the police have a role to play in the conduct of public meetings? (4.5 - 4.9)
8. Explain the statutory offences of (a) riot (b) violent disorder and (c) affray. (5.4, 5.9, 5.11)
9. What powers have the police in relation to processions? (5.18)
10. What are the main provisions of the Public Order Act 1936? (6.1)
11. To what extent may a person attending a meeting held on private premises be required to withdraw? (7.2)
12. What are the powers and duties of the police in connection with disputes and disorder at meetings on private premises? (7.4)
13. What is meant by a breach of the peace? (7.5)
14. What general rights have representatives of the press to attend meetings? (8.2)

Now try illustrative question 2 at the end of the Study Text

Chapter 3

THE CONDUCT OF MEETINGS

This chapter covers the following topics.

Introduction

This chapter is the first of several dealing with the conduct and management of meetings. Subsequent chapters deal in more detail with some of the topics introduced here: agenda is the subject of Chapter 4; motions, amendments and adjournments are covered in Chapter 5, minutes are discussed in chapter 6 and the duties of the chairman are dealt with in Chapter 7.

1 THE CONDUCT OF DIFFERENT TYPES OF MEETING **6/96, 12/99**

1.1 Much of the previous chapter dealt with aspects of public meetings. Characteristically, a random collection of people attend such meetings, and there is little formal organisation and procedure.

(a) The organisers may encounter **opposition** to their plans but it is they who decide how, in outline, the meeting will be conducted.

(b) The outcome of a public meeting is an **expression of opinion,** which may influence subsequent events but is not a binding decision.

(c) Partly because of the unrestricted right to attend and the lack of set procedure, a public meeting is more subject to the risk of **disruption** than other types of meeting.

1.2 There is no requirement that a private meeting shall be organised and conducted under set rules of procedure even if it is about a matter of public concern and leads to collective action. No one will thus be able to claim that the outcome of the discussion is invalid because of some procedural defect. Private meetings of this unstructured variety are not important in the context of a study of the law and procedure of meetings.

1.3 The more important type of private meeting however is that of an **established body**, such as a registered company, a club or association or a local authority. These meetings do produce binding decisions. As a safeguard to those who take part in them, in particular to a minority which disagrees with the majority view, it is always necessary to have elaborate regulations on the proceedings of the meetings.

1.4 These regulations may be standing orders, bye-laws, membership rules or articles of association. They vary according to the nature of the body which adopts them. For example, a company usually has a 'share capital' and members' votes are related to their shareholdings. Other bodies usually have a simple system of 'one man one vote'.

1.5 If there is a serious breach of those rules, the proceedings of the meeting are not valid and may be challenged.

2 REQUISITES OF A VALID MEETING

2.1 Regulations (of whatever type) for holding a meeting usually provide for:

(a) Properly **convening** the meeting

(b) How the meeting is **constituted**

(c) How the meeting is **conducted**

(d) Keeping a **proper record** of the proceedings, if the decisions reached at the meeting are to be applied later

2.2 The regulations do not deal with every detail, particularly as regards the course of debate at the meeting; generally accepted practice will usually be a sufficient guide for the organisers and chairman of the meeting. If the regulations do lay down specific requirements, however, they must be observed.

2.3 We will now go on to look at the convening, constitution and conduct of meetings in more detail.

3 CONVENING A MEETING: NOTICE 12/99

3.1 There are two main ways of convening or 'calling together' a meeting.

- '**Automatically**', without initiating action by the organiser on each occasion
- By **issuing a notice** of each meeting

3.2 If a meeting is one of a series or cycle of similar gatherings, it may simply be held at pre-arranged dates and times, and in the same place. A bowls club, for example, may adopt the practice of holding a meeting of members at the clubhouse at 10 am on the first Saturday of each month. Everyone knows that there will be such a meeting and it is unnecessary to issue a notice on each occasion.

3.3 Some company boards of directors adopt this kind of practice (though it is more usual to issue an agenda for each meeting, which also serves as a reminder and a notice that it is taking place).

Notice of meetings

3.4 The second option requires the organiser to 'call' each meeting by issuing a notice. In this case the regulations usually specify the following procedures.

(a) A notice to convene a meeting is to be issued on the authority of, say, the management committee (or board of directors of a company). It is also sometimes provided that:

- The chairman may convene meetings.

- Any member may require the managing body to call a meeting.

 The essential point is that a notice should only be issued by **proper authority**. If the secretary issues an unauthorised notice, it must be ratified before the date of the meeting.

(b) There may be a **minimum period of notice**, such as 21 'clear days' interval between the issue of the notice and the date fixed for the meeting. This is an important feature of company general meetings, for which the period of notice is fixed by law. In addition the Hampel report endorsed ICSA's recommendation that notice of the AGM should be circulated at least 20 working days in advance of the meeting.

(c) A notice is 'served' when it **reaches** (or is 'deemed' to reach) the person entitled to it. If it is sent by post, it is served when it arrives at the correct address, or after an interval specified by the regulations (eg 48 hours after posting). If notice is published by advertisement, notice board etc, it is served when it appears - no matter when the person concerned actually got round to seeing it.

(d) The notice must at least say **where and when** the meeting is to be held. Some information about the business to be done at the meeting may also be required, and the notice and agenda are often drawn up and distributed together.

(e) The notice must be **displayed or published**, or **copies sent** to individuals who are entitled to receive it, in the way prescribed by the regulations, eg through the post, by courier, by fax etc. The meeting may be invalidated if someone who is entitled to receive notice of the meeting has not received it: *Young v Ladies Imperial Club 1920.* The regulations should be specific on this point: they may, for example, provide that an accidental failure to send (or receive) notice of a meeting will not invalidate the meeting - though 'accidental' is likely to be open to interpretation.

3.5 Many organisations contain a statement in their constitutions that proof of posting of notice is conclusive evidence that notice was given. It is worth considering changing such regulations to read '**proof of sending**', since then more flexible means of notice, such as by fax, can be used. Without such a regulation the position is that notice by fax is only good service if it can be shown that the document was actually received, complete and legible, by the intended recipient: *Hastie and Jenkerson v MacMahon 1990.*

3.6 Unless a meeting is convened in accordance with requirements laid down, it is not a proper meeting and its proceedings may be invalid on that account.

4 CONSTITUTING A MEETING

4.1 A meeting which has been properly convened may only proceed to business if it has been properly 'constituted', that is if it is 'made up' in a certain way.

(a) A meeting must be **chaired**. We shall be using the term 'chairman' in this study text, referring equally to both sexes.

(b) A **minimum** number of persons (called a 'quorum'), as prescribed by the regulations, must be **present**.

5 QUORUM

5.1 A meeting ordinarily requires at **least two individuals** (who are entitled to take part in the proceedings) to be present.

5.2 In some exceptional situations company law recognises one person as a meeting. For example, if a company holds a 'class meeting' and all the shares of the class are held by one person, that person will be recognised as a meeting. A committee of one person may be appointed. One person may also constitute a meeting if the company is a single member private company.

5.3 The quorum for a meeting is fixed by the **regulations**, at the customary minimum of two or some higher figure. The regulations usually also permit a representative of an absent member (a 'proxy' in company law) to be counted when making up a quorum.

5.4 If the regulations do not fix a quorum, and none can be deduced from the usual practice of the body holding the meeting, the rule is that a quorum is that number which makes up **more than half the total membership**. So 8 would be a quorum if there were 15 members.

(You should note, however, that if powers are delegated to a committee, without fixing a quorum, the powers may only be exercised by all the members of the committee, who must assemble for that purpose.)

5.5 The mere presence of the number of persons required to make a quorum is sometimes not sufficient.

(a) The individuals who make up the quorum must attend with the **intention** of thereby constituting a meeting.

Baron v Potter 1914
The facts: There were only two directors of the company (B and P) and the quorum had been fixed at two. However P refused to attend board meetings. B waylaid P as he arrived at Paddington Station by train, called a meeting on the spot and purported to use his casting vote to carry a resolution as he chased P across the platform. P demurred.

Decision: As no proper notice had been given, P was entitled to say that his 'presence' did not amount to 'attendance' at a board meeting. As there was therefore no quorum, B's resolution had not been carried.

(b) A director of a company and a member of a local authority are often **disqualified** from voting on a matter in which they have a personal interest. If they are not allowed to vote, they **cannot** be counted towards a **quorum** for that item of business, unless the regulations provide otherwise.

5.6 The regulations usually provide that if there is no quorum at the appointed time for the meeting, there may be a brief delay to allow for late arrivals. If there is still no quorum, the meeting is **automatically adjourned** to another day, or dissolved altogether.

5.7 It is generally necessary to maintain a quorum throughout the meeting: the regulations should be specific on this point.

5.8 A meeting may have mustered a quorum when it commences or 'proceeds to' business, but may then lose it due to:

(a) The **departure** of one or more individuals, so that the number present is less than the quorum

(b) The **disqualification** of an 'interested party' from voting on a particular matter, leaving less than a quorum eligible to vote on that item of business

In such circumstances, the meeting should adjourn without completing its unfinished business, unless the regulations provide otherwise.

Exercise 1

Explain the importance of a 'quorum' in the context of the law of meetings and give examples of absence or inadequacy of the quorum.

Solution

In *Sharp v Dawes 1876*, a meeting was defined as a group of persons who have gathered together for a lawful purpose. From this brief description, we can draw certain conclusions about the nature of a meeting. The most obvious of these is that a meeting ordinarily requires at least two individuals to be present, both of whom are entitled to take part in the proceedings (although there are examples, such as a company class meeting where all the shares of the class are held by one individual, where one person can legally constitute a meeting). In addition to this basic rule, regulations (of one sort or another) will usually fix a minimum number of persons who must be present at a meeting of the particular organisation for that meeting to be validly constituted and therefore to have legal effect. This minimum number is called a *quorum*.

The number at which the quorum is fixed will vary from organisation to organisation. The standard quorum for a company meeting under the model Table A regulations is 'two persons entitled to vote upon the business to be transacted, each being a member or a proxy for a member or a duly authorised representative of a corporation'. However there is nothing to prevent the articles fixing a higher number. In the case of single member private limited companies, the quorum may be one. The normal quorum for a local government meeting is one-quarter of all the members; if there is no quorum fixed by the regulations, the rule is that it should be that number which makes up more than half the total membership.

The significance of a quorum is that, generally speaking, its absence will result in the meeting being improperly constituted and therefore without legal effect if its validity is challenged. For this reason, the regulations usually provide that if there is no quorum present at the time prescribed for the start of a meeting, a short period will be allowed for late arrivals, at the end of which (if there is still no quorum present) the meeting must be adjourned. The intention is, along with other provisions on the giving of proper notice, etc, to ensure that a meeting which is empowered to make decisions binding on all its members is a forum for proper discussion, not a mere vehicle for a small and possibly unrepresentative minority to enforce its views on the majority.

There are a number of examples of the absence or inadequacy of a quorum. They range from the obvious (where only one person or too small a number of persons are present) to the rather more subtle. One example is derived from *Baron v Potter 1914*, where a director waylaid another (who had been refusing to attend meetings) on Paddington station and purported to hold a meeting as the two ran along the platform. Although the quorum for board meetings was two, and two people were indeed present, there was no quorum because one of the directors had not attended with the intention of thereby constituting a meeting. It is therefore immaterial how many persons are present if they have been tricked into attending or are there by accident. Another situation might be where a number of directors are disqualified from voting on a particular motion at a board meeting due to having a personal interest in the matter under discussion, since such a disqualification also disqualifies them from being reckoned amongst the quorum. Should the situation be that the number of directors who may be reckoned in the quorum is below the required number, an interesting situation arises, by which the remaining directors can continue to act, but only for the purpose of filling vacancies or calling a general meeting. This is one of the rare occasions on which an inquorate meeting may continue to act, albeit with its powers severely curtailed.

6 AGENDA — 12/99

6.1 A meeting should (and can effectively) only discuss one subject at a time. If its business includes more than one item, the items will have to be taken in sequence. Hence it is standard practice to draw up a list (called 'an agenda' - Latin for 'things to be done') of the various items of business of a meeting.

6.2 The agenda is usually distributed to those participating in the meeting, so that:

(a) Everyone knows the **subject** of the business to be covered at the meeting, and can prepare speeches, questions etc accordingly.

(b) Everyone knows the **order** of business, and can if necessary arrange to attend only the relevant session of the meeting.

(c) The chairman can keep the meeting to a **schedule**, and within a framework for debate, of which everyone is already aware.

6.3 There are two ways of distributing an agenda.

(a) It may be sent out with the **notice** convening the meeting, or form part of the notice, if that gives the details of business to be done.

(b) Copies of the agenda may be **distributed** to members as they **arrive** for the meeting (though the chairman should have his special, annotated copy in advance).

6.4 The drafting of agenda of different types requires discussion and illustration, which are provided in a later chapter: it is one of the main tasks of a secretary.

7 MOTIONS AND RESOLUTIONS 6/96

7.1 It is always helpful if each item of business is put before the meeting in the form of a **proposal** which defines:

- The **matter** for discussion
- The **point** to be decided, in straightforward 'yea or nay' terms

If a decision is required, this becomes essential, so that those voting know beforehand exactly what is being proposed, and can confirm afterwards exactly what was decided.

7.2 Even an item of information laid before a meeting can be given in the form of a proposal: eg 'To receive the annual accounts for the year ended ...'.

7.3 The agenda may set out the proposal in full, or may simply indicate the subject on which a proposal will be made ('To elect members of the management committee').

7.4 The proposal put to a meeting is 'a **motion**' and if it is '**carried**' (approved) it becomes a '**resolution**' (decision). The 'original motion' is sometimes 'amended' (altered) in the course of debate and then carried in altered form as a 'substantive motion'. These points are considered in a later chapter.

8 CONDUCT OF DEBATE 6/96, 12/99

8.1 If there is more than one item of business on an agenda, and each is to be considered and voted on separately, the chairman's task is to **guide** the meeting through a sequence of short debates.

8.2 To begin a debate, the relevant motion must be **proposed**. It may fall to the chairman to do this, or it may be the task of some other officeholder, such as the treasurer. If the regulations permit, other members may propose motions *ad hoc*, as long as they are within the limits set by the notice for the business to be done at the meeting.

> *Choppington Collieries Ltd v Johnson 1944*
> *The facts:* The notice of a company general meeting listed its business to include 'election of directors' and indicated that the re-election of a director who was retiring by rotation would be proposed. At the meeting a member proposed the election of other persons as directors and this was carried.
>
> *Decision:* The motion was within the scope of the notice and had been properly proposed.

8.3 The regulations often require, however, that a member who intends to move a motion shall give **written notice** of it in advance of the meeting. It is in any case advisable that he should hand the chairman a written copy of his proposal, to prevent any misunderstanding of his meaning or intention.

8.4 Unless the regulations require it, there is no need to 'second' a motion for debate. But it is a convention that when a motion has been proposed, someone else formally declares his support, saying: 'I second the motion'. This may keep unsupported and time-wasting motions (obviously 'crackpot' proposals, or private hobby-horses of individual members) from cluttering up the agenda.

9 THE CHAIRMAN 6/96, 6/98, 12/99

9.1 The conduct of the general discussion is the most demanding test of a chairman's skill and judgement. He has some fundamental duties.

(a) Preserving order in the meeting, so that its business can proceed without hindrance, preventing people from growing frustrated or angry, interrupting or heckling etc

(b) Appearing fair and impartial

9.2 His task will be much more difficult if the meeting becomes antagonistic towards him or even loses confidence in his ability to keep the situation under control. He should be conciliatory but firm, perhaps letting some minor point of procedure pass unchallenged rather than provoke indignation.

9.3 In terms of procedure, the chairman should carry out the following.

(a) **Keep** the meeting to the **agenda**. Business should be taken in the set order - unless the meeting agrees on some variation. A topic should only be discussed when the motion is properly put to the meeting. Once before the meeting, a motion cannot be withdrawn without the consent of the meeting.

(b) Insist that only **one person** at a time may address the meeting. If more than one person at a time indicates that he wishes to speak eg by rising in his place or raising a hand, the chairman decides who is to speak next and usually calls on him by name. The other(s) must wait their turn. If opinion at the meeting is sharply divided, it may be tactful to call on speakers from each side in turn, so that neither side appears to be obtaining an unfair amount of time and attention.

9.4 The problems which may confront the chairman include the following.

(a) A speaker may be **provocative** or even abusive in his language, or may speak **at great length** (making the meeting grow restive) or may **stray** from the subject under debate. In any such case the chairman should give a warning and, if it is not heeded, require the speaker to be silent.

(b) If a speaker begins to address **someone other** than the chairman - 'I challenge Mr Smith to say ....' the chairman should intervene to remind him that all speeches should be addressed to the chair - 'Mr Chairman, I urge the meeting ....'.

(c) There may be **interruptions** of various kinds. If someone seeks to intervene in the debate, he must be told to wait until it is his turn to speak, or until the relevant motion comes before the meeting. Only if someone seeks to raise 'a **point of order**', which is an alleged procedural irregularity, should the chairman give a ruling at once. If there are disruptive remarks ('Rubbish' or even repeated cries of 'Hear Hear') the person who makes them should be warned that unless he is silent he will be asked to leave the meeting.

9.5 There can also be procedural problems over who is permitted to speak at the meeting.

(a) At some company meetings **proxies** or 'stand-ins' for absent members have the right to be present - but not to speak. The speaker's identity should therefore be established: it is in any case useful to require a speaker to give his name before he begins his speech. The chairman may sometimes find it tactful to allow a person who has no right to speak a brief opportunity to make his point.

(b) As a general rule no one may speak **more than once** in a debate on a particular subject. But:

 (i) The **proposer** of a motion (not of an amendment) is sometimes permitted to reply to the debate before the vote is taken.

 (ii) The chairman may request a speaker to give an **explanation**.

 (iii) Anyone may raise a **point of order** at any time.

(iv) If a large body, such as a local authority, '**goes into committee**' to discuss a document in detail, clause by clause, members may speak (at moderate length) more than once.

9.6 The purpose of a debate is to ascertain 'the **sense of the meeting**'. Hence the chairman, with an eye for the timetable and the number of remaining items on the agenda, may have to cut short the debate, once he considers that every point of view has had enough of an airing. If he wishes to do so, he may call on the proposer to reply to the debate, or he may sum up himself. Much depends on the regulations.

9.7 '**Procedural motions**', which are described in a later chapter, are a device by which the meeting itself may cut short a debate, if that is the wish of the majority. The chairman should take care, however, not to suppress a discussion which may still be constructive, and should also make sure that minority viewpoints have been allowed fair expression.

10 VOTING **6/96**

10.1 Voting is the means by which participants in a meeting may inform the chairman of their decision with regard to a motion.

Method of voting

10.2 In some small informal meetings it is not considered necessary to have a vote on the motion. At an amicable board meeting the chairman may look round the table, saying something like: 'Well, I think we are all agreed ...' and, unless there is dissent, the discussion will close at that point; the minutes will record that 'It was resolved'. Where everybody agrees - where there is unanimity - it is pointlessly time-consuming to take a formal vote.

10.3 If it is necessary (or usual in practice) to vote on a motion, there are the following alternative methods of doing so, the choice of which may be determined for the meeting by the regulations governing it.

(a) **Show of hands.** At the invitation of the chairman, those 'in favour' raise a hand (to be counted) and then 'those against' do so, and the chairman declares the result of his count of hands raised. This is a 'one man, one vote' system, obviously requiring the presence of the individual (or his appointed proxy, if the regulations allow). The chairman's declaration of the result is final, unless a poll is demanded.

(b) **A poll**. This is a feature of company voting procedures. Essentially each person who is entitled to vote does so in writing (on an individual voting paper or on a polling list), indicating the number of votes which he is casting, in proportion to his shareholding (not necessarily 'one man, one vote'). The recording of the vote in some documentary form is an essential feature of a poll: *R v How 1863*.

(c) **A ballot**. This is similar to a poll, but each voter completes an individual voting paper in secrecy, and puts it folded into a ballot box, to be counted later. Parliamentary and local government elections follow this procedure.

(d) **A division**. Those present rise from their places and walk into separate 'lobbies' ('For' and 'Against') where their numbers are counted by 'tellers' and reported to the chairman. This is the method used in Parliament and in the Synod of the Church of England.

(e) **A voice vote, or 'vote by acclamation'**. The chairman calls for those in favour to say 'Aye' and those against to say 'No' and determines the result by the apparent volume of votes. You will appreciate that the inaccuracy of this method makes it unsuitable for any business other than, for example, conventional votes of thanks, or matters on which there is almost certainly unanimous feeling.

10.4 Whatever the method of voting, the chairman **declares** the **result** and this should be entered in the minutes as a record. Once an item of business is concluded, it cannot be raised again, nor the debate re-opened, in the same meeting.

11 POINTS OF ORDER 6/96, 6/98

11.1 Once a meeting has commenced or 'proceeded to' business, and especially if that business includes binding decisions, it is essential to ensure that:

- The proceedings of the meeting are valid.
- The members are protected from the 'manipulation' of procedure by any party.

This is why the observance of the standing orders or regulations is so important. If any member finds or suspects some irregularity in the convening, constitution or conduct of the meeting, he can submit an objection to the chairman. This is called a **point of order.**

11.2 A point of order may be raised by any member (even if he has already spoken in the debate), at any time and without notice. The person speaking at the time must allow himself to be interrupted, and sit down. A point of order is not generally open to discussion, but the chairman may invite brief remarks from other members.

11.3 The decision on any allegations of irregularity rests with the **chairman**; his ruling must be immediate, and should be accepted by the meeting. (Legal proceedings may be instituted after the meeting to have a chairman's ruling annulled, but this is only likely if it can be proved that the chairman was not acting in good faith, and that hardship was caused by his ruling.)

11.4 The point of order is disposed of by the chairman's decision, and the member who was interrupted by it may simply resume, unless of course the ruling has been against his right to speak.

11.5 Common objections which may be raised as points of order include:

(a) A **defect in the convening** or constitution of the meeting: insufficient notice, or lack of quorum

(b) Other **breach of the regulations**; a motion has not been seconded as required; a member is attempting to speak or vote without the right to do so; the chairman is attempting to adjourn without the meeting's consent etc

(c) A **defect in the motion** or amendment before the meeting: it is beyond the scope of the notice, or outside the power or terms of reference of the meeting (*ultra vires*)

(d) The use of **improper language**

12 ACCEPTED RULES OF DEBATE 6/96, 6/98

12.1 The following is a useful checklist which shows the generally accepted rules of debate.

- The debate should be **related** to a **motion** which has been proposed for discussion.
- By convention, a motion is also usually **seconded** but this is not essential.
- Only **one person** at a time may address the meeting on the motion before it.
- The chairman decides on the **order** in which members are to speak.
- Speakers **address** themselves to the **chairman**, not directly to others.
- All present should **defer** to **rulings** by the chairman, such as on points of order.
- The business should be taken in the **order** in which it appears on the **agenda**. The chairman may propose and the meeting agree to alter the order of business.
- Each person present may speak **only once**; a proposer of a motion is allowed to reply.

- Unless motions are set out elsewhere, they should be **put forward in writing**.
- The **chairman decides** whether an **amendment** may be accepted for debate.
- A **point of order** may be taken at any time, for immediate decision by the chairman.

Exercise 2

Have you attended any meetings? Can you comment on their conduct compared to the contents of this chapter?

Chapter roundup

- If a meeting fails to follow the **rules** for the general conduct of a meeting, its validity may be challenged and its decisions nullified. Much depends on whether it is a private or a public meeting.
- Regulations generally require that a meeting, in order to be valid, should be properly *convened,* **constituted, conducted and recorded.** In these respects the common law rules as to notice, quorum, motions, debate and the role of the chairman, voting and points of order should be followed.

Test your knowledge

1 Outline some differences of procedure between public and private meetings. (see paras 1.1 - 1.3)

2 What is meant by saying that a meeting should be properly convened, constituted and conducted? (2.2, 3.1, 4.1)

3 By what means does a member become aware that there is to be a meeting on a given day? (3.2 - 3.4)

4 Explain a 'quorum' and how it relates to the principle that generally a meeting must be attended by at least two persons. (5.1, 5.2)

5 What is the result if there is no quorum (a) at the time appointed for the start of a meeting and (b) in the course of a meeting which was originally quorate? (5.6, 5.8)

6 Why do meetings normally have an agenda? (6.2)

7 What is a motion? When does it become a resolution? (7.4)

8 Explain what is meant by proposing and seconding a motion. (8.2, 8.4)

9 To what extent should a chairman permit persons to speak (in turn) at a meeting? (9.3, 9.5)

10 Illustrate the problems which may confront a chairman in promoting the proper conduct of a meeting. (9.4)

11 Describe the recognised methods of taking a vote at a meeting. (10.3)

12 What is a point of order? (11.1)

Now try illustrative question 3 at the end of the Study Text

Chapter 4

AGENDA

This chapter covers the following topics.

1 What is an agenda?

2 General content of the agenda

3 Order of items on the agenda

4 Types of agenda

Introduction

The agenda was mentioned briefly in the previous chapter, but it is an important document and so further detail is called for. There are different kinds of agenda, serving different practical purposes. An efficient secretary must be skilled in selecting the appropriate type of agenda; and including in it the items of business to be done, in a convenient order and in sufficient detail for the meeting's needs.

1 WHAT IS AN AGENDA?

1.1 Essentially, an agenda ('things to be done') is a programme. In this respect it must be distinguished from a notice issued to call members to a meeting and to inform them in advance of the general nature, and possibly the details, of the business to be transacted. The purpose of a notice is to enable those who receive it to:

- **Consider** whether **they wish** to **attend**
- **Prepare** their **contribution** to the discussion

However, it may well happen that the document issued as a notice will also serve, when the meeting is held, as an agenda, but this is merely a matter of convenience.

2 GENERAL CONTENT OF THE AGENDA **6/95, 6/96, 12/98, 12/99**

2.1 Some types of meeting are held mainly to enable those who manage the affairs of the relevant body to present reports on progress and to give members the opportunity of commenting and raising questions on the information given. Some decisions may be taken, but the main purpose of the meeting is **communication**.

2.2 Meetings of this type, held at regular intervals, tend to cover much the same ground each time. An agenda for such a meeting is adequate if it **lists the business** to be done, in the proper order. If detailed information is to be given in advance, it will probably take the form of an accompanying document, such as an attached report.

2.3 However, a management committee, including a board of directors, holds meetings both to **consider information**, and to **take decisions** as to what should be done. Some of the items requiring decisions may be 'special' non-recurrent business. It is helpful if those coming to the meeting are informed in advance of the decisions which they will be asked to take. They can then consider their position on each question and will not have to make any 'snap' judgements. In such circumstances, greater detail is obviously required on the agenda, perhaps including the full text of the formal resolutions.

2.4 As part of the preliminary planning process for a meeting with an non-routine agenda the secretary may:

(a) **Consult** the chairman or other colleagues as to whether they have items which they want to include in the agenda

(b) Keep a file, in which he puts **notes or copies** of papers which arise in relation to matters to be taken at the next meeting

(c) **Refer** to the **minutes** of the previous meeting (and perhaps of the meeting held at the same time in the previous year), to pick up any matters:

- Deferred on a previous occasion
- Recurring at long or regular intervals

(d) **Refer to standing orders** or other appropriate regulations which will stipulate recurring items such as the signing of minutes, election of officers etc.

2.5 Once the agenda has been drafted, the secretary should obtain the chairman's approval of its contents; it can then be issued to members.

AGENDA OF MEETING

1 Apologies for absence

2 Minutes of the last meeting

3 Matters arising from the minutes

4 Ordinary business

[eg (re-)election of officers, report and accounts, management progress reports, declaration of dividends, (re-)appointment of auditors]

5 Special business

[eg consideration of special reports, non-routine motions put before the meeting]

6 Any other business

7 Date of next meeting

3 ORDER OF ITEMS ON THE AGENDA

3.1 There is a logical order for some of the related items on any agenda. For example the accounts, showing the profits, would have to be considered before a decision was made about dividends. Otherwise, there is general agreement on the sequence to be adopted for the business of any type of meeting.

(a) The meeting should first dispose of **preliminary formal business**, which does not usually call for discussion but should not, by convention, be omitted. In this category are apologies for absence from those unable to attend, and the approval and signature of the minutes of the last meeting.

(b) The meeting should then move on to **matters arising from the minutes of the previous meeting**. This item should be confined to a brief report of further information obtained, action taken to implement previous decisions etc.

If some important topic considered at the previous meeting was left unfinished for further discussion later, it should be included at a later point in the agenda, as an item of business in its own right. Note also that 'matters arising' should not be used as an excuse to re-open and repeat previously decided debates.

(c) Next the meeting takes **ordinary business**, including recurrent items such as periodic management reports or financial statements. These items are routine - but they are also important, and may require discussion but not lengthy discussion, since the subjects are familiar and relate to established arrangements rather than new policies or developments.)

(d) If there are **special business items** (new projects, changes of policy etc.) which may require careful discussion, they are taken at this point, so that they do not 'crowd out' the earlier routine business, as they might if taken at the start. Motions for discussion and decision should usually be submitted in advance, and in writing.

(e) There may also be **matters to report**, which will not entail discussion. As examples, a board meeting of company directors might receive the report of the trustees of the employees' pension fund. These are matters of history; generally there is nothing to discuss, since the meeting has no direct or present involvement.

Matters of this kind may be placed earlier in the agenda (at (b) above), but as they are really 'appendices' to business already completed, they are often put at the end. If the meeting reaches this point, and finds that it is running out of time, nothing is lost by giving such matters the briefest formal consideration, so that they may simply be duly recorded in the minutes.

(f) Last of all come the **closing items**. Any other business is included to enable any person present to raise a short, quick point. It is not appropriate to use this item to introduce an important subject for discussion, since no notice will have been given, time may be short, members tired etc. Weighty matters should be deferred to the next meeting.

(g) If the **date of the next meeting** has not been arranged in advance it may be discussed and agreed at this point.

The 'bell curve' effect

3.2 Because an agenda, arranged in the sequence suggested above, begins with minor and routine items, passes on to larger topics, requiring longer discussion, and closes with routine items once more, it is sometimes said to have a bell curve structure, though this is hardly a very close analogy. If a graph were drawn, with a horizontal axis for time (the duration of the meeting) and a vertical axis for the importance of the business (and the attention required from the participants in the meeting), the line representing this type of agenda would appear as a bell-shaped curve.

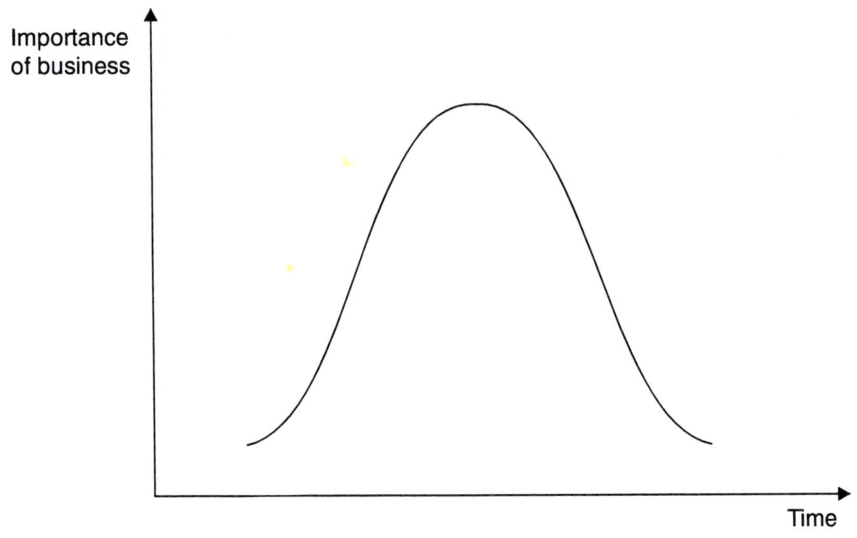

3.3 The underlying principle is to take routine first and special business later, and then round off with the final items of business. However this might vary according to circumstances. In particular, for 'political' reasons (for instance, if there is a power struggle between factions in the meeting), an agenda might be otherwise arranged to:

(a) **'Push through'** unpopular motions by scheduling them for discussion when time is short, or key opponents are absent

(b) **Suppress or delay motions** by placing them late on the agenda so that they will have to be deferred

3.4 An agenda might also be usefully drawn up to deal with more important matters earlier in the meeting, while members are fresh, especially if a long and heated debate is envisaged.

3.5 To fulfil its function, an agenda of this kind should be distributed **several days** before the meeting, with copies of as many of the papers relevant to the discussion as are then ready.

3.6 The agenda, issued in advance, may also serve as notice of the meeting appropriately headed with the nature of the meeting, and when and where it is to be held, for example 'The Annual General Meeting of the Company will be held at The Grand Hotel, Main Street, Ourtown on Wednesday 23 April 20X9 at 11.30 am, for the following purposes: .....'

4 TYPES OF AGENDA **12/99**

4.1 It is usual to distinguish between types of agenda in the following categories.

(a) A **skeleton agenda** is a mere list of the topics or items of business to be covered.

(b) A **detailed agenda** includes the text of any resolutions which the meeting is to consider.

(c) A **chairman's agenda** in its briefest form includes additional space, such as a blank right hand page or wide margin, on which the chairman may make notes. In its fullest form, this is a very detailed programme, giving guidance on what has to be done and by whom at every stage of the meeting. Background information may also be given, to help the chairman:

(i) **Guide** the meeting (with updates on past and current matters) x

(ii) **Control** it with tact (for example, if there is expected to be strong opposition to a particular motion)

Skeleton agenda

4.2 A skeleton agenda is suitable for routine or regular meetings which cover similar ground on each occasion. The characteristics of such a meeting are:

(a) **Routine business**

(b) **Communication of information** and opinion on basic topics, rather than decisions in detail

4.3 The annual general meeting of a non-commercial body, such as a club or association, will usually require only a skeleton agenda, which may be combined with the notice of the meeting, or distributed at the meeting itself.

Example of a skeleton agenda

Popplewell Cricket Club

Annual General Meeting

Saturday 10 October 20X9 at 7pm
at the Kings Head Hotel, Popplewell

Agenda

1 Apologies for absence

2 Minutes of the Annual General Meeting held on 9 October 20X8

3 Matters arising from the minutes

4 Report of the committee on last season

5 Annual accounts and Treasurer's Report

6 Possible increase of membership subscriptions

7 Any other business

8 Date of next meeting

Note. An agenda of this or any other type should always have a heading, giving the brief title of the meeting, and the date, time and place - even if it is not also serving as the notice of the meeting.

Detailed agenda

4.4 As explained earlier, a meeting which is concerned with management decisions or financial matters, or even a general meeting of members if there are financial reports to be considered, will need a detailed agenda. This should preferably set out the **draft resolutions** on the matters to be decided.

Example of a detailed agenda

Walter Wall Carpets Ltd

Meeting of the Board of Directors

on Tuesday 6 July 20X9 at 10am
at the registered office,
20 High Street, Popplewell

AGENDA

1 Sign minutes of meeting held on 4 June 20X8 (previously circulated).

2 Matters arising from the minutes:

(1) Report progress of negotiations for new lease of company's factory at Mill End Lane Minute 142).

3 Managing Director's monthly report for May 20X9 (attached).

4 Statement of cash and borrowings at 30 June 20X9.

5 Unaudited management accounts for half year to 30 April 20X9 (to be distributed at meeting).

6 Table attached draft service agreements for consideration between the company and (1) the Chairman and (2) the Managing Director for terms of three years from 1 January next.

7 Table report of sealings committee for the period since the last meeting of the Board.

8 Any other business.

9 Date of next meeting.

4.5 Each member of the board would receive a copy of the agenda, probably typed on A4 size paper. The chairman's copy, however, would be **typed** on the **left-hand** side of a double-page sheet, with the **right-hand** side left **blank**. As the meeting proceeds through the agenda, the chairman makes brief notes of the decision reached or the action taken on the right-hand side opposite the relevant item.

Exercise 1

Try to think of some typical notes which might appear on the chairman's copy of the specimen agenda given above, opposite each item.

Solution

Item 1	'Signed'
Item 2	'Reported'
Items 3 - 5	'Considered' (if no action or decision was necessary)
Item 6	'Resolved' (for the service agreements, if the draft resolution was adopted without amendment)
	'Committee to discuss clause 3 with solicitors' (say)
Item 7	'Tabled' would suffice.
Item 8	'None'; or, say,
	'Next month's board meeting to consider actuaries' report on pension fund', if this had been requested by one of the directors.

4.6 Chairman's notes of this type are merely a useful reminder to him and to the secretary of what was the outcome of each item on the agenda; they have no formal status.

4.7 The secretary himself would usually make more detailed notes, with particular reference to matters requiring any 'follow up' action by himself or by some member of the company's staff.

Chairman's agenda for a general meeting

4.8 This type of agenda for a general meeting, prepared specially for the chairman's use, is beyond the scope of this syllabus. In general, much depends on:

- The **size** of the meeting
- The amount of **publicity** given to it
- The **type and importance** of the **business** to be transacted
- The **temperament** and **experience** of the **chairman** himself

---

Exercise 2

Do you have access to agendas of meetings where you work? If you have, compare them to the content of this chapter.

Chapter roundup

- In this chapter we have seen the **form and function** of a meeting's agenda and the type of thing contained in it. Remember that the order of items contained in the agenda can be very important, in the light of the 'bell curve' effect.
- **Different types of agenda** are appropriate to different circumstances. A good secretary will not forget the importance of a chairman's agenda either; this is a vital tool to ensure that he can conduct the meeting as efficiently as possible.

Test your knowledge

1 What practical steps should a secretary take to ensure that items awaiting consideration at the next meeting of a board of directors are not overlooked? (see para 2.4)

2 Describe, with brief examples, the accepted sequence of subjects in an agenda. (3.1)

3 What is the bell curve effect? (3.2)

4 What types of agenda are there? (4.1)

5 What is a skeleton agenda? For what types of meeting is it sufficient? (4.1, 4.2)

6 Give three items which would usually be found in the agenda of a board meeting and place them in the correct sequence. (4.4)

Now try illustrative question 4 at the end of the Study Text

Chapter 5

MOTIONS, AMENDMENTS AND ADJOURNMENTS

This chapter covers the following topics.

1 Motions
2 Amendments
3 Formal or procedural motions
4 Adjournment

Introduction

This chapter explains how a meeting makes a formal decision and how a meeting can be formally interrupted. In each case it is important that the rules of the body concerned are followed. A **motion** is a proposal put before a meeting; a **resolution** is what a motion becomes if the meeting votes in its favour. An **amendment** is a proposal to alter a motion which has been put before the meeting, but has not yet been put to the vote. An **adjournment** is an interruption of the proceedings of a meeting before they have been completed.

1 MOTIONS

6/96, 6/98

1.1 People who come to a meeting for a common purpose usually want to be able to make a formal statement of the conclusions or decisions on which they have agreed. So a meeting usually proceeds by considering a sequence of specific proposals (called '**motions**' because they are 'moved' or proposed).

1.2 Generally, a motion relates to some **action** to be taken or **issue of policy** to be decided. For example, a director is elected by passing a motion to that effect. Even if the meeting is only dealing with information, that too is a form of action; a meeting is said to 'consider' a report, 'receive' annual accounts, or a document is laid before it ('tabled'). There are also procedural motions, by which a meeting regulates its own course of business.

1.3 If the motion is finally **passed**, it becomes a '**resolution**' (because the meeting so 'resolves' or decides).

1.4 A resolution, then, is a motion which has been carried. (In the Companies Act, the term resolution is also used to describe a motion, but for now we shall use different terms for what is proposed and what is carried). However it is not always the motion in the form in which it was originally proposed. The meeting may consider that the original motion should be altered (amended) to modify its effect, or to improve the language in which it is expressed.

1.5 Once carried, the resolution is recorded in the minutes as the final decision on the point which it covers: the matter cannot be raised again at the same meeting.

Drafting a motion

1.6 In moving a motion the proposer 'moves that ... [x should be done]' and if the meeting approves the motion it becomes a 'resolution that ... [x should be done]'.

Accordingly a motion (or resolution) should begin with the word 'That'.

1.7 The purpose of a motion is that something should be done or decided which would not be so otherwise: its purpose is creative, or positive.

Accordingly a motion should be affirmative and not negative.

1.8 There is no point in resolving that something shall *not* be done, since it won't be done unless a decision to do it is taken: those who don't want something done must simply vote against a positive motion, and get it rejected.

1.9 If the motion becomes a resolution, it will have to be implemented. Unless it is clear in its terms, there may be difficulty in deciding exactly what it was that the meeting intended. It is too late then to go back and ask for clarification because the matter is closed, and the meeting will probably have dispersed.

It is essential to **avoid ambiguity in drafting a motion.**

1.10 A couple of examples should illustrate how clear and specific the secretary (or any other individual) must be in composing a motion to be put before a meeting.

(a) A motion proposes that a committee be appointed to deal with a specified matter. It should state clearly whether the committee is to make recommendations to the body by which it was appointed, or whether it is authorised to go ahead and take executive action to implement its conclusions.

(b) A motion is proposed at a company annual general meeting for the payment of a dividend at a specified percentage rate on the issued shares. Fine. But when is the dividend to be paid? What provision is to be made for shares transferred just before the payment date: is the dividend to be paid to the shareholders on the register at the date of payment, or at some earlier 'record date'?

1.11 **A motion must always conform to the relevant regulations**, whether contained in general law or the constitution of the body holding the meeting.

1.12 The notice issued to convene a meeting defines the business which the meeting is to transact. Accordingly, any motion put before the meeting must be within the scope of the notice. For example, company law requires (s 378) that the **exact text of a special or an extraordinary resolution** shall be given in the notice. The secretary must note that the text of such a motion **cannot be amended**, as it would then no longer be the resolution of which notice has had to be given in advance.

1.13 Both at company and other meetings, however, the notice may be more flexibly expressed, so that it is possible to move any motion which remains within the topical limits set by the notice. In the *Choppington Collieries* case an unexpected resolution for the election of new directors (when only the 're-election' of a retiring director was contemplated by the company management) was held to be admissible, because the notice of the meeting only specified 'to elect directors' as the relevant item of business.

1.14 A more precise motion may be set out to include a phrase such as 'with such amendments and alterations as shall be determined upon at the meeting': *Betts & Co Ltd v Macnaghten 1910.*

1.15 Unless the regulations require advance notice, it is possible for the meeting to **frame a motion** (within the scope of the notice) at the close of a debate (at the meeting itself), to express the common intention which has emerged from the discussion.

Checklist 1

A motion:

- Is a proposal put to the meeting for action, decision or consideration
- Becomes a resolution when carried, and is recorded in the minutes as the final decision on the point which it covers

It must:

- Begin with the word 'that'
- Be positive rather than negative
- Contain sufficient detail to be unambiguous and easy to act upon
- Conform to any relevant regulations and/or statutes
- Be within the scope of the business indicated in the notice of the meeting

1.16 The Hampel report recommended that different proposals should **not** be **'bundled'** into the same resolution. Best practice is therefore to have separate resolutions for each substantially separate proposal.

Disposal of a motion

1.17 A motion is usually put to the vote, with or without discussion, or adopted informally by consensus. If put to the vote, it is either **'carried' by** whatever majority the regulations require, or it is **'defeated'** or rejected.

1.18 There are two situations in which a motion is said to be 'dropped', and therefore becomes a dropped motion.

(a) Once a motion has been proposed, it is under the **control** of the **meeting,** and no longer the 'property' of the person who brought it before the meeting. If the person who proposed it later wishes to withdraw it without a vote, he must seek the meeting's consent to do so.

(b) There is no **general requirement** for a motion to be **seconded** or formally supported by at least one person besides the proposer before it may be accepted for debate. But the regulations of some bodies do require a seconder and in that case, obviously, a motion which does not find a seconder is 'dropped' without debate.

2 AMENDMENTS

2.1 *An* **amendment** is a proposal to **alter** a motion which has been put before the meeting, but has not yet been put to the vote.

2.2 An amendment is a supplementary motion - it stands as a separate, additional proposal in its own right and must be disposed of accordingly. The regulations may impose specific requirements, for instance that a signed copy of an amendment must be handed in before the meeting.

2.3 There are the following general limits on the right to propose and withdraw an amendment.

(a) No person (including the proposer) who has already spoken in the debate on the original motion may speak a **second time** for the purpose of proposing an amendment to it.

(b) In proposing an amendment, the person concerned is using his opportunity to speak once in the debate: he cannot speak again to propose a second amendment. Note also that, unlike the original proposer of a motion, he may **not reply** to the debate on his amendment before it is put to the vote.

(c) A valid amendment, once submitted, 'belongs' to the meeting like any other motion, and may not be withdrawn without the meeting's consent.

2.4 The amendment must fulfill a number of criteria.

(a) **Relevant** to the original motion. An amendment must not seek to introduce some quite different subject.

(b) **In conformity** with previous decisions made by the meeting. An amendment may not be proposed in order to re-open a matter already decided by the carrying of an earlier motion.

(c) **Within the scope of the notice** of the meeting, and within the powers of the meeting. In particular, you might note that if an amount of a proposed financial commitment is specified in the notice, that places a ceiling on amendments: reduction would be possible, but *not* increase: *Betts & Co Ltd v Macnaghten 1910.*

(d) **Positive and not negative.** An amendment simply to insert the word 'not' is inadmissible. An amendment which would defeat the whole purpose of the motion, eg to reduce £1 million to £1, is treated as negative. A vote against the original motion would be a less time-wasting method of achieving the same effect.

(e) **In character** with the original motion. An amendment should not change the nature or importance of the motion expected by members (for example, by substantially increasing a financial commitment, or changing an 'ordinary' to a 'special' resolution, to which extra regulations apply in company law). People who decide not to attend what seems from the notice to be a routine meeting cannot be 'cheated' of the chance to vote on a motion which has been rendered crucial by some amendment.

2.5 An amendment may:

- Add words at any part of the motion
- Delete words at any part of the motion
- Replace part of the motion with different words
- Combine any of the above

Addendum and rider

2.6 An amendment which simply adds words to the motion is called an **addendum.**

2.7 It is also permissible, once a motion has been carried, to propose a **rider**, usually a recommendation of some kind, which does not alter the sense of the resolution on any original point. Thus a rider might be added to a resolution to engage 50 additional workers, asking that preference be given to candidates under the age of 21. This is merely an expression of opinion as to how the resolution should be implemented.

Procedural aspects of amendments

2.8 Amendments to a motion, especially if there are several of them, may present procedural problems to the chairman.

(a) He must consider whether a proposed amendment **conforms** to the various limiting conditions suggested above, and to the regulations for the meeting: eg if the amendment must be in writing, or have adequate notice given.

(b) There are the procedures for sorting out **multiple amendments,** voting on them in appropriate order and then voting either on the motion as amended, or on the original motion (if none of the amendments has been carried).

2.9 The chairman has an overriding power to **reject** an amendment which is merely frivolous. In case of doubt, however, it is wiser for the chairman to accept a doubtful amendment and allow it to go forward to a vote. If it is rejected, that disposes of the matter with no possibility of further challenge. The chairman may be challenged if he has rejected the amendment.

Henderson v Bank of Australasia 1890
The facts: The motion was to vary the rights attached to shares. The amendment (duly seconded) would have imposed additional restrictions on shares held by the directors of the company. The chairman consulted the company solicitor and on his advice ruled that the amendment was out of order and should not be debated. H challenged the chairman's ruling.

Decision: The amendment should have been accepted for debate, as it was relevant and within the scope of the notice convening the meeting. As there had been no opportunity to consider the motion in an amended form, the original motion had not been validly carried.

The popular method

2.10 If there is more than one proposed amendment to the same motion, the general practice (called the **popular method**) at the end of the debate is to put the amendments to the vote, one by one, in the order in which they will alter the sequence of words in the motion itself. Thus an amendment to the opening words of the motion will come before an amendment to the final words. As an example:

Original motion	That a committee of X and Y be appointed with plenary powers
Amendment No 1	Delete 'with plenary powers' and substitute 'to report to the board of directors with recommendations on future marketing policy in Southeast Asia'
Amendment No 2	Delete 'X and Y' and substitute 'X, Y and Z'
Order of voting	(1) Amendment No 2 (2) Amendment No 1 (3) Substantive motion (see below)

2.11 Each amendment is put to the vote. The result is treated as a decision on each amendment, and not on the entire motion.

(a) If an amendment is **rejected**, it drops out and the meeting proceeds to vote on the next amendment.

(b) If an amendment is **carried**, it is incorporated in the motion, which in its amended form is called '**the substantive motion**'.

2.12 Assume that, in the previous example, Amendment No 2 is carried, and then Amendment No 1 is rejected. The substantive motion is then:

'That a committee of X, Y and Z be appointed with plenary powers'.

2.13 When all the amendments have been put to the vote, the substantive motion is put to the vote.

2.14 If it is rejected, that is the end of the debate. The meeting cannot go back and vote on the original motion, since **the adoption of any amendment is by implication a rejection of the motion in its original form**. The original motion will only be put to the vote, therefore, if no amendment has been proposed, or if none has been carried.

2.15 **An amendment to an amendment** is not usually permitted, since it is likely to produce confusion. The proposer should put forward, as an alternative to the amendment which he wishes to modify, his own amendment to the original motion. For example, at the meeting of a club, a motion may propose the election of X and Y as officers for life. Josephine Bloggs proposes the first amendment - say, that X and Z be elected officers for life. A second amendment proposing that X and Z be elected officers for one year only would be put forward as an alternative amendment of the original motion.

2.16 If two or more amendments relate to the same part of the motion, and the meeting carries any one of them, the rest are by implication rejected without the need for a vote; the point has been decided by the first vote, and, as stated earlier, amendments may only be proposed in conformity with decisions already made.

2.17 As an example, suppose that the original motion proposes the creation of a post with an annual salary of £20,000. The first amendment is to substitute £18,000 for £20,000; the second is to substitute £15,000. When the matter comes to the vote:

(a) If £18,000 is approved, the other amendment (£15,000) is automatically **dropped**.

(b) If £18,000 is rejected, then £15,000 may be **put** to the vote.

(c) If **either** is carried, the **substantive motion**, which includes that amendment, is put to the Vote.

(d) If **neither** amendment is carried, the **original motion** (£20,000) is put to the vote.

Exercise

In considering whether to allow or reject an amendment, what factors should the chairman of a meeting take into account.

Solution

In considering an amendment, the chairman must first judge whether it complies with the various limiting conditions, both in its proposal and its substance. Briefly, these include the following.

(a) No person who has already spoken in the debate may speak for a second time for the purpose of proposing an amendment to the motion, nor may the proposer of one amendment propose another (since he has already used his one chance to speak).

(b) The amendment must be clearly relevant to the original motion, and must not seek to introduce some wholly new subject to it.

(c) The amendment must be in harmony with the previous decisions of the meeting; it may not be introduced if its effect is to re-open debate on a matter which has already been discussed and voted upon.

(d) The scope of both the notice for the meeting and the powers of the meeting must be wide enough to cover the matters dealt with in the amendment. If this is not the case, then the amendment is *ultra vires* and should not be accepted.

(e) The amendment must be positive, not negative - an attempt merely to insert the word 'not' into a motion should not be accepted. Similarly, a move to reduce £1,000,000 to 25p will be treated as negative. The reasoning is that a vote against the original motion would achieve the same effect and would be less time-consuming.

(f) The amendment must be in character with the original motion, so that its nature is not radically altered. For instance, an attempt to change an ordinary resolution to a special one will not be allowed, since members who have received notice of the meeting should not be cheated of their chance to influence a decision which has suddenly taken on a wholly new (and possibly more important) character.

---

3 FORMAL OR PROCEDURAL MOTIONS

3.1 Within the limits set by its regulations, the meeting may determine its own course of business. There are various motions which can be put forward in order to regulate or facilitate the business of the meeting: these are known as 'formal' or **procedural motions.** (They may also be known as 'interruptive' motions, since - like points or order - they are allowed to interrupt the course of business or debate at a meeting.)

3.2 Like any other, a procedural motion cannot be moved by anyone who has already spoken in the debate which it interrupts. Nor is it subject to amendment (to avoid pointless wrangling).

3.3 The meeting may resolve that it does not wish to listen to more discussion on a particular question, or to continue its session at all at that stage. A procedural motion may be passed in order to cut short the debate. (Deliberate prolongation of debate by a minority, to delay the moment when it loses a vote, is called a **filibuster**.) It also enables the meeting to 'take a break' for any reasonable cause, say for rest and refreshment, gathering of further information etc.

3.4 There is however sometimes a risk that a majority of members will resort to procedural motions to stifle debate on an embarrassing subject, or one on which they may not wish to disclose their unpopular views. This abuse is particularly characteristic of elected representative bodies, such as the House of Commons and local authorities. On the other hand, if a party in a meeting wishes to hold off the vote, or 'play for time' while it gathers support etc, a procedural motion may be used to delay business, say by shelving the debate until a later date, or interrupting it with a point of order. A motion used in such a way is called a **dilatory motion**.

3.5 The chairman has a general power to reject a procedural motion if he considers that:

- It is designed to **hinder** the progress of business.
- It is **against the regulations** laid down for the meeting.
- It will **prevent adequate discussion**, and particularly the expression of minority views.

He will often be bound by the regulations in this respect.

3.6 In any case, he should have regard to the **views** of the **majority**, expressed in the passing of a procedural motion, as to how the meeting should proceed. The minority should be fairly allowed to contribute, but they have no inherent right to take up the meeting's time, if all they are doing is publicising their views or disrupting other business.

3.7 The most drastic procedural step is to require that the motion shall, without further debate, be finally disposed of. For this purpose there are two types of procedural motions, previous question and closure.

Previous question: 'that the question be not now put'

3.8 The **previous question** motion is 'that the previous question be not now put', the 'previous question' being the original or substantive motion under debate when the procedural motion came up.

(a) If 'previous question' is carried, the debate on that motion is **ended** without a vote.

(b) If 'previous question' is put and rejected, the motion must **immediately** be put to the vote, without further debate. (This is because the **rejection** of a motion that 'the previous question be **not now** put' is a double negative, implying that the meeting has decided that the original or substantive motive **shall now** be put to the vote forthwith.)

Either way, the debate is ended immediately, so the chairman should not allow a 'previous question' motion if there has not yet been sufficient debate to allow the meeting to come to a considered decision.

3.9 'Previous question' incidentally demonstrates the exceptional case of a motion in negative form.

Closure: 'that the question be now put'

3.10 The **closure** motion is 'that the question be now put'.

(a) If it is **carried**, the **motion** previously under debate is put to the **vote**, without further discussion.

(b) If a closure motion is **rejected**, however, the **debate continues**.

3.11 This is a fairer method than 'previous question', since the debate is allowed to continue if that is the wish of the majority. The chairman may himself move to 'close' the debate, with the meeting's consent.

Other procedural motions

3.12 There are a number of other procedural motions by which debate is avoided or cut short for the time being, while still leaving open the possibility of resuming it later. However, an **indefinite postponement** is sometimes equivalent to outright rejection.

3.13 Other procedural motions include the following.

(a) **'That the meeting proceed to the next business'**.

This motion may be put to the meeting without discussion at the end of any speech. If it is passed, the item (whether a motion or amendment) is simply dropped, and the meeting proceeds to the next item on the agenda.

(b) **'That the motion be referred back to the committee'**.

This 'reference back' motion is suitable if the meeting considers that a report or recommendations of a committee are unsatisfactory in their present form, and should be reviewed. The matter may reappear on the agenda of a later meeting in a different form - but will not necessarily do so.

(c) **'That the debate be adjourned'**.

This is sometimes a useful means of interrupting a long debate, to enable the meeting to deal rapidly with some more urgent matter or to cool heated tempers. Adjournment of a debate, and of the meeting itself, is discussed in more detail below.

(d) **'That the meeting postpone consideration of the subject'** or **'That the motion lie on the table'**.

These motions are generally appropriate if the meeting does not wish to start a discussion of a matter at that session. It may be, for example, that opposed groups wish to have time to work out a compromise behind the scenes before entering on a public debate. The meeting retains the option of later resolving 'That the matter be taken from the table', and discussing the item if it wishes.

If any of these motions is put to the vote and **rejected**, the debate simply **continues** (or not, as the case may be).

Checklist 2	**Checklist 3**
Make sure you understand what it means for a motion to be:	Make sure you understand the common procedural motions:
'original' 'substantive' 'interruptive' 'dilatory' 'formal' or 'procedural' 'dropped'	closure previous question proceed to next business adjournment reference back let the matter lie on the table

4 ADJOURNMENT

4.1 An adjournment is an **interruption** of the proceedings of a meeting before they have been completed. It may be:

(a) An adjournment of a **debate**, to be resumed later in the same meeting

(b) An adjournment of the **meeting itself**, with a view to its resumption, and the completion of its business, at some later date (or possibly later on the same day - say when a meeting adjourns for lunch at midday)

4.2 It is not possible to cancel or postpone a meeting, once a notice to convene it has been issued: *Smith v Paringa Mines Ltd 1906*. If there are reasons for not holding it at the appointed time, the correct procedure is to hold the meeting but propose a motion for an adjournment before any business is done. (The secretary may issue an advance notice to members that the adjournment will be proposed, so that they do not waste time by coming to the meeting.)

4.3 Adjournment may be part of the planned programme of discussion.

(a) A meeting may start on a long agenda with the clear understanding that if it has not finished by an appointed time, there will have to be an adjournment to a **later occasion**.

(b) A meeting may adjourn **without prior arrangement**, if it seems only reasonable to do so, say because the chairman has suddenly fallen ill.

Power to adjourn a meeting

4.4 A meeting may be adjourned in various ways.

(a) By **passing a procedural motion** to adjourn - which the meeting has inherent power to do

(b) By the **chairman**, if he has powers to do it (usually very limited, as explained below)

(c) **Automatically**, in circumstances for which the regulations provide

4.5 There are usually express regulations to confer power to adjourn a meeting. If, however, there are *no* regulations on adjournment:

(a) The **general power** to adjourn is given to the **meeting**, which should pass a resolution to adjourn, if that is the wish of those present

(b) The **chairman** may adjourn a meeting for a short time, for the purpose of:

(i) Seeking to restore order: *John v Rees 1969*
(ii) Facilitating the business of the meeting by taking a poll: *R v D'Oyly 1840*

4.6 Except for the specific purposes mentioned above, the chairman has no inherent power to adjourn the meeting, if the regulations do not give the power to him.

Stoughton v Reynolds 1736
The facts: At a vestry meeting held to elect churchwardens, the vicar took the chair. Before the business had been completed the vicar adjourned the meeting. However those present remained behind and completed the election. The next day the vicar and others purported to resume the adjourned meeting, and elected a different candidate.

Decision: The right to adjourn was given to the meeting, and the vicar as chairman had no power to adjourn against the wishes of the meeting. (See also *National Dwellings Society v Sykes 1894* and *Byng v London Life Association 1989*).

4.7 In addition to these inherent (but limited) powers of the chairman, he may be given standard **express powers** of adjournment, illustrated by the model articles of association of companies as follows.

(a) The chairman may adjourn with the **consent** of the meeting (he may make the proposal himself, but he must obtain the consent of the meeting).

(b) The chairman must adjourn '**if so directed** by the meeting'.

4.8 Where the regulations contain only the formula in (a), but not (b), the effect is to restrict the inherent power of the meeting to adjourn: by implication it cannot adjourn if the chairman disagrees, and wishes to proceed with business: *Salisbury Gold Mining Co v Hathorn 1897*.

4.9 Accordingly the standard modern practice is to safeguard the meeting's own power to adjourn by including in the regulations an express statement that the chairman shall conform to the wishes of the meeting ((b) above) - though (a) already provides that he cannot impose his own wish to adjourn on the meeting if the majority wish to proceed with business).

4.10 Automatic adjournment under the regulations is not common. For company general meetings, however, there is a standard procedure in the model articles (Table A Article 41) if the meeting is inquorate, for adjournment until the same time and day the following week.

4.11 To sum up this rather complicated set of alternatives:

(a) It generally **rests** with the **meeting** to adjourn by passing a resolution to do so, either under its inherent powers, or under the standard express regulations.

(b) The chairman must **normally conform** to the wishes of the meeting over an adjournment. However he has power at common law to adjourn for certain purposes, and it is always advisable to refer to the regulations to consider what special powers (if any) he has to adjourn at his discretion.

Resumption of the meeting after adjournment

4.12 If there is an adjournment, there may be a pre-arranged date, time and place for resumption. If the meeting adjourns without having fixed when it is to resume, this is said to be adjournment **sine die** (Latin - 'without a day' fixed for resumption).

4.13 When a meeting is resumed after an adjournment it is treated as a **continuation** of the earlier session and not as a new meeting. It follows that it can only deal with the unfinished business of the adjourned meeting, of which the necessary notice has been given.

4.14 Notice of the resumed meeting to be held after an adjournment is not always required. However notice must be given:

(a) After an **adjournment sine die**, obviously, so as to give notice of the date, time and place of the resumed meeting

(b) If the **regulations** require that notice shall be given; this is normally a requirement if the interval between the sessions exceeds a certain minimum period, since the members may by this time need a reminder

4.15 There is no objection to convening a meeting to complete the business of the adjourned meeting and to deal with other new business. But it must be convened as a **new meeting,** and not as the resumption of the adjourned meeting.

Chapter roundup

- Remember that a **motion** is a proposal put before a meeting; a *resolution* is what a motion becomes if the meeting votes in its favour.
- Motions need to be very carefully **drafted** and there are certain rules to be followed in this respect. Most of all, it must be within the regulations of the relevant body.
- An **amendment** is a supplementary motion which can often present a problem to a chairman; the safest bet is to allow it to be voted on. Amendments once passed become part of the substantive motion. If this is then rejected it is not possible to go back and vote on the original motion.
- It is important for you to be able to identify **procedural motions** since these are often used in meetings and the secretary would be expected to understand the significance of each.
- The rules on **adjournment** are also significant; a meeting may be adjourned by the chairman or some other person authorised by the regulations, or by a procedural motion being passed.

Test your knowledge

1 What is (a) a motion (b) a resolution (c) a substantive motion and (d) a procedural motion? (see paras 1.1, 1.3, 2.11, 3.1)

2 What is meant by saying that a motion should be positive, not negative? Are there any exceptions? (1.7, 3.9)

3 How may (a) the regulations and (b) the notice of the meeting affect the proposing of a motion at a meeting? (1.11, 1.12)

4 What are the general rules on (a) seconding a motion and (b) withdrawing a motion? (1.18)

5 In what ways may a motion be altered by an amendment? (2.5)

6 Distinguish between an addendum and a rider. (2.6 - 2.7)

7 What is the 'popular method' of dealing with several amendments to a single motion? (2.10)

8 Explain (a) previous question and (b) closure as procedural motions. (3.8, 3.10)

9 What other procedural motions are there? (3.13)

10 In what circumstances may a chairman adjourn a meeting without first obtaining its consent? (4.5)

11 How do the powers of the meeting and the chairman interact with regard to adjournment? (4.11)

Now try illustrative question 5 at the end of the Study Text

Chapter 6

MINUTES

This chapter covers the following topics.

Introduction

You may have learned about minutes in your earlier studies for the module *Professional Administration.* Minutes are a written, indexed record of the business transacted and decisions taken at a meeting. Without them it would be difficult to act upon those decisions. The maintenance of accurate and timely minutes is one of the most important functions of a secretary.

1 THE IMPORTANCE OF MINUTES 12/99

1.1 Companies and local authorities are required by law to keep minutes of their meetings, being a **written record** of the business done at meetings. Other bodies may have regulations which impose a similar requirement. It is certainly the general practice of all established bodies to keep minutes, in case there is a later dispute as to exactly what was decided, or there is need to refer back to the business of a previous meeting.

Exercise 1

Consider why minutes of a meeting may be of value.

Solution

Minutes are likely to be of value to a body which holds meetings, as:

(a) A record of events for reference at a later date, or by members who missed the meeting. This will also be a useful control for the implementation of policy decisions taken at the meeting.

(b) Evidence of exactly what was decided, in case of later uncertainty or dispute. The minutes will be authenticated by signature as a true record of proceedings.

(c) A precedent and authority for future proposals. They provide confirmation of decisions taken and views expressed.

(d) An aid to compiling the next agenda. They can help picking up unfinished business, considering 'matters arising' etc;

(e) A check on ill-considered action at meetings. Participants are more accountable for views and decisions which are put into the minutes. They may also request to 'go on record' with views they hold particularly strongly, or wish to be recalled later (to prove the soundness of their judgement, after the event etc).

1.2 Minutes of a meeting should be distinguished from a report of a meeting. Newspaper reports often give more space to an account of the debate, and the personalities involved, than to the decision reached. By contrast minutes are a formal and complete record, in concise form, of **decisions taken** and **other things done**, but not usually of the course of debate.

1.3 An article by Susan Singleton in *Chartered Secretary* for December 1999 highlighted a number of practical issues that organisations should consider when deciding whether to minute meetings:

(a) Whether the meeting must be **minuted** or whether it is **preferable** that it is

(b) **Who** will **take** the minutes (there should not be different sets taken by different people)

(c) Should the meeting be **tape-recorded** (telephone calls including electronic attendance by telephone or video link should not be recorded without permission)

(d) Whether **draft minutes** will be **circulated** prior to approval, and if so by what means

(e) Who should be the **signatories** of the minutes

(f) For foreign meetings, what **languages** should be used, and which language should be taken as final if there are differences between translations in different languages

(g) What will be the **restrictions on circulation** of minutes

(h) Is the meeting held in a **particular form**, and is it clearly marked, for example 'without prejudice'

2 SECURITY OF MINUTES

2.1 Minutes are usually typed up from notes made by the secretary during the meeting, and preserved in minute books.

2.2 The simplest method is to paste typed sheets into a **bound book**, but this adds to the thickness of the pages and the book becomes unwieldy if there are many sets of minutes to be inserted.

2.3 The more convenient practice is to keep the minute book in **loose-leaf form**, adding one or more sheets as each set of minutes is prepared. If this is done, there should be precautions against:

- Removal of pages
- Other falsification by the substitution of pages without authority

2.4 The simplest precaution is to **number** the **sheets** in sequence and have each sheet initialled when the minutes which it contains are approved and signed. An alternative method is to use a **loose-leaf book** which can be **locked**, so that only the official who holds the key can insert or remove pages. In any event minute books should be kept safely in a locked cupboard, filing cabinet or safe.

3 THE FORM OF MINUTES **6/97, 6/99**

3.1 The minutes of each meeting should be headed to show:

(a) **What the meeting** was, such as the annual general meeting of a specified body.

(b) The **date** of the meeting and the place where it was held. It is not usual to record the time when the meeting began, but there is no objection to doing so.

(c) The **names** of the **persons present**, if this is practicable. In the case of a large meeting it may be better to invite those who attend to sign an attendance book or attendance sheets (with different sheets for eg. shareholders and other persons such as the press). The minutes then simply refer to the attendance record, which should be preserved;

(d) The **names** of those in **attendance**. Technically, the word 'present' in this context should be reserved for persons who have a right to be there. Thus in the minutes of a board meeting, only the directors are 'present'; the secretary, if he is not also a director, is 'in attendance'.

Note. If any person is present for only part of a meeting, say because he arrives late or leaves early, the minutes should, if possible, record the period when he was there. For example, 'Mr Smith during items 205 to 215'.

3.2 At the foot of the last (or only) page of the minutes of the meeting there is a space for the chairman's signature. This is sometimes marked for convenience as shown below.

....

Chairman

3.3 The body of the minutes should follow the order of business set out in the agenda, and should be divided into **paragraphs** and **numbered** for reference.

3.4 It is often good practice, in the minutes of a managing body which meets regularly, to run on the sequence of serial numbers, instead of starting at 1 for each meeting. Thus if item 59 is the last of one set of minutes, the minutes of the next meeting begin at 60.

3.5 If a minute of a later meeting picks up the subject of a minute of an earlier meeting, it may help to refer back to say 'Minute 312, 29 Mar 20X1'. In this way, the record of the various dealings involved in a long-running matter can be traced without difficulty.

3.6 Minutes may be set out as **action minutes**, with a slightly different format. A marginal column is provided, in which a note is made against any action to be taken, arising from an item of business, with the name of the person (if any) who is to be responsible.

Amount of detail in minutes

3.7 Minutes are of two kinds.

(a) **Minutes of resolution** are simple records of the decisions taken at the meeting, in the form 'It was resolved that ...'.

(b) **Minutes of narration** are records of things done at the meeting, other than passing resolutions, eg 'The actuaries' report dated ... on the staff pension fund was tabled'.

3.8 Minutes should always be concise, but sufficiently detailed to avoid ambiguity.

3.9 If a formal resolution has been passed, that resolution is the decision to be recorded - and it should be **recorded accurately** in full. The skill lies in framing the motion which is to be considered at the meeting, so that it contains all the details that may later be required.

3.10 It is generally not correct to include in a minute **any account** of the **discussion** leading up to a decision. The reasons or arguments advanced by one speaker may not, after all, be the factors which led others to vote in the same way. The decision is a collective act; each speaker speaks only for himself.

3.11 It is in any event always necessary to include in the minutes **sufficient detail** to enable a reader to understand the decision. If anything unusual has arisen, it is better that it should be mentioned.

3.12 In the minutes of managing bodies, such as a board of directors, it is not usual to record the names of the proposer and seconder of a resolution. In minutes of larger meetings, such as general meetings, it is sometimes done - but not essential. What has to be recorded is the decision of the meeting. It is not always important who among those present originated the proposal which later became the decision.

3.13 It is **unusual** to record the names of those who **vote** for and against a motion: in the case of a large meeting it is often not practicable to do so. However, if some person votes against a motion, or abstains from voting, and expressly requests that this be minuted, it is usual and courteous to comply with his request. This point is most likely to come up at a meeting of a board of directors, when an individual strongly disagrees with the decision of the majority, or wishes to have it recorded that he abstained from voting on a matter in which he had a personal interest.

4 MINUTES STYLE **6/97, 6/99**

4.1 In order for the minutes to fulfil their purpose, they should be:

(a) **Concise**, but sufficiently detailed to make the sense of the meeting clear

(b) **Precise** and **unambiguous**; factually accurate and fair in implication

(c) **Impersonal, impartial** and **uniform** in style - not 'coloured' by the 'author'

(d) Written in the **past tense** (with reported speech as appropriate ie: 'X requested that his Abstention be minuted', rather than 'X said: "I wish my abstention to be minuted"')

(e) **Clearly laid out**, paragraphed and cross-referenced

Example: minutes

4.2 At this point it is useful to set out a complete model, using the items of business set out earlier in the specimen agenda of a board meeting. These minutes would normally begin on a new sheet in the minute book, to keep them separate from the minutes of the previous meeting.

Walter Wall Carpets Ltd

Minutes of a Meeting of the Board of Directors
held on Tuesday 6 July at 20 High Street, Popplewell

CONFIDENTIAL

Present

Mr A Wun	Managing Director (Chairman)	*Distribution:*
Mr B Sting	Marketing Director	Directors
Mr C Schell	Finance Director	Secretary
Mr D Day	Production Director	

In attendance — *Action*

Mrs P A Searle — Secretary

202	Apologies for absence: Mrs I Shaw.	
203	The minutes of the meeting held on 4 June 20X8 were signed.	
204	Matters arising from the minutes: none	
205	The Secretary reported that the Landlord's Valuer would visit the factory next week to assess the market rent.	
206	The report of the Managing Director for May 20X9 was considered. It was resolved that the report should be accepted and attached to the minutes.	
207	Statement of cash and borrowings at 30 June 20X9 was considered. It was resolved that cash surpluses should be invested.	C Schell
208	Unaudited management accounts for half year to 30 April 20X9 were considered.	
209	Draft service agreements between the company and Mr A Wun and Mr B Sting for a term of three years in each case from 1 January 20Y0 were tabled and it was resolved that:	
	(1) The said agreements be approved subject to any modifications as provided below;	
	(2) A committee be established of Mr C Schell and Mr D Day, directors of the Company, with authority to approve any modifications to the said agreements which may be recommended by the Company's solicitors;	C Schell D Day
	(3) The said committee may authorise either of its members to sign engrossments of the said agreements on behalf of the company.	
	Mr Wun and Mr Sting did not vote on this resolution.	
210	Report of the sealings committee on documents sealed since 4 June 20X8 was tabled.	
211	Items for the next agenda:	
	(1) A progress report on the new production process	D Day
	(2) All regular items	
212	Date of next meeting: first Tuesday in August.	

....
Chairman

Note. In connection with the directors' service agreements it may be assumed (though it need not be recorded in the minutes) that one or both of the directors indicated that he would wish to raise some technical point. The other two directors (Schell and Day) are then in effect authorised to settle these points, in consultation with the solicitors, and to sign the fair copies (engrossments) on behalf of the company.

Minutes of resolution and minutes of narration

4.3 We mentioned minutes of resolution and minutes of narration above. The above example consists of a combination of the two, although the minutes of narration are very brief, eg:

> 'Unaudited management accounts for the half year to 30 April 20X9 were considered.'

4.4 Minutes of narration can go into more detail than this, particularly when it is helpful to put a resolution into context by summarising the discussion leading up to it.

> 'The question of replacing the company's computer was discussed and it was decided that the proposed purchase of .... should proceed with a view to the installation of the new computer as soon as possible.
>
> .... dissented from this decision and asked that his dissent be recorded in the minutes.'

4.5 As indicated above it would normally be incorrect to enter into details of the discussion. Some organisations, however, may require minutes of narration in further detail, including the recording of individual views expressed, for the following reasons.

(a) **Absent members** may wish to check a record of the discussion which took place.

(b) The chairman/managing director may wish to build up a **profile** of members' points of view and standpoints on certain issues.

4.6 Recording such minutes is fraught with difficulties, particularly if a debate became fairly heated, and it is generally better to avoid references to individual members or directors unless they wish their (usually dissenting) views to be recorded.

Other committee minutes

4.7 In most organisations of any size there are likely to be various committees which hold meetings, not only the board of directors or governing board. Minutes of such meetings must be kept, but they may be of a less formal nature than board minutes, depending on the nature of the organisation and the committee.

4.8 Given below is an example of the meeting of a sub-committee of a local authority. The same principles relating to minutes will apply to both the public and private sectors.

AT A MEETING of the JOINT MEMBERS' PANEL of the PLANNING AND TRANSPORTATION and EDUCATION COMMITTEES held at The Town Hall, Chester on 7th December 20X3

PRESENT
Councillors: R Barker, P T Basil, C J Clark, N Nash, P Sutherland, R T Thoms, P R Young

Councillors P Bone, L P R Haines and M Shah were also present.

1 APPOINTMENT OF CHAIRMAN

RESOLVED:

That Councillor P Sutherland be appointed Chairman.

P SUTHERLAND IN THE CHAIR

---

2 PARENT PARKING AT SCHOOLS

The Panel considered a report by the County Secretary (Item 2 in the Minute Book) concerning parent parking provision on school sites. A full discussion ensued, during which particular regard was paid to the following factors:

(a) General opposition to the principle of parent parking on the part of schools particularly because of concern for safety on school sites.

(b) Initiatives to alleviate the nuisance caused to neighbouring properties by traffic congestion outside schools at peak times.

(c) The Education Committee's concerns about the significant cost implications for its capital programme weighed against limited benefits.

Accordingly it was:

RESOLVED:

(i) That it be a RECOMMENDATION to the Planning and Transportation Committee:

That standards for parent parking provision be amended to a 'nil' requirement, only to be varied in very exceptional circumstances, subject to negotiation between the Education and Planning and Transportation Committees.

(ii) That the County Surveyor be requested to undertake a detailed analysis of the problem of nuisance caused to neighbouring properties by traffic congestion outside school peak times, with a view to identifying measures for alleviating the problem including action by Governors to discourage parents from using cars for home to school transport.

5 APPROVAL OF MINUTES — 6/97, 6/99

5.1 Immediately after the meeting the secretary should prepare minutes from his notes (referring, if necessary, to any notes made by the chairman of the meeting).

5.2 If he is competent, he can be reasonably sure that his version of the minutes will be accepted. He might show it to the chairman and then, with his approval, send copies of the minutes to each member of the board (in the case of a board meeting) or committee. It would be impractical to send minutes to all members of a large board or meeting, and they may be distributed or read at the next meeting instead.

5.3 The first business of the next meeting - (Minute 210 from our example above) - would be an **enquiry** by the chairman as to whether the meeting **agreed** to his signing the minutes in the form in which they had been circulated.

5.4 If any member requested a minor alteration, and this was agreed, the chairman would take the following steps.

- **Make** the **change** in manuscript on the minutes in the minute book.
- **Initial** the alteration.
- **Sign** the minutes.
- **Initial** any **previous page(s)** of the minutes for identification (in a loose-leaf book).

5.5 If a substantial alteration to the draft minutes was required, the chairman might defer signing the minutes until a retyped **fair copy** was available and have the revised version, as signed, tabled (or issued to members of the board) for record.

5.6 Signed minutes have some value as evidence. However unless the articles of association (or other regulations) provide that they are to be conclusive evidence, a person who later disputes their accuracy may still produce evidence to show that the minutes are not correct or are incomplete. The burden of proof though lies on him.

5.7 The practice of signing the minutes at the next meeting, after giving members an opportunity of commenting on them, is not a statutory requirement. It does **minimise** the **risk of dispute** arising about the accuracy of the minutes as a record. If a member was absent from the previous meeting, but does not object to the signing of the minutes of that meeting when it comes up at the next, this does not mean that he accepts responsibility for what was done at the meeting in his absence.

6 ALTERATION OF MINUTES **6/97**

6.1 The procedure for immediate correction of errors in minutes which are not yet signed has already been mentioned.

6.2 If an error is discovered once the minutes have been signed, or if a decision needs to be altered later, the **signed minutes must stand**, as the original record of the meeting. The correction or alteration of a previous decision should be dealt with as a **separate decision** of a later meeting, and should be minuted as such.

> 'With reference to Minute 209 of the meeting on 6 July 20X9 it was reported that the new service agreement with Mr A Wun would be for a period of 2.5 years only until Mr Wun attained the age of 70. It was resolved that the committee be authorised to approve and sign an agreement covering that period' *or*
>
> 'It was resolved that Minute 205 of the meeting on 6 July 20X9 should be corrected by the insertion of the words 'subject to arrangement' at the end of the minute.'

6.3 Note that the new minute **refers back** to the incorrect or amended minute of the previous meeting. The 'old' minute should also be cross-referenced to the 'new', so that a person consulting the minutes will be directed to the final decision or the correct facts. For example, a marginal note might read: 'See minutes of meeting dated ... for correction'.

Exercise 2

Do you have access to minutes of meetings at your place of work? Compare them with the contents of this chapter.

Chapter roundup

- The maintenance of **accurate and timely minutes** is one of the most important functions of a secretary. Since they are the formal record of decisions made at a meeting, it would be difficult to act on decisions without them.
- Minutes normally follow a **certain structure** of which you should be sure to be aware. Resolution minutes are generally much shorter than narration minutes, but it is good practice always to be concise.
- It is the secretary's duty to ensure that minutes are **kept securely** and in accordance with the organisation's regulations.

Test your knowledge

1. State the importance of the minutes. (see para 1.1, Exercise 1)
2. Describe the forms of minute book which are in common use. (2.2 - 2.4)
3. What items should be included in the heading of a meeting? (3.1)
4. How is it possible to trace the minutes relating to a single protracted question considered at different meetings of the same body? (3.4)
5. What is meant by (a) minutes of resolution and (b) minutes of narration? (3.7)
6. In what circumstances is it usual to record that a person present at a meeting voted against a resolution which was carried? (3.13)
7. Draft a minute relating to the formal consideration of a report presented to a board of directors. (4.2)
8. Describe the normal modern procedure for ensuring that the minutes, in the form signed by the chairman, have the agreement of other members. (5.2)
9. How may a correction be made to minutes (a) before and (b) after signature? (5.4, 5.5, 6.2)

Now try illustrative question 6 at the end of the Study Text

Chapter 7

CHAIRMAN AND SECRETARY

This chapter covers the following topics.

Introduction

As explained in the chapter on the conduct of meetings, the presence of a chairman to preside over proceedings is one of the essential elements of a properly constituted meeting. A meeting cannot regulate itself in the continuing sequence of debate. The secretary's duties are of an administrative nature, and should be viewed in the context of the working organisation of the body which from time to time holds meetings.

1 THE APPOINTMENT AND REMOVAL OF A CHAIRMAN 6/98, 6/99

1.1 An open public meeting would usually be presided over by a chairman appointed for the occasion by the promoter or organiser of the meeting. In the case of the more restricted and regular meetings of an established body, it is possible - and desirable - to aim for greater suitability, consistency and continuity in the chairmanship.

1.2 Accordingly, company regulations usually provide that:

(a) The managing committee, which meets frequently, shall appoint one of its members to be its chairman.

(b) He shall also be chairman of general meetings of the members of the body.

1.3 The chairman may be appointed for a **fixed term**, say one year, or he may be appointed to hold office **indefinitely**, until he vacates office or is removed.

1.4 If the regulations do not provide for the appointment of a chairman, a meeting has an inherent right to appoint a person present to be chairman of that meeting.

1.5 If the regulations do provide for the appointment of a chairman but:

- He is not present, at a meeting properly convened.
- He withdraws before the meeting has completed its business or adjourned.

the meeting may replace him with a chairman of its **own choice**: *National Dwellings Society v Sykes 1894*

> *Byng v London Life Association 1989*
> *The facts:* The annual general meeting of the company was duly convened at the Barbican Cinema in London. Due to the number of people attending, overflow rooms were used and the proceedings were linked by audiovisual technology. This failed halfway through, leaving approximately 1,000 angry members outside the meeting. Matters became difficult and the chairman walked out, declaring that the meeting would reconvene at the Cafe Royal that afternoon.
>
> *Deicision:* The chairman had the inherent power to adjourn the meeting but he exercised it unreasonably since the people who attended at the Barbican could not necessarily attend at the Cafe Royal in the afternoon. This would prevent them from voting since proxies could not be lodged in time. Hence the proceedings of the adjourned meeting were invalid.

1.6 If the chairman has been appointed under the **regulations**, which is the normal case, he can only be removed under the regulations: the meeting cannot usually vote him out of the chair. However a meeting which has properly chosen its own chairman may similarly remove him, by carrying a vote of no confidence and electing another chairman.

1.7 If there is some irregularity in the election of a chairman, **objection** should be made at once. (In particular, you might note that a person cannot chair a meeting while his own election as chairman is being debated and voted on; he must vacate the chair for the required period.) If the meeting proceeds under such a chairman, it will be taken to have waived the irregularity, and to have acquiesced in his appointment.

Exercise

The constitution of the Plant Protection Society is currently being drafted by its founding members. Advise them of the rules concerning the appointment and removal of the chairman.

Solution

Appointment of a chairman who continues in office should ensure the office is consistently exercised by a suitable person. This can be best achieved if the body chooses on individual, for his experience and personal qualities, to hold office as chairman for a certain period, and to take the chair at all meetings held within his period of office. This, then should be the starting point for the Plant Protection Society. Their regulations might provide that the managing committee shall appoint one of its members to be its chairman and that he shall also chair general meetings of the members of the body.

The chairman may be appointed for a fixed term, say one year, or he may be appointed to hold office indefinitely, until he vacates office or is removed.

Not providing regulations for the appointment of a chairman can be dangerous; if so, a meeting has an inherent right to appoint a person present to be chairman of that meeting.

If the regulations do provide for the appointment of a chairman but he is not present, at a meeting properly convened, or he withdraws before the meeting has completed its business or adjourned, the meeting may replace him with a chairman of its own choice: *National Dwellings Society v Sykes 1894*.

If the chairman has been appointed under the regulations, which is the normal case, he can only be removed under the regulations: the meeting cannot usually vote him out of the chair. But a meeting which has properly chosen its own chairman may similarly remove him, by carrying a vote of no confidence and electing another chairman.

Non-attendance of the appointed chairman

1.8 The chairman may not always be able to attend meetings, or he may unexpectedly be delayed or prevented from arriving at the time appointed for a particular meeting. In order to minimise disruption, the regulations usually provide either for:

- A **deputy chairman,** who takes the chair automatically in the absence of the chairman
- The **election** of a chairman for that meeting only

If the chairman arrives late, the person acting in his place vacates the chair, and the substantive (which means not the honorary, acting or temporary) chairman takes over.

2 QUALITIES OF A CHAIRMAN 6/99

2.1 Appointing an individual as chairman for a period enables the members (or the managing committee) to select someone who is likely to have and/or develop the required personal qualities for a position which can be rather demanding.

2.2 There are a number of recognised qualities of a good chairman (though common sense may dictate many others, varying with the circumstances of the meeting).

(a) He will have to give **immediate rulings** on points of dispute or doubt, so he should have:

(i) A sound knowledge of the relevant regulations

(ii) An ability to make up his mind without dithering

(iii) Skill in communicating his rulings clearly, but tactfully and in a courteous manner

(b) He should be, and be seen to be, **impartial.** There will be times when criticism is expressed which he personally may find unfair, or there is a strong clash of opinion between other members present. In either situation, whatever his personal views, the chairman should treat opponents with equal fairness. In particular he should treat his own opponents with as much consideration as his supporters.

(c) He should have the **discretion** to know when to insist on **strict observance** of correct procedure, and when a certain amount of **relaxation** will ease the tension. (If in doubt, proper adherence to procedure will be safer.)

(d) He should be **punctual** and regular in his attendance at meetings. If he cannot give his duties the appropriate amount of time and attention, he should consider resigning.

3 DUTIES AND POWERS OF A CHAIRMAN 6/96, 6/98, 6/99

3.1 Preceding chapters have incidentally illustrated many of the duties of the chairman in regulating the proceedings of a meeting, in:

- Preserving order
- Making sure that correct procedure is observed
- Ascertaining the 'sense' of the meeting on relevant issues

3.2 These are his main tasks. But a brief recapitulation may emphasise the personal contribution of the chairman.

(a) Before starting the meeting the chairman should be satisfied that it has been **properly convened** by notice and is **properly constituted** by the attendance of a quorum. He should be watchful to ensure that a quorum is maintained throughout the meeting, of persons entitled to vote on each item of business under discussion, if the regulations so require.

(b) He should do his best to **maintain order and harmony** (or at least courtesy). He should take appropriate action in face of disorder: his powers to do this are discussed below.

(c) He should **guide** the meeting through its business:

   (i) Making sure that each motion and amendment is valid and within the bounds of the notice convening the meeting

   (ii) Taking one subject at a time, in the order set out in the agenda (or any modification of it which may be agreed by the meeting)

   (iii) Making sure that only those who are eligible to speak are invited to do so, and that they speak only once during a debate (subject to the right of reply in some cases)

(d) He should **permit** an adequate amount of **discussion** on each motion, giving sufficient (but not excessive) opportunity for the expression of different points of view. He should deal firmly with irrelevance, long-windedness, interruption and signs of temper.

(e) If '**points of order**' are raised, that is complaints or queries regarding procedure, he should give **immediate rulings** on them.

(f) At the end of a debate he must **ascertain 'the sense of the meeting'** in an appropriate way.

   (i) At a small and informal meeting it may suffice for him to sum up the general agreement of the members on a particular conclusion.

   (ii) In case of disagreement, however, and at any larger or more formal meeting, he should put the issue to the vote. If amendments to the motion have been proposed, they should be put to the vote in the appropriate order, before the original or substantive motion finally comes to the vote.

   (iii) The chairman should count the votes (though this may be delegated to scrutineers in a vote on a poll at a company meeting) and to declare the result. Unless his declaration is challenged at the time, it cannot usually be disputed later (unless the declaration itself is glaringly wrong - eg. '4 in favour, 5 against, I declare the motion carried').

(g) When the minutes of the meeting have been prepared, the chairman should satisfy himself that they are an **accurate and complete record**. If he is satisfied, he should sign the minutes.

(h) In addition to his formal and public duties at the meeting itself, the chairman may have a part to play in the **preparations** for it. The secretary may seek his views in preparing an agenda, or may work with him on a statement which the chairman may be required to make at a general meeting of a public company or other large body.

The powers of the chairman

3.3 To some extent the duties of the chairman listed above also indicate his general powers to carry them out. The regulations may confer further express powers on him as indicated in earlier chapters, such as to adjourn the meeting, to decide that there shall be a vote on a poll or to decide how and when a poll shall be held.

4 THE MAINTENANCE OF ORDER — 6/96, 6/98, 6/99, 12/99

4.1 In the case of disorder at a public meeting, the chairman has statutory rights which are explained in Chapter 2 of this text.

4.2 In the case of a private meeting, he may **order** a **disorderly person to withdraw** and, if he refuses, order that he be removed.

4.3 If there are signs of serious disorder, the chairman has the right and duty (apart from any powers conferred by the regulations) to **order** a **short adjournment**.

John v Rees 1969

The facts: This was a meeting of a constituency political party, following an acute controversy in which the MP had just been expelled by the national executive of the party. In the course of heated and noisy argument there was 'bodily contact, but no real violence'. The chairman proposed a motion, of which no prior notice had been given, that the constituency party should continue to act in accordance with its constitution. When he failed to obtain acceptance of his motion, he adjourned *sine die*. The meeting however continued and passed a resolution to disaffiliate from the national party.

Decision: 'The first duty of the chairman is to keep order if he can', and if he cannot, 'to make earnest and sustained efforts to restore order'. It is proper for him to 'summon to his aid any officers or others whose assistance is available', but if this fails and 'people are put in fear' (more than 'mere punching and jostling') the chairman should adjourn. In doing so he should act in good faith, so that order may be restored and the meeting may continue. An adjournment for, say, 15 minutes would be appropriate - but an adjournment *sine die*, or to a later day, is likely to frustrate the purpose of the meeting and is more than would be required for a restoration of order.

4.4 In *Barton v Taylor 1886*, it was held that 'the same doctrine of reasonable necessity would authorise a suspension until submission or apology by the offending member'.

5 THE CHAIRMAN'S CASTING VOTE **6/99**

5.1 A chairman has no inherent right to a 'casting' vote, but he is not disqualified from casting an original vote as a member, merely because he is in the chair: *Nell v Longbottom 1894*. However, the regulations (for example a company's Table A Articles 50 and 88) usually give him an additional vote, which he may cast in order to resolve an impasse - equal votes for and against a motion.

5.2 Although there are no formal restrictions on the use of a casting vote, the general view is that the chairman, whatever his views on the motion, should endeavour to be impartial.

5.3 Unless he considers that the interests of the body (a) require that the motion be carried, and (b) would be prejudiced if it is not, he should normally use his **casting vote against the motion.** It is argued that, with the votes equal, there is no majority in favour of the proposed change in the existing situation, and the chairman should recognise that fact, even if he personally supports the motion. On that basis a tied vote should be treated as a failure of the motion, and the casting vote should be used to confirm this by defeating it outright.

5.4 Much depends on the circumstances, however. If the chairman acts in good faith in using his casting vote, no-one can accuse him of misusing it.

6 THE SECRETARY AND THE SECRETARY'S DUTIES

6.1 Much of the day-to-day work of a salaried secretary of an organisation is not concerned with meetings (and is studied in the context of Company Secretarial Practice), but work incidental to meetings is one of the most important recognised duties of a secretary.

(a) Duties **before** the meeting

- Fixing the date and time of the meeting
- Choosing and preparing the location of the meeting
- Preparing and issuing various documents

(b) Duties **at** the meeting: assisting the chairman, making notes

(c) Duties **after** the meeting: preparing minutes, acting on and communicating decisions

We will consider each of these duties below.

7 THE DATE AND TIME OF THE MEETING

7.1 One of the first steps to holding a meeting will be the appointment of a date and time for it.

7.2 An organisation will usually have an **established programme** of **meetings.** For example, the directors of a trading company may have decided to hold monthly board meetings on, say, the first Wednesday of each month, at a fixed time. The annual general meeting of any established organisation usually takes place at about the same time each year. In addition to this routine cycle of meetings, there may be special and non-recurrent meetings.

7.3 The time of day at which a meeting is held will vary according to the following.

(a) The **anticipated length of the meeting**. A long session should obviously start early in the day, if possible.

(b) The **anticipated stamina and attentiveness of the participants**. Members are unlikely to be at the peak of their energy and concentration if the meeting is held late in the day, or late in the week.

(c) The **location of the meeting.** Time must be allowed for members to get to the meeting, if they are not already gathered on the premises. Likewise, the meeting should finish early enough to allow them to get home (or elsewhere) conveniently.

(d) **Particular circumstances surrounding the meeting.** The urgency of a matter to be discussed by a meeting may dictate its timing; documents may have to be produced to meet the last post, decisions may have to be reached before another meeting etc. A small meeting may also be able to take into account the personal circumstances of its members, in determining when to convene.

8 LOCATION OF THE MEETING 12/99

8.1 A routine meeting of a management committee or board of directors usually meets in the same room on each occasion, but the secretary should ensure that the room is booked for the next meeting, if it is also used for other purposes.

8.2 An **annual meeting**, even if it is routine, is likely to require more elaborate preparation. Unless there are appropriate facilities for holding the meeting on the premises of the body itself, the secretary will have to make arrangements to book a hall or assembly room elsewhere.

8.3 If a guest speaker (or other important participant) will have to travel any distance to the meeting, the secretary may also be required to arrange:

- His transport to the location, and possibly overnight accommodation
- The refund of his travelling and/or other expenses

8.4 Ideally, the location of the meeting should be chosen for its **convenience** and **accessibility** to as many of the participants as possible.

Practical preparations for the meeting

8.5 The room must be set up for the meeting. In the case of a small, management committee meeting, this is unlikely to require much preliminary work, but at a public general meeting, the seating and other arrangements may include the following.

(a) There may be a long table at one end (possibly on a raised dais) on which the directors or members of a committee are seated in pre-arranged places, with the chairman in the centre (and the secretary alongside him).

(b) The press, if admitted, like to sit directly in front of the chairman and his colleagues, facing them. The press are likely to require a table on which to write their notes.

(c) The general body of the members attending the meeting are seated in the body of the hall facing towards the front. Alternatively, if the meeting is reasonably small, it may be possible to have tables set out as a ring, or four sides of a square, with members facing inwards.

(d) The needs of members will vary. It may be necessary to have 'Non-smoking areas'; depending on the type of meeting, tables may be provided for members who wish to make notes; drinking water may be set within reach etc.

(e) The secretary should take particular account of the needs of disabled attenders. These include making wheelchair access available, clear speaker systems, sign language and subsequent provision of written records of speeches for the hard of hearing, and minutes on audio tape or in Braille for the visually impaired.

(f) It may be necessary to install a public address (microphone) system if the room is very large. An overhead projector or other visual aid may also be required, unless the meeting is small enough to enable copies of relevant material to be distributed, or to 'gather round' a small visual display.

(g) The general suitability of the premises and its facilities will obviously vary according to the size and type of meeting. Attention should, however, be given to:

- The availability of toilets and refreshment facilities
- The availability of parking and access
- Lighting, heating and ventilation
- Decor (especially if the 'image' of the organisation is important)
- Safety (fire exits) and security

9 DOCUMENTATION AND PAPERS

9.1 Meetings inevitably generate a large amount of 'paperwork' for the secretary, along with the other general administrative duties required before, during and after the meeting. The various documents and other material that must be prepared, and either issued to members or brought to a meeting, include the following.

(a) **Notice and agenda.** It is usual to issue a notice and/or agenda in advance, with any attached papers that may be necessary. The chairman will need a special agenda with procedural information.

(b) **Reports and accounts**, which are the main business of most annual meetings. These must obviously be ready for issue at the appropriate time. The secretary may have to keep in close contact with colleagues who are preparing material, and perhaps with photographers, typesetters and printers. The material will usually be sent with the notice of the meeting, but the regulations may specify that the report or account, say of a small club, may simply be displayed on its premises for a period before the meeting. The secretary should in either case ensure that the appropriate procedure is observed.

(c) **Proxy forms**. Proxy forms (or cards) may also be sent out with the notice of the meeting, if the regulations allow for proxy voting: alternatively, the notice may state how and from whom a proxy form may be obtained. The forms will have to be prepared, and once they have been filled in and returned by members, they will have to be checked and summarised for the chairman (who usually 'casts' the proxy votes as directed). They should be brought to the meeting, preferably listed under, or bundled into, 'For' and 'Against', for ease of reference. (The Hampel report recommended proxies should be counted in advance of the meeting. Once a show of hands has taken place, and without a poll being demanded, the chairman should announce the total proxy votes for and against a motion.) Proxy voting will be described in detail later. Lists of members and proxies will also have to be prepared for checking admittance and voting rights at the meeting.

(d) **Polling lists or voting papers**. If it is anticipated that a poll will be demanded on some issue, and will be taken immediately, polling lists or individual voting papers should be prepared in advance.

(e) **Press announcements**. There may be publicity to arrange, including the reservation of space in newspapers for publication of advance information of the meeting in summary form.

9.2 All the above documents will require preparation to meet various deadlines - say in time for the issuing of the notice, or the date of the meeting - but the administrative effort does not stop there. The secretary may have to take papers with him for distribution at the meeting, and should make sure that everything likely to be required is ready at the venue on the day.

9.3 If confidential material is distributed to a board meeting, the secretary must also think about collecting up, at the end of the meeting, any copies left lying on the table. His own files and material must of course also be removed from the meeting place and returned to his office.

9.4 The secretary should generally bring to the meeting any **papers** he expects may be required for reference at the meeting.

(a) At a general meeting of a company, a copy of the register of **members**, so that voting rights etc can be sorted out on the spot if necessary

(b) A copy of **standing orders** or other regulations governing the meeting, to settle any questions of procedure: similarly, a copy of the Companies Act, the Memorandum and Articles of a company etc

(c) A copy of any **reports and accounts** (if not already circulated) that are to be considered

9.5 Certain documents (for instance the register of directors' interests) must by law be available for inspection before and during the meeting (as explained in a later chapter).

10 THE SECRETARY'S OTHER DUTIES BEFORE, DURING AND AFTER THE MEETING

12/99

10.1 If there is likely to be acrimony at the meeting, it may be wise to appoint **stewards**; they should be identified by badges. If necessary the police should be warned.

Duties of the secretary at the meeting

10.2 The main duty of the secretary at any meeting itself is to **take notes** from which he may later write up the minutes. If he is too much occupied with other things, the task should be delegated to a colleague, such as the assistant secretary (if any), as it does require undistracted and careful attention.

10.3 Large meetings pose their own problems. Apart from action in anticipation of disorder, there should be a **control of admission**. For this purpose a responsible member of staff should be posted at the doorway with an attendance list to be signed; there may be separate lists for members and others. The availability of the register of members enables a quick check to be made in case of doubt.

10.4 The secretary should arrange to receive, if possible, a **list of those present** at the start of the meeting, unless he knows them all by sight: it is useful to be aware when known 'supporters' or 'critics' have turned up. Later, of course, the secretary will need the attendance record for the minutes.

10.5 The chairman and his colleagues may have to make speeches, present reports and/or reply to questions. The secretary should have **anticipated** the **more likely questions** that might be put by the meeting, and brought sufficient reference material to find the information required. The secretary should be at the chairman's side to assist and advise in this capacity, being literally his 'right hand man'. The secretary should be supportive, without calling attention to the fact in such a way as to undermine the chairman's authority, for instance by loudly saying something like: 'Sorry, Mr Chairman, you seem to have forgotten the basic fact that ...'

10.6 At a large meeting, the voting is usually by **show of hands.** This may present no difficulties, but the secretary should silently make his own count of hands raised, in case the chairman's count is challenged. The usual response to a challenge on the count is to repeat it and count more slowly.

10.7 Certain documents may be required to be read aloud to the meeting (rather than just being 'taken as read') such as the notice convening the meeting or the previous minutes of a committee or board meeting. This will be the secretary's task.

Duties of the secretary after the meeting

10.8 The secretary's duties after the meeting include:

(a) **Writing** up the **minutes** in the minute book, and obtaining the chairman's approval

(b) **Noting,** and **acting on,** any **decisions** which require his own personal intervention, such as the amendment of documents, convening of a further meeting or other administrative tasks, for which there may be deadlines

(c) **Composing** a suitable **report** for the Press, if representatives were not present at the meeting

(d) **Communicating** the **decisions** of the meeting to colleagues, advisers and third parties

Chapter roundup

- Both chairman and secretary have vital roles to play in the operation of a successful meeting.
- This **chairman** must be validly appointed and should be aware of his duties and powers. Ideally he or she should be aware of the qualities which make a good chairman, and also of the extent of his or her powers to maintain good order at the meeting. A particularly important aspect is the chairman's possession of and use of a casting vote.
- The **secretary's role** in meetings is extensive; depending on the organisation, he or she may be solely responsible for setting the date and time of the meeting, its location and its preparation. It is important to take the right documentation and to be seen to be supporting the chairman.

Test your knowledge

1 How is the chairman of a meeting chosen? (see para 1.1)

2 How may a chairman be appointed if the regular chairman does not appear or withdraws? (1.5)

3 Give examples of the qualities which a good chairman should possess. (2.2)

4 Summarise the duties of the chairman in regulating the proceedings at a meeting. (3.2)

5 What powers has the chairman of a private meeting in the event of disorder? (4.2 - 4.4)

6 State whether a chairman has a casting vote and how he is expected to use it if he has. (5.1 - 5.4)

7 Give three examples of duties of a secretary before the day of the meeting arrives. (6.1)

8 What matters should be considered when setting the time of day for a meeting? (7.3)

9 Describe the normal seating arrangements at a general meeting of a large body. (8.5)

10 What documents is a secretary of a meeting required to prepare? (9.1)

11 How is it possible to (a) control admission and (b) ascertain who is present at a large meeting? (10.3, 10.4)

Now try illustrative question 7 at the end of the Study Text

Chapter 8

COMMITTEES AND CONFERENCES

This chapter covers the following topics.

Introduction

In this chapter we consider some specific types of decision making forum. **Committee** is a general term for a group of experts or interested parties to whom part of the main work of a larger body is delegated. They are more common in public sector and similar bodies, but may be found in large commercial organisations too. A *conference* is a means of bringing together a large number of people to discuss matters of current concern to them. Typically a conference will last several days.

1 REASONS FOR COMMITTEES 6/98

1.1 A large public or general meeting serves the purpose of:

- Providing information
- Permitting an expression of opinion
- Reaching agreement on the matters under discussion

However a meeting which is attended by a large number of people cannot effectually work on the details of a problem.

1.2 Sometimes, too, only a small group of experts is really competent to collect information and work out recommendations for dealing with complicated matters. Such specialised tasks may be 'remitted' or handed over to a committee.

1.3 There are other circumstances in which the committee system might be favoured.

(a) The need to remove routine business from the already crowded agenda of meetings which have important **special business** to attend to

(b) The convenience of appointing a small body, which can meet frequently, to **manage the affairs** of a disparate body, such as a sports club, with a large number of members

1.4 Whatever the advantages of remitting a subject to a committee, whether for a specific purpose or as a continuing responsibility, there are pitfalls, particularly associated with lack of communication and accountability. Careful consideration is needed of various factors.

(a) The definition of **what** it is **remitting** (the sphere of activity set out in the committee's terms of reference)

(b) Who are to be the **members** of the committee

(c) What **powers** to take action (if any) the committee is to have

In any event the committee is answerable to the body by which it is appointed, and should report back to it.

2 THE NATURE AND POWERS OF A COMMITTEE 6/95, 12/95

2.1 The essential characteristic of a committee is that a different, and usually larger, body delegates or entrusts certain tasks or responsibilities to it. A committee may consist of a single person, but it is more usual to appoint a committee of two or more members.

2.2 A committee's function may be:

(a) **Informative**; gathering and presenting information to the appointing body

(b) **Advisory**; informing the appointing body, and making recommendations or proposals, for decision by the body

(c) **Executive**; with powers to initiate and regulate action itself

Its function should be decided by the appointing body, and made quite clear in the terms of reference of the committee in question.

2.3 It is not essential that a committee should be given executive powers, though in some cases (eg a management committee of an association) the nature of the task requires the committee to have such powers. The body to which the committee is answerable is then bound by its actions, on the principle that a committee is acting as agent for the body (which is its principal).

Principal - Agent relationship

2.4 'A committee means a person or persons to whom powers are committed which would otherwise be exercised by another body': *Re Taurine Co 1882.*

2.5 However, the appointing body is not deprived of its own powers by delegating them to a committee; it may still, if it wishes, exercise those powers directly: *Huth v Clarke 1890.*

2.6 If powers are delegated to a committee, they are vested in all the members of the committee; in other words, it should **act collectively** (see *Cook v Ward* below). For convenience, however, it is common practice in appointing a committee to:

(a) **Fix a quorum** for committee meetings that is less than the full membership, so that meetings may be held without requiring every member to be present

(b) **Authorise a committee to delegate** its powers to an individual member or members

2.7 If there is dissatisfaction with the work of a committee, the proper course is to **revoke** or redefine its **powers** or to **alter** its **membership.**

Manton v Brighton Corporation 1951
The facts: A local authority acting under its standing orders appointed members of the authority annually to constitute standing committees with various tasks. Before the term of his annual appointment had expired the authority removed the plaintiff from the committees of which he was a member. He contended that the authority had no power to revoke his appointment in this way.

Held: The local authority was competent to revoke the delegated powers of an entire committee before its term of office had expired. It was therefore competent to remove a single member from a committee.

3 TYPES OF COMMITTEE **12/95, 12/98**

3.1 There are several different types of committee. We will look at each of these briefly in turn.

Executive committees

3.2 An executive committee is one which is appointed with full authority to manage the affairs of the body concerned. Often known in associations as a **management committee**, it performs tasks similar to that of a company board of directors. In particular, it will resolve when a full meeting of the body is to be held and will determine its agenda.

3.3 It is still responsible to the body from which it derives its powers, however, and must **report** on its conduct of the body's affairs. This is usually done by tabling, at meetings of the appointing body, either the minutes of committee meeting or a report compiled for the purpose by the committee.

Standing committees

3.4 The executive committee - and indeed the body as a whole - does not usually wish to take up its meeting time with matters which are either **strictly routine** or **highly specialised**. Instead, business of this type may be handled by a standing committee (or sub-committee), to which is delegated a continuing task or role.

3.5 The members of a standing committee may be appointed for a limited period but the committee itself, and its work, is continuous in nature. Its existence and functions may be formally and permanently recognised by the standing orders of the appointing body.

3.6 Again, the committee (or sub-committee) must report regularly to the appointing body. A standing committee which operates routinely and indefinitely will usually only be required to table the minutes of its meetings at a meeting of the appointing body.

3.7 As an example, most bodies find it useful to appoint a Finance Committee with authority to draw up estimates of income and expenditure. They are

(a) Either **submitted for approval** by the main body; or

(b) Or **approved** by the committee itself, by its delegated powers, and reported to the main body.

In any case the Finance Committee usually has delegated power to approve supplementary items of expenditure which are not included in the annual estimates. It may also be required to submit annual accounts to the main body.

Special or 'ad hoc' committees

3.8 A special committee is appointed to perform a **specific task**: having completed that task and made its report, it ceases to exist. Such a committee is also said to be appointed *ad hoc* (for that purpose only).

3.9 For example, a club might appoint an *ad hoc* committee to:

(a) **Gather information** on an important proposal, to aid the general meeting in making a decision

(b) **Review its regulations** and prepare a revised version for approval at a general meeting of the club

(c) **Organise** a one-off or annual **event** such as a dinner (if there is no standing committee in charge of such things)

3.10 It is less likely that executive powers will be delegated to a special committee, since the main body really requires proposals on which it can make its own decisions.

3.11 If some emergency is foreseen, it is also possible to provide for immediate consideration and decision by any members of the main body who are available at short notice.

Sub-committees

3.12 If it is authorised to do so, a committee may appoint a sub-committee, usually for a **specific, limited task.**

3.13 Thus a special committee appointed to make recommendations on a question of policy might decide that, as a first step, it would investigate the practice of other similar bodies. A sub-committee might be appointed to approach the other bodies and find out what they did and whether their practice was found satisfactory. This information would then be laid before the full committee.

3.14 A sub-committee is usually made up of selected members of the committee it is appointed to serve.

Joint committees

3.15 A joint committee is a **combined committee** appointed by **two or more main bodies**, with members drawn from them all. For example, if there is a project for a trade fair to be held in a particular town, the chambers of commerce and the trade associations might agree to appoint a joint organising committee to co-ordinate their plans.

3.16 A joint committee might also consist of representatives from various committees working side by side in a large organisation - for instance, in a trading concern, from the Sales, Production and Development committees - to 'pool' ideas and co-ordinate plans.

4 PROCEDURE IN CONNECTION WITH COMMITTEES 12/98, 6/99

4.1 A committee generally adopts the same basic meetings procedure as its main body, unless otherwise instructed. Thus it is usually unnecessary to lay down afresh procedures on notice to convene meetings, agenda, voting or minutes. But there are a number of matters which may require special consideration.

(a) **Quorum**. Unless a quorum is fixed at a lesser number, for convenience, all members must be present to form a quorum at committee meetings.

(b) **Voting**. Unless unanimous decisions are requested by the appointing body, a majority decision will suffice. If the committee cannot agree, the minority might:

- Ask that its dissent be recorded in the committee's report or
- Attach to the committee's report a statement of its own minority view

(c) The **chairman** is appointed by the members of the committee, unless the main body nominated a chairman when it established the committee itself.

(d) **Members** may only be **co-opted** (elected to the committee by the votes of its existing members) if the committee has the authority. Co-option is a common and useful way of bringing in expertise which the original members may lack. However it is usual to provide that co-opted members shall not vote; their function is rather to act as advisers.

(e) **Terms of reference** may be found in the regulations of the main body, in the case of a standing committee. Otherwise, suitable terms should be set out in the resolution by which the committee is appointed in general meeting. The terms should set out the nature and scope of the committee's task, its time-scale, powers and responsibilities.

(f) **Delegation of powers** to an individual member or members (as a sub-committee) is permissible only if the committee is given the authority for it: *Cook v Ward 1877*.

(g) A **report** is required, in the form of:

- Minutes of the committee meetings tabled at a meeting of the full body
- A formal report tabled for the consideration of the full body

(h) As an 'agent' of the appointing body, a committee must keep **proper accounts** of its doings, and of the body's property and funds (if these are at the committee's disposal). Members have a special duty:

- To have the body's interests at heart
- Not to make personal gain from their position on the committee
- Not to abuse any information they may gather in their work

(i) **Completion** of its task (or a report of its inability to complete it) is essential. Whatever the problems it encounters, a committee is agent of the main body, and cannot just abandon what it has been given to do.

(j) If the committee has made **proposals**, these may be considered and discussed by the full body, and adopted (or not). You may recall the standard procedural motion 'to refer back to the committee' the report which it has produced. This is in effect an instruction from the appointing body that the committee modify its proposals. It may sometimes also be an oblique way of dropping the whole scheme.

5 DISADVANTAGES OF THE COMMITTEE SYSTEM **6/00**

5.1 The main advantages of remitting subjects to committees were touched on in our introduction to this chapter.

5.2 We also mentioned earlier that a 'floating' committee might be provided for to deal immediately with matters arising in a particular situation. However, it cannot be said that the committee system is normally associated with prompt action. On the contrary, the appointment of a committee to investigate and report is an often-used device for putting off a difficult decision.

5.3 If a matter is referred to a committee, the body concerned should consider whether it can afford the added length of time before the matter is resolved - even if, as may often be the case, a better or wiser conclusion emerges from the committee.

5.4 A drawback of the use of committees, especially when it becomes the standard procedure for debating any matter of interest within a large body, is the **time** which it consumes.

5.5 Because committees can conduct their business informally, it is difficult to impose any restriction on the length of the proceedings and the number of times a single member can speak on a given subject.

5.6 The time of the members of the committee - particularly in companies, where they may be senior managers or consultants - is also costly.

5.7 Meetings of committees also require organisation, meeting facilities, and perhaps secretarial services.

6 EXAMPLES OF COMMITTEE SYSTEMS **12/97, 6/00**

Teaching organisations

6.1 For various reasons, teaching organisations make great use of committees. The following is no more than a selective illustration of the proliferation of committee work in a university.

(a) Each of the academic **departments** is likely to have **internal committees** to deal with such matters as syllabuses, lecture programmes, recommended reading lists, examination arrangements etc.

(b) The academic body as a whole usually has a **committee of all its members**, to discuss questions of academic and university policy. The parent committee will appoint a number of representative committees to deal with particular subjects, including junior academic and other staff appointments.

(c) The overall responsibility for the university is entrusted to a **senate**, board of trustees etc with members drawn from within and outside the university.

(d) On the **administrative side** of the university there will be a number of standing committees, and also *ad hoc* committees, to deal with the routine management of the university, its finances, external relations including appeals for funds, maintenance of buildings, library policy etc.

(e) If, as is usual, the university has received private endowments to provide scholarships or to finance research programmes, there will be **committees** both to decide how the **money** shall be used and to **oversee the investment** of the capital of the funds.

(f) Relations between the university and its student body and the trade unions which represent the various grades of staff may well lead to the establishment of **joint committees** of the two sides.

Professional organisations

6.2 Large professional organisations have fewer committees than teaching organisations. The membership tends to be larger and the meetings less frequent. But professions do perceive a need for consultation and policy-making by discussion: accordingly the committee system is a basic part of their structure.

6.3 As an example, the Law Society (the solicitors' professional body) has an elected Council at the apex of its structure. But the greater part of the work is done by committees, each of which is given responsibility for a particular aspect of the Society's interests, including:

- Current problems within the legal profession
- New legislation before Parliament
- Changes in public services such as legal aid (for litigants of limited means)
- Disciplinary proceedings for serious breaches of professional codes of conduct etc.

Committees in commercial organisations — 12/95, 12/98

6.4 Commercial organisations, such as large companies, use committees (typically boards of directors) for management and policy matters. Within such organisations, however, the general aim is usually to entrust the decision-making process to individual managers, with line responsibility from the chief executive downwards, and individual accountability (rather than blurring responsibility within a group).

6.5 The committee system has its merits - for brainstorming exercises, or staff relations - but it can be too time-consuming, costly in man-hours, and uncertain in effectiveness for the world of business.

6.6 The following is an example of a committee structure in an organisation and it demonstrates how and why committees are used by companies. Say that the board is serviced by five committees.

- Executive Management Committee
- Strategy Review Committee
- Audit Committee
- Remuneration Committee
- Nomination Committee

re. Cadbury report / Greenbury Report.

6.7 The last three of these will have been set up relatively recently to comply with the recommendations of the Cadbury Report on Corporate Governance and the Code of Best Practice from the Greenbury report (see Chapter 1). Effectively, compliance with these codes is or will be a requirement of a Stock Exchange listing.

6.8 We will consider the likely role of each of these committees in turn.

Audit committee

6.9 The Cadbury report contained a useful appendix showing specimen terms of reference for an audit committee. These are reproduced in full below.

'SPECIMEN TERMS OF REFERENCE FOR AN AUDIT COMMITTEE

For guidance only

Constitution

1 The Board hereby resolves to establish a committee of the board to be known as the audit committee.

Membership

2 The committee shall be appointed by the board from amongst the non-executive directors of the company and shall consist of not less than three members. A quorum shall be two members.

3 The chairman of the committee shall be appointed by the board.

Attendance at meetings

4 The finance director, the head of internal audit, and a representative of the external auditors shall normally attend meetings. Other board members shall also have the right of attendance. However, at least once a year the committee shall meet with the external auditors without executive board members present.

5 The company secretary shall be the secretary of the committee.

Frequency of meetings

6 Meetings shall be held not less than twice a year. The external auditors may request a meeting if they consider that one is necessary.

Authority

7 The committee is authorised by the board to investigate any activity within its terms of reference. It is authorised to seek any information it requires from any employee and all employees are directed to co-operate with any request made by the committee.

8 The committee is authorised by the board to obtain outside legal or other independent professional advice and to secure the attendance of outsiders with relevant experience and expertise if it considers this necessary.

Duties

9 The duties of the committee shall be:

(a) to consider the appointment of the external auditor, the audit fee, and any questions of resignation or dismissal;

(b) to discuss with the external auditor before the audit commences the nature and scope of the audit, and ensure co-ordination where more than one audit firm is involved;

(c) to review the half-year and annual financial statements before submission to the board, focusing particularly on:

(i) any changes in accounting polices and practices;
(ii) major judgmental areas;
(iii) significant adjustments resulting from the audit;
(iv) the going concern assumption;
(v) compliance with accounting standards;

(vi) compliance with stock exchange and legal requirements.

(d) to discuss problems and reservations arising from the interim and final audits, and any matters the auditor may wish to discuss (in the absence of management where necessary);

(e) to review the external auditor's management letter and management's response;

(f) to review the company's statement on internal control systems prior to endorsement by the board;

(g) (where an internal audit function exists) to review the internal audit programme, ensure co-ordination between the internal and external auditors, and ensure that the internal audit function is adequately resourced and has appropriate standing within the company;

(h) to consider the major findings of internal investigations and management's response;

(i) to consider other topics, as defined by the board.

Reporting procedures

10 The secretary shall circulate the minutes of meetings of the committee to all members of the board.'

6.10 The Cadbury report recommended that there should be a minimum of three members and that membership should be confined to non-executive directors, who should be independent of management and free from any business or other relationship which could materially interfere with their judgement.

6.11 ICSA published its own terms of reference for audit committees in October 1998. The major difference between these and those proposed by the Cadbury committee were that ICSA's terms included more details of the mechanics of meetings, covering:

- The calling of meetings
- Period of notice
- Quorum
- Provisions if the chairman is absent
- Keeping and circulating of minutes

Nomination committee

6.12 The nomination committee has the responsibility (in the words of the Cadbury report) 'of proposing to the board, in the first instance, any **new appointments**, whether of executive or non-executive directors.' Cadbury also recommended that it should comprise a majority of non-executive directors and be chaired by either the chairman or a non-executive director.

6.13 The committee presently should probably meet at least twice a year. It would be sensible if this committee could have a member or members in common with the Strategy Review committee, which ought to be able to supply input on future senior management needs of the business in the light of its intended long-term direction. For example, a director with a strong IT background might be considered desirable if the company as a whole were to become more reliant on computers.

Remuneration committee

6.14 The following guidelines are extracted from the Greenbury code as amended by suggestions made by the Hampel report.

(a) Boards of directors should set up remuneration committees of non-executive directors to recommend on their behalf, and on behalf of the shareholders, ... the company's policy on the framework of remuneration of directors, and should **determine executive remuneration** packages for each of the executive directors.

(b) Remuneration committees should **consist exclusively** of **non-executive directors** with no personal financial interest other than as shareholders in the matters to be decided, no potential conflicts of interest arising from cross-directorships and no day-to-day involvement in running the business.

(c) The **board** itself should **determine** the **remuneration of non-executive directors**, including members of the remuneration committee.

(d) Remuneration committees should **consult** the company chairman and/or chief executive about their proposals and have access to professional advice.

(e) The remuneration committee chairman should **attend the company's AGM** to answer shareholder's questions about directors' remuneration and should ensure that the company maintains contact as required with its principal shareholders about remuneration.

(f) The committee should consider each year whether the circumstances are such that the AGM should be invited to **approve the policy** set out in their report and should minute their conclusions.

Executive Management committee

6.15 The value of a **formally constituted** committee to **manage** the business is far more questionable. There is a strong danger that bureaucracy will strangle innovation at birth, or delay matters to such an extent that competitors are able to steal a march on us by responding more quickly to events. It would be more appropriate if the role of this committee was one of:

(a) Authorising expenditure between certain limits

(b) Considering more substantial capital expenditure proposals and submitting them to the board for approval if it sees fit

(c) Co-ordinating the activities of the separate operating divisions

(d) Considering divisional budgets prior to submission to the board for approval

(e) Monitoring the implementation of corporate strategy so far as it affects the three divisions in general

6.16 Meetings of this committee should be held at least monthly, prior to submission of papers to the monthly board meetings. Meetings may be needed more often than this in order to get quick authorisation for some ventures.

The Strategy Review committee

6.17 The functions of this committee are, essentially, **management functions** rather than corporate governance functions. Again, there should be as little bureaucracy as possible. Membership is likely to be, as a minimum, the chairman, the finance director, and at least one non-executive director. The suggested task of this committee would be to formulate proposals for the long-term direction of the company (for submission to the board), not simply to review current strategy. The review process is, of course, important too. The committee will focus on business reviews and acquisition proposals.

The board

6.18 Most important issues will still be primarily the responsibility of the board.

(a) Approval of accounts, communications and press releases

(b) Approval of terms of appointment and committee terms of reference

(c) Risk management strategy

(d) Divisional budgets (submitted after consideration by the Executive Management committee (EMC), which represent the short-term (one year) version of the long-term strategic plan)

(e) Capital expenditure proposals above a certain level, following consideration by the EMC

(f) Acquisition approvals after the Strategy Review committee has considered and submitted acquisition proposals

(g) Investment and treasury strategy

(h) Overall control of operating companies (in other words directing and monitoring their performance)

Exercise 1

What (if any) is the committee structure in the organisation you work for? Find out as much as you can about the roles, composition and actions of these committees.

---

7 CONFERENCES

7.1 A body which has a large membership spread over a wide area, such as a professional body or a trade union, may find conferences a useful means of improving contact between the organisation and the body of the membership.

7.2 A well-organised annual conference is a means of bringing together a much larger number of members to discuss matters of current interest or concern. It can 'bridge the gap', and give members a better understanding of what their organisation is trying to do for them and a greater commitment to it.

7.3 In a typical case, a conference lasts several days, sometimes spread over the long weekend of a public holiday: Easter is a favourite time for conferences. As the conference will entail hotel accommodation, it is often held at a seaside resort or inland spa which will have the facilities, and may provide them more cheaply 'out of season'.

7.4 There will be social events for the entertainment of members (and their spouses). The town chosen for the conference will usually encourage the organisation to come again by offering a civic reception or visits to places of interest. There may be a dinner for the conference delegates on one evening of the period. The social aspect adds to the preparatory work of the conference organiser.

Practical arrangements for a conference

7.5 A conference will always do some of its business (and in some cases, all of it) in full or 'plenary' session in a large room or public hall. Practical arrangements for the organiser(s) and secretary to consider include the following.

(a) **Admission**. Delegates should have tickets or badges to distinguish them from others. Admission is usually restricted to members, press representatives and invited visitors, all of whom must be identified.

(b) **Seating**. If the conference hall has numbered rows of seats, each delegate may be allotted his place for the duration of the conference. It is also necessary to decide who is to be seated on the platform (not necessarily the same individuals for the entire duration of the conference), and how they are to be placed. The chairman should, of course, have a central or otherwise prominent position.

(c) **Speeches.** Among other considerations:

(i) There may be standing orders which, for example, limit the length of speeches or require advance notice of the intention to propose a motion or speak in a debate.

(ii) It may be necessary to use a public address system, and to require speakers from the body of the hall to come to the podium to address the meeting.

(iii) Material may have to be distributed to the press about debates, before or after they have taken place.

(d) **Programme**. On these occasions, the number of topics which members wish to discuss, and the remarks which they wish to make on them, usually tend to exceed the time available. There should be a detailed schedule, to allocate time to each subject. It may be necessary to prepare in advance lists of speakers whom the chairman will call to speak in their turn. The chairman must politely but firmly keep the conference, and the individual speakers, within the limits set by the timetable and topical programme.

(e) **Motions**. The best means of keeping the proceedings under control is to confine each debate to discussion of a motion, which should be proposed and seconded, and if necessary put to the vote. The standing orders may well require it. If the members represent branches of the main body, as is often the case at trade union conferences, there should be effective means of taking 'card votes' and declaring the result.

(f) **Record of proceedings**. The minutes will not usually record the debate, only the result of votes. However, an organisation may have established the practice of publishing, in its members' journal, the full text of major addresses to the conference and/or a summary of the debate on each topic, with the names of the speakers. In this case, adequate notes must be taken, so that such a text can be prepared.

(g) **The press**. If press reporters are admitted to all or part of the proceedings of the conference, suitable facilities should be provided, such as reserved seats (usually at the front, below the platform), tables on which to write, accreditation cards to secure admission, and copies of the text of prepared speeches.

7.6 A **conference office** will be established, in or near the main hall, at which delegates may obtain copies of papers, ask for information, make complaints etc. Delegates will 'register' at the conference office when they arrive, so that their presence may be recorded, the initial issue of papers made, admission badges provided and information given of accommodation arranged for them. The conference office should be 'manned' during all working hours of the conference.

Other meetings in connection with conferences

7.7 As a national conference brings together in one place the most active and prominent members of the body, the body may wish to take the opportunity to arrange meetings of the **standing committees** of which they are members.

7.8 These meetings should be arranged so that they do not clash with major events in the conference hall. Committee rooms will be required, as well as the normal arrangements for such meetings: notice, agenda, minutes etc.

7.9 With the conference of a body whose members have a variety of special interests (such as a professional body with a membership in different working occupations) a number of ancillary meetings may be held during the conference. Groups with common interests may listen to an address by a distinguished specialist in their field, or discuss some topic of particular interest to them. The meetings do, however, form part of the conference programme and are usually open to all delegates to the conference. Obviously, this element of the conference adds considerably to the task of the organiser. In particular there may be papers to circulate or texts of speeches to record.

Costs and budgets

7.10 A conference of this type costs a large sum of money, in addition to the expenditure of time. The wages of the organising staff are paid by the main body, but the direct cost of the conference is usually recovered from the delegates who attend. This is reasonable, since not all members of the main body will attend a conference; the extra cash expenditure should be a charge on those who do come.

7.11 The first step is to **prepare** a **budget**, based on the costs of conferences in the recent past, with a margin for unforeseen and emergency expenses.

(a) The general overhead expenses of the conference, such as the hire of the hall or the printing costs, are averaged out as a 'conference fee' which all delegates must pay

(b) Some expenses, such as accommodation overnight at hotels, may more appropriately be recovered from the individuals to whom they relate: some delegates may not need accommodation, particularly if they live in the town where this year's conference is being held

(c) So also there may be a charge for a special outing, or a place at a conference dinner, if these expenses are not common to all delegates

7.12 Estimating, and then obtaining, payment of the charges due from each delegate is quite a considerable feat of accounting.

Exercise 2

Assume that your Institute is to hold a one day education conference at which lectures are to be given on topics of interest to members. Concurrent lectures are to be given so that members will have a choice as to which lecture to attend.

Draft a specimen programme for such a conference.

Solution

CONFERENCE

PHARMACEUTICAL PRODUCT LIABILITY AND USE OF LITIGATION

Conference Programme

9.00	Registration and coffee		
9.30	Introduction *Professor Angus Bogle, Duke's College, London*		
9.45	Plenary session: The Framework for Regulation *Rebecca Kingston, consultant in regulatory affairs*		
10.45	Coffee		
11.00	'The product is faulty' - protection against liability *Simon Halliday, Partner, Ironside & Mallone*	**11.00**	'Warnings of adverse reactions' *Professor Andrew Clutterbuck, Duke's College London*
12.15	'The common law and drug-related claims' *Marc Howe, Partner, Ironside & Mallone*	**12.15**	'The relationship with the CSM and DHS' *Professor Bruce Fleming, Duke's College, London*
1.00	Lunch		
2.15	'How to defend a drug adverse reaction case' *Simon Halliday, Partner, Ironside & Mallone*	**2.15**	'Extra-legal pressures' - Media and Action Groups *Professor Andrew Clutterbuck, Duke's College, London*

3.00	'Extra-legal pressures'- Media and Action Groups *Professor Andrew Clutterbuck, Duke's College, London*	**3.00**	'The common law and drug-related claims' *Marc Howe, Partner, Ironside & Mallone*
3.45	Afternoon tea		
4.00	Practical simulation and case study		
4.45	Plenary review and discussion *Simon Halliday, Partner, Ironside & Mallone* *Marc Howe, Partner, Ironside & Mallone* *Professor Andrew Clutterbuck, Duke's College, London* *Professor Bruce Fleming, Duke's College, London*		
5.15	Close		

Note. The programme above runs lectures concurrently, and allows for the bias of delegates. The left hand side column is clearly legally-based, whilst the right hand side column deals more squarely with medical matters. In the afternoon session, however two key lectures are repeated to allow those delegates who missed them in the morning to learn something of 'the other field'. The day begins and ends with plenary sessions, firstly to set the scene and secondly to 'tie up loose ends' and to allow the legal and medical themes to be brought together in discussion. Allowance has of course been made for lunch and refreshments.

8 JUDICIAL MEETINGS

8.1 A meeting is most likely to be exercising a judicial or quasi-judicial function if it is considering a possible **deprivation of existing rights**, for example by expelling a member of the body, or if it has to reach a decision on an application for the grant of rights, say admission to membership or the grant of a licence etc.

8.2 The rules of a club, society or other such body are regarded by the law as a kind of subordinate legislation set up by the club itself, which may be upheld in a court on the basis that a contract exists between the club and its members. The member agrees to be bound by the rules of the club, and the club in turn undertakes to apply its rules fairly and according to certain guidelines. Actions which are taken by the club or one of its committees which are in breach of the rules are *ultra vires* and therefore void; actions which are taken within the rules are subject to the principles of natural justice. A body acting in breach of these principles is subject to judicial review if it is exercising a judicial or quasi-judicial function.

Natural justice

8.3 The situation in which the rules of natural justice can be seen most clearly at work is in disciplinary matters. This is a judicial (or at least quasi-judicial) function, and it is to this sort of situation that the courts are most keen to apply the principles applied below.

8.4 The concept of natural justice is not well defined, and often seems to equate with a duty to act fairly; a number of individual rules can, however, be found and examined. These fall into three main categories.

Nemo iudex in sua causa

8.5 The principle is basically that no-one should be the **judge in his own case,** in other words that bias must be excluded from the decision-making process. Bias of a very general nature may not be objectionable (for instance, a plaintiff who was a member of the public suing a solicitor attempted to claim that any judge would be biased against him, but did not succeed in his claim: *Williams v Beesley 1973*), but the more specific and personal the bias becomes, the more likely the *nemo iudex* rule is to apply.

Metropolitan Properties Co (FGC) Ltd v Lannon 1969
The facts: The chairman of a rent assessment committee, which had to settle a dispute about a fair rent under the rent control legislation, lived in the same household as another tenant of the landlords involved in the appeal, and he had advised that tenant on his 'fair rent'.

Decision: The chairman had a personal interest in the current appeal, which rendered the committee's finding invalid.

8.6 Note that the principle is breached if the meeting includes a person who has an interest in its decision. Thus the court set aside a decision of a local authority committee on a planning application because one member was also a professional agent for the owner of the property, even though he took no part in the debate when the matter was before the meeting: *R v Hendon RDC ex parte Chorley 1973.*

8.7 A direct pecuniary interest is clearly established (for example *Dimes v Grand Junction Canal 1852)* as a ground for bias to be found, even if this interest is very small. Where the matter arises from a relationship with a party to a case - a 'challenge to favour' - the question is one of degree.

8.8 It is also worth mentioning that it is not necessary to prove that **bias** actually **existed**; the question is merely whether there are circumstances under which it might well exist.

Justice must be seen to be done

8.9 This is a basic principle in the area of **natural justice**. The question is not one of whether the proceedings were in fact fair, but whether they **seemed so**. Lawton LJ put this well in *Maxwell v Department of Trade 1974,* pointing out that 'doing what is right may still result in unfairness if it is done in the wrong way'.

8.10 Examples of the application of this principle can be found in *Re B (Adoption by Parents) 1975,* where a social worker retired with the justices whilst they considered their verdicts, and *Jeffs v NZ Dairy Product and Market Board 1967*, where the power of making decisions was improperly delegated to a person whose function was merely to gather information on which a decision was to be based. It is also clear from *Morris v Gestetner Ltd 1973* that all the members of a tribunal must participate in the decision if they are so entitled.

Audi alteram partem

8.11 The principle of a right to be heard covers a great range of matters, which will apply to some kinds of meeting and not to others. In some cases there will be a right to receive advance notice of the proceedings (*Cooper v Wandsworth Board of Works 1863)* and a right to legal representation: *Secretary of State for the Home Dept ex parte Tarrant 1984.*

8.12 The degree of disclosure of evidence required will vary from body to body, but in *R v Architects Registration tribunal, ex parte Jagger 1945,* the principle was laid down that a tribunal must afford a 'real and effective opportunity to the litigant to deal with or meet' the case against him. In *R v Board of Visitors of Blundeston Prison 1982*, the non-disclosure to the plaintiff of a witness to a prison disturbance was held to be a breach of natural justice.

8.13 Less often applied elements of the *audi alteram partem* rule include the possible right to **cross examination** in certain situations. This is not so frequently seen since tribunals as a whole are not bound by technical rules of evidence (as a court would be), or the necessity (or otherwise) for a tribunal to give reasons for its decisions.

8.14 Specific applications of the principle in case law include the following.

(a) The person whose case is to be decided is entitled to **know** of any **facts** or arguments which are adduced against him: he should know what the case is which he has to answer. This may involve the disclosure of evidence, and sometimes the formulation of a specific charge: *Santer v National Geographical Association 1973*.

(b) He should have the opportunity to **present** his own **case.** He must have time to prepare it and, if there is an oral hearing, he may usually bring a friend or advocate to put it for him. However, in some instances it may be sufficient to permit him to present his representations in writing. The meeting should not reach a decision, nor appear to do so, until the defendant or applicant has put his case in the appropriate manner: *Ex parte Ladbroke Group 1969.*

(c) If there is a **prescribed procedure** (as is often the case in disciplinary or dismissal proceedings) that procedure - with its safeguards for the person under threat - must be strictly observed.

(d) Sometimes, there is a **duty to inform** the parties (and witnesses) of all the possible outcomes of the tribunal's hearings: *Sheldon v Branfield JJ 1964.*

8.15 Unless procedure requires it, there is no general principle which requires a committee to give reasons for its decision when it is announced: the committee is presumed to have acted fairly unless it is proved otherwise.

> *Gaiman v National Association for Mental Health 1971*
> *The facts:* The council of the Association had a discretionary power to call on members to resign. The plaintiffs had been called on to resign because their membership of another body was believed by the council to be inimical to the interests of the Association.
>
> *Decision:* The court would not intervene since the decision appeared not to conflict with natural justice.

Ultra vires actions

8.16 A committee must be able to demonstrate that they have acted within the ambit of the powers which are granted to them by the association's constitution. If they have acted outside those powers then their actions are *ultra vires* and void.

> *Lee v Showmen's Guild of Great Britain 1952*
> *The facts:* A travelling showman was found guilty by the complaints committee of his Guild of having practised unfair competition and, on non-payment of a fine imposed under its rules, was expelled from the Guild.
>
> *Decision:* On the true construction of the rule under which the action was brought, the actions of the showman were not unfair competition at all, and the expulsion was therefore null and void.

8.17 The courts will intervene to declare such an expulsion *ultra vires*, and they will grant an injunction to prevent the expulsion if the livelihood or other proprietary right of the individual concerned is thus threatened: *Amalgamated Society of Carpenters v Braithwaite 1922*. However, a court will not grant an injunction to give a member a right of entry to a social club unless some kind of proprietary right is involved: *Baird v Webb 1890*. Expulsion from such a club does give rise to natural justice, however (*Faremus v Film Artists Association 1964*), and public policy may also play a part, as in *Nagle v Feilden 1966.*

8.18 A committee must therefore ensure that it construes its rules correctly, so that it keeps within its jurisdiction and it applies the rules correctly to the facts.

9 ACCESS TO DOCUMENTS AT COMMON LAW

9.1 At common law, a member has the right to inspect such documents as are necessary to enable him to carry out his duties properly: *R v Birmingham City Council ex parte O 1983*. Such a reason may be found in membership of a committee, whilst a 'need to know' would be necessary in relation to information from other committees: *R v Sheffield City Council ex parte Chadwick 1985*.

Chapter roundup

- **Committees** are generally used to work on the details of a problem when the full meeting of the body would be inadequate for the task. Generally they have such powers as they need, given by the general meeting. You should be sure to distinguish the different types: executive, standing, special/ad hoc, sub- and joint committees.
- **Committee meetings** have rules as to quorum, voting, minutes and general conduct as do other types of meeting.
- Secretaries and administrators are involved in setting up **conferences** and this is a practical topic which requires a common sense approach.
- The **principles of natural justice** often arise in examination questions. The key points to remember are that: no-one should judge his own case, justice must be seen to be done and everyone has a right to be heard.

Test your knowledge

1 What powers (if any) does a committee possess and how may they be exercised? (see paras 2.2 - 2.5)

2 Explain the difference between a standing and a special or *ad hoc* committee. (3.4 - 3.9)

3 What is (a) a sub-committee and (b) a joint committee? (3.12 - 3.16)

4 Give three instances of procedural matters incidental to the work of a committee. (4.1)

5 What are the advantages and disadvantages of remitting a problem to a committee for examination and report? (5.2 - 5.7)

6 Give some examples of the use of the committee system:

(a) by an educational or professional body;
(b) in an annual conference. (6.1, 6.6, 7.7 - 7.8)

7 What is the likely role of a remuneration committee? (6.14)

8 What are some of the practical considerations involved in a big conference? (7.5)

9 What are the three main principles of natural justice? (8.5, 8.9, 8.11)

Now try illustrative question 8 at the end of the Study Text

Part B
Corporate information needs

Chapter 9

THE USES AND APPLICATION OF INFORMATION AND DATA

This chapter covers the following topics.

1 Data and information

2 Sources of data and information

3 Information and technology

Introduction

The next topic in the syllabus concerns 'The uses and application of information, data and technology as corporate resources in the contemporary organisation'. In this chapter we introduce the topic of data and information, looking at what they are and what they are used for. This will mainly be revision of material covered in your earlier studies, but note the comments about exam questions in Exercise 2.

Note also that information is to be regarded as a resource - an asset - of the organisation and that it needs to be managed as such. In Chapter 10 we shall go on to look at how information resources can be managed by using technology.

1 DATA AND INFORMATION

1.1 First, some definitions: in normal everyday speech the terms data and information are used interchangeably. However, in the context of data processing and information systems the terms have distinct meanings.

(a) **Data** is the raw material for data processing. Data relates to facts, events, and transactions and so forth.

(b) **Information** is data that has been processed in such a way as to be meaningful to the person who receives it.

Exercise 1

This distinction should be very familiar from your earlier studies. Can you provide a business example?

Solution

A pile of weekly timesheets is an example of *data*. These may be processed in the wages office to produce a payroll analysis printout, which shows the same sort of detail as individual payslips. To the wages clerk, the payroll analysis is *information*. It shows, among other things, how much money needs to be included in each pay packet when these are made up.

However, one person's information is another person's data. The personnel director may wish to assess how likely the company is to fall foul of potential legislation restricting the number of hours an employee may work. She wants to know about staff who have worked more than ten hours' overtime in the period. She does not have time to leaf through the payroll analysis looking to see who has worked overtime, and even less will she wish to flick through the pile of timesheets, which have in any case already been authorised by departmental managers. Both of these are data to her. She receives information in the form of an *exception report* showing all staff who have recorded over ten hours' overtime.

If you struggled with this you may need to return to your earlier study material and do some revision.

For this topic we recommend the BPP Study Text on Pre-professional level *Managing Information Systems*. There is an order form at the back of this book if you are worried about whether you *really* possess the knowledge that underpins Professional level *Administration of Corporate Affairs* and want some more study material.

Data processing system model

1.2 Any data processing system might be described as follows.

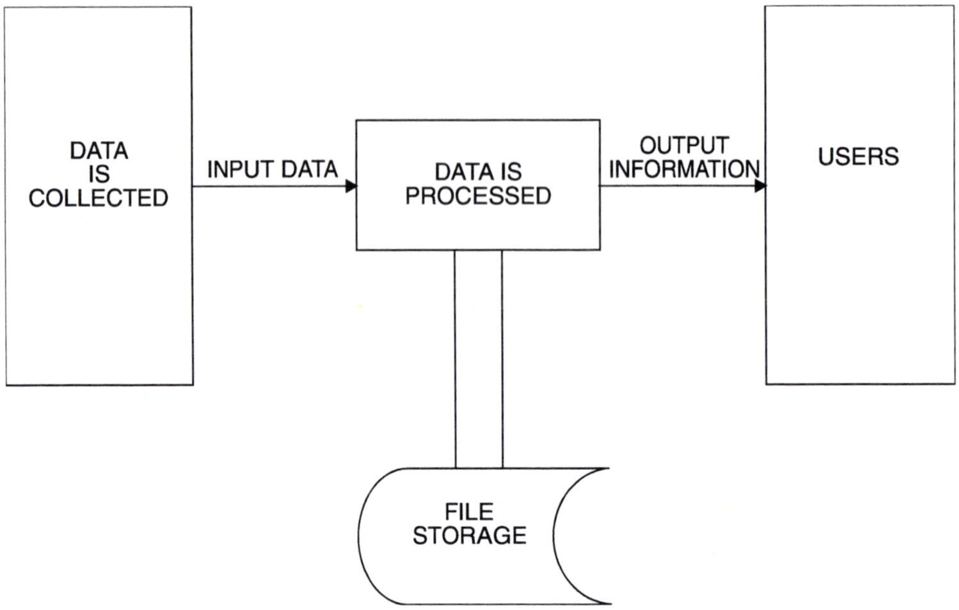

1.3 Processing data can be said to have the following features for both manual and electronic data processing.

(a) Data is **collected**. There must be data to process and this may arise in the course of operations. There has to be a system or procedure for ensuring that all the data needed for processing is collected and made available for processing. The quality, accuracy and completeness of the data will affect the quality of information produced.

(b) Data is **processed** into information, perhaps by summarising it or classifying it and/or producing total figures. For example, a sales system might be required to process data about goods despatched to satisfy customer orders so as to:

- Produce invoices
- Record the invoices produced in the customers' personal ledgers
- Produce a report of the total value of invoices sent out in the day/week etc
- Record new information in the marketing database about customer's tastes

(c) Data is **communicated**. The invoices are sent out to customers. Communication might involve the **routine dissemination** of information to users. Communication also involves the provision of **non-routine information** to users on request, for example a list of how many customers buy red coloured products as opposed to green ones.

(d) Files are **updated** to incorporate the processed data. Updating files means bringing them up to date to record current transactions.

Storage and retrieval of data and information

1.4 There is no reason why processed information should be used straightaway. It might be kept for later use. If it is, it must be stored, or filed away, and then retrieved when it is eventually needed.

1.5 Storage and retrieval of data are two interrelated aspects of holding data for a later use because data must be stored in such a way that it can be found again when it is eventually wanted. To assist with storage, data (or information) is often stored in a pre-sorted order (for example alphabetical order). Alternatively, it is given a reference number and filed in reference number order. Sometimes, an index helps the storage and retrieval process.

Timescale for information use

1.6 Information can be **collected** and **stored** for future use, although presumably there will be a limit to its useful life.

(a) Some information might have been gathered several years previously and used eventually to analyse past trends in order to predict the future. In other words, forecasting the future is often based on an analysis of historical information.

(b) Information which is several years old might also be used to compare past and current performance - for example to compare today's return on capital employed and profit/sales ratio with what was being achieved a few years before. Comparisons of this sort are useful for control purposes because they help to identify possible weaknesses in current performance.

(c) Information used by junior managers and supervisors usually has a short life span. Supervisors need to know what is going on now.

Good information

1.7 The qualities of good information are as follows.

(a) It should be **relevant** for its purpose.

(b) It should be **complete** for its purpose.

(c) It should be sufficiently **accurate** for its purpose.

(d) It should be **clear** to the user.

(e) It should be **consistent** - prepared using the same methods from one period to the next.

(f) It should be **reliable**. Reliability is linked to collection methods and accuracy.

(g) It should be communicated to the **right person**, through the **right channel** of communication.

(h) It should be **concise** - its **volume** should be manageable.

(i) It should be **timely** - communicated at the most appropriate time.

(j) It should be **cost-effective** - provided at a **cost** which is less than the value of the benefits it provides.

Exercise 2

Again, these qualities should be very familiar to you from your earlier studies: see if you can expand each of points (a) to (j) to explain what, say, 'sufficiently accurate' or 'user confidence' mean. If not, return to your earlier study material.

Exam questions in *Administration of Corporate Affairs* will not ask you such basic questions as 'what are the qualities of good information', but you should always keep the basics in mind. Many of the above points, for example are relevant to a question that asks you about 'the provision of information to senior management'.

Much of the rest of this chapter should be read in the same spirit. It is essential background but you will not be able to reproduce it *verbatim* as an exam answer: questions will require you to *apply* your knowledge in a particular scenario.

Users of information

1.8 The information generated by an organisation can be valuable to many different people. Users of an organisation's information can be **external or internal**.

1.9 Internal users of information include (by status) the following.

(a) The board of the company, or the equivalent of a board in other organisations

(b) Directors with functional responsibilities

(c) Divisional general managers, reporting to these directors

(d) Divisional heads

(e) Departmental heads

(f) Section leaders or foremen

(g) Discretionary employees, those who are expected to act on their own initiative to some extent

(h) Non-discretionary employees, who work under instruction all the time with little scope for initiative

Internal users of information can also be classified by department.

Exercise 3

It is important to bear in mind that information may be relevant to people outside the organisation as well as to its internal management and employees. In fact, decisions relating to an organisation can be taken by outsiders. Give four examples of decisions which may be taken by outsiders.

Solution

There are many possible suggestions, including those given below.

(a) The organisation's **bankers** take decisions affecting the amount of money they are prepared to lend.

(b) The **public** might have an interest in information relating to an organisation's products or services.

(c) The **media** (press, television etc) use information generated by organisations in news stories, and such information can adversely or favourably affect an organisation's relationship with its environment.

(d) The **government** (for example Companies House) regularly requires organisational information.

(e) The **Inland Revenue** and **HM Customs and Excise** authorities require information for taxation and VAT assessments.

(f) An organisation's **suppliers** and **customers** take decisions whether or not to trade with the organisation.

---

2 SOURCES OF DATA AND INFORMATION

2.1 Data and information come from sources both inside and outside an organisation, and an information system should be designed so as to obtain all the relevant data and information from whatever source.

Internal information

2.2 Gathering data/information from **inside** the organisation involves the following.

(a) **Establishing a system** for collecting or measuring transactions data - for example measuring output, sales, costs, cash receipts and payments, asset purchases, stock turnover etc. In other words, there must be established procedures for what data is collected and how it is processed, and filed or communicated

(b) Relying to some extent on **informal communication** of information between managers and staff (for example, by word-of-mouth or at meetings)

(c) **Communication between managers**

2.3 Most management information systems (MIS) are not designed, but grow up informally, with each manager (depending on his drive and initiative) making sure that he gets all the information he thinks he needs to do his job. Such an informal system works best in small companies, but is inadequate in a large company, especially one which spreads over several industries, areas or countries.

2.4 The consequences of a poor MIS might be **dissatisfaction** amongst employees who believe they should be told more, a **lack of understanding** about what the targets for achievement are and a **lack of information** about how well the work is being done. Some information systems are designed or planned, often because the introduction of computers has forced management to consider its information needs in detail.

2.5 Management should try to design the management information system for their enterprise with care. For example, without formal planning and design of the MIS, the following situations are likely.

(a) Some managers will prefer to keep **data in their heads** and will not commit information to paper. When the manager is absent from work, or is moved to another job, his stand-in or successor will not know as much as he could and should about the work because there would be no information to help him.

(b) **Not all data** is **collected** and processed that ought to be, and so valuable information that ought to be available to management would be missing from neglect.

(c) Information is **available** but **not communicated** to the managers who are in a position of authority and so ought to be given it. The information would go to waste because it would not be used. In other words, the wrong people would have the information.

(d) Information is **communicated late** because the need to communicate it earlier is not understood and appreciated by the data processors.

2.6 Whether a management information system is formally or informally constructed, it should have certain essential characteristics.

(a) The **functions of individuals** and their areas of responsibility in achieving company objectives should be **defined**.

(b) **Areas of control** within the company should also be clearly **defined**.

(c) **Information** required for an area of control should **flow** to the manager responsible for it.

External information

2.7 Obtaining information from **outside** the organisation might be entrusted to particular individuals, or might be 'informal'.

2.8 **Formal collection** of data from outside sources includes the following.

(a) A company's tax specialists will be expected to gather information about changes in tax law and how this will affect the company.

(b) Obtaining information about any new legislation on health and safety at work, or employment regulations, must be the responsibility of a particular person - for example the company secretary - who must then pass on the information to other managers affected by it.

(c) Research and development (R & D) work often relies on information about other R & D work being done by another company or by government institutions. An R & D official might be made responsible for finding out about other R & D work.

(d) Marketing managers need to know about the opinions and buying attitudes of potential customers. To obtain this information, they might carry out market research exercises.

2.9 **Informal gathering** of information from the environment goes on all the time, consciously or unconsciously, because the employees of an organisation learn what is going on in the world around them - perhaps from newspapers, television reports, meetings with business associates or the trade press.

Exercise 4

An exam question might ask you about the problems of handling information collected by, say, a nationwide sales force.

Imagine that you are the information manager of a large company such as an insurance company or a consumer electronics manufacturer. Think about what sort of information the sales force might collect and how it could be relayed to the head office and disseminated to others in the organisation.

Environmental scanning

2.10 Management information is available from a wide range of external sources. These may be electronic, as for example, Reuters' services to the financial sector, or non-electronic, as for example, newspapers and magazines. Some examples are provided below.

Teletext

2.11 There are several different Teletext systems in the UK. The most widely received are currently **Ceefax** (provided by the BBC) and **Teletext** (provided by the independent television companies). Users must have a **television set** with a teletext facility; otherwise they pay no fee for use of the service.

2.12 The information is broadcast on pages over the air, dealing with items such as weather reports, news, sports reports, subtitles for certain television programmes and other items of general interest. Teletext allows some information to be provided as advertising at a low cost to the advertiser. Ceefax and Teletext both provide a 'City' news service and also offer advice to viewers in 'Your money' columns.

Value Added Network Services (VANS)

2.13 **VANS** is a collective term for the range of computer services provided by external organisations, which are used in conjunction with the telephone network or another (private) communications network. The term 'value added network services' derives from the idea that by combining a computer system with a communications network, the service is able to provide something extra (ie an added value) to the user, greater than the sum of its individual component parts.

2.14 Examples of VANS are as follows.

- Electronic mail services
- Information services, such as Reuters and the Stock Market (Topic)
- Bibliographic database systems
- Videotex/viewdata services such as Prestel
- Electronic data interchange

2.15 Most of these services have now been relaunched on the Internet. The Internet or World Wide Web is a vast network linking up millions of computers across the world via telecommunications links. Information can be found on virtually any topic using a network browser, and the net can also be used to exchange information.

2.16 The Internet is described in more detail in the chapter on Technological Developments.

3 INFORMATION AND TECHNOLOGY

3.1 Information systems may be manual, computerised or a combination of the two. What are the advantages of the use of information *technology*?

- The **accuracy** of information is improved.
- The **volume** of information which can be processed is increased.
- The **speed** at which information becomes available is higher.
- The **workforce** is freed up for more skilful and judgmental work.
- There is greater **access** to information available to more people.

Exercise 5

What are the disadvantages of the use of information technology in an organisation?

Solution

You may well have examples of your own, based on experience. Some suggestions are given below.

(a) There may be a tendency to produce information for its own sake, rather than because it is required.

(b) Users may not be able to cope with complex technology, resulting in reduced efficiency.

(c) Development staff and users may not communicate well with each other, so that user requirements are not properly met.

(d) Wider access to data increases the risk of threats to security, particularly where data is transmitted between sites.

3.2 Information technology can be broadly defined as the convergence of **computer** technology and **communications** technology.

3.3 Many of an organisation's activities are enhanced through the use of information technology. Cheap computer hardware, based on microchip technology with ever-increasing power and capacity, has been harnessed to an extensive telecommunications network.

3.4 Computers are able to '**talk**' to each other over telecommunications links, or can transmit data to and from remote terminals. Small computers have spread rapidly in the home and the office. Information technology also involves other equipment and information transmission systems, not just computers; for example, there is electronic mail, facsimile transfers, cable television, teletext, electronic telephone exchanges, satellite communications and data transmission using laser technology.

3.5 The emergence of the **electronic office** means that management information can be provided more quickly and cheaply than before, and that managers can obtain greater involvement in information production and report design. Some typical applications are:

- Text processing (word processing systems, graphics)
- Computing (cheap PCs)
- Telecommunications and networks
- Data storage and reference (databases)

Presentation of information

3.6 For example, modern technology has greatly expanded the techniques for displaying management information. Management information can be presented in a number of ways.

Computer printouts

3.7 Management information can be presented in **printed computer reports**, or summaries. For relatively simple information this is cheap and easy to prepare. Once the information becomes complicated, rows of figures become harder to use.

Desktop publishing

3.8 More advanced printing technology has greatly expanded the scope and flexibility for the visual presentation of management information. **Graphs, charts, maps** and so forth can be used to enhance the subject.

VDU

3.9 Much management information is computer-generated. Managers can access information with a VDU and keyboard. The advent of powerful graphics software means that the information can be **manipulated, converted** into graphical format, and **made easier to understand**. Electronic mail is another way of distributing management information from computer to computer.

Verbally

3.10 Remember that management information, especially of the more unstructured nature, can be distributed on the 'grapevine'.

Group information

3.11 Some management information will be presented in a group context.

(a) If senior management wish to communicate, say, a change in strategy to middle management, this can be achieved by group presentations. Videos, for example, can be used to present this type of information. Moreover, some computer graphics packages are able to manipulate video-based information so that a combination of graphics and pictures can be prepared relatively cheaply.

(b) Another source of information is the '**bulletin board**' which becomes possible with e-mail systems, so that managers can communicate information to all their colleagues. This is a good way of sharing ideas. Computers are arranged in a network, and everybody has access to the bulletin board. eg. BP plc ⇒ "Quickplace"

Why share information?

3.12 There are lots of different and separate activities within an organisation, which is why organisations are organised into **departments** or **functions**. For example, a manufacturing organisation will have amongst other things, a production department, as part of operations, and a sales department. The sales department liaises with customers. The production department makes the goods. These activities appear completely distinct.

3.13 However, these two functions are vitally linked, and, to different degrees in different organisations, each activity depends on linkages to other activities to function effectively.

(a) The sales and production departments need to exchange information about their requirements and capacities. Put another way, there needs to be a **flow of data.**

(b) The sales and production departments are, as it were, mini-organisations in their own right within the organisation as a whole, yet inevitably, they must be linked in some way. Most organisations therefore display some sort of **structure**, with varying degrees of formality, linking the various forms of activity within the organisation.

(c) Most organisations are a lot more **complex** than our simple example. What do you think is the link between, say, the research and development activity and the production activity, or the research and development activity and the marketing activity?

(d) It was mentioned that a selling price would have to be determined. This means that **decisions** must be taken about quantity of goods produced and the price at which they are to be sold.

Business Process Re-engineering (BPR)

3.14 A modern trend, that uses information systems to cut across traditional organisation structures, is known as Business Process Re-engineering. The main writing on the subject is Hammer and Champy's *Reengineering the Corporation* (1993), from which the following definition is taken.

> Reengineering is 'the fundamental rethinking and radical redesign of business processes to achieve dramatic improvements in critical contemporary measures of performance, such as cost, quality, service and speed.'

3.15 The key words here, as identified by Hammer and Champy, are '**fundamental**', '**radical**', '**dramatic**' and '**process**'. The first two indicate that BPR starts by asking basic questions such as 'why do we do what we do', without making any assumptions or looking back to what has always been done in the past.

3.16 The most important word, however, is 'process', by which Hammer and Champy mean 'a collection of activities that takes one or more kinds of input and creates an output that is of value to the customer.' For example, order fulfilment is a process that takes an order as its input and results in the delivery of the ordered goods. Part of this process is the manufacture of the goods, but under BPR the aim of manufacturing is not merely to *make* the goods. Manufacturing should aim to **deliver** the goods that were **ordered**, and any aspect of the manufacturing process that hinders this aim should be re-engineered. The first question to ask might be 'Do they need to be manufactured at all?' (Could somebody else manufacture them?)

Example: BPR

3.17 Ford once employed huge numbers of staff to perform the standard accounting task of matching goods received notes with orders and then with invoices. About 80% of their time was spent trying to find out why 20% of the set of three documents did not agree.

One way of improving the situation would have been to computerise the existing process to facilitate matching.

This would have helped, but BPR went further and asked: why have invoices in the system at all? Now all the orders are entered onto a database on the computer. When goods arrive at the goods inwards department they simply agree to goods that have been ordered or they don't. Goods that agree to an order are accepted and paid for. Goods that are not agreed are **sent back** to the supplier. There are no files of unmatched items and time is not wasted trying to sort out these files.

Information technology and BPR

3.18 Hammer and Champy are keen to emphasise that simply throwing IT at a problem does not cause it to be re-engineered, as illustrated by the Ford example above.

3.19 IT is not the solution in itself, it is an **enabler.** BPR uses IT to allow a business to do things that it is *not* doing already. For example teleconferencing facilities might be introduced with the idea of cutting down on the costs of travelling to meetings, but a re-engineering approach takes the view that teleconferencing allows **more frequent meetings**. As Hammer and Champy put it, 'It is this disruptive power of technology, its ability to break the rules that limit how we conduct our work, that makes it critical to companies looking for competitive advantage.'

3.20 Here are the examples given by Hammer and Champy. (We explain databases, expert systems and so on in more detail in the next two chapters.)

(a) **Shared databases** mean that information can appear simultaneously in as many places as it is needed.

(b) **Expert systems** mean that a generalist can do the work of an expert.

(c) **Telecommunications networks** mean that businesses can simultaneously reap the rewards of centralisation and decentralisation.

(d) **Decision support tools** mean that decision making is part of everyone's job.

(e) **Wireless data communication and portable computers** mean that field staff can send and receive information wherever they are.

(f) **Interactive videodisks** mean that personal contact with buyers can be replaced by *effective* contact with buyers.

(g) **Automatic identification and tracking technology** means that things (such as distribution vehicles or any asset) tell you where they are, without you having to find out.

(h) **High performance computing** means that plans get revised instantaneously, not periodically.

Exercise 6

Read through the above list again and see if you can think of examples of how IT enables a *bank* to do things that it could not do before.

(A bank is an easy example: you may like to repeat the exercise for other sorts of organisation, including your own.)

Chapter roundup

- **Data** is the complete range of raw facts and measurements which exist within and outside an organisation. Information is data which has been processed in some way so as to make it meaningful to the person who receives it. Conversion of data into information occurs when the data received by the user enhances his or her knowledge or understanding of a situation. Good information has a number of specific qualities.
- Data can be **collected** from **within** and **beyond** an organisation.
- **Environmental scanning** is a process of obtaining information from external sources. Externally generated information may be more difficult to assimilate or to input into an information system, but is just as important to management as internal information, perhaps *more* so at senior management level.
- All parts of the organisation need to **exchange information** so that activities can be co-ordinated and decisions can be made. **Information technology** allows information to be processed more quickly and accurately and to be shared more easily. It is increasingly cutting across traditional organisation structures. **Business Process Re-engineering** entails a radical rethink of business processes and uses IT to *enable* a business to do things that it is not doing already.

Test your knowledge

1 What are the features of data processing? (see para 1.3)

2 Who uses organisational information? (1.8 - 1.9)

3 What does internal information gathering entail? (2.2)

4 List four sources of external information (2.10 - 2.16)

5 What is information technology? (3.2)

6 How can information be communicated to groups? (3.11)

7 What is BPR? (3.14)

8 Why is technology disruptive? (3.19)

Now try illustrative question 9 at the end of the Study Text

Chapter 10

INFORMATION MANAGEMENT

This chapter covers the following topics.

Introduction

In this chapter we look at a wide variety of issues concerning the way information is managed in organisations. Again you will have studied much of this material before, although you will not have seen it organised in this way before. We shall consider ways of organising the machines that underlie modern information management. Then we look at the handling of the 'raw material' data. Next we consider a variety of *uses* of data and information by management. Finally, we look briefly at the problem of integrating information systems.

1 INFORMATION MANAGEMENT

Information management

1.1 Information must be managed just like any other organisational resource. Information management entails the following tasks.

(a) **Identifying** current and future information **needs** (see Chapter 9)

(b) **Identifying** information **sources** (see Chapter 9)

(c) **Collecting** the information

(d) **Storing** the information

(e) **Facilitating** existing methods of **using** information and identifying new ways of using it

(f) **Ensuring** that information is **communicated** to those who need it, but *not* to those who are *not* entitled to see it.

1.2 Technology has provided **new sources** of information, new ways of **collecting** it, **storing** it and **processing** it, and new methods of **communicating** it. This in turn has meant that information needs have changed and will continue to change as new technologies become available.

Exercise 1

Think in these terms if you are faced with a question on how information management can be improved. How can information be *collected* more efficiently? Can it be *stored* in a way that improves access without jeopardising security, or allows data previously held separately to be matched up?

Apply these and similar questions to different types of business.

So far in *Administration of Corporate Affairs* exams, questions have been set on: a distribution company handling leisure wear; a plc's Company Secretarial department; a manufacturing organisation (three times); the head office of an industrial holding company with worldwide interests (twice); a financial services company; a textile company; a hotel and leisure organisation; and a life assurance company.

Information needs

1.3 The term **management** information system (MIS) can be defined as follows.

> 'A system to convert data from internal and external sources into information and to communicate that information, in an appropriate form, to managers at all levels in all functions to enable them to make timely and effective decisions for planning, directing and controlling the activities for which they are responsible.'
>
> (Lucey, *Management Information Systems*)

1.4 An MIS, therefore, presents information to management. However, this is not the only function of an organisation's information systems. A number of tasks might be performed simultaneously.

- Initiating transactions
- Recording transactions as they occur
- Processing data
- Producing reports
- Responding to enquiries

1.5 A good MIS will **satisfy** all the **informational needs** of management from the most junior of supervisors to the managing director. Whether this is possible will depend to some degree on the nature and type of information provided. An MIS is good at providing regular formal information gleaned from normal commercial data. For example, an MIS relating to sales could provide managers with information on the following.

- Gross profit margins of particular products
- Success in particular markets
- Credit control information (aged debtors and payments against old balances)

1.6 It may be **less efficient** at **presenting information** which is relatively unpredictable, or informal, or unstructured. So, for example, an MIS could not provide much-needed information relating to the sudden emergence of a new competitor into the market.

1.7 While an MIS may not, in principle, be able to provide all the information used by management, it should however, be sufficiently flexible to enable management to **incorporate unpredictable,** informal or unstructured information into decision-making processes. For example, many decisions are made with the help of financial models (such as spreadsheets) so that the effect of new situations can be estimated easily.

1.8 A table showing typical inputs, processes and outputs at each level of a management information system is provided below.

	Inputs	*Processes*	*Outputs*
Strategic	Plans Competitor information Market information	Summarise Investigate Compare Forecast	Key ratios Ad hoc market analysis Strategic plans
Tactical	Historical data Budget data	Compare Classify Summarise	Variance analyses Exception reports
Operational	Customer orders Programmed stock control levels	Update files Output reports	Updated files Listings Invoices

2 NETWORKS 6/95, 6/96

Centralisation and decentralisation

2.1 An important design issue is whether the information processing system ought to be centralised or decentralised.

(a) Centralised processing means having the data/information processing done in a central place, such as a **computer centre** at head office. Data will be collected at 'remote' offices and other locations and sent in to the central location, by post, by courier or by telecommunications link. Processing could be in either batch processing mode or on-line. At the central location there will be:

  (i) A central computer, possibly a large mainframe computer
  (ii) Central files, containing all the master files and reference files for the system

(b) Decentralised processing means having the data/information processing carried out at several different locations, away from the 'centre' or 'head office'. (distributed processing). Each region, department or office will have its own processing systems, and so:

  (i) There will be different and unconnected computers in the various offices.

  (ii) Each computer will operate with its own programs and its own master files and reference files.

2.2 The advantages of centralised processing are as follows.

(a) There is **one set of files**. Everyone uses the same data and information.

(b) It gives **better security/control** over data and files.

(c) **Head office** is in a better position to know what is going on.

(d) An organisation might be able to afford a **central computer** which is **very large**, with extensive processing capabilities that smaller 'local' computers could not carry out.

(e) There are **economies of scale** available in purchasing computer equipment supplies.

(f) Computer staff are in a single location, and **more expert staff** are likely to be employed. Career paths may be more clearly defined.

2.3 The disadvantages of centralised processing are as follows.

(a) Local offices might have to **wait** for data to be processed centrally, especially if processing is done by batches.

(b) **Reliance on head office.** Local offices have to rely on the central processing unit to provide the information they need.

(c) If the central computer **breaks down**, or the software develops a fault, the entire system goes out of operation.

Exercise 2

What are the advantages and disadvantages of *decentralised* processing? (You should remember this from Pre-Professional level *Managing Information Systems*.)

Solution

Advantages

(a) Each office can introduce an information system specially designed for its individual needs.

(b) If data originates locally it might make sense to process it locally too.

(c) Each office has control over its own files and data.

(d) There is likely to be easy/quick access to information when it is needed.

(e) Any breakdowns in the system are restricted to just one part of the system.

(f) It fits in with the organisation structure and responsibility accounting systems (profit centres).

(g) It allows staff to concentrate on business objectives rather than being constrained by IT objectives.

Disadvantages

(a) Many different and uncoordinated information systems will be introduced.

(b) Decentralisation encourages lack of co-ordination between departments.

(c) One office might be unable to obtain information from the information system of another office.

(d) There might be a duplication of data, with different offices holding the same data on their own separate files.

2.4 Information systems do not have to be entirely centralised or entirely decentralised, and a suitable mixture of centralisation and decentralisation can be used.

(a) Local offices can have their **own local systems**, perhaps on PC, and also input some data to a centralised processing system.

(b) Computer systems can be **networked**, and there might be a multi-user system and a distributed data processing system in a local area network (LAN) or wide area network (WAN). Networks of interconnected but autonomous computers are becoming more common.

Local area networks

2.5 A local area network (LAN) is a system of **interconnecting PCs** and other devices over a small area, typically within a few hundred metres.

2.6 Several sorts of networks exist, giving a variety of speed/cost/capacity trade-offs. The accepted definition of a local area network states that its distinctive characteristic is that systems are **linked** by **direct cables** (such as Ethernet), rather than via telecommunications lines. This means that a LAN will usually be located on a single site, and does not need modems. This characteristic distinguishes LANs from wide area networks.

2.7 Most LANs include a **server computer** (or file server). This may be a powerful PC or a minicomputer. As its name implies, it serves the rest of the network offering a generally-accessible hard disk file for all the other PCs in the system and sometimes offering other resources, such as shared printers for the network. Networks can interface with users in two ways.

(a) The **file server model**. In this way, the server sends entire files down the network to users. This means that a file might be temporarily unavailable to other users. However information and applications are shared without being duplicated.

(b) The **client server model** works in a different way. The server machine does not transfer entire files to the workstation on the network. Instead, it only sends the data requested.

 (i) It reduces network communications costs.

 (ii) It allows the central computer to be used for administrative tasks such as network management.

 (iii) The technological flexibility of this type of system allows the use of sophisticated applications such as multimedia and DIP.

Wide area networks

2.8 Wide area networks (WANs) are networks on a wide geographical scale. WANs use minicomputers or mainframes as the 'pumps' that keep the data messages circulating, whereas shorter-distance LANs normally use PCs for this task. A wide area network is similar to a local area network in concept, but the key differences are as follows.

(a) The **geographical area** covered by the network is greater, not being limited to a single building or site or country.

(b) WANs will send data over **telecommunications links**, and so will need modems or digital telecoms links (ISDN). LANs, in contrast, will use direct cables only for transmitting data.

(c) WANs will often use a **larger computer** as a file server.

(d) WANs will often be larger than LANs, with **more terminals or computers** linked to the network.

(e) A WAN can link two or more LANs, using **gateways**.

 (i) Connections may be **leased**. This is the preferred option when there is a high volume of inter-office communication.

 (ii) Connections may be made over the **public telephone network**. Standard call charges will apply, so this is beneficial where communication levels are relatively low.

Advantages of networks 6/97, 6/98

2.9 The advantages of using a network are as follows.

(a) Networks have been made available to computer users at a fairly **low price**.

(b) There is **greater flexibility** in system design. The system can cater for both the specific needs of each local user of an individual computer and also for the needs of the organisation as a whole, by providing communications between different local computers in the system.

(c) Networks have a significant knock-on effect on the **human element** of office work. They provide speedy communication and quick responses to enquiries, both of which reduce traditional areas of user dissatisfaction.

(d) **Data files can be shared** by all the PCs/terminals in the network. With stand-alone PCs, each computer would have its own data files, and there might be unnecessary duplication of data. A system where everyone uses the same data will help to improve data processing and decision-making. The value of some information increases with its availability.

(e) **Each PC/terminal** in a network can do the **same work**. If there were separate stand-alone machines, A might do job 1, B might do job 2, C might do job 3 and so on. In a network, any PC (A, B or C) could do any job (1, 2 or 3). This provides flexibility in sharing work-loads.

(f) **Peripheral equipment** can be **shared**. For example, in a LAN, five PCs might help to share a single on-line printer, whereas if stand-alone PCs are used, each PC must be given its own separate printer.

(g) Since data files can be held locally, **data transmission** is **restricted** because each computer maintains its own data files which provide most of the data it will need. This reduces the costs and security risks in data transmission.

(h) The effect of **breakdowns** is **minimised**, because a fault in one computer will not affect other computers in the system. With a centralised processing system, a fault in the mainframe computer would put the entire system out of service.

(i) The fact that it is possible to acquire powerful PCs at a 'cheap' price enables an organisation to **dedicate** them to **particular applications**. This in turn means that the computer system can be more readily tailored to the organisation's systems, rather than forcing the organisation to change its systems to satisfy the requirements for a mainframe computer.

(j) Decentralised processing may **facilitate** greater **user involvement** and increase familiarity with the use of computer technology. The end user must accept responsibility for the accuracy of locally-held files and local data processing.

(k) There is no need for costly air-conditioning or filtration units or for high voltage electricity supplies.

2.10 Networks have certain disadvantages, some of which might be overcome by future technological developments.

(a) Minicomputers and PCs have **not had a large storage capacity** in the past. This disadvantage is now being eliminated by the development of ever more powerful small machines.

(b) There may be a **duplication of data** on the files of different computers. If this is the case, there may be some unnecessary storage costs incurred.

(c) A distributed network can be **more difficult** to **administer** and to maintain with service engineers.

(d) The items of equipment used in the system must, of course, be **compatible** with each other.

Modern mainframes

2.11 Mainframes, dominated by the IBM S/390 system, are by no means dead, especially in businesses with very high volumes of transactions such as banks. Recent studies indicate that for organisations with 200 or more users mainframes are a good deal cheaper than competing technologies to run over the medium term, not least because management and support costs need to be included.

2.12 Mainframes are also considered to offer greater reliability, functionality and data security than distributed systems. Even if the network option is preferred, mainframes can be used with advantage as powerful server computers in large businesses.

Exercise 3

A major issue that may lead more companies to adopt networked PCs in preference to what, in reality, are perfectly adequate existing systems is the millennium. Why?

Solution

You should have read about this in the newspaper and in *Company Secretary* magazine. Many older computers run on software that ignores the first two digits of the date, so year 2001 could only be entered as 01 and the system would assume that 1901 was meant. This is especially problematic where dates are used to do calculations such as producing analyses of aged debts or performing interest calculations (a deposit made in 1999 and withdrawn in 2001 would earn 01 – 99 = –98 years of interest!)

Some estimates put the world wide cost of repairing the year 2000 bug at over £645bn. Many companies have been slow to realise that their systems cannot cope.

3.1 The database concept is based on considering what **data** can be **provided** and then suiting that to the **needs** of **particular applications**, rather than beginning with the needs of particular applications. An organisation might easily end up with separate files and processing subsystems for each area of the business. However, in many cases the underlying data used by each application might be the same. A major consequence is that data items are duplicated in a number of files.

3.2 The disadvantages of application-specific files are as follows.

(a) Data is **duplicated** (data redundancy).

(b) Data can **only be used** in a **limited way.** For example, a payroll system is a program which only uses payroll data to produce output which has been determined in the program; other than simple file enquiries, it would be necessary to write a new computer program to select certain items of data which share one characteristic in common, say, for personnel administration purposes.

Integrated systems and databases

3.3 The problem of data redundancy is overcome, partly at least, by an **integrated system**. An integrated system is a system where one set of data is used for more than one application. In an administrative context, it might be possible to integrate parts of the payroll system, the personnel systems and the production job costing system, so that data input to the production system, such as hours worked, updates the wages due automatically.

3.4 The integrated systems approach, where different applications update each other, is a half-way house between a system based on separate application-specific files and a database approach. Broadly speaking a database is a file of data organised in such a way that it can be used by many applications. Using the example of hours worked given above, the following situations are possible.

(a) The employee's hours are input twice, once to the job-costing application, once to the payroll system, in a non-integrated system of **application-specific files.**

(b) In an **integrated system**, the data would have been input to the job-costing application. The job-costing application would have been used to update the payroll application.

(c) In a **database system** the data would only be input once and would be immediately available to all systems.

The database and the DBMS

3.5 It might be useful to give definitions of the terms database and database management system.

(a) A database is a collection of **structured data**. The structure of the data is independent of any particular application. Any item of data can be used as a subject of enquiry. The concept is that programs are written around the database rather than files being structured to meet the need of specific programs.

(b) **A database management system (DBMS)** is the software that builds, manages and provides access to a database. It is a system which allows a systematic approach to the storage and retrieval of data in a computer.

3.6 A database provides a comprehensive file of data for a number of different users. Each user will have access to the same data.

3.7 The introduction of information systems incorporating a database and DBMS is more than simply about the technical efficiency of different file structures. The use of a database system is a first step in **controlling** and **managing** an organisation's use of data. Many business functions have been computerised piecemeal. The different functional systems may have used similar data, but the data definitions may not have been identical, or may have been slightly different. The same data items may have been given different names.

3.8 As well as integrating files and avoiding data redundancy, a database system requires a great deal more thought as to what data needs to be **captured**, and the **relationships** between different data items.

3.9 Summary of objectives of databases

(a) **Avoid data duplication** (or redundancy) by allowing a single data element to be used in a number of applications

(b) Make **data independent** of the programs which use it

(c) **Ensure consistency** in an organisation's use of data

Exercise 4

If you are only familiar with PC-based products such as Microsoft Access, see if any of your friends or colleagues can describe larger systems to you. The following article gives you an idea of the leading products and current developments.

'Computer Associates object-orientated database, Jasmine, will eclipse the company's relational database product, CA-OpenIngres, in terms of numbers of users within two years...'

CA is concentrating its development efforts on Jasmine, because the ability to handle objects has become critical to databases.

Users are demanding databases which can store complex video and audio files – something a relational database cannot effectively cope with.

Oracle, Informix and Sybase have adopted a hybrid approach to handling objects by combining relational and object database technology. However, CA has developed Jasmine as a 'pure' object database in collaboration with Japanese computer giant Fujitsu.

Computing, September 1996

The objectives of a database system

3.10 A database should have four major objectives. (features?)

(a) **It should be shared.** Different users should be able to access the same data in the database for their own processing applications, and at the same time if required. This removes the need for duplicating data on different files.

(b) **The integrity of the database must be preserved**. This means that one user should not be allowed to alter the data on file so as to spoil the database records for other users. However, users must be able to update the data on file, and so make valid alterations to the data.

(c) **The database system should provide for the needs of different users,** who each have their own processing requirements and data access methods.

(d) **The database should be capable of evolving,** both in the short term (it must be kept updated) and in the longer term (it must be able to meet the future data processing needs of users, not just their current needs).

Creating a database structure

3.11 The most crucial operation involved in setting up and using a database is the creation and structure of the database file or files. The person creating the database file must first carry out an **analysis of all the data** for processing and filing, because a full and accurate analysis of data in the system is crucial to the construction of complete and workable database files.

The database management system (DBMS)

3.12 The database management system is a system which organises the **storage of data** in the most appropriate way to facilitate its storage, retrieval and use in different applications. It is a piece of software which provides the interface between the logical data and the physical data. The user does not need to know anything about the physical location of data on the storage medium. Indeed, he may actually be prevented from doing so. The user simply requires the set of definitions used to describe the data items he wishes to retrieve and use.

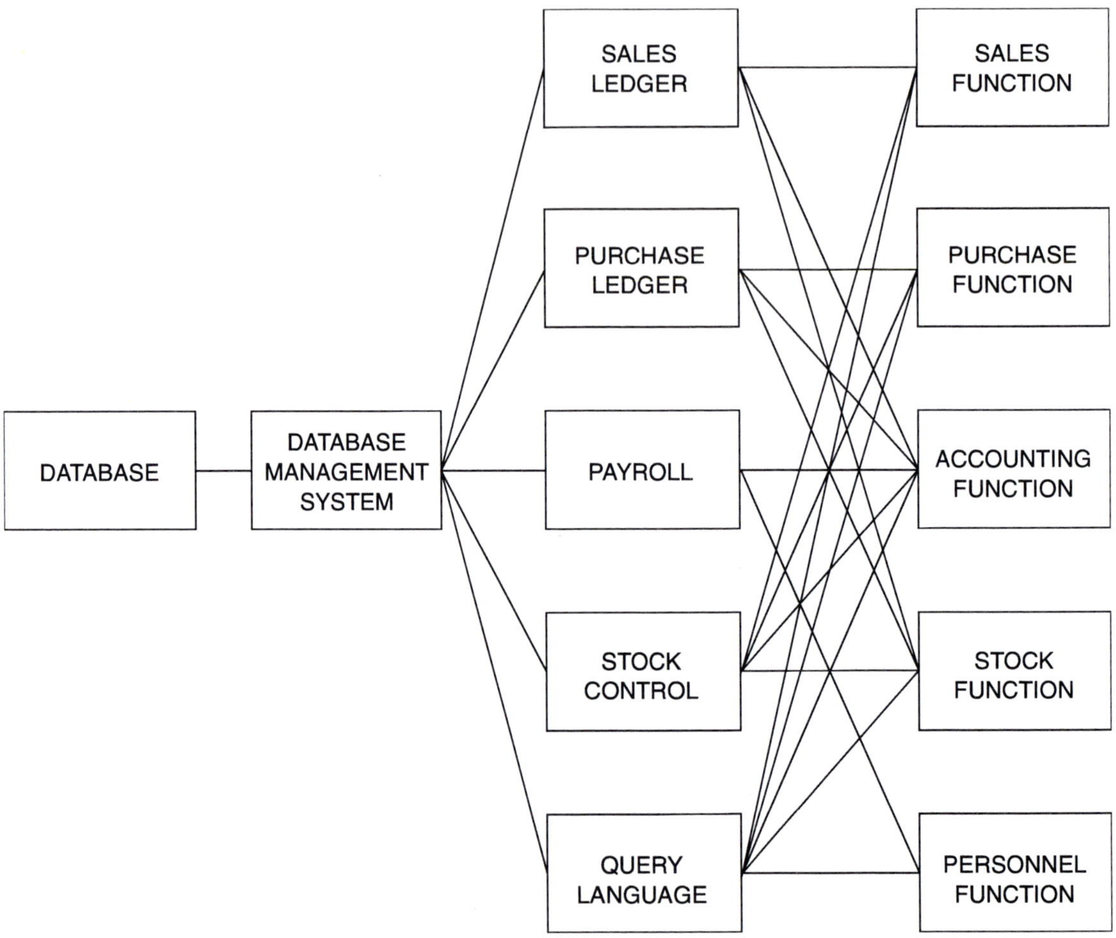

3.13 The use of database systems has permitted programmers and users to focus more intently upon the **logical relationships** which are of greater importance for using the information. The database system then takes over the mechanics involved in handling the physical storage of data and accessing it as needed.

Database administration and maintenance

3.14 The database should be **dynamic**. The contents of the data records will be continually changing, and the types of data and the relationship between the items will also occasionally change. The DBMS will automatically re-index the records according to the changes made and provide the interface with the application programs which transfer the input and output to and from the database. The application programs should be independent, as far as is possible, of the actual organisation of the database. The DBMS has to protect data from unauthorised access and from corruption during processing. By keeping a record of data items accessed the DBMS can identify redundant items that can be removed from the database.

3.15 A database administrator will often be appointed to look after the structure, physical storage and security of the data in the best interest of all users. He is responsible for **maintenance** of all aspects.

(a) The **database** itself, including the addition of new data (liasing with users, the systems analysts and programmers) and ensuring there is no duplication

(b) A **dictionary** describing the data items

(c) **Manuals** for users describing how to use the facilities of the database

(d) Overseeing the **security** of the database and ensuring that individual privacy is not encroached

(e) Ensuring that the requirements of the **data protection legislation** are complied with

(f) Setting **standards** for the **input** of data, definitions, **storage** structure, system **performance**, **security** and **integrity** of data, and **back-up** and **recovery** strategies

A database for company secretarial work — 12/95, 6/98

3.16 The best-known database product for company secretaries is BLUEPRINT 2000 *Company Secretary for Windows* produced by ICSA Software. Features of BLUEPRINT include the following.

(a) It is capable of **printing** all the forms, registers and minutes required to be produced by statute, not only in the UK and the Republic of Ireland, but also in many other jurisdictions worldwide. There is the facility to see a graphical representation of forms on screen, prior to editing and printing, and to print company logos on reports and registers. All company reports and registers can be customised: the user can choose what is shown in a printout. A compliance diary, allowing users to monitor outstanding statutory work, is also available.

(b) The database approach ensures that there is one **consistent source** of information, which can also be used to provide a range of group and company reports.

Data can easily be exchanged with other commonly-used office software packages such as Microsoft Word, Excel and Powerpoint. BLUEPRINT can also can link with existing database systems and for the core of an extensive management information system, where information is collated into reports from different database applications on different software platforms.

(c) On the one hand **fields can be defined** by the **user** (useful, for example, if it were important for a particular company to record non-standard information such as favourite colour on the main directors' personal details screen).

(d) On the other, it is possible to **control user access** to each field and button in the system, so that users can be prevented from changing information in a certain field or even from seeing the field altogether. There is also a utility that allows the user to assign certain companies to groups. The groups in turn can be assigned to individual users so that certain users can only see certain companies. This is particularly useful where the software is being used on a wide area network with several office sites accessing a central database.

(e) Information that people across the company may need to consult can be made available in *intranet* form (see Chapter 11).

3.17 ICSA Software also produce a Windows version of a product called *Rolls*, which is the market-leading package for the administration of employee share schemes.

Data warehousing

3.18 A 'data warehouse' is a **database** on a very **large scale**: a database that collates data stored on other separate databases. This is especially important for companies that have developed a number of databases over the years using incompatible technologies. Data warehousing tools allow the end user to access, query, view and link up data held in different locations and formats.

(a) Retail chains such as Tesco find data warehouses useful to keep up with what is selling by analysing cash register data and linking it to data derived from loyalty cards. The result is a list of the names and addresses of customers and of what they buy, and where and when they buy it.

(b) International hotel chains use data warehouses to record the preferences of every guest and so have the little extras that individual clients always request (three extra pillows, a mini-bar full of pineapple juice, or whatever) ready to hand.

(c) British Airways in conjunction with other airlines use data warehouse information to help to work out what range of fares should be offered on particular routes.

3.19 An often-quoted example is the discovery, using a data warehouse, by an American retailer, Wal-Mart, that there was a strong correlation between the sales of nappies and beer. Wal-Mart found that both tended to sell at the same time, just after working hours, and concluded that men with small children stopped off to buy nappies on their way home and picked up some beer at the same time. If the two items were put in the same shopping aisle, sales of both should increase. Wal-Mart tried this and it worked.

4 DECISION SUPPORT SYSTEMS

4.1 Decision support systems are used by management to assist in making decisions on issues which are **unstructured**, with high levels of uncertainty about the true nature of the problem, the various **responses** which management would undertake or the likely impact of those actions. These highly ambiguous environments do not allow the easy application of many of the techniques or systems developed for more well defined problems or activities.

4.2 Decision support systems are intended to provide a wide range of **alternative information gathering** and **analytical tools** with a major emphasis upon flexibility and user-friendliness.

4.3 Decision support systems **do not make decisions**. The objective is to allow the manager to consider a number of **alternatives** and evaluate them under a variety of potential conditions. A key element in the usefulness of these systems is their ability to **function interactively**. This is a feature, for example, of spreadsheets. Managers using these systems often develop scenarios using earlier results to refine their understanding of the problem and their actions.

Models

4.4 A model can be defined as an **abstract** of a **real system** which permits the exploration of the behaviour of the system under various different circumstances. The term 'simulation model' is used to describe any model which somehow represents a 'real' system. The main type of simulation model that managers use is a **symbolic** or **mathematical model**, in which variables in the 'real' system are represented by mathematical symbols and equations.

4.5 A model is used to provide managers with information for decision-making. A model is used in most cases because it would be impossible to experiment with the physical, 'real-world' system itself.

4.6 Many models which are built relate to a particular area of a company's operations.

(a) **Market** models may be used to forecast sales demand. The variables which affect demand must be identified, quantified and set in some mathematical relationship with each other, so as to build a sales forecasting or market model. The variables affecting demand include:

(i) Past and current sales, where trends or cycles are discernible

(ii) Market conditions - ie size of the market, market segments, taxation, new technology

(iii) Consumer spending patterns

(iv) Competition

(v) Sales promotion and advertising expenditure

(vi) Market research findings, product design and development, etc

(b) **Cost prediction** models and financial models (for example cash flow models)

(c) **Transportation** models, or models to help decisions about siting factories

(d) **Departmental** models, covering the design of products, production scheduling and control, stockholding, distribution and sales within a department or division

(e) **Technical** models used, for example, in product design

Budget models

4.7 A budget is a model for a **medium-term plan**. A budget model can be computerised, quite possibly using a spreadsheet package on a PC in the case of smaller organisations.

4.8 Budget models allow managers to **assess alternative plans**, or to carry out sensitivity analysis to test what would happen if certain variables turn out differently from the way assumed in the budget. Computerised models allow managers to change their assumptions and re-formulate their budgets quickly, by making minor input amendments.

4.9 Budget models can also be used for **management control**. If a budget has been prepared using a computer model, it is usually a simple extension of the model to include a facility for recording actual results, period by period, and to produce budgetary control reports, such as:

- Variance analysis reports
- Profit centre profitability statements
- Revised forecasts of future achievements over the budget period

Strategic planning models

4.10 In large groups of companies, it is not uncommon for the strategic planning process to begin at the subsidiary company level, or sub-subsidiary level, with individual companies preparing their own business plans using a strategic business planning computer model, and then for the plan to be fed into the planning model of the parent company, which can co-ordinate the plans of its different subsidiaries, and amend them as necessary. Modelling helps to **speed up** the **co-ordinating** and **decision-making** process between companies in the group.

Econometric models for medium-term forecasting

4.11 Econometrics is the study of economic variables and their interrelationships, using computer models. Short-term or medium-term **econometric models** might be used for forecasting. Such models, incorporating mathematical techniques such as regression analysis, may well be useful for medium-term forecasting.

Forecasting packages

4.12 **Software packages** that prepare forecasts from historical data are available for all sizes of computer, from mainframe to PC, varying in **complexity** (and cost). These packages take historical data fed in by the computer user, and conduct correlation analysis and regression analysis to produce forecasts and information about the degree of confidence that can be placed in them.

Optimisation models

4.13 Once long-term forecasts have been made, and the framework of strategic plans agreed, managers will know what **assumptions** they are expected to make about future environmental conditions and resource availability. Given such assumptions about the constraints within which the organisation will be operating, other types of models, referred to collectively as either mathematical programming models, or optimisation models, can be used.

4.14 Examples of optimisation models are:

(a) **Linear programming models**, which seek to maximise the value of an objective function (usually profits or sales revenue) or minimise its value (usually costs), given certain constraints, such as a known limitation on the availability of resources

(b) **Economic order quantity models**, which seek to minimise costs of stockholding by identifying the least-cost size of order for raw material and component supplies, or for production quantities in batch production systems

(c) **Critical path analysis, or PERT analysis**, which seeks to minimise the timescale for completion of a project, perhaps within the framework of resource limitations and/or cost controls

Ad hoc decision models

4.15 A further type of model is a decision model, which can be used to enable managers to make 'ad hoc' or '**one-off' decisions**, as distinct from routine and repetitive decisions such as budget planning. Examples of decision models are the following.

- Discounted cash flow (DCF) models for capital expenditure appraisal
- Lease versus buy decision models
- Models to enable decisions to be taken about new products or new markets
- Shutdown decision models to decide whether to close down an operating division
- Models for sell-off decisions or acquisition decisions
- Game theory models

Behavioural models

4.16 Some experiments have been carried out to develop behavioural models which attempt to analyse and **predict customer** or buyer behaviour by:

(a) Recognising what **factors influence** a buyer's purchasing decision, and assigning a points 'score' or weighting to each factor within the behavioural model

(b) Assessing how well the organisation's products and marketing mix can tap the buyer's **purchasing motives**

4.17 The model can then be used to experiment with the marketing mix to decide what mix is most likely to be successful in creating sales.

Exercise 5

What are the benefits of modelling?

Solution

Note that there was a question on benefits of IT-based budgeting and forecasting (amongst other things) in the Specimen Paper for this topic.

In broad terms, the advantages of models in terms of corporate information needs are:

(a) The ability to explore more alternatives
(b) Improved decision making
(c) More effective planning

(d) Faster decision making
(e) More timely information
(f) More accurate forecasts
(g) More extensive information, and ready access to information
(h) Flexibility in the production of control reports
(i) Cost savings, possibly as a result of the other benefits

5 EXECUTIVE INFORMATION SYSTEMS

5.1 An executive information system (EIS) provides the executive with the underlying performance facts and figures which have traditionally been under the control of middle managers. It is a type of decision support system, and takes the form of computer workstations on top of executives' desks. An EIS is likely to have the following features.

(a) Provision of **summary-level data**, captured from the organisation's main systems (which might involve integrating the executive's desk top PC with the organisation's mainframe)

(b) A facility which allows the executive to '**drill-down**' from higher levels of information to lower

(c) **Data manipulation** facilities (for example comparison with budget)

(d) **Graphics**, for user-friendly presentation of data

(e) A **template** system. This will mean that the same type of data (eg sales figures) is presented in the same format, irrespective of changes in the information required

5.2 The basic design philosophy of executive information systems is as follows.

(a) They should be **easy to use** ('idiot-proof' not just user friendly) as an EIS may be consulted during a meeting, for example.

(b) They should **make data easy to access**, so that it describes the organisation from the executive's point of view, not just in terms of its data flows.

(c) They should **provide tools for analysis** (including ratio analysis, forecasts, what-if analysis, trends).

(d) They should **provide presentational aids** so that information can be conveyed 'without bothering the executive with too many trivial choices of scale, colour and layout.'

5.3 At the heart of an executive information system is a **corporate model**, which holds key information about the organisation, such as organisational structure including consolidation and sub-consolidation groupings, performance indicators including ratios, and reporting cycles as appropriate. This model provides the interface between the database and the executive, who as a result does not have to define how information should be displayed.

6 EXPERT SYSTEMS

6.1 Computer systems are now recognised as suitable for use in the decision-making process in a number of areas.

(a) Computerisation itself has enabled a given volume of data to be processed at a **cheaper cost** than with manual methods of processing.

(b) Database methods for storing information enable it to be **retrieved in any format**. With the increased volume of information available, the ease with which desired information can be selected and defined in advance has given the virtue of flexibility to information access and retrieval.

(c) Modelling systems enable data to be **used in a number of ways** to evaluate the effect of changes in one variable on changes in another, according to the relationships between them which have been determined by the model-maker.

6.2 However, the role of the computer in actually taking decisions is in fact largely passive. The computer will give you the information you want (providing that it is requested in the right way), and it will process it according to the instructions given (specified rigorously in advance), but it cannot do the following.

(a) Tell the user how to take the decision.

(b) Replace the hunches or rules of thumb based on past experience which may determine how decisions are taken in the first place.

(c) Weigh up the qualitative factors in taking a particular decision.

(d) Weigh up the relative value of two different pieces of information.

(e) Handle uncertainty very well.

(f) Assess whether the result derived from the execution of its programmed instructions is adequate to a problem.

6.3 For example, a doctor may take one patient's description of his or her symptoms less seriously than another's owing to the former's reputation for hypochondria. This condition is something the doctor would learn about over time. It is hard to include such reasoning into the prescriptive logic of a computer program. However certain features of the diagnosis can arguably be put in a computer form to simulate the type of deduction that the doctor would make.

6.4 **Artificial intelligence** is the concept that computers can be programmed to imitate certain features of human reasoning. Artificial intelligence has led to the creation of expert systems.

Exercise 6

Why do you think organisations need to automate reasoning or decision-making tasks which humans are naturally better able to perform than computers?

Solution

(a) The primary reason has to do with the relative cost of information. An expert can spend a great deal of time acquiring a specialised body of knowledge, but the commercial value of this expertise ceases with the expert's retirement or departure from the labour force.

(b) Secondly, enshrining an expert's accumulated wisdom in a computer system means that this wisdom can be accessed by more people. Thus, the delivery of complicated services to customers, decisions whether or not to extend credit and so forth, can be made by less experienced members of staff if the expert's knowledge is available to them. If a manufacturing company has a complicated mixture of plant and machinery, then the repair engineer may accumulate a lot of knowledge over a period of time about the way it behaves: if a problem occurs, the engineer will be able to make a reasoned guess as to where the likely cause is to be found. If this accumulated expert information is made available to less experienced staff, it means that some of their learning curve is avoided.

An expert system is advantageous because it saves time, like all computer systems (in theory at least) but it is particularly useful as it possesses both knowledge and a reasoning ability.

6.5 Expert systems have been used in a number of situations.

(a) The first expert system, MYCIN, was used to diagnose patients.

(b) Tax advice is also provided by expert systems.

(c) Expert systems are used in some areas of the law.

(d) Expert systems are used in engineering systems. The Royal Bank of Scotland has employed an expert system to diagnose faults in its extensive computer networks.

(e) Expert systems can be used in banking and financial services.

(f) In some database systems they can speed up the process of retrieving data from a database file.

(g) Diagnostic systems can identify causes of problems, for example in production control systems, or in medical applications.

(h) In some decision support systems they can provide advice to a decision maker. Expert systems can give facts, but they can also indicate to the user what a decision ought to be in a particular situation, and in this respect, expert systems can be a form of decision support system for managers in business.

6.6 An organisation can use an expert system when a number of conditions are met.

- The problem is **reasonably well defined.**
- The expert can **define some rules** by which the problem can be solved.
- The problem cannot be solved by **conventional** processing or data handling.
- The **expert could be released** to more difficult problems.
- The **investment in an expert system** is cost **justified.**

6.7 Expert systems are computer programs which allow users to benefit from **expert knowledge and information**, and also **advice**. An expert system is therefore a program for which the master/reference file holds a large amount of specialised data, for example on legal, engineering or medical information, or tax matters. The user keys in certain facts and the program uses its information on file to produce a decision.

Exercise 7

Read the following extracts.

(a) 'Direct Line's speed of response and cost advantage derive from its policy of only accepting low risk business and the use of sophisticated computer systems which allow telesales staff to key in essential details and respond to applications for insurance instantly rather than having to spend days waiting for a decision from an underwriter.'

(b) 'Know-How has set out to formulate and make accessible a wealth of internal information. The map references to such information previously existed only in the heads of experienced solicitors. Now, documents are analysed before data entry by experts who predict how they are likely to be of use in the future and encapsulate carefully-coded keywords in the text.

Typically, the information on the system is used to shed light on new situations and interpret them in the light of previous experience.'

(c) 'Instant access to summary information, the potential for highlighting exceptions or variances with budget and the ease with which executives can find the reasons for a variance, in terms of an individual salesman's performance, have thrown up major implications for entire organisations'.

Which of these extracts describes a decision support system, which an executive information system and which an expert system?

Solution

The point of exercises like this one is to bring some real life to the factual information in the main body of the text, and to make sure you are paying attention. The answers are (b), (c) and (a) respectively.

Strategic planning packages

6.8 A variety of software packages exist to help with strategic planning. Some are commercially available, while others have been developed by larger businesses in-house, or by management consultants.

Advantages and disadvantages of strategic planning packages

6.9 The advantage of tools such as these is that they force managers to **think** about **strategic** issues, and they draw upon ideas that managers might not know about.

6.10 Disadvantages are as follows.

(a) A package is only as good as the **rules contained** within it; some might be invalidated by new ideas.

(b) The analysis depends on the user giving **accurate answers** to questions, many of which are very impressionistic ('rate your business's ability to do X on a scale of 1 to 10').

(c) Brilliant new ideas are often born because their inventor has the ability to **break away** from conventional thinking.

7 SYSTEMS INTEGRATION 6/00

7.1 As you may have gathered by now, many organisations will have a whole variety of computer systems built up over time.

7.2 Many of these items of equipment will have been manufactured by different suppliers. For example, it would be quite typical for a large organisation to have an IBM mainframe, DEC minicomputers and a range of IBM-compatible PCs manufactured by different companies.

7.3 The main problem is that the marketing rules which applied for mainframes no longer apply for a market which is far more diversified.

(a) Mainframe manufacturers made their profits by **'locking-in' customers** to their own proprietary systems. This made it difficult if not impossible to connect machines made by different manufacturers. Upgrades (moving to a bigger mainframe) were difficult, because applications could not simply move up to the new machine; they had to be rewritten, as manufacturers even produced incompatible operating systems for differing products.

(b) Customers, on the other hand, faced with a wide choice in the PC market wanted **more flexibility**. They wanted to be able to 'mix and match' equipment and software from any supplier.

Interoperability

7.4 **Interoperability** means that any company, individual or institution can readily **share** and **exchange information** and **facilities** with any other company, individual or institution. Moreover, they can do so without having to use the same service provider as the other party, or without having to use the same technology platform; they need have only a minimum of concern about data structures. There is a minimum need for new skills when using new applications and technologies.

Backward compatibility

7.5 A new version of a **program** is said to be backward compatible if it can use files and data created with an **older version** of the same program. Computer **hardware** is said to be backward compatible if it can run the same software as **previous models**.

7.6 Backward compatibility is important because it **eliminates the need to start afresh** when upgrading to a newer product. A backward-compatible word processor, for instance, allows users to edit documents created with a previous version of the program. In general, manufacturers try to keep their products backward compatible. Sometimes, however, it is necessary to **sacrifice** backward compatibility to take advantage of a **new technology**.

Legacy system

7.7 A legacy system is a computer system or application program which **continues to be used** because of the **prohibitive cost of replacing or redesigning it** and often despite its poor competitiveness and compatibility with modern equivalents.

7.8 **Legacy software** may only run on antiquated **hardware**, and the cost of maintaining this may eventually outweigh the cost of replacing both the software and hardware.

Open systems

7.9 Organisations develop computerised systems over a period of time, perhaps focusing on different functions at different times, and a number of consequences are likely to become apparent.

- They may have networks or other equipment supplied by a **range of manufacturers**.
- **Data is duplicated** in different areas of the business.
- **Software** may have become **inefficient and out of date**.

7.10 **Open systems** aim to ensure compatibility between different makes of equipment, enabling users to choose on the basis of price and performance. An open systems approach has a number of characteristics. The first is **vendor independence**. Applications can be 'ported' from one system to another. An open systems infrastructure supports **organisation-wide functions** and allows interoperability of networks and systems. Authorised users would be able to access applications and data from any part of the system.

Case example: Pure Java v Microsoft Java

Depending on who you talk to, Java is three things. Firstly, it is a programming language: a scaled down version, some would even argue a derivative, of C++. Java has the benefit of being a write-once-run-anywhere language, or so its creators claim.

Secondly, Java is a platform all of its own. It runs on any computer that has a Java Virtual machine - embedded code that recognises and reads Java code as it is downloaded onto the machine. Java is a single unifying platform for organisations with heterogeneous computing environments, which is most companies. Finally, Java has assumed the role as the ultimate IT panacea, 'Java-as-lifestyle'.

[A number of] industry heavyweights are jostling for position in their attempts to dominate the Java field. First up, naturally, is Sun. Creator and progenitor of Java, Sun appears to be betting the company jewels on Java. Definitely belonging to the 'Java-as-lifestyle' element, Sun has even committed itself to a '100% Pure Java' initiative, a bid to get programmers to write for and in native Java without calling on any local machine code, such as Windows APIs, for extra functionality.

Behind the Java evangelists are the two companies with most to gain from Java as a platform: IBM and Oracle. Although IBM has publicly chided Microsoft for not supporting the 100% Pure Java initiative, it is the Java as middleware idea that would appear to drive IBM's interest. Firstly, it has many different platforms to unify. Vendors are also increasingly wary of committing to proprietary security, messaging and transaction software from IBM, because they have been burned in the past and because they now demand the inter-operability and openness that the Internet exemplifies. ...

And then there is Microsoft, both contrary and dominant simultaneously. Microsoft has been anything but slow in developing Java. Its own Java VM is the fastest available. Yet Microsoft insists that Java is just a language. And to demonstrate its ambivalent attitude towards Java, it will make its breakaway move whilst attempting to win plaudits for development the fastest Java VM. ... This sort of commitment to developing Java tools and code for its other products, but endless re-iteration of how Java itself is only a poor rival to C++, is why so many of Microsoft's opponents accuse it of hypocrisy.

Microsoft came under more scrutiny when UK manager Jeremy Gittins commented on the likelihood of Microsoft splitting from the Java standard. Although Microsoft has yet to endorse these comments, it seems that the company is gearing itself up for a split. Microsoft claims publicly that the Sun standard for Java will only run on 42 per cent of systems before making calls to the operating system, and that the cross-platform Java claim is simply not true except for trivial applets. So, the 'Java-as-extension-of-Windows' model is one that Microsoft appears committed to follow.

Source: *Information Week,* September 1997

UNIX

7.11 The UNIX operating system was developed as a **non-proprietary** (ie not specific to one manufacturer) **multitasking** operating system that could be portable to different computer architectures. By the 1980s it had been developed far enough for commercial users to take an interest in it.

7.12 UNIX works equally well in a PC network environment as in a mainframe system. Particular areas where UNIX has demonstrated its capabilities are **communications**, where the ability to accommodate PC operating systems in the UNIX environment supports the use of electronic mail, and **engineering**, where UNIX's capabilities are suited to driving high-resolution graphics systems.

7.13 There are two main versions of UNIX, one called **System V,** the other **BSD**.

PC operating systems

7.14 In the PC market there is a sort of *de facto* open systems arrangement, given that there are so many 'clones' of the PC originally developed by IBM, all of which use versions of a Microsoft operating system, *Windows* or, on older machines, *MS-DOS*.

Windows

7.15 Early incarnations of Windows, culminating in **Windows 3.1** and **Windows for Workgroups 3.11**, were not genuine operating systems in their own right, but were really an operating environment for an older Microsoft system called **MS-DOS**. This meant that MS-DOS, which is very hostile to beginners, was always running underneath any applications and users were therefore still constrained by, for example, **eight-character file names** and various problems relating to the conventional memory of a PC.

7.16 In 1993, Microsoft launched **Windows NT**, a complete operating system in its own right, designed for **networks**, and now providing strong competition for other network operating systems like Novell Netware. Subsequently Microsoft launched Windows 95 and Windows 98. A new version, **Windows 2000** was released in mid-2000.

7.17 Features of Windows 98 and Windows NT include the following.

Feature	Comments
User friendly interface	User interface enhancements include easier navigation, such as single-**click launching** of applications, icon highlighting, forward/backward buttons, and an easy to customise Start Menu. (See the next section of this chapter for more on the 'user interface'.)
Desktop	Disk drives, folders (directories) applications and files can all be placed on, and **accessed** from, the desktop.
Task bar	Including a start button and buttons showing and enabling access to every open application.
Long file names	No longer are file names restricted to eight characters. Meaningful file names can now be given (up to 256 characters).

Feature	Comments
Recycle bin	For **easy recovery** of 'deleted' files.
Multitasking	'True' or pre-emptive multitasking, under which each program is allocated a **time slice** and tasks switch whenever the operating system dictates.

Web integration	A variety of features are designed to **enhance Internet access** and use of Internet facilities and technologies, and integrate them with the users system. For instance it is possible to access a website directly from the 'Explorer' file management system (see Chapter 2).
Multimedia	Windows 98 has better **graphics** and **video capabilities** and better support for games hardware such as joysticks. It supports digital video disks (DVD) and technologies connected with digital television.
More manageable for businesses	Built in tools such as Dr. Watson and System Information Utility make it easier for IT support staff to **diagnose** and **correct problems**. Easy integration with networking software is possible.

7.18 Although it has bugs and irritations for the experienced user, Microsoft Windows provides a **comprehensive working environment**, managing programs specifically written for it by other software companies (WordPerfect for Windows, Lotus 1-2-3 for Windows etc) as well as older versions which were written for MS-DOS. This makes it easier for beginners to learn how to use PCs, as most new applications tend to look and 'feel' the same as existing ones.

Apple Macs

7.19 There is still a minority of microcomputer users, particularly those working in design and graphics, who prefer the Apple Macintosh system, claiming that Windows 95 merely does what 'Apple Macs' have done for years. For an organisation that already has many Apple Macs and many staff familiar with them the best option may be to continue to use them.

7.20 The majority of Apple users have an operating system called System 7, which does indeed pre-date Windows 95 and to which Windows 95 bears a striking resemblance. A new version, System 8, was released in 1997.

Case example: UNIX v NT

From small businesses to large multinationals, companies are ditching their UNIX and Novell NetWare and buying into a Microsoft idea of one 'total solution' - NT across the enterprise. One indication of the rise of NT has been the sudden increase in membership of the Windows NT User Forum over the last six months. According to Grant Pearson, managing director of the Forum: 'Among the people that are signing up for the User Forum are those who have been using Windows 3.11 and never really trusted Windows 95 for their workstations. NT seems to have come of age and users are bypassing 95 and installing NT.'

Pearson notes, however, that very few NT users are opting for total NT solutions. According to Forum figures, almost a third are still running UNIX, and another third use NetWare alongside NT, because many users don't totally believe Microsoft's marketing message, and are installing NT only in areas where there are sound technology reasons.

'There is no doubt that NT is a good operating system, but it is just as good as anything else. UNIX handles applications better and NetWare has a better file and print system, for example,' he says.

NT's success stems from Microsoft's marketing machine, which has managed to convince users that it is more compatible with the rest of its software, according to Pearson. 'If your company was using Exchange or Office, then the Microsoft marketing machine would convince you that NT would bring the whole thing together.'

Microsoft's marketing has certainly convinced users that it is more appealing than its rivals. 'NT is forcing its way into the corporate market on the basis of its sex appeal. NT looks like 95 for users who are Windows-comfortable. But UNIX does not look as friendly and NetWare is not as pretty.'

But Pearson feels that UNIX will hold its ground among customers, because it has a solid following among IT staff. 'Certainly on application servers it is a lot more powerful than NT,' Pearson says.

(Source: *Information Week,* October 1997)

Chapter roundup

- **Information management** entails identifying information needs and sources, collecting and storing information, facilitating methods of using and communicating information and ensuring that it is protected. Management information may range from lists of transactions, used to monitor day-to-day operations, to market and competitor information for strategic planning.
- **Centralised and decentralised information systems** each have advantages and disadvantages. The current trend is towards networks which can be built up gradually from relatively low start-up costs and offer greater flexibility, easier data-sharing, and more computer power for individual needs.
- **Databases** avoid data redundancy, make data independent of programs (and so easier to share) and ensure consistency of data. Careful initial design and careful control and maintenance of the database are essential. ICSA's BLUEPRINT is a good example of an off-the-shelf database application.
- **Decision support systems** are used by management to **provide assistance** in decision-making. Spreadsheet models are common examples. Packaged models exist for tasks such as forecasting, predicting customer behaviour, strategic planning and so on.
- **Executive information systems** are a form of information system designed to give senior executives easy access to data. They typically include a 'drill-down' facility, graphics and data manipulation facilities.
- **Expert systems** use artificial intelligence to deal with problems that can be reasonably well defined and solved by reference to set rules. For instance strategic planning packages may draw on the work of experts such as Porter and Kotler.
- **Interoperability** means that it is possible to share and exchange information and facilities with others without having to use the same service provider or technology platform and with a minimum of concern about data structures, and a minimum need for new skills. A key issue in the *open systems* debate at present is the choice of *UNIX or Windows NT* as an operating system.
- The diversity of systems that have been developed means that **incompatibility** has been a serious problem. Unix and Windows are *de facto* standards in the market at present.

Test your knowledge

1 How can information management be improved? (See para 1.1, Exercise 1)

2 What is the role of a server in a LAN or WAN? (2.7)

3 What are five advantages of networks? (2.9)

4 What is the difference between an integrated system and a database system? (3.4)

5 What are the objectives of a database? (3.9)

6 What are the responsibilities of a database administrator? (3.14)

7 What does BLUEPRINT do? (3.16)

8 What sort of computer models may be used to help with decisions? (4.6)

9 What features is an EIS likely to have? (5.1)

10 In what situations might an expert system be used? (6.5 -6.6)

11 What is the point of open systems? (7.10)

12 Name six features of Windows 98. (7.17)

Now try illustrative question 10 at the end of the Study Text

Chapter 11

TECHNOLOGICAL DEVELOPMENTS

This chapter covers the following topics.

1 Collecting information
2 Storing and retrieving information
3 Using information
4 Communicating information
5 The Internet
6 Electronic commerce

Introduction

In this chapter we shall review a wide selection of recent and forthcoming technological developments that will help with information management. This chapter is structured along the lines suggested as the key issues in information management at the beginning of the previous chapter, so besides considering some now common office packages used for processing information, we look at better ways of collecting data, such as FutureTags which may replace barcodes in time, better ways of storing and retrieving data, such as recordable CDs and DIP, and especially better ways of communicating information, in the so-called 'decade of telecommunications'.

The Internet has come about through the combination of many of these developing technologies and it is also the subject of constant media attention, so to round off this chapter we devote a section to this important new phenomenon in corporate information.

Awareness of technological developments is very important in this paper. Both questions in December 1999 involved a discussion of the benefits of new technology.

1 COLLECTING INFORMATION **6/96, 12/99**

1.1 Data capture or data collection can suffer from a number of problems.

(a) It may be **time-consuming,** especially when a large volume of data must be input for processing.

(b) It is **costly,** because of the labour time needed to collect, transmit, prepare and input the data and also because of the costs of the equipment and data documents and files needed to do the work.

(c) It risks being **error prone,** especially where the collection of data is done largely by manual methods.

(d) It is sometimes **inconvenient**, especially when data has to be despatched, perhaps by security van, to a distant computer centre where it will be processed by a mainframe computer, and then returned with the output information, also perhaps sent by security van.

1.2 The ideal methods of data collection and input are therefore those which minimise:

- The time needed to record, transmit, prepare and input data
- Costs
- Errors

- The 'turnround time' between submitting data and receiving output

1.3 The challenge in implementing new technologies is to find the optimum balance between:

- The **cost** of data collection, control and accuracy
- Achieving the degree of **control** and accuracy required

Case example: Collecting data

'When customers of Hertz return their rented cars to Heathrow and 12 other locations in Europe, they are met by Hertz representatives wielding hand-held radio data terminals. Details of the vehicle registration number, rental agreement, mileage and fuel level are keyed in and sent via base stations and computer links to the Hertz mainframe in Oklahoma City. Within 60 seconds the customer receives an itemised receipt from a printer attached to the terminal. This time saving innovation is an example of an emerging trend in wireless radio frequency data communications (WDC). An increasingly common feature of warehouses and distribution centres for food, pharmaceutical and other industries, they are beginning to make inroads in manufacturing, ports and container-handling terminals and other applications.'

Source: Financial Times, August 1996

Keyboard input

1.4 By far the most significant advantage of direct input via keyboard is that a computer user can have **interactive processing** using a keyboard and VDU. Interactive processing is when data can be input to a computer, output information received quickly, and where appropriate further input keyed in and output received. The computer user gets the information he or she wants 'instantly'.

1.5 However, direct keyboard input is **unsuitable** for **large volumes** of transaction data and it is likely to be error-prone because the only data verification that can be done is a visual check of the data on the VDU screen before input. There might also be security problems because there is a possibility that unauthorised users can gain access to a keyboard terminal in an office (or that unauthorised people can gain access from their own personal terminal to someone else's computer). For this reason businesses are keen to develop new ways of inputting data.

Pen based computers

1.6 Pen based computers, ranging from pocket-sized devices to A4-sized 'notepads', are being used increasingly in applications where the user would conventionally have taken **written notes** and then transferred them onto a computer by conventional keying in at a later date. For example, police officers in the City of London use a pen based computer to produce electronically generated parking tickets. The computer then simply needs to be plugged into the main system when back at the office to download all the data recorded on the move. Other examples are in retail, distribution, and insurance.

Document reading methods

1.7 Document reading methods of data collection involve the use of a source document that both humans and computers can read. Document reading methods reduce human 'intrusion' into data capture and cut out the need to transcribe manually-prepared data on to a computer-sensible input medium.

Magnetic ink character recognition (MICR)

1.8 MICR is the recognition by a machine of special formatted characters printed in **magnetic ink.** The main advantage of MICR is its **accuracy**, but MICR documents are **expensive** to produce, and so MICR has only limited application in practice. The largest application of MICR is in the banking system. Cheques are pre-encoded with certain data and, after use, post-encoded with the amount of the cheque.

Optical character recognition (OCR)

1.9 OCR is a method of input involving a machine that is able to read characters by **optical detection** of the **shape** of those characters. Optical (or laser) scanners can read **printed documents** at up to 300 pages per hour. The advantage of OCR over MICR is that the computer can read ordinary typed or printed text, provided that the quality of the input document is satisfactory. In practice the difficulty of distinguishing between O and 0, and I and 1, means that OCR applications are limited.

1.10 The technology now exists for computers to **recognise handwriting**. Devices that allow the user to write on the screen and have this handwriting converted into computer sensible form are being used in warehousing and stock control.

Optical mark reading (OMR)

1.11 Optical mark reading is generally used for **numeric** characters. Values are denoted by a pencilled (graphite), ballpoint pen or typed line or cross in an appropriate box, whose position represents a value, on the preprinted source document (or card). Applications very familiar to many readers will be **National Lottery** entry forms and answer sheets for **multiple choice exam questions**! The main drawback (especially in exams!) is that the users can easily put their marks in the wrong place.

Turnaround documents

1.12 OCR and OMR methods of character recognition can make use of a turnaround document. A turnaround document is a document that is initially **produced** by **computer**. It is then used to collect more data and then **re-input** to the **computer** for processing. Many mass market companies include a **payment counterfoil** with their computer-produced bill, which is returned with payment and then used for inputting payment data to a computer.

Scanners

1.13 Computers can read words and pictures from a 'hard-copy' page, using a scanner. Scanners have some uses for publishing work. A scanner looks at a whole printed page of input, and records and stores a pattern of dots, according to whether the paper original is black or white. Publishers can therefore put illustrations into a scanner. The image will be fed in to the computer, where it can be enlarged or reduced, and 'cut and pasted' into position alongside printed text on a page. Another use of scanning is to 'read' a document and store the text on a complete file.

Bar coding

1.14 Most large retail stores have introduced electronic point of sale (EPOS) devices, using bar coding, which act both as cash registers and as terminals connected to a main computer. This enables the computer to produce **useful management information** such as sales details and analysis and stock control information **very quickly**. The provision of immediate sales information (for example, which products sell quickly), perhaps analysed on a branch basis, permits great speed and flexibility in **decision-making** (certainly of a short-term nature), as consumer wishes can be responded to quickly.

FutureTags

1.15 A FutureTag is a postage-stamp-sized device which can be **scanned** by a reader up to three metres away. It is read using low-power radio waves. This means, for example, that if products carry Future Tags rather than barcodes it would be possible to scan an entire supermarket trolley full of shopping in one go. Information can also be transmitted to a FutureTag, so that if you had, say, a container full of car wings you could tell one that it was going to be painted green, another red and so on.

Card reading devices

1.16 **Magnetic stripe cards** have machine-sensible data on a magnetic stripe, which is a thin strip of magnetic recording tape, about 1.2 cm wide, stuck to the back of the card. A magnetic card reader can convert this information into directly computer-sensible form.

1.17 The widest application of magnetic stripe cards is as bank credit or service cards, for use in cash machines. Also many retailers have now introduced systems for the **electronic funds transfer at the point of sale (EFTPOS)**. Customers in shops and at petrol stations can use a plastic card (usually a credit card or debit card) to purchase goods or services, and using an EFTPOS terminal in the shop, the customer's credit card account or bank current account will be debited automatically. EFTPOS systems combine point of sale systems, which many retail organisations now use, with electronic funds transfer.

1.18 A **smart card** is a plastic card in which is embedded a microprocessor chip. Besides basic account data, a smart card would typically contain a memory and a processing capability. The smart card is used in a similar way to magnetic stripe cards for money transmission. One of the principal economic advantages of smart cards over magnetic stripe cards is that they are **harder to duplicate**, and so are more secure.

Voice recognition

1.19 Computer software has been developed that can **convert speech** into computer sensible form, using a microphone. At present, affordable versions of the software require users to speak very slowly; however the technology is improving. A voice-enabled version of the Sage Line 50 (formerly Sage Sterling) accounting package is planned soon.

2 STORING AND RETRIEVING INFORMATION 12/99

Disks

2.1 In the mid-1990s disks of various types may be regarded as the main backing storage medium of the present and future, because they offer direct access to data, an extremely important feature.

Hard disks

2.2 A modern business PC invariably has an **internal hard disk**, but external disks may be used too. External disks sit alongside the computer in an extra 'box', with its own power supply and plug socket. Internal disks are incorporated inside the PC itself.

2.3 In larger computer systems **removable disk packs** (several flat disks mounted on a spindle) may be used, or a **Zip Drive**, suitable for **back-ups,** mass storage or moving files between computers.

Floppy disks

2.4 Modern PCs will also have one or two floppy disk drives. The floppy disk provides a cost-effective means of **on-line storage** for small business computer systems. Floppy disks are used in the smallest PC systems as well as with minicomputers, and are particularly useful in providing a means of decentralised processing.

2.5 Floppy disks do not require special storage conditions, and indeed, they are often stored or filed in open trays. However, data on them can be **easily corrupted**. In particular, they are subject to physical wear, because the read/write head actually comes into contact with the disk surface during operation. This is not the case with other types of disk. Because they can be left lying around an office, they are also prone to **physical damage**, such as having cups of coffee spilled over them. As the disks tend to be less reliable than hard disks, administrative procedures should be instituted to protect them (for example the use of steel filing cabinets and careful handling).

Tape storage

2.6 Like an audio or video cassette, data has to be recorded **along the length** of a computer tape and so it is **more difficult to access** (compare the time it takes to find your favourite song on an audiocassette compared with the time it takes with a vinyl record or CD).

2.7 It follows that magnetic tape as a file storage medium is only practical when every record on the file will be **processed in turn**. For example a supermarket's stock records might have movements in every item of stock every day, and so tape would be a suitable for backing up at the end of the day.

2.8 Tape cartridges have a **larger capacity** than floppy disks and they are still widely used as a backing storage medium. Fast tapes which can be used to create a back-up file very quickly are known as **tape streamers.**

2.9 Like any other storage medium tapes can get lost, or the data on them can get corrupted. Since tapes can only be **updated** by producing a completely new carried forward tape this provides an automatic means of **data security**. The brought forward tapes can be kept for two or three 'generations' to safeguard against the loss of data on a current file. This '**grandfather-father-son**' technique allows for files to be reconstructed if a disaster should occur. Once the stipulated number of generations has passed, the former 'grandfather' tape can be purged and used again for other processing.

CD-ROM and CD-R

2.10 Optical disks, which use similar technology to the laser-based compact disc audio system, are being used increasingly for data storage. The capacity of optical disks is **very high** compared with other media and they are **more difficult to damage**. The latest PCs are now automatically supplied with a CD-ROM drive and some software packages are now only available on CD-ROM. Larger systems use what is known as a juke box, which can hold hundreds of CDs and load up the one required in seconds.

2.11 The initials ROM stand for **read-only memory**. This means that all data is implanted onto the disc when it is made, and subsequent users can only **retrieve** information, they cannot alter or overwrite or delete what is already on the disk.

2.12 CD **recorders** are now available for general business use (for under £500) with blank CDs (CD-R). CD-Rs are not reusable in the way that floppy disks are. Rewritable CDs (CD-RW) have just been launched in the UK.

DVD-ROM

2.13 The CD format has started to be superseded by DVD. CD-ROMS hold 650 megabytes of data, which only a few years ago was considered enough for any application. However, the advent of multimedia files with video graphics and sound encouraged the development of a new storage technology.

2.14 **Digital Versatile Disk (DVD)** ROM technology can store almost 5 gigabytes of data on one disk. Access speeds are improved as is sound and video quality.

2.15 DVD is sometimes referred to as Digital Video Disk. Many commentators believe DVD will not only replace CD-ROM, but also VHS cassettes, audio CDs and laser discs.

Document image processing

2.16 Document image processing is an electronic form of filing. In a DIP system, a document is passed through a **scanner,** translated into **digital form** and a digitised image is then stored on a storage device (perhaps an optical disk). (This can then be retrieved at will and shown on a computer screen). One optical disk could contain at least 60,000 pages of A4.

2.17 Some DIP systems not only store the electronic image of a document, but allow the stored documents to be used in other office systems. It might be possible to display, on the VDU, both the scanned document, and keyed-in text commentary (for example notes of a subsequent phone conversation). The advantages are as follows.

- **Reduced space** is needed for files
- The same file can be viewed by **different users** simultaneously
- Files **cannot be 'lost'** as the original image is on disk
- There is **faster retrieval** of files than with a manual system

2.18 The main cost savings of using DIP over paper are in **storage and retrieval,** as the time taken to hunt for a file is eliminated. In order for these savings to be achieved, documents must be scanned as soon as they are received.

2.19 A possible disadvantage of DIP is that a lot more information is stored than is strictly necessary. So, organisations installing a DIP system should bear in mind the following.

(a) The **importance** (or criticality) of the documents, if their loss would be a major disaster.

(b) **How often** documents are **accessed**. If a document or file is greatly in demand, document imaging might be a useful technology.

(c) The **volume** of documents is an issue. Small volumes of documents probably do not justify the expense of a DIP system. Large volumes, in saved storage space, almost certainly do.

(d) The **uses** to which a document is put. If a document is altered (eg a design), it might help to have one 'master' copy so that all can refer to it.

2.20 Applications of DIP include **electronic data exchange, desktop publishing** (by enabling photographs, for example, or other images to be stored) and management of **accounting transactions**. All the documentation relating to an accounting transaction can be referenced to the ledger record; an entry in the sales ledger, for example, could be accompanied by images of all related paperwork.

3 USING INFORMATION **6/95, 12/99**

Office software

3.1 PCs and modern packages such as Microsoft Office offer the average office worker computing power undreamed of only a few years ago. Microsoft Office Professional consists of four user-friendly applications.

(a) The **Word** word-processing package, used for simple letters or memos, or to design, create, and index whole books, such as this one

(b) **Excel**, a hugely powerful and versatile spreadsheet package

(c) **Access**, a database package that can be used for applications ranging from simple customised mailing lists to something as elaborate as ICSA's BLUEPRINT, described in an earlier chapter

(d) **PowerPoint,** a presentation package that can take simple headings and bullet points and turn them into highly effective animated coloured slide presentations

---

Exercise 1

(a) What are the advantages of word processing over a manual or simple electronic typewriter for producing text?

(b) Describe the features typically found in a spreadsheet package such as Excel.

Solution

(a) The advantages of word processing for producing text include the following.

- (i) The ability to produce personalised letters of a standard type
- (ii) The ability to amend, correct or update text on screen easily
- (iii) A low error rate in the text
- (iv) Speed of keying in text, and corrections
- (v) Easy formatting of text
- (vi) Quality is improved
- (vii) Security may be enhanced

(b) We would expect you to have mentioned features such as formulae, cell replication, spell checking, macros, graphics facilities and so on.

Return to your earlier study material if you struggled with either of those questions.

Example: using spreadsheets

3.2 Spreadsheets are particularly useful at the **tactical** level of management.

(a) At **operational** level, decisions are more structured and routine and therefore more suited to specific application packages.

(b) At **strategic** level, decisions are less structured and relevant factors are less likely to be able to be incorporated into a computer package.

(c) Much tactical management, however, involves the **analysis and interpretation** of operational information. The '**what if?**' manipulation of data, for example, is probably the most important facility in a spreadsheet package.

As a simple illustration, a manager planning activities for the next six months might want to know how his department's cash flow would be affected if interest rates changed. It is a simple matter to set up a spreadsheet so that the interest rate is entered in a separate cell and treated as a variable in the cash flow calculations.

Drawbacks of using spreadsheets

3.3 Spreadsheets are immensely popular and can be used for a very wide range of modelling tasks. However, because they are essentially **single-user packages** and because each one is designed from scratch, the information manager needs to be aware that there are risks in their use.

(a) Although users are sometimes trained in how to use a spreadsheet, they are rarely trained in **spreadsheet discipline** or **best practice**. This means that spreadsheets may be badly designed, increasing the risk of errors or inefficiency.

(b) Users are unlikely to **document** the workings of their spreadsheet, as they consider it 'obvious'. This makes it difficult for other staff (temporary replacement or permanent successor) to understand, use or modify the model.

(c) The '**macro**' is an important feature of all but the simplest spreadsheets. Macros can be **difficult to write and to understand** and are not as conducive to tight control as the use of a programming language.

(d) The **lack of a proper audit trail** can be a disadvantage. Because the user works with a spreadsheet in memory (RAM), only saving it at certain intervals, it is unlikely that a record of the intermediate stages will be maintained, even if output from the intermediate stages is important.

Presentation software — 6/96

3.4 Programs for presentations allow the user to build up a series of graphical displays or images which can be used for presentation. With additional hardware, this type of software can be used to produce **35 mm slides** for an on-screen slideshow or storyboard (which can be synchronised with a sound track). The slides that your lecturer uses on the overhead projector may well be produced by similar means using, for example, the Microsoft PowerPoint package.

Exercise 2

What other part of the Administration of Corporate Affairs syllabus might this be relevant to?

Graphics software

3.5 Graphics software comes in a variety of forms and may provide any of the following facilities (in ascending order of 'sophistication' or complexity).

- The facility to interpret and represent data in a simple graphical form
- The facility to interpret and represent data in an enhanced graphical form
- Presentation graphics
- Free-form graphics

A widely used 'office' package is CorelDraw.

Exercise 3

Some programs with a graphics facility allow the user to display data in a simple graphical form. What types of graph or diagram might you wish to prepare using a graphics package?

Solution

(a) Line graphs (for example a time series graph, showing sales and profits over a period of time)

(b) Bar charts

(c) Pie charts

(d) Scattergraphs which plot the value of pairs of data

(e) Maps (in two or three dimensions)

(f) Architectural drawings

(g) Organisation charts

In fact, (a) to (e) can easily be done with a spreadsheet package rather than special graphics software.

Desktop publishing

3.6 Desktop publishing software packages vary in complexity. Some are suitable for the general PC user producing an occasional document. Others are appropriate for full-time in-house publishing departments, with sophisticated photography and artwork for output onto professional typesetting printers.

3.7 DTP systems **pull graphics and text** together from other programs. However, with one or two exceptions, DTP programs are not good programs with which to **create text** or graphics. DTP's main function is that it enables the page, both graphics and text, to be seen as the 'artwork' image for editing and production. A space for a picture can be moved around the page, like 'cut and paste' artwork. This **cuts out the intermediate stage in publishing** or sending material to a phototypesetter to make up pages for printing.

Exercise 4

Give examples of how a business organisation can use DTP.

Solution

(a) Design of management reports

(b) Design and preparation of the annual report

(c) Design of external documentation, such as press releases and mailshots

(d) Design of advertisements

(e) Publication of in-house magazine

(f) Design of an organisation's standard documentation (for example order forms and quality assurance manuals)

Project management software

3.8 Project management software packages have been available for a number of years. An example is Microsoft Project.

3.9 Software might be used for a number of purposes.

(a) **Planning**

Network diagrams (showing the critical path) and Gantt charts (showing resource use) can be produced automatically once the relevant data is entered. Packages also allow a sort of 'what if?' analysis for initial planning.

(b) **Estimating**

As a project progresses, actual data will become known and can be entered into the package and collected for future reference. Since many projects involve basically similar tasks (interviewing users and so on), actual data from one project can be used to provide more accurate estimates for the next project. The software also facilitates and encourages the use of more sophisticated estimation techniques than managers might be prepared to use if working manually.

(c) **Monitoring**

Actual data can also be entered and used to facilitate monitoring of progress and automatically updating the plan for the critical path and the use of resources as circumstances dictate.

(d) **Reporting**

Software packages allow standard and tailored progress reports to be produced, printed out and circulated to participants and senior managers at any time, usually at the touch of a button. This helps with co-ordination of activities and project review.

Groupware

3.10 Groupware is software that is intended to help **groups work together** by sharing information and controlling workflows. Examples include project management software, e-mail and shared databases. The best known example is Lotus Notes.

Multimedia **6/95, 6/96**

3.11 Multimedia is a style of computing that allows users access to a **range of different styles** of information in addition to conventional computer data like words and figures. Still pictures or graphics, sound and video clips can be stored and played back, and can be linked together so that, for example, the user might be able to point to a name on a personnel database and, by clicking on it, see a picture of the individual and hear them speak a short message such as their name.

3.12 Applications of multimedia

- Video phones and video conferencing
- Home shopping
- Distance learning and internal training across geographically dispersed sites
- Security systems
- User-friendly presentation of complex data

4 COMMUNICATING INFORMATION **12/95, 6/96, 12/97, 12/99, 6/00**

4.1 The telephone is still the most important method of communication in the office, and in this area there are continuing major advances in technology. Some people have referred to the 1990s as the 'telecoms revolution'.

Telecoms strategy

4.2 Studies in the UK indicate that most companies see telecoms as integral to business development, principally as a means of **cutting costs** and **improving customer service**. The telecommunications business in the mid 1990s is highly competitive and this is forcing prices down and broadening choice. For instance, some service providers offer a huge diversity of services, others provide strong back-up protection in case telecoms lines go down, others offer individually negotiated contracts, or centralised billing and consolidated management reports providing a comprehensive view of telecoms usage.

4.3 A recent global pact on telecoms **liberalisation**, involving 53 countries, is likely to bring still lower prices, better services, and more advanced technology.

4.4 The developments are all good for telecoms users, but it makes it increasingly difficult for telecoms managers to keep up with the technology, to ascertain current and future business communications needs and to select the best option from the wide range available.

Case example

Rhône-Poulenc

Telecommunications is of growing strategic importance to many large companies and there comes a day when they face a stark choice: continue running telecommunications as an internal function or hand over to a more experienced outsourcing partner.

For French chemicals giant Rhône-Poulenc, that day came at the end of 1996.

The company recently awarded the contract to run its worldwide data communications to Equant, a global networks provider. Voice services are not included.

Cost savings have traditionally been a powerful motivator for outsourcing but in the case of Rhône-Poulenc, this was not the most important factor. 'Cost is a long-term issue, particularly as regards the investment required to expand in new countries, but it is not the most important driver,' says Mr Beer-Gabel.

Rhône-Poulenc relies increasingly on data communications to connect its plants and subsidiaries around the world. It was looking for a vendor to provide it with a 'seamless' network that could be fully managed and supported from a single source.

In addition to the RP-Net data network, RPT also provide value-added services to most of the companies within the Rhône-Poulenc group. These services include e-mail, file transfer, electronic data interchange (EDI), remote access and, most recently, a corporate intranet.

Today, the intranet covers half the company's sites and about two-thirds of its 68,000 employees, but it will ultimately be extended to reach everyone. The growing importance of the intranet was another reason for outsourcing RPT to Equant.

Source: Financial Times, June 1998

Public transmission links

4.5 In the UK, British Telecom and Mercury are the principle providers of services for the transmission of data (although no longer the supply of some of the equipment used) and can supply public or private lines for direct data links.

(a) Public lines use the ordinary telephone network and the cost is **dependent** upon the **service used** and the **time** the telephone **link is maintained** (as for any ordinary telephone call). If an organisation only requires occasional communication links, it will probably use public lines, with links being set up to transmit a message and closed when the transmission is completed.

(b) Private lines also use the telephone network but a **special line** is provided at a **fixed charge** per annum. Private lines are sometimes referred to as leased lines. If an organisation requires frequent or constant communications links, it will be more likely to lease private lines.

4.6 New technologies require transmission systems capable of delivering substantial quantities of data at great speed. For data transmission through the existing 'analogue' telephone network to be possible, there has to be a device at each end of the telephone line that can convert (MOdulate) the data from digital form to analogue form, and (DEModulate) from analogue form to digital form, depending on whether the data is being sent out or received along the telephone line. This conversion of data is done by devices called **modems**. There must be a modem at each end of the telephone line.

(**Digital** means 'of digits or numbers'. Digital information is information in a coded (binary) form. Information in analogue form uses continuously variable signals.)

Integrated Systems Digital Networks (ISDN)

4.7 An important development in the 1990s is the introduction, by both British Telecom and Mercury, of **Integrated Systems Digital Networks(ISDN)**, which in effect will make the entire telephone network digital – it will therefore be possible to send voice, data, video and fax communications from a single desktop computer system over the telecommunication link, without using a modem. Advantages of ISDN are that:

- Computer networks can be extended to small branch offices.
- A number of services can be sent over the link at one time.

4.8 There are various other new technologies associated with companies need to send or receive large amounts of data. As the demand for sending and receiving large graphics files, video, voice and other multimedia data services increases these will become increasingly important.

(a) **Synchronous Digital Hierarchy (SDH)** offers data speeds from 155 megabits per second (Mbps) to as much as 10 gigabits per second, and it can carry ATM and frame relay (see below) too.

(b) **Asynchronous Transfer Mode (ATM)** is capable of sending data at speeds of 155 Mbps or more.

(c) However, at present most companies find a speed of about 1.5 Mbps perfectly adequate: **frame relay switching** is a slower but cheaper technology than ATM that can cope with such requirements.

Exercise 5

You will *not* be tested on the technical details of technologies such as ATM in the *Administration of Corporate Affairs* exam. The examiner positively discourages the use of technological jargon in exam answers.

Nevertheless, for practical purposes in your work you will find it useful to understand some of the terminology when reading articles on technological developments, or worse, being asked to take decisions on corporate telecommunication needs.

What do you understand by the terms 'megabit', 'packet' and 'switching', in a telecoms context?

Solution

(a) *Bit* stands for BInary digiT. A bit is the smallest unit of information in any computer system. Each individual storage element in a computer's memory consists of a simple circuit which can be switched ON or OFF. These two states can be conveniently expressed by the numbers 1 and 0 respectively. Any piece of data or instruction must be coded in these symbols. Each 1 or 0 is a bit. Bits are grouped together in groups of eight to form *bytes*.

A *mega bit* is about 1 million bits (representing, for instance, about 30 pages of this book).

(b) A data message is divided up into 'packets' of data of a fixed length and transmitted through the communication network in these separate packets. Each packet contains control data, which identifies the sender of the message and the address of the recipient. At the receiving end the packets of data are re-assembled into their full message, which is transmitted to the recipient. ATM divides data traffic into packets of 53 bytes.

(c) 'Switching' is simply a matter of directing the data traffic along the right routes, like trains have to be 'switched' between different railway lines (not a perfect analogy, but sufficient for our purposes).

'Packet switching' enables data to be transmitted more quickly because the packets are of fixed length: a short message is not unduly delayed by having to wait for a longer message to cross its path (again, think of trains).

If you feel you need to know more about the technical side of IT, refer to the BPP Study Text on Foundation level *Information Systems*.

Virtual Private Networks

4.9 A Virtual Private Network, uses 'intelligent' switching equipment, and is able to give customers the equivalent of a leased line for the cost of a call over the public switched network. New locations can simply be 'plugged in' as required.

Mobile communications

4.10 Radio networks for portable telephone communications, also known as **'cellular phones'**, started up in the late 1980s and have boomed in developed countries in the 1990s, as you are no doubt aware from the deluge of advertising on television and radio.

4.11 Again, digital networks are being installed and likely to supersede the early transmission systems in the not-too-distant future. These are better able to support data transmission then the older analogue networks, with higher transmission speeds and less likelihood of data corruption. This means that a salesperson out on the road, say, can send or receive a fax simply by plugging a lap-top PC into a mobile handset. A combined palmtop computer and cellular phone is already on the market.

4.12 In theory it is now possible to do any kind of 'office' activity outside on the move, although limitations in battery power impose restrictions. The mobile services available are increasing all the time. Here are some examples.

(a) **Messaging services:** voice mail; short message service which allows messages of up to 160 characters to be transmitted over a standard phone and paging services.

(b) **Call handling services** such as: call barring, conference calls and call divert.

(c) **Corporate services** such as: integrated numbering, so that people have a single contact number for both the phone on their desk and for their mobile; and virtual private networks that incorporate mobile phones as well as conventional desktop phones, so that users can dial internal extension numbers directly.

(d) **Internet access** is possible, the speed of transmission when downloading information is relatively slow at present, but improving. **Wireless Application Protocol (WAP)** technology will make parts of the Internet accessible using a mobile phone.

(e) Satellite technology enables some mobile phones to '**roam**' (ie be used) in many countries around the world - rather than in the 'country of issue'.

Case example: Mobile telecoms

Tesco, the UK's leading supermarket chain, has equipped staff at its Southampton depot with cordless telephones to improve internal and external communications. ... In older depots Tesco uses the more conventional radio and public address communications systems but has found that they are inefficient. When people are called over a public system they have to find the nearest phone extension and wait for the incoming call to be diverted to it. This takes too much time and the call can be lost before it is picked up, which in turn causes unnecessary waste of time and the extra expense of calling back. With the new cordless system staff can now be contacted easily anywhere within the depot by head office, local stores or business partners.

Source: Financial Times, June 1996

Fax

4.13 Fax (or facsimile transmission) involves the transmission by data link of exact duplicate copies of documents. The original is fed into the fax machine, which 'reads' it and converts it into electronic form so it can be transmitted over the telephone. It is printed by the recipient's fax machine.

4.14 Fax has largely **superseded** systems such as telex and the computerised equivalent 'teletex' (not to be confused with 'teletext').

4.15 The latest fax machines can also be used as **scanners** to scan data into a PC, as printers for PC output and as **photocopiers**. Faster machines are being developed that will cut down the time to send an A4 sheet from six seconds to one to two seconds.

4.16 Alternatively a PC can be fitted with a **fax modem**, allowing data to be transmitted directly from the PC without going through a separate fax machine. Manufacturers of stand-alone fax machines point out that the sender tends to assume that there is a standalone machine at the receiving end. Also users of PCs fitted with fax modems may easily forget that when they switch off their machine at the end of the day it will **not be able to receive fax messages**, unlike a standalone machine, which tends to be left on-line 24 hours.

Electronic mail (E-mail) 12/98

4.17 The term 'electronic mail', or **e-mail**, is used to describe various systems of sending data or messages electronically via a telephone or data network and a central computer, without the need to post letters or place memos in pigeon-holes or despatch documents by courier. It has the following advantages.

(a) **Speed** (transmission, being electronic, is almost instantaneous). E-mail is far faster than post or fax. It is a particular time-saver when communicating with people overseas.

(b) **Economy** (no need for stamps etc). E-mail is reckoned to be 20 times cheaper than fax.

(c) **Efficiency**. A message is prepared once but can be sent to thousands of employees at the touch of a button.

(d) **Security**. Access can be restricted by the use of passwords.

(e) Documents can be retrieved from **word-processing** and graphics packages.

(f) Electronic **delivery** and **read receipts** can be requested.

(g) E-mail can be used to send **documents** and **reports** as well as short memos.

4.18 Typically information is 'posted' by the sender to a central computer which allocates disk storage as a 'mailbox' for each user. The information is subsequently 'collected' by the receiver from the mailbox.

(a) Senders of information thus have **documentary evidence** that they have given a piece of information to the recipient and that the recipient has picked up the message.

(b) Receivers are **not disturbed** by the information when it is sent (as they would be by face-to-face meetings or phone calls), but collect it later at their convenience.

4.19 Each user will typically have **password protected access** to his own inbox, outbox and filing system. He can prepare and edit text and other documents using a word processing function, and send mail using **standard headers and identifiers** to an individual or a group of people on a prepared **distribution list.**

4.20 E-mail systems may serve one department or the whole organisation. It is also possible to connect an e-mail system to outside organisations. Despite problems of hacking and security, this is becoming an immensely popular means of communication. The security problems involved in e-mail are discussed further in Chapter 13.

Voice mail

4.21 Voice mail (or v-mail) systems enable the caller's message to be recorded at the recipient's voice mail box similar to a mail box in an e-mail system. The main advantage of the system is that it only requires a telephone to be used. No typing or keying in is necessary. A voice mail message is basically a **spoken memo**.

4.22 Some companies allow their clients to use their voice mail network to leave messages for company representatives. The advantage of voice mail messages, compared to cellular radio or mobile communications, is that it is relatively cheap. However, it is not suitable for conversations. Voice mail can be used for different situations.

- To contact sales representatives **'in the field'**
- To **leave messages** in departments in different time zones
- In organisations where employees might be **working away** at a client's premises

Voice messaging (IVR)

4.23 This is a kind of **switchboard answerphone** that takes the place of a human receptionist, or at least relieves the receptionist of the burden of dealing with common, straightforward calls. Typically, when a call is answered a **recorded message** tells the caller to dial the extension they want if they know it, or to hold if they want to speak to the operator. Sometimes other options are offered, such as 'press 2 if you want to know about X service and 3 if you want to know about Y'.

4.24 Such systems **work well** if callers frequently have **similar needs** and these can be accurately anticipated. They can be **frustrating** for callers with **non-standard enquiries**, however, and many people find the impersonality of responding to an answerphone unappealing. Badly set up systems can result in the caller going from one recorded message to another and never getting through to the person they want to deal with.

Case example: Interactive voice response (IVR)

Several pharmaceutical companies have installed sophisticated interactive voice response systems to deal with enquiries from doctors, chemists or patients. For example some allow the caller to press a number on their handset and have details of possible side effects sent back to them by fax.

Computer Telephony Integration (CTI)

4.25 Computer Telephony Integration (CTI) systems **gather information** about callers such as their telephone number and customer account number or demographic information (age, income, interests etc). This is stored on a customer database and can be called up and sent to the screen of the person dealing with the call, perhaps before the call has even been put through.

4.26 Thus sales staff dealing with hundreds of calls every day might **appear to remember individual callers** personally and know in advance what they are likely to order. Order forms with key details entered already can be displayed on screen automatically, saving time for both the sales staff and the caller.

4.27 Alternatively a busy manager might note that an **unwelcome call** is coming in on the 'screen pop' that appears on her PC and choose to direct it to her voice mail box rather than dealing with it at once.

4.28 As another example, a bank might use CTI to **prompt sales people** with changes in share prices and with the details of the investors they should call to offer dealing advice.

Computer conferencing

4.29 A computer conferencing system is similar to e-mail but more expensive, in that there is a huge central mailbox on the system where all persons connected to the system can **deposit messages** for everyone to see, and, in turn, **read what other people have left** in the system. Computer conferencing can be appropriate for a team of individuals at different locations to compare notes. It becomes a way of keeping track of progress on a project between routine team meetings.

4.30 Computer conferencing systems can become **organisation-wide bulletin boards**, where members can leave messages of general import. A bulletin board might encourage new ideas to be developed informally, and so is a way by which companies can tap their employees' creativity and expertise.

Videoconferencing 6/96

4.31 Videoconferencing is the use of computer and communications technology to **conduct meetings** in which several participants, perhaps in different parts of the world, are linked up via **computer** and a **video system**. Conference calls on a telephone system, where several people can converse at the same time, are a precursor of teleconferencing.

4.32 Videoconferencing has become increasingly common as the ready availability of chips capable of processing video images has brought the service to desktop PCs at reasonable cost. More expensive systems feature a **separate room** with **several video screens**, which show the images of those participating in a meeting. Even if the technology used is expensive, it is far **cheaper** when compared to the cost in management time and air fares of business **travel**.

4.33 Videoconferencing allows far more frequent face to face contact between people who are spread widely across the world, but it does present some difficulties.

(a) **Cultural differences** might be **forgotten**. For example the US representatives may not realise that when the team from Spain 'sign off' for lunch they are unlikely to return for several hours, although then they will be prepared to work far later into the evening than their UK counterparts.

(b) The **technology** currently offered by some providers of videoconferencing facilities is **far from perfect**. Frequently there are problems with the synchronisation of lip movement and speech (lip synch), and with normal body language such as hand movements, which may appear to be blurred or jerky and convey unintended messages. In any case, the telecom links can only be as good as the telecoms infrastructure in the different locations.

(c) The systems tend to be **voice-activated,** and this means that the camera gives priority to the person speaking the loudest. The system will also have difficulty coping if more than one person speaks at once.

(d) It is more **difficult** and time-consuming (although possible), to **pass round** copies of *ad hoc* **data** that has been brought to the meeting.

(e) There are few of the usual **signals** that **constrain** behaviour in meetings (for example sitting at the head of the table) and this may mean that the leading role shifts from person to person and site to site.

(f) Research suggests that people feel **less need to participate** when attending this sort of meeting.

Electronic data interchange

4.34 Electronic data interchange is a form of computer-to-computer data interchange, and so another form of electronic mail. The general concept of having one computer talk directly to another might seem straightforward enough in principle, but in practice there are two major difficulties.

(a) Each business wants to produce documents (and hold records on file) to its own **individual requirements** and structure. Thus a computer of X Ltd could not transmit data to a computer of Y Ltd because the records/data transmitted **would not be in a format or structure** to suit Y Ltd.

(b) Businesses may work to **differing time schedules,** especially when they are engaged in international trade. If a London company's computer wants to send a message to a computer in San Francisco, the San Francisco computer might not be switched on or otherwise able to receive the message.

Compatibility is less and less of a problem as businesses adopt common standards and set up sites on the Internet.

4.35 Successful implementation of EDI depends on a number of factors.

- Deciding which categories of information are to be sent or received
- Adapting internal systems, so that they match up with the EDI translation software
- Changeover

4.36 The advantages of EDI extend to purely internal uses, too.

- If an organisation is decentralised, EDI can expedite internal billing.
- If an organisation's paperwork is intricate and complex, EDI can speed it up.
- EDI can be used to create files of historical information.

Electronic Funds Transfer

4.37 Electronic Funds Transfer describes a system whereby a computer user can use his computer system to **transfer funds** - for example make payments to a supplier, or pay salaries into **employees**' bank accounts. Since businesses keep most of their cash in bank accounts, electronic funds transfer must involve the **banks** themselves.

SWIFT

4.38 A system for the electronic transfer of funds **internationally between banks** themselves is known as SWIFT (the Society for Worldwide Interbank Financial Telecommunications). If X Ltd in the UK wishes to make a payment to a company in, say, Germany, and if his UK bank and the German company's bank are members of the SWIFT network (all the UK clearing banks are members), the settlement between the banks themselves can be made through the SWIFT system. (Each bank holds accounts with 'correspondent' banks in other countries, and those accounts are used to settle such payments, but the authorisation to transfer the funds is given via the SWIFT system).

CHAPS and BACS

4.39 Interbank settlements by the clearing banks **within the UK** are also made by electronic funds transfer, using the CHAPS system (Clearing House Automated Payments System). Many large companies now pay the salaries of employees by providing computer data to their bank, using the **BACS (Bankers' Automated Clearing Services)** or BACSTEL service. Switching to BACS can save approximately 90% on transaction charges.

EFTPOS

4.40 **Electronic funds transfer at point of sale** (EFTPOS) aims to handle, electronically, the high volume, **low value transactions** which make up the bulk of the payments by number which banks currently have to handle and process in paper form. EFTPOS systems integrate the retailer's POS system, which might consist of bar-code scanning or involve a sophisticated computerised cash register, with an electronic payment system.

4.41 More and more large retail stores are introducing electronic point of sale devices which act both as cash registers and as terminals connected to a main computer. This enables the computer to **produce useful management information** such as sales details and analysis and stock control information very quickly. Many use bar coding or direct keyboard entry.

5 THE INTERNET **6/98, 12/99**

5.1 The **Internet** is the name given to the technology that allows any computer with a telecommunications link to exchange information with any other suitably equipped computer.

5.2 Terms such as 'the net', 'the information superhighway', 'cyberspace', and the 'World Wide Web (www)' are used fairly interchangeably, although technically the '*web*' is what makes the 'net' *user-friendly* (rather like Windows did for MS-DOS).

Case example: How world-wide is the web?

Overall about 100m people in 150 countries already have access to the Internet and this figure is expected to reach 250m by the end of the century.

Two out of three major European firms are currently using the Internet for business, and one in five reports higher sales as a result, according to a Gallup survey commissioned by the Wall Street Journal and IBM.

While the survey indicates that web usage is still immature (most companies are using the web to gather information and communicate with customers), 37 per cent of wired companies are actually conducting electronic commerce over the net. The Internet has even influenced some companies to change their corporate strategies.

When broken down by country, the survey documents clear disparities in web usage by Europe's three biggest economies. Germany has the most net-connected companies with 74 per cent of the companies contacted saying they were using the Net for business, compared to 70 per cent in Britain and 55 per cent in France.

Access to the Internet will become easier and easier: most new PCs now come pre-loaded with the necessary software, cheaper Internet devices are about to hit the market, and developments in telecommunications networks will eventually render modems unnecessary. The UK is in the forefront of all of these developments.

Websites

5.3 As you are no doubt aware, most companies of any size now have a *'site'* on the Net. A site is a collection of screens providing information in text and graphic form, any of which can be viewed simply by clicking the appropriate button, word or image on the screen.

5.4 The user generally starts at the site's **'home page'**, which sets out the contents of the site. For instance, **here is Microsoft's home page.**

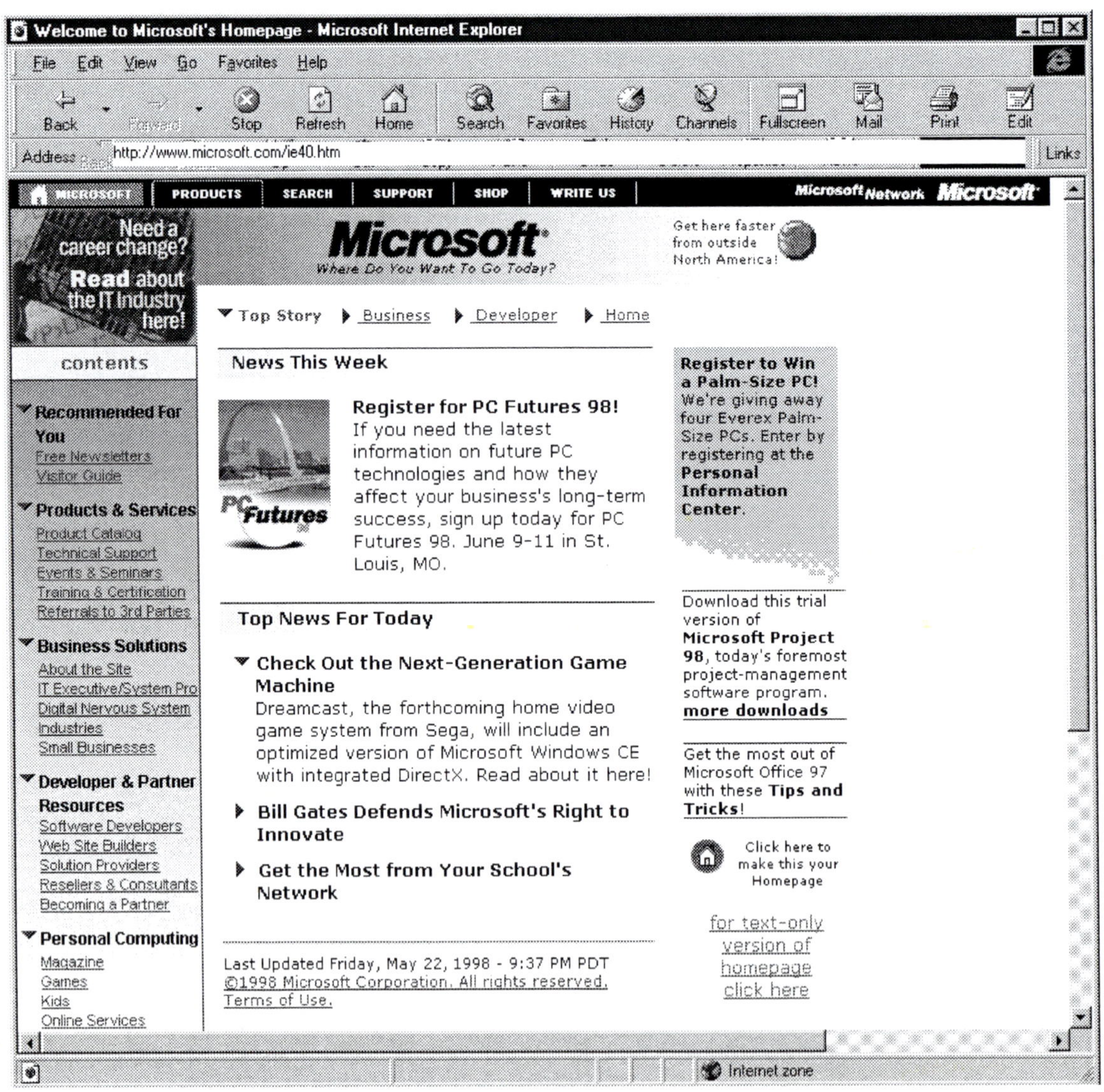

5.5 The main part of the page offers *news* about what is happening at the company. The buttons in the black bar across the top of the page take the user to other pages where they can:

(a) Find out more details about individual Microsoft **products**

(b) Carry out a **Search** of the whole site to find Microsoft web pages connected with the information they are looking for

(c) Consult pages that offer technical **Support** for Microsoft products, perhaps including **FAQs** (frequently asked questions and their answers) and files to *download* such items as **free demonstrations** of products or *fixes* for problems with Microsoft software

(d) Order products directly (**Shop**) or find out the names of retailers in their local area

(e) Contact Microsoft directly (**Write Us**) to ask questions or make comments about Microsoft and its products

5.6 A further set of *links* is provided in the frame on the left of the page. These are fairly self-explanatory.

Internet Service Providers (ISPs)

5.7 Connection (if not available through a user's organisation) is made via an Internet Service Provider (ISP). The user is registered as an Internet subscriber and may pay a small monthly fee (some providers do not charge this fee) together with **local telephone call charges,** even if contacting other users on the other side of the world.

5.8 ISPs such as **CompuServe, America Online (AOL)** and **Microsoft Network** provide their own services, in addition to Internet access and e-mail capability. For instance, AOL also offers a main menu with options such as Life, Travel, Entertainment, Sport, Kids. It is rather like a quality Sunday newspaper, except that the sections are updated at least daily, and it provides **much larger information resources** (one option in the travel section, for instance, is to find out about train and plane timetables throughout the UK or worldwide).

5.9 The number of ISPs has recently grown rapidly, with many now offering free access to the Internet, meaning users only pay the local telephone charges incurred during connection. Free ISPs include Virgin Net, Dixons Freeserve and Freedom online.

Browsers and search engines

5.10 Most people use the Net through interface programs called **browsers** that make it more user-friendly and accessible. The best known are **Netscape Navigator** and Microsoft **Internet Explorer.**

5.11 Surfing the Net is done using a **search engine** such as Yahoo!, Excite or AltaVista. These guide users to destinations throughout the world: the user simply types in a word or phrase like 'beer' to find a list of thousands of websites that contain something connected with beer.

5.12 Companies like Yahoo! make money by **selling advertising space**. For instance if you type in 'beer', an advertisement for Miller Genuine Draft will appear, as well as your list of beer-related sites. If you click on the advertisement you are taken to the advertiser's website.

5.13 The advertiser may get you to **register your interest** in the product so that you can be directly targeted in future.

5.14 An Internet development that has created a good deal of excitement is known as '**push**' **technology**, because instead of having to search for individual pieces of information the user simply accesses a '**channel**' and watches as information is sent down the line.

(a) For instance **PointCast** has attracted more than 1m regular viewers to its Web news channel, which automatically delivers content from newspapers and magazines at regular intervals. It retrieves information from selected sources on the net and presents it, with advertisements, headlines and stock prices, on a screen saver.

(b) **Marimba** allows users to download a 'tuner' and select content channels, very much like switching channels on TV.

5.15 Browser software packages provide a facility to **store Internet addresses** so that users can access frequently-visited sites without having to go through a long search process. In business use, workers who **regularly need up-to-date information,** say, on stock market movements, can simply click on the appropriate entry in a personal 'favourites' directory.

Exercise 6

'You can't yet be born on the net but you can order your coffin from the Carlos A Howard funeral home and you can have a virtual memorial forever in cyberspace. You can job-hunt, house-hunt, be diagnosed by your doctor, worship with the congregation in a church, find a spouse, buy groceries, a car and insurance, and read your virtual newspaper on a virtual beach on your virtual holiday.

So far, with the exception of the odd gimmick, the net has been about word, images and more recently sounds. Now it is about to get physical. Already a prototype glove exists enabling two people, anywhere in the world to share physical sensations. Soon, while at work in your office, you will be able to cook the dinner at home, record a TV programme, let in the gasman and keep an eye on him on your screen, and even feed the cat.

What are the business implications of all this?

Going directly to an Internet address (URLs)

5.16 You may know the precise address of an Internet site that you wish to visit, perhaps because you have seen or heard it on TV or radio or read it in a newspaper or magazine. Typically the format is something like '**http://www.bbc.co.uk**'.

5.17 The address is called a **URL** or **Uniform Resource Locator**

URL element	Explanation
http://	**Hypertext Transfer Protocol,** the protocol used on the World-Wide Web for the exchange of documents produced in what is known as 'hypertext mark-up language' (HTML). A common alternative to **http** is **ftp** (file transfer protocol) explained briefly later. The two forward slashes after the colon introduce a 'host name' such as *www*.
www	This stands for **World Wide Web**. As noted before, to put it simply the web (via its use of HTML), is what makes the Internet user-friendly
bbc	This is the **domain name** of the organisation or individual whose site is located at this URL
co	This part of the URL indicates the type of organisation concerned. The Internet actually spans many different physical networks around the world including commercial (**com** or **co**), university (**ac** or **edu**) and other research networks (**org, net**), military (**mil**) networks, and government (**gov**) networks.
uk	As you can probably guess, this indicates that the organisation is located in the UK

5.18 The idea behind an '**intranet**' is that companies set up their own mini version of the Internet, using a combination of the company's own networked computers and Internet technology. Each employee has a browser and a server computer distributes corporate information on a wide variety of topics, and also offers access to the global Net.

5.19 Potential applications include daily company newspapers, induction material, online procedure and policy manuals, employee web pages where individuals post up details of their activities and progress, and internal databases of the corporate information store.

5.20 Most of the *cost* of an intranet is the staff time required to set up the system, which is often quite small. The *benefits* of intranets are diverse.

(a) A considerable amount of money can be saved from the **elimination of storage, printing and distribution of documents** that can be made available to employees on-line.

(b) Documents on-line are **more widely used** than those that are kept on shelves, especially if the document is bulky (for instance company information handbooks, finance manuals and procedures manuals) and needs to be searched. This means that there are **improvements in productivity and efficiency**.

(c) It is much **easier to update** information in electronic form.

(d) Wider access to corporate information should open the way to **more flexible working patterns**. For instance if bulky reference materials are available on-line then there is little need to be in the office at all.

Case example: Groupware and intranets

The original idea of a 'personal' computer was to allow people to work together and share information across a network through a mainframe computer'. However, users became so frustrated at their inability to get what they wanted from mainframe systems that they welcomed the IBM PC, used in stand-alone mode, with open arms.

This meant in turn that groupware (software designed to let users work together and share information through computers) had to be invented. (Examples are Lotus Notes (now Lotus Domino), Novell Groupwise, and Microsoft Exchange.) Groupware technology has been widely used to enable people to communicate, to share information, to work together and, most importantly, to carry out business processes and execute transactions, often using unstructured data.

The current fashion for intranets has given new impetus to these ideas, and all of the major products have now adopted Internet-type standards. Such products may have an advantage over intranets built from scratch because they recognise and address the problems of bringing about the *cultural* changes needed to get better business processes and generate competitive advantage.

Case example: Swiss Bank Corporation

'One of the biggest users of intranets is Swiss Bank Corporation. In fact it has so many - around 100 - that it has just appointed a head of intranets to co-ordinate them all.

At Swiss Bank Corporation intranets are used for:

Corporate accounting and credit information
Publishing research internally, and to a select group of 50 external clients
Trading information
Ordering information technology equipment
IT project management
Informing staff of regulatory changes

The job of Marie Adee, the company's new head of intranets, is to unify the disparate sites so that employees can find information easily. The sites will also be given a common look and feel. All the company's sites can be searched using the Netscape Navigator Web browser, but the company is also standardising on Lotus Domino software.

This software will sit on the server computers that store the intranet information. Domino incorporates Lotus Notes information sharing software. So employees will be able to input information to Web sites either through Notes or through their Web browsers. It will also be possible for SBC to set up workflow applications - which control the flow of work between users in a team.

File Transfer Protocol

5.21 **File Transfer Protocol (FTP)** is the facility on the Internet that allows users to **copy files from one computer to another across the network**. Using an FTP program, information and applications residing on distant computers can be accessed and retrieved. A wide range of files are available via system called 'Anonymous FTP'. This lets users connect to a remote computer and **download files** from a public area of its disk. Many companies maintain such a site to allow customers to download new versions of software and product information.

5.22 An **extranet** is an intranet that is partially accessible to **authorised outsiders.** Authorised outsiders are allocated a username and password, which allows entry and determines which parts of the extranet are able to be viewed. Extranets are becoming popular means for business (eg customer and supplier) to share information.

Commercial use of the Internet 6/98

Marketing

5.23 Besides its usefulness for tapping into worldwide information resources businesses are also using it to **provide information** about their own products and services. The Internet offers a **speedy and impersonal** way of getting to know the basics (or even the details) of the services that a company provides. For businesses the advantage is that it is **much cheaper** to provide the information in electronic form than it would be to employ staff to man the phones on an enquiry desk, and much **more effective** than sending out mailshots that people would either throw away or forget about.

marketing

5.24 Thus business use of the Internet is set to grow for any product or service about which **customers** are liable to engage in **information seeking**; in other words for most **intermittent**, relatively **high value purchases** such as washing machines, hi-fi and TVs, motor cars and the like.

Sales

5.25 Interactive **electronic purchasing**, has grown rapidly in the last two years. Initial concerns over the security of Internet purchasing using a credit card and or debit card have reduced somewhat due to the development of 'secure sites'.

5.26 Further **technological developments** will provide whatever reassurance is needed, and once people are used to this method of buying it is likely to become the *norm* for many transactions that are presently conducted by post, fax or phone.

Distribution

5.27 The Internet can be used to get certain products directly into people's homes. Anything that can be converted into **digital form** can simply be uploaded onto the seller's site and then **downloaded** onto the customer's PC at home. The Internet thus offers huge opportunities to producers of **text, graphics/video, and sound-based products**. Much computer software is now distributed in this way.

Problems with the Internet

5.28 To a large extent the Internet has grown organically **without any formal organisation**. There are specific communication rules, but it is **not owned** by any one body and there are no clear guidelines on how it should develop.

5.29 Speed is a major issue. Data only downloads onto the user's PC at the speed of the slowest telecommunications link, as at present downloading data can sometimes be a time-wasting procedure. However, future developments will mean that speeds will improve.

5.30 So much data is available on the Net that employers worry that their staff will **spend too much time** browsing, possibly through irrelevant or non-work-related websites. The quality of much of the information on the Internet leaves much to be desired.

5.31 **Security** is perhaps the biggest worry of all. Security aspects of the Internet are discussed in Chapter 14.

6 ELECTRONIC COMMERCE

6.1 Electronic commerce or e-commerce has increasingly been used to describe the use of the **Internet** and Websites in the sale of products or services.

Setting up an e-business

6.2 Components of an e-business

(a) **Telecommunications infrastructure**

On average a leased line will cost about £700 to install and about £200 per month to rent. A large business such as a financial institution might require greater capacity, and greater fault tolerance – which will cost significantly more.

(b) **Hardware**

A powerful PC or server capable of handling web traffic will cost between £1,500 and £10,000. A bank needing a server capable of handling 50,000 transactions or more a day might spend as much as £1m.

(c) **Software**

Most e-businesses opt for a combination of packaged software such as Microsoft Site Server and other customised applications. Much depends on the extent to which the e-business needs to link in to **existing** transaction processing systems.

As a minimum the website itself will need to consist of the following.

(i) An **online catalogue.** This should give comprehensive descriptions of the products and services on offer, using images and other details that will be of interest.

(ii) **Shopping cart software.** This is software that allows the customer to pick items, keep as running total, amend their order and calculate delivery charges, VAT and so on.

(d) **Services**

As a minimum these might consist fees for web developers (£300 to £600 per day), who in turn need to work in conjunction with graphic designers and marketing staff.

(e) **An SSL certificate**

A SSL (Secure Sockets Layer) certificate can be obtained from a 'trusted party' who has the authority to issue certificates. When a user enter a '**secure**' section of the site their browser sends a 'hello' message to the site server together with a unique string of numbers. The site server responds by sending back a 'server certificate' and a second unique string of numbers. The browser checks that the server certificate is genuine and then creates a 'master secret' based on the two unique strings of numbers. This is then used to encrypt all data that is sent between the browser and the web site server.

(f) **Transaction processing**

Some e-businesses are therefore still clearing credit card payments manually, just as if the order had been received in the post. Minimum needs are:

(i) A **merchant agreement** with a bank or credit card company. This allows the e-commerce site to accept credit card payments.

(ii) **Credit card authorisation.** This guarantees the seller payment and gives the customer an assurance of credit card confidentiality. The seller does not actually see the customer's credit card details; these are sent to a third party who then sends the seller an authorisation code.

(g) **Order fulfilment**

There needs to be a reliable mechanism for delivering products to customers.

(h) **Customer registration**

This allows the seller to collect information about customers for future marketing and planning.

(i) **Feedback mechanism**

Customers should be encouraged to comment on the site and on the service they receive.

(j) **Promotion and maintenance**

Promotional efforts have to continue after the technology is in place. It is not enough to market the business online; conventional advertising will still be necessary to make people aware that the service exists. Maintenance is essential because the more traffic a site gets the more technical services are needed to keep the site running.

Disadvantages of e-commerce

6.3 E-commerce involves an **unusual mix of people** – security people, web technology people, designers, marketing people – and this can be very difficult to manage. There may be a lack of evidence of desirable controls. The e-business needs supervision by expensive specialists.

6.4 At present, in spite of phenomenal growth the market is still fuzzy and undefined. Many e-businesses have **yet to make a profit,** the best-known example being **Amazon.co.uk** the Internet book-seller.

6.5 Unless the e-business is one started completely from scratch any new technology installed will probably **need to link up with existing business systems**, which could potentially take years of programming. Under-estimating the time and effort involved is a common obstacle.

6.6 E-commerce suffers from a lack of **trust**. The lack of a **physical presence** on the Internet discourages some people from conducting transactions. Large, reputable businesses are less affected than smaller entities. Concerns over providing credit and debit card information over the Internet have been addressed to a certain extent through the development of 'secure sites' utilising encryption technology. There is also the issue that existing commercial law has not fully caught up in various ways with e-transactions. Problems may arise through a lack of documentation.

Chapter roundup

- **Data collection methods** ideally collect data with 100% accuracy at minimum cost. Typically this means eliminating human intervention as far as possible. Examples include document reading methods and bar codes.
- **Data storage Issues** are instant retrieval of data by diverse users and minimisation of storage space requirements. Optical disks are the most efficient storage medium currently available.
- **Office software packages** allow modern workers to produce greater volumes of work much more efficiently than in the past and to a standard of presentation that would have been difficult to imagine only a few years ago. The main danger with office packages is that they are so easy to use that bad habits can develop.
- The 1990s has been described as the decade of **telecommunications**. There is far more choice, both in terms of technologies available and providers. Particularly important developments for the information manager are digital networks, e-mail, mobile telecoms, Computer Telephony Integration, and cheap videoconferencing.
- The **Internet** connects millions of computers worldwide and is having a major impact on ways of communicating and doing business. Companies are setting up their own intranets using the same technology.

Test your knowledge

1 What are the advantages of keyboard input of data? (See para 1.4)

2 Describe four ways in which collection of information can be improved by machine readable data. (1.7-1.15)

3 Why are disks more versatile as a storage medium than tapes? (2.1, 2.6)

4 What are the advantages of DIP? (2.17)

5 What are the drawbacks of using spreadsheets? (3.3)

6 What is presentation software? (3.4)

7 How might multimedia be used in business? (3.12)

8 Why is increased transmission capacity of the telecoms network of relevance to information management? (4.7, 4.8)

9 What sort of mobile telecoms services are now available? (4.12)

10 What are the advantages of e-mail? (4.17)

11 What is CTI? (4.25)

12 What sort of problems may occur with electronic meetings? (4.33)

13 What is an Internet service provider? (5.7 - 5.9)

14 Describe what is meant by an 'intranet'. (5.18 - 5.20)

15 How can the Internet be used commercially? (5.23 - 5.27)

Now try illustrative question 11 at the end of the Study Text

Chapter 12

THE MANAGEMENT OF TECHNOLOGICAL CHANGE

This chapter covers the following topics.

Introduction

In this chapter we shall be looking at the impact of technological change on the organisation. This can give rise to human problems such as fears about job security, disruption of existing (informal) groups, and fear of depersonalisation. It can also be counterproductive in work terms if the change is not properly controlled at each stage of the development of the system.

1 TECHNOLOGICAL CHANGE AND THE WORKING ENVIRONMENT 12/99

1.1 Technological change is rapid, and organisations must adapt themselves to it. Technological change can affect the activities of organisations as follows.

(a) **The type of products or services that are made and sold**. For example, consumer markets have seen the emergence of home computers, compact discs and satellite dishes for receiving satellite TV. Technological changes can be relatively minor, such as the introduction of tennis and squash rackets with graphite frames, or fluoride toothpaste.

(b) **The way in which products are made**. There is a continuing trend towards the use of modern labour-saving production equipment, such as robots. The manufacturing environment is undergoing rapid changes with the growth of advanced manufacturing technology. These are changes in both apparatus and technique.

(c) **The way in which services are provided**. High-street banks encourage customers to use 'hole-in-the-wall' cash dispensers, and shops are now using computerised Point of Sale terminals at cash desks.

(d) **The way in which markets are identified**. Database systems make it much easier to analyse the market place.

(e) **The way in which employees are mobilised**. There is some discussion that computerisation encourages 'delayering' of organisational hierarchies, and greater workforce skills. Using technology frequently requires changes in working methods. This is a change in organisation.

The working environment

1.2 The consequences of technological changes are particularly felt in the world of work.

(a) Semi-skilled jobs will be taken over by **robots and computers**. There will be fewer jobs or more part-time jobs, and so less need for supervision.

(b) There may be **degrading of old skills**, or an ending to the need for old skills. New skills will be needed, and:

   (i) There will be more pressure on managers to provide training or re-training for staff.

   (ii) Management development will be more important, to keep managers up-to-date, and to motivate them as advancement gets harder.

(c) As equipment becomes simpler to use, there could be opportunities for greater **flexibility in manning**, with one worker able to carry out more varied tasks. In manufacturing, there may be more continuous shift work working (24 hours a day), to keep expensive assets in constant use.

(d) Since more jobs will be part-time, there will be **less need** for **full-time employees**. More work will be sub-contracted, and full-time jobs axed.

(e) Better communications systems, portable computers etc reduce the need for people to work together in an office. There will be **more working at home**. Several managers can then share the same small office, and go into work only occasionally. Hotdesking.

(f) Working at home is likely to speed up the progression towards '**sub-contracting**', and some managers might become self-employed consultants with a 'main client' (their erstwhile employer) and a number of smaller clients who are picked up as the individual gradually markets his services more widely. "Virtual office"

(g) Improved information systems should help managers to **plan and control work** more effectively.

(h) Better information systems open up opportunities for **more centralisation** of decision making by top management and a reduced need for middle managers.

Human problems

1.3 The human problems with systems design can fall into several different categories.

Job security and status

1.4 Employees might think that the new system will put them out of a job, because the computer will perform routines that are currently done manually, and so reduce the need for human intervention. An office staff of, say, 10 people might be reduced to 8 say, and the threat of being out of work would **unsettle the entire office staff**. Even when there is no threat of losing a job, a new system might make some staff, experienced in the existing system, feel that all their experience will be worthless.

1.5 In some cases, the resistance to a new system might stem from a fear that it will result in a **loss of status** for the department concerned. For example, the management of the department concerned might believe that a computer system will give 'control' over information gathering and dissemination to another group in the organisation. **Dysfunctional behaviour** might therefore find expression in interdepartmental squabbling about access to information and a tendency to disregard the new sources of information.

Career prospects

1.6 In some instances, managers and staff might think that a new system will **damage** their **career prospects** by reducing the opportunities for promotion. On the other hand, today's successful manager should be able to adapt to information technology, and to develop a career means having to be flexible, accepting change rather than resisting it.

Social change in the office

1.7 New systems might **disrupt** the established 'social system' or '**team spirit**' in the office. Where possible, new systems should be designed so as to leave the 'social fabric' of the workplace undamaged. Group attitudes to change should then be positive rather than negative.

1.8 Another aspect of change is **ergonomic change**, changes in the way space is used including a reduced working area, and having to share a desk if the changes lead to a shift system being introduced.

Health and safety

1.9 Staff may have worries about the effect on their health of increased computer work, including Repetitive Strain Injury and eye problems.

Bewilderment

1.10 It is easy for individuals to be **confused** and bewildered by change. The systems analyst must **explain** the new system fully, clearing up doubts, inviting and answering questions, etc from a very early stage in systems investigation onwards through the design stages to eventual implementation.

Fear of depersonalisation

1.11 Staff may be afraid that the computer will 'take over' and they will be reduced to being operators chained to the machine, losing the ability to introduce the 'human touch' to the work they do. This is not wholly unrealistic.

1.12 Dysfunctional behaviour might manifest itself in the **antagonism** of operating staff towards data processing specialists who are employed to design and introduce a computer system. It might take the form of:

(a) An unwillingness to explain the details of the current system, or to suggest weaknesses in it that the new system might eradicate

(b) A reluctance to be taught the new system

(c) A reluctance to help with introducing the new system

1.13 A new system will reveal weaknesses in the previous system, and so another fear of computerisation is that it will show up exactly how poor and inefficient previous methods of information gathering and information use had been. If individuals feel that they are put under pressure by the revelation of any such deficiencies, they might try to find fault with the new system too.

1.14 In extreme cases, dysfunctional behaviour might take a more drastic, aggressive form. Individuals might show a marked reluctance to learn how to handle the new equipment, they might be deliberately slow keying in data, or they might even damage the equipment in minor acts of vandalism.

Teleworking

1.15 Advances in communications technology have, for some tasks, reduced the need for the actual presence of an individual in the office. This is particularly true of tasks involving computers.

- The worker can, for example, do '**keying in**' tasks at home or on the move.
- The keyed-in data can be **sent over a telecommunications** link to head office.

1.16 Homeworking is often known as **telecommuting** or **teleworking** if it involves IT.

1.17 The **advantages** to the organisation of teleworking are as follows.

(a) **Cost savings on space**. Office rental costs and other charges can be very expensive. If firms can move some of their employees on to a teleworking basis, money can be saved.

(b) A **larger pool of labour**. The possibility of working at home might attract more applicants for clerical positions, especially from people who have other demands on their time (eg going to and from school) which cannot be fitted round standard office hours.

(c) If the teleworkers are **freelances**, then the organisation avoids the need to pay them when there is insufficient work, when they are sick, on holiday etc.

1.18 The **advantages to the individual** of teleworking are as follows.

(a) **No time is wasted commuting** to the office. Perhaps commuting time is more a problem of the congested metropolis of London than in some other areas, but commuting can often take three to four hours a day.

(b) **The work can be organised flexibly** around the individual's domestic commitments (eg school trips) or business travel requirements.

(c) **Jobs which require concentration** can sometimes be done better at home without the disruption of the office.

1.19 The problems for the organisation are chiefly problems of **control**. Managers who practise close supervision will perhaps feels a worrying loss of control. Managers might view teleworking as an opportunity for laziness and slack work.

1.20 However, these problems of control are partly illusory. Studies show that many people welcome teleworking. Instead, the 'problems' for the organisation might be as follows.

(a) **Co-ordination** of the work of different teleworkers. The job design should ensure that teleworkers perform to the required standard.

(b) **Training.** If a teleworker needs a lot of help on a task, this implies that the task has not been properly explained.

(c) **Culture**. A teleworker is relatively isolated from the office and therefore, it might be assumed, from the firm. However, questions of loyalty and commitment do not apply for an organisation's sales force, whose members are rarely in the office.

1.21 Problems for teleworkers are as follows.

(a) **Isolation**. Work provides people with a social life, and many people might miss the sense of community if they are forced to work at home.

(b) **Intrusions**. A teleworker is vulnerable, by definition, to other interruptions (eg from members of his or her family forgetting that the worker is **working at home**, in time that the employer is paying for).

(c) **Adequate space.** It is not always possible to obtain a quiet space at home in which to work. Having a separate work space does make it easier to manage.

(d) In practice many teleworkers, especially if they are freelances, have **fewer employment rights**. They are not entitled to sick pay or holiday pay. They have limited security, as the firm can dispense with their services at whim.

Exercise

Your MD has asked you to produce a paper on 'Changing over to teleworking: management issues'.

Produce an outline of the main points you would make.

Solution

This question was addressed by Alan Fowler in the 7 March 1996 issue of *People Management* magazine. Here are some of the key points, in summary.

Employer benefits: reduced office space; access to alternative labour markets; increased staff retention.

Job design: pattern of work, task variety, extent of checking, need for interaction and teamwork.

Equipment required: specification and cost of equipment and data transmission facilities (in the long term); loss of in-house flexibility; health and safety issues.

Recruitment and induction: how does the organisation judge whether external recruits are suitable if it cannot 'keep an eye on them' in their initial employment period? How are employees immersed in the organisation culture?

Control: conventional controls such as monitoring and timekeeping do not apply. Measurable outputs and targets are needed.

Communication: consider newsletters, home visits, regular meetings of groups of teleworkers to instil a sense of belonging, and to identify shared problems.

Training: teleworkers need training just as much as conventional office workers.

Pay: should be equivalent to office-based staff doing the same job; pay for output rather than for completing set hours.

2 OVERCOMING THE HUMAN PROBLEMS

2.1 To overcome the human problems with systems design and implementation, management must recognise them, and do what they can to resolve them. There is a key role here for the **company secretary**, whose responsibilities frequently cut across organisational divisions.

Information

2.2 Employees should be kept **fully informed** about plans to install the new system, how events are progressing and how the new system will affect what people do. It should be explained to staff that 'change is for the better' with the reasons why this is so.

Participation

2.3 User department employees should be encouraged to **participate fully** in the design of the system, when the system is a tailor-made one.

(a) Their suggestions about problems with the existing system should be fully discussed.

(b) The systems analyst's ideas for a new system should be discussed with them, and their views considered.

(c) Their suggestions for features in the new system should be welcomed.

Participation should be genuine.

Skills

2.4 Staff should be informed that they will be **spared boring, mundane work** because of the possibility of automating such work and so will be able to take on more interesting, demanding and challenging work.

2.5 Employees should be told that they will be able to **learn new skills** which will make them more attractive candidates either for internal promotion or on the external labour market.

Planning

2.6 A **training** programme for staff should be **planned** in advance of the new systems being introduced. If there are to be job losses, or a redeployment of staff, these should be arranged in full consultation with the people concerned.

2.7 Careful attention should be given to:

(a) The design of work organisation

(b) The developments or preservation of 'social work groups' - the new technology and systems should not leave individuals feeling cut off from their fellow workers

(c) The inter-relationship between jobs and responsibilities in the new system

2.8 Change should be planned and managed. Reductions in jobs should be foreseen, and redundancies can be avoided if plans are made well in advance (eg staff can be moved to other job vacancies in the organisation). Training of staff should be organised.

Advice

2.9 A member of the staff should be appointed as the **office expert** or 'guru' in the system, to whom other members of staff can go to ask for help or advice. When the software is bought as an off-the-shelf package, this office expert should be made the person who contacts the software supplier about any problems with the system.

Management

2.10 When systems are designed in-house, the company secretary may need to persuade those responsible for the design to do the following.

(a) Introduce changes **gradually**, giving time for personnel to accept the changes before their implementation.

(b) Build up a **good personal relationship** with all the people they have to work with. They must listen sympathetically to their ideas, and encourage constructive thoughts and suggestions.

(c) Give **sound guarantees** for the future, as regards job retraining, redundancy payments etc.

(d) Work towards getting employees to **accept change** as a matter of course. Frequent changes (resulting from new technology) become more acceptable.

(e) Be willing to **listen to criticisms** of the system he or she is designing, and do something to meet them.

2.11 The system should not be introduced in a rush. Users of the system should be given time to become familiar with it.

3 MANAGEMENT OF CHANGE 12/99

3.1 It has been suggested that change management should be properly thought out:

(a) A **sponsor** is a person (or group), preferably a senior manager, who gives some direction to the change, making it legitimate in the eyes of staff, in that it has the support of somebody in a position of seniority.

(b) A **change agent** actually executes the change.

(c) The **target** is the person or group expected to change.

3.2 One way of assessing whether change can be made successfully is to carry out the following steps.

(a) **Describe** the **change** to all parties concerned.

(b) **Assess the sponsor's commitment** to the project. If the sponsor is lukewarm or busy elsewhere, his or her lack of interest will undermine the change.

(c) **Evaluate the support** or resistance of the targets. If the targets are in favour, it will be easy. If they are vehemently opposed, the change will be hard to implement.

(d) **Assess the change agents' skills.** If the change agents are well qualified for the task, then change will be easy. Change which is managed incompetently loses the support of senior management, who do not like to be associated with failed projects, and staff, who suffer rather than benefit.

3.3 Inadequacies in any one of these factors (senior management commitment, the abilities of change agents, staff attitudes) can sabotage the change so that it is disruptive .

3.4 The purpose of change management is to 'involve users as much as possible in system development to ensure that when the system is installed, the users will feel that they are its owners'.

4 CONTROLLING SYSTEMS DEVELOPMENT

4.1 When a computer system is developed from scratch, there should be controls over systems design, development and testing. The main objectives of systems development controls are as follows.

(a) Ensure that new computer systems are developed only if they appear to be **beneficial**, on the grounds of favourable cost-benefit analysis or other performance criteria.

(b) Ensure that each system under development has **clear, specified objectives**.

(c) Control the **scheduling** of development work.

(d) Ensure that suitable **operational and administrative controls** are built into the system design when it is being developed.

(e) Ensure that users acquire an **understanding** of the new system.

(f) Ensure that the system is **properly tested**, and provides a suitable degree of control and also achieves its objectives.

(g) Establish a basis for **management review** of the system.

(h) Ensure that systems and programs are **maintained** when the system goes operational.

(i) Ensure that **proper and complete documentation** of the system is created and maintained.

4.2 The authorisation of each stage in development must be documented. For example:

(a) The authorisation of the **feasibility study recommendation** should be recorded in the minutes of the meeting of the steering committee and/or board of directors where the authorisation is given.

(b) Users formally authorise the **specification of requirements**.

(c) The authorisation of the system specification is recorded in the specification itself.

Controls of costs, progress and system design amendments

4.3 Costs, progress and planned amendments must be reviewed at each phase of the development to ensure tight control.

4.4 **Control of costs** can be achieved in three ways, all of which should be used.

(a) Control over **system development costs**, using budgets and budgetary control variance reporting.

(b) **Monitoring changes** in the expected future costs and benefits of the system. Costs already incurred should be ignored, and the future development costs, expected system running costs and expected benefits should be the factors which determine whether it is worthwhile continuing with the system development.

(c) The **post-implementation review** of a project should study the actual development costs, system running costs and system benefits, to determine:

(i) Whether the system is currently justifiable, or should be abandoned even at this late stage

(ii) Whether the original decision to develop the system was a good one, with the benefit of hindsight

(iii) By how much actual costs and benefits differed from expectation, the reasons for these differences, and whether there are any lessons to be learned for the future

4.5 **Control over progress** can be achieved through techniques such as critical path analysis or Gantt charts.

4.6 Controls must be maintained over **amendments to the system design**. Once a system development has started, it is all too easy for the systems analysts or user department managers to think of new features to add to the system, or 'improvements' that can be made, with the result that amendments get written into the system as the design work progresses. Some amendments might be desirable; others might not be worthwhile.

4.7 Controls should be exercised over amendments, so that if any amendments are proposed which are not included in the system specification, they must be authorised at a suitable managerial level (eg by the steering committee) and the authorisation and details of the amendment should be included in the amendments section of the system specification.

Testing

4.8 Program testing, systems testing and the user department's acceptance tests are all important ingredients in development controls, to ensure that the programs are free of bugs, and that the system appears to work and meet its objectives.

System handover: training of users

4.9 The handover of the computer system from the computer experts to the computer user's non-technical staff must be done in such a way that the computer users are able to learn as much about their system as they need to know. Training of the user's staff will be necessary, backed up by involvement in acceptance testing, but there should also be full, clear and non-technical documentation of the system in a **user's manual.**

Control by users over system development

4.10 A common complaint relating to systems development is that, when finally installed, the system does not do what users want it to do, in the ways users want. It is important that users are consulted at every stage.

(a) Users' problems and requirements are **documented.**

(b) These are **referenced** to the **requirements specification**, which is agreed and authorised and approved by users.

Chapter roundup

- **Human problems** arising from changes in technology include worries about job security and status, career prospects, social changes, bewilderment and fear of depersonalisation. Working at home or teleworking gives rise to new issues of control and motivation.
- To overcome this staff should be kept **fully informed** and **allowed to participate** in systems development. Training and advice should be provided as required. Management need to learn to trust and empower staff.
- IT empowers workers but arguably it **disempowers middle managers**, and so it may have a fundamental impact on the organisational hierarchy and culture.
- Change management aims to **involve users as much as possible** in the system development so that they feel they are *owners* of the system when it is up and running.
- High standards of **control** are needed over systems development. Costs, progress and planned amendments should be carefully monitored. The systems analysts should build controls into the system. Testing is vital and file conversion should be tightly controlled. Users should be consulted at every stage.

Test your knowledge

1 What are the consequences of technological change on the working environment? (see para 1.2)

2 What is dysfunctional behaviour? (1.12)

3 What are the advantages of teleworking? (1.17, 1.18)

4 How can management plan to overcome human problems? (2.6, 2.8)

5 What parties are involved in change management? (3.1)

6 What are the objectives of systems development controls? (4.1)

Now try illustrative question 12 at the end of the Study Text

Chapter 13

CONTROL AND SECURITY

This chapter covers the following topics.

Introduction

The final syllabus topic under the heading 'Corporate information needs' is 'Security and integrity of information and data including the control of access'. The senior administrator is most likely to be concerned with general controls over the computer environment, rather than with detailed 'application' controls over data processing. A secure environment is one that ensures that risks, ranging from spilled coffee to terrorist bombs or industrial espionage, are minimised. There is some overlap here with Parts C & D of the syllabus (risk and asset management).

1 ADMINISTRATIVE CONTROLS

1.1 Administrative controls are controls over data and data security that are achieved by administrative measures. They should be applied in the information systems department, where an organisation is large enough to have one, and in the computer user's offices. With PC-based systems, the computer user's administrative controls will include controls over handling the computer hardware, software and files.

Personnel selection

1.2 Controls related to **personnel**, which were developed before the advent of computers, include the following.

(a) **Checks and balances** so that a security violation must pass through several steps before being implemented

(b) **Segregation of duties** (division of responsibilities, see below)

(c) **Job rotation**, so that employees change jobs at random intervals, thus making it uncertain that an individual will be able to set up a breach of security in the time available

(d) Enforced **vacations**

(e) Access to information granted not on rank in the management hierarchy or precedent, but on a **need to know basis**

(f) Careful **selection** of personnel, DP staff being recruited with care and references taken up

(g) **Termination procedures,** employees about to leave should have their access to sensitive data restricted

1.3 Some employees, (for example the systems analyst, and the computer security officer if one is appointed) are always in a position of trust. However, a well-designed security system puts as few people in this powerful position as possible. In particular, the role of **database administrator** (DBA) is central to the security of an information system based on a DBMS, as the DBA controls the access of other members of staff to the database or parts of it. The computer security officer's nightmare when it comes to personnel is when a member of staff who has expertise in the design of the system (and so knows of its vulnerabilities) and a member of staff who uses the information system (and so has day to day procedural knowledge as to how it works, other personnel involved) combine to create a breach of security.

Cost control

1.4 DP management and management in general, should be encouraged to appreciate the cost of processing by computer, and so should be aware of the need to restrict purchases to situations where the benefits obtainable exceed the costs.

Division of responsibilities

1.5 Organisation controls are the controls that arise from having an organised structure of jobs in the DP department - ie. that work is divided between systems analysts, programmers and operating staff, and that operations jobs are divided between data control, data preparation and computer room operations etc. The functions of an organisation structure, as far as control is concerned, are twofold.

(a) To **assign** the **responsibility** for certain tasks to specific jobs and individuals. A person in a given job has the responsibility for ensuring that certain controls are applied. Some jobs are specifically control jobs. These are the jobs of the data control clerks and, to a large extent, of the file librarian.

(b) To **prevent deliberate error**. It is easier for a person to commit fraud if he can input data, write programs and operate the computer all by himself. By dividing up the work, it is more difficult to commit fraud or tamper with data, except in collusion with others.

1.6 Organisation controls can be applied by creating a **division of duties** into at least three parts.

- Data capture and the authorisation of data processing work
- Computer operations work
- Systems analysis and programming work

1.7 In other words, the following duties should be **segregated**.

(a) Staff who are responsible for data capture and data entry should not be allowed to do any computer operations work or systems analysis and programming work.

(b) Staff who are responsible for computer operations should not be allowed to do any data capture or systems analysis and programming work.

(c) Staff who are responsible for systems analysis and programming should not be allowed to do any data capture or computer operations work.

1.8 In addition, within the computer operations section, the computer operators should ideally not be given responsibilities for data control, nor should they be given responsibility for looking after the computer file library. Note that these controls are hard to implement in an environment of end-user computing.

Organisational controls in user departments

1.9 The Institute of Chartered Accountants in England and Wales' IT Statement on security of data suggests that there are three types of management responsibility for the security of data, below top management level, in every organisation that uses computers.

Data security management

1.10 This involves setting up and **monitoring data security procedures** which all departments will be expected to follow - eg locks on rooms or keyboards, password procedures, fire safety measures, security codes for access to buildings etc.

Data

1.11 'Shared use of computing resources **erodes physical security** and, given the limitations of many operating systems, may provide easy opportunities for users to have access to data which management did not intend to be available to them. It is therefore necessary to identify some individual or department with primary responsibility for the security of each element of shared data. Each element of data should therefore have a defined owner'. The responsibilities of a data owner include:

- Keeping the **data accurate** and up-to-date
- Deciding who should have **access** to the data
- Developing **security procedures** in conjunction with the data security manager

Use of data

1.12 There is a responsibility for using the data operationally in such a way that the requirements for data security are met. This is a responsibility of all line managers who use computerised data in any way.

Computer centre

1.13 The most important points of control in a computer centre are as follows.

- Access to **source documents** should be **restricted** to data preparation and control staff.
- Access to the **computer** should be **restricted** to operating staff.
- Access to **master files** should be **restricted** to the librarian (or control clerk).
- Computer operators and programmers must **not originate live entries**.
- Control staff in a computer centre should have **no other DP duties**.

1.14 Achieving these organisational controls will be helped by drawing up an **organisation chart** and procedure manuals. It is then the task of the manager to ensure that these procedures are obeyed.

1.15 Obviously, in the case of PC-based operations these organisational controls do not apply. The same person who operates the computer also inputs data, and may even write his or her own programs for it. In these cases, however, it is still essential that the data being processed is not such as to have a bearing on the assets of the business. For example, if a PC were to be used for a sales ledger system or payroll system, the person responsible for data input and operating the PC must not be allowed to design the system nor write its programs, and there must also be suitable internal (and external) audit checks of the system.

Underpinning knowledge

Much of this should be familiar from your earlier studies for Pre-Professional *Managing Information Systems*. If you learnt that material thoroughly you may regard this chapter as revision and speed through it.

Note, however, that security issues are regularly examined in the *Administration of Corporate Affairs* exam, and the final sections of this chapter on disaster planning and backup could also be relevant to questions on Part D of the syllabus, Management of corporate assets.

2 PERSONNEL ISSUES

2.1 The establishment and maintenance of a security framework should be made the responsibility of a **computer security officer**.

2.2 The role of a computer security officer is less concerned with investigation and more with prevention. The officer will be responsible for creating and monitoring a secure computing environment.

(a) Employees should be made aware, and reminded at regular intervals, of their responsibilities.

(b) Employees should realise that the environment is conducive to fraud detection and that any perpetrator is likely to be discovered.

Job sensitivity analysis

2.3 Every individual in an organisation has some opportunity to commit fraud. The potential which they will have to do so depends on a number of factors.

- Ability to gain **access** to critical resources
- **Time available** to plan and carry out fraudulent activities
- **Skill and motivation**

2.4 Job sensitivity analysis is a system of **review** by the **security** and **personnel functions**, which seeks to identify risks by performing an analysis of each job and the potential for fraudulent behaviour inherent in the design of that job. It involves identification of valuable assets, for example portable computers, payments made to customers or postings to suspense accounts, and considers all those staff who might have an opportunity to cause loss.

2.5 There are a number of indications, or warning signs, which may suggest that an employee's behaviour should be investigated more closely. Many can be contained under the heading of evidence of **unduly lavish lifestyles**.

- Unexplained wealth, enabling for example purchase of a new car or house
- Higher than usual spending patterns, on holidaying entertainment, gambling etc.
- Liaisons with staff from rival businesses
- Lack of respect for the organisation, for example, expressions of insubordination
- Regular working 'after hours' even when this does not seem necessary

2.6 There may of course be perfectly rational explanations for any of these indicators. The key is that any suspicions should be handled with utmost sensitivity. Unfounded accusations of dishonesty can at best ruin the individual's career, and a loss of staff morale is also likely. At the same time, a 'softly softly' approach may warn the fraudster that he or she has been placed under suspicion. Absolute secrecy should be maintained while investigators set to work.

(a) A review of **historical data** can bring to light changes in performance or in key indicators, which may be evidence of some sort of fraud.

(b) A comparison of **performance** of similar departments, branches or business units might produce a significant variance in the performance of one unit.

3 SECURITY AND RISK 12/95, 12/99, 6/00

3.1 **Security** can be defined as follows.

> 'The protection of data from accidental or deliberate threats which might cause unauthorised modification, disclosure or destruction of data, and the protection of the information system from the degradation or non-availability of services'.
>
> (Lane: *Security of computer based information systems*)

3.2 The concept of **privacy** is narrower, being closely related to the idea of confidentiality, or the need to prevent unauthorised disclosure of data. Privacy is the right of the individual to control the use of information about him or her, including information on financial status, health and lifestyle.

3.3 Related concepts are as follows.

(a) **Data integrity** in the context of security is preserved when data is the same as in source documents and has not been accidentally or intentionally altered, destroyed or disclosed.

(b) **Systems integrity** refers to system operation conforming to the design specification despite attempts to make it behave incorrectly.

(c) **Threats** created by a person or an event are a potential danger to a component of an information system, which as a consequence of the threat may have its functional purpose modified or destroyed.

(d) **Vulnerabilities** are weak points in an information system allowing the system to be abused, and the data or services to be compromised.

(e) **Loss** is the undesirable end-result of a threat such as the added expense or non-availability of services.

(f) **Risk** is a quantified assessment of loss.

3.4 The consequences of a breach of security may be:

- **Loss of integrity**, as defined above
- **Loss of availability** of computer services (for example as a result of fire)
- **Loss of confidentiality** (for example through hacking)

3.5 A breach of security can be accidental or deliberate. Threats can be caused by the information system itself (for example component malfunction or a bug in the software), people, or natural disasters.

3.6 Security, it can be seen, covers a wide managerial remit, as it refers to technical issues related to the computer system, psychological and behavioural factors in the organisation and its employees, and protection against the unpredictable occurrences of the natural world. Human errors or omissions can be just as dangerous as deliberate acts.

3.7 Security, therefore, can be subdivided into a number of separate functions in the organisation.

(a) **Prevention**. It is in practice impossible to prevent all threats cost-effectively.

(b) **Detection**. Detection techniques are often combined with prevention techniques: a log can be maintained of unauthorised attempts to gain access to a computer system.

(c) **Deterrence**. As an example, computer misuse by personnel can be made grounds for dismissal.

(d) **Recovery procedures.** If the threat occurs, its consequences can be contained (for example checkpoint programs).

(e) **Correction procedures.** These ensure the vulnerability is dealt with (for example, by instituting stricter controls).

(f) **Threat avoidance.** This might mean changing the design of the system.

Risk

3.8 With so much more data being held in magnetic form, and much higher investment in IT, some organisations might embark on a security evaluation. This will identify **threats** to an organisation's information systems. **Risk** has been defined as a quantified assessment of potential loss. A further investigation may be made of particular information systems. For example, some information in some applications may be more 'sensitive' than others.

3.9 As we shall see in more detail in Part C, there are four ways of coping with risks.

- **Avoidance** (for example modify a system so it is not vulnerable)
- **Reduction** (security measures reduce risk to an acceptable level)
- **Nothing** (as risk is insignificant)
- **Transfer** (the financial consequences are transferred to an insurance company)

Developing a security policy

3.10 Information security is an important responsibility for all levels of management. A security policy is needed, not simply a collection of measures adopted ad hoc. Developing security policy would involve the following stages.

- Identification of risks
- Quantification of risks
- Placing of risks in order of potential loss
- Identification of counter-measures
- Costing of counter-measures
- Selection of counter-measures
- Implementation of counter-measures
- Draw up contingency plans (eg backup if counter-measures are ineffective)
- Review and monitor security

3.11 Security is the responsibility of all levels of management.

Organisation level	*Responsibility*	*Examples*
Top management	Organisational control environment	Initiate and approve **contingency plan**. Act on all incidents of known violation of management security policy (such as illegal and unethical transactions).
User management	Data integrity	Establish **procedures** (for example, segregation of duties or authorisation procedures). Strive to employ, train and develop **competent** and **trustworthy personnel** with clear lines of authority and responsibility

Organisation level	*Responsibility*	*Examples*
	Confidentiality and data integrity	Establish **physical and access controls** to assets and data. Establish and maintain check points and balances. Monitor compliance with controls through scheduled and unscheduled audits.
Data processing manager	Confidentiality, integrity and computer services	Ensure that hardware, software and computer operations **meet security requirements**
Personnel departments	Organisational control environment	Establish **terms of employment** and screening procedures consistent with company and department security aims

BS 7799

3.12 BS 7799 is the British Standard *Code of Practice for Information Security Management*, issued in 1995. It is divided into ten sections. What follows is only an outline of a lengthy document.

(a) **Security policy**. A written document setting out the organisation's approach to information security should be available to all staff.

(b) **Security organisation**. It should be clear who has responsibility for the various aspects of information security.

(c) **Asset classification and control**. Information is an asset, just like a machine, building or a vehicle, and security will be improved if information assets have an 'owner', and are classified according to how much protection they need.

(d) **Personnel security**. This covers issues such as recruitment of trustworthy employees, training and also reporting of security-related incidents.

(e) **Physical and environmental security.**

(f) **Computer and network management**. Particularly important is protection from viruses.

(g) **Systems access control.**

(h) **Systems development and maintenance**.

(i) **Business continuity planning**. This means that there should be measures to ensure that if something does go wrong, the business will not be completely unable to function.

(j) **Compliance** with any relevant legal requirements and also with organisational policies in standards. There is no point in having them if they are not enforced.

3.13 Try the following exercise, in case you get an exam question that asks you to produce a report or memo on IT security matters that need to be addressed in an imaginary company.

Exercise 1

A survey of medium and large companies (reported in March 1996) found the following statistics.

(a) 98% of organisations have not implemented BS 7799.

(b) 67% of businesses have no business continuity plan.

(c) Only 45% have a written computer security policy.

(d) Fewer than one-third of policies address Internet security.

(e) Only one in five require formal security compliance from business partners.

(f) Computer passwords are not changed often enough.

(g) Back-ups and disaster plans are untested.

(h) Compliance reviews are rare.

(i) Only 25% of organisations have a security officer, and only half of those report to the board.

(j) Only 36% regularly back up data held on PCs.

Try to fix these facts in your mind by finding out to what extent they are true of your own organisation. Better still, if they are true, *do* something about it.

4 THREATS TO THE ORGANISATION 12/95, 12/98, 12/99, 6/00

4.1 Broadly speaking a threat combines with a pre-existing vulnerability in the information system to produce a breach of security, resulting in a loss.

What can happen to make controls necessary?

4.2 Threats might arise from events which are accidental or deliberate. Data processing by computer creates extra problems for control because of its special characteristics, which are as follows.

(a) Large volumes of data are concentrated into files that are physically **very small** - much smaller than a corresponding manual filing system would be to hold the same data.

(b) The **processing** capabilities of a computer are **extensive**, and enormous quantities of data are processed without human intervention, and so without humans knowing what is going on. This places great reliance on the accuracy of programs and of data on file.

(c) It is **easy to lose** data on file. Equipment can go wrong and malfunction, data files can become corrupt and store meaningless data, bits of information can get lost when files are copied, and data files are always susceptible to loss through theft, flood or fire in a way that manual files are not.

(d) Unauthorised people can **gain access** to data on files, and **read classified data** or tamper with the data on file (for example insert bogus data). This is a particular problem with on-line systems because access to a computer program and master file can be from any remote terminal. It is even possible for 'hackers' to use their home computers to gain access to the files and programs of other systems.

(e) Information on a computer file **can be changed** without leaving any physical trace of the change. In comparison, a change to a manual file would often involve leaving a trace - eg crossing out data on a card file to insert new data etc.

4.3 It does not help matters that computers **lack judgement**, and errors in data processing by computer can go undetected when this would not be the case with manual data processing. For example, a payroll system might produce a salary cheque for an employee of £0.00 or for £1 million, and would not know that it had done something wrong. (This sort of problem can be overcome by building range checks/reasonableness checks into a program as a data validation routine.)

4.4 A further problem is that programmers are experts, and with careful planning, a dishonest programmer can tamper with a program to his own benefit. A case has been recorded, for example, of a programmer who arranged for all halfpennies in salaries to be paid into a bogus bank account which the programmer opened and from which he took the money. Several thousand halfpenny payments mounted up over time into substantial sums of money.

4.5 **Accidental error** can cause problems too. What is to stop a computer operator from using a file containing master file data as an output file in a different program? If this were done, the data on the master file would be wiped out. This is such an important source of potential error that controls to prevent this from happening should be built into any computer system.

4.6 Computer systems controls must be maintained regardless of the size of application or method of processing (batch or real time). If certain controls are difficult to establish in a PC-based system (eg division of responsibilities), more emphasis has to be placed on other control areas (eg procedural and processing controls).

Exercise 2

How common do you think security lapses are? Have you had personal experience of any such losses in the organisation for which you work?

Solution

The following article gives an indication of the scale of the problem.

> 'Lapses in IT security have reached epidemic proportions, affecting over 80% of UK users. ...
>
> Computer security lapses cost UK industry at least £1.2bn last year, £100m more than two years ago. ...
>
> These worrying statistics are the key findings of the latest survey of 850 UK corporations by the Department of Trade & Industry, the National Computing Centre and ICL.
>
> The survey found 71% had suffered a physical security breach with 57% reporting a breakdown in logic security involving software viruses or hacking. This compares with 1992 figures of 40% and 35% respectively.
>
> The cost of the average security breakdown has also shot up dramatically in the last two years. In 1992, each lapse in security was estimated at £2,000 - the average has now soared to £9,000. ...
>
> The largest single breach of security reported was a £1.2m fraud, and one virus attack affected three large local area networks at a cost of over £100,000.
>
> The survey found that users' greatest security fear was fire, but that equipment failure was far more common.' (*Computing*, April 1994)

The risks to data

4.7 The risks to data are set out in the ICAEW's Information Technology Statement No 1, as follows.

Human error

4.8 'This is the risk with the highest incidence. Examples of human errors are entering incorrect transactions, failing to correct errors, using wrong data files during processing, and failing to carry out instructions in respect of security procedures.'

Technical error

4.9 'This is probably the second most common risk after human error. Technical error can involve malfunctioning of hardware, system software, application software or communications software. System software includes the operating system, file management software and database software. Hardware includes not only computers and disk drives but communication equipment, normal and emergency power supplies and air conditioning units.'

Natural disasters

4.10 'Fire, flooding, explosion, impact and lightning are examples of natural disasters, the possible consequences of which should be foreseen.'

Deliberate actions

4.11 'The scope for **fraud** needs particularly careful consideration if data is held on magnetic media, because such data is not immediately legible and it may therefore be difficult to obtain evidence of improper data amendment. Also, there is a wide variety of different methods by which such fraud can be committed.'

Commercial espionage

4.12 'When considering the value of data to competitors the organisation should consider how a particular item of data might **complement other data** which a competitor has obtained from publicly available sources.'

Malicious damage

4.13 'There are many cases of disaffected employees destroying data or software. Sabotage also falls under this heading.'

Industrial action

4.14 'The more concentrated the processing and storage of data the more vulnerable an organisation can be to industrial action.'

Exercise 3

The risks to data set out by the ICAEW are relevant to manual as well as computerised systems. With computers however, the risks are greater, because data is held on magnetic files, and cannot be seen or read by the human eye. What risks do you think are particularly relevant to data storage on a magnetic medium?

Solution

The dangers associated with information storage on a magnetic medium include:

(a) Physical security. Tapes or disks can be stolen or mislaid or damaged or destroyed by fire, flood or vandalism.

(b) Environmental security. Tapes and disks are susceptible to magnetic fields, dust and extremes of temperature and humidity. Although in modern mini-computer and PC-based systems the problems of environment have been reduced, they are still quite important.

(c) Loss of confidentiality. Information stored in magnetic files may be accessed by unauthorised persons. This is a particular problem in larger systems with remote terminals, or in time sharing/computer bureau applications.

(d) Processing the wrong file. Since data is in magnetic form, and not visible, the wrong file could be read, or a file overwritten when its data is still needed.

(e) Hardware or program corruption. Hardware or software faults may damage or destroy the information on the files, as can updating a file with incomplete or inaccurate data.

---

5 MINIMISING PHYSICAL THREATS **12/97, 12/98**

5.1 Physical security comprises two sorts of controls.

- Protection against **natural** and man made **disasters**, such as fire, flood or sabotage
- Protection against **intruders** gaining physical access to the system

5.2 **Fire is the most serious hazard** to computer systems. Destruction of data can be even more costly than the destruction of hardware. A proper fire safety plan is an essential feature of security procedures, in order to prevent fire, detect fire and put out the fire. Fire safety includes:

(a) **Site preparation** (for example, appropriate building materials, fire doors)

(b) **Detection** (for example, **smoke detectors**)

(c) **Extinguishing** (for example, **sprinklers**)

(d) **Training** for staff in observing **fire safety procedures** (for example, no smoking in computer room)

5.3 **Water** is a serious hazard. **Flooding** and water damage are often encountered following **firefighting** activities elsewhere in a building. This problem can be countered by the use of **waterproof ceilings and floors** together with the provision of **adequate drainage**. In some areas flooding is a natural risk, for example in parts of central London and many other towns and cities near rivers or coasts. **Basements** are generally not regarded as appropriate sites for computer installation.

5.4 **The weather may be a threat**. Wind, rain and storms can all cause **substantial damage** to buildings. Many organisations make heavy use of **prefabricated** and portable offices, which are particularly vulnerable. **Cutbacks in maintenance** expenditure may lead to leaking roofs or dripping pipes, which can invite problems of this type.

5.5 Lightning and electrical storms can play havoc with power supplies, causing **power failures** coupled with power **surges** as services are restored. Minute adjustments in power supplies may be enough to affect computer processing operations (characterised by lights which dim as the country's population turns on electric kettles following a popular television program). One way of combating this is by the use of **uninterrupted (protected) power supplies.** This will protect equipment from fluctuations in the supply. Power failure can be protected against by the use of a **separate generator**.

Backing up

5.6 Files should be backed up regularly.

Maintenance

5.7 All computers are covered by some kind of **warranty** from the manufacturer when they are bought new. Warranty periods range in length, typically up to one year. But what should the computer user do after the warranty period has expired?

(a) The user can decide to do nothing until the computer has a **breakdown** or other fault, and then ask a third-party computer repair company to come in and do the repair work. The drawbacks to this approach are that:

(i) Repair companies give **priority** treatment to **contract customers.** The waiting time (or 'call-out' time) for a non-contract customer might be very long.

(ii) One-off repair **charges** will be very **high**.

(b) Instead, the user can arrange a **maintenance contract** with the manufacturer or a third-party repair company. The cost of these contracts will be quite high (perhaps 10% - 20% of the hardware cost per annum) and cost varies on the agreed call-out time.

(c) A third option is **breakdown insurance**, which provides insurance cover against breakdown and certain consequential losses. Insurance provides cover against expense, but the computer user is left with the operational problem of how to get the repair work done within a reasonable time - eg with a short call-out time and the provision of a replacement machine while the repair is being carried out, which is what maintenance contracts can provide.

Exercise 4

You are the assistant accountant in your organisation. The company is in the process of installing a minicomputer, and because your department will be the primary user, you have been co-opted onto the project team with responsibility for systems installation. You have a meeting at which the office services manager will be present, and you realise that no-one has yet mentioned the risks of fire or flooding in the discussions about site selection. Make a note of the issues which you would like to raise under these headings.

Solution

(a) Fire. Fire security measures can usefully be categorised as preventative, detective and corrective. Preventative measures include siting of the computer in a building constructed of suitable materials and the use of a site which is not affected by the storage of inflammable materials (eg stationery, chemicals). Detective measures involve the use of smoke detectors. Corrective measures may include installation of a sprinkler system (water-based or possibly gas-based to avoid electrical problems), training of fire officers and good siting of exit signs and fire extinguishers.

(b) Flooding. Water damage may result from flooding or from fire recovery procedures. The golden rule is to avoid siting the computer in a basement.

6 PHYSICAL ACCESS CONTROL 12/97

6.1 The other main issue of physical security is access control, to prevent intruders getting near the computer equipment or storage media. Methods of controlling human access range from:

(a) **Personnel** (security guards)

(b) **Mechanical devices** (eg keys, whose issue is recorded)

(c) **Electronic identification devices** (eg card-swipe systems, where a card is passed through a reader)

6.2 Obviously, the best form of access control would be one which **recognised individuals** immediately, without the need for personnel, who can be assaulted, or cards, which can be stolen. However, machines which can identify a person's fingerprints or scan the pattern of a retina are still, for practical purposes, cost prohibitive.

6.3 It may not be cost effective or convenient to have the same type of access controls around the whole building all of the time. Instead, the various **security requirements** of **different departments** should be estimated, and appropriate boundaries drawn.

6.4 Guidelines for data security which should be applied within the office are as follows.

(a) **Fireproof cabinets** should be used to store files, or **lockable metal boxes** for floppy disks. If files contain confidential data, they should be kept in a safe.

(b) Access to the data should be made difficult (ideally, impossible) for an unauthorised user. Programs which make use of **passwords** should be used. Computer terminals should be **sited** to minimise the risk of unauthorised use. Computers with **lockable keyboards** can be used.

(c) The password systems should **not** be operated in a **lax** way. Passwords can be next to useless if the overall system is abused. Employees can be encouraged to change passwords every so often and never to 'lend' them to a colleague.

(d) If computer printout is likely to include confidential data, it should be **shredded** before it is eventually thrown away after use.

(e) **Disks** should **not** be **left** lying around an office. They can get lost or stolen. More likely still, they can get damaged, by spilling tea or coffee over them, or allowing the disks to gather dust, which can make them unreadable.

(f) The **computer's environment** (humidity, temperature, dust) should be properly controlled.

PINs

6.5 In some systems, the user might have a special **personal identification number**, or PIN, which identifies him or her to the system. According to what the user's PIN is, the user will be **allowed** access to certain data and parts of the system, but **forbidden** access to other parts.

6.6 An example of authorisation systems with PINs is cash cards for bank or building society cash dispensers. The cash dispenser checks the PIN code on the magnetic strip of the cash card against the code number keyed in by the cardholder, and the two codes must match before the cardholder is allowed to withdraw any cash.

Door locks

6.7 Conventional door locks are of value in certain circumstances, particularly where users are only required to pass through the door a **couple of times a day**. If the number of people using the door increases and the frequency of use is high, it will be difficult to persuade staff to lock a door every time they pass through it. Similarly, other points of entry into the room/complex must be as well protected, otherwise the intruder will simply use a window to gain access.

6.8 One difficulty with conventional locks is the matter of **key control**. Inevitably, each person authorised to use the door will have a key and there will also be a master key maintained by security. Cleaners and other contractors might be issued with keys. Practices such as lending out keys or taking duplicate keys may be difficult to prevent. One approach to this is the installation of **combination locks**, where a numbered keypad is located outside the door and access allowed only after the correct 'code', or sequence of digits has been entered.

Card entry systems

6.9 This is a more sophisticated means of control than the use of locks, as **cards can be programmed** to allow access to certain parts of a building only, between certain times. These allow a high degree of monitoring of staff movements; they can for example be used instead of clock cards to record details of time spent on site. Such cards can be incorporated into **identity cards**.

Computer theft

6.10 A problem which is related to the problem of physical access control is that of equipment theft. As computer equipment becomes **smaller** and **more portable**, it can be 'smuggled' out of buildings with greater ease. Indeed much equipment is specifically designed for use off-site (for example laptops, notebooks, handhelds, bubblejet printers) and so control is not simply a question of ensuring that all equipment stays on site.

6.11 A **log of all equipment** should be maintained. The log should include the **make, model** and **serial number** of each item, together with some other organisation-generated code which identifies the **department** which owns the item, the **individual** responsible for the item and its **location**. Anyone taking any equipment off-site should book it out and book it back in.

6.12 Computer theft may be carried out by persons who have official access to equipment. It may equally be carried out by those who do not. **Burglar alarms** should be installed.

6.13 **Smaller items** of equipment, such as laptop computers and floppy disks, should always be **locked securely away**. Larger organisations may also employ site security guards and install closed circuit camera systems.

Exercise 5

You are the chief administrative officer at your company. Your department, located in an open-plan office, has five networked desktop PCs, a laser printer and a dot matrix printer.

You have just read an article suggesting that the best form of security is to lock hardware away in fireproof cabinets, but you feel that this is impracticable. Make a note of any alternative security measures which you could adopt to protect the hardware.

Solution

(a) 'Postcode' all pieces of hardware. Invisible ink postcoding is popular, but visible marking is a better deterrent. Soldering irons are ideal for writing on plastic casing.

(b) Mark the equipment in other ways. Some organisations spray their hardware with permanent paint, perhaps in a particular colour (bright red is popular) or using stencilled shapes.

(c) Hardware can be bolted to desks. If bolts are passed through the desk and through the bottom of the hardware casing, the equipment can be rendered immobile.

(d) Ensure that the organisation's standard security procedures (magnetic passes, keypad access to offices, signing in of visitors etc) are followed.

---

7 PASSWORD SYSTEMS 12/97, 12/98

7.1 A password is 'a set of characters which may be allocated to a person, a terminal or a facility which are required to be keyed into the system before further access is permitted.' (CIMA: *Computing terminology*)

7.2 Passwords can be applied to data files, program files and to parts of a program.

(a) One password may be required to **read a file**, another to write new data.

(b) The terminal user can be **restricted** to the use of certain files and programs (eg in a banking system, junior grades of staff are only allowed to access certain routine programs).

7.3 In order to access a system the user needs first to enter a string of characters. If what is entered **matches** a password issued to an authorised user or valid for that particular terminal the system permits access. Otherwise the system **shuts down** and may record the attempted unauthorised access.

7.4 Keeping track of these attempts can alert managers to **repeated efforts** to break into the system; in these cases the culprits might be caught, particularly if there is an apparent pattern to their efforts.

7.5 The restriction of access to a system with passwords is effective and widely used but the widespread and growing use of PCs and networks is making physical isolation virtually impossible. The wider **use** of information systems requires that access to the system becomes equally **widespread and easy**. Requirements for system security must be balanced by the operational requirements for access: a rigidly enforced isolation of the system may significantly reduce the value of the system.

Problems with passwords

7.6 Passwords ought to be effective in keeping out unauthorised users, but they are by **no means foolproof**.

(a) By **experimenting** with possible passwords, an unauthorised person can gain access to a program or file by **guessing** the correct password. This is not as difficult as it may seem when too many computer users specify 'obvious' passwords for their files or programs. In addition **computer programs** are available that run through millions of possible combinations at lightning speed until the correct one is found.

(b) Someone who is authorised to access a data or program file may **tell an unauthorised person** what the password is, perhaps through carelessness, or because it seems convenient on a particular occasion.

(c) An unauthorised person may simply observe someone else keying in their password. Most systems display **asterisks** instead of the actual characters typed, to try to prevent this, although this may not help if the password is a short simple one and the user types very slowly.

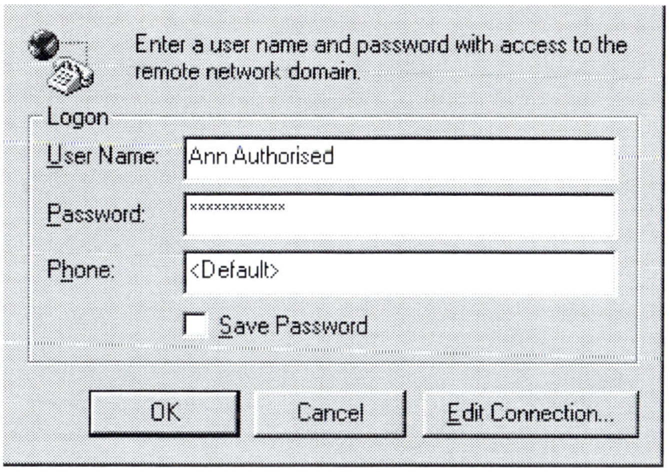

(d) Many password systems come with **standard passwords** as part of the system, such as LETMEIN. It is essential for these to be removed if the system is to be at all secure. Such common passwords become widely known to people in the industry using similar packages.

(e) Password systems rely upon users to use them **conscientiously**. Users can be extremely sloppy with their security control. Passwords are often left in plain view or 'hidden' beneath keyboards or inside desk drawers where virtually anyone could readily find them. A password system requires both a software system and strong organisational policies if it is to be effective.

(f) A good password, in a form such as f146PQzH7364 (numbers and letters, upper and lower case), would be very difficult to guess, but it is also very **difficult to remember**! Valuable information may become totally inaccessible if the user assigns a password (to a spreadsheet or database, say) and then forgets it.

Ways of avoiding this include using **mnemonics** for the letters and using numbers that are **significant** to the user for another reason (a cash card PIN number in reverse, say), but not easily guess-able by others.

Exercise 6

Draw up a checklist of points to be observed by computer users to whom passwords have been allocated.

Solution

The following should contribute to the effective operation of password security.

(a) Keep your password secret. Do *not* reveal it to anyone else.

(b) Do *not* write it down. The second easiest way of revealing a password is to write it on an adhesive label and stick this to the VDU, the desk beneath the keyboard, the inside of a desk drawer or the underside of an overhead filing cabinet.

(c) Change your password regularly.

(d) Change and use your password discreetly. Even though a password does not show up on screen, it is easy for onlookers to see which keys are being used. (FRED is a popular password for this reason; the relevant keys are close together on a QWERTY keyboard.)

(e) Do not use an obvious password. (FRED is an obvious password.)

(f) Change your password if you suspect that anyone else knows it.

Database controls

7.7 **Databases** present a particular problem for computer security. In theory, the database can be **accessed by large numbers of people**, and so the possibility of alteration, unauthorised disclosure or fraud is so much greater than with application-specific files.

7.8 It is possible to construct complicated password systems and build a set of privileges into the system, so allowing authorised users with a particular password to access more information.

7.9 However, there are problems ensuring that individuals do not circumvent the database by means of **inference**.

7.10 For example, the database forbids you to ask if John is employee Category A. However, if you know there are only three employee categories, A, B, and C, and there is no prohibition on asking about categories B and C, you can work out the members of category A by process of elimination (ie neither B, or C, therefore A). So-called **inference controls** exist to make this difficult by limiting the number of queries, or by controlling the overlap between questions.

8 HACKERS, ENCRYPTION AND VIRUSES — 12/95, 12/97, 12/98

Telecommunications dangers

8.1 When data is transmitted over a network or **telecommunications link** (especially the **Internet**) there are numerous security dangers.

(a) Corruptions such as **viruses** on a single computer can spread through the network to all of the organisation's computers. (Viruses are described at greater length later in this chapter.)

(b) Staff can do damage through their own computer to data stored on other computers. For example, they may try to transfer a file from their own hard disk to a colleague's hard disk without realising that their colleague has a file with the same name. Unless care is exercised it is easy to **overwrite somebody else's data.**

(c) Disaffected employees have much greater potential to do **deliberate damage** to valuable corporate data or systems because the network could give them access to parts of the system that they are not really authorised to use.

(d) If the organisation is linked to an external network, persons outside the company (**hackers**) may be able to get into the company's internal network, either to steal data or to damage the system.

Systems can have **firewalls** (which disable part of the telecoms technology) to prevent unwelcome intrusions into company systems, but a determined hacker may well be able to bypass even these. (There is more on hackers below.)

(e) Employees may **download inaccurate information** or imperfect or **virus-ridden software** from an external network. For example 'beta' (free trial) versions of forthcoming new editions of many major packages are often available on the Internet, but the whole point about a beta version is that it is not fully tested and may contain bugs that could disrupt an entire system.

(f) Information transmitted from one part of an organisation to another may be **intercepted**. Data can be 'encrypted' (scrambled) in an attempt to make it unintelligible to eavesdroppers, but there is not yet any entirely satisfactory method of doing this. (The problem is being worked upon by those with a vested interest, such as credit card companies, and will no doubt be resolved in time.)

(g) The **communications link itself may break down or distort data**. The worldwide telecommunications infrastructure is improving thanks to the use of new technologies, and there are communications 'protocols' governing the format of data and signals transferred (see below). At present, however, transmitted data is only as secure as the medium through which it is transmitted, no matter what controls are operated at either end.

Protocols

8.2 One of the big problems in transmitting data down a public or private telephone wire is the possibility of **distortion or loss of the message**. There needs to be some way for a computer to:

(a) Detect whether there are **errors in data transmission** (eg loss of data, or data arriving out of sequence, ie in an order different from the sequence in which it was transmitted).

(b) Take steps to **recover the lost data**, even if this is simply to notify the computer or terminal operator to telephone the sender of the message that the whole data package will have to be re-transmitted. However, a more 'sophisticated' system can identify the corrupted or lost data more specifically, and request **re-transmission** of only the lost or distorted parts.

8.3 The mechanism used to detect and usually then to correct errors is known as a **communications protocol**. Factors covered by a protocol include the following amongst many others.

- **Speed** of transmission
- **Format** of the data
- **Error detection** and correction procedures

Hacking

8.4 A hacker is a person **who attempts to invade the privacy of a system**. Hackers are normally **skilled programmers**, and have been known to crack system passwords with consummate ease. The fact that billions of bits of information can be transmitted in bulk over the public telephone network has made it **hard to trace** individual hackers. Hackers, in the past, have mainly been concerned to **copy** information, but a recent trend has been their desire to corrupt it. The Computer Misuse Act 1990 addresses the problems of hacking, but cannot *prevent* it: see the next chapter.

8.5 Phone numbers and passwords can be guessed by hackers using **electronic phone directories** or number generators and by software which enables **rapid guessing** using hundreds of permutations per minute.

8.6 **Default passwords** are also available on some electronic bulletin boards and sophisticated hackers could even try to 'tap' messages being transmitted along phone wires (the number actually dialled will not be scrambled).

Encryption

8.7 When data is transmitted over a telecommunications link or network, there are three security dangers.

- A **hardware fault**
- **Unauthorised access** by an eavesdropper
- **Direct intervention** by an impostor who sends false messages down a line

8.8 **Encryption** is the only secure way to prevent eavesdropping (since eavesdroppers can get round password controls, by tapping the line or by experimenting with various likely passwords). Encryption involves scrambling the data at one end of the line, transmitting the scrambled data, and unscrambling it at the receiver's end of the line.

8.9 **Authentication** is a technique of making sure that a message has come from an authorised sender. Authentication involves adding an extra field to a record, with the contents of this field derived from the remainder of the record by applying an algorithm that has previously been agreed between the senders and recipients of data.

8.10 **Dial-back security** operates by requiring the person wanting access to the network to dial into it and identify themselves first. The system then dials the person back on their authorised number before allowing them access.

8.11 All **attempted violations of security** should be automatically **logged** and the log checked regularly. In a multi-user system, the terminal attempting the violation may be automatically disconnected.

Viruses

8.12 A virus is a piece of software which infects programs and data and which replicates itself.

8.13 Viruses **need an opportunity** to spread. The programmers of viruses therefore place viruses in the kind of software which is most likely to be copied. This includes:

- Free software (for example software downloaded from the Internet)
- Pirated software (cheaper than original versions)
- Games software (wide appeal)
- E-mail attachments (quick to spread)

8.14 The problem has been exacerbated by the **portability of computers and disks**. Many employees **take disks home** and may work on them on their own personal PCs. Office PCs may be taken home and the opportunity taken to try out games or other software. It is consequently very difficult to keep control over **what disks** are inserted into an organisation's computers and similarly **what computers** may be used to retrieve data from or store data to office disks. Some organisations go so far as to disable the floppy disk drive on PCs.

The effect of viruses

8.15 Many viruses may be present for years with no noticeable effect; some, however, may cause **random damage to data files** (sometimes insidiously, over a long period) or attempt to **destroy files and disks**.

8.16 Others cause **unintended damage**. Even benign viruses (apparently non-destructive viruses) cause significant damage by occupying disk space and/or main memory, by using up CPU processing time, and by the time and expense wasted in detecting and removing them.

8.17 An activated virus can **show itself** in a number of ways.

(a) The **Jerusalem** virus **slows down** the operation of the infected machine so much that it becomes virtually unusable, then deletes files.

(b) **Cascade** causes letters on the **screen** to 'fall' to the bottom of the screen and may reformat the hard disk.

(c) **Casino** displays a one-armed bandit game on screen; if you fail to win the jackpot, your **hard disk is wiped**.

(d) The **Melissa** virus infects Microsoft office documents, making them unusable.

(e) The '**Love-bug**' virus detects various files from the operating system, and corrupts other files. It also sends itself on to all addresses held in the users on-line address book.

8.18 The most serious type of virus is one which **infects an operating system** as this governs the whole execution of a program.

8.19 Viruses can spread via data disk, but have been known to copy themselves over whole **networks**. When transmitted over a network into a clean system, the virus continues to reproduce, thus infecting that system.

Identification of a virus

8.20 There are two ways of identifying a virus. The first is to identify it before it does any damage. The second is to identify it when it is activated.

8.21 It is difficult for the typical user to identify the presence of a virus. There are sometimes **tell-tale signs**, such as slight changes in file lengths as displayed in the directory, or additional disk activity before a program is run, but **more sophisticated controls** than this are needed.

(a) **Anti-virus software** such as Dr Solomon's is capable of detecting and eradicating a vast number of viruses before they do any damage. Upgrades are released regularly to deal with new viruses. The software will run whenever a computer is turned on and will continue to monitor in the background until it is turned off again.

(b) Organisations must have **procedures** to guard against the downloading of unauthorised files to their systems. Many viruses and trojans have been spread as files attached to e-mails (eg Melissa, Love-bug).

(c) Organisations, as a matter of routine, should **ensure that any file received from outside** (whether on disk or attached to an e-mail) **is virus-free** before the file is downloaded.

(d) Any **flaws in a widely used program** should be rectified as soon as they come to light.

Exercise 7

Many organisations have introduced PC operating standards which include provisions designed to minimise the risk of introducing viruses. Draw up a checklist of administrative procedures to be followed to prevent infection.

Solution

Administrative procedures which can be followed are set out below.

(a) Prevent others from using your hardware and software.

(b) Do not share programs or data files with other.

(c) Do not use pirated software.

(d) Do not use public domain or shareware software, unless this has been checked or guaranteed.

(e) Use write protect tabs on floppy disks.

(f) Do not use games on any office computers.

(g) Do not use home computers for office work.

(h) Only use anti-virus software which is supplied from a reputable source.

9 E-MAIL 12/98

9.1 E-mail can pose the following problems for organisations.

(a) **Legal**. E-mail leaves a permanent record and can be sent out very easily. It could mean that people give advice that they are not authorised to give or make comments that could be the subject of other legal proceedings such as libel. In the case of *Western Provident v Norwich Union 1997* the plaintiff successfully sued for defamation, after the defendant had spread false rumours by e-mail that the plaintiff was in financial trouble. The court made an order that hard copies of the offending e-mail messages should be made available.

Some commentators have argued that this is more likely to occur because e-mail encourages people to use a more open manner, the sort that would be used in telephone conversations rather than written material. In addition the Business Names Act requires business letters to give details of names and addresses.

There have also been a number of reported cases of harassment or discrimination (through downloading of pornographic material) by e-mail, and organisations may be liable if they do not prevent this.

(b) **Security of data**. E-mail systems are not secure, and confidential information could be intercepted. The organisation may also face proceedings under data protection legislation if sensitive data about individuals is intercepted, and may have problems abroad if information is sent to certain countries contrary to local laws.

(c) **Viruses**. These can be introduced to computer systems by unauthorised attachments.

9.2 To combat these risks, organisations should enforce strict policies.

(a) **Limits** should be imposed on the personal use of e-mail. A blanket prohibition may not work, as employees will use web services instead. A possible solution would be to provide a secondary personal e-mail address, usable from desk computers, but with limitations such as a prohibition on attachments.

(b) The policy should prohibit the sending of defamatory, abusive, sexist or racist messages, or downloading offensive material.

(c) E-mails to external customers should give the **company's name, address, telephone number** and fax number and full name of the person sending the e-mail. They should include a disclaimer.

(d) The sending of **confidential information** to external sources should be **prohibited** as far as possible. If confidential information has to be sent, it should be encrypted or password-protected.

(e) Ideally **external e-mails** should contain **matters of fact** only.

(f) Employees should be advised that e-mails may have to be **disclosed** in court, and hence they should not delete sensitive e-mails from the system, and should keep hard copies of sensitive e-mails. If there is a legal dispute, employees should not discuss it over e-mail.

(g) All **attachments** to e-mails received should be **copied to disks**, and **checked** for viruses.

(h) Security software should be used to **analyse attachments** for viruses and e-mails themselves for sensitive words or abusive language. Electronic limits can also be placed on the types of attachment specific users can send out.

10.1 The preparation of a contingency plan is one of the stages in the development of an organisation-wide security policy. A **contingency plan** is necessary in case of some terrible disaster occurring to the system, or if some of the security measures discussed elsewhere fail. We can say that a disaster occurs where the system for some reason breaks down, leading to potential losses of equipment, data or money. The victim, however, cannot simply wait before continuing operations.

10.2 Minor system breakdowns occur regularly and require a *short term* recovery plan. Disasters which result in the destruction of a major computer facility or installation require a *long-term* plan. Disaster planning can be defined as follows.

> 'Contingency plans drawn up by an organisation to ensure recovery in the minimum time following a major disaster such as fire or flood damaging the core computing resources. Such plans may involve the temporary use of another company's installation or the use of a standby computer in a separate location. The policy for off-site storage of back-up data is likely to be fundamental to disaster planning.' (CIMA, *Computing Terminology*)

Exercise 8

Give as many circumstances as you can think of which might cause a systems breakdown.

Solution

System breakdowns can occur in a variety of circumstances, for example:

(a) Fire destroying data files and equipment
(b) Flooding if the computer room is in a basement), or other natural disasters
(c) A computer virus completely destroying a data or program file
(d) A technical fault in the equipment
(e) Accidental destruction of telecommunications links (eg builders severing a cable)
(f) Terrorist attack
(g) System failure caused by software bugs which were not discovered at the design stage

---

10.3 A **contingency plan** is therefore an exercise in damage limitation. A contingency can be defined, in this context, as 'an unscheduled interruption of computing services that requires measures outside the day to day routine operating procedures'.

(V P Lane: *Security of Computer Based Information Systems*)

10.4 Any contingency plan must therefore provide for the following.

(a) **Standby procedures** so that some operations can be performed while normal services are disrupted.

(b) **Recovery procedures** once the cause of the breakdown has been discovered or corrected.

(c) The **personnel management policies** to ensure that (a) and (b) above are implemented properly.

10.5 The contents of a contingency plan will include the following.

(a) **Definition of responsibilities.** It is important that somebody (a manager or co-ordinator) is designated to take control in a crisis. This individual can then delegate specific tasks or responsibilities to other designated personnel.

(b) **Establishment of priorities.** Limited resources may be available for processing. Some tasks are more important than others. Priorities must be established in advance. Similarly, the recovery program may indicate that certain areas must be tackled first.

(c) **Backup and standby arrangements**. These may be: with other installations; with a company (eg a computer bureau) that provides such services; manual procedures.

(d) **Communication with staff.** The problems of a disaster can be made worse by poor communication between members of staff.

(e) **Public relations**. If the disaster has a public impact, the recovery team may come under pressure from the public or from the media.

(f) **Risk assessment**. Once the problem is contained, a skeleton service might be resumed but resources will still need to be thrown at the problem.

11 BACK-UP AND RECOVERY 12/97

Back-up procedures

11.1 An overriding concern of the system designer will be to provide the required services continuously without a break or deterioration in performance.

11.2 This will require that data be made secure by making **back-up files**. **Back-up** means to make a copy in anticipation of future failure or corruption. A back-up copy of a file is a duplicate copy kept separately from the main system and only used if the original fails.

11.3 The **purpose of backing up data** is to ensure that the most recent usable copy of the data can be recovered and restored in the event of loss or corruption on the primary storage media.

11.4 A related concept is that of **archiving.** Archiving data is the process of moving (by copying) data from primary storage, such as a hard disk, to tape or other portable media for long-term storage.

11.5 Archiving provides a legally acceptable **business history,** while freeing up **hard disk space**. If archived data is needed, it can be restored from the archived tape to a hard disk. Archived data can be used to recover from site-wide disasters, such as fires or floods, where data on primary storage devices is destroyed.

11.6 How long data should be retained will be influenced by:

- Legal obligations
- Other business needs

11.7 Data stored for a long time should be tested periodically to ensure it is **still restorable** – it may be subject to **damage** from environmental conditions or mishandling.

11.8 In a well-planned data back-up scheme, a copy of backed up data is delivered (preferably daily) to a secure **off-site** storage facility.

11.9 A **rotation scheme** can provide a restorable history from one day to several years, depending on the needs of the business.

11.10 A well-planned **back-up and archive strategy** should include:

- A plan and schedule for the **regular back-up of critical data**
- **Archive plans**
- A **disaster recovery plan** that includes off-site storage

11.11 As with archiving, regular tests should be undertaken to **verify that data backed up can be successfully restored.**

Standby hardware facilities

11.12 Similarly hardware duplication also will permit a system to function in case of breakdown.

11.13 The provision of **back-up computers** tends to be quite costly, particularly where these systems have no other function. Many organisations will use several smaller computer systems and find that a significant level of protection against system faults can be provided by shifting operations to one of the systems still functioning. Where an organisation has only a single system to rely upon this ready recourse to a backup facility is unavailable. In these instances one response would be to negotiate a maintenance contract which provides for backup facilities.

11.14 Available standby hardware facilities include the following.

(a) **Computer bureaux** can agree to make their own systems available in the event of an emergency. Such an arrangement has to be specified in advance, as there might be other demands on a bureau's resources.

(b) Co-operating with **other organisations** in the locality, through a mutual aid agreement, may be a way of pooling resources. However, these other organisations themselves might not, in the event, be able to spare the computer time.

(c) **Disaster standby companies** (operating specially set up computer rooms only used for the purpose) are becoming more widespread as computer users are made more aware of the potential dangers of a major disaster. These companies offer office premises with desks, telephones and storage space which are equipped with hardware, including terminals, of the same type as that used by their customers. In the event of a disaster, the customer can 'invoke' standby procedures and load backups of software to carry on essential business. Disaster standby companies generally offer services to users of one hardware manufacturer's equipment only, and clearly require a number of subscribers if they are to offer a cost effective service. The upper limit on subscribers is governed by the probability that two customers require facilities at once; this is determined by insurers.

Chapter roundup

- **Administrative** controls are designed to support the smooth continuing operation of systems. They include controls over personnel selection, costs and division of responsibility.
- Certain personnel will always be placed in a **position of trust**. This means that systematic controls over their roles cannot be maintained, however a number of measures are possible. Job sensitivity analysis seeks to identify the opportunity to commit fraud which is inherent in each post in the organisation.
- **Security** is the **protection of data** from **accidental** or **deliberate threats** and the protection of an information system from such threats. Privacy is the right of the individual not to have information about him or her disclosed in an unauthorised manner.
- The first steps in developing a **security policy** are the **identification** and **quantification of risks**. Controls cost money to develop and operate, and so the response to risk will not always be the implementation of a control.
- The **risks to data** may be classified as human error, technical error, natural disaster, deliberate action, commercial espionage, malicious damage and industrial action.
- **Physical threats** to security may be natural or man made. They include fire, flooding, lightning and storm.
- **Physical access control attempts** to stop intruders or other unauthorised persons getting near to computer equipment or storage media. Important aspects of this type of control are door locks and card entry systems. Computer theft is becoming more prevalent as equipment becomes smaller and more portable. All computer equipment should be tagged and registered, and portable items should be logged in and out.
- **Passwords** can be applied to data files. A password is a set of characters which are required to be keyed into a system before further access is permitted. Although password systems can be extremely sophisticated, they all depend on user discipline.
- A **hacker** is a person who attempts to invade the privacy of a system by circumventing logical access controls. When data is transmitted over telecommunications links, there are a number of security risks. One method of preventing eavesdropping is encryption. Authentication ensures that a message has come from an authorised user.
- **Viruses** are currently the cause of much concern. A virus is a piece of software which corrupts the operation of programs and, given the opportunity, replicates itself throughout a system. Virus protection should be a standard part of the internal control system of any organisation.
- **Disaster recovery** ought to be supported by contingency planning, consisting of standby procedures to maintain essential services, and recovery procedures to restore normal operations. Contingency plans should set out responsibilities clearly, establish priorities, and provide for enhanced communications, both internally and externally.
- **Back-up procedures** are necessary to enable file data to be recreated when a file is lost or corrupted. **Standby facilities** permit a system to continue to be operated in the event of a major breakdown. Back-up is a prerequisite for successful use of such facilities.

Test your knowledge

1 List four controls over personnel selection. (see para 1.2)

2 What are the two functions of organisation structure? (1.5)

3 What is the role of a computer security officer? (2.1, 2.2)

4 What is job sensitivity analysis? (2.4)

5 What stages are involved in the development of a security policy? (3.10)

6 What security responsibilities do different levels of management have? (3.11)

7 What are the major aspects of a fire safety policy? (5.2)

8 How can human access be controlled? (6.1)

9 What are the drawbacks inherent in the operation of a password system? (7.6)

10 What is an inference control? (7.10)

11 What is encryption? (8.8)

12 What type of protection can be had against viruses? (8.21)

13 What controls should organisations have in place over use of their e-mail systems? (9.2)

14 What should a contingency plan contain? (10.5)

15 What is a disaster standby company? (11.14)

Now try illustrative question 13 at the end of the Study Text

Chapter 14

LEGAL ISSUES

This chapter covers the following topics.

1 Data protection legislation

2 The Computer Misuse Act 1990

3 Other issues

Introduction

The ICSA Syllabus Expansion Notes make it clear that you are expected to know about 'The legislative requirements which affect information, data and technology in the organisation and the guidelines for best practice to meet corporate information requirements'. In this chapter we deal with these and associated issues. Note that legal issues surrounding, the Internet are largely untested and it is well worth watching the newspapers for developments, especially in the area of security.

1 DATA PROTECTION LEGISLATION

1.1 Privacy is the right of the individual to control the user of information about him or her, including information on financial status, health and lifestyle (ie prevent unauthorised disclosure).

Why is privacy an important issue?

1.2 In recent years, there has been a growing popular fear that **information** about individuals which was stored on computer files and processed by computer could be **misused.**

1.3 In particular, it was felt that an individual could easily be harmed by the existence of computerised data about him or her which was inaccurate or misleading and which could be transferred to unauthorised third parties at high speed and little cost.

1.4 In the UK the current legislation is Data Protection Act 1998. This Act replaced the Data Protection Act 1984, although there is a transitional period.

The Data Protection Act 1998

1.5 The Data Protection Act 1998 is an attempt to protect the **individual**. The terms of the Act cover data about individuals - **not data about corporate bodies**.

Definitions of terms used in the Act

1.6 In order to understand the Act it is necessary to know some of the technical terms used in it.

(a) **Personal data** is information about a living individual, including expressions of opinion about him or her. Data about other organisations (eg supplier or customer companies) is not personal data, unless it contains data about individuals who belong to those other organisations.

(b) **Data users** are organisations or individuals who control the contents of files of personal data and the use of personal data which is processed (or intended to be processed) automatically - ie who use personal data which is covered by the terms of the Act.

(c) A **data subject** is an individual who is the subject of personal data.

The data protection principles

1.7 There are certain Data Protection Principles which registered data users must comply with.

DATA PROTECTION PRINCIPLES (1998 ACT)

Schedule 1 of the Act contains the revised data protection principles.

1 Personal data shall be processed fairly and lawfully and, in particular, shall not be processed unless:

(a) at least one of the conditions in Schedule 2 is met (see item (d) above), and

(b) in the case of sensitive personal data, at least one of the conditions in Schedule 3 is also met (see item (e) above).

2 Personal data shall be obtained only for one or more specified and lawful purposes, and shall not be further processed in any manner incompatible with that purpose or those purposes.

3 Personal data shall be adequate, relevant and not excessive in relation to the purpose or purposes for which they are processed.

4 Personal data shall be accurate and, where necessary, kept up to date.

5 Personal data processed for any purpose or purposes shall not be kept for longer than is necessary for that purpose or those purposes.

6 Personal data shall be processed in accordance with the rights of data subjects under this Act.

7 Appropriate technical and organisational measures shall be taken against unauthorised or unlawful processing of personal data and against accidental loss or destruction of, or damage to, personal data.

8 Personal data shall not be transferred to a country or territory outside the European Economic Area unless that country or territory ensures an adequate level of protection for the rights and freedoms of data subjects in relation to the processing of personal data.

1.8 In July 1995, however, the European Parliament adopted a new Directive on Data Protection, with two main purposes.

(a) To **protect individual privacy**. Previous UK law only applied to computer-based information. The directive applies to **all personal data, in any form.**

(b) To **harmonise data protection legislation** so that, in the interests of improving the operation of the single European market, there can be a free flow of personal data between the member states of the EU.

The coverage of the Act

1.9 Key points of the Act can be summarised as follows.

(a) With certain exceptions, all **data users** have had to register under the Act with the Data Protection Registrar.

(b) **Individuals** (data subjects) are awarded certain **legal rights.**

(c) **Data holders** must adhere to the **data protection principles**.

Registration under the Act

1.10 The Data Protection Registrar keeps a Register of all data users. Each entry in the Register relates to a data user or computer bureau. Unless a data user has an entry in the Register he may not hold personal data. Even if the data user is registered, he must only hold data and use data for the **purposes** which are registered. A data user must apply to be registered.

The rights of data subjects

1.11 The Act establishes the following rights for data subjects.

(a) A data subject may seek **compensation** through the courts for damage and any associated distress caused by the **loss, destruction** or **unauthorised disclosure** of data about himself or herself or by inaccurate data about himself or herself. A data subject may also ask the Commissioner to check whether processing is being carried out in accordance with legislation.

(b) A data subject may apply to the courts for **inaccurate data** to be put right or even **wiped off** the data user's files altogether. Such applications may also be made to the Registrar.

(c) A data subject may obtain **access** to personal data of which he is the subject. (This is known as the 'subject access' provision.) In other words, a data subject can ask to see his or her personal data that the data user is holding.

Case example

In July 1997 the Data Protection Registrar issued an enforcement notice to British Gas Trading Limited. The notice sought to restrain BGTL from using personal data held in connection with the supply of gas to domestic customers, or derived from that data, for the promotion of non-gas related products or services without the consent of customers. British Gas appealed against the notice to the Data Protection Tribunal, but lost the case in May 1998.

BGTL sent out a leaflet to existing customers inviting them to opt-out of disclosure of data. However, the tribunal took the view that it was unfair of BGTL to assume that those customers who failed to respond to the leaflet were silently consenting to disclosure of their personal data to other companies or to the use of their personal data for marketing non-energy related products or services.

1.12 Features of the 1998 legislation are:

(a) Everyone now has the right to go to court to seek redress for **any breach** of data protection law, rather than just for certain aspects of it.

(b) Filing systems that are structured so as to facilitate access to information about a particular person now fall within the legislation. This includes systems that are **paper-based** or on **microfilm** or microfiche. Personnel records meet this classification.

(c) Processing of personal data is **forbidden** except in the following circumstances.

(i) With the **consent** of the subject (consent cannot be implied; it must be by freely given, specific and informed agreement)

(ii) As a result of a **contractual arrangement**

(iii) Because of a **legal obligation**

(iv) To **protect the vital interests** of the subject

(v) Where processing is in the **public interest**

(vi) Where processing is required to exercise **official authority**

(d) The processing of '**sensitive data**' is forbidden, unless express consent has been obtained or there are conflicting obligations under employment law. Sensitive data includes data relating to **racial origin, political opinions, religious beliefs,** physical or mental **health, sexual proclivities** and **trade union** membership.

(e) If data about a data subject is **obtained from a third party** the data subject must be given.

   (i) The identity of the **controller** of the data
   (ii) The **purposes** for which the data are being processed
   (iii) **What data** will be disclosed and to whom
   (iv) The existence of a right of subject **access** to the data

(f) Data subjects have a right not only to have a **copy of data** held about them but also the right to know **why** the data are being processed and **what is the logic** behind the processing, and who are the recipients of the data. They also have the rights to prevent processing that is likely to cause damage and distress or that is for the purposes of direct marketing, and the right not to have significant decision's solely based on the results of automatic processing.

1.13 The new Act provides for a transitional period which data controllers can bring existing systems into line with the new law. Manual and automated data where processing was already underway before 24 October 1998, will not have to comply with the new Act until 2001.

1.14 The Data Protection Act 1998 will have a large number of practical consequences, and you should watch the press for details of these. One example is **surveillance of employees**. The Data Protection Registrar plans to implement a code which will prevent organisations disciplining staff where the evidence available is solely derived from automated systems such as surveillance cameras, computer systems (in particular e-mails) or telecommunication systems.

Exercise

Your MD has asked you to recommend measures that your company, which is based in the UK, could take to ensure compliance with data protection legislation. Suggest what measures should be taken.

Watch the newspapers for details of further developments in data protection legislation.

Solution

Measures could include the following.

(a) Obtain consent from individuals to hold any sensitive personal data you need.

(b) Supply individuals with a copy of any manual files you have about them if so requested.

(c) Consider if you may need to obtain consent to process personal data, on computer, paper or microfiche.

(d) Consider how you will be able to meet the notification requirements of the Directive in situations where you obtain personal data about individuals from third parties.

Once initial arrangements are in place, ongoing controls will be required to ensure compliance with the eight data protection principles. Organisations should have checks in place to ensure that processing is being carried out in accordance with the purposes stated in the Register of Data Controllers, and that communications from the data subjects are dealt with in accordance with their rights.

Protection of data

1.15 The *Copyright and Rights in Databases Regulations* 1997 came into force on 1 January 1998.

(a) Databases are defined as a collection of **independent works,** data or other materials arranged in a systematic or methodical way and individually accessible by electronic or other means.

(b) Databases include **literary, artistic and manual collections,** and also other collections of data such as texts, sounds, images, numbers and facts. The 'protected' part is the headings or categories or structure of the database, not the information itself (which may be copyright works in their own right).

1.16 Most organisations operate databases that fall within these criteria (a list of customers would seem to fit the description), but usually such databases are for internal use only and so copyright will not be an issue. It only becomes an issue if the owner of the database tries to exploit it for profit.

1.17 On the other hand, it is increasingly likely that organisations will be opening up a database of some sort to the public because of the commercial need to have a presence on the Internet.

Junk communications

1.18 Legislation to protect consumers and businesses against receiving unwanted faxes and phone calls, the Telecommunications (Data Protection and Privacy) (Direct Marketing) Regulations, came into force in May 1999. The rules:

(a) **Ban** the **unwanted sending** of junk faxes to individuals (including sole traders and partnerships) and allowing companies to opt-out

(b) Enable people to **opt-out** of receiving unwanted phone calls by registering their name on a central list

(c) Require marketers to offer **contact details** so that people can contact them to ask to be removed from their databases

The Regulations will be enforced by the Data Protection Registrar.

2 THE COMPUTER MISUSE ACT 1990 12/95

2.1 The Computer Misuse Act 1990 was enacted to respond to the growing threat of hacking to computer systems and data. There was some dispute as to whether hacking was a crime. For example, if you had illegally copied data, this could not be classified as theft, as the original data was not stolen. To a certain degree the law of copyright could be used. The Act has created three new criminal offences.

Unauthorised access

2.2 This means that a hacker, who, knowing he or she is unauthorised, tries to gain access to another computer system. It is the **attempt** which is the crime: the hacker's success or failure is irrelevant.

Unauthorised access with the intention of committing another offence

2.3 This results in **stricter penalties** than unauthorised access alone. However, it might be a suitable charge if a hacker had been caught in the early stages of a fraud.

Unauthorised modification of data or programs

2.4 In effect this makes the deliberate introduction of computer **viruses** into a system a criminal offence. However, this does not apply to the simple addition of data, just its corruption or destruction. Guilt is based on the **intention to impair** the operation of a computer or program, or prevent or **hinder access** to data.

2.5 Methods of combating the risks from hackers should be addressed in any organisation's security policy. Relevant points include the following.

(a) Hierarchical access structure allowing users to reach only those parts of the system they need to use.

(b) Multi-level password system.

(c) Access control logs to record unauthorised attempts to gain access.

3 OTHER ISSUES 6/98, 12/98

3.1 Establishing a presence on the Internet has certain legal implications which may not occur to managers in the IT department and the marketing department in their enthusiasm to get on-line. On the other hand much existing business law is likely to apply to communication on the Internet: the problem is that very little has yet been tested in the courts.

Addresses

3.2 For example, **Internet addresses** should be recognised as assets in themselves and companies should therefore register their names and brands and trade marks, before others with similar names do so. A solicitor called Mr Coke or Ms McDonald, for example, would find it difficult to register their surname as part of their Internet address because the global companies with those names have beaten them to it. (In fact a US computer magazine was the first to register the name McDonalds, before the fast food chain thought of doing so, to test the issues raised.)

3.3 However, if Mr Coke or Ms McDonald had got there first and started selling fizzy drinks or burgers over the Internet as a sideline, they could be sued for passing off or infringement of trade marks in the normal way.

Libel

3.4 Libel laws apply and therefore care should be taken that e-mail messages, bulletin boards and the like do not contain comments about colleagues or business contacts that could be considered libellous. A careless or off-the-cuff remark may be more widely broadcast than was ever intended.

Copyright

3.5 **Copyright** in information put onto the Internet rests with the writer of the information or their employer. Technically, therefore, unless permission to copy is expressly given (as it usually is), **printing** and **downloading information** is a **breach of copyright.** If users then try to gain commercially by using the downloaded material they are liable to face an action for infringement of copyright.

Case example

In late 1996 the *Shetland News* was prevented by interim interdict (the Scottish version of an interlocutory injunction) from using hypertext links from its Web site to the Web site of the *Shetland Times.*

The latter placed news articles from its hard copy newspaper onto its Web site. The *Shetland News* copied a number of headlines from the *Shetland Times* onto its own Web site, and then set up hypertext links from these headlines directly to the corresponding article on the *Shetland Times* Web site. Accordingly, when a user clicked on one of these headlines in the *Shetland News* Web site, the user was linked directly to the corresponding article without going through the front page of the *Shetland Times*' site. A significant concern of the *Shetland Times* was that its potential to advertise was being undermined by these direct hypertext links which resulted in visitors to its Web site bypassing the front page.

Patents and commercially sensitive information

3.6 The ability to obtain a patent is lost if the information is in the public domain, and information put onto the Internet is considered to be in the **public domain**. This has clear implications for research scientists and product developers who wish to communicate over the Internet. Companies need to decide whether they regard the Internet as a secure medium for communication and issue instructions to staff on when and when not to use it. Some e-mail providers claim to offer a service that gives protection from hackers who might wish to steal commercially sensitive information.

International law

3.7 It may be an offence in one country to put **certain kinds of information** onto the Internet, but not in another. It would be very easy for an unwary marketing department to breach another country's laws on, say, advertising to children. Appropriate advice should be sought if there is any doubt about the information that is to be made available.

Misleading information

3.8 The usual provisions regarding accuracy of information in marketing material apply to the Internet. For example, Virgin Atlantic neglected to update the fares advertised on its Internet site when the season changed from off-peak to peak, and found itself liable to pay a fine to the US Department of Transport as a result.

Case example: the Internet and the law

The Internet has developed a reputation as a law-free zone, beyond the writ of national jurisdictions and the influence of law enforcement agencies.

As a result, there is much clamour from governments, law enforcers and business for a unified legal framework.

While governments and law enforcers are concerned about crime and taxation, business wants global agreements covering issues such as data protection, intellectual property protection, and legal liability, to allow it to trade with confidence. Inevitably, business favours the lighter touch of self-regulation, rather than having to operate under a heavy-handed criminal law regime.

One of the key stumbling blocks in framing Internet laws is the conflict between the needs of governments and the needs of business. This is exemplified by arguments over the use of encryption, with companies saying they should be allowed to protect information - one of their most valuable assets - by encrypting it, and governments arguing that in the fight against crime, they must have the right to control the use of encryption, and to monitor and decrypt Internet traffic.

There have been a number of moves by commercial interest groups to clarify the legal status of information and transactions on the Internet.

Last November, the International Chamber of Commerce (ICC), in Paris, published guidelines for a legal framework to prove that electronic messages are sent by the organisation claiming to send them, and thus are legally valid.

The guidelines cover the use of digital certificates and certification authorities, both areas where a number of governments are currently contemplating legislation.

The ICC, which represents 63 national chambers of commerce, said it wanted to set up a system of self regulation on behalf of business world wide to pre-empt the establishment of regulatory barriers by national governments.

Financial Times, April 1998

Electronic Communications Act 2000

3.9 The major provisions of the Act are:

(a) **Electronic signatures** are recognised in questions relating to the authenticity or integrity of the communication of data.

(b) **Obstacles** to electronic communication in other legislation are removed.

(c) Businesses providing **cryptography** services are to be legally approved.

Chapter roundup

- The Data Protection Act 1984 is a piece of UK legislation which protects individuals about whom data is held on computer. Data users must register with the Data Protection Registrar and announce the uses to which the data will be put. The Act contains eight data protection principles, to which all data users must adhere.
- The Computer Misuse Act 1990 was enacted in the UK to respond to the growing threat to computer systems and data. While it cannot *prevent* hacking, it recognises a number of offences and provides certain punishments. A hacker is a person who attempts to invade the privacy of a system by circumventing logical access controls.

Test your knowledge

1 Under the Data Protection Act 1998, what is personal data? (see para 1.6)

2 What rights does a data subject have under the Data Protection Act 1998? (1.11)

3 What is unauthorised modification of data or programs under the Computer Misuse Act 1990? (2.4)

4 Why should businesses register on the Internet? (3.2)

5 When is it acceptable to make multiple copies of information found on a Website? (3.5)

Now try illustrative question 14 at the end of the Study Text

Part C

Pensions, insurance and risk

Chapter 15

RISK AND RISK MANAGEMENT

This chapter covers the following topics.

Introduction

In this part of the Study Text we deal with the various topics mentioned in the *syllabus* under the heading Pensions, Insurance and Risk. You will be required to answer one question from a choice of two on this area in your examination, worth 30 marks in total.

In this chapter we deal with risk, a topic that you may have met in your earlier studies for *Professional Administration* and in your current studies for *Corporate Finance*. Specifically, however, the syllabus expects you to know about 'The control and management of business risks.'

Finally in this chapter we include some information on the way in which the insurance industry shares out the burden of risk - not normally a concern for the insurance-buying public, but certainly useful knowledge for a risk manager attempting to obtain insurance for a substantial risk.

In the next chapter we shall consider the features of insurance law - utmost good faith, indemnity and so on.

1 TYPES OF RISK — 6/95, 6/96, 6/97, 6/98

1.1 A risk is a potential source of loss. There are various types of risk that exist in business and in life generally.

(a) **Fundamental risks** are those which affect society in general, or broad groups of people, and are beyond the control of any one individual. For example there is the risk of atmospheric pollution which can affect the health of a whole community but which may be quite beyond the power of an individual within it to control.

(b) **Particular risks** are risks over which an individual may have some measure of control. For example there is a risk attaching to smoking and we can control that risk by refraining from smoking.

(c) **Speculative risks** are those from which either good or harm may result. A business venture, for example, presents a speculative risk because either a profit or loss can result.

(d) **Pure risks** are those whose only possible outcome is harmful. The risk of damage to property by fire is a pure risk because no gain can result from it.

1.2 In this case we are concerned with risk and the need for **insurance** which has been defined very broadly as an arrangement by which one party (the **insurer**) promises to pay another party (the insured) a sum of money if something which is subject to a risk of happening actually does happen. The insurer charges the insured a **premium** for accepting the liability to pay out if the specified happening does occur.

Insurable risks

1.3 Not all risks can be insured. Usually four factors are required.

(a) **Pure risks** are generally the only type that can be insured (otherwise businesses would never fail, for example).

(b) **Widespread risks** are necessary so that the insurer can fill up the insurance pool (see Section 8) with many individuals exposed to the same risk.

(c) **Measurability** in monetary terms (or the possibility of agreement in advance of a monetary value in the case of life assurance), is required for the operation of the principle of indemnity (the preservation of the insured's financial position).

(d) **Unintentional** or **accidental** loss must be the outcome that is being insured against. You will clearly have no interest in protecting the insurer's interests if you want to lose or damage the insured property.

Exercise 1

Risks can be described as insurable and uninsurable. What do you think are the principal characteristics of insurable risks?

Solution

Think about this before you go on, do a short answer now and bear this question in mind as you read the rest of the chapter.

---

2 RISK MANAGEMENT WITHIN AN ORGANISATION 6/95, 6/96, 6/97, 6/00

The risk manager

2.1 A risk manager's job is **handling the risks** (that is, perils, such as the possibility of the death of a breadwinner, or of destruction of property) likely to harm a person or organisation, in the most appropriate manner. Whether a specialist is employed depends on the amount of work involved, and the time and expertise which the person, or the organisation's officers, have available for it.

2.2 Large companies, or groups of companies, have a person or section to deal with risks full time. In many organisations, however, detailed risk management functions are **divided** among those officers whose jobs are related to them. The office manager may deal with fire precautions, and the managing director with buying insurances, for example, and each may call in experts to assist with these functions; while the transport manager may manage the motoring risks by himself.

2.3 In much smaller organisations, all such jobs are naturally dealt with by the executive manager, who may well have an outside expert such as an insurer's inspector or broker's account handler to do much of the technical planning.

Specialists

2.4 Most individuals have little time for looking after their personal safety and security, still less for searching the market for the most suitable insurances; they frequently employ agents to help manage some of their risks.

2.5 A **specialist** advising on management of personal risks can work only as well as the client allows. A good specialist will ask for information and for co-operation with the expert surveys which enable him to provide a proper service; he will ensure that the client understands what safety measures are required and he will see that they are put into practice.

2.6 The client will usually require some information about **available insurances**, expect a policy to do particular things, and want a courteous service and immediate results for minimal cost. Neither's expectations can be fulfilled without the other's unstinted co-operation.

Co-operation and teamwork

2.7 The success of an insurance policy also depends on **co-operation**. For example the cost and extent of cover under fire insurance bought by the managing director will be affected by the office manager's fire precautions, which in turn may be modified by the fire insurer's requirements.

2.8 Risk management involves **all aspects** of an organisation's existence, so a risk manager works with personnel at all levels and needs a sufficient understanding of the business as a whole to be able to co-ordinate the activities of specialists effectively. Everyone in an organisation is affected by its risks to some extent, and is also in a position to help manage them. Risk managers may also find that many people react with deep suspicion to enquiries into such matters as what their jobs involve, and can react unfavourably to suggested safety measures. Tact, diplomacy and patience, and knowledge of who should be approached first are therefore essential, as is the ability to explain clearly and briefly why the required information about an individual's work is relevant and necessary.

2.9 S 7 of the Health & Safety at Work Act 1974 makes all employees at work responsible for:

(a) Their own safety

(b) That of other people who could be affected by their work

(c) Co-operating with management in fulfilment of their relevant statutory duties (reporting accidents, keeping premises safe for anyone in them, and so on)

This recognises that any effective risk identification, loss prevention or loss reduction measures must involve everyone in the organisation, from the machine operative, who should not neglect wearing safety clothing, to the directors, who should be seen to co-operate with fire drills, and to give proper priority to risk management measures in the organisation's budgets.

2.10 All successful risk management programmes therefore depend on **teamwork**. This extends to co-operation with police, fire brigade, and other specialists who can help to reduce the chance of losses occurring, and ensure that those which do happen are kept small.

3 IDENTIFICATION AND ANALYSIS OF RISK — 6/95, 6/96, 6/97, 12/98, 6/99, 6/00

Identification

3.1 No-one can manage a risk without first being aware that it exists. Some knowledge of perils, what items they can affect and how, is helpful to improve awareness of whether **familiar risks** (potential sources and causes of loss) are present, and the extent to which they could harm a particular person or organisation. The risk manager should also keep an eye open for **unfamiliar risks** which may be present.

3.2 Risk identification is a continuous process, so that new risks and changes affecting existing risks may be identified quickly and dealt with appropriately, before they can cause unacceptable losses.

3.3 Means of identifying risks (potential sources of loss) include:

(a) **Physical inspection**, which will show up risks such as poor housekeeping (for example rubbish left on floors, for people to slip on and to sustain fires)

(b) **Enquiries**, from which the frequency and extent of product quality controls and checks on new employees' references, for example, can be ascertained

(c) **Checking** a copy of every letter and memo issued in the organisation for early indications of major changes and new projects

The methods used depend on the conditions in the organisation at any given time.

Exercise 2

What sort of risks might a company face?

Solution

Make your own list, specific to the organisations that you are familiar with. Here is a list extracted from an article by Tom Jones 'Risk Management' (*Administrator*, April 1993).

- Fire, flood, storm, impact, explosion, subsidence and other hazards
- Accidents and the use of faulty products
- Error: loss through damage or malfunction caused by mistaken operation of equipment or wrong operation of an industrial programme
- Theft and fraud
- Breaking social or environmental regulations
- Political risks (the appropriation of foreign assets by local governments, or of barriers to the repatriation of overseas profit)
- Computers: fraud, viruses, and espionage
- Product tamper
- Malicious damage '

Risk analysis

3.4 It is not always simple to forecast the financial effect of a possible disaster, as it is not until *after* a loss that extra expenses, inconveniences and loss of time can be recognised. Even then it can be difficult to identify all of them. If your car is stolen, for example, and found converted to a heap of scrap metal, in addition to the cost of replacing it you can expect to pay for some quite **unexpected items**:

(a) Fares home, and to and from work until you have a replacement

(b) Telephone calls to the police, your family, your employer, and others affected

(c) Movement and disposal of the wrecked car

(d) Increased grocery bills from having to use corner shops instead of a distant supermarket

(e) Notification of DVLC that you are no longer the owner

(f) Work you must turn down because you have no car

(g) Hire purchase charges on the new car because you have insufficient funds to buy one, when all this happens

(h) Your time (which is difficult to value)

3.5 Organisations will probably keep more detailed records of their activities and the unit costs involved, but it is unlikely that any organisation can predict the full cost of every loss which might befall it with certainty. The calculation will involve numerous factors, of which those noted in the following paragraphs are only suggestions.

3.6 **Organisation charts** will be needed if a manager is taken ill, for example to calculate which personnel will have extra work in his and other departments, how much need be paid in overtime rates and whether additional expertise may have to be brought in temporarily. The personnel department may be asked for lists of employees with appropriate skills and experience who are prepared to help out.

3.7 **Production flow charts** must be used to discover the extent to which a factory's production will be affected by one machine breaking down, and whether alternative machines can be obtained or constructed, or alternative processes used.

3.8 **Supplies flow charts** and forecasts will help to assess how long a factory can maintain some or all of its production if any particular supplier suffers a major fire, or bankruptcy, and whether there are alternative suppliers.

3.9 Details of **major customers** can be monitored to identify those whose bankruptcy could damage the organisation.

3.10 **Published accounts, internal accounts and budgets** are a fertile source of information. The more carefully costs are allocated to each department, the easier it should be to calculate additional costs which would be incurred in a given emergency, which budgets will be affected and how quickly necessary funds can be made available.

3.11 Detailed **plans of site and buildings** will show potential bottlenecks in fire escape routes, obstructions which might make difficulties for fire engines and problems of access which could occur for both the site and its neighbours from fire, explosion, or escaping gas.

3.12 **Physical inspection** should be carried out regularly. Potential backup storage space and other possible emergency measures may be spotted, which may not appear in records.

Loss measurement

3.13 From this exercise is derived both the **average size** of a loss, and the **largest predictable** loss, to which the organisation could be exposed by a particular risk.

3.14 The risk manager must also be able to estimate the average and maximum probable sizes of **direct loss** from each cause, as some of the financial effects which he needs to consider cannot be insured against (as discussed in a later chapter). It is the latter figures which will therefore interest insurers.

3.15 The maximum figures for direct damage and insurable indirect losses are known as MPL or MFL (maximum possible loss, or maximum probable loss or maximum foreseeable loss). To avoid confusion, we shall use the term recommended by the Reinsurance Offices Association, **Estimated Maximum Loss** (EML), which emphasises the subjective element in the figure.

3.16 The likely **frequency** of losses from any particular cause can be predicted with some degree of confidence, from studying available records. Even recent records of the risk in question can be used to predict future losses with only a degree of statistical accuracy. This confidence margin can be improved by including the likely effects of changed circumstances in the calculation, once they are identified and quantified. Risk managers must therefore be aware of the possibility of the increase of an existing risk, or the introduction of a new risk, affecting the probability and/or possible frequency of losses from another cause.

3.17 The effect of any particular cause of loss on an organisation can be crudely forecast as N × L where

N = number of forecast losses in a given period, and
L = the average total forecast financial effect of one loss to the organisation.

This is an over-simplification, however, because:

(a) An organisation may be able to absorb the cost of one, or perhaps N, losses, and yet be in such a position that **one more** would result in restricted cash flow, a need to increase borrowing, substantial loss of market share, and other unacceptable financial effects.

(b) The **average size** of loss experienced can be **larger than** that predicted.

(c) There may be **cross-effects** of coincidental and serial losses occurring in a relatively short time.

3.18 The risk manager should therefore take the following steps.

(a) He should have some measure of the value of N for each risk which, in one or more occurrences, may be capable of precipitating loss of unacceptable proportions.

(b) He should have a means of **recording losses** from those causes. This will indicate when the accumulation of successive losses (especially above-average sized losses) and/or the cross-effects on the organisation of several kinds of loss occurrence are approaching unacceptable levels.

(c) He should keep the **calculations up-to-date**. Such factors as inflation, management policy or credit facilities can affect the size of a single loss (of whichever type) and the total size of multiple losses within a year that the organisation can absorb without serious consequences.

3.19 Thus equipped, the risk manager will be in a position to advise on risk reduction measures, as he can demonstrate whether the time and effort involved in any particular measures would be excessive, compared to the probable benefit those measures would bring the organisation in the shape of reduced losses.

3.20 The following extract from an article in the *Administrator* (now *Chartered Secretary*) in December 1990 provides a good simple example of risk identification and analysis. The writer, John Whitefield, is discussing losses from shoplifting.

> 'There's little point in insuring such losses, since the premium will inevitably overtake the loss cost to the extent of insurers' administrative expense in settling such losses. The obvious solution, ignoring risk management measures, is to decide on the figure to be budgeted against such losses, build it in to the sales price and restrict insurance to the possibility of an unacceptably high volume or cost of such losses.
>
> However, new ranges of product or shelf layout may call for a recalculation of probable losses. Unless production and sales directors are aware of the bearing these may have on the insurance programme, they may not advise or consult the secretariat in advance, so the latter's insurance plans may be over generous or inadequate until study of the loss experience reveals the discrepancies.'

4 RISK REDUCTION 6/95, 6/96, 6/97, 6/99, 6/00

4.1 Once a risk is identified and analysed, the person or organisation likely to be affected by it can investigate whether any measures can be taken to reduce it. Some risks are not susceptible to reduction at all, and others (for example natural disasters) are only so within the limitations of current technology.

4.2 Moreover, the **acceptability** of suggested measures depends on any number of factors, and risk managers must acknowledge **other people's assessments** of the priorities involved. If the logging of telephone calls is so destructive of employee morale (because they feel it demonstrates distrust or meanness) that absenteeism starts to rise and extra hours are no longer worked, then the cost of the risk reduction measure may be greater than its intended saving.

Regulations

4.3 Some of the risk reduction work should already have been done, not just in the interest of economy (which does not always conflict with safety) or common sense, but under such legislation as the Factories Acts, the Offices Shops and Railway Premises Act 1963 and their appendant regulations. The government has consolidated this complex system of safety rules gradually under the umbrella of the Health and Safety at Work Act 1974.

4.4 The risk manager should be familiar with those regulations which apply to the types of activity followed in his own organisation, not just because they are designed to **prevent accidents** (and losses), but also because infringement can sometimes lead to **unlimited fines** (another form of loss) and provide anyone injured with an additional right of action for damages against management.

Planning and review

4.5 Risk reduction measures can require considerable planning, and their effectiveness needs periodic review. A useful example is **recall programmes** for products found to have potentially harmful defects. The programme must be communicated to wholesalers, retailers and people who have bought the products. Practice exercises can be costly and time-consuming, but an inefficient programme could produce thousands of claims for damages from customers who have been injured, or had their property damaged, by those products. The resulting bad publicity could reduce sales.

4.6 Food manufacturers who can identify each tin from a batch, and record its destination for accounting purposes, start with a cost and effort advantage. A car manufacturer who advertises in the press and on radio and television that its 1986 Camomiles were faulty, and that owners should contact their nearest dealer for new brakes to be installed free of charge, will avoid damages claims and will in the process improve its public relations.

4.7 Risk reduction methods can be identical to economy and efficiency measures, or can work against them: for example, locking up tools to prevent theft can reduce working time. In either case, risk reduction can obviously affect many people in the organisation, so must involve teamwork from the planning stage onwards.

Contingency planning

4.8 In its widest sense the whole of risk management can be described as '**contingency planning**'. Here, however, we are concerned with the narrower sense of what is to be done when, in spite of the efforts that have been put into measures to reduce the possibility of a serious loss, the loss actually occurs.

4.9 Contingency planning involves identifying the **post-loss needs** of the business, **drawing up plans** in advance and **reviewing them regularly** to take account of changes in the business. The process has three basic constituents.

(a) **Information**. How, for example, do you turn off the sprinklers once the fire is extinguished? All the information that will need to be available during and after the event should be gathered in advance. This will include names and addresses of staff, details of suppliers of machinery, waste disposal firms and so on. The information should be kept up to date and it should be circulated so that it will be readily available to anyone who might need it.

(b) **Responsibilities**. The plan should lay down what is to be done by whom. Duties should be delegated as appropriate; deputies should be nominated to take account of holidays and sickness. Those who hold responsibilities should be aware of what they are, how they have changed, who will help them and so on.

(c) **Practice**. Unless the plan has been tested there is no guarantee that it will work. A full-scale test may not always be possible; simulations, however, should be as realistic as possible and should be taken seriously by all involved. The results of any testing should be monitored so that amendments can be made to the plan as necessary.

4.10 Neil Crockford *(An Introduction to Risk Management)* distinguishes between the emergency plan and the recovery plan.

(a) The **emergency plan** should be designed to ensure that action at the time of the event is swift, certain and decisive. Everyone should know where to go, what to do, when to do it and when to stop.

(b) The **recovery plan** comes into play once the initial crisis is dealt with and is intended to make sure that the business gets back on its feet as soon as possible. If a serious loss of market share will result from a temporary inability to produce and supply goods the recovery plan must aim to make 'temporary' as temporary as possible.

Loss reduction

4.11 Control of losses also requires careful advance planning. Crockford identifies two main aspects to good loss control, the physical and the psychological.

(a) There are **many physical devices** that can be installed to minimise losses when harmful events actually occur. Sprinklers, fire extinguishers, escape stairways, burglar alarms and machine guards are obvious examples.

It is **not enough** however to **install such devices**. They will need to be **inspected** and **maintained** regularly, and back-up measures will be needed for times when they are inoperational. Their adequacy and appropriateness in the light of changes to the business also needs to be kept under constant review. Periodic checks should be made to ensure that they are being operated correctly: for example machine guards may hamper efficiency and there may be a temptation not to use them.

(b) The key psychological factors are **awareness** and **commitment**. Every person in the business should be made aware that losses are possible and that they can be controlled. Commitment to loss control can be achieved by making individual managers accountable for the losses under their control. Staff should be encouraged to draw attention to any aspects of their job which makes losses possible.

conflict between security & safety (eg locked doors).

4.12 The success of the loss reduction system depends upon **co-ordination** and **co-operation**. To some extent specialist fire prevention, safety and security officers are needed for efficiency's sake, but the overall loss control system should be capable of cutting across such boundaries. The security aspect, for example, must not be allowed to conflict with the safety aspect: locked fire doors are an obvious example.

4.13 **Communication** between managers with different loss reduction responsibilities is essential; a policy statement setting out the overall philosophy and explaining the links between individual duties will help to promote understanding.

4.14 **Loss reduction** and **risk reduction measures and planning** overlap, and have many supporting organisations in common. It may be very difficult to decide whether something can be classified as one or the other. Medical organisations can both identify susceptibility to disease and assist its cure, and in curing a contagious disease may reduce its victim's loss of time and faculties, and reduce the chance of other people contracting it. It is, however, advisable to consider the two exercises separately. There may be separate measures which should be considered for loss reduction: even if there are not, it is helpful to consider working with the effects of different degrees of loss/ destruction as an aid to planning for disaster.

5 OPTIONS FOR DEALING WITH RISK

Avoidance of risk

5.1 The first option for dealing with a risk which should be considered is whether the risk can be avoided and if so whether avoidance is desirable. That is, will the possible savings from losses avoided be greater than the advantages which can be gained by not taking any mcasures, and running the risk?

5.2 Often risks can be avoided in part, or reduced, but not avoided altogether. For example, if public transport in your area is inadequate for your needs, you will probably be unable to avoid the risks associated with car ownership, but you might:

(a) **Transfer** to an insurer most of the risk of liability to pay for damage and injury you do to others with your car (the 'third party' risk)

(b) **Retain** the risk of injury to yourself

(c) **Self-insure** against the cost of repairing the damage to your car by setting money aside for the eventuality

Retaining or transferring risks

5.3 The decision of whether to retain or transfer risks depends first on whether there is anyone to transfer a risk to. The answer is more likely to be 'no' for an individual than for an organisation, because:

(a) Individuals have **more small risks** than do organisations and the administrative costs of transferring and carrying them can make the exercise impracticable for the insurer.

(b) The individual has **smaller rcsources** to find a carrier.

5.4 Organisations, however, can have such large and unattractive risks that few insurers would accept them at economic rates and terms, or at all. This would be unusual for individuals. In the last resort organisations usually have customers to pass their risks or losses to, up to a point, and individuals do not.

5.5 Decisions should not be made without careful checking to ensure that as many influencing factors as possible have been included in the assessment. A decision not to rectify the design of a product, because rectification could be as expensive as paying any claims from disgruntled customers, is in fact a decision to transfer the risk to the customers without their knowledge: it may not take into account the possibility of courts' awarding exemplary damages to someone injured by the product, to discourage people from taking similar decisions in the future.

Self-insurance

5.6 An option sometimes associated with retaining risks is **self-insurance**. In contrast to non-insurance, which is effectively gritting one's teeth and hoping for the best, self-insurance is putting aside funds of whatever size, in a lump or at intervals, in a reserve dedicated to defraying the expenses involved should a particular sort of loss happen.

Exercise 3

You are the Secretary of a medium sized manufacturing organisation. Your chairman is concerned at the substantial outlay, in this and recent years, in respect of terms of insurance premiums and is querying the merit of going self-insured.

Draft a concise report setting out the advantages and disadvantages of self-insurance.

Solution

Some of your answer can be drawn from Section 5 above, but you will need to think about the possible disadvantages of self-insurance for yourself. As food for thought, some local authorities have considered self-insurance following the collapse of the leading local government insurer, MMI. Can you think of any disadvantages in such a case?

6 TRANSFER OF RISK **6/96, 6/99**

6.1 Alternatively, risks can be transferred - to suppliers, customers, insurers or even to the state. Contract and tort law allow customers' claims, concerned with defective or dangerous goods, to be passed on to the supplier of defective components, designs or formulae, or materials which may have caused the problem; however, the law does not prevent trade agreements in which one party agrees to reimburse the other for any claims for damages.

Hold harmless agreements

6.2 Such **indemnity** or **hold harmless agreements** can be useful. They:

- Reduce the price of goods for a party who takes on extra responsibility
- Preserve good trading relations by avoiding arguments
- Preserve good public relations if efficiently and sympathetically operated

6.3 Well-known examples of hold harmless agreements, where legal liability falls on one party but claims are dealt with and paid by another, are construction contracts involving builders, civil engineers, or electrical or mechanical engineers. Standard forms of contract are published, providing for agreed distribution of liability for injury, loss and damage under various headings, as well as (usually) for insurance of particular items and liabilities by one party, frequently in both their names.

Limitation of liability

6.4 Some contracts, in which one party accepts strict liability up to a set limit, or liability which is wider than the law would normally impose, follow very ancient customs. Many are governed by statutes, such as the Hotel Proprietors Act 1956. This makes the hotelier strictly responsible for loss or damage to staying guests' property within limits, and only in most cases up to £50 per article or £100 per guest. A notice about the limitation must be properly drawn to the guests' notice on or before arrival. Other examples are contracts for carriage of passengers or goods by air or sea.

Government

6.5 Government departments also accept risks:

(a) By entering into standard contracts or variations of them

(b) In cases where extraordinary circumstances cause losses which insurers cannot carry, or demand measures which will cause individuals crippling loss

Examples of such circumstances are:

(i) War involving the UK (in which case the government can write insurances and reinsurances for property on land, and goods in transit by sea or air, which will be administered by underwriters and companies)

(ii) Specified epidemic diseases among farm animals or in crops, which require the destruction of whole herds or acres of crops under various regulations, in which case the relevant Ministry pays a fixed rate of compensation

Legal and other restrictions on transferring risks

6.6 The first restriction is that a supplier or customer may **refuse** to enter a contract unless your firm agrees to take a particular risk. This depends on the trading relationship between the firms concerned, and not a little on economics: how many firms could supply the item or service in question, for example, and how great is your firm's need for the item?

6.7 This presupposes that the larger the firm you are negotiating with, the **less** it will consider **accommodating** your individual requirements, and that government bodies will behave like extremely large firms. This is not always the case, however, as some small firms have demonstrated.

Terms of trade

6.8 Secondly, there is the limitation imposed by '**standard terms of business**', or '**usual terms of trade**', which firms adopt partly to simplify their trading. Some are drawn up by trade associations, for example terms for the hire of large equipment when the hirer frequently takes responsibility for its safety, and any damage or injury caused by the machine or the operator supplied with it.

Regulation

6.9 Last but not least, business contracts with consumers are very closely regulated. The modern legislation, consumer complaints organisations, and trading standards offices try to protect consumers to achieve the follwing ends.

(a) Consumers **know** what they are buying.

(b) They are **made aware** of any **complications** affecting the ownership of what they buy.

(c) Goods will be both **suitable** for their intended purpose, and of **reasonable** ('merchantable') **quality**.

6.10 A consumer must not be expected to take the risk of anyone's being injured or killed by defective goods or inadequate services (Unfair Contract Terms Act 1977, s 2(1)). Although consumers have accepted goods and services subject to other risks, for example if they are firmly told that goods may have minor defects, such restrictions would be ineffective if the defect was in fact dangerous, or serious.

6.11 For example if a cosmetic preparation causes a dramatic and unexpected change of complexion, or shoes fall apart after two weeks wear, this would be considered 'unreasonable' under s 2(2) of the 1977 Act. The goods themselves might also be judged as not of merchantable quality (s 14(2) of the Sale of Goods Act 1979). Other contracts, such as for leasing or repair, were brought into the net by the Unfair Contract Terms Act and the Supply of Goods and Services Act 1982.

6.12 The Consumer Protection Act 1987 affects practically all contracts with consumers for, or involving, supply of goods, except complete buildings or unprocessed agricultural produce. The Act makes manufacturers, 'own label' retailers, and others whose work on a product may have caused a defect in it, **strictly liable** for death or injury, and loss and damage to property (except land) which it causes. It thus outlaws the transfer of many product-related risks to consumers.

7 THE CAPTIVE OPTION **6/99, 12/99**

What is a captive?

7.1 A captive, or captive insurer, is an insurance company **wholly owned** by a commercial organisation, and usually **dedicated solely** to the underwriting of its **parent company's**

risks. Its primary purpose, therefore, is to be a vehicle for transfer of the parent company's risks.

7.2 Like many other good ideas, captives have been abused.

(a) Organisations have set up 'captives' from time to time to which they have dictated premiums and terms, rather than allowing the captive's underwriters scope to do their work.

(b) Captives in sunny climates can provide facilities for most agreeable 'business' trips to reward successful executives.

(c) 'Claims' have been paid which are little more than subsidies to the parent.

(d) Excessive premiums, far larger than necessary for the risks insured, have been paid to captives in tax havens, for purposes of investment rather than insurance, in the hope of evading taxes on profits.

Students of economics may appreciate that such practices are ultimately expensive for that majority of companies who obey normal rules of business. The publicity is bad for the rest of the market.

7.3 Most captives, however, write insurances responsibly, and usually successfully. Many extend their activities to **writing business** for other companies, some even for the public, and a few have become viable members of the open insurance market. Market insurers may be irritated by losing written premiums to them. However a captive is unlikely to absorb all of its parent's insurances. Indeed, some established insurers and insurance brokers provide an advisory service, investigating and reporting for companies on whether a captive would be a viable project for them, and the best way for them to establish one.

Why have a captive?

7.4 An organisation with a risk which it cannot carry, which cannot find one or more insurers to take the bulk of that risk from it, may form a captive insurer to carry that risk. The captive insurer has all the parent's experience of the horrible risk to call on, so its premiums will not be unnecessarily large, and its policy terms will be reasonable.

7.5 In the 1960s it became fashionable to form captives. In some cases this was because the parent company hoped to exchange a regular large expense on premiums for a profit centre.

(a) **Premiums** remitted to the captive (tax deductible as business expenses) can be **invested** by the captive to earn dividends etc.

(b) The captive's **underwriting**, even if restricted to the parent's risks, can be **profitable**.

(c) As premiums and claims are paid back and forth between countries, **payments** can be **timed** to some extent so that profits can be made in currency exchange.

(d) A foreign captive can work on a **smaller initial investment**, and with lower taxes on its profits, than a British insurer. (This may be reflected in the size of premiums it quotes.)

(e) If the company trades in several different countries with local regulations, it often becomes apparent that the buying power associated with a large group is **not reflected** in **premiums obtainable** in individual countries. Furthermore the local policy conditions will often fall short of the cover required by the group that may well then have to take out a further policy to cover the 'difference in conditions'. A captive is one way to solve this problem.

7.6 In other cases, companies subject to large risks, but wishing to retain a sizeable slice of that risk (a large excess, or deductible) were **unable** to **find insurers** in the market who would allow such a large 'excess'. If they did, those insurers were reluctant to allow a sufficiently large discount on the premium. The dissatisfied companies formed captive insurers to write business on terms more acceptable to their parents.

7.7 There are various other advantages of using a captive.

(a) Using a captive insurance company should have the dual advantages of **minimising costs** and **ensuring conformity of cover**. This is particularly useful in sensitive, and therefore potentially expensive, areas of risk such as environmental pollution, product liability and professional indemnity.

(b) Premiums will purely reflect the group's **own claims experience** rather than the industry as a whole that may be tainted by more reckless operators.

(c) Costs and **administration** are more easily **controlled** with smaller overheads than a large insurance company and the commercial profit element removed, though the captive should not make losses. There is also a direct management link between the insurance of the business and its operations with a powerful incentive for effective risks and claims management.

(d) The captive can link into the **re-insurance market**. This enables a significant part of the risk to be 'laid off' with re-insurers at comparatively low rates.

Joint captives

7.8 If a captive is set up, there will be a loss of the **expertise** that was previously obtained from using a professional insurance company. Choice of staff and professional advisers will be critical.

7.9 The captive may also be vulnerable if it faces a **large claim** in its early years before sufficient premiums have been built up. The company would have to bear the losses itself. It is therefore normal practice for a captive to cover only a set proportion of the risk until premiums have been built up.

7.10 Captives are not always owned by a single organisation or company. It is becoming increasingly common in the UK to find groups of companies forming joint captives.

7.11 The principal reason for joint captives seems to be that the initial outlays required are too large, and the projected premium available too small, for a company to support a captive alone. These captives have the following other advantages.

(a) The **risks** they write can be **smaller** (if they belong to small businesses) and will be more numerous than if they had a single parent.

(b) The **claims** they pay will generally be **smaller** and less likely to exhaust their funds.

(c) There is likely to be a **larger number of risks** insured which do not produce claims in any one year.

(d) Where the individual premiums are worth hundreds of pounds, increased numbers of risks do **not involve incurring** an **unacceptably large ratio** of administrative expenses to premium.

Location of captives

7.12 There are about twenty countries where captives are registered. The initial attraction of a foreign location, especially for UK parents, was low rates of local company taxation. These may not remain constant, but small countries attracting large volumes of such business are unlikely to increase their taxation to unattractive levels.

7.13 A second, but very important, consideration is the **political stability** of the country considered: the risk of a new regime nationalising the business, or imposing restrictive exchange control, must be small.

7.14 Setting up a captive abroad is easier initially if:

(a) **Local laws facilitate** setting up a firm.

helpful & knowledgeable.

(b) **Local officials** are **helpful** and know what is involved.

(c) The **local facilities**, from communications and electricity supplies to office personnel available, are at least **adequate**.

8 HOW INSURANCE HANDLES RISK

8.1 The idea of insurance is one that is probably very familiar to you from personal experience. You may though have never considered how insurance actually works. This section looks briefly at the principle of the insurance pool and then we spend some time looking at how premiums are decided in different cases. This introduces you to the various different types of insurance. The chapter after next goes into more detail.

The insurance pool

8.2 The basic principle of an insurance fund is that it is made up of all the **insureds' premiums**. These form an 'insurance pool' from which money can be drawn to reimburse an insured who suffers loss. Each member exchanges the risk of suffering losses of unpredictable size, number and occurrence pattern for a contribution of known size due on a set date.

ie. insurance traded for a premium

Characteristics of the pool

8.3 Pooling risks works well, provided that the pool has the following characteristics.

(a) There must be **enough insureds** or members contributing for the 'law of large numbers' to apply: that is, for the number and average size of claims on the pool to be reasonably close to what was anticipated. If not the fund will become bankrupt.

(b) The **contributions** made must be **adequate** to pay the claims on the pool, if not every year, then at least on average over a number of years. Again, if not, the fund will become bankrupt.

(c) The insureds' **loss experience** must be more or less **homogeneous**: that is, no one insured or small group of insureds claims amounts significantly greater than the others, especially over a period of time. If not, insureds who present fewer, smaller claims ('good risks') will feel that the contributions asked of them are too large considering the benefit they derive from the pool and in comparison to contributions they would be charged by other pools.

The descending spiral

8.4 A descending spiral can result as illustrated below.

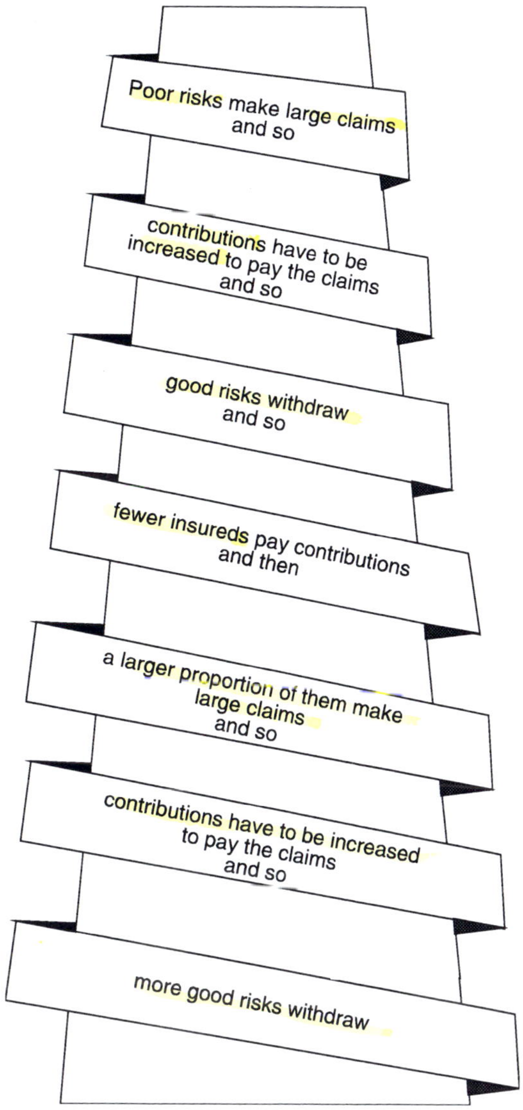

This goes on until the only people who wish to join are poor risks who expect to make claims at least as large as their contributions.

8.5 Obvious measures to halt the spiral are to ask the 'poor risks' to withdraw from the pool or to charge larger contributions to the 'poor risks'.

Risk spreading

8.6 We have mentioned the insurer's need to give as much play as possible to the operation of the **law of large numbers** by constructing risk portfolios consisting of many similar items. This is just one of several ways in which the insurer will seek to diminish his risk by ensuring that it is well spread.

(a) The insurer will be concerned to **pool items** from different locations to provide a geographical spread. This avoids the possibility of abnormal losses resulting from localised incidents.

(b) The insurer's risk will also be **spread** in a **chronological sense**, by building up reserves to be used against losses in the future. This is easier for the insurer than for individual companies because the insurer is permitted to make transfers to reserves of this kind out of pre-tax profits.

Exercise 4

Why should an administrator have any interest in the insurance pool?

Solution

The administrator who handles his or her organisation's insurance needs to understand the consequences of being seen as a bad risk. A reckless attitude to risk management is financially naive and socially irresponsible.

(a) It is likely to lead to serious loss or damage to assets.
(b) It may increase insurance premiums, perhaps for all, not just the reckless.

(You can probably add to this list.)

A second good reason is that the better his or her understanding of insurance the better the administrator will be able to negotiate with insurers.

Premiums

8.7 A risk manager will need a basic understanding of how premiums are calculated, and of the likely effects on the premium of features which underwriters have found make an individual risk better or worse than other risks.

(a) Such knowledge will assist him or her to **assess** the **priority** that should be given to various possible risk improvement measures.

(b) It also helps in appreciating why proposal forms include particular questions and which **items of information** an insurer will need, and in understanding different types of reinsurances.

(c) It also assists in appreciation of the **characteristics of risks and perils** which are insurable.

Pure risk premium

Probability => 0 → 1

8.8 **Probability** is measured on a scale of 0 (impossibility) to 1 (certainty). For example, the likelihood or chance of your falling overboard if you never go on a boat is 0, and the chance or probability of anyone dying is 1.

8.9 The measure of probability can be affected by circumstances; hence regulations on the maximum length of a 'shift' for airline pilots and coach drivers to reduce the possibility of their making fatal mistakes because of fatigue can be ineffective if a pilot's or driver's attentiveness is affected by stress at home.

Types of premium

Office premium and loading

8.10 Commercial insurance companies have operating expenses such as accommodation, wages and commission to pay, as well as their insureds' claims. Those expenses (at least) which are directly related to writing insurances (variable costs) should be defrayed by the premiums written, and so a **percentage load** is added to each pure risk premium to achieve this. The loaded pure risk premium is called the **office premium**, or sometimes the **gross premium** or **top line**. It is then adjusted, if required, to reflect the degree of risk presented in each individual proposal.

8.11 Small risks, and alterations to large ones, often attract a **minimum premium**, which represents not so much the degree of risk it presents as the cost of administering the policy. **Flat rate premiums** often reflect this: a fixed charge is made per item insured, which varies in many cases according to the risk's location, but which is seldom varied for individual risks unless they have an unusually large loss record, or other very special characteristics.

An example is block insurances for letters and packages, providing their individual value do not exceed an agreed amount.

Fire insurance premiums

8.12 Fire insurance premiums are calculated on the basis of the losses paid for a class of risks plus the loadings described above compared to the value of the property insured in that class (as a percentage). The resulting percentage is the basic premium rate to be charged per £1,000 (per mille), or occasionally per £100 (per cent) of the sum insured for each risk in the class: that is, to each normal risk. A **normal risk** is about half way between the best risk and the average for the class.

Business interruption premiums

8.13 Flat rate premiums are still occasionally found in business interruption insurance (see Chapter 17), applied per mille to turnover, fee income, or even the number of a factory's machines if this is the most suitable measure of the probable loss. The 'basic rate' used for the premium is normally, however, based on the **fire insurance rate** for the insured's **contents,** which experience has shown to be the most satisfactory measure of the risk. The **indemnity period** must be sufficient (ie the period the insurer must pay for lost profits, output etc, after the event) and wages should be covered for staff unable to work.

Motor insurance premiums

8.14 Rating of motor insurance for large fleets of vehicles is usually based on a basic formula: the fleet is divided (commercial vehicles by type, and cars by use) and the formula applied to each group, its claims experience for the last three to five years being taken into consideration.

8.15 Some insurers still rate goods-carrying vehicles according to the **location** of their base of operations and the radius of operation from their base, but the **type of goods carried** is very important, as third party claims for damage and injury caused by goods exploding, liquids in a tanker spilling, long loads smashing windows or falling off, and so forth, are covered by the motor policy. Whether the insured **owns** the goods is also important.

Life assurance premiums

8.16 Life assurance provides cover against the **risk of death**. The related premium consequently brings into account the estimated chances of the life assured dying during each of the successive years of the policy's term. These estimated chances are derived from appropriate mortality tables based on relevant risks. With **endowment assurances** the premium additionally brings into account the estimated chance that the life assured will survive to the maturity date.

Personal accident insurance premiums

8.17 Personal accident insurance premiums are calculated principally on the **size of benefits** chosen and the **proposer's occupation,** which usually represents the principal exposure to the insured risk. Desk-bound occupations attract lower premiums than manual occupations. Again, group insurances offer larger benefits without medical examination. However some offices offer lower premiums in respect of individuals who agree to complete separate proposals and undergo a medical if required.

Suiting premium to risk

8.18 Where the insurer uses different rates of premium, for example for different age groups, or different areas, more information is needed. At the far end of the scale, very complex proposal forms and survey reports can be required for non-standard commercial risks, such as fidelity, business interruption and fire insurances.

8.19 In most cases (apart from life insurance) the insurer has a **vested interest** in the quality of care exercised by the insured party. This applies to others involved in the care of the insured risk. Obviously, their management of it affects its susceptibility to most of the perils that it can be insured against.

Adjustments to basic rating

8.20 **Basic premium rating** is **subdivided** to allow for common characteristics known to have a bearing on the susceptibility of various types of risk to loss. Rating of fire and private motor risks, for example, has acquired the additional step of basic rates for common subgroups being set out in rating guides, with lists of loadings and discounts for additional standard features of those risks which are applied to the basic rate or 'top line'.

Moral hazard

8.21 A highly individual feature of any risk is the chance that it may be influenced for the worse by **moral hazards** (as opposed to physical hazards). These have been classified as carelessness, fraud, a 'difficult' attitude to claims settlements, and the general trend of external socioeconomic events and pressures on the insured. With business risks, this can apply to the carelessness, disaffectedness or dishonesty, for example, of one or more employees as well as to management.

8.22 Underwriters presented with signs of moral hazard, in one or more answers in a proposal, will apply their usual methods of levelling-out their exposure to the risks concerned with even more severity: loading premiums, imposing special terms and so forth. Alternatively, they may **refuse** an otherwise '**normal**' **risk** in these circumstances.

8.23 This illustrates the importance of the risk manager's job in ensuring that even such mundane items as regular rubbish disposal are properly attended to.

Liability insurance

8.24 Liabilities are real and serious potential sources of loss, but most of them cannot be valued. You cannot normally say 'I know how much I shall be asked to pay people for the damage, loss or injury I shall cause them in the next twelve months through using my car, or running my factory'. Sometimes you may be able to limit your liability.

(a) You could **limit your liability** for **damage** done to **goods** you **repair** or process to the cost of replacing the goods (so your customer must bear his own loss of use, loss of business costs).

(b) You could **limit your liability** for **goods** you **carry** to a maximum figure per package or per ton.

Even then, however, there can be exceptions, such as your own or your employees' gross negligence, which can make the limits ineffective. Besides, you have no means of knowing how many disgruntled customers will wish to claim compensation from you.

Employers' liability

8.25 Different occupations represent **different exposures** to risk for liability insurers, and attract different rates of premium. Employees who clean windows outside tall buildings are more exposed to risk (as well as to wind and weather) than clerks. The rate must then be applied to a factor which measures the extent of exposure to the particular risk. Salespersons' cars are driven many more miles per year than the average private car, and so motor insurance may charge double the basic 'social, domestic and pleasure' rate as a basic premium for cars used by the sales force.

8.26 In employers' liability, the factor can be the **number of employees** on the payroll (including directors and others who are paid fees rather than wages). The annual wage bill may be a preferred indicator. The exposure represented by products or services can be measured by turnover, output of products, gate receipts or the seating capacity of a building. Sometimes the limit of liability (see below) is used instead, especially if it is unusually large.

8.27 **Fidelity guarantee insurances**, which give assurance for individuals' trustworthiness (and sometimes their competence), are also rated on a variety of factors. These can impose a maximum amount guaranteed, limit ease of access to money and the sums for which the individual may be responsible, and dictate the extent and methods of supervision. So the sum of premium charged per cent of guarantee may be twice as much for a rent collector as for a manager.

Extent of liability

8.28 Insurers, therefore, have to estimate the extent to which they are exposing themselves to the risk of paying your claims if they insure one of your liabilities. They have two measures.

(a) The limit to claims payments under the policy

(b) The extent to which you are exposed to the risk of receiving the particular type of claims from other people ('third parties')

8.29 Policies do not always contain a limit of liability (limit on the amount the insurer will pay you). Important exceptions are as follows.

(a) **Employers' liability:** the Employers' Liability (Compulsory Insurance) General Regulations 1971 require insurers to provide indemnity of at least £2m per employee per accident, but most of the policies give unlimited cover.

(b) **Private motorists' liability to third parties** is covered without limit, (although commercial motor policies may have a limit on third party claims).

8.30 Examples of how limits are applied:

(a) Per accident or per occurrence (the insured bearing any extra cost)

(b) Per claim

(c) Per batch of a product

(d) For all claims arising from a single cause, for all units of a product which have a similar defect

(e) Per year

(f) Per £n per claim (or whatever) and 2 × £n (or $2^1/_2$ ×, or 3 ×) per year

You must therefore read any policy offered to you, and ask sufficient questions to ensure that you understand the extent of the cover it gives.

8.31 Another important point is whether claimant's costs and expenses (legal costs and other incidental expenses) are to be reimbursed in addition to settlement of the claim.

Co-insurance

8.32 Your organisation may propose an insurance greater than an insurer can cover prudently. In such a case the cover might be provided by several insurers who agree to share in agreed proportions. This is known as **co-insurance**.

8.33 The insurer with the greatest proportion of the cover is called the **lead insurer** or **carrier** or the **leading office**. The lead insurer is responsible for carrying out a survey and preparing a collective policy on behalf of all the insurers involved.

8.34 Co-insurance must not be confused with re-insurance.

(a) **Co-insurance** involves a **direct relationship** between the **insured** and the **co-insurer** and if a claim is made each co-insurer is separately responsible for meeting it.

(b) **Re-insurance**, on the other hand, does **not involve** the **insured.**

Reinsurance

8.35 Insurers who take a burden of risk direct from the public (with or without the assistance of intermediaries) may reduce their net expense on claims by **ceding (passing on)** parts of the **risk** to reinsurers.

8.36 Reinsurers' main functions are protecting the direct insurer's **stability,** and **increasing** the market's **capacity** for carrying risks. Their solvency is therefore important, and they protect it as insurers do theirs, by reinsuring slices of their portfolios: this is called retrocession. The retrocession market is mainly concentrated at Lloyds of London.

Effects of reinsurance on insurance

8.37 Reinsurance is designed to reduce the effects of unacceptably frequent and/or large losses. Therefore:

(a) The ceding office can **take on more**, and larger, direct risks than it could otherwise consider (the direct market's capacity is increased).

(b) Reinsurance **evens out fluctuations** in the ceding office's loss experience, and so helps prevent violent premium fluctuations which could lead to the descending spiral.

(c) Direct insurers have **more freedom** to invest their reserves, as they should not need to cash so many of their investments, possibly when their market value is low, to pay large claims.

(d) Because reinsurance improves the ceding office's stability, **adequate reinsurance** is a statutory requirement.

Chapter roundup

- In this chapter we have looked at the nature of **risk** and found that only pure risk can be insured against.
- We then saw that **risk management** depends on teamwork. We found that identification of risks is only the first step. Measures can then be taken:
  - Ascertain the consequences of risk by analysis
  - Mitigate those consequences (risk reduction)
- If the **risk cannot be avoided** altogether the organisation must choose whether to retain it, to ask an insurer to cover it, to pass it on to someone else, or to cover it themselves. In certain circumstances it may even be worth forming a captive insurance company.
- It is useful to understand how insurance deals with risk. The **insurance pool principle** is very simple but very important. Remember the consequences of taking on too many poor risks.
- The sections on **premiums** give background information and introduce you to some of the terminology used in insurance and to certain types of insurance. Later chapters cover individual areas in more detail.

Test your knowledge

1 List four types of risk. (see para 1.1)

2 Who might be involved in the job of risk management? (2.8)

3 List some possible means of identifying risk. (3.3)

4 What sort of records are likely to be consulted to analyse a risk? (3.6 - 3.11)

5 Explain the process of contingency planning. (4.9)

6 Give four options for dealing with risk. (5.1, 5.2)

7 How does legislation restrict the passing on of risk to customers? (6.9 - 6.12)

8 Why might an organisation form a captive insurance company? (7.4 - 7.7)

9 Explain the descending spiral of results. (8.4)

10 Why do risk managers need to understand how premiums are calculated? (8.7)

11 What is an office premium? (8.10)

12 Why is reinsurance so important to the insurance industry? (8.37)

Now try illustrative questions 15 and 16 at the end of the Study Text

Chapter 16

INSURANCE LAW

This chapter covers the following topics.

Introduction

In this chapter we look at a range of terms and principles that are crucial to the understanding of insurance. In essence we will be discussing what the insurer needs to be told, what can and cannot be insured within the law, and what sort of compensation the insurer is liable to pay you in different circumstances.

1 UTMOST GOOD FAITH

1.1 Insurances involve payment of a premium and a promise to conduct matters connected with the contract in particular ways, in exchange for promises to provide payment and services, often in circumstances when the recipient will be very vulnerable. For the contract to operate successfully, each party must be able to rely on the other's co-operation.

1.2 A customary rule has therefore evolved to this effect, accepted into common law as the technical principle **uberrima fides**, or utmost good faith. Justice May described it in *March Cabaret Club and Casino Ltd v London Assurance 1975*: 'it arises outside the contract; it applies to all contracts *uberrimae fidei* and is not limited to insurance contracts; it also applies, for instance, to contracts of partnership, contracts of surety, certain family settlement contracts and other similar types of contractual relationship'.

1.3 The principle amounts to a duty imposed on both parties to disclose all facts material to the contract.

Duty of disclosure

1.4 The proposer (or 'prospect', in life assurance) must appreciate which **risks** the insurer is willing to cover and accept any **restrictions** on the cover and any special duties which the underwriter requires within reason. The insurer must be aware of the individual characteristics of the risk offered, and the extent of liability which will attach to it on completion. Utmost good faith therefore operates even before the contract is completed, by imposing a duty of disclosure on both parties.

1.5 The duty of **disclosure** has been analysed in many cases, and was codified for the convenience of the marine market in the Marine Insurance Act (MIA) 1906 ss 18-20. S 18(1) describes the effect of a proposer's breach of the duty, which underlines its importance to insurance contracts.

> 'The assured must disclose to the insurer, before the contract is concluded, every material circumstance which is known to the assured, and the assured is deemed to know every circumstance which, in the ordinary course of business, ought to be known by him. If the assured fails to make such disclosure, the insurer may avoid the contract.'

The duty of the insured

1.6 It is impossible for insurers to ask about every material fact which might be presented in any risk, even in cases where proposal forms are required for submission of details of new risks. Technology, for example, may often alter risks in ways which are outside insurers' experience, and the scope of their imagination. Thus, as Lord Justice Stephenson put it in *CTI v Oceanus 1984*:

> '(The underwriter) cannot expect to be told everything, every minute detail ... He can expect to be given a fair summary (of the risk presented), and can assume that placing files which he has an opportunity of examining contain nothing exceptional or unusual'

1.7 In other words (he quoted from *Zurich Insurance Co v Morrison 1942*):

> 'Accordingly, it is for the insured to give the underwriter the material; it is not for the underwriter to ask for it. It is not of itself a good answer to say "if it was material why did you not ask?"'

1.8 Additionally, it is possible to answer all questions truthfully, but still leave the insurer with an erroneous overall impression. This, too, is misrepresentation, or **non-disclosure** of the true state of affairs: many cases on this point turn on the proposer's subjective description of facts, such as a series of costly repairs referred to as 'not serious'.

Agents and intermediaries

1.9 An insurer is deemed to know facts which its agents have seen and heard in the course of acting for it. Consider the pair of cases *Woolcott v Sun Alliance & London Assurance Ltd 1978* and *Woolcott v Excess Insurance Co 1978*. Besides having an interest in the building society's block policy with Sun Alliance, Woolcott also held his own buildings and contents insurance with the Excess, arranged by a broker. The broker knew that Woolcott had a conviction for robbery. The conviction was a surprise to both insurers when the property was destroyed by fire, and both refused to indemnify Woolcott for his loss, for nondisclosure: convictions for dishonesty are considered to have an important bearing on the moral hazard in household risks.

1.10 It was held that Sun Alliance were entitled to repudiate liability for Woolcott's claim. The courts, however, imputed the broker's knowledge of the conviction to the Excess, holding the broker to be its agent for the purposes of issuing the policy. As the Excess were presumed to have the information, they could not plead that it had not been disclosed to them.

1.11 Whether an intermediary is acting for the insurer or the proposer (or insured) in carrying out any particular part of his or her work depends on which rules it is most appropriate to apply in the circumstances. There are a few basic rules. For example, although Lloyd's brokers are responsible to underwriters for payment of premium under the Lloyd's Acts, the

Acts state that they are the insured's agents, especially in handling claims. However, the Lloyd's Acts may not govern even a Lloyd's broker's dealings with an insurance company.

1.12 **Life assurance proposals** include a **declaration**, which is agreed by the proposer in the act of signing the form, that the proposer is the principal of anyone else who completes the proposal for him or her.

1.13 Financial services legislation makes independent intermediaries agents of members of the public whom they act for. On the other hand, proposers and assureds are entitled to rely on cover notes which agents issue on behalf of insurers - motor insurers, at least. By a common law extension of this rule, they can also rely on such agents' statements that a risk is on cover.

1.14 The courts can apply the various principles to make the insurer or the intermediary responsible for paying the insured's claims, where the agent was given sufficient indication of the existence of information which must be disclosed to the insurer.

Insurer's duty of disclosure

1.15 If the insurer discovers a **material circumstance** which the insured may not be aware of, it has some duty to tell the insured.

1.16 Cases on insurers' duty of disclosure are few. A recent example is *Banque Keyser Ullman & Others v Skandia & Others 1986*, which concerned credit insurances purchased to protect banks by one Ballestero, as a precondition of their lending money (partly secured on overvalued jewellery) to four companies he owned.

1.17 The Lloyd's broker entrusted with placing insurance of 97.3m Swiss Francs split the risk into three layers, but was unable to place the last 27½% of the second excess (top) layer before the loans' completion date. He nevertheless signed cover notes which certified to the banks that the risk was placed, and the first loan was completed. The underwriter who accepted the whole primary layer and most of the second excess layer became aware of the deception some six months later. Further loans were then given, for which he wrote insurances, before and after he moved to another insurance company. His silence about the deception might have been unnoticed, but Ballestero disappeared with the loan money.

1.18 The insurers avoided the policies, as the fraud clause covered the broker's deception, and there seems to have been no 'mortgage protection' clause.

1.19 The banks then sued the insurers for damages, alleging breach of duty of care (tort), and breach of utmost good faith.

1.20 The court held the banks to be entitled to recover their financial losses, for breach of the rule in *Hedley Byrne v Heller & Partners 1964*, the duty of care owed by professionals who are aware that people are likely to rely on their skill and care. It also held the insurance companies (vicariously) liable for their underwriter's nondisclosure, and the traditional remedy for breach of utmost good faith (avoidance of the policy and return of the premium) inadequate. As the banks had not proved that the material fact would have led them to avoid the first loan, they were awarded damages for the subsequent loans.

2 LIMITATIONS ON THE DUTY OF DISCLOSURE

2.1 The duty of disclosure is therefore very strict, but it has limits. MIA 1906 s 18(1) restricts disclosure to material circumstances or facts. There are numerous definitions of what a material fact is, including Lord Justice MacKinnon's in 1942:

'that which would influence the mind of a prudent insurer in deciding whether to accept the risk or fix the premium.'

The question as to whether a particular fact is material is decided in each case, in the light of the individual circumstances.

2.2 In addition, the law does not consider that the underwriter needs protecting against accidental or intentional concealment of facts in certain circumstances.

(a) They are **common knowledge** (eg there are 366 days in a leap year).

(b) The insurer should know them from the **ordinary course of its business** (eg the claims record of an insured with the insurer's own office).

(c) They are the subjects of **express** or implied **warranties**.

(d) The insurer **waives information** about them (eg the usual question in motor proposals about the proposer's motoring convictions, which restrict the information required to incidents up to three or four years old).

(e) They **diminish the risk** (eg that a private house has a burglar alarm system).

Waiver of information

2.3 As mentioned above, the insurer often waives its right to be given particular information: the proposer then has no duty to disclose it.

2.4 If a proposal form question is left unanswered, however the insurer will normally return the form for completion, even if it is aware that this will reveal nothing exciting. To ignore the omission would be to waive its right to have the information, or to complain if it had erroneously concluded that that aspect of the risk was normal.

2.5 Information is sometimes waived by restricting the extent of detail requested. For example a motor insurance proposal might do this as follows.

(a) Have you been convicted or charged with any offence in connection with a motor vehicle in the last 5 years?

(b) Give details of any motor accidents and losses in the last 4 years.

Here the insurer waives information which relates to older incidents, to any other sort of criminal charges, and to losses and claims on any other class of policy.

2.6 Insurers in some other classes of insurance require more general information: for example, household and theft insurers are interested in any criminal charges connected with dishonesty (which might indicate increased moral hazard), whether or not they ask for information specifically.

What is truth?

2.7 There is yet another limit on the scope of the duty of disclosure. Scientific 'truth' consists of propositions and theorems built on facts as understood by the observer at the time. Insurers, too, need to know what is meant by **'truth' of representations** about the characteristics of individual risks. Common law restricts the truth which it is the proposer's duty to disclose. In *Joel v Law Union and Crown Insurance Co 1908* a judge gives the example of a man with a headache, who, not having a brain specialist's knowledge, cannot be expected to realise that it is a symptom of 'hidden mischief' which would be material to a life assurer. He comments:

'You cannot disclose what you do not know. The obligation to disclose, therefore, necessarily depends on the knowledge you possess.'

So the proposer's answer to the philosophers' question 'what is truth?' is: 'what it is reasonable for me to believe is the truth, in the light of what I know, or ought to know in my particular circumstances'.

Criminal convictions

2.8 The Rehabilitation of Offenders Act 1974 caused some anxiety at first. It expunges criminal convictions from people's records for almost all purposes except:

- Subsequent criminal proceedings
- Care and other proceedings affecting minors
- Other proceedings as necessary to avoid injustice

It is an offence to take information about rehabilitated offences into consideration, when assessing a risk, or to pass on such information to anyone else. The **rehabilitation period** begins when a sentence is imposed. The time it lasts until the offence is expunged depends on the severity of the sentence (eg 5 years' rehabilitation for a fine, 10 years for a term of imprisonment of between 6 and 30 months) and (of particular interest to motor insurers) it lasts the same length of time as a period of disqualification or prohibition.

2.9 Insurers can still take note of offences which are sufficiently serious to merit more than 30 months' imprisonment, as such sentences are excluded from the Act's provisions.

Time limits for disclosure

2.10 The duty of disclosure is sometimes said to exist until the first premium is accepted and the contract is complete. Occasionally, however, a life policy may include a requirement to disclose a **particular change** in the life assured's circumstances, such as emigration to an unfamiliar climate. If the relevant change occurs and the insurer is not notified, the insurer is entitled to repudiate the claim, and need not return premium instalments paid since the change.

2.11 In most general insurances, the insurer needs to be informed of **changes in material circumstances** during a policy's currency, and notice of some such changes may be the subject of specific warranties. It seems to be questionable whether duties or implied warranties, when reinforced by express warranties. Examples of circumstances which, if they occur during the currency of a general insurance, will need to be declared to the insurer, include:

(a) Changes which **increase the risk** to an appreciable extent (such as a building being extended, where the work and presence of the workmen increases the risk, and the sum insured should be increased)

(b) A change in the insured's **interest in the risk**, for example if an insured item is sold

Consequences of non-disclosure

2.12 Failure to disclose an alteration in a material circumstance, whether the duty to disclose is contractual or extra-contractual, will entitle the **insurer** to **avoid** the **whole policy** if the matter is sufficiently important to the particular insurance; the insurer keeps any premiums received.

2.13 If the fact is less important, but still material, or the insurer has other reasons for not avoiding the policy (such as insufficient proof of deliberate concealment of the fact, and a desire to avoid libel suits), there are practical remedies.

(a) The insurer can **refuse to pay** a claim (or just not pay): the insured can only obtain payment of the claim by starting legal proceedings, and can only succeed if innocent of deliberate concealment.

(b) The insurer can **cancel as prescribed** in the cancellation clause, and will not have to give a reason for cancellation, although it will have to return the unearned proportion of the premium.

Duty to take care

2.14 In general insurances, including personal accident, personal accident and sickness, and permanent health insurance, it is probable that, even in the absence of specific warranties and exclusions, the insured is bound to take reasonable care to:

- **Avoid insured loss**
- **Protect** the **insurer's position** if an insured loss occurs

2.15 Insured and insurer both benefit from the preservation of the subject matter, but this may well require a higher standard of care, in some circumstances, than the insured normally exercises. If it were not so, it would not be necessary for insurers (or even local authority inspectors) to have premises inspected at intervals to ensure, for example, that goods or rubbish are not being stacked against emergency exit doors, and that building site workers are supplied with adequate headgear.

3 OBTAINING ACCURATE INFORMATION

Proposal form

3.1 Sometimes insurers make the **accuracy** of any information given to them about a risk, in a proposal form for example, material. This is done in proposal forms by adding a declaration or memorandum asserting that all the statements in it are true.

3.2 In *Dawsons Ltd v Bonnin 1922* the policy stated that the proposal form would be the basis of the contract (hence the name 'basis clause'), and be held as incorporated in the policy. The court held the insurers entitled to repudiate the claim (for a lorry destroyed by fire in its garage), because the garage was in the outskirts of Glasgow, whereas the proposal had not given an address where the vehicle was kept, just the insured's address in central Glasgow. The declaration made the garage address a material fact, even though it would have shown the insurers that the risk was less than they thought, and worthy of a lower premium than had actually been levied.

Information required

3.3 Whether or not a proposal form is used, the insurer will need sufficient information for a number of purposes.

- **Identify** the **proposer** and the risk
- **Ascertain** the **type**, extent and size of cover required
- **Provide** a **clear description** of the risk
- **Describe unusual characteristics** which make it susceptible to more, or larger, claims than similar risks

Information required for calculating the premium, commonly called 'rating factors', must be 'material facts' as described above, by definition.

Surveys and medicals

3.4 **Commercial property** and **liability risks**, being for the most part larger and more complex than personal risks, are usually surveyed, even if a proposal is used.

3.5 Proposals for life **assurance** or **personal accident** or health insurance include a sentence by which, on signing the form, the proposer gives the office permission to ask his personal medical attendant (PMA) to submit a report on his medical history, and current ailments and treatment (if any). For larger sums assured in particular, a very thorough medical examination by a specialist diagnostician is required.

3.6 Whoever carries out a survey or medical is the insurer's eyes and ears, and must be given the whole truth in response to his or her questions. Even an independent expert is the insurer's agent in preparing a report for the insurer to rely on, so misleading the expert is effectively the same as misleading the insurer.

3.7 **Survey reports** might include:

- Detailed plans of buildings (or their contents) which are proposed for insurance
- Adequacy of risk reduction measures, with suggestions for improvements
- Suggested appropriate rates of premium
- Any special warranties which should be added to the policy

3.8 Specialist medical attendants will give tentative prognoses of the **development** of any **medical condition** or injury a proposed individual may have, and may include an estimate of his or her life expectation. However it is no longer market practice to ask PMAs to forecast life expectation; this is considered a specialist skill.

3.9 If the insurer's initial impression has not prompted it to reject the risk, it is usually prepared to grant reduced cover pending receipt of surveys or medical reports. In some cases, however, no cover is given unless and until a satisfactory report is received. Property insurers, in particular, may require proof that recommended devices (such as a specified safe) have been installed before they will go on risk; in such cases the surveyor's recommendations become conditions precedent to the contract.

Confidentiality

3.10 If proposers or insureds could not rely on information being kept confidential (for example with regard to the temperature at which a new process operates), they could not afford to risk allowing the insurers' experts to make thorough inspection.

3.11 Insurers and their surveyors concerned with general insurances understand the importance of confidentiality for secret processes, price sensitive information on financial performance and so on.

3.12 In addition, they have an interest in keeping such information secret: if a competitor should get hold of it the **insured's business** could be **damaged**, the values of its insurable risks would be reduced, and the insurer could lose the business. Medical reports, too, are highly confidential; they are not even disclosed to the subject.

Exercise 1

This chapter mentions a number of statutes. As a means of reviewing the chapter so far and previewing what is to come, find out where and why the following are mentioned (some are mentioned several times).

(a) The Marine Insurance Act 1906
(b) The Financial Services Act 1986
(c) The Rehabilitation of Offenders Act 1974
(d) The Theft Act 1968
(e) The Gaming Act 1845
(f) The Sex Discrimination Act 1975
(g) The Race Relations Act 1976
(h) The Married Women's Property Act 1870
(i) The Riot (Damages) Act 1886

---

4 ILLEGAL INSURANCES

4.1 Insurances, although they have some specialist rules, are basically ordinary contracts, and so cannot operate on illegal subject matter, or where performance of the contract would be illegal.

4.2 The rule where the insured is an innocent party to an illegal insurance is that the premium should be **returned**. If an insured is aware of its illegality, however, the premium is only returnable if he or she repudiates the policy. No premium will be returned if the behaviour of the insured or his agent has been fraudulent.

4.3 Insurances can be illegal if the insurer is not licensed to write them under the Insurance Companies Acts.

4.4 The two examples below are clearly instances of illegal insurances which have been effected without the insurer's compliance or knowledge.

(a) One might pay contributions to a personal pension scheme which amount to more than 17½% of one's 'net relevant earnings' in one tax year, and so obtain a larger share of a tax-exempt savings fund than one is entitled to receive tax relief on under Inland Revenue regulations. This can obviously happen accidentally, as many people make contributions before their exact tax liability can be ascertained when the tax year ends. In such cases, the insurer will return the excess contribution immediately the mistake is discovered.

(b) One might insure property which one is not entitled to have, such as stolen property, or property subject to import duty which has been evaded. Again, it is possible for accidents to happen. For example, where large volumes of goods are moved and stored, the insured is not always aware if an item has been omitted from a customs declaration. The insurer would certainly require the position to be rectified as soon as it is discovered, however, otherwise the item is technically not the insured's, being liable to be confiscated.

Gambling

4.5 One of the most important categories of illegality for the insurance industry is gambling, forbidden generally by the Gaming Act 1845, which made all gaming and wagering contracts void, and therefore to the courts' mind non-existent. Policies 'gambling' on the safety of other people's ships and cargoes have been illegal (void) since the Marine Insurance Act 1745, and the rule was extended to people's lives and other property by the Life Assurance Act 1774.

Discrimination

4.6 It is, generally speaking, illegal for UK insurers to discriminate, in their acceptance of proposers or the terms on which they offer cover, on grounds of:

- **Sex** or **marital status** (under the Sex Discrimination Act 1975)
- **Race, religion** (Race Relations Act 1976)
- **Disability** (Disability Discrimination Act 1995)

- except when justifiable on basis of actuarial statistics – eg. women live 4 yrs longer than men (✗)

The 1975 Act, however, allows discrimination which can be justified from actuarial or other statistics obtained from a reasonably reliable source, provided the discrimination is appropriate in each individual case.

Sex

4.7 There is ample statistical evidence, for example, that **women live**, on average, approximately four years **longer** than men. Translated into long-term policy premiums, this means that a woman is very often asked to pay the same life assurance premium (for the same type of policy, with the same sum assured) as a man two to four years younger than she is. Conversely, a life pension payable to a woman would be paid, on average, for a longer period than for a man, so women have to pay larger contributions than men to obtain the same level of benefit.

4.8 In annual personal accident and sickness policies and permanent health insurance, however, statistics show women as having **greater morbidity** than men; this can be reflected in a premium loading of 30% to 100%, and sometimes a seven day 'waiting period' (time excess) before benefit becomes payable, applied onto women's policies.

4.9 Another result is insurance offices' general reluctance to include sickness and disability related to pregnancy in their cover, although a few PHI offices will pay benefit for such a disability if it lasts more than three months longer than the pregnancy.

4.10 Traditional sociological differences between men and women also have their effect on those policies. Weekly or monthly benefits are calculated to replace earned income lost through incapacity, so household skills practitioners (of either sex) and others without predictable regular earned income are regarded by many offices as not having a potential loss to insure against. Other offices will consider proposals for benefits of a reasonable size to pay for their indirect expenses arising from significant disability, such as wages for a replacement housekeeper.

Race

4.11 Insurers do not, any more than practitioners in any other profession, wish to discriminate against paying customers on grounds of race. Unfortunately there are particular instances where a person's background is such that it would be unfair to other insureds with similar policies if apparently discriminatory terms were not offered.

4.12 Notable examples are again to be found in **motor insurance**: premium loadings, for example, are imposed on people without at least twelve months' accident-free driving in the UK, and some insurers even include a UK driving licence in this description. The idea is to give someone used to less congested traffic conditions, different standards of driving manners and/or driving on the right hand side of the road time to become accustomed to driving safely in UK road conditions.

4.13 Another important instance is the effect on a person's health of **prolonged exposure** to a climate very different from that to which he or she is accustomed, which can sometimes affect the underwriting of long-term policies. Under some life policies, and most permanent health insurances, for example, cover for UK policyholders only extends for three or six months' residence in any one year outside listed countries with temperate climates. In some cases, special terms can be arranged for longer periods.

4.14 Some diseases are known to be **genetically linked**, such as sickle-cell anaemia and haemophilia, but underwriters consider such cases individually, as they do diabetes and dwarfism, which are not always hereditary.

Other aspects of illegality

4.15 An insurance which is legal at its inception, but becomes illegal because of changes in laws or circumstances, is automatically **cancelled.**

4.16 **Wholly illegal insurances** should be distinguished from those containing **illegal clauses.** Some such clauses make the whole policy unenforceable at law (eg PPI clauses, see below) but most have no effect, either in themselves or on the rest of the policy.

4.17 It was the market's fear that arbitration clauses would be held ineffective, as attempts to oust the jurisdiction of the courts, which prompted the adoption of a standard arbitration clause.

4.18 The standard clause restricts the use of arbitration to disputes over quantum where the insurer has already agreed to make some payment for a claim, but the arbitrator may still decide that there should be no payment.

4.19 Illegal clauses are **ineffective**, and therefore ignored, whether or not there can be other consequences, such as fines. Similarly, if a whole policy is illegal, no part of it can be enforced: and if it becomes illegal, from that moment the courts will regard it as cancelled, and neither party can oblige the other to perform any more of their duties under it.

5 INSURABLE INTEREST

5.1 Insurers may require proof that you have a **measurable financial interest** in something before they agree to insure it for you, although they often make do with a proposal form or survey which will demonstrate your interest. They need to know the extent to which you will be financially prejudiced if the subject matter of the insurance dies, or is lost or destroyed, as it cannot be insured for a larger sum than that. In some cases, however, interest is hard to value: but so long as there is a real financial value insurers and insured agree on a reasonable sum to insure it for.

5.2 The need for insurable interest has different effects on the main branches of insurance, as follows.

General insurance

5.3 In general insurances, the insured must continue to be at **risk of suffering loss** from the thing insured throughout the policy year. Once a firm has sold its factory, that firm will not be affected if the factory is burnt to the ground, the loss will be the concern of the new owner. The first firm must therefore tell its insurers that the factory is being sold. Although the insurers may agree to carry the risk for the new owners, it is usually most practical to cancel the old cover and start again.

Land

5.4 When land (including houses, factories etc on it) is sold in England and Wales, there is a period between the written agreement to sell and completion of the sale contract under seal, when both parties are interested in the property.

(a) Buyers are well advised to insure the property themselves during this period, and a sort of 'contingency insurance' is often used, to take effect if there is insured damage which the seller's policy does not cover.

(b) As the sale price is normally fixed at the exchange of contracts, however, any damage to the building during this period would be the seller's loss, so fire and perils policies contain a 'change of interest' clause which provides for any benefit from the policy for this damage to be paid to the buyer. This is a convenient way of protecting the insured seller.

Liabilities

5.5 To be able to insure an interest in anything, you must be able to value it in **terms of cash**, but there are exceptions. Unless it is the value of property left in the insured's charge, a potential liability can only be valued when the amount of a **third party's claim** is **agreed**, or fixed by a court. Most liability insurances, therefore, do not have sums insured, just 'limits of liability' showing the maximum the insurer will pay.

Life assurance

5.6 Life assurance itself provides a major complication; how much is your life worth to you? The courts' work includes finding practicable interpretations of statutes. They solved this problem by deciding that interest can be presumed, and cannot be valued:

(a) If it is one's **own life**, in *Wainwright v Bland 1835*

(b) If it is a **wife's interest** in her **husband's life**, in *Reed v Royal Exchange 1795*

(c) After the Married Women's Property Act 1870 had enabled a married woman to own property in her own right, if it is a **husband's interest** in his **wife's life**, in *Griffiths v Fleming and Others 1909*

You can therefore insure your own or your spouse's life, or part of it, for as much as life offices will agree to, subject only to the amount you can afford for premiums.

5.7 To insure anyone else's life, however, you will first need to show **proof** of an **interest** with a financial value, such as a debt owed to you or which you owe the person whose life you propose. It was held in 1902 *(Simcock v Scottish Imperial)* that an employer's interest in the life of an employee is insurable to the extent of wages payable to the employee during the period of notice.

5.8 This has led to a question mark over the validity (so far apparently untested at law) of **key-man insurances**. Businesses use these policies to insure against the considerable loss of turnover or profits, and/or large extra expense, should a valuable employee die, or become disabled. It is likely that should such a policy be tested, the decision in Simcock would be confined to its own facts, and the 'key-man' policy found enforceable.

5.9 S 1 of the Life Assurance Act 1774 says it is illegal to make assurance on any life unless you have an insurable interest in it. In the life assurance field this has been interpreted literally, to mean that your interest need only exist when the policy is effected: *Dalby v India & London Life Assurance Co 1854.*

5.10 As a result, most life policies can be assigned to creditors as **collateral** for loans. Ordinary branch assurances can normally be assigned at will, but 'industrial assurances' on specified close relatives' lives ('burial policies') cannot: the potential moral hazard is such that the relations which can be insured are listed in the Industrial Assurance Acts, and the sum insured is limited to £30.

5.11 Ordinary branch policies must be **assigned in writing,** either by endorsement on the policy or on a separate paper. The insurer should also be notified, to protect the assignee's priority should there be other claimants to the policy benefit. The assignment will then be 'legal', that is, entitling the assignee to claim in person, even if only part of the benefit is assigned (since the Policies of Assurance Act 1867, which governs these assignments, does not require the assured to part with the whole of it).

Marine insurance

5.12 Marine insurances are the exact opposite. In marine policies it is enough, at the inception of the policy, to be **reasonably certain** that you will have an interest in the thing insured before it is lost or damaged, as it is only necessary to prove your interest if and when there is a loss.

Gentlemen's agreements and PPI policies

5.13 Insurable interest must be **legal, valuable, definite,** and **immediate or future.** (Non-marine insurances can be arranged to come into force when a future interest attaches. It would be difficult to collect a new car if this was not so.)

5.14 Ordinary commercial contracts do, however, occasionally contain a clause stating that they are **not enforceable** in the courts, for various practical reasons. The courts respect the parties' wishes, and do not take any notice of them (so long as they are legal in other respects). This means that each party must be confident that the other will perform his or her contractual duties, and the contracts are often called 'gentlemen's agreements'.

5.15 Occasionally businessmen put money at risk in circumstances where they cannot demonstrate their interest, although it is otherwise legal, or the subject matter is a financial interest which could be totally destroyed before it can be valued. Insurable interest rules preclude legal insurance in these cases but, provided the insurer is satisfied that the interest (present or future) is real, a policy will occasionally be issued.

5.16 In marine insurance these policies are known as **policy proof of interest (PPI) policies**, and are identifiable by the clause in which the insurer waives proof of the interest or its value. This clause makes the policy void, but it will be honoured unless the insurer receives proof of fraud.

6 PROXIMATE CAUSE

The rules of causation

6.1 The insurer will not pay a claim unless the loss or accident in question is covered by the policy. It is therefore necessary to discover the true cause of the loss. Specialists in this field are known as 'loss adjusters'.

6.2 Even very simple demonstrations of the cause of a loss involve use of the **rules of causation**.

6.3 The rules are basically extremely straightforward: a *cause* (for example an unexpected sneeze) produces an **effect** (spectacles fall off your nose onto a concrete floor, and break). That is an example of a 'chain of causation'.

6.4 However, the insurer who pays for the spectacles under an 'all risks' policy, for example, might discover that a flaw in the spectacle frames (or the fitting of the lenses) caused them to break, and was the reason why the shock was sufficient to shatter the lenses: that would be an **intervening cause (novus actus interveniens)** breaking the chain of causation, and wholly responsible for the loss. It would give the insured a right of action against the manufacturers for replacement (or the value) of the spectacles.

6.5 On the other hand, the insurer might examine the **cause** of the sneeze, and be able to prove that it occurred as the insured's involuntary reaction to sniffing glue, which (in the imaginary circumstances) would bring the loss within a policy exclusion of 'losses occurring while the insured is under the influence of alcohol or unprescribed prohibited drugs'.

6.6 There is a limit, however, to how far back in the **chain of causation** it is necessary to go. As you can see from the above example, the answer to the question 'do I need to look any further back?' depends on the reason why you are looking. An insurer covering the peril 'fire' without any qualification will not need to discover whether it was caused by malicious persons, and would not look for a cause of the fire unless presented with some indication that it may have been caused by the insured. If there are exclusions which may apply, the insurer will need to be satisfied as to the *efficient cause* of the fire.

Proximate cause

6.7 **Proximate cause** may be considered as the active and efficient cause of loss which sets in motion a train of events which brings about a result without the intervention of any force started and working actively from a new and independent source.

6.8 No insurance claim can succeed unless the loss is proximately caused by a **peril insured against**. According to the case of *Pawsey v Scottish Union and National 1907*, the proximate cause of loss is not the most recent cause but the 'active, efficient cause which sets in motion on a train of events which brings about a result, without the intervention of any force started and working actively from a new and independent source'.

6.9 The determination of the proximate cause of loss should be by common sense principle: in the legal case of *Leyland Shipping Corporation v Norwich Union Insurance Corporation 1918* a ship which had been previously torpedoed sank in a storm. It was held that the torpedoing was the proximate cause of loss.

6.10 Sometimes there are **two separate causes** of an accident or loss. If both are 'efficient' causes, and one is not insured or is excluded, it will be necessary to try and identify the separate damage caused by each.

6.11 Where damage cannot be separated, the following rules apply.

(a) If one cause is insured and the other is *not* excluded, the policy will pay.

(b) If one cause is insured and the other is excluded, the claim must be rejected: to do otherwise would make nonsense of the policy.

Inquests

6.12 Death certificates usually give at least some guidance as to cause, for example in the case of claims for capital benefits under personal accident policies. If the cause of a death is not shown on the certificate, and sometimes even if it is, an **inquest** ('fatal accident inquiry' in Scotland) will be held, largely at public expense, to determine the circumstances of the death.

6.13 Inquests are also required to determine the cause of fires in London, and a verdict of arson could exclude a claim for fire damage from cover in some circumstances (if the insured or the insured's employee was found to be responsible, for example, or in some cases if the fire comes under the heading of 'malicious damage').

6.14 Inquest verdicts are findings of fact which bind insurers as well as the general public.

6.15 Most motor policies also provide for '**manslaughter cover**' - representation on criminal charges involving reckless or careless driving causing death.

Coverage

6.16 It should be apparent that it is as important to ascertain exactly what a policy covers, as to discover the exact cause of a loss. 'Rules of construction' govern these decisions. Examples are as follows.

(a) **Lists** followed by a **general term** ('ducks, geese and other fowl') are construed as referring only to items of the same kind as those listed: the example might not include a hawk, as it is not domesticated.

(b) **Express** terms overrule **implied terms** (for example, although taking reasonable care of the subject matter of an insurance, so as to avoid loss, is implied in all policies, insurers can amend this by requiring inspections of insured property at regular intervals).

Exercise 2

Explain the doctrine of proximate cause quoting the leading case on the subject and explain its practical relevance to claims under Personal Accident policies.

Solution

Pawsey is the leading case. It would improve your answer to quote other cases too. Personal accident insurance is dealt with in Chapter 18, but its name is self-explanatory so you should be able to attempt the second part of the question. It is seldom appreciated that the operative cause of most of these policies require the event to result from accident solely and independently of any other cause.

7 INDEMNITY

7.1 'Indemnity' in common parlance means **compensation** for a loss incurred. In insurance it refers to a payment that restores the insured as far as possible to the financial position that he was in before he suffered any loss or damage.

7.2 **Indemnity** and **insurable interest** are **interlinked**: the indemnity principle prevents an insured from recovering a sum greater than his insurable interest.

7.3 All insurance policies other than life and personal accident insurance are subject to the principle of indemnity. The measure of indemnity for pecuniary insurances and liability insurances is simply the **value of the loss**, however that is arrived at. For property insurance the position is not as straightforward because what constitutes the restoration of the insured's previous financial position is open to interpretation.

Limits of indemnity

7.4 Where there is a limit of indemnity, there is always the chance that a claim will be larger than the limit. Insurers normally include a term explaining that should this happen, they can at any time pay the insured a **sum equal to the limit** and allow the insured to continue negotiations and defence, and to bear any expense in excess of the limit.

Assessors

7.5 For claims in excess of a certain amount, if the claimant is unhappy with the loss adjuster's recommendation, it could be worth his while to **engage** his own **assessor** (another loss adjuster) to make his own assessment of the value of the claim and negotiate a settlement with insurers.

Total or partial loss?

7.6 The distinction can be important, especially for property insurances which, in the absence of a condition to the contrary, achieve their purpose in full by paying for a total loss, and must be started again from scratch to cover replacement property. In marine cargo insurances, the answer will have a bearing on whether an excess applies: but the policy may provide for settlement on the basis of 'total loss of part', where the insured consignment consists of several packages, barrels or the like, and one of them is lost or destroyed.

The circumstances of the insured

7.7 The measure of indemnity to be paid for a claim depends on the circumstances of the loss. Estimates for reinstating an uninhabitable building, insured for £1m (reinstatement value), may vary, say, from £500,000 for replacing it with one of modern design, to £750,000 for rebuilding it to its original specification.

Exercise 3

What is the indemnity principle? Give a practical example of one of the main insurance classes where it will operate.

Describe two examples of property insurance policies where the principle is modified.

Solution

Indemnity applies to all policies of insurance except life and personal accident insurance on your own life or your spouse's. Look back in the text for an example.

Indemnity may be modified if no clear measure of indemnity can be agreed, or to allow the insured to receive more than a 'fair' amount (eg 'new for old') or to allow the insurer to provide less than indemnity.

8 EXCESS AND FRANCHISE

8.1 Insurers have a great fear: that people who are insured will be less careful to avoid loss and damage to whatever is insured, than they would be if they carried the risk themselves. One means of combating this tendency is imposition of an **excess**, which makes the insured responsible for the first £x of each claim.

8.2 Excesses are useful underwriting tools. In most instances, a proposal from the insured to carry a larger excess than the prescribed minimum will be rewarded by a discount in the premium quoted.

8.3 An alternative means of engaging the insured's interest in avoiding small losses is a **franchise**, which excludes any claim from cover unless it is worth more than a fixed sum: any claim larger than that sum will be paid in full.

8.4 There is a second reason for excesses and franchises, that the **cost of** administering and paying a claim can be much more than the settlement cheque, so if insurers receive a lot of small claims, the expenses element of premiums will tend to increase premium rates.

9 UNDERINSURANCE

9.1 Sometimes it is considered unnecessary, or uneconomic, to insure an article for its full value. It may be thought highly unlikely that thieves would be able (or willing) to remove 100% of the contents of a stock room.

First loss

9.2 In these cases a first loss policy can be helpful, to **restrict** the **maximum cover** to the reduced level required. It is important that insurers should be given an accurate valuation as if the property were to be insured in full. The premium will be calculated on the declared (full) value. A discount is then allowed, whose size depends on:

(a) The office/class of business

(b) The extent of underinsurance agreed on

(c) Contemporary practice, for example:

Insured percentage of full value	*Scale of discount from full cover premium*
90%	0.5%
85%	5.0%
75%	10.0%
50%	30.0%
25%	50.0%

Insurers' sanctions

9.3 Insurers also employ sanctions to protect their adequately insured risks against underinsured or undervalued risks. The simplest example is a **warranty** that property will be insured for its full value; underinsurance amounts to misdescription of a rating factor, which entitles insurers to avoid a (commercial) policy, if the underinsurance is serious enough.

Average

9.4 A more common sanction used against underinsurance is **average**, not in the marine sense but in the sense of a reduction of the sum payable on the claim as follows:

> 'such proportion of the said loss as the sum insured by this policy bears to the total value of the said property'.

The formula for calculating the amount payable on the claim is:

$$\frac{\text{Sum insured (SI)}}{\text{Full value (FV)}} \times \text{loss}$$

9.5 Average is not a suitable practice for some insurances (especially liability insurances) where the criterion is not 'full insurance' but 'how much cover do I need, and how much cover can I get?' Where the claimant's costs and expenses are paid in addition to the limit of liability, however, this item can be the subject of a proportional settlement with the insured.

9.6 Thus if a claim is settled (or damages are awarded) for an amount which exceeds the limit of indemnity, the practice in some cases is for the insurer to pay the same percentage of those additional costs and expenses as they pay of the settlement or award, for example:

Limit of indemnity £1m
Damages awarded £1.5m
Claimant's costs and expenses (incurred with the insurer's written consent) £6000

Insurer pays towards damages £1m
Insurer pays towards claimant's costs and expenses £4000

Under some policies, however, claimant's costs would be paid in full.

9.7 Average cannot apply in life assurances and similar, as they are not, strictly speaking, contracts of indemnity.

10 SUBROGATION

10.1 Subrogation is the right of one person to stand in the **legal place** of another and avail himself of all the rights and remedies of that other. If the rights have already been exercised, subrogation entitles one only to the proceeds.

10.2 For example, if your car is damaged by another motorist's negligence you can claim compensation from your insurers and from the negligent motorist. Normally you would simply claim under your insurance policy. Your insurers are then **subrogated** to your rights against the third party and they can recover any money paid to you under your policy.

10.3 The case usually cited is *Castellain v Preston 1883.* Preston's house burnt down after he had completed sale of it and he received the loss from the insurer. He also obtained the full purchase price from the buyer and therefore obtained the value of the loss twice. The insurers, standing in the place of their chairman, Castellain, sued and recovered their money.

10.4 As stated above, subrogation rights are only acquired after an **indemnity** has been provided and therefore the principle is only applicable where indemnity applies.

10.5 The common law position is usually modified in general insurance policies. In these the subrogation clause repeats the insurer's right to exercise its insured's rights, but enables the insurer to take any necessary steps in such an exercise before it pays the relevant claim (provides indemnity). This enables the insurer, for example, to obtain witnesses' statements and have writs issued to protect third party money or property.

Waiver of subrogation rights

10.6 In theory insurers would very frequently find themselves having to exercise subrogation rights against another insurer. Because of the administrative inconvenience and cost it is often the case in practice that insurers enter into agreements to waive subrogation rights against each other. The theory is that rights forsaken are likely to be balanced by claims not pursued. The best-known example is the '**knock-for-knock agreement**' on motor insurance.

11 CONTRIBUTION

11.1 The chief respect in which '**universal average**' (the use of average conditions in all policies) would simplify claims handling is when two policies are **called into contribution** in payment of a loss. In this context, contribution is the process by which a loss is shared equitably (or as is dictated by their conditions) between two or more insurers who are both (or all) responsible for paying at least some of that loss to the same insured. The circumstances which must exist before contribution can occur are as follows:

(a) All the policies must protect the **same insured**.

(b) They must be **in force** when the loss occurs.

(c) They must **cover the property** which is the subject of the claim against that same peril which has operated to cause the loss, and be liable to pay something for the claim.

11.2 Two or more policies which do exactly the same job are concurrent. However if one of them covers additional property, additional insureds, different perils, and/or does so under different conditions which affect the claim in question, it does not rank concurrently with the other policy or policies.

Contribution and indemnity

11.3 A **rule is necessary**, to prevent an insured recovering more than the amount of a loss, when, by accident or otherwise, the insured is protected by several policies which are all liable to pay the same loss.

Apportionment

11.4 Contribution is a very old principle: its application to various commercial and other circumstances was reviewed in *Harbert's Case 1584*, and summed up in *Dering v Earl of Winchelsea 1787*:

> 'the law requires equality; one shall not bear the burden in ease of the rest '

Narrower range policies

11.5 The first 'contribution' clauses provided that whichever policy concerns itself **most exclusively** with the property in question should pay for the loss, the prime candidate being a policy which covers no other property, thus deserving the description narrower range.

11.6 A common example of its application occurs when a car with **comprehensive insurance** is broken into, or involved in an accident. If a carriage clock belonging to the driver or a passenger, just collected from the repairer's, perhaps, is stolen (or damaged in the crash), the motor policy would pay up to a fixed sum for its loss under the 'rugs, coats and personal effects' section (unless especially valuable items are excluded).

11.7 If the owner has 'personal effects all risks', or 'contents all risks including temporary removal from the house' cover under a household policy which covers the loss, the household insurer will pay the claim. Household cover could well be adequate to reimburse the full value lost, too, leaving the small motor policy extension to deal with, for example, the week's shopping stolen (or mashed beyond recognition) at the same time.

Contribution and excess

11.8 A later clause adopted by the market, and still common, particularly in certain types of liability insurances, turns the policy into an excess policy if another insurer is also liable to pay the claim in question.

11.9 The clause compels the insured to **claim** from the **other policy first**. However if that insurer's claim payment is inadequate to cover the loss, the clause allows the insured to make a second claim under it, for a sum to make up the balance of the loss. This is sometimes called a '**co-existing cover**' clause.

Contribution and average

11.10 Where one policy is subject to average, it often happens that another, which is not (but is also liable for the same loss), contains a clause which '**imports average**' into it, so that both policies calculate the amount payable on the same basis.

11.11 In some cases, for example where policies are not subject to average, the maximum liability basis is used, contributions being calculated in proportion to the separate sums insured.

Non-contribution

11.12 **Non-contribution clauses** are also common; they mean what their name says. They are used notably, but by no means exclusively, to prevent a policy's being called into contribution with what would otherwise be a non-concurrent policy (of necessity, as both would not cover identical lists of perils) in another branch of insurance.

11.13 Contribution in these circumstances (in particular) can be extremely complicated, and as, for example, the loss could be valued on different bases, a matter for a skilled independent loss adjuster. The mutual exclusion of each other's specialist risks by public liability insurers and motor insurers (who exclude some of the risks of loading and unloading commercial vehicles, loading and unloading except by the driver), is an example of a much more straightforward market approach.

11.14 However a commonsense answer may be employed, with both insurers paying an equal proportion of the third party's claim.

Market agreements

11.15 Market agreements governing insurers' contributions to the same claim are a simpler, and therefore cheaper, method of resolving the complexities of incompatible contribution provisions. They are used especially where policies in **two branches of insurance** are liable to pay one claim.

11.16 Other examples of such solutions are as follows.

(a) Claims which might either belong to a **public liability** or an **employer's liability policy**, or a motor policy or an employer's liability policy. The employer's liability insurer pays.

(b) **Multiple motor accidents** where several insurers receive a claim for injury from someone who was not driving a car insured by any of them. Insurers share the claim equally.

(c) The notorious '**knock for knock**' **agreement** which, in the simplest circumstances it governs, provides for each of two motor insurers to bear the cost of their own insureds' damage claims under their comprehensive policies. Several insurers have now withdrawn from this arrangement.

11.17 The main disadvantage of such market agreements is that **not all insurers** who may be involved in such situations are **parties** to the agreements.

11.18 Note that many policies contain a warranty that **no other insurance** will cover the property or liability in question, unless insurers' permission has been obtained. There are many reasons why insurers find this useful, and permission is sometimes a formality. However if a proposer neglects to declare the existence of another relevant policy (providing it is actually in force), the insurer using this warranty will be entitled to avoid its policy.

Exercise 4

Explain, with appropriate examples, each of the following:

(a) Utmost good faith
(b) Proximate cause
(c) Subrogation

Solution

Look back to sections 1, 6 and 10 of this chapter.

Chapter roundup

- **Utmost good faith** is a duty imposed on the two parties to a contract to disclose all facts material to the contract. The duty is very strict, although there are limits. Insurers take various steps themselves to ensure that they have all the information they need.
- Insurances cannot operate on **illegal subject-matter**, and they cannot *discriminate* on grounds of sex or race.
- The **insurable interest** is the extent to which the insured will be financially prejudiced by a loss. This cannot be measured in advance in the case of liabilities and so limits of liability are agreed. It also cannot be measured for life assurance where the value of the cover is directly related to the premiums paid.
- **Proximate cause** is the active and efficient cause of loss which sets in motion a train of events which brings about a result without the intervention of any force started and working actively from a new and independent source.
- **Indemnity** restores the insured to the financial position that he was in before he suffered any loss. There can be difficulties in applying indemnity depending upon the class of insurance, the circumstances of the insured, and the extent of the loss.
- **Underinsurance** is sometimes expedient from the insured's point of view. Insurers are likely to apply 'average', reducing the sum payable in the event of a loss.
- **Subrogation** allows the insurer to exercise the rights of the insured.
- **Contribution** is the process by which a loss is shared equitably between two or more insurers who are covering the same insured item.

Test your knowledge

1 Explain the duty of disclosure. (see paras 1.4, 1.5)

2 When is the underwriter not protected by the law against accidental concealment of facts? (2.2)

3 What information (in brief) does an insurer need? (3.3)

4 Explain what is meant by insurable interest. (5.1)

5 Explain what is meant by indemnity. (7.1)

6 How will an insurer deal with underinsurance? (9.3, 9.4)

7 Define subrogation. (10.1)

8 Explain the circumstances that must exist before contribution can occur. (11.1)

Now try illustrative question 17 at the end of the Study Text

Chapter 17

CLASSES OF GENERAL INSURANCE

This chapter covers the following topics.

Introduction

We have already had reason to mention various different kinds of insurance. In this chapter we look at the different classes in more detail, following the structure of the classes identified in the EC Directive on the topic.

In the following chapter we go on to consider the various types of insurances of the *person* that are relevant in a business context. Here we are concerned with the insurance of *things*.

Much of the material is also highly relevant to Part D of this Study Text on the Management of Corporate Assets.

1 CLASSES OF INSURANCE 12/96, 6/99, 12/99

1.1 Insurances for things (real and personal property, cash and negotiable instruments etc), and choses in action (rights enforceable at law) are insured in separate categories initially because of their very different characteristics and behaviour.

1.2 In the schedules to the Insurance Companies Act 1982 general insurances (mostly insurances for **things**) are sorted into seventeen classes, as required by EC Directive 73/239. The Department of Trade and Industry can authorise insurers to write insurances, and minor incidental covers, under one or more of these seventeen separate headings. They can be grouped in several ways.

The classes

1.3 The EC's classes of insurance can be grouped to be more easily memorable, for example as follows.

(a) There is one class for **accidents** which cause death or injury, or **diseases** which incapacitate (class 1).

(b) Five classes consist of specific sorts of **property** which are insured (land vehicles, railway rolling stock, aircraft, ships and goods in transit (classes 3 to 7 inclusive).

(c) Three describe **perils** which can cause restricted sorts of loss: sickness insured against for terms less than five years (class 2); fire, explosions, subsidence and natural perils causing damage to property not in group 1.4(b) (class 8), except for hail, frost, theft and other occurrences, which have their own class (class 9).

(d) Four relate to **liabilities** (motor, aircraft and ships, separated from 'own damage' (classes 10 to 12), with class 13 for any other liabilities.

(e) Four are for purely **financial** losses: credit insurances (class 14); guaranteeing people who have given guarantees, and the provision of bail bonds etc (class 15); legal expenses policies (class 17); and miscellaneous financial loss insurances, and anything not included in other classes (class 16).

2 INSURANCES OF PROPERTY: FIRE INSURANCE

Material damage insurances 12/96

2.1 Most material damage policies protect either **buildings** (including their fixtures and fittings) or **moveable property**, as 'contents' of buildings, or on its own. In most cases those policies cover the insured's loss from loss of or damage to the property by fire and/or usual perils, or all risks, that is all perils of a kind described in the policy and not excluded from it.

Coverage and exclusions

2.2 It is very important to ensure that you know what a policy will and will not cover, and the exclusions which will reduce or negate its cover, before you decide to rely on it. For example, the list of '**usual perils**' or '**additional perils**' added to commercial fire policies, and normally included in personal property insurances, can vary. Moreover, insurers may require an additional premium for protection against a particular peril, if a proposer is particularly exposed to it.

Standard Fire Policy

2.3 Whether damage is covered depends on the **circumstances** involved and the **terms** of the policy in force. The Standard Fire Policy (Material Damage) pays reference to loss, destruction or damage not only specifically from fire but also from lightning and explosion.

Fire insurance

2.4 Fire insurance covers the cost of **repairing fire damage** to material property, which was not intended to be burnt; or, if the property is too badly damaged to be an economic proposition for repair, the insurer will pay to the insured in money the **value** of the **whole property** (not exceeding the sum insured). 'Fire' insurance also includes cover for:

(a) Consequential damage, such as smoke damage from actual ignition or damage caused by falling debris

(b) Incidental expense, for example on necessary debris removal

(c) Fees to architects and surveyors

2.5 More remote financial loss, such as loss of profits, is not covered, however. Some more remote consequential losses may be included automatically or by extension (see below).

2.6 **Loss reduction measures** themselves are included in the cover, such as damage and loss caused by:

- Attempts to stop the fire or save property from it
- Water damage by the fire brigade's efforts or from sprinklers activated by the fire
- Damage caused by rescuers breaking in
- Property damaged to prevent the fire spreading, or while being removed to safety

These, too, are examples of **direct consequential damage.**

Extensions

2.7 A common extension, not always optional, covers increase in the cost of reinstating the property due to **local councils' requiring changes** in location or design (provided they ask for these after the fire, and not because of any shortcomings unconnected with the fire). This expense is often included in the sum insured, but can have a separate sum provided for it.

2.8 Cover against **sprinkler systems** operating or leaking through damage, unusual heat, a passing pipe smoker, mechanical defects not found by regular inspections and the like has been available as a fire insurance extension since 1978. **Sprinkler leakage policies** or extensions carry detailed requirements as to maintenance, and how they must be left if the premises is unattended for an extended period.

3 PERILS **6/96, 12/96**

3.1 Over the decades fire insurers have been asked to cover property against other common or memorable perils. Insurers:

- Offer a selection of these as **one or more optional extensions** to a fire policy
- Include them in a single **fire and perils** cover
- Include them as a normal part of a **package policy**

Lightning

3.2 Lightning is one of the causes of loss covered in the Standard Fire Policy (Material Damage). It is mentioned separately because it can cause extensive damage to buildings, or to electrical equipment, without actually starting a fire: any associated scorching may not be sufficient evidence that **actual ignition** (necessary for a fire claim) followed the strike.

Earthquake

3.3 While most people have some idea of what an earthquake is and does, it surprises some of us that small ones happen on average a couple of times a year in the UK, though they are seldom strong enough to shake things off shelves. Some earth movement is also due to subsidence caused by mining, however. It is therefore sensible to obtain some official confirmation, if possible, that an **earthquake** occurred in the same time and place as the damage you wish to claim for under this cover, before actually submitting the claim, as **subsidence** is a separate peril.

Subsidence, landslip and heave

3.4 **Subsidence** became a popular additional peril in the early 1970s, when building societies asked for it to be added to the list of standard perils in household insurances. There was a spate of claims due to a series of dry summers lowering the water table, causing foundations in shrinking soils (particularly clay) to move and break. It frequently keeps company with

landslip cover, which is especially desirable and difficult to obtain in areas subject to coastal erosion. **Heave** is useful where, for example, buildings replace recently removed hedges and woods: the ground, recovering from the persistent drying action of generations of deep roots, swells, tilting and breaking foundations.

Flood, storm and tempest

3.5 Flood, storm and tempest are often excluded or added in together.

(a) '**Flood**' to insurers is **water overflowing** or **breaking out** from natural watercourses, reservoirs, canals and the like, but **not pipes or tanks** (as bursting or overflowing of pipes and tanks is another peril, frequently written for both water and oil tanks).

(b) '**Storm**' has been held to mean **wind plus rain or snow**, at least one of them severe, but 'windstorm' cover is also available, which should mean just high winds.

Frost

3.6 Frost insurance is particularly useful for **crops** liable to such damage, although frost can also ruin partly erected buildings as it freezes any water in concrete, cracks, or containers, causing the water to expand. Frost is, however, sometimes found among 'usual perils'.

Impact

3.7 Impact frequently covers **collision** with **moving animals**, and sometimes even trains, as well as road vehicles. Commercial covers may exclude damage by the insured's vehicles.

Riot

3.8 Riot is another peril with a technical meaning. (See Chapter 2)

3.9 Riot damage is considered to be the **responsibility** of the **police**, as they must have failed in their duties to keep the peace and protect property. The Riot (Damages) Act 1886 allows claims for such damage, provided they are presented to the police in writing within 14 days of the event. This is why insurers usually require notice of riot damage claims within 7 days: there is still 7 days for the insurer (or insured) to give the police notice that they will be asked to pay for the damage. Insurers exclude the cover for Northern Ireland risks. A claim on the insurer is more advisable than a direct claim on the police because it may transpire that the event was not a riot, and then the claim will be for **malicious damage**, if the policy covers that peril.

Malicious damage

3.10 Someone may do (or omit to do) something without a lawful excuse, knowing that damage or destruction of another person's property will (or not caring that it could) result, causing malicious damage (or 'criminal damage' or 'arson').

3.11 Policy wordings vary, but policies covering risks in Northern Ireland **exclude malicious damage**. This is a standard market exclusion; the government pay compensation for damage connected with terrorist organisations.

Accidental damage

3.12 Almost *all* insurances protect against accidental damage (or injury) and loss. This means that there must be **visible physical** results arising from an external cause and involving a degree of force (which can be vestigial, for example if poison is accidentally left in reach of livestock), and that the insured **must not expect** (or at least intend) it to happen. Assaults and malicious damage are 'accidents' in this sense.

3.13 Accidental damage, qualified by exclusion of some of its causes, can be an additional peril applied to particular types of property covered by a policy (such as fixed glass and pottery fixtures in a building). It can be the principal or only basis of cover under some policies on contents, or on individual items of property.

Other perils

3.14 Other causes of damage commonly found among 'usual perils' are falling aerials and masts, aircraft and other artificial flying objects, and occasionally trees. Theft can be in the list, or it can be a separate option, or under a separate policy.

Exercise 1

In January 1993 an article appeared in the *Administrator* on 'Insurance and the computer'. Describe the sort of cover you think ought to be taken out to protect an organisation's computer system.

Solution

Your list should have been a long one. The article notes that perils include fire, flood, theft, accidental damage, deliberate sabotage and viruses. The downtime may result in lost sales; there will be a cost for reconstructing the data lost. Both hardware and software should be covered. Laptop or notebook computers should be covered both on and off the premises. Insurers generally require the insured to take certain precautions (back-ups, passwords etc).

---

4 THEFT 12/96

Definition

4.1 Theft means **temporarily** or **permanently relieving** another natural or legal person of his, her or its property, intentionally, and without permission or legal excuse.

Classification

4.2 This comprises a very wide range of activities indeed, in respect of possession of, or rights to, both tangible and abstract property. Insurers classify losses from theft into various different policy types, chiefly according to the characteristics of the **type of material** at risk.

(a) **Cash, negotiable instruments,** and **tokens** are either **excluded** from 'theft' insurances or **dealt with under separate terms**, as they are easy to move and dispose of, and can be very difficult to identify and so recover.

(b) **Insurance** of **abstract property** such as patents, which are more easily stolen by copying or by other actions done at a distance than by removing items from the insured's possession, is a **separate,** small specialist area. Newspapers, broadcasters and the like can protect themselves against **unintentionally committing** theft of this sort (and so having to pay damages) by expensive specialist liability policies.

4.3 Insurance also classifies theft according to the **status of the thief**.

(a) Theft by an **insured** will **not** be **covered** under a 'theft' insurance; nor if committed by an insured's **employees** or **members** of his or her **household** (the policy affords them indirect protection, and it is possible but very difficult to prove that the insured could have been in collusion).

(b) Insurance of theft of a **commercial insured's money** or **stock by employees** (or even members of an insured partnership) requires quite different loss reduction measures from other kinds of theft. As it more frequently involves manipulation of figures in the books or computer records, than physically breaking into a place, the risks are rated differently too. Such thefts are therefore dealt with under:

(i) **Fidelity guarantee** (FG) insurances, covering the insured's property (see later in this chapter)

(ii) **Money had and received** policies, covering money which the insured holds in trust, usually for customers such as premiums held by insurance brokers to pass on to insurers

Most organisations handling **customers' money** will normally have both covers.

Personality

4.4 Theft cover for **portable material property (personality)** is generally under a separate theft policy, or occasionally included in a list of 'usual perils' added to a fire insurance. In either case, cover is restricted to thefts in which the thieves use force or violence either to gain entry to the insured buildings or leaving the premises.

Attractiveness

4.5 Property insured against theft is classified according to its **attractiveness to thieves**, and this is reflected in proposal forms, schedules and the percentage rate of the sum insured charged for premium. Generally speaking, small items with high value to weight ratios are most attractive, but shortages, market price fluctuations, fashions, and occasionally motivation have a bearing on an article's attractiveness.

Pilferage

4.6 Pilferage is not generally insurable because:

(a) It is **difficult to identify** what has been stolen as distinct from losses caused by errors in, say, stock records.

(b) The thief could, possibly, be an **employee** of the insured, in which case the loss falls under 'fidelity guarantee'.

(c) Most **losses**, whoever is responsible, are **so small** that they are disproportionately expensive to claim for, let alone for the insurer to process and reimburse. Nevertheless pilferage overall can be a major source of loss and can reduce an organisation's competitiveness: reduction measures should be reviewed frequently, although losses are generally transferred to customers. It has been said that this increases shop prices by 3% in some areas.

Loss reduction measures

4.7 An important part of a commercial theft insurance contract is the insured's continual use of prescribed **loss reduction measures**. The initial survey ensures that if locks, bars, safes and burglar alarms are not of suitable type and in working order, the insurer will ask for appropriate repairs and replacements to be done. If any insured premises is protected by a burglar alarm, its proper use and maintenance is specifically required in the policy.

Buildings

4.8 It must be difficult to steal a building unless by illicit manipulation of paperwork or by 'squatting' in it; the first method does not involve physical destruction, and the second should be excluded by insurers' requirements for care of unattended buildings to prevent squatters gaining access, although if they do, damage they cause could be described as 'malicious'. So why are buildings insured against theft? Thieves frequently cause malicious damage, but they may also steal **fixtures**, and, perhaps more importantly, they can cause considerable **damage** in breaking in, or attempting to do so.

4.9 In the case of buildings theft cover protects against the following.

(a) Theft of fixtures

(b) 'Consequential' damage from successful or attempted thefts

(c) Incidental malicious damage if that is not excluded (or unless that peril is specifically covered)

Money insurances

4.10 'Money' insurances, which protect **cash** and **near cash**, take account of the things firms habitually do with money, such as counting it into wage packets, keeping some of it to hand to provide change, or allowing collectors and specified employees to keep it at home overnight when it would be inconvenient or difficult to do otherwise. Money kept in any such circumstances is insured up to a **set sum**, the sizes of the different limits reflecting the different degrees of risk involved.

4.11 Only a short period will be available for reporting losses to be claimed for. This reflects the necessity of reliable systems for regular checks on sums held. As in most cases, insurers' required measures for reducing the risk are a reflection of sound commonsense business practice. They will wish to know about the quality of the safe or strongroom in which money is kept and to have details of audit procedures and regularity of checks.

5 ALL RISKS 12/96

5.1 All-risks policies offer wider cover than that provided by the Standard Fire Policy. Several types are available, including the following.

5.2 **Industrial all-risks policies** extend the basic cover to such items as sprinkler leakage, water damage, subsidence, theft and so on. Some losses, for example war risks, are still excluded however.

5.3 **Contractors all-risks policies** cover building and engineering contractors against loss or damage to the works for which they are made responsible by their contracts of hire. Such contracts contain insurance clauses requiring contractors to insure both the works and themselves from injury.

5.4 Other types of all-risks cover in various circumstances are mentioned in the following sections.

6 TRANSPORTATION INSURANCES: GOODS IN TRANSIT 6/96

The need for insurance

6.1 Transit risks reflect the **different ways goods** are **carried** by air, ship, inland waterway, road and (by whatever means) in the post.

6.2 Suppose it is a matter of whether your own goods, conveyed from between your sites to another in your own transport, should be insured. You would assess the risk of loss and damage from known possible causes, and consider whether the premium would be a good investment in the particular circumstances, as opposed to retaining the risk of loss. Similarly, you would compare the additional cost and inconvenience involved in sending the goods in small consignments at intervals, with the resulting reduction in possible size of unit loss.

6.3 If you are transporting other people's goods, you would be primarily interested in the terms of the **contract of carriage**, and in particular the following.

(a) The possibility of **occurrences** of a sort for which the contract would render you **liable** to compensate the goods' owner for loss or damage.

(b) The **limits** of your **liability** per package, unit of weight, or whatever, imposed by the contract.

(c) The chance that the circumstances of any occurrence may invoke **proviso terms,** or make you liable outside the contract's terms, so that you would be liable for the full value of lost and damaged goods, and perhaps for fixed penalties or compensation for consequential losses too.

Contractual liability

6.4 You could contract on the basis that the goods' owner or other customer carries all the risks to the goods, in full; this could be reasonable for commercial customers, if your freight charges (fees) were commensurately reasonable. You could modify this by agreeing to pay compensation for loss or damage which the customer proves is due to someone's wilful misconduct for which you, as the employer, are responsible. Like the Post Office, you might not accept any liability except under special forms of contract, such as registered post.

6.5 You could accept liability (which need not be limited to the value of the goods) for failing to deliver at all, if the customer can show this is due to your negligence, but you could refuse to accept liability in cases where you could prove it was caused by an event outside your control, such as the following.

(a) **Customers' fault**, including mistakes, inadequate packing, or failing to produce the consignment for carriage, or to make adequate arrangements for their collection within a reasonable, or a specified, time

(b) **Legal confiscation or seizure**, which might cover anything from requisition for emergency services, confiscation by HM Customs & Excise, to seizure by court order as security for damages in a pending action

(c) **War**, with other degrees of conflict, riot and strikes specified in the same way as insurers specify them

(d) **Acts of God,** provided they are the sole cause of loss or damage

6.6 Additionally, you could protect yourself by limiting the compensation you are prepared to pay.

(a) Your limit could be **per package** (you might even provide a choice of limits, attracting different freight charges).

(b) You could relate the maximum figure per consignment to its **gross weight** (multiplying this by £800 or £2,000 per metric tonne, say), and using the resulting figure to calculate your limit for partial loss (or damage) claims.

(c) You could agree to carry consignments with **higher liabilities** for compensation provided you could choose in advance what items to carry, and could be paid an additional payment.

Commercial carriers

6.7 Whether commercial carriers carry insurance is generally a matter of choice. Where the customer chooses to carry all or most of the risks, it is the customer's choice whether to insure them, provided insurance is available: it may not be, for carriage of attractive goods in areas where there is a high risk of theft. The carrier may have a special scheme or agency to provide cover. British Rail and the Post Office accept some liability for most types of goods they carry, up to a specified amount.

The cover available

6.8 We outline above the distribution of losses between carrier and customer in inland contracts of carriage. If this is under a **standard form of contract** such as Road Haulage

Association, British Transport Commission or 'CMR' (Contrat de Merchandises par Route) terms, insurers are familiar with it; they will need to read non-standard contracts first, but if satisfied that the additional liability is acceptable, they will extend their cover to include it.

6.9 Insurers may **exclude high value** items such as jewellery; an additional premium may secure cover, or, as is the case with carriers' customary exclusion of dangerous goods (one list of which includes cattle) the carriers could put the same exclusions into their contracts. Such items require special handling, so many carriers will not accept them.

6.10 Cover can be arranged **per package, per consignment** (which can be several packages), or **per year**. It can cover:

- Specified perils
- 'All risks'
- Your liability or contractual liability to compensate your customers

6.11 'All-risks' cover in this context can **exclude delay, consequential loss, inherent vice** of the goods and **vermin damage**, and of course war and radioactive contamination. Conditions may apply such as:

- Suspension of cover between certain hours in certain high risk areas
- Use of secure lorry parks
- Disabling unattended vehicles
- Requiring your new drivers to provide references

The transfer of risk

6.12 If goods are to be delivered in the course of their sale, the question of whether there is insurance, and if so who arranges it and who pays for it, is normally answered by the contract of sale. Remember that passing of ownership or payment need have no connection with transfer of the risk.

(a) **FOB (free on board):** the seller is responsible until goods are delivered over a ship's rail: or, in a 'home' (UK) FOB sale, to the first carrier. The buyer arranges transit, and insurance if needed.

(b) **CIF (carriage insurance & freight):** the seller arranges carriage to an agreed port or depot, and insurance, and provides the buyer with a bill of lading (proving shipment) and insurance policy or certificate, with the invoice for the goods. The risk passes to the buyer when the goods arrive at the port of destination.

(c) **C & F (carriage & freight)** is a useful version of CIF, especially for UK sales, for example when a buyer of valuable, dangerous or other goods which are difficult to insure has a policy to which the shipment can be added.

Standard forms of contract are frequently varied in individual cases.

Successive carriers

6.13 Many consignments travel by several different forms of transport and thus generally in the charge of a succession of carriers. Insurers normally write policies covering the whole transit; cover depends, largely, on whether they are written in the marine market or the non-marine market.

6.14 A standard Companies/Lloyd's policy is in use covering 'CMR' conditions of carriage, which apply to goods shipped from or to countries which have ratified the 1956 Convention on the Contract for the International Carriage of Goods by Road - which came into UK law under the Carriage of Goods by Road Act 1965.

6.15 At present 'roll-on-roll-off' ('RORO' vessels) commonly carry vehicles plus their loads by sea, so an international 'road' transit can begin or end in the UK, and thus all carriers concerned with it are governed by CMR conditions of carriage, whether or not they are aware of this. CMR needs a liability rather than a property cover; liability is more extensive than that usually accepted by inland carriers.

6.16 CMR terms can be used voluntarily, but if they must apply to a contract, its own terms cannot be less generous than CMR terms.

Items in transit

6.17 Items of contents in transit from one insured premises to another, or given into temporary storage, or even, sometimes, being moved about for business use off the premises, may be covered for all or some of the policy's perils.

6.18 The cover may be **restricted** to **removal** for cleaning, repair or similar purposes. It is likely to exclude stock or materials in trade, which should have their own separately rated 'all risks' extension.

7 MOTOR INSURANCE — 6/96, 12/96

The need for motor insurance

7.1 Not all motor vehicles are used on roads to a sufficient extent to require licensing.

(a) **Public liability insurers** will cover third party risks from use of stacker trucks, detached trailers, and the like on premises where the public do not have access.

(b) A **fleet motor policy** (unless small enough to cover specified vehicles) will usually pay third party claims caused while these vehicles are on roads, but may require their types and numbers to be declared and a reasonably small flat rate premium.

(c) **Mobile cranes, excavators** and other special types of vehicle can also be insured under a motor fleet policy, or separately if required, but each type is **rated separately**.

Road Traffic Act insurance

7.2 Although motor **insurance** began as a **property insurance**, since 1930 its **liability cover** against third party claims for death and injury (RTA cover) has been its corner stone. The Road Traffic Act 1991 says that: Must have insurance to use a motor vehicle on the road.

> 'it shall not be lawful for a person to use, or cause or permit any other person to use, a motor vehicle on a road unless there is in force in relation to the use of the vehicle by that person ... a policy of insurance ... or a security '

7.3 Anyone who owns a motor vehicle, or hires it under a long-term contract, is its user; and anyone driving it also commits an offence unless protected by RTA cover (the user's or his own), except for employees of the user who are confident that their employer has insurance to protect them.

7.4 By the EC Directive on third party motor insurance, compulsory cover now extends to third party property damage at a specified level.

Who is protected?

7.5 Note that the Act does **not require** insurance to **compensate** the **driver** of a motor vehicle for possible injury received in connection with its use. The common law rule applies here: a volunteer, accepting a risk that he or she is aware of (unless helping with an emergency), cannot complain if hurt. Logically, either the injury is the driver's fault, in which case one cannot normally claim damages from oneself, or it is the fault of another person, who can be claimed against, and who (assuming the injury was caused by that person's use of a vehicle) should have RTA cover to meet the claim.

7.6 The owner becomes a third party to his own motor policy, however, while someone else is driving. Lord Porter explained in *Digby v General Accident Assurance Corporation 1943*:

> ' "Third party" is merely a useful description of a particular type of insurance and does not mean that "any claim by any person" must be confined to a third person who is not a party to the contract.'

Thus the insurer also contracts by implication with authorised drivers, like Digby the chauffeur.

7.7 Motor policies also protect people **in charge** of the vehicle but not driving it, the insured's employer or partner, and (at the insured's request) passengers, provided the people in those categories are acting with the insured's permission.

Types of motor insurance

7.8 Most motor insurances can be classified by the **basis of cover**: third party; third party, fire and theft; or comprehensive (see below). There is also a classification by the **use of the vehicle** which the policy permits. Starting with the cheapest (equivalent to a 'normal risk'), the standard uses for motor cars are as follows. Note that the probable annual mileage (and therefore exposure to risk) is larger in successive classes.

(a) Social, domestic and pleasure (will usually allow the insured to drive to and from his/her place of work)

(b) Class (a) plus the insured driving in the course of his, or his employer's business (for low risk businesses the extension is free and often included automatically)

(c) Classes (a) and (b) plus other people driving on the insured's or his employer's business

(d) Classes (a) and (b) plus commercial travelling

Common exclusions are towing for reward (even for commercial vehicles) and road testing, racing and rallying.

7.9 **Commercial risks** and **fleets** use the same basis as cars, but with additions.

(a) Carrying passengers for reward (classified as private hire)

(b) Plying for hire (taxis)

(c) Self-drive hire (the owner normally has a block policy and customers may need to pay a premium for cover)

(d) Coaches, grouped by number of seats

Other commercial vehicles (CVs) are classified by their **weight**, as a guide to the extent of damage they can cause: tankers, and 'special types' like mobile cranes, count as separate classes.

Third party cover

7.10 Third party cover protects against **damage** and **loss** that third parties may claim for, normally up to a limit per claim if the insured vehicle is a commercial vehicle (a van, lorry, or heavy vehicle, or a car which carries passengers for reward). 'Third party only' policies are usually considerably cheaper than policies which include material damage cover for the vehicle, and are therefore popular, especially for fleets, whose owners can retain the risk of damage.

7.11 Policies commonly have an **extension**, which covers the insured for **third party** (TP) **risks** while driving a vehicle which is neither his or on long-term hire to him. Under a market agreement, this extension does not operate while the policyholder is driving another person's car as a named additional driver, or as 'any other person with the owner's permission'.

7.12 The extension is normally omitted from commercial vehicle policies and fleet policies. Many private motor cycle policies, on the other hand, cover either the policyholder riding any machine his licence will permit, or specified machines for a specified group of riders, such as a firm's employees.

Third party, fire and theft

7.13 The cheapest form of policy to cover **'own damage'** is third party, fire and theft cover, to which **accidental damage** cover can sometimes be added, for example for high value commercial vehicles or 'special types'. The theft cover includes damage caused by thieves or attempts to steal.

7.14 Private car policies (PC policies) cover not only **articles** which thieves have to detach from the car, but also its **parts** while detached and scattered about in its garage. In risky areas however a flat rate additional premium is payable if no lockable garage is used, or theft cover may be deleted altogether.

7.15 Incidentally, insurers consider **locking the garage** while it is unattended to be taking reasonable care. The car should also be locked whilst in the garage. CVs not housed in a garage overnight will not normally be insured against malicious damage or frost, or, often, theft.

7.16 Own damage also covers the **reasonable cost** of **protecting** the **vehicle** following damage, of necessary temporary repairs, and of hauling it to the nearest competent repairer.

Comprehensive cover

7.17 Comprehensive cover for PCs is much more extensive than mere protection against fire, theft and accidental damage. Some examples follow, beginning with the more usual.

(a) **Personal accident** generally covers policyholder and spouse, and sometimes passengers, for injury caused by the insured vehicle; wider versions may include other forms of transport, or even unspecified accidents in the UK. There may be age limits. The cover is occasionally found on CV policies.

(b) **Medical expenses** cover up to, say, £50 per person injured in the insured vehicle.

(c) **Rugs and coats** cover up to, say, £50, excluding cash and similar, and sometimes high value items such as furs.

(d) **Fire damage to garage** while the consumer's car is in it, covers up to say £200, unless the damage is covered by another policy.

(e) **Road fund tax** covers unexpired tax which cannot be recovered if the car is a write-off (ie total loss), or is stolen.

(f) **Loss of use** covers two weeks use of a hired vehicle, but this is rare.

(g) **Legal expenses** are very unusual, as there are now separate policies for motorists.

Exclusions

7.18 The usual **exclusions** from motor insurance cover are as follows. The words in italics here are to help you remember the excluded items: they are *not* accepted equivalents.

(a) **Illegal driving.** This is use by 'authorised drivers' who are not entitled to driving licences.

(b) **Should be under another policy.** This is employers' liability claims; liability for damage to a person's property if he is also entitled to protection as an insured (for example if someone borrows a car and crashes it into his own fence, claiming for the damage would be claiming against himself); such a person's claim if he is also able to claim under another policy (this is a market agreement); also for rugs, coats etc, (a policy specifically covering them should pay for them).

(c) **Reinforcing the policy terms**. This is use for a purpose outside the insured class of use; people insured claiming if they have not complied with policy terms.

(d) **Own damage exceptions.** This is loss of use; depreciation (a financial loss); wear and tear (depreciation); mechanical or electrical failures; breakdowns (wear and tear with no external cause, therefore not accidental); damage to tyres from braking or road punctures, cuts and bursts (but not malicious damage to tyres); policy excess.

(e) **Usual property/liability exceptions**. This covers war and the other organised conflicts (and for using a vehicle in Northern Ireland, riot and civil commotion), and sonic bangs.

(f) **Term applying to use of a vehicle abroad.** If there is any doubt about whether the loss or damage was caused by earthquake, riot or civil commotion, the insured must prove it was not.

Insurance for the motor trade

7.19 The description 'motor trade' covers a multiplicity of activities, from sale of cars on commission to carrying out complex repairs with heavy equipment. The perils are frequently grouped under two separate policies.

(a) **Internal risks policies** cover:

- (i) Vehicles owned by the policyholder and his family against accidental damage
- (ii) Vehicles in the insured's custody against liability for damage caused by negligence or defects in the premises or plant
- (iii) Liability for injury or death, excluding the policyholder and his family and employees

The **exclusions** can be results of fire, explosion, theft, defective or careless workmanship, lifting machines, alterations and installation of equipment, waterborne vessels, work away from the insured's premises, the usual contractual liability, radioactivity, earthquake, war and riot, and use on roads.

(b) **Road risks policies** are very similar to CV policies: there is a limit on cover for liability for damage, as for CVs, except that liability for property held in trust by the insured (especially applying to customers' vehicles!) is commonly not excluded. Both comprehensive and third party, fire and theft versions are written, as well as a 'combined' or 'road and garage' version incorporating both. Some policies can be extended in suitable cases, to cover:

- (i) Product liability incurred in sales or servicing (for injury and damage)
- (ii) Unintentional 'detinue' (wrongful detention) and wrongful conversion to new ownership of a vehicle when it transpires that the seller was not the full owner
- (iii) Damage (including from breakdown) to petrol pumps
- (iv) A range of more usual business risks

Exercise 2

Summarise the main areas available for motor insurance and commercial on their respective merits.

---

8 AVIATION INSURANCE

8.1 Aviation insurance is available to aircraft owners, operators and manufacturers and to airport authorities. Of particular interest is **aviation liability** insurance because of its international nature and the potential extent of damage and loss.

Passengers

8.2 The Warsaw Convention makes aircraft operators liable for injury to passengers and damage to their property. There is no need for passengers to prove that the operator was negligent.

Third parties

8.3 The Civil Aviation Act 1982 requires aircraft operators to **pay compensation** in respect of injury or damage to persons or property on the ground. Cover in this category might also include passengers on other aircraft in the event of a collision.

Manufacturers

8.4 Aircraft manufacturers will have **product liability insurance** to provide cover in the event of claims arising from defective aircraft or aircraft components. This type of insurance is dealt with later in this chapter.

Airport authorities

8.5 Airport authorities engage in many activities such as retailing, catering, baggage-handling, servicing aircraft and so on. They will need both public liability insurance and product liability insurance: see later in this chapter.

9 INSURANCES OF LIABILITY

9.1 As the world becomes more crowded and its people pursue more activities, chances of causing injury to other people and destruction or damage to their property increase.

9.2 It is now possible for an individual's claim to be worth over £1m. As hundreds of people can be affected by one product or accident, the practice of offering a global sum to be divided among a group of claimants is more familiar. Such a claim, and its attendant legal fees, can cripple a small company, and could unbalance the budget arrangements in a large one.

9.3 Insurance has become such an important method of handling '**third party**' **risks** that firms for whom it has become uneconomically expensive, or unobtainable, have resorted to setting up their own captive insurers, and clubbing together in mutual indemnity schemes.

9.4 Liability to third parties can arise in a number of ways, as you will remember from your studies of English law.

(a) **Negligence** is causing loss by a failure to take reasonable care when there is a duty to do so. It is the most important and far-reaching of modern torts.

(b) **Strict liability** arises in law in some circumstances even where reasonable care has been exercised. For example the Consumer Protection Act 1987 extends product liability so that whenever injury is caused to an individual, or damage to property, as a result of a defect in a product, the manufacturer or importer is liable even if they can show they took reasonable care.

(c) **Nuisance** (private or public) is unlawful interference with the use of someone's property or with his health and comfort or convenience. Examples are noise, fumes, vibrations, obstructions and so on.

(d) **Trespass** to the person may be assault, battery or false imprisonment. Trespass to land is interference with the possession of land.

(e) **Statutory liabilities** are those imposed by legislation.

(f) **Contractual liability**. Liabilities under contract are any additional liabilities assumed under the terms of contracts entered into with third parties.

10.1 The risk of receiving third party claims from employees made sick or injured (or relatives of those fatally injured), must be insured **by law** in a great number of countries. This has been superseded in the UK by a simpler concept, 'Employers' Liability' (EL), made compulsory by the Employers' Liability (Compulsory Insurance) Act 1969 for almost everyone employed in the UK.

Extent of cover

10.2 Policy wordings are short, covering claims from employees for death, injury and disease arising in the course of the insured business, and for which the insured is liable, including claimants' costs and expenses. The **minimum cover** permitted under the regulations is **£5 million**, but this is rather small in many circumstances, and most policies provide unlimited cover. A copy of the certificate of insurance must be displayed in every location (or depot) where the insured firm's employees work (or work from).

10.3 Rates of premium vary according to **employees' activities**, so insurers require numbers or annual wages paid to those in clerical and supervisory work, those in manual work, those operating machinery and so on, separately: often a very detailed list.

10.4 It can be difficult to tell whether a person is an employee or not in law, so insurers prefer everyone to be on risk to avoid a gap in cover.

Indemnity for other persons

10.5 Like motor policies, EL policies provide **indemnity** for other people, besides the insured, who may be liable for an insured claim, for example:

(a) Directors, partners and employees in the business

(b) People occupied in the firm's in-house services

(c) Officers for whom employees do a spot of home decorating and the like (which falls within some employees' job description)

10.6 The insured may be **vicariously responsible** for liability any of these people incur in their work for the firm, so it would be invidious not to provide the cover automatically (unless the extension refers to work of a very different character from that of 'the business'). Some policies only indemnify these people at the insured's request.

10.7 Agreements in the insurance market

(a) **Share claims** for illness which may have been caused in one of several former employments

(b) **Cover claims** for deafness due to work in foundries etc

(c) **Pick up claims** where there is doubt as to whether they fall under EL or another of the insured's liability policies (for example when travelling as a passenger in the insured's vehicle might or might not be 'in the course of employment')

Restrictions on cover

10.8 There is no 'safety net' arrangement equivalent to the motor insurance market's Motor Insurers' Bureau to pay claims against employers who had no insurance when the injury or disease was caused. In addition limits of indemnity under such old policies look tiny today, and some firms cannot find a record of who did insure them, so long ago.

10.9 As with motor insurance, the insurer reserves the right to **obtain repayment** from the insured of any settlement of a claim which would have been repudiated for breach of policy terms (for instance if the insured fails to take proper care to avoid accidents, or to give sufficiently prompt notice of an accident), had repudiation not been outlawed by the regulations to protect the third party. The injured employee must get his compensation unhindered by arguments as to whether the insurer is liable to pay it under the policy's terms.

10.10 Employer's liability policies, like motor policies, operate within **specified territorial limits** (the UK including its islands), and cover employees working abroad for short periods. They often include a form of jurisdiction clause, limiting insurers' liability in such cases to the amount of damages which would have been awarded under UK law.

10.11 Having already restricted the cover by defining the claimants the place where and circumstances under which liability may arise, there is very little which an EL policy excludes in its exclusions.

11 PUBLIC LIABILITY POLICIES **6/96, 12/96, 6/99**

11.1 Public liability (PL) policies cover civil liability incurred in the conduct of the insured business. Occasionally cover may be restricted to claims for death and injury. There is a limit of liability per claim, but different limits may apply to liability for injury and for property damage. Limits for policy extensions may be different again. The insured business is described as including its usual in-house services: indemnity to other persons is as in EL.

Exclusions

11.2 PL policies normally clarify the extent of cover given by use of exclusions, including the following.

(a) **Should be under another policy**

- (i) EL risks
- (ii) RTA risks and any liability connected with the use of any vehicle, watercraft or aircraft
- (iii) Engineering liability risks, especially passenger lifts and any boilers or pressure vessels
- (iv) Professional indemnity risks, excluded as 'design or advice', except normal in-house services, and sometimes minor work ancillary to a firm's work
- (v) Medical and chemists' professional indemnity and products risks
- (vi) The cost of putting right defective workmanship, on items being worked on: there are specialist markets for separate 'extended warranty' (motor) and 'breakdown' guarantees (for electrical and mechanical products)
- (vii) Radiation liability risks. Operators of nuclear installations should either self insure or obtain cover through the British Insurance (Atomic Energy) Committee. Liability from use of isotopes for inspection or measurement is usually covered as part of the normal conduct of firms' business

(b) **May be included for additional premium**

- (i) Contractors' risks, except 'indemnity to principal'
- (ii) Weakening of support (mainly a construction risk, if insurable)
- (iii) Pollution
- (iv) Injury and damage caused by defective products, whether the defects were caused in the insured's business or not
- (v) Defective design or advice (if it concerns, say the packaging of a product)
- (vi) Product recall exercises undertaken to avoid a real risk of loss

(vii) Libel and slander (normally a separate specialist risk)

(c) **Own damage exceptions**

The insured's own property, and other people's in the insured's custody and control. The insured cannot normally claim damages against itself, so this should be under a material loss and damage policy, except that employees' personal effects are often specifically included in the PL cover.

(d) **Some usual property/liability exclusions**

(i) War and other organised conflicts
(ii) Appropriation under some official authority
(iii) The excess applying under the appropriate section

Vehicles

11.3 Loading or unloading vehicles is **usually excluded** by **CV policies** and covered by an exception to the motor exclusion.

11.4 Insureds whose employees use their own vehicles on company business will need '**motor contingency' insurance**, which can be written by a motor insurer or as a further PL extension. It only protects the insured from third party claims for injury and damage caused by employees whose own current motor insurance covers use for the insured's business.

Premises

11.5 The Defective Premises Act 1972 makes a landlord, owner or occupier of a dwelling liable to subsequent owners and occupiers for loss, damage or injury due to defective workmanship. An insured who has disposed of premises may, in some cases, receive claims up to fifteen years after the defective work was finished (Latent Damage Act 1986). Cover is provided by an automatic extension in appropriate cases.

Financial loss cover

11.6 Other extensions can include **financial loss cover**. The contingency PL policies cover is accidental injury or damage to a third party or third party property. Claims from third parties suffering just financial loss as a result of an insured occurrence will generally fall within the scope of the cover, provided they are sufficiently closely connected with the occurrence to attach civil liability to the insured for the loss. Where there is no damage or injury from an occurrence, the insured may still be liable for third parties' losses it causes, so a 'financial loss' extension is sometimes needed to protect against those claims.

11.7 For example, suppose weedkiller is accidentally packed in babyfood bottles: consumers noticing the food has the wrong smell and consistency might return it for replacement, and the insured would want the wholesalers and retailers to return all the bottles from the faulty batch. They might claim for loss of bargains and the cost of exchanging the product for a more expensive equivalent, even though no claims for poisoning are received.

12 PRODUCT LIABILITY 6/99

12.1 Product liability insurance provides cover in the event of successful claims for injury or damage caused by goods supplied, sold, tested or repaired by the insured. A person who suffers injury in connection with defective or dangerous goods may have remedies as follows.

(a) If he is the purchaser he can probably **recover damages** from the insured vendor for breach of the statutory implied conditions of quality imposed by the Sale of Goods Act 1979 (goods must be fit for the purpose for which they were sold and be of 'merchantable quality' and so on). If he deals as consumer he cannot be deprived of these safeguards; in any other case an attempt to exclude or restrict them is void unless it satisfies a test of reasonableness: Unfair Contract Terms Act 1977.

(b) If he **suffers personal injury or damage** to property by a defective product he may be able to recover damages for negligence from the manufacturer. Any attempt to exclude liability for personal injury or death due to negligence is void and exemption from other liability is usually subject to a test of reasonableness: Unfair Contract Terms Act 1977.

But in either case the insured may dispute liability and in any case the claimant must prove breach of contract or negligence as the case may be.

12.2 Although a supplier has, at present, no general duty at common law to take care in examining and if necessary remedying defective products supplied to him by a manufacturer, a dealer in goods which are secondhand or otherwise likely to be defective by their nature has such a duty.

The Consumer Protection Act 1987

12.3 The Consumer Protection Act imposes **strict civil liability**, and this liability cannot be excluded by any disclaimer. (The Consumer Protection Act 1987 repealed a number of earlier Acts, including the Consumer Safety Act 1978.)

12.4 Prior to the 1987 Act, the consumer could still have sued the retailer without proving negligence, but there were disadvantages, in that only the actual purchaser could make a claim, and if the seller had disappeared, no remedy was available.

Strict product liability

12.5 Claims for losses caused by defects in a product may be brought against the following.

- The manufacturer of the end-product
- The manufacturer of a defective component
- An importer into the EC
- An 'own-brander'
- A supplier, who is usually a retailer

Because of the potential liability of the parties above, it is usual for a supplier only to be liable if he will not disclose the identity of the importer or manufacturer.

12.6 The burden of proof is on the consumer to prove that:

- The product contained a defect.
- He suffered damage.
- The damage resulted from the defect.
- The defendant was either the producer or some other person listed above.

Proving causation on the balance of probabilities, remoteness of damage and reasonable foresight has the same difficulties as under the law of tort.

'*Defective*' *product*

12.7 A product will be found to be **unsafe** where it is not as safe as it is reasonable to expect. This standard of relative safety requires a court to take into account all circumstances surrounding the product - the way it is advertised, the time at which it was supplied, its anticipated normal use, the provision of instructions for use, even its likely misuse - in establishing the standard required. Also the benefit to society and the cost of making the product safer can be considered.

12.8 The products covered by this legislation include all goods, such as raw materials, components and packaging, plus electricity, except non-processed agricultural products and buildings.

Scope of the Act

12.9 Consumers and other users, but not business users, can claim compensation for **death, personal injury** or **damage** to other property. There is unlimited liability but:

(a) A claim must be brought within three years of the fault becoming apparent.

(b) No claim may be brought more than ten years after the original supply.

(c) Where the claim is for damage to property, it must not be business property which is damaged and the amount of the damage must be more than £275.

Defences

12.10 The defendant in a case under this Act has six possible defences.

(a) 'Development risk' - the state of knowledge at the time of manufacture and supply was such that no manufacturer could have been expected to detect the fault.

(b) The defect did not exist in the product when originally supplied.

(c) The product complied with mandatory statutory or EC standards.

(d) The supply was otherwise than in the course of a business.

(e) More than 10 years have elapsed since the product was first supplied.

(f) The defect was wholly attributable to the design of a subsequent product into which the product in question was incorporated.

12.11 The Act is a significant step towards protection against unsafe goods. Producers and other distributors now have to ensure that they are protected by insurance in their business contracts; careful record-keeping is also required so that the other people in the distribution chain are adequately identified.

13 PROFESSIONAL INDEMNITY 12/96

13.1 Over recent years there has been a marked increased in the number and size of actions brought against members of professions, and professional indemnity insurance is usually now very expensive and sometimes difficult to obtain.

13.2 **Professional indemnity insurance** is a requirement for the practice of solicitors and accountants, for example. It differs from the normal public liability policy in that it includes purely financial loss. The precise details of the cover will depend upon the liabilities that may be incurred by different 'professions'.

13.3 Here are some examples from an article on the subject in the February 1992 *Administrator*.

(a) A biotechnical consultant designed a waste treatment plant which allegedly failed to operate to the required standard, resulting in discharge levels into a nearly river being higher than permitted.

(b) A fuel economy consultancy was allegedly negligent in their design of a factory heating and lighting system.

(c) A bingo game designed by a computer consultant produced too many winners.

Directors' and officers' insurance (D & O)

13.4 This is really a development of professional negligence cover for a specific, very common class of professional. Directors and the senior management of a company are constantly exposed to the risk of claims for loss resulting from a **failure to manage** the affairs of the company properly.

13.5 Take up of D & O has increased sharply in the UK and about 40% of UK public companies now buy it. This is no doubt due to the difficulties companies have experienced during the recession and concerns over accusations of wrongful trading.

14 PECUNIARY LOSS 12/96

14.1 In a sense, all liability insurances protect against pecuniary loss, that is pecuniary compensation which the insured is liable to pay to third parties with valid claims. Some insurers, however, offer **'economic loss' extensions** to product liability extensions in public liability insurances. These are carefully expressed to cover cases where a third party claim is not covered by the product liability extension, because the claimant has suffered no damage or injury. Basic public liability and product liability exclusions, the cost of recalling, replacing or repairing the product, or making good defective workmanship, still apply.

14.2 An insured's business can suffer financial loss from many causes. In many cases, protection against financial loss may be had by insuring against those causes.

(a) Traditionally, insurers insist that the 'direct' physical loss or damage be the subject of a material damage policy too, but there are some cases where this is not appropriate, for example 'key-man' insurances and 'contingency' insurance (for example weather being unsuitable for an outdoor project).

(b) In some other cases, the value of the item itself is insignificant compared to the consequential loss which will be caused by its damage, as can be the case with a roll of film which is damaged in processing.

14.3 The insured's *profit* can be included in loss and damage insurance in a few cases.

15 BUSINESS INTERRUPTION 12/96, 6/99

15.1 The major category of 'own loss' insurance against financial loss is business interruption (BI), so called as its former names ('loss of profits' and 'consequential loss') can be misleading.

Material damage and financial loss

15.2 BI insurance is written by fire insurers, engineering insurers and others, according to which perils are to be insured The premium is usually calculated from the corresponding **physical damage/loss rate**. Payment of BI claims is conditional on payment of a loss or damage claim, except under the common extensions covering, for example:

(a) **Loss of access** to the insured premises (in case, say, neighbouring premises catch fire)

(b) Communicable **diseases** (a cook found to be a typhoid carrier, or a guest with plague, could close a hotel)

(c) **Murder** (as the police would prevent access to the room concerned for a time)

Measuring the loss

15.3 The interest insured under BI is basically loss to a business during a fixed period following an insured occurrence (called the **indemnity period**). The loss is the difference between a reasonable projection of the insured business's financial performance over that period, and its actual performance as reduced by the insured occurrence. The insurer covers that difference, up to a limit per year, during the indemnity period, which should be sufficiently long for the business to recover from the effects of the insured peril on its performance.

15.4 The subject matter insured for BI may be defined as 'trading loss ... the rate of gross profit on any shortfall in expected sales', described as:

profit as % of gross sales × shortfall in gross sales

15.5 Other methods of calculating gross profit include the **difference basis.**

	£	£
Annual turnover		X
Closing stock at year end		X
		X
Less: opening stock at beginning of year	X	
cost of purchases	X	
variable charges	X	
		(X)
Gross profit		X

This automatically includes wages and overheads of a profitable organisation in the cover. Variable charges reduce as business slackens, and are not insured. An older method, the difference basis can take more calculating. It can be summarised as:

	£
Net profit	X
Standing charges	X
	X

or, in the absence of profit,

Standing charges	(X)
Less trading loss	(X)
	(X)

15.6 Although there are standard accounting practices, methods of calculating the above items must vary between firms, because the processes and trading practices differ. There are cases, however, where the accountants' figures present a true picture of trading, but do not relate very easily to a real loss of production claimed for (for example if this relates to parts of several orders, and the orders will not all appear in the same accounting year). In such circumstances, the loss adjuster will use the most practical and equitable method available to quantify the loss.

Increased cost of working

15.7 Most BI policies have a separate item covering **increased cost of working** (ICOW), which represents abnormal items of expenditure incurred in loss reduction. Examples of expenses counting as ICOW are: renting alternative premises during repair of the insured's damaged building; wages for temporary staff helping to restore records, and hire charges for a replacement for a damaged machine.

Wages and salaries

15.8 It is not always expedient to include all wages in the sum insured for BI. While it is not uncommon to find separate BI limits for distinct areas of a firm's operations, it is quite common to find **payroll cover** given separately according to the circumstances. This is most often for wages paid to retain skilled and experienced staff, who might find other permanent employment if made redundant during a period of interrupted work.

16 FIDELITY GUARANTEE INSURANCE 12/96

16.1 Fidelity guarantee insurance (sometimes called **commercial guarantees**) covers losses arising from the dishonest actions of a supposedly responsible person. Modern policies cover theft of the insured's property, in addition to traditional embezzlement risks. Auditors' fees for proving a loss is a common optional extension. Insured losses happen

fraudulent diversion of funds.

during an identified employee's uninterrupted employment, or are discovered up to six months after he or she leaves, is dismissed, retires or dies.

16.2 Types of policy include the following.

(a) Policies issued on **specified employees**, or on the holders for the time being of particular jobs, or on groups of employees (named or not) with varying degrees of access to and control over the employer's money and assets

(b) Policies for **partnerships**, which specifically protect the firm against theft by a partner

(c) '**Collective**' **policies**, covering groups of staff, which do not include details of names and duties

(d) '**Blanket**' **policies**, covering all staff

Some advantages of blanket policies are that the insured does not practice selection against the insurer, and that the insured is protected against theft by any employee whose job is not supposed to entail access to computer records, safe keys, goods, or cash.

Conditions of cover

16.3 The insured is required to take **all possible steps** to recover stolen money or goods (or their value); anything belonging to an employee in question can be appropriated for this purpose: outstanding wages, shares in the firm, or craftsmen's tools left in their lockers.

16.4 There is a good deal that an employer can do himself to **reduce the risk** and commercial fidelity guarantee insurers' proposals and surveys will therefore take special interest in:

(a) Supervision of employees who work with (or near) cash or accounts records, and systems of check to spot any irregularities

(b) The backgrounds and previous employment records of employees (hence job application references should be checked thoroughly)

(c) The firm's relevant loss and insurance history, and the basis for the firm's selection of individuals or groups to be insured (unless it is a blanket policy)

(d) Physical inspection of the risks

(e) Systems of check and physical arrangements for handling of cash and records, perhaps the most unexpected being a requirement that employees must take a minimum of ten consecutive days' holiday each year

Reputedly a valued employee had not had a day's absence for sickness or holidays for forty years. When he retired, his successor discovered that he had systematically edited small sums out of the accounts for as long as could be checked, and had disappeared as a rich man.

Exercise 3

You are the Company Secretary of a major food manufacturer. Your chairman is considering the merits of Business Interruption Insurance which the company has not previously used.

Advise the chairman in general terms as to the mode of operation and the importance of such insurance for this type of business.

Chapter roundup

- In this chapter we have looked at the *ECs* **seventeen classes of insurance**, which may be grouped as follows.
    - One class for **accidents** which cause death or injury, or **diseases** which incapacitate (class 1).
    - Five classes consist of specific sorts of **property** which are insured (land vehicles, railway rolling stock, aircraft, ships and goods in transit (classes 3 to 7 inclusive).
    - Three describe **perils** which can cause restricted sorts of loss: sickness insured against for terms less than five years (class 2); fire, explosions, subsidence and natural perils causing damage to property not in group 1.4(b) (class 8), except for hail, frost, theft and other occurrences, which have their own class (class 9).
    - Four relate to **liabilities** (motor, aircraft and ships, separated from 'own damage' (classes 10 to 12), with class 13 for any other liabilities.
    - Four are for purely **financial losses**: credit insurances (class 14); guaranteeing people who have given guarantees, and the provision of bail bonds etc (class 15); legal expenses policies (class 17); and miscellaneous financial loss insurances, and anything not included in other classes (class 16).
- It is very important to know **what is** and is **not covered** under your organisation's policies. Look carefully through your own organisation's policies.

Test your knowledge

1 List the departments commonly found in large insurance companies. (see para 1.3)

2 What is covered by 'fire' insurance? (2.4)

3 List five 'perils'. (3.1 - 3.14)

4 Define 'theft'. (4.1)

5 Briefly explain three ways of risk reduction with respect to goods in transit. (6.4 - 6.6)

6 Explain the terms FOB, CIF, C&F. (6.12)

7 Is motor insurance required for all motor vehicles? (7.1)

8 List the risks likely to be covered by comprehensive motor insurance. (7.17)

9 What is the most important source of liability in business? (9.4)

10 What sort of risks are covered by employers' liability insurance? (10.1)

11 List a selection of the items likely to be excluded from public liability cover. (11.2)

12 What effect has the Consumer Protection Act 1987 had upon the liability of product manufacturers? (12.3)

13 When might professional advice give rise to liabilities? (13.1 - 13.3)

14 How is the loss measured in business interruption insurance? (15.3)

15 What do you understand by the term 'fidelity guarantee'? (16.1)

Now try illustrative question 18 at the end of the Study Text

Chapter 18

INSURANCES OF THE PERSON

This chapter covers the following topics.

Introduction

Perhaps the most valuable and important assets that organisations employ are its people. Many enlightened organisations realise this and insure against the possibility of loss or damage to human resources in the same way that they take care of their physical assets.

1 INSURANCES OF THE PERSON AND INDEMNITY

1.1 Insurances of the person differ from most other insurances in that they do not provide indemnity, even if many of them look as if they do. This has important practical effects.

(a) In theory you can **insure your own** or your **spouse's life** for benefits of unlimited amount.

(b) If an insurer pays a claim under a life assurance or a personal accident policy for death or injury caused by a third party's fault, the insurer has **no interest** in any compensation which that third party may be liable to pay for the death or injury.

Benefits

1.2 Although insurances of the person are not policies of indemnity, that does not say that the size of benefits they pay are not related to the size of the insured's loss. In insurances against sickness and disability, and insurances effected by one person on the life of another, the **size of the benefit** is normally related quite closely to the **size of the loss.**

First party policies

1.3 In contrast to property and liability insurances in general, payment of the benefit under a 'personal' insurance is the end of the story. The insurer has no procedures for recovering the outlay from wrongdoers whose actions or inaction may have made it necessary. In contrast to 'third party' (liability insurance) policies, 'insurances of the person' are **first party policies,** because they protect the party they insure against direct loss from his or her own death, injury or sickness, rather than against claims from third parties for their losses.

2 PERSONAL ACCIDENT INSURANCE 12/95

2.1 The purpose of PA policies is to pay specified benefits when the insured is injured by an **accidental cause.** As mentioned earlier, an accident is considered to be caused by some external, unexpected force.

2.2 Personal accident insurance cover lasts for one year. At the end of the year the insurer may refuse renewal (for example, if the risk involved is no longer acceptable to him), or he may increase the premium.

Extent of cover and benefits

2.3 Insurances may be had for loss of or damage to other parts than just limbs and eyes: a small market exists which covers dancers' legs against injury, actresses against scarring, singers against injury or even illness causing loss of voice. Such detailed schedules of benefits are known as **continental scales.**

Employers' arrangements

2.4 The lack of a ceiling on life assurance payouts allows employers to arrange **group (or single) life and PA policies** on employees' lives to benefit the employees' dependants without regard to whether the employee has arranged any such cover for him or herself, or which may attach through the employee's membership of a club or trade union.

2.5 The cover which the employer can arrange is limited by the employee's wages or salary for tax reasons. It is not though uncommon in medium and larger firms to find employees provided with both life assurance and at the least PA death benefits during their terms of service, often provided as part of the remuneration package. In addition, employees with mortgages on their homes, or cars on hire purchase, will almost invariably have life assurances at least large enough to pay those debts outstanding at their deaths, plus (very often) additional policies to protect their surviving families' financial security.

Group personal accident cover

2.6 Group PA cover can be arranged for all employees, or for selected groups (such as those paid monthly or less often, or for those in clerical and managerial positions). Modern schemes frequently include all full-time staff, divided into groups by 'salary bands'. However insurers still apply **classification by occupation**, charging higher rates of premium for members whose work involves increased risk of accidents. Other details an employer needs to declare for each member (or annually in large schemes) besides the number of employees covered in each group, are their ages, sex and sometimes their names.

2.7 Schemes with at least ten members may not require **medicals,** except:

(a) Where individual employees complete proposals (when the premiums are slightly lower)

(b) For an employee insured for disproportionately large benefits compared to other members

(c) Occasionally for an individual whose impaired health may increase the likelihood of suffering an accident

Waiver of medicals means little, if any, premium loading for such 'bad risks'

2.8 In exchange for a large spread of lives in a group scheme, and reduced paperwork, the insurer quotes **reduced premiums.** Employers can offset PA premiums against corporation tax as a business expense. Large group schemes may also include provision for **profit sharing** (the return of a percentage of the premium, if the claims/premium ratio for any year is below an agreed level).

2.9 PA **medical expenses** cover is generally unimportant for UK based employees. For directors and staff engaged in foreign travel, however, medical expenses become far more important.

Business travel insurance

2.10 Although reciprocal national insurance agreements operate with most European countries, benefits provided locally vary considerably, and usually involve payment in cash. Firms may however insure this risk through an annual **business travel package** arrangement. Like a holiday package, this will usually include PA, 'all risks' cover for baggage and personal effects, personal liability insurance and (provided cover is effected sufficiently early) cover against cancellation due to, say, illness.

3 SICKNESS INSURANCE 12/95

3.1 **Sickness insurance** is frequently found in combination with PA. Like PA on its own, is basically an **annual insurance**. It usually replaces earnings lost through some degree of incapacity caused by illness, or by specified illnesses. For this reason, and because younger adults are generally less susceptible to illness than other people, most insurers provide cover for people between the ages of 15 and 60 or 65 years.

Extent of cover

3.2 Cover against **specified illnesses** is cheaper than 'all sickness' insurance, but offices offer it to proposers who are rather bad risks for 'all sickness' cover. Where proposers opt for it there is a large chance that 'selection against the insurer' is operating (that is, the proposers choose to insure against the diseases which they are most likely to contract).

Benefits

3.3 The insured is entitled to benefit for each week's total disablement from an insured (or not excluded) illness after, say, its first seven days, or the first two or four weeks. Coverage lasts for up to a maximum period of, say, two years from when the incapacity starts (or, of course, until the insured recovers, after a shorter time). The insured may receive payment for each week sick providing the illness lasts for a continuous period of more than, say, 14 days.

3.4 The initial '**waiting period**' or '**deferred period**' bars small claims, which are expensive to administer. Alternatively, no benefit is payable for the weeks in the deferred period (like a 'time excess' in a general insurance). As in general insurances, opting to increase the extent of this 'time excess' or waiting period will usually bring a reduction in premium.

3.5 The scheduled periodic benefit is approximately equivalent to the insured person's current wages, and the benefit paid is normally restricted to 75% of that, or 90% less any NI sickness benefit and other income received because of the incapacity.

3.6 An important reason for the restriction of benefit size is, again, statistical: apparently people whose income does not fall by more than about 40% while they are sick take longer to recover than those in more straitened circumstances, which, it is supposed, is not entirely unrelated to moral hazard. The insurer is entitled to require a medical report from its nominated physician to check the progress of the insured's recovery in cases of doubt.

Total and partial disablement

3.7 Definitions of total and partial disablement may rely on the insured person's **being unable to attend** to any of his business or occupation, or a substantial part of it, respectively. A variety of definitions is in use for the insured contingency in sickness insurance. Total incapacity is often incapacity to perform the duties of the occupation pursued immediately before the onset of disability, for instance, and reinforced by the requirement that the insured person is not carrying out any other paid work. Partial disablement, which carries a proportion of the total disablement benefit, can depend on a medical practitioner's certifying the insured person as less than 50% capable in his or her usual occupation (due to the illness). Sometimes total incapacity means being confined to bed, and partial incapacity means being confined to the house.

Information required

3.8 As benefits are payable for disablement, **proposers' ages and occupations** are at least as important to underwriters as they are in PA, and so are their hobbies. Even minor injury or sickness can result in inability to follow some occupations.

3.9 **Location of residence** is more important than for PA, at least in part because morbidity statistics and NHI medical and hospital facilities vary from region to region. The insurance is generally restricted to temperate climates.

3.10 Proposal forms include questions about the **proposer's current state of health,** and whether he or she suffers from any physical defect, disorder or weakness, especially anything affecting sight or hearing. Illness arising within a specified time after a new policy's inception is excluded, to ensure that the policy covers only illness contracted *after* the insurer goes on risk, as far as possible. Known recurrent illnesses, whose effects are not serious enough to merit refusing the proposal as a whole, are specifically excluded.

Aids

3.11 As offices are now beginning to feel the effects of claims from sufferers of the Human Immunodeficiency Virus (Aids) in claims ratios for several classes of insurances of the person, it is likely that, besides introducing questions into proposals about recent advice, tests or treatment connected with Aids, offices will take steps to exclude Aids-related illnesses from cover, in view of the effect of the condition on a person's propensity to contract illness and ability to recover from it. It is also possible that offices will not wish to offer renewal to an insured who is found to be HIV-positive during a policy year.

Sex

3.12 The sex of insureds is interesting to insurers, because statistics show that **women have greater morbidity** than men - or at least, government statistics show that, for example, at the end of the 1960s, single women made about 1½ times as many claims for sickness benefit, and married women 15 times as many, as men in equivalent age groups. This is, naturally, reflected in:

- Premium rates
- Increased minimum waiting periods
- Reduced benefits
- Maximum benefit periods
- Any combination of them, depending on the office concerned

Group cover

3.13 Group or occupational scheme proposals require **less detailed information** about the members to be insured, and have more generous terms, in similar manner to PA insurance (as discussed above). Some insurers apply the exclusion of claims within a set time from the inception of a new policy only to employees who were not at work on the date when cover started, for instance.

4 PERMANENT HEALTH INSURANCE

4.1 Permanent health insurance (PHI) policies, which may be individual or on a group basis, are designed to **replace earned income** lost through physical incapacity to earn, caused by accidents and sickness, if necessary for many years' incapacity.

4.2 Permanent health insurance, however, is a 'long-term' cover like life assurance: its term, from its inception to the insured's anticipated retirement date, can run for many years. Like life assurances it is **non-cancellable**. This means that the insurer cannot cancel the policy except in the event of fraud, or if the policy terms include provision for cancellation in specific circumstances.

4.3 **Occupational PHI** or **life assurance schemes**, however, are administered like **annual contracts** with the employer, although life offices generally guarantee to renew them if the insured firm requires. The insurer's liability is also potentially 'long tail', as for liability policies covering risks of third party injury and professional negligence. Once an insured employee falls sick, the office will continue to pay for the claim, until that employee reaches retirement age if necessary, whether or not the policy is renewed.

Benefits

4.4 The definition of the benefits can be **arranged to suit the insured**, but the income limit during incapacity is unlikely to exceed 75% of previous salary, and benefits are subject to deduction of tax under PAYE. Proportional benefits can be payable when an employee becomes able to perform alternative, lower paid, work, even if with another employer.

4.5 The deferred period is seldom shorter than 26 weeks (except for individual policies for self-employed) to correspond with the length of the maximum period for which NI sickness benefit is payable. It is a very useful means of suiting cover to abnormal risks, and can often be reduced or increased for a suitable premium adjustment. Policy wordings can vary considerably.

Group schemes

4.6 With group PHI schemes it is the **employer** who **pays** the **premiums** to the insurance company, but employees are *not* assessed for tax on these premiums. An employer may feel that he has obligations to his employees should they suffer severe illness and the liability for continued payment of salary could be heavy. By arranging a group PHI scheme with an insurer the employer replaces possible heavy outlay at indeterminate times by premium payments at known regular intervals at a relatively stable rate.

4.7 The benefits are then payable by the insurance company to the employer who then passes them on to the disabled person.

4.8 The disabled person generally **remains an employee** of the employer, and so may then continue to remain a member of the company pension scheme throughout his incapacity with the employer continuing to pay pension scheme contributions. The pension scheme contributions of both the employer and the employee might be insured alongside the disablement benefits under the PHI scheme.

4.9 As for PA&S cover, schemes covering a large percentage of a firm's staff, especially if membership is automatic, may provide **'free cover'** (that is, without evidence of members' health) providing benefits subject to specified limits even (in large schemes) for members of any age. The free cover (or 'non-selection') limit is not likely to apply in schemes where there are fewer than, say, 50 members. Benefits above the limit will only be available where evidence of good health is provided.

The cost of private healthcare

4.10 Private medical insurance has become increasingly common over the past 20 years: about 12% of British people now have it, mostly via corporate schemes. As interest in health issues has risen employees have become more likely to claim on policies and some abuse of the system has been found.

4.11 Consequently many companies are trying to find ways of cutting down on claims in return for lower premiums.

(a) Employees may now be asked to pay an **excess** - say the first £100 of any treatment.

(b) **Administration** is being tightened and central controls introduced.

(c) Claims are **vetted** by senior managers.

(d) The **cost** of surgery or hospital stays is more **closely monitored**. Special arrangements may be made for bulk purchase of administration and accommodation with private or NHS hospitals.

(e) Employees may be encouraged to use **NHS facilities** wherever possible.

Exercise 1

What is the scope of cover for permanent health insurance and what practical value is it to policy holders?

---

5 KEY-MAN INSURANCES

5.1 A firm may effect personal accident and sickness insurance on the health of its employees, but for its own benefit, for example to fund the firm's sick pay scheme. Another, increasingly important, use is to **replace loss** to the business due to the death or incapacitating illness of a **key man**: specified directors, departmental managers, or project leaders for instance.

5.2 For a key-man policy the insurer requires completion of a different, much longer proposal, giving details of the business's trading figures for the last few years and projections for the next year or two, as would be required for a business interruption policy covering a property risk. This is because of the difficulty of assessing the size of the risk and of any loss claimed for, and because some underwriters are still anxious about the legal validity of insurances on employees' lives, for sums assured in excess of the total wages payable to the employee during his or her period of notice.

5.3 Total wages payable was the court's assessment of the value of the employer's interest in an employee in *Simcock v Scottish Imperial 1902*. To counter this possible limitation the sums insured under today's key-man insurances are therefore set as closely as possible to the key employee's **demonstrable financial value** to the business. Dicta in other cases, however, suggest that insurers' fears may be groundless.

Kidnap and ransom insurance

5.4 The value of key men to their employers has sometimes been tested by kidnappers who have demanded (and received) enormous ransoms running into millions of pounds. Insurance to cover this risk is not available in some countries (for example Ulster) or cities since it is thought that it may encourage kidnapping.

5.5 A strict condition of kidnap and ransom cover is that its existence is not **disclosed**. Such policies will usually be subject to a **large excess**, perhaps 10% of any ransom paid. As mentioned in an earlier chapter, insurers will be concerned about risk reduction measures such as employing bodyguards and training chauffeurs.

5.6 A related risk, applying in particular to retailers and manufacturers of food or drugs, is that of **extortion** by actual or threatened contamination of the product on the shelf. The costs in terms of damaged sales and the need to recall and inspect stocks may be considerable.

Exercise 2

This question tests you on material from the previous chapter as well as from this one. Note that you are asked for a report, if you write out a full answer.

Your chairman has requested you to advise him as to whether Fidelity Guarantee insurances and Key Man insurance would be desirable for your company, and as to the merits of such covers. Your report should include a brief summary of the cover that is available.

---

6 LIFE ASSURANCE

Types of life assurance

6.1 There are three basic types of life assurance, term assurance, endowment assurance and whole life assurance.

(a) **Term assurance**, or temporary insurance, is for a fixed term and pays the agreed benefit (sum assured) if the life assured dies within the term.

(b) **Pure endowment assurance** pays the sum assured if the life assured survives to the end of the term, that is, to the policy's 'maturity'.

6.2 A common form of policy, which is useful for investment, is the **endowment assurance**, which is a combination of the other two, and pays either on the life assured's death, if this occurs within the term or at the policy's maturity. It is most important not to get their names confused.

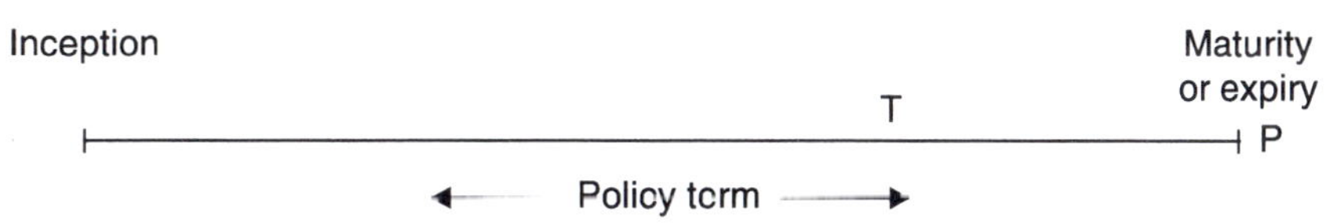

6.3 T is the point at which a claim may occur on a **term assurance** (at any point during the term). If there is no claim, the policy expires at the end of the term. P is the point at which a claim may occur on a **pure endowment**, ie only if the life assured survives until the policy matures. An **endowment** policy pays either on death at T or survival to maturity at P.

6.4 The third basic form, **whole life assurance**, pays the sum assured on the life assured's death (W), and has no fixed term.

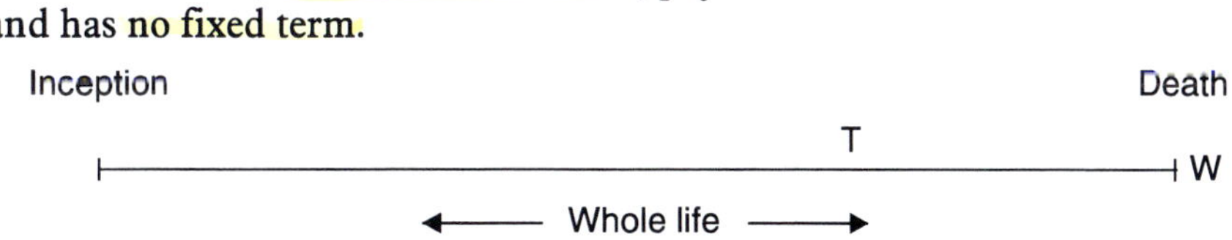

6.5 There are in practice a number of variations on the above. One is the **Family Income Policy** which is effectively a form of term assurance. Should the life assured die during the stipulated term the sum assured becomes payable, not as a lump sum, but as a series of instalments spread over the policy's outstanding term. Thus such policies can provide valuable income to a family.

6.6 A **double accident** benefit extension will double the sum assured on a whole life or term assurance, if the life assured dies in an accident.

Premiums

6.7 Premium rates for normal lives are charged according to the life assured's age at inception. With a few exceptions, premiums are payable in equal instalments at inception and the policy's anniversaries throughout the policy's term. Examples of exceptions are as follows.

(a) **Temporary premium loadings** imposed for some substandard lives. The loading becomes smaller in stages or simply stops after a certain date, by which the abnormal aspects of the risk should have abated.

(b) **Decreasing term policies.** These are term assurances with a sum assured which gets smaller, and the premium may shrink over the term, too. These policies often protect creditors whose loans are repaid in stages, the outstanding debt reducing at approximately the same rate as the sum assured.

(c) **Single premium policies**, for which the whole premium is payable at inception.

Non-profit and with-profits

6.8 Conventional life assurance policies are broadly of two forms, either **non-profit** or **with-profits**. However, policies under which a significant reserve does not build up during the policy's term, for example temporary assurances, are customarily written only on a non-profit basis.

6.9 The calculation of life assurance premium rates for conventional long term policies involves estimates of future **mortality rates**, future **interest rates** and future **expenses**. These rates are not easily predictable. Thus for non-profit policies (those where the sum assured and the premium are guaranteed on a fixed relationship basis) the life office has to be prudent when deciding upon the actual mortality and interest rates.

6.10 Thus in practice, life offices prefer to transact conventional long term ordinary life assurance contracts on a with-profits basis, the premiums on which are greater than the corresponding non-profit premiums, because with-profits premiums Surplus, as defined by the life office is returned to the with-profits policyholders on a non-contracted basis.

Bonuses

6.11 The consequence is that with-profits policies tend to give **better value for money** than non-profit policies although this is at the expense of some loss of guarantees. The bonuses usually take reversionary form, that is they are calculated as a percentage addition to the sum assured.

6.12 Recently, to reflect special experience, such as exceptionally high interest rates and/or capital appreciation earnings, **reversionary bonuses** have been augmented by special bonuses and/or terminal bonuses. **Special bonuses** may make, say, an extra percentage additional to the sum assured for each year the policy has been in force.

6.13 **Terminal bonuses** are also declared as percentage additions to the sum assured, but apply only to claims (whether by death or maturity) within a short time period not exceeding one year following the declaration. Thereafter they may be held, increased or decreased. Terminal bonuses may be regarded as reflecting surplus from capital appreciation which will not necessarily recur.

Types of with-profits policies

6.14 The with-profits system has proved valuable in the development of certain contracts. The following are some examples.

(a) **Low-cost whole life assurances.** These operate on the normal with-profits system, but they have the added feature of a guaranteed death benefit which is greater than the basic sum assured, and which is payable until the basic sum assured plus allotted bonuses exceeds it.

(b) **Low-cost endowment assurances**. These operate similarly to low-cost whole life assurances. The guarantee, however, attaches only to the death benefit; the amount payable at maturity is the basic sum assured plus allotted bonuses as for a straight with-profits endowment assurance.

(c) **Low-start endowment assurances**. These are effectively low-cost endowment assurances modified to allow premiums to start at a low level and then to increase yearly over a period of years.

(d) **Flexi-endowment assurances**. A feature of these policies is that they grant a very favourable guaranteed surrender value should the policy be encashed during the first ten years of its term, although they are normally written, with profits, for a much longer term.

Unit-linked assurances

6.15 The **distribution of surplus** under the with-profits system can be regarded as fair and reasonable, as is its determination. The latter aspect may however not be readily understood by all policyholders, and the extent of participation in, for example, capital appreciation of investments, may not be entirely explicit. Thus the life offices introduced unit-linked policies. With these policies the benefit payable is linked to the value of units in a unit trust or linked with a unitised segregated internal fund operated by the issuing office.

6.16 Under a **unit-linked endowment assurance**, each premium may be used partly to purchase units in a fund of the policyholder's choice, partly to ensure a guaranteed death benefit, and partly to incur management charges. The division is on an explicit basis. Should a death claim arise either the guaranteed death benefit or the bid value of the units allocated to the policy, whichever is the higher, becomes payable. On the maturity of the policy it is the bid value of the units allocated which become payable.

Life assurance and saving

6.17 People save for various reasons and some form of life assurance is frequently the vehicle used for the purpose. The role of insurance in the pensions industry has been discussed in the first part of this Study Text. Other examples include the following.

House purchase

6.18 The 1980s saw a considerable growth in the use of **endowment life assurance policies** to repay mortgage loans such that this is now the most common method for new mortgages.

School fees

6.19 School fees plans usually involve purchasing with-**profits endowment life assurance** which matures at the time when fees are due to be paid. The proceeds may be paid out in instalments on, say, a termly basis.

Lump sum investment and bonds

6.20 For those who wish to save a lump sum for capital growth or to generate income insurers offer a variety of single-premium life assurance policies known as bonds.

(a) **Guaranteed bonds** provide guaranteed benefits with a maturity of five to ten years. Most commonly they are based on single-premium life assurance contracts with guaranteed annual bonuses. **Income bonds** give a guaranteed income and a maturity value roughly equivalent to the initial investment. **Growth bonds** reinvest the income element so as to provide capital growth up to maturity.

(b) **Investment bonds** are unit-linked single premium endowment or whole life policies. The premium is invested in units or funds which may be specialised or consist of a mixture of investments. Further tailoring to individual investment objectives is possible by means of **minibonds** where a personalised fund is set up within the insurer's fund.

Surrender values

6.21 With unit-linked policies encashment during the term of the policy is again on the basis of the bid value of the allocated units. However, with conventional types of life assurance the position is necessarily different.

6.22 **Temporary assurances** which provide cover only against death do not normally require any surrender value on discontinuance.

6.23 With other types of conventional policy, such as whole life assurance and endowment assurance, the **initial expenses** and **commission payment** are relatively **heavy** so that generally no surrender value accrues, under an annual premium policy, during the first two years. Thereafter, in the further early years of the policy's duration the life office might use as a surrender value basis an accumulation of all premiums paid, less all expenses incurred, less the cost of the death cover provided. In later years the life office might use as a surrender value basis the discounted value of all future benefits and expenses expected, less the discounted value of all expected future premiums.

6.24 As an alternative to surrendering a conventional life assurance policy, the policy may be converted into a paid-up policy. Then no further premiums are payable and the policy remains in force for a reduced sum assured.

6.25 The Income and Corporation Taxes Act 1988 charges to income tax (but usually only at the higher rate) gains which arise from life assurance policies in some circumstances (known as chargeable gains). This affects all life policies effected after 19 March 1968 and policies effected before then if they are varied after that date so as to extend the term or increase the benefits. But with 'qualifying policies' (as under s 15 of the Income and Corporation Taxes Act 1988), only gains in the first ten years are taxable.

6.26 Life assurance policies are normally exempt from capital gains tax.

Chapter roundup

- **Personal accident insurance** covers injury by some external, unexpected force. Group PA cover can be arranged for all employees or selected groups. It is often found in combination with sickness insurance.
- **Permanent health insurance** is similar to personal accident and sickness cover except that it is a long-term form of insurance rather than an annual insurance.
- **Key person insurance** may be taken out for specified personnel such as directors or project managers. In some cases kidnap and ransom insurance may also be advisable.
- Be sure that you can **distinguish** between term assurance, endowment assurance and whole life assurance and between non-profit, with-profits and unit-linked policies.

Test your knowledge

1 Why are insurances of the person not policies of indemnity? (see para 1.1)

2 What sort of cover is available under personal accident insurance? (2.3)

3 Distinguish between total and partial disablement. (3.7)

4 Why might an employer provide a group permanent health insurance scheme? (4.6)

5 What doubts surround the insurability of 'key' employees? (5.2)

6 What is the difference between term assurance and whole life assurance? (6.1 - 6.4)

7 Explain the various types of bonuses that are declared under with-profits policies. (6.11 - 6.13)

8 What is an investment bond? (6.20)

Now try illustrative question 19 at the end of the Study Text

Chapter 19

THE INSURANCE MARKET

This chapter covers the following topics.

Introduction

In this chapter we give a quick overview of the main suppliers of insurance in the UK - basically insurance companies and brokers. We also include notes on how the various bodies are controlled by regulation.

1 MARKET STRUCTURE

1.1 Suppliers of insurance are of two main types: **producers**, that is insurance companies of various types, and **intermediaries**, the common term for brokers and agents.

Proprietary and mutual insurance companies

1.2 Within the UK most insurance business transacted through companies is written with **proprietary companies**, that is offices owned by shareholders who are entitled to a share of the profits of the company by way of dividends on the shares they own.

1.3 **Mutual companies**, on the other hand, are owned by their policyholders who share in profits either through lower premiums or through bonuses (in the case of life policy holders).

Friendly societies

1.4 The mutual organisations known as 'friendly societies' usually specialise in **life, annuity, personal accident, permanent health and/or medical expenses** business, and a few in commercial insurances (some for very specialised, if large, markets), especially P&I clubs (Protection & Indemnity clubs) which write commercial marine liability risks.

Industrial assurance companies

1.5 In addition, there are industrial assurance companies, dedicated to or specialising in **small life policies** of specified sorts, which are distinguished by their collectors, who call on their insureds to collect premiums at least once every two months. Friendly societies writing this sort of business are known as collecting societies.

Captive insurance companies

1.6 Captive insurers are a fairly small factor in the British insurance market as few are registered in the UK. Their average premium income appears to be relatively small but they do make a valuable contribution to the **capacity** of the market and they also provide direct capacity and some expertise for the insurance of some very unattractive risks, such as public liability cover for explosives manufacturers and manufacturers.

Reinsurance companies

1.7 Most direct insurers also operate **reinsurance departments** or reinsurance subsidiaries and much business is transacted via reciprocal exchange with other direct insurers. There are specialist reinsurance companies (professional reinsurers) however, and a large volume of reinsurance business is placed at Lloyd's.

Groups of insurers

1.8 Insurers themselves form collective bodies to insure and reinsure difficult risks. Examples are:

(a) The **life assurance pools** set up in the early 1950s for sufferers from diabetes, coronary disease, and hypertension

(b) The **British Insurance (Atomic Energy) Committee**, set up in 1957 to manage the insurance public liability and material damage risks for UK nuclear installations, currently shared by approximately 57 companies and 224 Lloyd's syndicates

(c) The **Motor Insurers' Bureau**, which manages statutory claims (which will be shared by all UK motor insurers) for injuries caused by uninsured or untraced motorists

Division by specialisation

1.9 The market picture as regards specialisation is considerably complicated by the mergers and takeovers of the last century or so, specialist organisations having broadened their scope to underwrite related and other business. A principal factor in this has been the wish to provide for all their customers' needs, cutting out other insurers' chances of attracting away their customers as far as possible. What was originally a fire and perils specialist might therefore have taken over a plate glass replacement specialist and a liability insurance specialist, and now offer a wide selection of commercial insurances.

1.10 Despite increasing diversification by larger insurers, **many specialists** remain, however, and the main divisions of the market from this angle are:

- Life assurance (and/or pensions)
- General insurance (whether or not specialised)
- The composite companies which write classes of insurance in both those branches

Some specialist classes, owing to the relatively small volume of business available, are written by a mere handful of insurers (which do not necessarily restrict themselves to the speciality), for example aviation insurance and weather insurance.

1.11 A notable development in the 1990s, particularly in motor insurance, is the success of companies which **sell direct** to customers (such as Direct Line), usually concluding business by telephone, rather than via high street brokers. These companies do not employ large numbers of highly trained underwriters but instead use underwriting software which automatically produces a quotation when information is keyed in by telesales personnel.

*This is an example of an EXPERT SYSTEM (see Part B).

Choosing an insurer

1.12 Unless the available market is very small, and the risk you present such that it will be carried by several insurers, it pays to **shop around**.

1.13 On the other hand, a good relationship with a few reliable insurers over a long period pays dividends, as their staff and yours will get to know each others' methods and problems, which can mean smoother working relationships, and save time and expense in emergencies. Discounts may be available for long-term agreements.

1.14 The best approach is a combination of both practices, because it is unlikely that any insurer will always be the most competitive, or be able to write all the insurances a developing or complex business may need.

Regulation

1.15 Insurers are regulated under the Insurance Companies Act 1982 which specifies the constitution of new UK insurers, limits their activities, sets minimum financial requirements and requires all managers and their seniors to be 'fit and proper persons'.

2 LLOYD'S OF LONDON

2.1 The Corporation of Lloyd's provides only accommodation and central services; the insurance business is conducted by individual broking firms (intermediaries, discussed later in this chapter) and underwriting members.

Underwriting members

2.2 There are about 20,000 Names, that is **underwriting members** of Lloyd's; they are individuals who accept risks in return for a premium and meet any claims under policies underwritten.

2.3 'Names' group into syndicates of which there are some 400, thereby enabling larger sums to be underwritten than could be done individually. A Name may be, and often is, a member of more than one syndicate. It is customary for each syndicate to accept a particular type of risk such as marine, motor etc. The syndicates are run by professional managing agents. The responsibility for negotiating and accepting the risks of any one syndicate is delegated to one or more active underwriters.

2.4 Each Name has **unlimited personal liability** for the payment of his share of his syndicate's policies; the share is proportional to the capacity he has contributed to the syndicate compared with its total capacity for writing premiums in a year. A name must show net assets of £250,000 generally excluding the main residence, and some other specified assets. A deposit of at least 20% of the overall premium limit must be made to Lloyd's and additionally funds equal to 30% of the overall premium limit must be held at Lloyd's.

2.5 The potential financial gains that can be made by Lloyd's names are enormous, but so is the personal risk. Some syndicates have fared particularly badly in recent years implicating their members in vast losses.

3 BROKERS AND INTERMEDIARIES

3.1 Intermediaries are of two main types, agents and brokers, but in between may be found a range of advisers with various specialisations, and extent of authorisation.

Agents

3.2 Agents, or 'part-time agents' **write insurances** as an **additional service** to their customers. Examples are car sales firms, which introduce their customers to motor and vehicle breakdown insurers, and solicitors, accountants and other professionals who introduce their clients to life and pensions offices.

Brokers

3.3 Insurance brokers must be registered with the Insurance Brokers' Registration Council (IBRC). (The Financial Services Authority is taking over this responsibility.) Among other specialisms, they normally practice insurance full-time. Brokers give advice and provide a wide range of services including the following:

- Placing and extending insurance cover
- Making arrangements for surveys of risk and insurance
- Dealing with claims
- Liasing with loss adjusters
- Advising on business contracts
- Crisis management services

3.4 **Remuneration** arrangements for brokers vary. Some brokers use the long-standing method of charging clients the gross premiums required by underwriters and then deducting commission on the premiums received. More common nowadays is a system of charging net premiums plus a management fee agreed in advance with the broker according to the services provided.

3.5 Even if the organisation uses an insurance broker, it will still retain **certain responsibilities** including providing information on experience of losses and risks, and advising on material changes to its circumstances.

3.6 When choosing a broker an organisation should consider the following factors:

- Knowledge of the industry, markets and areas of relevant insurance
- Proof of their presence in key areas
- Standard policy wordings
- Extent to which they provide risk management advice
- Ancillary services such as training
- Methods of processing claims

Intermediaries and insurers

3.7 There are some insurers which accept all their business through intermediaries: in exchange for a fee (a percentage of the premium for each insurance written), the intermediaries undertake some of the advertising and administration involved.

3.8 At the other extreme, there are producers who, although they do not refuse business introduced by intermediaries, treat them as mere **introducers of business**, preferring to control the quality of their sales and service through the training and supervision of their own staff, who do all the work.

3.9 Most insurers, however, while maintaining agency contracts of various types, are also accustomed to **writing business direct**. Both the extreme descriptions of producers tend to be specialist organisations, writing life assurance or particular types of general insurance.

Choosing an intermediary

3.10 Buyers of insurance should therefore be aware that even in these days of electronic gadgets which select the best quote for risks such as private cars, it is impossible for any one intermediary to have agencies with all the insurers who might accept a risk. If time allows, advice from several intermediaries and a selection of 'direct only' insurers will produce a range of quotations and terms.

Exercise 1

Set out the main divisions of the United Kingdom insurance market.

Regulation of intermediaries

3.11 No intermediaries should offer services beyond their competence, and the better qualified and experienced the intermediary is held out to be, the higher the standards of service which should be provided, and the better trained and supervised their staff.

3.12 It is useful to remember that, although the intermediary usually receives commission from the insurer for placing your insurance, the intermediary himself has a common law duty to exercise reasonable care and skill in recommending, placing and handling the business. The House of Lords held in *Hedley Byrne v Heller & Partners 1964* that breach of this duty is actionable if it causes mere financial loss.

3.13 Intermediaries who charge their clients **fees**, for example for placing and renewing insurances or for arranging surveys, making inspections and reporting on the safety or best methods of handling risks, also have a **contractual relationship** with the client who pays them; this can allow a disappointed client an additional choice of legal remedies.

Code of conduct

3.14 The IBRC (Code of Conduct) Approval Order 1978 provides fundamental principles for insurance brokers.

(a) Conduct their business with **utmost good faith** and integrity at all times

(b) Put their **clients' interests** first, satisfying their insurance requirements as far as possible and, subject to this, to have proper regard for others

(c) Ensure that **advertising** by them or on their behalf does not involve misleading or extravagant statements

3.15 The code of conduct is reinforced by examples of acceptable behaviour, from provision of objective independent advice, to adequate description of the premiums and fees charged to their clients, and warnings to clients to check the accuracy and adequacy of documents. A broker's gross or repeated negligence may amount to misconduct deserving removal from the register. The IBRC accepts complaints, and can help resolve disputes.

Exercise 2

Most of the insurance arrangements of X Ltd are handled by a broker. What responsibilities does X Ltd have in the relationship?

Solution

Garry Shillingham 'Broker service agreements' (*Administrator*, October 1994) says that the client makes all final decisions and specifically is responsible for the following:

(a) Designating the person to whom the broker will report

(b) Providing the broker with information on loss experience, risk exposures and any other data requested

(c) Advising changes in the business operations and the nature of the business

(d) Reviewing insurance policies placed by the broker to ensure that the terms, conditions and policy limits are satisfactory

4 FINANCIAL SERVICES LEGISLATION

4.1 The Financial Services Act 1986 regulated the activities of those selling investment contracts and therefore it affects all insurance companies and insurance intermediaries who advise on or sell life assurance (other than purely 'protection' policies), and/or pensions and other savings-linked contracts. Although the government decided that compulsory licensing would be a costly means of conveying a (possibly unwarranted) impression of depth of knowledge, and that it was therefore inadvisable, these agency and advice activities are a criminal offence unless the intermediary is authorised.

4.2 The Financial Services and Markets Act 2000 received Royal Assent on 14 June 2000. The act will replace not just the Financial Services Act 1986, but other acts relating to specific institutions. The Government has stated a target of about a year for completion of the necessary subsidiary legislation, and other preparations for the implementation of the Act.

5 LOSS ADJUSTERS

5.1 Firms of independent specialist loss adjusters have grown up to serve the insurers' need to **investigate large claims**, especially in the areas of property, marine and aviation insurance. They can give valuable advice on the various measures that can be taken to mitigate a loss, for example by salvage, repairs and plant hire.

Exercise 3

What principles of insurance law would be of particular relevance to a loss adjuster?

Solution

Proximate cause and, of course, indemnity.

6 THE INTERNATIONAL MARKET

6.1 Insurance may be international in the sense that the policy is placed with an overseas insurer or that the insured item travels internationally.

6.2 **Cross-frontier business** (or services business) is the term used when the insured purchases insurance from an insurer who is established in a different country. **Establishment business** involves the purchase of insurance from an admitted insurer, that is one who is established in the same country as the insured but whose head office is overseas.

Cross-frontier business

6.3 Reasons for conducting business on a **cross-frontier** basis

(a) It may be that cover cannot be obtained locally.

(b) It may be cheaper to use an overseas insurer.

(c) It may be convenient or advantageous to do so because of foreign currency considerations.

(d) It may be desirable to spread the risk as widely as possible via reinsurance.

Establishment business

6.4 Reasons for transacting insurance through an **overseas branch**

(a) Cross-frontier business is not permitted by the country in question.

(b) Obviously, setting up an overseas branch is one way in which insurance companies can expand.

(c) Insurers may find that establishment business is more profitable than business conducted on a services basis.

The European Union

6.5 There is already total '**freedom of establishment**' for insurers within the EU (formerly the EC): in other words insurers in one member state can set up a branch in another member state and carry on business on the same terms as domestic insurers. Likewise there is freedom to provide reinsurances on a cross-frontier basis. Over the last few years insurers have been building up pan-European alliances to take advantage of the opportunities presented by the single European market.

7 ACQUISITIONS AND DIVESTMENTS 12/99

7.1 One practical area in which the company secretary may well be involved is considering the consequences for insurance cover of businesses acquired and disposed.

7.2 A **detailed review** of **risk** and **current insurance cover** should be carried out on all businesses acquired. Areas of particular concern may include condition and valuation of assets and on insurance taken out on staff. Full information should be provided to the organisation's current insurers if they will be undertaking responsibility for the acquired business. Warranties should be obtained as appropriate.

7.3 To smooth the necessary changes, policies are generally on a declaration basis, with cover being amended on the basis of subsequent declaration. However problems may arise if the proposed amendments are not insurances of a similar risk.

7.4 Important considerations on the sale of the business include **arranging the date** on which the selling organisation ceases to be responsible for cover. The acquirers will want a summary of the acquired business's cover and recent insurance history, and there should be the appropriate warranties in the agreement of sale. Return premiums should be obtained for unexpired periods of insurance. Appropriate documentation should be passed over or retained, and appropriate declarations made, if policies are on a declaration basis.

Chapter roundup

- The **UK domestic market** can best be summarised by way of a diagram. See the next page.
- The opening up of the **European insurance market** is likely to lead to changes in the coming years. Watch the press for details.
- **EC directives** have a direct impact on UK insurance legislation as the UK must implement all EC directives.

Test your knowledge

1 What is the difference between a proprietary and a mutual insurance company? (see paras 1.2, 1.3)

2 Explain how Lloyds underwriters are organised. (2.2, 2.3)

3 What is the part of an agent in the insurance market? (3.2)

4 What fundamental principles should insurance brokers follow? (3.14)

5 What does a loss adjuster do? (5.1)

6 Distinguish between cross-frontier business and establishment business. (6.2)

Now try illustrative question 20 at the end of the Study Text

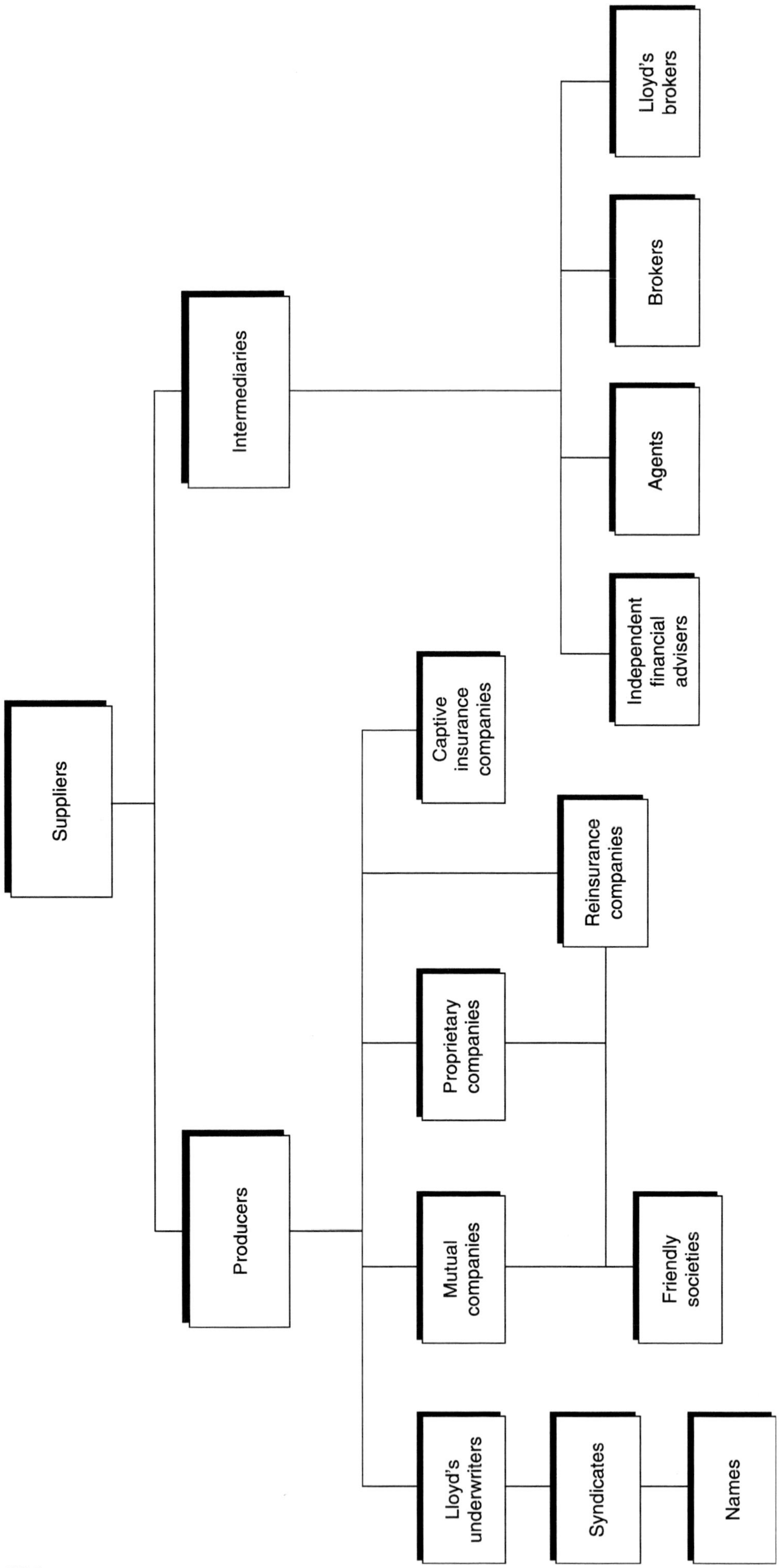

Suppliers
Intermediaries
Producers
Independent financial advisers
Agents
Brokers
Lloyd's brokers
Captive insurance companies
Reinsurance companies
Proprietary companies
Mutual companies
Friendly societies
Lloyd's underwriters
Syndicates
Names

Chapter 20

PENSION SCHEMES AND TRUST LAW

This chapter covers the following topics.

Introduction

'Pensions' is a highly complex area of study. Not surprisingly most companies leave the detailed management of their pension fund with specialist fund managers such as Mercury Asset Management, Phillips & Drew and Prudential.

In your role as Company Secretary and Administrator, however, it is highly likely that you will be expected on the one hand, to deal with fund managers, and on the other, to explain aspects of pensions to senior and junior colleagues. This and the following chapters aim to equip you with the basic knowledge that you will need.

Much of this first chapter on pensions should be revision of a topic covered on your earlier studies - Trust Law. Even if so, do not neglect sections 1, 6 and 7, otherwise you will struggle with the material that follows.

1 THE CONSTITUTION OF PENSION SCHEMES 6/96

1.1 The subject of pensions seems daunting because of its apparently endless and impenetrable jargon and because of the maze of rules, regulations, and statutes that has grown up around it. At the centre of the maze, however, is an extremely simple concept, and one that you should always keep in mind, especially if you feel that you are starting to get lost: a pension scheme is a set of arrangements made now in order to secure an income later.

1.2 The remainder of this part of the text explores the ramifications of that statement. What arrangements can be made? Do they involve money now or are they merely a promise? Who makes the arrangements? Who provides the money? How much money is provided? How much is needed? How large is the income later, and who is entitled to it? When? And the question to be dealt with in this section is perhaps the most important of all. What guarantee is there that present expectations will be met: how *secure* is the promise of an income later?

Statutory and company schemes

1.3 There are a number of ways in which **security** can be **achieved**. For example pension arrangements could be constituted on a **discretionary basis**. When an employee gets to an appropriate pension age the employer could then consider paying the employee a pension in the same way as he had previously paid the employee his salary. This is, in fact, the basis on which statutory schemes, such as those for civil servants operate.

1.4 The position of employees under such statutory schemes is, however, quite different from that of employees under company schemes. Statutory schemes have the **national credit** behind them since the Government always has the necessary powers to raise revenue by taxation and uses this to pay salaries and pensions to government servants.

1.5 However, the future of individual companies is not guaranteed. If an employer were to adopt the statutory method of financing pensions by leaving the cost to be met until the employees reach pension age, he would risk failing to provide an adequate measure of security. If his company went out of business before it had made any specific commitment to pay pensions then no pensions would be forthcoming to its employees.

Pooled pay-as-you-go system

1.6 Under this system groups of companies can be formed for pension arrangements, the respective groups covering all companies within a whole industry. The logic is that whilst individual companies might fail it is unlikely that a whole large industry will do so. The system's weakness is a **demographic** one: more and more people are living for longer and longer, such that the balance is likely to shift and there will be more people living off pensions than there are in employment to pay for them.

Pensions funding and the book reserve system

1.7 Instead of waiting until individual employees attain pension age and financing those pensions then, pensions could be promised in advance of pension age. Pensions could be considered to be subject to a **building-up process** year by year during each employee's period of active service. The necessary money to meet the associated liabilities attaching to the pension promises, as they accrue year by year, could be accumulated. This is known as **pensions funding**.

1.8 Such a funded pension arrangement could be transacted by an employer as part of his business; the fund which is being built up forming part of the overall assets of the business and being identified by a special reserve in the accounts of the employer. This is known as the **book reserve** system.

Trusts

1.9 In the UK it is felt that the security of private 'occupational' pensions schemes is best achieved if pension arrangements are set up and maintained by individual employers, but in such a way that they are divorced from the employer's business interests, and hence the risk of the employer failing.

1.10 Under English law, it has long been believed that the best way of setting up and maintaining a group occupational pension scheme, which is to be paid for largely by the employer but is divorced from his business interests, is to constitute it under a **trust**. This is recognised by the Inland Revenue who, as we shall see in Chapter 22, are only prepared to grant full tax reliefs to schemes that are set up under a trust.

2 TRUSTS AND TRUST LAW 6/95

2.1 You should be familiar with trusts and trust law from your earlier studies. The following sections are intended to remind you of the salient points, although aspects that particularly impinge upon pensions schemes are picked out.

Definition

2.2 No formal definition of a trust exists although the definition given by Sir Arthur Underhill is most commonly quoted. It states that a trust is:

> 'an equitable obligation, binding a person (who is called a trustee) to deal with property over which he has control (which is called the trust property), for the benefit of persons (who are called beneficiaries or *cestuis que trust*), of whom he may himself be one, and any of whom may enforce the obligation.'

2.3 A completely constituted trust, on the other hand, may be **enforced** by the **beneficiaries**, even though they may learn of the existence of the trust only long after it has been created. Thus a pension scheme set up as a trust can be enforced by members who were not even alive when it was established. The use of a trust to set up a pension scheme enables the beneficiaries to enforce their rights.

2.4 **Trustees** are those persons entrusted by the person who sets up the trust, to **administer** the trust for the **benefit of beneficiaries** and with a pension scheme the trustees hold the assets for the benefit of the members and pensioners.

The three certainties

2.5 An express trust will only be valid if the three certainties as laid down in *Knight v Knight 1840* are present.

(a) **Certainty of words**

The words used to declare a trust need not be formal; indeed there is no obligation for a settlor to use the word 'trust'. However, the words must be imperative and show that a trust was intended.

(b) **Certainty of subject**

The property which is the subject of the trust must be certain and the interests of the beneficiaries in that property must be ascertainable.

(c) **Certainty of objects**

The 'objects' of a trust are the beneficiaries. 'Certainty of objects' means that the settlor must identify or supply the means of identifying the persons whom the trustees are to recognise as the beneficiaries.

The beneficiary principle

2.6 The beneficiary principle is that, with the exception of charitable trusts, a trust must be for the **benefit of individuals**. It cannot be just for a purpose or an object since then the court could not enforce and control the trust. But trusts set up for the purpose of, for example, providing a sports ground may still be valid since the court will identify persons who will be interested in the trust: the people who will use the ground.

Profits from trusts

2.7 It is a strict rule of equity that a trustee or other person in a fiduciary position is **not entitled** to make a **profit** from his trust. If he does make such a profit he will hold it on constructive trust.

Generally

3.1 Any person capable of holding property may act as a trustee, apart from criminals, bankrupts and directors who are disqualified by statute. The following special cases should be noted.

(a) A **corporation** may be appointed. It is usually advantageous if it is a **trust corporation**. A trust corporation is a body corporate which satisfies the following three conditions.

(i) It is registered and constituted under the law of any member state of the European Community and has a place of business within the European Community.

(ii) The memorandum authorises it to undertake the business of acting as a trustee and of acting as a personal representative.

(iii) It has an issued capital of not less than £250,000 of which not less than £100,000 must have been paid up in cash (or equivalent amounts for other European Community countries).

(b) Certain **persons** are granted the status of trust corporation. They are:

- Any company appointed by the court
- Certain charities
- Certain public officers (such as The Public Trustee)
- Certain local and public authorities

3.2 Some persons would not normally be appointed trustees by the court, although they may be appointed by the settlor. These persons would include **beneficiaries** for trusts which are not pension schemes, but so long as conflicts of interest can be avoided it is generally seen as a positive advantage in the case of pension schemes that some trustees should be drawn from the employee membership (see the OPB's views below).

Appointments

3.3 In creating a settlement the settlor appoints the first trustees and they are usually parties to the trust deed to signify their acceptance of the appointment. The trust deed may also provide for the appointment of replacement trustees when need arises.

3.4 A trust is **not allowed** to **fail** for **lack of a trustee**. There is a statutory power (s 36 TA) to appoint a trustee as replacement for another who:

- Dies, retires, or is removed
- Remains out of the UK for more than 12 months
- Refuses to act
- Is unfit to act or is incapable of acting
- Is a minor
- Is a corporation which is dissolved

3.5 The replacement trustee may be appointed, in writing, by:

(a) Persons named in the trust deed; or if none (or none willing to act)

(b) Other trustees, or personal representatives of the last trustee if he is dead (they may appoint themselves in an emergency, for example, when there is only one trustee and two are required to sell land)

3.6 The **court may appoint** trustees under s 41 TA whenever it is inexpedient, difficult or impracticable to appoint trustees without the assistance of the court, whether or not there are remaining trustees. The beneficiaries or the trustee may apply to the court for an appointment to be made (s 58 TA) and the desires of the beneficiaries will be taken into account. However, the court will not exercise this power of appointment to interfere with appointments made by others entitled to do so.

3.7 After appointing the first trustees the **settlor** has **no power** to appoint replacement or additional trustees unless the trust instrument reserves that power to him. A person who has the statutory power of appointment may appoint himself as a replacement trustee but not as an additional trustee. In selecting a person for appointment as trustee he should do what is conducive to the interests of the trust.

3.8 A **beneficiary** has **no inherent power** to appoint trustees nor any right to be consulted about appointments: *Re Brockbank 1948*. However in certain circumstances he may be able to terminate or reconstitute the trust. If all beneficiaries are *sui juris* and absolutely entitled to the trust property, then acting together they may terminate the trust: *Saunders v Vautier 1841*.

3.9 **Additional trustees** (not replacing retiring trustees) may be appointed under s36(6) TA subject to the following limitations.

(a) The number of trustees may not be increased above four.

(b) No additional trustees may be appointed if the existing trustees include a trust corporation.

(c) The appointor may not appoint himself: *Re Power's Settlement Trusts 1951*.

3.10 A trustee is appointed **in writing** (except where he becomes trustee by operation of law). It is standard procedure to make the appointment by deed in order to effect an automatic transfer to the trustee of trust property.

3.11 No one can be compelled to accept appointment as trustee, which may be a burdensome office. A prospective trustee is invited to be a party to the deed of appointment so that it is clear that he has accepted office. If he refuses he is said to **disclaim**. It is normal practice to execute a deed of disclaimer. If the matter is left in doubt and the designated person interferes with the trust property in any way, he risks being deemed to have accepted office by his conduct in acting as trustee.

The termination of a trustee's office

3.12 A trustee may **retire** from his office:

(a) Under a provision in the trust instrument

(b) Under an order of the court

(c) With the consent of all the beneficiaries, all being *sui juris* and absolutely entitled

(d) Under s 36 TA, on the appointment of a new trustee

(e) Under s 39 TA, without a new appointment, provided that:

(i) The request to retire is by deed.

(ii) He obtains the consent of the other trustees by deed.

(iii) He obtains the consent by deed of anyone named in the trust instrument as having power to appoint new trustees.

(iv) There will remain at least two trustees or a trust corporation, either already in office or appointed on his retirement.

3.13 A trustee may be **removed** from his office:

(a) Under a power contained in the trust deed

(b) By the court under s 41 TA for any reason if for the benefit of the beneficiaries (for example if a trustee becomes bankrupt)

(c) Under s 36 TA, where the trustee has remained out of the UK for more than 12 months, or refuses to act or is unfit to act or incapable of acting

The number of trustees

3.14 There is no general maximum or minimum number, but if the trust property includes **land**, the maximum number of trustees is **four** (s 34 TA).

3.15 Unless the trust instrument expressly requires a minimum of two trustees, a **single trustee** is sufficient to administer a trust (except if the trust includes land).

The vesting of property in trustees

3.16 The settlor must **vest** the property in the **first trustees**, otherwise the trust may be incompletely constituted.

3.17 Property vests automatically in new trustees under s 40 TA where the appointment of a new trustee is by deed, except for:

(a) Mortgages of land (where trustees have lent money on the security of land, the mortgage must be transferred into the names of the new trustees)

(b) Leasehold land held under a covenant not to assign without consent (which must be assigned, or transferred and the new owners registered)

(c) Stocks and shares (which must be transferred and the new owners registered)

Special trustees

3.18 A custodian trustee is one in whom property is vested for greater security, but with the administration of the trust being carried on by the ordinary trustees. The Treasury Solicitor, trust corporations and local authorities may be custodian trustees.

3.19 On application by the settlor, a trustee or a beneficiary the court may appoint, at its discretion, any fit and proper person as a **judicial trustee**. This procedure may be useful where the administration of the trust has broken down. The judicial trustee is under the control of the court.

3.20 The Public Trustee, who is a public official, may be appointed as a trustee in various circumstances.

Pensions Act 1995: member-nominated trustees

3.21 In future, scheme members will have the right to choose **at least one third** of the scheme's trustees. A minimum of two trustees (called 'member-nominated' trustees) will have to be chosen in this way, except in schemes with less than 100 members when there will have to be at least one.

3.22 Schemes will be able to devise their own rules for selecting **member-nominated trustees**. These rules will have to be approved by the scheme members under a statutory consultation procedure. Employers will be able to propose alternative arrangements to having member-nominated trustees. Any proposal will have to be approved by scheme members under the statutory consultation procedure.

3.23 Employers are required to allow member trustees to have time off work to attend meetings and to receive training.

4 THE DUTIES OF TRUSTEES 6/95, 6/96, 6/98, 6/00

Outline

4.1 In January 1992 the Occupational Pensions Board issued a brief guide for pension trustees. This usefully summarises the duties of a pension scheme trustee as follows.

(a) To act in accordance with the **trust deed** and **rules** of the scheme, within the framework of the law

(b) To act **prudently, conscientiously** and honestly and with the utmost good faith

(c) To act in the **best interests** of the beneficiaries and strike a fair balance between the interests of different classes of beneficiary

(d) To take **advice** on technical matters and any other matters which the trustee does not understand

(e) To **invest** the funds

General duties

4.2 A trustee's duties are imposed by the trust instrument and by general law. Sometimes a trustee can use his discretion (for example investing in particular securities) and then he must **act honestly** and with the **care** that a prudent man of business would exercise in the management of his own affairs. He should also use any special skills he possesses.

4.3 A pension scheme trustee must **familiarise himself** with the **trust deed and rules** of the scheme, for it is his duty to administer the pension scheme impartially in accordance with the rules. Furthermore, so as to be properly informed regarding the scheme, a trustee should obtain a list of the scheme's investments and their valuation; and details of members, those in active service, those with pensions in the course of payment, and deferred pensioners. Also he should study the annual reports of the scheme and the minimal valuation reports.

4.4 Trustees should see that **money owed** to the scheme is **paid** and that transactions and proceedings of the scheme are properly recorded. This means that proper accounts must be kept, and that the scheme accounts must be audited. They are also responsible for ensuring schemes fulfil their taxation liabilities.

4.5 The trustees hold the assets of the scheme for the **benefit** of the **members** and the trustees must carry out their duties with reasonable care and in good faith. This involves obtaining and considering professional advice in areas where the trustees themselves are not experts.

4.6 Trustees should of course act in the **best interest** of **beneficiaries**, and should also be impartial between different classes of employee. In practice this may involve balancing the interests of a number of different classes.

Discretionary powers

4.7 Scheme rules cannot cover every possible happening. Therefore trustees may be given **discretion** in some areas to deal with certain matters not covered by the rules or only covered in general terms. One such power would indeed be amendment of the scheme rules.

4.8 These discretionary powers may involve decisions in principle or also for individuals. As examples, there may be discretionary powers to the trustees in connection with permissible late entry to the scheme, to the re-entry of a leaver from the scheme, or as regards permissible early retirement. For individuals, trustees may have discretion to decide to whom death benefits should be paid.

Accounts

4.9 Trustees have a duty to **keep accounts** of all transactions for which they are responsible as trustees. No particular form is required by law for trust accounts generally, but for pension schemes there are detailed requirements.

The personal advantage of trustees

4.10 A trustee may **not secure** any personal advantage (**'profit'**) from his position as trustee, unless one of the exceptions applies. It is the duty of a trustee to avoid any situation or transaction where his personal interest and his duty of disinterested service may conflict. If he does secure an illicit profit he holds it in trust or, in certain cases, the transaction is voidable.

Trustees' remuneration

4.11 In principle a trustee is not remunerated for his services. But the principle is so impractical that there are numerous exceptions to it.

(a) Remuneration is allowed where the trust deed authorises it: *Webb v Earl of Shaftesbury 1802*.

(b) Remuneration may be allowed by order of the court if the trust is more onerous than the trustee reasonably expected when he had accepted appointment: *Re Duke of Norfolk's Settlement Trusts 1981*.

(c) Remuneration may be obtained by contract with the beneficiaries provided they are all *sui juris*.

(d) The Public Trustcc and custodian trustees have a statutory right to remuneration.

(e) A solicitor trustee may charge for work done in legal proceedings on behalf of all trustees (see below).

(f) A trust corporation appointed by the court may charge a fee if the court so authorises.

(g) Remuneration is allowed where the trust property is situated abroad, the foreign law permits payment and the payment was received without the trustees' volition.

4.12 In modern practice every **trust instrument** includes a clause by which an individual trustee, if he carries on a profession, may charge for time spent on trust work and a corporate trustee may charge in accordance with its current standard scale.

Purchases of trust property

4.13 While the rules on purchases of trust property have the effect of preventing a trustee from profiting from his position, they achieve this by subjecting trustees to certain disabilities (*Tito v Waddell (No 2) 1977*).

4.14 If a trustee purchases trust property, any beneficiary may within a reasonable time after the purchase apply to the court for an order to set aside the sale. The trustee must then return the property but is repaid the purchase price with interest.

4.15 The objection is to the conflict of interest. Accordingly the purchase is voidable even if:

(a) There are other trustees whose decision to sell was entirely disinterested.

(b) The price paid was based on an independent valuation or can otherwise be shown to be a fair price.

(c) The sale is advantageous to the trust, for example because it needs to raise money for other purposes.

4.16 The trustee may not evade the rule by a **sale** to his own **nominee** or to his partner. A sale to the trustee's spouse or to a company of which he is a member will be closely investigated and the sale may be set aside.

4.17 A purchase of trust property by a trustee will be valid and binding if:

(a) The trust instrument **authorises** it.

(b) The **beneficiaries** give their **consent** (with no fraud or concealment by the trustee) or lose their right of objection by failing to object within a reasonable time.

(c) The trustee obtains **leave of the court**, though the court is likely to withhold approval until attempts to sell the property to another buyer have proved unsuccessful.

(d) The trustee **retires** from his trusteeship and a long interval ensues before the purchase (12 years was an acceptably long period in *Re Boles & British Land Company's Contract 1902*).

(e) Before the beneficiaries intervene, the **trustee** has **re-sold** the property to a third party who was unaware of the breach of trust, but the beneficiaries may be able to recover from the trustee his profit on re-sale.

4.18 A trustee may **purchase** from a **beneficiary** the latter's interest in the trust. But the trustee must disclose all the material facts to the beneficiary (*Hill v Langley 1988*) and must pay a fair price. A trustee is in a better position if the beneficiary has taken the initiative in proposing the purchase: *Coles v Trecothick 1804*. If the trustee takes unfair advantage of his position, the sale may be voidable.

Profits obtained by trustees from their position

4.19 A trustee is entitled to be **reimbursed** out of the trust funds for any out-of-pocket expenses properly incurred in the execution of his duties (s 30(2) TA). He also has the right to a personal indemnity for his expenses from a beneficiary who is *sui juris* and absolutely entitled.

Delegation

4.20 Except for the provisions below, a trustee cannot delegate his duties unless he is given authority by the trust instrument to do so.

4.21 By s 23 TA trustees **may employ and pay an agent** (for example, a solicitor or a stockbroker or, in the case of a pension scheme, a life assurance office) to transact any business or do any act required in the execution of a trust including the receipt and payment of money. The agent, who need not necessarily be a professional person, is unable to make the basic decisions required of a trustee but may implement those decisions. The trustees must, however, select the agent themselves (*Re Weall 1889*), and the agent must be acting within his usual business (*Fry v Tapson 1884*).

4.22 Trustees are entitled to be **paid charges** and **expenses** incurred in employing an agent. They are not responsible for the default of any agent employed in good faith.

4.23 By s 25 TA, as amended by s 9 of the Powers of Attorney Act 1971, a trustee may delegate all or any of his discretionary powers by power of attorney, but:

(a) This is the only occasion on which he may delegate his discretionary powers.

(b) The delegation cannot be for a period exceeding 12 months.

(c) The trustee must give written notice of the delegation within seven days to each of the other trustees, and to any other person who has power to appoint new trustees.

(d) The trustee may not delegate to a sole co-trustee unless it is a trust corporation.

(e) The trustee is liable for every act or default of his delegate.

Joint action by trustees

4.24 As a general principle, trustees are required to exercise their **powers jointly**. Hence they must act unanimously and a majority decision is not generally binding.

4.25 Difficulties may arise from a disagreement among the trustees as to what they should do.

(a) If the matter at issue is a duty, for example to distribute all the income of an exhaustive discretionary trust, the court will if necessary order the trustees to perform that duty even against a dissenting majority.

(b) If, however, the trustees have a discretionary power, for example to make advances of capital to beneficiaries, the court will not overrule a minority of trustees who object. The power cannot then be exercised.

(c) If the trustees are at loggerheads or in dispute over their legal position, the majority may apply to the court for an order to pay the trust moneys into court so that the trustees' responsibility is ended: s 63(3) TA.

Handing over trust property

4.26 Trustees have a duty to **hand over trust property** to beneficiaries in accordance with the terms of the trust. If they pay the wrong people, they will only avoid liability to pay again (to the right people) if they paid to an apparent beneficiary on the face of the trust document without notice of any facts or documents which might indicate that some other person was entitled. If in doubt, they should apply to the court for directions.

4.27 In practice it would seem unlikely that payment to the wrong beneficiaries would arise in the case of pension schemes. There is a problem, however, when a scheme and its beneficiary lose touch. The Social Security Act 1990 (SSA 1990) requires all pension schemes to register with the Pensions Tracing Registry so that lost pension benefits can be traced more easily. The Occupational Pensions Advisory Service (see below) believe that there are millions of pounds of unclaimed benefits left frozen in company pension schemes.

Pensions Act 1995

4.28 Specific duties the Act imposes include the following:

(a) Keeping proper books and records, including records of trustee meetings

(b) Obtaining audited accounts

(c) Making a statement of investment principles

(d) Preparing schedules of contributions and other expenses payable, and reporting when contributions are not paid in accordance with the schedule

(e) Establishing procedures for dealing with member complaints

(f) Ensuring that member-trustees are recruited in accordance with the regulations made under the Act

(g) Exercising powers to make payments to employers

4.29 The Occupational Pensions Regulatory Authority (OPRA-see below) has powers under the Pensions Act 1995 to impose a wide range of penalties on trustees. These include suspension and disqualification of trustees, obtaining restitution orders, and imposing other penalties. OPRA can also appoint trustees if necessary.

restore to its proper owner/ repair damage.

4.30 OPRA also has the power to direct trustees to take specific actions such as paying benefits or distributing information to members.

4.31 New legislation is due to be brought in shortly, marking the biggest change in the law relating to trustees since the Trustee Act 1925.

(a) Trustees will have a duty to **exercise reasonable skill and care,** taking into account individual specialist skill and knowledge.

(b) Trustees will be able to **invest trust property** as if they were absolutely entitled to the assets themselves.

(c) Trustees' **power** to **appoint nominees** and custodians will be confirmed by statute.

Secretary to the trustees

4.32 The role of secretary is increasingly important. The secretary will be involved in **ensuring compliance** with legal requirements, **co-ordinating communications**, liaison with external advisers and **organising trustee training**. The secretary will need a good knowledge of scheme rules and an awareness of the differing responsibilities of trustees and employer.

5 TRUSTEES AND INVESTMENTS 6/95

5.1 The investment of the money of a pension fund necessarily has to conform with any legal restrictions and those responsible for pension fund investment must be quite certain that they are acting within their authority. The ultimate responsibility for the investment of pension fund money rests with the trustees.

Broader powers

5.2 Most pension schemes are set up with the trust deed worded so as to permit broad powers of investment. Trustees should however still consider their **powers** and **responsibilities** in accordance with the principles of trust law. Where appropriate there should be reliable advisers to ensure that the powers are not used unwisely.

5.3 Nevertheless, in certain circumstances there are other regulations laying down the categories of investment which may be made use of and the investment limits in each category (PSO/OPB Memorandum No 93). Restrictions are not applied to investments in assurance policies and annuity contracts, authorised unit trusts, EC government securities, bank deposit and share accounts, and building society shares. Limits do apply to other investments.

5.4 As examples, the proportion of scheme resources which may be invested in land is restricted to 25%. For securities listed on a recognised stock exchange in a member state of the EC (except EC government securities and investment trust companies) the limit on the proportion of scheme resources which may be invested in the securities of any one issuer is either 5% or up to 10% so long as the total of such investments greater than 5% is not more than 40% of the scheme resources.

Types of investment in practice

5.5 The basic criteria for investment are that the safety of the fund is protected by **spreading the risk** across the different types of investment available (and also within each category) and that the best possible return is achieved. The whole portfolio must be considered each time a new investment is made to ensure that these criteria will continue to be met.

5.6 Other matters to be considered include the amount of money available, the period over which individual investments can be held, the needs of the fund for cash, and the administrative burden of reclaiming tax deducted at source where applicable.

Equities

5.7 Equities will generally form the **largest proportion** of the fund because of their potential for capital growth and because returns will be higher than those available from fixed interest stocks, reflecting the relative degrees of risk. A good spread is essential and the performance of the chosen companies and sectors must be closely monitored.

Gilts and other fixed interest stocks

5.8 Government stocks are considered to be **risk-free** in terms of payment of interest and capital in accordance with the terms of issue, and they are also the most marketable form of investment. A wide range is available and it is possible to deal in very large sums of money. Other types of fixed interest stock include debentures or bonds issued by large public companies, preference shares and convertible stocks. The principal disadvantage is the lack of a hedge against inflation. It is this that has caused the shift in emphasis to equities in recent decades.

Overseas investments

5.9 Investing overseas **increases** the **options** available and **spreads** the **risk** further; it also provides a hedge against a fall in sterling. Against these advantages must be set the possibility of political unrest abroad, lack of investment information and volatility of overseas markets. In practice the US and Japan are seen as the most attractive homes for funds invested overseas but there is no guarantee of safety. Further considerations are the attitude of political parties or unions who are unfavourably disposed towards overseas investment, and the impact upon the liquidity of the fund.

Property

5.10 Investments in property may be made either directly or through property companies and property unit trusts. Investment would tend to be long-term and would be seen as a hedge against inflation. There may be diversification within the portfolio (shops, offices etc).

very un-liquid, tho'

Self-investment

5.11 For some time the question of whether pension funds should be allowed to invest in or make loans to the employing company which set up the scheme has been a matter for concern. The issue was brought into the public eye in the aftermath of the death of Robert Maxwell.

5.12 Self-investment can take several forms, ranging from holding **shares** in the employing company to **purchasing company property** or **making a loan** to the company. In principle there is nothing wrong in this, and for a small business in its early years it offers a very effective means of providing finance. In such circumstances the members of the pension scheme are likely to be active participants in the employer's business and also to be fulfilling the role of trustees, and thus they bear the consequences of their own decisions.

5.13 For larger schemes, however, the practice is far more questionable. The National Association of Pension Funds concluded in 1988 that 'self-investment is an undesirable practice which creates potential conflicts of interest, irresolvable pressures and arguments between trustees and company managements'.

Restrictions on self-investment

5.14 Inevitably there have been calls for government action to outlaw self-investment altogether. Regulations under the Social Security Act 1990 came into force in March 1992 **limiting self-investment to 5%** of a scheme's assets. Existing holdings of property or equity in private companies may be retained but no further self-investment will be allowed. A total exemption from the regulations is available for 'small self-administered schemes'.

Ethical investment

5.15 Ethical investment means that certain sectors are avoided or that there is discrimination against or in favour of certain companies for **social, moral or political reasons**. Typically a fund run on ethical grounds will avoid companies involved in armaments, tobacco, alcohol and gambling, and companies in, or with interests in, countries whose political regimes are seen as undesirable. More recently companies with **environmentally-friendly policies** have been favoured.

5.16 The first ethical unit trust in the UK was established in the UK in 1984 and the trend is still an increasing one, with green issues in particular coming to the fore.

5.17 The problem with this approach is its restrictiveness: although most ethical and green funds have performed at least as well as their non-ethical counterparts so far, it is too early to judge how well they will perform in the long term. In the meantime, trustees have a duty to ensure that they achieve the **best possible return**.

Judgement re Mineworkers Pension Scheme 1984

5.18 The above principle is well illustrated by a judgement in April 1984 in respect of an application for a declaration that an investment scheme suggested by the fund managers should not be vetoed. The application was made by the trustees of the scheme who were appointed by the National Coal Board.

5.19 The veto of the scheme had been applied for by the five remaining trustees appointed by the National Union of Mineworkers. The defendants rejected the investment scheme on the grounds that the fund could and should invest more of its assets in the United Kingdom rather than overseas and it should not invest in industries which compete with the coal industry (in particular, oil companies).

5.20 Judgement was that there was no justification in attempting to discriminate in favour of present members and against pensioners in subsidising the coal industry. The following points were also made.

(a) The investments should be made in the **best interests** of the **beneficiaries** and these are normally their financial interests.

(b) The trustees should **not reject** certain investments for **social, moral or political reasons** if the investments are more beneficial to the beneficiaries.

(c) In exercising his power of investment the duty of the trustee is to act as a **prudent man** making an investment for other people for whom he is morally bound to provide and in doing so he must seek advice and not reject it without good reason.

(d) **Diversification** of investments should be considered by the trustees.

Performance measurement

5.21 The trustees must monitor the performance of their fund to ensure that the investment strategy is on course. There are a number of methods of measurement.

(a) The '**money-weighted return**' **(MWR)** and the '**time-weighted return**' **(TWR)** method are both used. The latter is more accurate because it takes into account new money invested and the time when it was invested.

(b) The fund may be **compared** with an **index**, for example the FT Actuaries All Share Index.

(c) The fund may be **compared** with **other funds**. Firms of actuaries and stockbrokers offer performance measurement services comparing the results of their own clients.

Exercise

What is a Trustee? Explain the importance of a Trustee in terms of pension scheme constitution and describe the main functions of such a person.

Solution

The first part of this question can be answered by reference to Paragraph 2.4 above. The second part could be answered in a variety of ways (depending upon how much you overlap with the third part) but you should certainly have mentioned that trusts cannot exist without a trustee, and that a pension scheme cannot get full tax relief unless it is constituted as a trust. You should also point out that scheme members depend on trustees to prevent foul play or incompetence on the part of the employer and professionals. The main function of a pension fund trustee is to look after the assets on behalf of the beneficiaries, and various aspects of 'looking after' could be developed (custody, investment, disclosure of information etc).

You will be much better equipped to answer this question once you have studied the remainder of this part of the Study Text.

Pensions Act 1995

5.22 The Act has introduced the following requirements.

Minimum funding requirement

5.23 A statutory **minimum funding requirement (MFR)** will be introduced for salary related schemes. Trustees will be responsible for ensuring that a MFR valuation is carried out by the actuary at least once every three years. This will be in addition to the current formal valuations. The effective date of the first MFR valuation must be no later than three years after that of the last formal valuation carried out before April 1997.

5.24 Following the MFR valuation, a **schedule of contributions** must be set up. This must show the rates of contributions and when payment should be made over the next five years. The schedule must be revised after each valuation. It should be certified annually by the actuary to confirm that the contribution rates will:

(a) Keep the scheme funding at least at the level of the MFR over the period covered by the schedule

(b) If the scheme is below the MFR, reach the MFR by the end of the period covered by the schedule

Statement of investment principles

5.25 In future, trustees of occupational pension schemes will have a duty to explain in a written statement the **principles** which govern their investment decisions.

5.26 The statement's contents will be for **trustees to decide**, but it must include their policy for making sure the scheme can comply with the MFR. It must also include:

- Their policy on the kinds of investments to be made
- The balance between those different kinds of investments
- The expected return on investments
- The degree of risk in the investments

5.27 In preparing or revising the statement, trustees must obtain and consider the written advice of someone who is suitably qualified to advise them on their pension scheme investments and liabilities. They must also consult the employer who is sponsoring the scheme.

5.28 Each year, the trustees must declare, in the scheme's annual report, that they have a **statement of investment principles** and that this is available to any member who wants a copy. They must also include in the report details of whether investments are in accordance with the statement, explain the reasons for any departures from the principles and identify the investments involved.

6 EXTERNAL SUPERVISION

The Pension Schemes Office and the Occupational Pensions Regulatory Authority

6.1 The Pension Schemes Office (PSO) (formerly the Superannuation Funds Office (SFO)) is the branch of the Inland Revenue whose approval is required in order to ensure that the scheme is tax effective. Scheme approval is dealt with in Chapter 22. The PSO is not to be confused with the Occupational Pensions Regulatory Authority established under the Pensions Act 1995.

The Occupational Pensions Regulatory Authority (OPRA)

6.2 OPRA was established by the Pensions Act 1995 to **monitor** and **supervise** the implementation of the statutory pensions regime. However it does not have sole responsibility for pensions and must co-ordinate with the other statutory bodies.

6.3 OPRA's main focus is on **schemes in difficulties** that are brought to its notice and the protection of the interests of the members of those schemes. Scheme members and advisers may report concerns to OPRA; scheme actuaries and auditors must report to OPRA matters that are of **material significance to OPRA**.

6.4 OPRA has many powers, including the following:

(a) Appointing, removing and disqualifying trustees

(b) Imposing fines and bringing criminal proceedings

(c) Applying to the court for protection of scheme assets

(d) Winding up or modifying schemes

(e) Checking that statutory requirements are met before a refund is given to an employer

(f) Directing schemes to carry out specific activities, for example communication with members

(g) Appointing inspectors to investigate a scheme's activities

6.5 OPRA's remit however does not extend to issues such as unfair treatment of members or training of trustees.

Scheme administrator

6.6 In addition to the other parties involved it is a requirement that there be a scheme administrator. The Inland Revenue's *Practice Notes* state the following.

(a) The legislation lays certain **duties** upon the **administrator** of a scheme, and defines him as the person or persons having the management of the scheme.

(b) The administrator will often be the trustee of the scheme or may be, or include the employer, or may be a committee of management, and may be named in two documents or deduced from their terms.

(c) If the administrator is resident abroad the scheme will not be approved unless there is a person resident in the United Kingdom who will be responsible for discharging the duties laid upon the administrator.

(d) If an **administrator defaults**, disappears or dies, the **employer** becomes **responsible** in his place and when the employer is resident outside the United Kingdom any branch or agent in the United Kingdom is equally responsible.

The Ombudsman

6.7 The SSA 1990 brought into being a Pensions Ombudsman. The duties of the Ombudsman are to **conduct investigations** into allegations of injustice arising from maladministration by the trustees or managers of an occupational pension scheme, and to **make determinations** in relation to such complaints. The Ombudsman is also able to investigate and determine any disputes of fact or law between an authorised complainant and the trustees or managers of a scheme. For the purposes of investigation, the Ombudsman has the same powers as a court in respect of the attendance and examination of witnesses and the production of documents. The Ombudsman may seek to enforce his decisions through a court of law. The powers of the Ombudsman are extended by the Pensions Act 1995 to include complaints by trustees/managers against employers or vice versa, or the trustees/managers of one scheme against the trustees/managers of another.

The Pensions Registry

6.8 The SSA 1990 has also brought into being a Registrar of Occupational and Personal Pension Schemes, and the setting-up and operation of a register of occupational and personal pensions. The purpose of the Registry is to enable individuals to **trace past preserved pension rights**.

Occupational Pensions Advisory Service

6.9 OPAS was formerly a charitable organisation but in April 1991 it became a grant-aided non profit-making company. Its function is to offer **free and independent advice** to pension scheme members and beneficiaries who have just cause for complaint. Its scope has now been extended to take in personal pension schemes.

Pensions Compensation Board

6.10 A Pensions Compensation Board was set up to administer a **compensation scheme** in cases where the employer becomes insolvent and the scheme's assets have been reduced by theft, fraud or misappropriation of assets. The scheme does not cover losses arising from poor administration or investment. The amount of compensation is likely to be 90% of the assets lost.

Independent trustee

6.11 OPB Announcement No 38 states that requirements have been introduced by SSA 1990 where an employer has become insolvent. These overriding provisions impose a duty on an insolvency practitioner (or the official receiver) who commences to act in relation to an employer participating in an occupational pension scheme to ensure that at least one of the trustees of the scheme is an **'independent' person**.

6.12 The Independent Trustee Regulations state that the independent trustee provisions in SSA 1990 do not apply:

(a) To a scheme which provides only money purchase benefits or death in service benefits

(b) If each scheme member is a trustee

(c) If all scheme members are secured by policies under which the benefits are earmarked for particular employees

(d) Where an insolvency practitioner or the official receiver started to act in relation to the employer before 12 November 1990

Department of Trade and Industry

6.13 The DTI deals with the authorisation of insurance companies and is concerned with their financial solvency. Annual returns and details of actuarial valuation have to be submitted by the insurance companies to the DTI. The many pension schemes which are transacted through life assurance offices are thus covered by this overall supervision.

7 RECENT EVENTS 6/95, 6/96, 12/96

7.1 The world of pension schemes was struck by a thunderbolt when it was discovered that the Mirror Group Newspaper (MGN) Pension Funds had lost between £300m and £400m as a result of the apparently fraudulent activities of at least one of those entrusted with fiduciary responsibility for them. This was in spite of the fact that the main provisions of the Social Security Act 1990, which sought to protect pensions, were already in force.

7.2 In the subsequent debate, several weaknesses in the regulation of pension schemes came to light. One of the most significant flaws is the problem of trust law. Trusts are only effective in separating the assets of the pension scheme from those of the employer company as long as trustees honour their trusts.

Problems with pension funds

7.3 In practice, under a pension trust the **employer commonly appoints** the **trustees**, and may include himself, directors of a parent company or anyone else he likes. The employer decides how much to pay in and he can structure the scheme in such a way that trustees cannot really exercise any discretion without his consent and yet are obliged to carry out his decisions. The actuary who assesses the position of the scheme is appointed by the employer and is not accountable to the beneficiaries. In practice, the employer also frequently appoints the fund's auditors and legal advisers. The potential scope for abuse is immense.

7.4 The law on the running of pension schemes is a combination of the general law of trusts and occupational pension legislation which has been introduced on an *ad hoc* basis in successive social security acts. The existence of the latter could be regarded as implicit recognition that trust law is inadequate *on its own* to cater for pensions funds.

7.5 The main areas of concern can be summarised as follows.

(a) The then current accounting (annual) and actuarial (triennial) reporting requirements were ineffective to prevent abuse, because the information contained in them was out of date at the time of publication.

(b) Requirements of accountability to scheme members were susceptible to manipulation.

(c) Third parties who handled pension fund assets did not have to be bonded (a type of insurance) and were generally entitled to retain the proceeds of fraud if they received them in good faith.

(d) There was no fit and proper person test for the trustees of occupational pension schemes.

(e) Confronted with dishonest trustees, even well informed scheme members were prevented from taking effective action by financial constraints and lack of adequate information.

(f) The investment and administration of pension funds was subject to the vagaries of the law of trusts and the expense of High Court proceedings. Conflicts of interest between employers and beneficiaries were built into the system.

(g) Pension fund members whose benefits could not be paid ranked as unsecured creditors in an insolvency and the receiver/liquidator who was appointed over the employer owed them no duty whatsoever. In addition, administrative receivers and liquidators who might have encountered some of the more obvious cases of abuse were under no clear statutory duty to report such abuse. It was not usually within their powers to pursue those responsible for committing the abuse if there was no hope of recovering assets for the creditors.

7.6 The area of **transfers** between pension schemes, particularly in a take-over situation, also gave cause for concern. There was no requirement that transfer values be earmarked for the benefit of transferring employees, and so any surplus over the cash equivalents might be used by the buyer for a contribution holiday, a loan or a straightforward return of surplus.

7.7 In a take-over situation, the buyer and seller companies will include the pension scheme as part of the consideration. This undermines the independence of the trustees: the trust is supposed to separate the assets of the scheme from that of the company.

Pensions Act 1995

7.8 The Pensions Act 1995 has now been passed, although it will not be fully implemented until the next century (see below). There are six components of this enormous piece of legislation.

- 'Post-Maxwell' security measures
- Sex discrimination in pensions
- Equalisation of retirement ages
- Terms governing contracting out from SERPs
- Treatment of pension rights and divorce
- Miscellaneous matters

7.9 The key points are as follows.

(a) The Act set up a new watchdog body called the **Occupational Pensions Regulatory Authority** as described above.

(b) The Pensions **Ombudsman's duties** are to be extended as noted above.

(c) The **Pensions Compensation Board** was set up.

(d) The Occupational Pensions Board was wound up and its duties are to be transferred to the **Occupational Pensions Regulatory Authority** and the DSS.

(e) The Act introduced a **minimum solvency requirement** for final salary schemes with trustees being required to agree a schedule of contribution payments which is certified by the actuary as adequate to maintain the minimum solvency level.

(f) The Act required that arrangements for **member-nominated trustees** set up. The arrangements must provide for at least one-third of the trustees to be member-nominated, subject to a minimum of two (or one for schemes with less than 100 members).

(g) The Act spells out **trustees' duties regarding investments,** and places a duty on the trustees to consult with the employer in determining investment policy. Effectively it makes clear that the requirements of the Trustee Investment Act 1961 (see also below) apply equally to pension scheme trustees. Trustees will have to maintain a written statement of investment principles.

(h) The idea of **Limited Price Indexation** (introduced in SSA 1990) finally comes into force. This means that all pensions in payment earned after an appointed day (probably 6 April 1997) must, when they come into payment be increased in line with price inflation subject to a maximum of 5% per year.

(i) The Act requires all occupational pension schemes to comply with the **equal treatment provisions** of European law.

(j) **State Pension Age** is to be **equalised for men** and women at 65. This will be introduced progressively over a 10-year period starting on 6 April 2010.

(k) The Act will **restrict the ability to make changes** to a scheme which would affect members' rights. The trustees must approve such changes and members must give their consent unless an actuary certifies that they will be no worse off.

(l) The Act will **specify** the order of **winding-up liabilities** in a final salary pension scheme and spell out what is to be done in the case of a deficiency or a surplus on winding up.

(m) A **new procedure** will be followed for the provision of transfer value quotations to members of salary-related schemes to avoid a situation where a member receives a transfer payment less than the amounted quoted due to market fluctuations over time.

(n) The **links** between **SERPS** and **contracted-out schemes** will be **broken**.

(i) Employees who are contracted out will lose their future entitlement to SERPS in full from an appointed day.

(ii) Contracted-out persons will not be entitled to a top-up in line with inflation: at present they are entitled to a top-up for any excess of inflation over the 3% increase applied to GMPs.

(iii) GMPs will cease to accrue on or after the appointed day. Thereafter schemes that contract out will only be required to ensure that they provide benefits of a good enough standard to satisfy the government.

(iv) Because of the need to provide higher levels of pension increases for contracting out, the NI rebate will be calculated at a higher level than before. It will be *age-related* for money purchase schemes and personal pensions to make contracting out more attractive across the age range.

Chapter roundup

- You should make sure that you understand why **UK pension schemes** are usually constituted under trusts and what alternatives there are.
- It is most important that you revise the **statutory rules** governing trustees and investments, but equally important that you realise that most pension schemes are set up so as to permit much broader powers. Whatever the case, the overriding consideration is the **security of the trust property**: this is the aim of the statutory provisions and this should still be the aim if the trust deed lays down its own powers of investment.
- Most of the existing external supervisory bodies have been introduced **relatively recently**. Again, you should watch the press for any reports of their activities. The importance of the PSO and OPRA will become apparent in the chapters that follow.
- Keep up to date with changes to the law and regulation of pension funds by reading the **Chartered Secretary** and trade journals like **Pensions World**. In particular you should watch out for changes in the implementation timetable, indications of how implementation has affected schemes and case law that pertains to the new legislation.

Test your knowledge

1 List four ways in which a pension scheme could be constituted. (see paras 1.3 - 1.10)

2 What is the usual definition of a trust? (2.2)

3 What sort of person may be appointed as a trustee? (3.1)

4 How may a trustee vacate office? (3.12, 3.13)

5 Summarise the general duties of a trustee. (4.1 - 4.6)

6 What is meant by 'ethical investment'? (5.15)

7 Which government bodies regulate pension schemes? (6.1)

8 What are the main provisions of the Pensions Act 1995? (7.9)

Now try illustrative question 21 at the end of the Study Text

Chapter 21

THE STATE SCHEME AND CONTRACTING OUT

This chapter covers the following topics.

Introduction

In this chapter we tell you what you need to know about the UK state pension scheme and what 'contracting out' means.

1 BACKGROUND

1.1 The intention behind the State arrangements has never been to provide fully for all that an individual might need in retirement, but is rather to provide a **basic level of benefit**, which will meet essential needs. Those who are able to, are expected to make additional provision for themselves, in order to improve their overall financial position in retirement.

1.2 The impact of State pension provision seems set to decrease still further into the future. The benefits payable are increased each year, at least in line with the increase in the RPI, and this protects the purchasing power of benefits. However, because earnings tend to increase faster than prices, the effect of providing benefits which are indexed to prices only, is to decrease their level relative to earnings.

1.3 In addition, as explained later in this chapter, the benefit formula itself under the earnings related part of the State scheme is being scaled down. This will further reduce the impact of the State scheme on retirement planning.

1.4 Further changes to State pensions are planned, and were announced in the Government Consultation paper *Partnership in Pensions* published in December 1998. This aims in particular to focus State provision on the lower paid, by moving from an earnings related basis to a flat-rate basis over a period of years. These changes are discussed further in section 8 of this chapter.

2 FUNDING STATE PENSIONS

2.1 Much of the reason for the decision to decrease the level of State provision for the future, springs from the **changing population structure** of the nation as a whole. These 'demographic' trends indicate that in the future, the relationship between the number of people working and the number of people in retirement will change significantly. Essentially the working population is likely to remain broadly constant or decrease whilst the number of people in retirement is set to increase by something like 50% over the next 30 years.

Pay as You Go

2.2 The importance of this lies in the fact that the State scheme is designed on a Pay as You Go basis rather than on a funded basis. This means that the benefits which are currently being provided by the State are funded by the **National Insurance Contributions** currently being received from those working. There is no invested fund underlying the State pension scheme.

2.3 Thus the continued availability of State benefits is dependent on the **willingness** of **future generations** to continue to fund the contributions.

2.4 A major weakness of this approach is that the **level of contributions** required from individuals during their working career does **not reflect** the **level of benefits** which they themselves expect to receive, but instead is related to the benefits currently being provided to an older generation.

2.5 Clearly the contributions required are affected by the level of benefit provided to each pensioner, but crucially, also by the relationship between the number of people working and the number receiving benefits. This is often referred to as the **Support Ratio**. As the number receiving benefits increases, so the requirement for National Insurance Contributions escalates.

2.6 At the present time, the Government is continuing to encourage individuals to contract out - in other words to make private provision instead of relying on the State scheme - but on a voluntary basis. This may well make the transition to a funded scheme more achievable in the future, and certainly it reduces the extent of the potential problems which are likely to arise in the future as a result of the projected demographic changes.

3 STRUCTURE OF THE STATE SCHEME 6/99

Basic pension: flat rate, revalued each yr with RPI.
SERPS = 2nd tier pension relating to "band earnings" (earnings between stipulated lower/upper earnings limit).

3.1 The State scheme consists of two components, the basic pension and the State Earnings Related Pension Scheme (SERPS). Subject to certain earnings and contribution requirements, the basic pension is available to all those with earned income, whilst SERPS is available only to employees.

State Pension Age

3.2 Currently, State Pension Age is 65 for men and 60 for women.

3.3 This is however to be equalised in the future, to allow men and women to draw their State pensions at the same age. A number of different approaches have been considered and discussed, but the basis adopted is that State Pension Age for both sexes will be 65.

Exercise 1

Don't worry too much about the details given above at this stage but take note of the terminology and make sure you understand the basic distinction between a SERPS pension and a contracted out arrangement.

3.4 It is possible to **defer** taking a State pension for up to five years after State Pension Age, but it is not possible to take benefits early. The pension is increased by 7.5% for each year of deferment.

3.5 From April 2010, it will be possible to defer drawing State pension indefinitely, and the rate of increase will rise to 10.4% per year.

Basic pension

3.6 Payment of the full basic pension is dependent on the individual's **National Insurance Contribution** record, and to qualify, the individual must normally have paid NICs for at least 90% of his working career. Benefits are reduced on a proportionate basis where the contribution record is not sufficient to provide a full pension.

3.7 Where National Insurance Contributions are not paid, they will be credited as paid in certain cases, for example where the individual is unable to work because of sickness, is unemployed, is taking part in an approved training course or is receiving certain Social Security benefits including Maternity Allowance and Disability Working Allowance.

4 STATE EARNINGS RELATED PENSION SCHEME (SERPS) 6/99

4.1 SERPS was introduced in April 1978, with the intention of providing a significant level of earnings related pension benefit on top of the basic State pension described above.

4.2 Broadly the concept was (and is) that SERPS should provide a **partial replacement** of earnings within a defined band. This band lies between the Lower Earnings Limit (LEL) and the Upper Earnings Limit (UEL). The Lower Earnings Limit is broadly equivalent to the level of State basic pension provision, whilst the Upper Earnings Limit is approximately seven and a half times the Lower Earnings Limit.

Eligibility

4.3 Not everyone is a member of SERPS, and it is therefore important to establish precisely who will qualify for benefits.

4.4 First of all, those whose earned income is **less that the Lower Earnings Limit** will pay no National Insurance Contributions and will not qualify for basic pension, nor for SERPS benefits.

4.5 Secondly, SERPS provides **benefits** only for **employees**, not the self-employed.

4.6 It is also possible for employees to be **contracted out of SERPS**, either through an occupational pension scheme or through a personal pension arrangement, and this is considered in more detail below. In these cases, although some SERPS benefits are lost in respect of periods of time during which the employee is contracted out, there will be benefits provided in their place under the private pension arrangement.

5 CONTRACTING OUT

5.1 When SERPS was introduced in 1978, it was recognised that the occupational pensions industry was already well established, and that many occupational schemes provided benefits which were often significantly better than those which could be accrued under the State arrangements. If SERPS had been made compulsory, many employers might have chosen to abandon their own schemes entirely, and instead, rely solely on the State scheme.

5.2 It was therefore recognised that it would be better if a **partnership** between the **State** and the **private sector** were established, by means of allowing schemes which provided benefits at a certain level to contract out of SERPS. Contracting out means that the employees concerned give up benefits under SERPS, but instead are granted benefits under a private arrangement.

5.3 In return, **National Insurance Contributions** are **reduced**.

5.4 Contracting out is allowed only from SERPS, not from the State basic pension. It is therefore an option which applies only to employees, since only employees are eligible for SERPS.

5.5 In 1978, in order to contract out, employees had to be provided with a **guarantee** that the benefits under the private arrangement to which they belonged would at least equal those given up under SERPS. This guarantee is necessarily benefit related, and is open-ended, since the cost of providing such benefits can only be estimated in advance. It could not therefore be provided under a money purchase arrangement.

5.6 This meant that contracting out was only possible using an occupational pension scheme, and generally one which provided benefits on a final salary basis.

5.7 The level of benefit which had to be promised in order to ensure that the employee was no worse off is known as the **Guaranteed Minimum Pension (GMP)**.

5.8 In practice, most private schemes provided benefits considerably in excess of GMP. There was in fact an additional requirement which schemes needed to meet in order to achieve contracted out status, the **Requisite Benefit Test**. In most cases this meant that only schemes which provided benefits at least equal to 1/80th of final salary for each year of service were able to contract out.

Contracting out since 1997

5.9 The original Requisite Benefit Test was abandoned some years ago. Its removal was intended to be part of a general drive towards the simplification of contracting out, but this did not really succeed because it was the GMP test rather than the Requisite Benefit Test which led to the majority of complications. The changes to contracting out which result from the introduction of the Pensions Act 1995 will remove the GMP test from April 1997, and will re-introduce a revised form of Requisite Benefit Test. However GMP benefit already earned will not be affected by this change and will therefore remain a feature of the benefit structure of many schemes for many years.

5.10 The regulations govern **Contracted Out Basic Salary Schemes (COSRSs)**. The key test is that a COSR must be 'broadly equivalent to a reference scheme', as defined by the Pensions Act 1995. Features of a reference scheme include a normal retirement age of **65** and the accrual rate being **1/80th** of **final salary** for each year of scheme membership. The maximum length of membership is 40 years. The spouse of the member must be entitled to a 50% pension on death in service prior to retirement (calculated on service completed to the date of death), and the spouse must also have the right to a 50% pension on death after retirement.

5.11 The scheme's actuary must state that at least **90% of members** and **spouses** of deceased members will **receive benefits** that are at least broadly equivalent to those of the reference scheme. The actuary should confirm this is the case at least every three years, and also do so if there is a significant change in the formula for calculating benefits.

5.12 Under this basis an employee gives up *all* his entitlement to SERPS benefits.

Money Purchase Test

5.13 The changes to SERPS introduced by the Social Security Act 1986 have already been discussed. At the same time however, changes were made to the basis upon which employees could be contracted out, with the general objective of making it easier to contract out.

5.14 No change was made as far as defined benefit occupational schemes were concerned, but two other methods of contracting out were introduced.

5.15 Firstly, **money purchase occupational schemes** were allowed to **contract out**. The basis of contracting out (the Money Purchase Test) was simply that the reduction in National Insurance Contributions which results from contracting out should be invested to provide benefits in place of those which would otherwise have been provided by SERPS.

5.16 Occupational schemes which contract out on this basis are known as **Contracted Out Money Purchase Schemes (COMPS),** and they have certainly had the effect of widening the availability of contracting out. This is because smaller employers have been reluctant to take on the open-ended promise involved in a defined benefit scheme, but can now contract out without doing so.

Exercise 2

What do you think a small employer would gain by establishing a COMPS as opposed to a money purchase scheme which is not contracted out?

Solution

The advantage is to be seen to establish a pension scheme, but to have the contributions subsidised by the NI rebate for contracting out. Most small employers would not be able to take on the open ended liability of a defined benefit scheme, and so would not have been able to achieve this situation before the introduction of the money purchase test.

5.17 There remained many individual employees whose employers were either not willing to establish a scheme at all, or were not prepared to take on the administration involved in contracting out. In order to enable these individuals to contract out if they so wished, it was also decided to allow contracting out using **personal pension arrangements**. (PPs which offer the facility for members to contract out are known as 'Appropriate PPs'.) PPs & APPs

5.18 The basis of contracting out is broadly similar to that which applies to COMPS arrangements, in that the saving in NICs resulting from contracting out is used to provide benefits to replace those given up under SERPS.

5.19 The **rebate** is dealt with differently however. Under a COMPS, the level of NICs paid by the employer and employee are immediately reduced. This is the same system that would apply under a defined benefit scheme.

5.20 With a personal pension arrangement, the level of National Insurance Contributions paid month by month or week by week is unaffected, but the **rebate** is calculated and **paid direct** to the **pension provider** by the DSS after the end of the tax year to which it relates.

Although this means that there is a delay before the rebate is invested, it also means that the employee can choose freely whether to contract out or not, and does not need the agreement or co-operation of his employer.

SERPS benefits

5.21 Anyone who was contracted out under the money purchase test was entitled to residual SERPS benefits for periods up to 5 April 1997. Employees contracted out on a money purchase basis have however lost all entitlement to SERPS benefits for the periods *after* 6 April 1997.

Tax credits

5.22 The Chancellor's decision to take away from pension schemes the **right** to **reclaim tax credits** on UK dividends impacted on all pension funds, but particularly affected decisions about contracting out. As the taxation change meant that the return on the investments of pension funds would reduce, therefore the amount of **contracting out rebate** needed to be **higher** to persuade people to contract out. The various changes were thus made to rebates to increase their attractiveness from April 1999.

Making the decision

5.23 Under a personal pension arrangement, whether to contract out is essentially a decision which is based on an arithmetic consideration of the **value** of the **rebate**, and what it could provide if invested until State Pension Age. On any given set of assumptions, it is possible to calculate whether contracting out is an attractive proposition at any particular age.

5.24 It should however be emphasised again that contracting out on this basis carries a **risk**. There is no guarantee that the benefits provided will exceed those which would otherwise be provided by SERPS, and this risk needs to be taken into account in making the decision. Contracting out will be more attractive to the young than to the old, but also will appeal more to those who have an optimistic view of likely future investment returns.

5.25 **Earnings levels** are also important, because the size of the rebate depends on earnings. Most Personal Pensions include charges which impact to a greater extent proportionately on arrangements with low levels of input, and this may mean that contracting out is unattractive for individuals earning less than say, £10,000 per annum, irrespective of their age.

5.26 Under a COMPS, the decision will be made by the **employer** rather than by the employee, since it will be the employer who decides the basis upon which employees join the scheme and the categories which are or are not contracted out.

5.27 From a theoretical point of view, under the current flat rate rebate arrangements, it is likely to be attractive to contract out employees below a certain age and then to contract back in at that age.

5.28 For individuals contracted out under personal pensions, the decision is essentially one which can be made for each tax year. With the flat rate rebate, it is commonplace for employees to contract out up to the pivotal age, and then to contract back into SERPS. With the introduction of age related rebates, it will probably become more usual for employees to remain contracted out throughout the bulk of their working career.

6 CONTRACTING OUT PROCEDURES

Notice of intention to contract out

6.1 Before the employer can make an application to the Department of Social Security he must consult with all the recognised trade unions concerned and give **at least three months notice** of his intention to the employees concerned, the trade unions which are recognised as representing them for the purposes of negotiation, and the trustees (if any) and administrators of the scheme.

6.2 The notice must be **in writing** and must either be given to **all employees**, or **displayed** conspicuously on a notice board with each employee's attention drawn to it in writing, for example by insertion of a slip in his pay envelope. The notice must:

(a) State the employer's intention to contract out

(b) Make clear which jobs covered by the pension scheme will be included in the contracting-out certificate

(c) Describe the scheme benefits and any contributions which the employee has to pay to the scheme

(d) Explain any changes there will be in the scheme's benefits and employees' contributions in order to contract out

(e) Explain the effect of contracting out on state scheme benefits and contributions

(f) Give particulars of people to whom representation may be made

Sufficiency of the scheme's resources

6.3 Before the DSS can issue a contracting-out certificate it must be satisfied about the **sufficiency of resources** in the scheme concerned. For this purpose the DSS place considerable reliance on a certificate which is prepared by the scheme's actuary concerning the situation that would arise were the scheme to be wound up within a five year period (or such shorter period as may be stated in the certificate).

Money purchase schemes

6.4 For the purposes of the DSS's supervisory procedures money purchase schemes are regarded as falling into two categories, 'insured' and 'self-administered'.

6.5 For **insured schemes** the DSS require a Life Assurance company's certificate at the date of the election to contract out. Thereafter the DSS require annual confirmation about the procedures relating to the payment of premiums and the other requirements relating to the receipt and investment of minimum payments. The annual return is given by the life office direct to the DSS.

6.6 For **self-administered schemes** the DSS require an employer who has a COMP scheme to obtain an annual statement signed by a trustee of the scheme or the scheme administrator relating to receipts, payments, investments, the scheme accounts and their audit.

6.7 Trustees must be satisfied that all minimum payments in respect of a member are applied so as to provide money purchase benefits for or in respect of that member except so far as they are used to defray administrative expenses or to pay commission.

7 FUTURE DEVELOPMENTS

7.1 The Government published a consultative paper entitled *A New Contract for Welfare: Partnership in Pensions* in December 1998. This contained proposals for a significant reform of State pension provision. The ideas in the consultation paper have now been followed through in the Child Support, Pensions & Social Security Bill.

7.2 The main intention behind the changes is to **focus benefits** to a greater extent on the **lower paid**, by replacing SERPS with a **new State Second Pension** (S2P). It is anticipated that those on higher earnings will be better served by contracting out (possibly through **stakeholder pensions**), whilst the S2P will cover primarily those on lower pay (particularly those earning up to £9,500 per year).

7.3 The change to the S2P will be in two stages. The first stage will see benefits still linked to earnings above the Lower Earnings Limit, but enhanced for lower earners. This will be done by:

(a) Doubling the SERPS rate of accrual on earnings up to **£9,500** per year

(b) Treating those earning less than £9,500 per year, but more than the Lower Earnings Limit, as if they earned £9,500 per year

7.4 It is also intended to bring **carers** (including mothers looking after young children) into the scheme, with benefits provided as if they were earning £9,500 per year.

7.5 Benefits for those earning between **£9,500** and around **£21,600** will be increased as a result of the doubling of accrual on the first £9,500 of earnings, though the effect is less significant. Those earning above this level will be no worse off than under SERPS.

7.6 Increased contracting out rebates will be introduced to encourage higher earners to make private provision rather than rely on the State. The second stage will be the conversion of the S2P to a **flat rate scheme** (additional to the existing basic pension), but this will not occur until the Government is confident that arrangements are in place to encourage an increased take-up of contracting out. The flat rate scheme will in effect treat all members as if they were earning **£9,500** per year.

7.7 The initial changes cannot start to be made after legislation is passed. The earliest implementation date is 2002, and the new scheme will not be fully mature until the middle of the 21st century. The **monetary figures** (£9,500 etc) will be **increased** to reflect rises of earnings generally up to the time S2P comes into operation.

Chapter roundup

- **State pensions** are provided on a pay as you go basis, and costs are subject to demographic pressures as well as changes in benefits.
- State Pension Age for **men** and **women** is in the process of being equalised at 65, but this will not be fully effective until 2020.
- The basic state pension is a **flat rate amount** payable from state pension age to all who have a sufficient NIC record.
- **SERPS** provides earnings related benefits for employees, but not the self-employed.
- The **original basis** of SERPS was a maximum benefit of 25% of revalued band earnings, averaged over the best 20 years.
- The **SERPS formula** has been reduced to 20% of revalued band earnings, averaged over the whole of an employee's working lifetime, but the change is being phased in gradually, starting in the year 2000.
- **Contracting out** can be achieved by means of occupational schemes, either on a defined benefit or defined contribution basis, or under a Personal Pension.
- From 1997, the **NI rebate** for contracting out varies according to age under Personal Pensions and COMPS, where contracting out is on a money purchase basis.

Test your knowledge

1 What does the expression 'Support Ratio' mean? (see para 2.5)

2 For how long after state pension age can benefits be deferred? (3.4, 3.5)

3 What NI contributions do the employed and self-employed pay? (3.8)

4 Who is eligible to receive benefits under SERPS? (4.4 - 4.6)

5 Whom will the State Second Pension primarily cover? (7.2)

Now try illustrative question 22 at the end of the Study Text

Chapter 22

SCHEME MANAGEMENT

This chapter covers the following topics.

Introduction

This chapter brings together a variety of topics mentioned in the syllabus guidance notes (though not specifically in the syllabus). Most are dealt with only in outline since full details would take up several chapters, whereas 'Pensions' only represents about 10 - 15% of the *Administration of Corporate Affairs* syllabus.

1 DOCUMENTATION

1.1 Trusts are created by a written document and so occupational pension schemes are usually set up by a **deed**, although sometimes they are set up by resolution of a company's board of directors.

1.2 Two kinds of document are used for setting up a group occupational pension scheme:

- An interim trust deed
- A definitive trust deed and rules

Interim trust deed

1.3 The interim trust deed gets the scheme off the ground in a short space of time. It contains **basic trust provisions** relating to, as examples, investment, appointment and removal of trustees, winding up provisions. An announcement is issued to all concerned, indicating the setting up of the scheme, its broad provisions and who is eligible to join. A booklet is also published and distributed to all concerned, giving the broad provisions of the scheme, its benefits and contributions payable.

1.4 The Inland Revenue will not formally grant the pension scheme tax approval before the definitive trust deed and rules are executed. The Inland Revenue will, however, grant provisional relief from tax on employees' contributions and will not treat, for tax purposes, contributions paid by the employer as part of the remuneration of the employees concerned.

Definitive trust deed and rules

1.5 The definitive trust deed and rules should be **completed within two years**, although the Inland Revenue are sometimes prepared to extend this time period.

1.6 The definitive trust deed and rules - which should be approved by the employer, the trustees, the Pension Schemes Office and the Occupational Pensions Regulatory Authority - contain full details of the scheme. Typically the trust rules will cover the following matters.

(a) The trustees' powers of delegation, decision making and so on, and their indemnity provisions

(b) Contributions payable by the employer and the members

(c) The benefits provided to members

(d) Death benefits, both for death in service and death after retirement

(e) Normal retirement age, and provisions for early or late retirement

(f) Transfers into and out of the scheme

(g) Investment policy

(h) The procedure to be followed when amending the scheme

(i) The procedure to be followed if the scheme is wound up

(j) All the provisions required by legislation such as the limits on maximum benefits, the preservation of benefits for scheme leavers, and so on

2 SCHEME APPROVAL

2.1 Retirement benefit schemes should be **submitted** to the **Pension Schemes Office (PSO)** of the Inland Revenue for approval. Approval is given only if certain requirements are met and relevant legislative provisions are fulfilled.

2.2 Taxation advantages principally make approval desirable; approval gives valuable tax reliefs. If an employer establishes a scheme to which the Income and Corporation Taxes Act 1988 (ICTA 1988) applies **without obtaining approval** of the scheme the employees are disadvantaged. With an unapproved scheme the employees who are members of the scheme are taxed on the employer's contributions paid to the scheme on their behalf as if those amounts had been paid to them as salary or wages.

Exempt approval

2.3 If a retirement benefit scheme is granted merely **bare approval**, the effect is to remove the taxation disadvantages to employees as stated above in connection with non-approval. However, the PSO also grants **exempt approval** and it is only exempt approval which gives rise to all the valuable tax concession for a retirements benefits scheme. Customarily, therefore, it is exempt approval which is sought.

2.4 If exempt approval is granted the tax reliefs obtained are, put simply: income tax reliefs on employees' contributions, tax reliefs on employers' contributions, and tax relief on investment income of the fund.

The earnings cap and unapproved schemes

2.5 An earnings cap applies to tax-approved occupational pension schemes. This is £91,800 for 2000/2001. The cap means that the maximum pension payable from an approved scheme is the cap × 2/3 and the maximum tax-free lump sum that can be given is the cap × 1.5.

2.6 It is also possible to set up a scheme that is *not* approved to provide further pension benefits, but this has no favourable tax treatment.

Approval under the simplified procedure

2.7 A simplified procedure for the approval of pension schemes exists. Applications for approval must be made on the prescribed forms and model documents are available. If these model documents of the Inland Revenue are used without amendments the resulting scheme will normally be approved automatically.

2.8 There are two types of scheme which may qualify for the simplified approval procedure.

(a) A simplified 'final salary' scheme, the benefits from which are subject to Inland Revenue limits

(b) A simplified 'defined contribution' scheme which offers only money purchase benefits and to which no limits on benefits apply but which imposes an overall limit on contributions

3 CHANGES TO PENSION SCHEMES

3.1 **Statutory changes** to pensions law and regulations issued by government departments override any scheme rules, whether the scheme's constitution is formally altered or not. Obviously it is preferable for the rules to match what is legal and it is the responsibility of the pensions administrator to keep up to date with changes in the law.

Contracting out or contracting in

3.2 This is the most fundamental change that can occur.

Other changes

3.3 The trust deed will have a provision setting out what needs to be done if it is desired to **change** the **scheme** in some way. For example:

(a) It might insist upon the members' approval for any proposed changes.

(b) It might simply require members to be notified of any changes.

(c) It might permit alterations only on the condition that they do not have an adverse effect on members existing rights.

Disclosure

3.4 The foregoing sections will have made it plain that any alterations will need to be submitted to the PSO and OPRA to determine whether the status of the scheme is jeopardised.

Takeovers and mergers

3.5 At one time the pensions manager would not be involved in takeover or merger negotiations until after the sale had been agreed. Problems such as funding deficiencies or dubious provisions for senior employees were often only discovered after the event. Now the pensions manager is likely to play a much more prominent role, working closely with the actuary to assess the funding position and structure of the other company's pension scheme, developing a strategy for bringing the various schemes together, liaising with personnel and payroll departments and ensuring that uncertainty among the workforce is minimised.

Takeovers

3.6 If an entire business changes hands it may be that the pension scheme attached to the business simply goes with it. In these circumstances there is no need to upset the existing arrangements: the members can stay in their own separate scheme within the new company. This is not to say that there will not be any changes in a takeover situation. For example, the acquiring company may not want to contribute to the 'old' scheme, or it may want to bring its new employees into its own scheme. There are a number of options, exactly as for mergers.

3.7 A distinction should be made between the **sale** of a **company** and the sale of a company's **business and assets,** without the company itself. In the former case the sale may set off the winding-up provisions of the scheme, so that members become entitled to a share of the fund including any surplus. The latter situation may merely involve the termination of the members' service (and an offer of a job with the 'new' company) making available to them only the leaving service entitlements.

Mergers

3.8 Besides the question of the value to be transferred there may be other respects in which the merging companies' schemes differ. The following are possible solutions.

(a) A **facsimile scheme** could be set up by the controlling organisation, that is, a new scheme but one which is the same in every way as the one out of which the new employees have had to transfer.

(b) The new employees could join the controlling organisation's scheme but on special terms which maintain their previous position. This is sometimes known as **red circling**.

(c) A **completely new scheme** for everyone involved in the merger or takeover could be set up. This is probably the simplest solution, especially where the two existing schemes are very different. It is also likely to be cheaper in terms of administrative costs. It would, however, involve the winding up of the existing schemes.

Discontinuance

3.9 A scheme might be discontinued for a number of reasons.

- In the case of a **merger** or takeover, as noted above
- Because most of the employees have decided to make their **own arrangements**
- Because the company itself is being **wound up**
- An **order** from OPRA

IR uses "discontinuance" to apply to freezing or winding up of scheme.

3.10 In these circumstances a scheme can either be **frozen** or it can be wound up itself. (The term **discontinued** is used by the Inland Revenue in either case.)

Frozen pensions

3.11 The Practice Notes explain the implications of freezing a scheme as follows.

> 'All contributions cease, but the assets of the scheme continue to be held by or on behalf of the administrator, and are applied to provide benefits according to the rules when existing members retire, or die, or withdraw from service.'

Closing down the scheme

3.12 The **scheme rules** will set out exactly what is to be done if the scheme is closed down. The main consideration is who takes priority in the distribution of the funds.

3.13 Typically the rules will prioritise as follows.

(a) Pensions in payment

(b) 'Guaranteed minimum pensions' (as defined by statute)

(c) Members benefits in general

(d) If there is anything left over, everyone will get the same proportion of his full entitlement

(e) If full entitlements have been provided for any surplus is returned to the company

Pension deficits

3.14 When a pension scheme's assets are **insufficient** to meet its liabilities it is said to have a 'deficit'. Any such deficiency in a scheme that is wound up is treated as an ordinary debt which must be **made good** by the **employer**. This is in accordance with the Occupational Pension Schemes (Deficiency on Winding Up etc) Regulations 1992.

Winding up the company

3.15 If the company is wound up its pension scheme must be wound up too. Members' **accrued benefits** must either be **transferred** to another scheme or else the funds must be used to **buy a deferred annuity**.

3.16 The pension scheme is a **preferential creditor** in a liquidation and therefore any outstanding contributions will be paid up if there are funds available.

Disclosure

3.17 Obviously the PSO and OPRA must be told if a scheme is being discontinued. The beneficiaries must in addition be informed of the amount of benefit due to them.

4 MEMBERSHIP

Category of member

4.1 An individual employer may wish to provide pensions for several categories of employee. (The terms are outmoded but convenient.)

(a) The executive category for whom maximum benefits approvable have frequently been the target

(b) The 'white-collar' or staff category for whom it is often considered desirable to provide fairly generous pension benefits, albeit not always up to the approvable maximum

(c) The 'blue-collar' or works category for whom collective bargaining with the trade unions is often a feature

(d) Salespersons

(e) Weekly and monthly paid staff being distinguished and so on

In the past it has not been all that uncommon for separate schemes to be set up for the different categories of employee to meet their different circumstances.

4.2 The conditions for eligibility into a company scheme might also have regard to:

(a) **Minimum** age of entry

(b) The **length** of the period to be served with the company before eligibility to the company scheme is permitted

(c) A possible **maximum eligibility age**

4.3 Employers are likely to have good business reasons for wishing their employees to be members of their company pension scheme rather than making pension arrangements elsewhere, and so it would seem reasonable that they should impose as few restrictions as possible on employee eligibility.

Criteria for membership

4.4 The Practice Notes state that membership of an approved scheme must be confined to employees of the employers participating in the scheme. The term 'employee' is interpreted fairly broadly.

Voluntary membership

4.5 Employees have had three choices.

- They can **join their employer's scheme** if there is one, or leave it if they choose.
- They can take out a **personal pension** policy.
- They can **participate fully** in the **State Earnings Related Pension Scheme**.

(This has been complicated by the introduction of stakeholder pensions, discussed further in the next chapter.)

Discretionary membership

4.6 It is not necessary that membership should be open to all the employees in the employer's service or to any particular category of them; as noted in an earlier chapter a scheme may in fact relate to a single employee or to individuals selected on a discretionary basis. Some discretionary schemes are still set up, such as top-up schemes for senior executives.

Directors

4.7 All directors may be included in an occupational pension scheme, subject to certain conditions, but only in respect of their Schedule E remuneration. There are various categories of director.

(a) A **controlling director** is a director of a company in which the directors either directly or indirectly control more than 50% of the voting shares and who personally controls more than 5% of the voting shares. A controlling director, as such, may be eligible to join an occupational pension scheme unless he is a 20% director when certain restrictions apply.

(b) A **20% director** is one who has at any time after 16th March 1987 and within ten years of retirement been a director and either on his own or with one or more **associates** beneficially owned or been able to control directly or indirectly or through other companies 20% or more of the ordinary share capital of the company. inc. spouses, children, etc.

The term **associates** includes any relation (ie spouse, forebears, issues and siblings) partners, and the trustees of any trust in which the director has been involved.

(c) Directors **appointed for life** clearly cannot fulfil the requirement for approval of having a normal retirement age. Nevertheless, subject to the certain conditions, they can be included in a scheme providing only death-in-service benefits.

Equal rights

4.8 The general feeling, nowadays, is that in the area of retirement benefits provision there should be **equality of treatment** between men and women.

Equal pay

4.9 The first English statute to have a positive effect on equality was the Equal Pay Act 1970. This introduced the concept of equal pay for equal work, a concept already accepted by the then European Economic Community and included in the Treaty of Rome 1957. This was also incorporated into English law in the European Communities Act 1972. Equal pay had regard to basic wages plus any other consideration, direct or indirect.

4.10 The Equal Treatment directive by the EEC in 1976 stated that equal pay for equal work means **equal pay for work of equal value**. The Equal Pay Act of 1970 accordingly was amended in 1983.

Equal access to pension schemes

4.11 The requirements regarding equal access of men and women to membership of occupational pension schemes are contained in the Social Security Pensions Act 1975 (the equal access requirements) and there are parallel provisions in the Sex Discrimination Act 1974 and the Employment Protection Act 1974. Membership of the scheme must now be open to both men and women on terms which are the same as those pertaining to the age and length of service needed for becoming a member. Schemes with different normal pension ages for men and women have been permitted to allow different maximum age limits for admission to apply to men and women. This maximum age limit has been lower for the sex with the lower normal pension age.

4.12 The Equal Treatment directive issued by the EEC in 1986 meant that for **new entrants** in occupational pension schemes there should now be no discrimination between men and women as regards access to membership, contribution payments, and benefits. However, pension *ages* may remain different while state pension ages remain different (see below).

The Sex Discrimination Act 1986

4.13 The Sex Discrimination Act 1986 requires that contracts of employment must specify the **same retirement ages** for men and women doing the same jobs. It is to be noted that whilst the same retirement ages must be specified, **different pension ages** may remain.

Non-discriminatory pension benefits

4.14 Women in the UK have not always been able to retire at a younger age than men. It was the Old Age and Widows Pension Act 1940 which lowered the state pension age for women only from 65 to 60. All present problems result from that alteration.

Barber v GRE 1990

4.15 The issue is one that has seriously vexed the pensions industry in recent years. It was brought to a head by the decision by the European Court of Justice in the case of *Barber v Guardian Royal Exchange 1990*. Mr Barber belonged to the Guardian Royal Exchange pension scheme which had normal pension ages of 62 for men and 57 for women. He was made compulsorily redundant and under the terms of the scheme he was not entitled to an immediate pension although a woman of the same age would have been entitled. He took the matter to court and eventually won his case.

4.16 The European Court ruled that pensions fall within the provisions of Article 119 of the Treaty of Rome which requires that men and women should receive equal pensions as well as equal pay for equal work.

4.17 The court also ruled that 'with effect from 17 May 1990' (the date of the judgement) individuals have an enforceable right to non-discriminatory pension benefits. Until very recently the problem envisaged for pension schemes and the companies providing them was to know exactly what was meant by 'with effect from 17 May 1990'.

4.18 The position has been clarified as a result of a protocol to the Treaty of Rome approved at the Maastricht summit in December 1991. The protocol says that companies will not be required to provide equal pension benefits for men and women for any period of service prior to 17 May 1990. A man halfway through his working career will be eligible for improved pension benefits only for the period **beginning 17 May 1990**. This was recently affirmed by the European Court's decision in the *Ten Oever* case which dealt with related issues. It is also a provision in the Pensions Act 1995.

Equalising state pension age

4.19 The Pensions Act contains the provisions which lead to the **equalisation** of State Pension Age at 65. These proposals have been the subject of wide publicity and debate for some time now, and there are no amendments to the proposals originally put forward.

4.20 The changes will only be fully effective from the year 2020, but all women born after 5 April 1950 will be affected at least to some extent, and those born after March 1955 will, as a result of the changes, not reach State Pension Age until their 65th birthday.

Maternity benefits

4.21 A provision of the Social Security Act 1989 came into effect on 1 January 1993, whereby a women will continue to accrue pension benefits during paid maternity leave. Benefits will accrue based on the remuneration she would have been paid if she had been working normally, but she will only be required to pay contributions on the contractual pay or statutory maternity pay actually received.

5 FINANCING

The role of the actuary

5.1 A pension scheme's actuary is concerned with matters such as recommending a contribution rate to be paid into a pension scheme and in carrying out from time to time (usually triennially) valuations to ascertain the financial position of the scheme.

5.2 The actuarial considerations are well set out in the accountancy bodies' Statement of Standard Accounting Practice 24 (SSAP 24) *Accounting for pension costs* which reads as follows, slightly abbreviated, and with emphasis added.

> 'In defined benefit schemes, the choice of assumptions and the choice of valuation method can both have a major affect on the contribution rate calculated at each valuation. The choice of assumptions can be as significant as the choice of method.
>
> 'The assumptions which the actuary must make in carrying out his valuation will be about matters such as future rates of *inflation* and *pay increases*, increases to *pensions in payment*, earnings on *investments*, the number of *employees joining* the scheme, the *age profile* of employees, and the probability that employees will *die*, or *leave* the company's employment before they reach retiring age. The actuary will view the assumptions as a whole; he will make assumptions which are mutually compatible, in the knowledge that if experience departs from the assumptions made, the effects of such departures will be offsetting, notably in the case of investment yields and increases in prices and earnings.
>
> 'The *funding methods* developed by actuaries are designed to build up assets in a prudent and *controlled* manner in advance of the retirement of the members of the scheme, in order that the obligation of the scheme may be met without undue distortion of the employer's cash flow. The actuary's main concern is that the present and estimated future contribution levels should be at least sufficient to provide security for the payment of the permitted benefits.

"In practice it is common for actuaries to aim at a *level contribution rate*, as a proportion of pensionable pay in respect of current service. The contribution rate thus determined depends on the particular actuarial method used and the assumptions made regarding new entrants to the scheme. In broad terms, in projecting a stable contribution rate, *accrued benefits methods* rely on the assumption that the flow of new entrants will be such as to preserve the existing average age of the work force; *prospective benefits methods*, on the other hand, normally look only to the existing work force and seek a contribution rate which will remain stable for that group despite its increasing age profile until the last member retires or leaves.

'From time to time it may be necessary to improve the level of funding because of *deficiencies* where these are not expected to be offset by future *surpluses*. This may be done by an increase in the ordinary annual rate of contribution or by additional special payments over a limited period. Conversely, a previously high level of funding may be lowered by reducing or interrupting the contributions.'

Funding assumptions

5.3 It is to be appreciated that estimates involve the adoption of assumptions. These various assumptions, termed in pensions work the **funding assumptions** include the following.

(a) **Valuation rate of interest**. A very important assumption is the rate of interest or future dividend growth used in the actuarial calculations to obtain present values.

(b) **Mortality rates**. These are the rates the actuary will incorporate in his calculations to reflect his estimates of the members of his fund surviving or dying in successive years. He might use different mortality rates for pensioners and those in active service. Possibly he may use different mortality rates according to type of retirement; for example, mortality rates for those who have retired on pension early because of ill-health will be different from those of normal retirement pensioners, to reflect possible heavier mortality of the former group.

(c) **Increase in pensionable remuneration.** Many pension schemes relate a person's pension to his final pensionable remuneration, which is of course unknown in advance. The actuary then has to make an estimate of how the current pensionable remuneration of a member, which is known, is likely to increase each year from his current age to his retirement age. Salary increases arise both because of general increases in the rate of pay in the economy and because of promotional or merit increases as individuals acquire greater experience and status. A salary scale reflecting the likely experience of the scheme may be adopted.

↑Salary from ↑wage inflation or from promotion.

(d) **Increases to pensions**. Assumptions have to be incorporated into the funding calculations to reflect estimated increases to be made to pensions. In this connection it is important that all statutory requirements are properly allowed for. It may also be that the scheme trustees have discretionary powers to increase pensions in payment above any statutory requirements.

(e) **Other items**. Other items which the actuary may introduce into his funding calculations include early retirement dates, late retirement dates and dates of withdrawal, and anything else considered appropriate from the experience of the scheme.

5.4 It is not the absolute level of each assumption that determines the result of the valuation but their level relative to each other.

5.5 The assumptions actually adopted can significantly affect the calculation of contribution rates. Furthermore they can significantly affect the apparent financial position of the scheme, in particular the extent to which it is **solvent**.

Methods of funding

5.6 We now need to look in more detail at the methods used to determine what contribution rate will be sufficient to **fund** the scheme to its required **value**.

5.7 The extract from SSAP 24 quoted above distinguished between **accrued benefits methods** and **prospective benefits methods**, which differ in that only the former take account of future entrants. There are, in fact, five main methods of funding a **defined benefit scheme**, under which pensions are related to final remuneration.

5.8 First, however, you should study the diagram below which, although an extremely simplified picture, should make what follows a good deal more digestible.

Actuarial liability

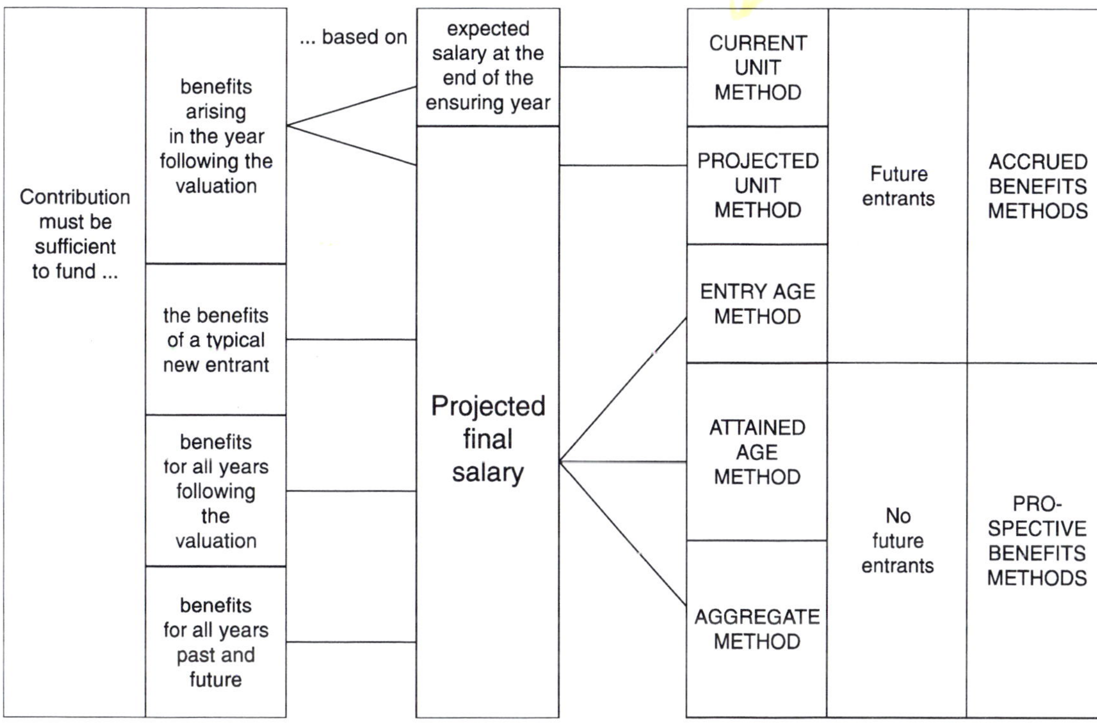

5.9 Note that account has to be taken of the value of assets built up from past contributions, relative to the present value of benefits which have accrued in respect of past service up to the valuation date. Thus in each case an **actuarial liability** has to be calculated from which can be assessed an appropriate modification to be made to the **standard contribution rate** to arrive at the **recommended contribution rate**.

Entry age method

5.10 Under this method, the standard contribution rate, expressed as a percentage of earnings, is found by **dividing** the **present value** (PV) of all future benefits by reference to projected final earnings for a member entering at a normal age **by** the **PV** of his **total** projected **earnings** throughout his expected future membership.

5.11 An actuarial liability is calculated by **deducting** from the **PV of total benefits** (based on projected final earnings for members in service) the value of the **standard contribution rate multiplied** by the **PV of total projected earnings** of all members throughout their expected future membership.

5.12 The recommended contribution rate, expressed as a percentage of earnings, is obtained by **modifying** the **standard contribution rate** to reflect the difference between the value placed on the scheme assets for valuation purposes and this actuarial liability.

Attained age method

5.13 Here the standard contribution rate, expressed as a percentage of earnings, is found by **dividing** the **PV of all benefits** which will accrue to present members after the valuation date by reference to service after the valuation date and projected final earnings **by the PV of total projected earnings** for all members throughout their expected future membership.

5.14 An actuarial liability is calculated by **summing** the **PV of all benefits accrued** at the valuation date (based on projected final earnings for members in service).

5.15 The recommended contribution rate is obtained by modifying the standard contribution rate in a similar manner to that used for the entry age method.

Projected unit method

5.16 The standard contribution rate, expressed as a percentage of earnings, is found by **dividing** the **PV of all benefits** which will **accrue in the year** following the valuation date by reference to service in that year and projected final earnings *by* the **PV of members' earnings** in the year.

5.17 An actuarial liability is calculated by summing the **PV of all benefits accrued** at the **valuation** date (based on projected final earnings for members in service).

5.18 The recommended contribution rate is obtained as before.

Current unit method

5.19 The standard contribution rate, expressed as a percentage of earnings, is found by **dividing the sum** of both:

(a) The **PV of benefits** which will **accrue in the year following** the valuation date, by reference to service in that year and projected earnings at the end of that year, *and*

(b) The **PV of the benefits accrued** by the valuation date multiplied by the expected percentage increase in earnings over the next year

by the PV of members' total projected earnings over that year.

5.20 An actuarial liability is calculated by **summing** the **PV** of **all benefits accrued** at the **valuation** date. Accrued benefits are calculated as if no further benefits will accrue thereafter, based on earnings at the valuation date for members in service but with allowance made for increases in actual benefits after the valuation date in accordance with the provisions of the scheme and statutory requirements.

5.21 The usual modification procedure is then carried out to obtain the recommended contribution rate.

Aggregate method

5.22 The fifth basic method of valuation is the aggregate method. Under this method a recommended contribution rate expressed as a percentage of earnings is obtained directly by **dividing the excess** of the **PV of all benefits** which have **accrued** and will accrue (based on total service and projected final earnings for members in service) *by* the value placed on the scheme assets for valuation purposes. The result is then divided by the **PV of total projected earnings for all members** throughout their expected future membership.

Surplus regulations

5.23 In the preceding paragraphs reference has been made to the possibility of an actuarial valuation revealing a **deficiency or surplus** in the scheme. Actuarial valuations are based on a number of assumptions, but even where the objective is to achieve precisely 100% level of funding, it is unlikely that those actuarial assumptions will materialise precisely in practice over the period of years up to the next valuation. Thus at the next valuation date, the funding level revealed by the valuation may well be different from 100%. If it is greater then we say that the scheme is **overfunded** or that it is **in surplus**; if less, the scheme is **underfunded** or in **deficit.**

5.24 The position of exempt approved pension schemes in terms of taxation is so favourable that, when circumstances so suited him, an employer might find it desirable to overfund his pension scheme for his employees.

5.25 Because of the favourable position of exempt schemes, regulations apply to the actuarial valuation of schemes.

(a) An actuarial valuation must be carried out **at least once** in **every 3 years**.

(b) If **assets exceed 105%** of the **liabilities** of the scheme then steps should be taken to reduce the assets to this level.

These provisions do not apply to schemes with less than 12 members.

5.26 FA 1986 suggested possible corrective action to reduce a surplus to the required level, the trust deed and rules permitting, may be as follows.

(a) A **contribution holiday** by the employer and/or the employees for up to 5 years.

(b) An **increase in benefits** for past service within Inland Revenue limits. However, since the surplus should normally be eliminated over 5 years benefits for future service can be improved but this will only affect the liabilities in respect of benefits accruing within 5 years of the valuation.

There are limited exceptions to the requirement that surpluses should be eliminated over 5 years.

(c) A **payment of surplus** to the **employer**, to be taxed at 40%. This option is not permitted, however, when on its own or in combination with (a) or (b) it would reduce the surplus in the scheme to less than 5%. (It is relevant to mention here that the position has been affected by the Social Security Act 1990. Schemes are now precluded from making payments to the employer until provision has been made in the scheme rules for pensions to be increased in line with the rise in prices up to a ceiling of 5% pa. This is explained in greater detail in the next chapter.)

5.27 If action is not taken to reduce surplus, as the regulations require, then the Inland Revenue will specify an appropriate proportion of the fund's income and capital gains to be taxed, that is taxation will be imposed on the proportion of the fund in excess of the 105% level.

Deficiencies

5.28 The position is further affected by the Pensions Act 1995 (see Chapter 20, Section 7). This provides that approved defined benefit schemes will have to meet a **solvency standard**. The market value of assets must cover 100% of the cash equivalents (transfer values) of the members accrued benefits. A fall below 90% must be restored within three months, and below 100% within three years.

Disclosure of information regulations

6.1 It has for many years been a requirement that if a retirement benefits scheme is to be approved, every member and every employee who has a right to be a member must be given written particulars of all essential features of the scheme which concern him.

General requirements

6.2 The specified persons to whom the required information is to be supplied are:

(a) **Members** and prospective members of the scheme

(b) The **spouse** of any members or prospective members

(c) Independent **trade unions** recognised to any extent for the purpose of collective bargaining in relation to members and prospective members of the scheme

6.3 The regulations are to keep such persons informed of:

(a) The pension scheme's **contributions**

(b) The pension scheme's **administration** and finance

(c) The **rights which** arise or may arise under it

(d) Any other matters which appear to the Secretary of State to be relevant to occupational pension schemes of a description to which that scheme belongs

6.4 There are also requirements regarding an annual report, audited accounts and an actuarial valuation and statement.

6.5 Responsibility for disclosure rests with the trustees, or if a scheme has no trustees, with its managers.

Basic information about the scheme

6.6 The trustees must provide certain basic information about the scheme to every person who becomes a member. This information must be given to **every new member** within 2 months of joining.

(a) The categories of persons who are **eligible** to be members of the scheme

(b) The **conditions** of membership

(c) The **period of notice** (if any) which a member of the scheme must give to terminate his pensionable service

(d) Whether, and if so upon what conditions (if any), a member of the scheme whose pensionable service has terminated before normal pension age, may **re-enter pensionable service**

(e) How **members' contributions** are calculated

(f) How **employer's contributions** are calculated

(g) The arrangements made for the payments of **additional voluntary contributions**

(h) Whether the scheme is a **tax approved scheme**, and if not whether an application for the scheme to become a tax-approved scheme is under consideration by the Inland Revenue

(i) Which of the relevant employments are, and which are not, **contracted-out employments** within the meaning of the Social Security Pensions Act 1975

(j) Except in the case of a simplified defined contribution scheme, **normal pension age** under the scheme

(k) What **benefits** are payable under the scheme and how they are calculated. When changes are made members should be informed beforehand or, if this is not practicable, within one month afterwards

(l) The **conditions** on which benefits are paid

(m) Which benefits, if any, are payable only at some person's **discretion**

(n) The effect of s 149 of the 1995 Act on **accrued rights**

(o) **The short title of the statute (if any) which provides for:**

   (i) The setting up of the scheme
   (ii) The determination of the rate or amount of the benefits under the scheme

(p) Whether there is power under the scheme rules to **increase pensions** after they have become payable, and if so what it is, who may exercise it, and whether and to what extent it is discretionary

(q) Information about the **acceptance of cash equivalents** and provision of transfer credits

(r) A summary of how **transfer values** are calculated

(s) What arrangements are made, and in what circumstances, for estimates of a member's:

   (i) Entitlement to a cash equivalent

   (ii) Statements of entitlement to a guaranteed cash equivalent

   (iii) The refund of contributions

   (iv) The preservation or transfer of the accrued rights where the relevant employment or pensionable service in relevant employment terminates before he reaches normal pension age

(t) A statement that a **scheme annual report** can be requested

(u) The **address** to which enquiries about the scheme generally or about an individual's entitlement to benefit should be sent

(v) The procedures the scheme has for the **regulation of disputes**

(w) Information about the **roles** of the Occupational Pensions Regulatory Authority, Pensions Ombudsman and the Occupational Pensions Advisory Service including the addresses at which they may be contacted

(x) Whether information about the scheme has been given to the **Registrar of pension** schemes

Information to individuals

6.7 The disclosure regulations also require certain information to be made available to individuals. Under the regulations, members have the right to request annually information about benefits payable if service terminates either at normal pensionable age, or within one month of the date information is made available. The information should also include the date on which pensionable service began, the pensionable remuneration at a specified date, and details of how benefits and deductions are calculated. Members of money purchase schemes have the right to receive details of contributions credited, and the value of protected and accrued rights.

6.8 Most trustees fulfil this requirement by sending **benefit statements** to all members automatically. These benefit statements may also include details of additional voluntary contributions paid, and other benefits such as health insurance.

6.9 In addition members are entitled to **receive details of benefits** they are to receive when they are about to start collecting those benefits. If members leave service they should be told their rights and options on leaving, details of their refund of contributions or of their transfer value, and their rights to discretionary benefits.

Pension scheme booklets

6.10 As well as fulfilling the above statutory requirements, trustees should also make a booklet available to members, containing information about the scheme in 'plain English'. The booklet might include the following items:

(a) Introduction
(b) What pension terms mean
(c) Membership of the scheme
(d) Benefits under the State Scheme
(e) Contributions
(f) Additional contributions
(g) Reckonable service
(h) Pension benefits
(i) Death before retirement
(j) Family benefits
(k) Benefits after the death of a pensioner
(l) Pension increases
(m) Joining the scheme
(n) Leaving the scheme
(o) Re-employment and re-entry
(p) Time limits
(q) Services to members
(r) Where to obtain further information

Annual report

6.11 With the exception of public service schemes, trustees of schemes to which the regulations apply must, in relation to each scheme year, make available copies of an annual report.

6.12 The content of the annual report is governed by The Occupational Pensions Schemes (Disclosure Of Information) Regulations 1996, and the Statement Of Recommended Practice *Financial Reports Of Pension Schemes* (the SORP).

6.13 **The annual report**

(a) **Fund account.** This includes contributions, transfers in, benefits payable, payments to leavers, administrative expenses and returns on investment (including investment income and increases in the market value of investments);

(b) **Net assets statement.** This includes a split between investment assets, and other fixed and current assets and liabilities. Money purchase assets should be included in the net assets statement as appropriate;

(c) **Notes to the accounts**. These include transactions with related parties, employer-related investments, contributions not paid over and additional voluntary contributions. The notes will also include some of the large amount of detail required to supplement the fund account and the net assets statement;

(d) **Trustees' report**

(i) Trustee details(names and appointment and removal provisions)

(ii) Names of professional advisers and banks and custodians

(iii) Address for enquiries

(iv) Beneficiary numbers

(v) Whether the accounts have been prepared and audited in accordance with the Pensions Act 1995

Other details to be included if applicable are:

(i) An explanation if the scheme could not offer the full statutory cash equivalents together with a statement of when these were likely to become available

(ii) Reasons for not calculating cash equivalents in accordance with social security regulations

(iii) Failure by the employer to keep up recommended funding levels

(iv) Reference to the actuarial report if the scheme is likely to be wound up and the accounts therefore prepared on a discontinuance basis

(e) **Investment report**

(i) Names of investment managers

(ii) The extent to which trustees have delegated responsibility

(iii) Details of whether the trustees have produced a statement of investment principles and have complied with it

(iv) Review of investment performance over recent years

(v) Custody arrangements for the scheme's assets

(vi) Investment in the employer

(vii) The extent to which investment policy is determined by social, environmental and ethical considerations

(viii) Their policy regarding the exercise of rights (in particular voting rights) attaching to investments

(f) **Compliance statement** including details of pension increases, discretionary benefits and tax approval status, and also a statement if there have been no employer-related investments;

(g) **Audit report**

(h) **Actuarial statement** of the results of the last valuation, the ability of the resources of the scheme to meet liabilities as they fall due and the methods and assumptions used.

The actuary should also update the results of the last valuation, by making a statement about the adequacy of the contributions and relevant changes since the last valuation.

The accounts should also contain certain general details including compliance with the SORP and an explanation that the accounts do not take account of liabilities to pay benefits after the year-end. There are also the usual requirements for accounts generally such as comparatives, explanation of accounting policies and so forth.

6.14 For many pension schemes, a simplified annual report is often sent to members. This statement is designed to supplement the annual benefit statement, and focuses on the value of the fund, the security it provides, the management of assets, and what has happened during the year.

6.15 The SORP suggests that trustees might consider including the following items in their simplified annual report:

(a) **Trustees' report** containing details of trustees and membership movements during the year

(b) **Investment report** including organisation of investments, performance objectives and returns, asset allocation at the end of the year and custody arrangements

(c) **Financial report** containing details of contributions and benefits and any special circumstances

(d) **Benefits**

(e) **Statements by auditors and actuary**

(f) **Contact name and address**

Other considerations

6.16 A well-managed fund will not restrict the occasions when it communicates with its members to those that are required by legislation. Somebody in the organisation should have the responsibility of communicating face to face with members whenever they so desire. Many companies give regular presentations (using audio-visual aids and so on) for new members. Posters and pay-packet inserts can be used to announce changes in the scheme or in the law. Companies that have in-house newspapers might have a regular pensions section. Retired members can be kept in touch by means of a newsletter. Some funds like to send Christmas cards to their members.

6.17 In 1980 the National Association of Pension Funds introduced the Golden Pen Awards as a means of stimulating improved standards of communication by pension schemes with their members. Apparently there has been a 'marked shift in the pattern of communications with an increasing number of schemes placing greater emphasis on popular reports to members, rather than relying on the formal annual report and accounts, which is distributed by many only on request.

Exercise

What matters should normally be covered in a pension scheme's trust deed?

Answer

Look back at paragraph 1.6

Chapter roundup

- Two kinds of document are used for setting up a group occupational pension scheme - the **interim trust deed** to get the scheme off the ground, and a *definitive trust deed and rules* containing full details of the scheme.
- Approval by the Pension Schemes Office means that a scheme is entitled to the substantial **taxation advantages** available for a retirement benefits scheme. The many conditions for approval are set out in the Income and Corporation Taxes Act 1988.
- **Takeovers and mergers** present a variety of options although there is no need to upset the existing arrangements. Discontinuance may occur because of a merger or takeover or because most employees leave the scheme or because the company itself is being wound up. The scheme rules will set out exactly what is to be done.
- Membership of a company pension scheme is **voluntary**: employees may choose to have a personal pension policy instead or remain in SERPS. **Equal rights** to pension benefits are now more or less secured in European law and the UK state pension age will be equalised (at 65) very gradually starting in the next century.
- There are **five main** methods of **funding** and **valuing** a pension scheme. They differ in the benefits they take into account, the basis upon which those benefits are calculated and whether they take account of future entrants to the scheme. If a valuation reveals a surplus or deficit action must be taken to rectify the situation.
- Members of pension schemes have a right to know how their future pensions are being handled. Regulations cover specific matters to be **disclosed** to members and there is a requirement to produce an annual report. Plain English is to be encouraged, as in all communication.

Test your knowledge

1 Why is it desirable for a scheme to be approved? (see para 2.2)

2 Must all schemes be approved? (2.5, 2.6)

3 What problems arise as a result of takeovers or mergers? (3.6 - 3.8)

4 In what ways is membership of an approved scheme restricted? (4.2, 4.4, 4.5)

5 In what respects is sex discrimination in pensions illegal and what is the relevance of the Barber judgement? (4.11, 4.13, 4.15 - 4.18)

6 List five actuarial assumptions. (5.3)

7 How should a surplus be dealt with? (5.26)

8 List twelve items of information that must be given to a new member of a scheme. (6.6)

Now try illustrative question 23 at the end of the Study Text

Chapter 23

TYPES OF SCHEME

This chapter covers the following topics.

Introduction

This chapter concludes our lightning tour of the pensions scene by looking at the various types of scheme that exist. To some extent we will be going over ground already covered, but from a different perspective that will hopefully help your understanding of the previous chapters.

1 GROUP OCCUPATIONAL PENSION SCHEMES 6/97, 6/99

1.1 A group occupational pension scheme is one set up by an employer for a **group of employees**. It is thus distinct from various individual arrangements that can be made, most notably the personal pension scheme.

1.2 Occupational pension schemes can be classified according to employer: there are public sector schemes and private sector schemes. Private sector schemes can be very large ones arranged on an industry-wide basis or relatively small ones for individual employers. They can also be classified according to how they are administered. First, however, we shall consider the two broad bases for the calculation of benefits.

Money purchase schemes (defined contribution schemes)

1.3 Money purchase schemes involve a **fixed rate of contribution** from the employer being allocated to each member. This fixed rate is usually a fixed percentage of the employee's salary. The contributions are invested and accumulate for each member. The resulting pension is that which can be purchased with the accumulated value of the contributions at the retirement date. Under this system the **retirement pension** does **not** have a **direct relationship** with the employee's final salary. Contributions paid in shortly before retirement have less time to accumulate than contributions paid in for a member in earlier years. Contributions paid by an employee accumulate in the same way as those paid by his employer.

Final salary schemes (defined benefit schemes)

1.4 The commonest type of defined benefit scheme is the final salary scheme where **benefits** are **related** to the **length** of an **employee's service** and his salary at or near his retirement. By this system retirement benefits cover earnings growth, including that due to inflation, during the employee's service, and the benefit is geared realistically to immediate pre-retirement earnings.

1.5 Where benefits are guaranteed the **cost** to the **employer** is **unknown**. This contrasts with the money purchase system where the cost to the employer, expressed as a percentage of payroll, is fixed, but the emerging benefits to his employee are unknown.

1.6 Although this sounds very dangerous, defined benefit schemes have been operating for many years, and actuaries are able to predict costs with a reasonable degree of certainty, based on statistical analysis, and past experience.

1.7 For the employer who feels able to take on the commitment of such a scheme, there are definite advantages. The function of a pension scheme is to replace earnings when the employee retires, so a link to final salary is certainly desirable.

Hybrid schemes

1.8 As noted in an earlier chapter, a money purchase scheme may be advantageous for young employees because contributions made on their behalf will accumulate over a long period. On the other hand a final salary pension scheme is likely to be of advantage to those employees relatively close to pension age. Now that scheme membership is voluntary some employers have introduced hybrid schemes to provide some encouragement to employees to join the company pension scheme, rather than take out a personal pension. Hybrid schemes may be seen as **final salary schemes** (for the benefit of members who stay in the scheme until retirement or who serve long periods of qualifying service) **underpinned by money purchase scheme** benefits for earlier leavers.

Which type of scheme to choose

1.9 The most important consideration, namely certainty of cost against certainty of benefit has been discussed above.

1.10 Other important factors relating to final salary schemes

(a) It is easy to include benefits on **disability** or death within the scheme design, and also integrate state pension provision.

(b) The employer is able to **control** how the scheme is funded, and build in provisions for future contingencies.

(c) Investment surpluses can be used to **reduce pension costs** or improve benefits.

(d) **Early leaver benefits** are **less valuable** than retirement benefits, and this can create a conflict of interest between those entitled to receive a benefit and those that are not.

(e) Final salary schemes are most attractive when **employees** have a **steadily rising income**, but this is less guaranteed with increased labour flexibility.

(f) There may be **conflict** over the use of surpluses.

(g) The provisions of **pensions legislation**, particularly as regards solvency and funding requirements, impose significant burdens on employers and trustees.

1.11 A number of considerations should be taken into account when assessing whether to set up a money purchase scheme.

(a) **Employees** have **greater control** over how their monies are invested. On the other hand however employees bear the risks of poor investment returns and some may not feel able to decide how their monies should be invested.

(b) The schemes appear to **treat employees equally**. However schemes cannot take into account the increased costs of pensions with age, unless age-related contribution rates are used, which may appear to be unfair.

(c) Employers can offer an **extra salary contribution** in return for benefits foregone.

(d) It can be **difficult to include** provisions for **dependants' benefits** within the framework of the scheme.

Other private sector schemes

Average salary schemes

1.12 With these arrangements retirement benefits are not based on final salary but are expressed as a percentage of the employee's salary in each year. The pension is thus related to the **employee's average earnings** over his whole career.

Revalued average salary schemes

1.13 These are similar to average salary schemes but with each year's salary **revalued** in line with an increase in an index such as the RPI or the earnings index, the latter being the more appropriate. For employees who reach their maximum earnings rates in mid career, for example salespersons and those engaged in heavy manual work, such schemes may be able to provide more satisfactory benefits than schemes which have benefits based on final salary.

Graded scale schemes

1.14 In the past instead of adopting an average salary scheme some employers would divide salaries **into bands**, for example one band might be salaries from £10,000 to £15,000, the next band being for salaries from £15,000 to £20,000 and so on. The scheme would then provide a unit of annual pension for each band of earnings.

Flat rate schemes

1.15 These schemes are inappropriate today and are rarely, if ever, adopted. The concept underlying them was that every employee would receive the same flat rate pension of a fixed amount, subject to completion of a specified number of years service with the employer. An alternative was to provide a pension of a fixed amount for each year of service completed with the employer.

2 SELF-ADMINISTERED SCHEMES 12/95

2.1 Group occupational pension schemes may be run on an entirely self-administered basis. As previously indicated they are constituted by a **trust deed** and **rules**; trustees are appointed who are responsible for the running of the scheme in a proper manner. With complete **self-administration**, the **trustees**, in co-operation with the employer, **carry out all the administrative work** in connection with the operation of the scheme, collecting contributions from the employer and employees, paying benefits as and when they arise, and so on.

2.2 The **fund** built up from the accumulation of the contributions is **invested** under the authority of the **trustees** of the scheme, the trustees seeking investment advice. Subject to such advice, and to meeting any legislative requirements, the trustees have control over the investment policy, choosing one which in their judgement is in the best interests of the beneficiaries of the scheme.

2.3 The scheme clearly needs **professional services**, however, and the trustees will usually engage an independent solicitor to carry out all the legal work, an independent chartered accountant to carry out the audit of the accounts, and an independent actuary to perform the necessary actuarial duties.

2.4 In practice self-administration works completely satisfactorily. It is an extremely popular method of running a pension scheme, particularly for larger schemes.

Pension scheme management 12/95, 12/98

2.5 If a pension scheme was run **entirely in-house**, it would be the **pension scheme manager**'s **responsibility** to ensure that all benefit calculations are carried out strictly in accordance with the scheme rules. Payments need to be made promptly (which means careful cash management) and correctly.

2.6 The scheme manager also needs the skills and knowledge to **operate** the **scheme** in compliance with legal and tax regulations. This includes knowledge of trust law and the ability to understand and interpret lengthy and complex legal documents such as the trust deed and rules. It also means understanding the requirements of the Pension Schemes Office of the Inland Revenue and OPRA.

2.7 There are various **secretarial duties** to be done to support the trustee function.

(a) Submitting annual returns, accounts and complying with other statutory requirements

(b) Preparing papers for meetings, arranging AGMs and EGMs, taking and distributing minutes

(c) Dealing with appointments and resignations of trustees

(d) Making allowances for the different communication needs of different trustees: member trustees who work on the shop floor will be far less comfortable with board room procedure than members for whom formal meetings are a normal part of their job

2.8 The manager needs to oversee the mechanisms that are used for:

(a) Collecting, banking and investing money from employees and the employer

(b) Ensuring that the contributions paid are those recommended by the actuary

(c) Ensuring that income from investments (including tax reclaims) is available for reinvestment as soon as possible

2.9 **Broker skills** may be needed, such as purchasing annuities from insurance companies, and arranging group or individual life assurance, and perhaps other insurances such as personal accident policies or medical insurance.

2.10 The pensions manager needs to be a **good communicator**, able to convey information to members, pensioners, members' representatives and a variety of professionals such as actuaries, accountants, solicitors, bankers and brokers. Intercompany communications also need to be strong. Close liaison with the personnel and payroll departments is necessary.

2.11 The manager will also be involved in **appraising** the company's **pension policy** from a strategic point of view: ensuring that it remains competitive compared with benefits offered by other companies, and assessing the impact of changes in the statutory environment such as the recent legislation to equalise the state pension age.

Cost implications and management resources: internal vs external management?

2.12 To carry out *all* of the above duties in-house would usually require a full time PMI **qualified pensions manager,** and administrative support. There will be an annual cost in terms of salaries plus expenses to cover the costs of equipment, office space and so on, although these costs may well be incurred in any case and should be ignored if so. The cost of professional advisers such as solicitors and actuaries would be significantly reduced, but the precise change would depend on the quality of the manager appointed.

2.13 At the other extreme, if as many as possible of the above duties were carried out by a third party there would be an **annual fee.** This may be cheaper than in-house management, but it may be somewhat misleading, because it does not include *all* aspects of scheme management: the company may wish to retain some of the secretarial responsibilities, for example, and would need to get involved in the communication aspects. The personnel and payroll administration aspects of the scheme would either be duplicated, or else would have to be considered for outsourcing, too: this may not be acceptable.

Information and computer systems

2.14 Standard **modern office software** (such as spreadsheets for certain calculations and word processors for the large volume of fairly standard correspondence needed) takes much of the administrative chore out of pensions scheme management, although it needs to be carefully controlled. There are also many off-the-shelf pension administration packages. For a small scheme a standard package should be perfectly adequate, so long as it remains compatible with the systems used by personnel and payroll.

2.15 **Good record keeping** is vital: many authorisation documents, insurance policies, certificates of birth, death and marriage and so on need to be held. A third party offers economies of scale because it would be able to justify the expense of more powerful software. The auditability of third party systems is an issue to consider, however.

Meeting members needs

2.16 Arguably this is the most important consideration of all, though a more balanced view would also take account of the organisation's needs.

(a) The use of a **suitable third party** would no doubt mean that specialist expertise and equipment could be brought to bear on our scheme. This could only be to the advantage of members.

(b) Members might welcome the fact that the **management** of the scheme was in the hands of a **reputable third party,** who might be perceived as more likely to act objectively and independently.

(c) Alternatively, the move to **outsourcing** might be taken to indicate a lack of commitment to the scheme on the part of the organisation: it may seem as if we are washing our hands of the scheme.

3 INSURED SCHEMES

3.1 As an alternative to self-administration a group occupational pension scheme can be insured, with virtually all the duties mentioned above in connection with self-administration being handed over to a Life Assurance company. Insured schemes are still set up under a trust with rules, and trustees are appointed as for self-administered schemes.

3.2 There have been various types of insured scheme all of which can be transacted through the pension business fund of the life office, which operates on a tax free basis in the same way as does a self-administered fund.

Non-profit group deferred annuities

3.3 Under the non-profit group deferred annuity approach **premium rates** are **guaranteed** for a limited period of years. Thus when premiums are paid they purchase a certain amount of pension, that is, the contributions can be applied to purchase pensions of individual members on an accurate basis.

3.4 When costing a non-profit group deferred annuity scheme it is customary to consider future service pensions and past service pensions separately.

With-profits group deferred annuities

3.5 A development of the non-profit group deferred annuity approach has been the with-profits form. The distinctive factor of with-profits group deferred annuity schemes is that the benefits contain a **bonus element** which is not guaranteed. This unknown profits element means that future benefits cannot be costed with precision and the methods adopted for non-profit group deferred annuity schemes are impracticable. Instead an **aggregate costing method** is adopted.

Deposit administration

3.6 Whilst group deferred annuity schemes have merits, it is claimed by pension fund managers that their method of operation is not altogether explicit. In consequence life offices introduced deposit administration. Under deposit administration when the premiums are received by the life office they are merely **left** in a **pool** to accumulate with interest. When benefits need to be purchased for members, for example when a member is due to retire, money is taken out of the pool to purchase the benefit.

3.7 The method is explicit in that expense charges in connection with the scheme are specifically stated. Moreover the rate of interest credited to the pool of investments, and hence to the individual pension schemes in it, is specifically announced each year. The rate of interest normally comprises a guaranteed basic rate set at a low level with bonus interest, dependent on actual experience each year, added. Contributions payable into a deposit administration arrangement are calculated by an aggregate method similar to the one used for with-profits deferred annuity schemes.

Managed funds

3.8 With deposit administration investment of the pool of funds is left entirely to the life office concerned. Some fund managers prefer to have rather more say in investment policy. Life offices have therefore introduced managed funds. Contributions to be paid by trustees of individual schemes are again based on assumptions; these include estimates of the earnings of the fund, rates of mortality, and salary trends. The method of operation is for contributions available for investment to be **applied** in all or any of several **unitised funds**: payments into the fund are applied to buy units whose values are affected by accumulation of interest and alterations in capital value. In other words they operate on the unit trust principle.

3.9 A life office usually has several managed funds, one for equities, another for fixed interest securities, one for property and so on. Whilst the constitution of the individual funds is left to the life office, individual pension schemes can choose the proportion of trust contributions which they wish to have allocated to each separate fund. When benefits need to be paid out to individual scheme members they are purchased from cash taken out of the funds.

3.10 Managed funds are designed for pension scheme managers who wish to retain a **direct stake in investment performance** and to obtain the widest possible spread of investments by pooling their assets with those of other pension funds.

Segregated funds

3.11 Some life offices are prepared to go beyond the scope of managed funds by operating segregated funds, that is **separate funds** for **individual pension schemes** subject to a minimum size of scheme. The investment policy for such a segregated fund is agreed with the trustees from time to time, either in general terms or in detail.

Self-administered schemes and life offices

3.12 It is not essential for a group pension scheme either to be 100% self-administered, or 100% transacted through a life office. A self-administered scheme might otherwise retain all relevant services under its own control but place some of its investments with a life office managed fund in order to obtain added diversification, for example in property or in overseas equities.

3.13 A self-administered scheme might wish to **self-administer** the **retirement pensions element** and **insure** the **death-in-service benefits**. An adverse mortality experience in a particular year could result in an unusually large outlay in lump sum death-in-service benefits, conceivably so much so as to exhaust all income of the fund for the year and necessitate the realisation of assets. This could be at an inconvenient time for the scheme. Thus, depending upon the size of the scheme and its previous claims experience, the transfer of this risk to a life office is sometimes considered desirable.

Exercise 1

There is enough material in the preceding sections to enable you to try the following question from the June 1992 examination.

You are responsible for the in-house management of a substantial pension fund.

It has come to your chairman's notice that some of the very large UK pension funds have switched to external fund management. You have been requested to provide him with a briefing paper on the merits of such a change in the case of your own company. Outline the most important points.

Exercise 2

Here is a series of extracts from an article in a *Financial Times* survey on Pension Fund Investment.

> 'By the end of last year the top six external investment management companies controlled UK pension fund portfolios worth £110bn. If you add in the top few in-house managers, led by PosTel with £20bn, it is likely that only about 10 or a dozen managers control half the £370bn total value of UK pension funds.'
>
> 'But, as fewer and fewer managers come to dominate, their big bets can have a disproportionate impact, sometimes for good but with worrying longer term implications. Excessive concentration could increase the risks of investment and create distortions. The focus of the problem changes from time to time, however. A few years ago institutional investors were being roundly attacked for too readily supporting aggressive takeovers, and for helping to generate undue short-termism. But at present there are scarcely any contested takeover bids so the criticism has shifted, concentrating for instance, on the pressures exerted on British companies for excessive dividend payments.'
>
> One other cloud on the horizon is being anxiously watched. It is the possibility that the present overwhelming predominance of final salary based pension schemes in the UK might be disturbed by a swing towards money-purchase schemes which sidestep the controversy over surpluses.
>
> A widespread switch to money-purchase schemes would pose big challenges to fund managers. Instead of having a single very long-term client in each scheme they would have thousands of individual, shorter-term investors. They would need to invest in lower risk assets, to address the needs of scheme members approaching retirement.
>
> Moreover, the greater participation of individual scheme members and, probably, trade unions, would require investment managers to act much more like retail institutions offering

simple, but flexible products and seeking to build customer-friendly images. It would be a major change of approach for institutions, such as Mercury Asset Management and Phillips and Drew Fund Management, which are highly successful at dealing with professional pension consultants and trustees but scarcely have high profiles as far as the public at large is concerned.'

In the light of the above and of what you have learnt in this chapter and the preceding ones what type of pension scheme options would you recommend to a new and fairly high tech medium-sized organisation of which you are the company secretary?

Solution

It is for you to make the decision, but you will be influenced by articles such as this and your own confidence and experience in dealing with pension matters and pension providers.

---

4 OTHER ARRANGEMENTS

Individuals and small groups

4.1 Employers often wish to set up a group scheme for their employees, but occasions can arise when a **one-man scheme** is desired. Subject to the normal requirements a scheme for one person can be approved by the Inland Revenue under ICTA 1988. Executive pension schemes are in fact used by employers quite often for key employees. An individual arrangement can provide confidentiality and flexibility. Such contracts are insured and generally they operate on a money-purchase basis.

4.2 Arrangements might also be made through a life office for a **small group** of senior executives as selected by the employer, a group policy then being issued. By such an arrangement an employer may be enabled to reward those key employees who have contributed most to the success of his business with attractive fringe benefits.

Hancock annuities

4.3 The case of *General Reversionary and Investment Company v Inland Revenue 1919* established an important precedent. As a result an employer is entitled to tax relief on a single premium to purchase an immediate annuity for a retired employee or for a dependant of a deceased employee. The conditions include one requiring that the pension must be non-commutable and non-assignable.

4.4 They are termed **Hancock annuities** because Hancock was the name of the Inland Revenue Inspector involved in the case.

Purchased life annuities

4.5 These are life annuities purchased through a life assurance office; they are transacted through its general annuity fund, not as portfolio pension business. A pension from a group occupational pension scheme is taxed as income, but with a purchased life annuity (when a lump sum is paid for an annuity to an individual) the annuity payments are taxed only on their interest content. In effect the annuity payments are considered to comprise two elements,

(a) A **capital element** (obtained by dividing the single payment by the expectation of life, according to a specific mortality value, of the annuitant at the date of purchase)

(b) An **interest element**

4.6 Thus in certain circumstances a purchased life annuity can prove to be a valuable tax efficient investment. It is to be noted that any pension annuity or Hancock annuity provided in connection with an approved superannuation scheme does *not* qualify as a purchased life annuity.

4.7 There are, however, cases in connection with an occupational pension scheme where part of the pension is **commutable at retirement**. If that commuted lump sum is then reapplied to buy a life annuity through an assurance office that annuity can be treated as a purchased life annuity. By this means the retiree replaces part of his pension which is wholly taxable as income by a pension which is taxable only on its interest content.

4.8 A number of different types of annuity are available; the type chosen will depend on individual circumstances including family history of longevity and health.

5 INDUSTRY-WIDE AND SIMILAR SCHEMES

5.1 A scheme open to the employees of more than one employer may be approvable. Examples of this would be where one employer is a **subsidiary** company of the other; where the shares of two companies are held by individuals but one group of shareholders is in a position to control both; or where the scheme is established by a **professional** or **trade association** on behalf of a group of employers in that profession or trade. It may also be possible to approve a **centralised scheme** for employers who are not related either by trade or profession. In all cases the Inland Revenue must be satisfied that the scheme will be properly administered and that the financial arrangements to be adopted are sound.

5.2 It will not usually be possible, without very complicated rules, to allow employees to be members both of a centralised scheme for non-associated employers and of another scheme set up by their employer.

Funding

5.3 Normally the basis of funding will be such that each employer will provide the **benefits** for his **own employees** exclusively but the Inland Revenue will be prepared to consider the use of controlled funding where the employers accept that, taking one year with another, substantial cross subsidies will occur.

Benefits

5.4 Pensions at normal retirement age must not be greater than **1/60th of final remuneration** with the last employer, for each year of membership of the scheme up to 40 years. The last employer may, nevertheless, augment the final pension up to the limit allowed under normal approval where up to **1/30th of final pay** may be provided for each year (up to a maximum of 20 years) with the last employer, benefits from previous employment being taken into account.

5.5 Final remuneration with the last employer, however, is not an acceptable criterion for compounding the lump sum benefit for members who have moved from one employment to another. The lump sum available by right will generally have to be computed by reference to each employment separately on the basis of **3/80th of final remuneration** from the employer in question for each year of service with him.

Association of schemes

5.6 To be accepted as associated the employers must be linked so closely that they are treated as carrying on a **single trade or undertaking**, or they must all belong to a group of companies forming a single financial unit. Alternatively, even though no parent/subsidiary relationship exists, there may be enough links between the employers to warrant a centralised scheme based on close association through a permanent community of interests.

5.7 A scheme for associated employers may adopt any **method of funding** which would be acceptable for the scheme of a single employer.

5.8 A centralised scheme for associated employers may provide **benefits** based on the employer's final remuneration up to the normal Inland Revenue limit. The employee's total service within the group, irrespective of moves from one participating employer to another is regarded as constituting a single unbroken employment.

5.9 The advantage of a centralised scheme for the employer(s) is the **saving in administrative costs**; for the employee his career choices will be enhanced because a possible deterrent to changing jobs while remaining within the associated group as a whole is removed if he can be sure that his pension will not be affected.

6 PUBLIC SECTOR SCHEMES

6.1 These comprise schemes established under statutory powers such as those for the armed forces, the civil service and the police; and schemes constituted under a trust deed and rules and conforming with Inland Revenue requirements.

Contributions and benefits

6.2 Public sector schemes are often **non-contributory**. Indeed non-contributory pensions were extended to the whole of the Civil Service under the Superannuation Act 1834.

Funding

6.3 Schemes for the armed forces, civil servants, police, fire service are not funded; they are financed on a pay-as-you-go system.

6.4 Another system of financing in the public sector is that of **notional funds**. Under this system contributions by employees and the employers are paid into the Exchequer and benefits are paid from the Exchequer. An account is kept of these contributions and benefits but no actual investment of the contributions is made. Instead mere notional investment in government securities is assumed with notional interest being credited to the pension scheme.

7 RETIREMENT ANNUITIES

7.1 Many are entitled to become members of a group occupational pension scheme by reason of their being in the employment of an employer who has set up such an arrangement for the benefit of his staff. On the other hand there are many others, such as the self-employed who are not eligible for such an arrangement. The latter category used to make appropriate provisions for their own retirement and various ways of saving for that purpose are available to them. Nevertheless, substantial taxation advantages result from taking out a pensions contract which is approved by the Inland Revenue Authorities.

7.2 The Finance Act 1956 introduced provisions whereby the self-employed, or those in non-pensionable employment, would receive tax relief on the whole of the premiums paid to provide a retirement annuity, although certain conditions of approval were attached.

7.3 These 'retirement annuity schemes' are **money purchase** arrangements. The maximum amount of premium paid in any year eligible for tax relief, is limited to a fixed percentage of the policyholder's **net relevant earnings** (see below) for that year.

7.4 No new retirement annuity schemes may be effected; they have been superseded by personal pension schemes.

8 PERSONAL PENSION SCHEMES

8.1 Personal pensions, which supersede retirement annuities, became available from 1 July 1988. They are **money purchase** arrangements. The concept of personal pensions has been developed from that set out in the Social Security Act 1986 by the Finance Acts of 1987, 1988 and 1989. The main legislation is contained in ICTA 1988 ss 630 - 655.

Definition

8.2 The Social Security Act 1986 defines a personal pension scheme as:

> 'any scheme or arrangement ... to provide benefits, in the form of pensions or otherwise, payable on death or retirement to or in respect of employed earners who had made arrangements with the trustees or managers of the scheme for them to become members of the scheme.'

Approval

8.3 Personal pensions need to be **approved** by the Inland Revenue Authorities. When approved a personal pension scheme obtains the same taxation advantages as are granted to exempt approved occupational schemes.

8.4 A personal pension scheme can be based on **insurance policies** with an insurance office or friendly society, on **units in an authorised unit trust scheme**, on **shares or deposits** with a **building society**, or on an **interest-bearing account** with a **bank**. Within limits personal pension scheme providers may allow individuals to specify their own portfolio of investments.

Eligibility

8.5 Individuals aged 16 to 74 who have net relevant earnings, as defined in ICTA 1984, may effect a personal pension, where such individuals are either employed but not members of a pension scheme or self-employed. Also a personal pension scheme may be set up in respect of a person without net relevant earnings, to accept a transfer value from an employer's scheme but without any further contributions.

8.6 A person may have more than one personal pension scheme, but only one may be chosen to receive **minimum contributions**, in any one tax year, in connection with a contracted-out personal pensions scheme.

Net relevant earnings

8.7 To summarise the Finance (No 2) Act 1987, **relevant earnings** means all earnings from employment or self-employment which are chargeable to income tax for the year in question and which are not earnings as a controlling decision of an investment company. To arrive at **net relevant earnings** specified deductions are made. These are the deductions which would be made in computing the taxable trading profits of the individual.

Allowable contributions

8.8 The following percentages of net relevant earnings may be contributed to a personal pension scheme, in any tax year.

Age at beginning of tax year	*Percentage of net relevant earnings*
16 to 35	17.5
36 to 45	20.0
46 to 50	25.0
51 to 55	30.0
56 to 60	35.0
61 to 74	40.0

8.9 Net relevant earnings are restricted to a maximum equal to the **earnings cap** (£91,800 for 2000/2001).

8.10 Neither an individual nor his employer is allowed to contribute to a personal pension scheme if he is already a member of an occupational pension scheme, unless that scheme provides certain benefits only.

8.11 An employer is not required to contribute to a personal pension scheme but should he do so the total contributions to all personal pension schemes by a person, and by his employer in respect of him, are subject to the overall limits given in the above table.

Minimum contributions

8.12 Any minimum contributions by the Department of Social Security to a contracted-out personal pension scheme are **additional** to the limits quoted in the table given above. Minimum contributions comprise the **NI rebate**, income tax relief at the basic rate on the employer's share of the net rebate, and the **incentive payment** for those who qualify for it.

Unused relief

8.13 A **carry-forward option** and a **carry-back option** are available. The former involves carrying forward any shortfall between contributions paid and the maximum allowable, thus enabling a person to pay higher contributions than the maximum normally allowable in a particular year. The carry-back option allows a contribution to be treated for income tax purposes as having been paid in a previous tax year (subject to the overall limits); tax relief is then given at the rate in force in the previous year.

Cessation of contributions

8.14 On cessation of contributions by choice or by lack of continued eligibility the **benefits** may be **preserved** until retirement, or transferred either to another personal pension scheme or to an approved employer's scheme which is both willing and able to accept a transfer value.

Transfers

8.15 Transfers can be accepted by personal pension schemes from another personal pension scheme, an occupational pension scheme, a statutory scheme, a buy-out policy, a free standing additional voluntary contribution scheme, or a retirement annuity policy.

Benefits

Pension age

8.16 The age at which benefits, in excess of protected rights (see below), can be chosen by the member to be paid may be any age between **50 and 75**. The amount of pension which can be paid to a member of pension age is not restricted. The restriction under a personal pension scheme arises only from the limitation placed upon contributions.

Lump sums

8.17 At pension age the member can choose to take a **pension** for himself only or a **pension** for himself combined with a **lump sum** and/or a dependant's pension following his death. Under personal pension schemes 25% of the accumulated fund may be taken as a tax-free lump sum.

Death

8.18 Should the member die *before* pension age the lump sum payable under a term assurance effected in connection with the personal pension scheme may be paid and either a return of the accumulated fund may be given as a lump sum, or dependants' annuities may be bought with the amount of the accumulated lump sum.

Group personal pension schemes

8.19 Although a personal pension scheme is an arrangement between a provider and an individual, group arrangements are sometimes set up by an employer. This sometimes happens when the employer does not operate a company pension scheme. By operating on a group basis, with the employer collecting and remitting contributions, savings in costs can often be made and this sometimes enables the scheme provider to offer slightly more favourable terms.

9 FREE STANDING ADDITIONAL VOLUNTARY CONTRIBUTIONS

9.1 The Inland Revenue will, since 1987, approve retirement benefits schemes to which employers do not contribute, but through which their employees can buy relevant benefits additional to those provided by the employer's scheme. Such schemes are referred to as **Free Standing Additional Voluntary Contribution Schemes (FSAVCs).**

9.2 The right to contribution to an FSAVC scheme is available only to members who are **simultaneously accruing benefits** under an approved scheme (except one approved under the simplified procedure) or a statutory scheme of their present employer or to which that employer contributes. The Social Security Act 1986 requires every employer's occupational pension scheme to provide an 'in-house' AVC facility from 6 April 1988. It is thus up to the employee contemplating paying AVCs to choose which of the alternatives he considers to be most favourable to him.

9.3 For example there is a 'cash flow' consideration in that the relief is not given through the net pay system. Basic rate relief is obtained by paying over to the provider only the net amount but higher rate relief must be obtained by application to the Inland Revenue.

9.4 However the choice of FSAVC schemes available is much wider than the one or two options likely to be offered by the company AVC scheme. The FSAVC scheme as a whole may be more costly; the employer remains responsible for monitoring both the amounts put in and the retirement benefits and may also make a charge for providing information to the FSAVC scheme. However, this does not apply where contributions are less than £2,400 per annum. As with company AVC schemes, if benefits arising are in excess of the allowable limits, the excess will be returned to the employee (subject to a tax charge).

Requirements

9.5 An FSAVC scheme can be approved only if it is **established** by an **insurance company**, a **building society**, a **bank**, or a unit trust. There are a number of requirements.

(a) There must be a named administrator.

(b) The sole purpose must be the provision of income in retirement, not tax-free lump sums.

(c) The scheme must be established by irrevocable trusts.

(d) Apart from death benefits FSAVC schemes must operate on a money purchase basis.

(e) An employee must not contribute to more than one FSAVC scheme in any one tax year.

(f) '20% directors' are not eligible.

(g) The total of an employer's contributions to all schemes must not exceed 15% of his remuneration in any one year (although minimum contributions paid by the DSS do not count towards this limit) and total benefits must not exceed the earnings cap.

(h) The rules must prohibit any contributions or contribution from a member's employer.

(i) The normal retirement age must be the same as that under the employer's scheme. On early retirement, benefits under the FSAVC scheme must commence at the same time as under the employer's scheme.

(j) The rules should not permit the acceptance of transfer values into an FSAVC scheme except from another FSAVC scheme.

SERPS

9.6 An FSAVC scheme may be used to **contract out** of SERPS, but in this case the employee's share of the minimum contribution does not qualify for grossing up for tax relief.

Transfers

9.7 A member leaving an FSAVC scheme may require the value of his accrued benefits to be applied to spare transfer credits under a scheme of his current employer, or an approved scheme of a subsequent employer of which he has become a member, or another FSAVC scheme. A transfer may also be made to a personal pension scheme if he is no longer accruing benefits, other than death benefits, in an employer's scheme.

Benefits

9.8 For maximum approvable benefit purposes the benefits from FSAVCs are **aggregable** with those **under the employer's scheme**, but this does not apply if the employer's scheme is a simplified defined contribution scheme.

9.9 To ensure that aggregate contributions do not produce benefits in excess of approvable benefits, the maximum contribution rate may be calculated so that the capitalised value of future payments of AVCs shall be equal to the excess of:

(a) The **capitalised value** of the **maximum approvable benefits** in relation to service with the current employer at normal retirement age

(b) The **amounts credited** in respect of that employment in free-standing or other money-purchase AVC schemes

10 STAKEHOLDER PENSIONS

10.1 The Government announced its intention to introduce 'stakeholder pensions' as part of the overall reforms described in the consultation paper *A new contract for welfare: Partnership in Pensions* published in December 1998.

10.2 Stakeholder pensions are primarily aimed at employees who earn between **£9,500** and **£20,000** and have no access to occupational schemes; their only option therefore for private saving has been a personal pension scheme.

10.3 The legal framework has been enacted under the Welfare Reform and Pensions Act 1999, and the tax treatment will be governed by the Finance Act 2000, and subsequent regulations. Stakeholder pensions will be introduced from **6 April 2001**, and will provide an additional pension choice.

10.4 The **tax treatment** will be modelled on the existing treatment of personal pensions, but with some changes. The revised regime will then apply to stakeholder pensions, personal pensions and, if they so elect, occupational schemes on a defined contribution basis.

10.5 The intention is to simplify the existing regime. The contribution limits will be the **greater** of **£3,600** per year or the **age** and **earnings related** figure from the existing personal pension scale. The result of this will be that those who have no earnings will be able to contribute up to £3,600 per year. (Members of an occupational scheme will generally not be able to contribute unless the scheme is a defined contribution arrangement which has opted for the new regime to apply.)

10.6 Contributions will qualify for **tax relief** at the **individual's highest rate**(s) and both employees and the self-employed will pay contributions net of basic rate tax relief.

10.7 The investment fund will be **free** from **tax** on **capital gains** and **income**, except that (as at present) dividend tax credits will not be reclaimable.

10.8 At retirement, up to 25% of the fund, excluding protected rights, can be taken as a tax free **lump sum**, and the income benefit will be taxed as earned income, under PAYE. **Phased retirement** and **income withdrawal** will be permitted.

10.9 There are **no limits** on **benefits**, apart from the restriction relating to the maximum proportion of the fund available in cash.

10.10 To ensure the widest possible accessibility of these schemes, **minimum contribution levels** will be kept low. The minimum acceptable contribution must **not exceed £20**, and there must be no requirement for regularity. This means that a one off contribution of £20 must be acceptable.

10.11 The terms of stakeholder pensions must also be very **flexible**. Contributions can be varied, or stopped, without penalty, and transfers in and out must be permitted without extra charge or exit penalty.

10.12 It will be possible to use stakeholder pensions to **contract out** of SERPS, and, when it is introduced, S2P. For the first year of the operation of stakeholder pensions, the basis will be the same as currently applies to personal pensions, and the rebates will be the same. The rebates will be the subject of a review starting in the summer of 2000, with the intention of determining new rebate levels to apply from April 2002.

Responsibilities of employers

10.13 The government has chosen to use employers to bring in the scheme as this will make it easy for employees to join, and part of the cost will be borne by employers. The basic requirement is that employers should **provide access** to a stakeholder pension for employees, allowing at least one scheme to be promoted through the workplace and collecting contributions through payroll.

10.14 Although the employer will be involved in promoting the scheme, there will be **no compulsion** for the employer to **contribute**, though this will be permitted if the employer so wishes.

10.15 The requirement for employers to provide this access will come into effect in October 2001, to give time for employers to choose a suitable scheme after the first availability of stakeholder pensions in April 2001. The employer is not responsible for the performance of the scheme and will not be regarded as having given investment advice as a result of making the choice. This is specifically covered in the Welfare Reform and Pensions Act 1999. In practice, employers are likely to enlist the help of a **suitably qualified financial adviser**.

10.16 Some employers will be exempt, but the grounds for exemption are limited. They are that:

- The employer has **fewer** than **5 employees**; or
- All employees are offered **membership** of an **occupational scheme**; or
- All employees are **offered membership** of a **group personal pension arrangement** with an employer contribution of **at least 3%** of earnings (defined as basic salary) and with no exit charges; or
- All employees **earn less than** the **Lower Earnings Limit**.

10.17 If the occupational scheme exemption is used, this will not be affected if the scheme has a 'waiting period' prior to entry, provided this does **not exceed one year**, and it is also possible to exclude employees who are aged under 18, or are within 5 years of retirement.

10.18 Where the exemptions do not apply, access to the designated stakeholder pension must be made available within three months of an employee entering the employment.

10.19 Employers have a number of responsibilities.

(a) **Designate a scheme**. All stakeholder schemes have to be registered with OPRA.

(b) **Discuss with employees**. The workforce must be consulted, and employers must consider how queries that are raised should be answered.

(c) **Provide access.** Employers will have to provide information to enable employees to contact the scheme.

(d) **Payroll deduction.** Employers will have to deduct contributions and pass them onto the designated scheme. Employers can specify that they be determined either as a flat monetary amount, or a percentage of earnings (or offer a choice of either). The employee can vary the level of deduction, but the employer can restrict the ability to vary to once every six months.

(e) **Maintain compliance**. The requirements are the same as for occupational schemes.

10.20 Clearly there will be costs to employers; the government is however proposing a 1% of the fund cap on the charges for administering the scheme and providing basic advice.

11 FUTURE DEVELOPMENTS

11.1 The government's Green Paper in December 1998 proposed the following changes for occupational pension schemes:

(a) The introduction of a more flexible contracting-out procedure

(b) Allowing employers to make membership of an occupational pension scheme compulsory, unless the employees can show that they are making sufficient alternative provision

(c) Removing from employers the right to opt-out of the member-nominated trustee provision (subsequently introduced in the Child Support, Pensions and Social Security Bill 1999)

(d) Reviewing the minimum funding levels

(e) Reviewing entitlement to benefits from insured schemes and AVCs

(f) Increased exemptions from the provisions of the Pensions Act 1995 for small self-administered and money purchase schemes

(g) Requiring trustees to disclose details of ethical investments policy (now enacted)

(h) Strengthening the sanctions for late payment of contributions and failing to disclose information to OPRA

Chapter roundup

- The various types of **occupational scheme** may helpfully be summarised in diagrammatic form (see the following page).
- **Personal pension schemes** were at the centre of the so-called 'Pensions revolution' which took place in the second half of the 1980s. Companies offer their own pension schemes as a means of attracting and retaining high-calibre employees.
- It is essential to be aware of the alternatives that its scheme is now required to compete with. You should therefore make sure that you are aware of and are able to offer information about the features of personal pension schemes.

Test your knowledge

1 Distinguish between a money purchase scheme and a final salary scheme. (see paras 1.3, 1.4)

2 Distinguish between a self-administered scheme and an insured scheme. (2.1, 3.1)

3 Distinguish between non-profit and with profits schemes. (3.3, 3.5)

4 Explain what is meant by deposit administration. (3.6, 3.7)

5 Why might a one-man scheme be set up? (4.2)

6 What is an associated centralised scheme? (5.1, 5.6)

7 What methods of funding are used for public sector schemes? (6.3, 6.4)

8 Who is eligible for a personal pension scheme? (8.5)

9 What is the position regarding transfers into and out of personal pension schemes? (8.15)

10 What are the conditions for approval of an FSAVC? (9.5)

Now try illustrative question 24 at the end of the Study Text

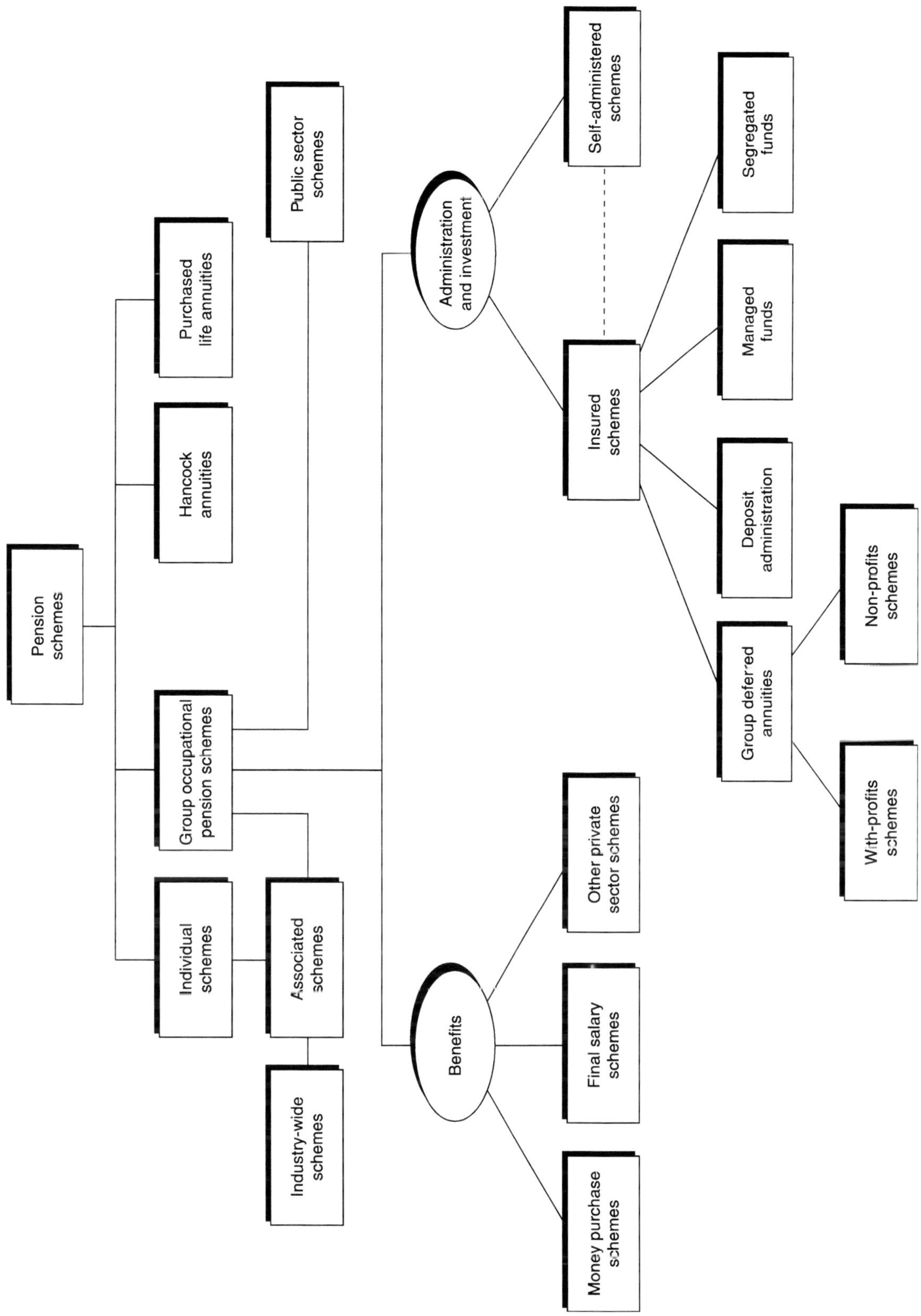
Pension schemes
Individual schemes
Group occupational pension schemes
Hancock annuities
Purchased life annuities
Public sector schemes
Associated schemes
Industry-wide schemes
Benefits
Money purchase schemes
Final salary schemes
Other private sector schemes
Administration and investment
Insured schemes
Self-administered schemes
Group deferred annuities
Deposit administration
Managed funds
Segregated funds
With-profits schemes
Non-profits schemes

Part D

Management of corporate assets

Chapter 24

IDENTIFICATION AND PROTECTION OF ASSETS

This chapter covers the following topics

Introduction

In this chapter we address the question of the identification and protection of assets from a legal point of view, concentrating principally on intangible assets and intellectual property. This is a quite a difficult area of the law and one that *has* been examined, so we go into a certain amount of depth, even though you should have studied this at Pre-Professional level.

In the next chapter we move on to consider more practical matters concerned with the management and security of assets that you can *touch*, especially buildings.

1 ASSETS AND COMPANY WELL-BEING

The definition of an asset

1.1 Assets have been defined in many different ways and for many purposes. For instance an asset has been described as:

> 'Any tangible or intangible possession which has value.'

An asset is so called because it is **owned** by someone who **values** it.

1.2 In the Accounting Standards Board's FRS 5 assets are defined as follows.

> 'Assets are rights or other access to future economic benefits controlled by an entity as a result of past transactions or events.'

1.3 The term '**future economic benefits**' refers to future cash flows expected from the use or disposal of the asset. Control implies the ability to obtain future benefit or to restrict others' access to it. Control is normally based on legally enforceable rights but these are not essential.

1.4 The Companies Act 1989 says that:

> 'fixed assets' means assets of a company which are intended for use on a continuing basis, and current assets means assets not intended for such use.

A current asset is an asset like cash or debtors. Examples of fixed assets are given below.

1.5 Fixed assets may contribute in various ways to an organisation's prosperity.

Exercise 1

Study the table below. This suggests various ways in which assets contribute to corporate prosperity, but it is not meant to be comprehensive. See if you can think of other ways and further examples.

Asset	Future (economic) benefit
Development costs (The costs of using existing scientific or technical knowledge to produce new (or substantially improved) products or systems, prior to starting commercial production operations).	These will lead to income when the new products or systems go into production. Commercial viability is one of the key criteria for treating such expenditure as an asset.
Concessions, patents, licences etc Described in more detail later in this chapter.	These generally give the organisation the right to do something in preference to a competitor, for example the right to market a certain drug. They are thus a source of competitive advantage and therefore profit.
Land and buildings Offices, factories, shops. Farm land, mines, reservoirs etc.	Buildings are used to house and protect other human and physical resources which themselves are used to add value to resources and generate profits. Land may be used to grow saleable products or may give them up when mined. Both land and buildings may be rented out to others or sold at a profit. There may also be non-economic benefits: a prestigious building or a scenic location may boost staff morale, for example.
Plant and machinery An oil refinery, an assembly line, a crane, a fleet of vehicles etc.	These may be used to process other resources to add value and make a profit, or to *save* expenditure on other resources such as time and money in the case of a salesman's company car. Delivery vehicles can also be used as a 'free' medium for promotion. Company cars motivate salespeople.
Fixtures, fittings, tools and equipment The interiors of buildings, office and factory infrastructure, furniture, computer equipment, drills, saws, handtools etc.	These are used to process and add value to other resources such as raw materials or raw data or to save the resource of time. Again there are also psychological benefits.

Asset	Future (economic) benefit
Investments Subsidiary companies, or shares bought on the stock market held for the long term.	In a sense investments are a 'package' of the other assets listed above. These are held to generate income in the form of dividends, interest and management charges and also perhaps to make capital gains. Savings may be derived from economies of scale, for example a retailer that buys a manufacturer-supplier.

Legal considerations: property and ownership

Underpinning knowledge

A distinction may be made between real property (land owned in perpetuity), *choses in possession* (moveable tangible property such as a bicycle), and *choses in action* (intangible things such as bank accounts).

Ownership of land is transferred by deed, chattels are transferred by mere delivery of possession and choses in action are transferred by assignment (usually a written transfer).

The owner of property has various rights of ownership. He may usually do with his property what he pleases: use it or not use it, lend it, give it away etc.

These ideas are not likely to be directly examined in *Administration of Corporate Affairs* exams, but they may be fundamental to a question on asset management and protection. Consider whether you need to revise your earlier law papers.

Intangibles: industrial and intellectual property 12/95

1.6 Although it is deemed to be in the public interest that **ideas** in general should be allowed to be exploited rather than subjected to monopolistic control, the law has developed as a combination of statutory principles, common law rules and equitable principles to provide protection to certain specific categories of industrial and intellectual property. Three main categories can be distinguished.

(a) A **patent** is a monopoly right to exploit an invention for a stated period of time. By registering a patent an inventor makes it an offence for other people, without his consent, to cash in on the fruits of his intellectual efforts.

(b) A **trade mark** is a distinctive word, name or other mark which is used to indicate a connection in the course of trade between goods or services and their owner. By registering a trade mark, the owner of the mark makes it an offence for other people to use it.

(c) **Copyright** protects authors, artists, composers etc from being deprived of their rewards by unauthorised copying of their works. Unlike patents and trade marks, copyright is not subject to any system of registration: it comes into effect automatically when a work is created.

2 PATENTS 12/95

2.1 The law relating to patents is contained in the Patents Act 1977 and the Copyright, Designs and Patents Act 1988. The Patents Act sets out a system by which inventors may register their discoveries. In return they are granted a period in which they have a **monopoly right** to exploit them and may prevent all others from making use of them in the country in which the patent is granted. There is of course no obligation on an inventor to register his idea; he may prefer not to publish it and to rely on secrecy as his safeguard against competitors.

2.2 Certain things are specifically declared not to be inventions for the purposes of the Act. They include scientific theories, aesthetic creations (literary, musical or artistic works) and computer programs. The Act also specifies that patents will not be granted for inventions which might encourage offensive, immoral or anti-social behaviour.

Underpinning knowledge

What follows is an abbreviation of material that you should have studied for Pre-Professional *English Business Law.* We have simplified the legal language somewhat for the purposes of this Study Text. *Administration of Corporate Affairs* is more interested in broad issues than in the nitty gritty detail of the law.

Refer back to your earlier study material if you want a fuller account.

Criteria for patentability

2.3 Under the Patents Act the criteria which an invention must satisfy before the issue of a patent can be considered are as follows.

- The invention must be **new**.
- It must involve an **inventive step**.
- It must be capable of **industrial application**.

2.4 In practice the Patent Office examination is mainly restricted to prior British patent specifications. The result of this is that patents may often be granted where the criteria are not satisfied. The validity of such patents may be challenged.

Novelty

2.5 'An invention shall be taken to be new if it does **not** form part of the **state of the art**' (s 2(1). As noted much earlier, when discussing the Internet, this means that an invention is *not* new if, before the date of filing the patent application, any processes, products or information relating to it had freely been made available to the public. This can lead to problems in fields where many inventors are at work simultaneously. The rule is that if two or more inventors file similar applications, the earlier application is deemed to be included in the state of the art when the later application is being considered.

Encourages 'patent races', which can be economically inefficient.

Inventive step

2.6 'An invention shall be taken to involve an inventive step if it is **not obvious** to a person skilled in the art, having regard to any matter which forms part of the state of the art' (s 3). This is an area where there is a great deal of case law. When a patent is challenged many years after it was granted, the state of the art may have made great advances in the meantime. It may appear, looking back, that the new development was obvious enough, and therefore not an inventive step. However the use of hindsight in this way may well be unfair to the patentee and the courts have tried to recognise that what seems a simple step today may not have been so obvious ten years ago.

2.7 Merely to 'collocate' known products or processes in a new way will not normally constitute an inventive step, even though the result may be novel, such as to produce a pen which is also a torch. However if the collocation produces some real advance or involves the exercise of inventive ingenuity it is patentable. For example, the Black & Decker 'Workmate' was essentially a combination of known devices but it was nevertheless patentable.

Industrial applications

2.8 An invention shall be taken to be capable of industrial application if it can be **made or used** in any **kind of industry** (s 4). For this purpose, agriculture is included as an industry. This provision means that surgical or therapeutic processes and diagnostic methods used in medicine cannot be patented.

The rights of the patentee

2.9 A patent gives the owner a virtually exclusive monopoly to exploit a product or process for a period of **20 years**, provided renewal fees are paid on time. After four years the monopoly is enjoyed annually on the payment of **renewal fees**. Failure to renew the patent results in the lapse of rights.

2.10 The original patentee or any subsequent owner of a patent may exploit it themselves or, more usually, they will **grant licences** to others. Others may become interested either through perusal of Patent Office publications or by responding to information about inventions in international journals and on databases or from invention exploitation enterprises.

Infringement

2.11 A patent is infringed if a person, **without the consent of the proprietor**, takes any of the following actions.

(a) If he **makes, disposes of, uses** or **imports** a **patented product** or **keeps** it, for disposal or otherwise.

(b) If he **uses** a patented process or he offers it for use when he knows that this would be an **infringement** of the patent.

(c) If he **disposes** of, **uses** or **imports** any **product obtained directly** by means of a **patented process** or keeps any such product, for disposal or otherwise.

2.12 However, an act is not an infringement in a variety of circumstances, notably if the act is done **privately** and **for non-commercial purposes**, or if it is done for **experimental purposes** relating to the subject matter of the invention.

2.13 If an infringement is judged to have taken place, the patentee may apply for an **injunction**, or for **damages**, or for **surrender** of any products infringing the patent, or for all of these. He may also apply for an account of the defendant's profits derived from the infringement and for a declaration that the defendant has been guilty of an infringement.

Patent exploitation

2.14 The Act encourages exploitation of the patent by 'licences of right' and 'compulsory licences'.

Licences of right

2.15 A patentee may apply to the Patent Office for an entry to be made on the **register** that licences under patent are to be available **as of right**; any person will then be entitled to a licence on terms agreed with the patentee or, failing that, by the Patent Office.

Compulsory licences

2.16 After three years from the grant of a patent any person may apply to the Patent Office for a licence. There are a number of grounds on which an application may be granted; most require evidence that the invention is not being exploited to a reasonable extent in the light of the demand of the public or industry or commerce. The threat of compulsory licences is an incentive to patentees to exploit inventions themselves and very few compulsory licences are granted.

Employee inventions

2.17 An invention made by an employee is taken to belong to his employer for the purposes of the Patents Act 1977 if:

(a) It was made in the **course** of the **employee's normal duties**, or in the course of other duties specifically assigned to him, and the circumstances were such that an invention might reasonably be expected to result.

(b) It was made in the **course** of the **employee's duties** and the employee, because of the nature of his duties and the particular responsibilities arising from them, had a **special obligation** to further the interests of his employer's undertaking.

All other employee inventions belong to the employee.

2.18 An employee may apply for a ruling that his invention, for which a patent has been granted, is of outstanding benefit to the employer and that it is just that compensation should be paid to him by the employer.

3 TRADE MARKS — 12/95, 6/00

3.1 It would be unfair if a newly formed business attempted to capitalise on the goodwill built up by another business by making out that its own products or services were those of the established business.

3.2 Anyone who suffers financial loss as a result of an offence of this kind is entitled to bring a **passing off action** in the courts claiming compensation for his loss and asking for an injunction against continuance of the deception. Such actions suffer from the disadvantage that the related offence is very hard to prove. An injured party is in a stronger position if he can rely on the law relating to **trade marks**; it may be easier to prove that an infringement of a registered trade mark has taken place.

3.3 A trade mark is a mark used to indicate a **connection** in the course of the trade or business between the goods and the proprietor or registered user of the mark. It is defined by the Trade Marks Act 1994 as follows.

> Any sign capable of being represented graphically which is capable of distinguishing goods or services of one undertaking from those of other undertakings.

3.4 The TMA provides for the maintenance (at the Patent Office) of a **register of trade marks.** Unless a mark is registered, the owner will not be able to institute proceedings for an infringement, though of course he may still have an action for passing off. Trade marks can only be registered in respect of **particular goods** or **classes of goods**. Once a trade mark has been registered, its owner is given the exclusive right to use the mark in respect of the goods concerned.

Note that:

> A trade mark may, in particular, consist of words (including personal names), designs, letters, numerals or the shape of goods or their packaging.

Exercise 2

Give some examples of things that you think would be registrable trade marks.

Solution

You should remember some examples from your earlier studies of *Business Law*.

(a) *Devices* (eg the Mercedes three-pointed star)

(b) *Names* (eg 'Esso')

(c) *Words* known or invented (eg 'Crest'; 'Kodak')

(d) *Letters* (eg 'BPP')

(e) *Numerals* (eg '4711')

(f) *Smells* (which computers can now depict graphically to establish their uniqueness)

(g) *Colour combinations,* although a trade mark is usually registered for use in any colour

(h) *Sounds*, such as the cavalry charge jingle of the Direct Line red telephone on wheels

(i) Some *three-dimensional figures*, such as the Rolls Royce *Spirit of Ecstasy* silver lady

(j) *Three-dimensional shapes* such as the traditional glass Coca-Cola bottle

The register of trade marks

3.5 To be registered a mark must satisfy the definition given above.

3.6 Signs that show no distinctiveness cannot be registered, for example if they consist of signs that have become customary in the current language or established practices of the trade. Some signs cannot be registered no matter how distinctive they are, for example if the shape derives from the very nature of the goods, or if they are contrary to accepted principles of morality. Signs cannot be registered if they are identical with or similar to an earlier trade mark and liable to cause public confusion, or undermine the earlier mark.

Collective and certification trade marks

3.7 **Certification trade marks** are granted to owners who do not trade in the goods themselves, but authorise others, in accordance with regulations approved by the Trade Marks and Department of Trade and Industry Consumer Affairs Division, to use the mark as a certificate of compliance with certain standards. Examples are the pure wool and wool blend marks of the International Wool Secretariat and the Harris Tweed mark.

3.8 A **collective mark** is a mark distinguishing the goods or services of members of the association which is the proprietor of the mark from those of other undertakings, for example distinguishing ICSA members from members of the ICAEW.

The rights of the owner of a trade mark

3.9 The owner of a trade mark has an **exclusive right to use** of the mark. The right is infringed if any other person, without the owner's consent, uses the mark itself or a mark closely resembling it in the course of trade (not in a song, a painting or an instruction manual for instance). The infringement will occur if the offender uses the mark either as a trade mark applying to his own goods, or in less blatant circumstances.

3.10 If the owner of a mark succeeds in his action against an infringement, he is entitled to an **injunction** to prevent the infringement being repeated, to **damages and compensation**, or to an **account of profits**.

Counterfeiting

3.11 The Act contains important anti-counterfeiting measures. It is an offence for a person to try to benefit by applying a **mark resembling** a registered trade mark to goods when that person is not entitled to use the mark in question and the goods are not connected with a person who is entitled to use it.

Trade mark licensing

3.12 Trade marks have become an indicator of the **quality** of goods rather than (as originally) an indicator of the origin of the goods. Legislation has influenced this trend, as it allows trading in the mark without the attachment of a relevant part of the business. This means that there does not have to be a single place of origin of the goods: they can be sourced from different locations. This promotes licensing of trade marks. Character merchandising is a phrase used to describe the position where a trade mark is applied to a wide variety of different goods or services. This is particularly common with children's products: *101 Dalmatians* pyjamas, *Wallace and Gromit* wallpaper and so on.

Exercise 3

Why should a manufacturer of goods, who is the registered owner of a trade mark, wish to license the trade mark?

Solution

(a) Licensing can help expansion.
(b) Licensing can ensure protection of the goods.
(c) Long-term brand loyalty can be encouraged.
(d) Access to additional manufacturing capacity can be obtained.
(e) Access to new outlets can be obtained without the owner having to manufacture there.

3.13 Once a license is registered, any licensee may call on the owner of the registered trade mark to commence infringement proceedings, or failing that, bring them in his own name.

4 COPYRIGHT

4.1 The basic notion of copyright is the **exclusive right** to **use one's own work**, and to stop others from exploiting the skill and labour which has gone into the production.

4.2 The right has been extended to **unauthorised performances** of literary and musical works and (because of technological advances) broadcasts and cable transmissions of literary and dramatic works where copying plays no significant part.

4.3 An important consequence of the definition is that there must be some form of work or product. An **idea**, which has no tangible product, is not protected from being copied.

Scope of copyright legislation

4.4 The relevant legislation is the Copyright, Designs and Patents Act 1988, as recently modified by the Duration of Copyright and Rights of Performances Regulations 1995. CDPA states that copyright is a property right which subsists in the following works.

- Original literary, dramatic, musical or artistic works
- Sound recordings, films, broadcasts or cable programmes
- The typographical arrangement of published editions

Original literary, dramatic, musical and artistic works

4.5 **Original** means that the work emanates from the author and is not copied, although a derivative work, such as a translation, which involves distinct skill and labour, gives rise to a new form of copyright. The term can be taken to mean that skill, judgement and effort should have been taken in producing the work.

4.6 A **literary** work is any work, other than one which is dramatic or musical, which is written, spoken or sung. It includes not only novels, poems and plays but also such diverse items as a computer program and a timetable. **Dramatic** works include those which involve dance or mime. However copyright in a literary, dramatic or musical work does not subsist until it is recorded, in writing or otherwise. A **musical** work does not include the words or actions which accompany it. Hence the composer of a West End musical has copyright in the music and the lyricist has copyright in the lyrics.

4.7 **Artistic** work is defined in the Act as being any of the following.

(a) A graphic work, photograph, sculpture or collage, irrespective of artistic quality

(b) A work of architecture, being a building or a model for a building (the plans are protected as a graphic work)

(c) A work of artistic craftsmanship

Sound recordings, films, broadcasts and cable programmes

4.8 Sound recordings include recordings on any **medium**, such as audio cassettes or compact discs. Films include **'still' photographs** from films. Broadcasts include any sound or pictures transmitted by means of a broadcast, in other words by wireless telegraphy. Cable programs include transmissions which are not 'broadcasts', for example cable television programmes.

Typographical arrangements of published editions

4.9 Often editions of plays, poems or musicals have a distinctive typographical page layout. Copyright can exist in this for a publisher even though the copyright in the work itself has expired.

Authorship and ownership of copyright

4.10 The 'author' of a work is the person who **creates** it. This simple definition is extended as follows.

(a) Sound recordings or films; the principal director jointly with the producer

(b) A broadcast; the person who makes the broadcast

(c) A cable programme; the person providing the cable programme service in which the programme is included

(d) A typographical arrangement of a published edition: the publisher

(e) A literary, dramatic, musical or artistic work which is computer-generated: the author shall be taken to be the person by whom the arrangements necessary for the creation of the work are undertaken

4.11 The author becomes the first owner of any copyright as soon as the work is created and without any formality, subject to certain provisions. In particular, where the work has been made by an employee in the course of his employment, his employer is the first owner.

4.12 **Joint ownership** is possible, for example where a work is co-produced.

Copyright assignment

4.13 It is possible for the normal provisions of 'first ownership' to be set aside by the **assignment** (transfer of ownership) of copyright in a work *prior* to its creation. It is *always* possible to assign copyright *after* the completion of the work. A valid assignment must be in writing and signed by or on behalf of the copyright owner.

Copyright licensing

4.14 No formalities are required for the **licensing** of a **copyright** unless it is to be an exclusive licence, in which case the same formalities are required as for an assignment of ownership.

A licence, which may be implied, allows the licensee to use the work subject to the owner's copyright. In most cases a person who commissions a work for a particular purpose, such as a graphic illustration for a textbook, has an implied licence to use it.

Duration of copyright

4.15 The period of copyright in different works expires as follows (as recently modified by the new regulations).

(a) **Literary, dramatic, musical or artistic works**: at the end of the period of 70 years from the end of the calendar year in which the author dies. If the work is of unknown authorship, it expires at the end of the period of 70 years from the end of the calendar year in which it was first made available to the public. If the work is computer-generated, it expires at the end of a period of 70 years from the end of the calendar year in which it was made.

(b) **A film or sound recording**: from when the work was released to the end of the period of 70 years after the last to die of the principal director, the author of the screen play, the author of the dialogue, or the composer of music specifically created for and used in the film.

(c) **Broadcasts or cable programmes:** at the end of the period of 50 years from the end of the calendar year in which the broadcast was made or the programme included in a cable programme service. Copyright in a repeat expires at the same time as the original broadcast or cable programme.

(d) **The typographical arrangement of a published edition**: at the end of the period of 25 years from the end of the calendar year in which the edition was first published.

Revived copyright

4.16 The usual period was formerly 50 years in the UK, but the changes under the Duration of Copyright and Rights in Performances Regulations 1995 mean, for example, that the works of Rudyard Kipling, Kenneth Grahame and Edward Elgar, which were out of copyright, are now *back* in copyright! However, no act done before 1 July 1995 will be regarded as an infringement. Revived copyright is treated as licensed subject to the payment of a reasonable royalty, set by the Copyright Tribunal in the UK if the parties cannot agree. (In some cases the return to copyright has been a brief one. Thomas Hardy for example, who returned to copyright in 1995, went out of copyright again on 1 January 1999.)

Rights of the copyright owner

4.17 The copyright owner has the exclusive right to do any of the following in the UK.

- **Copy** the work.
- **Issue copies** of the work to the public.
- **Perform**, show or play the work in public.
- **Broadcast** the work or include it in a cable programme service.
- Make an **adaptation** of the work or do any of the above in relation to an adaptation.

4.18 The underlying right is the same in each case. It is a right of the owner to prevent others from reproducing his work. This amounts to an exclusive right to reproduce the work for a fixed period.

Moral rights

4.19 The Act provides for certain additional rights which apply to certain works only, and can be asserted by the author, director or commissioner of a work, whether or not he is the owner of the copyright.

(a) '**Paternity**' refers to the right of the author of a copyright literary, dramatic, musical or artistic work and the director of a copyright film to be identified as the author or director of the work whenever the work is published commercially, performed in public, broadcast or included in a cable programme, or copies of a film or sound recording are issued to the public.

(b) '**Integrity**' is the right to object to derogatory treatment of the work. The author of a copyright literary, dramatic, musical or artistic work, and the director of a copyright film, have the right not to have their work subjected to derogatory treatment.

Exercise 4

Turn to the introductory pages of a modern novel and find the page containing information about the publisher (the verso page). What copyright information can you see?

Solution

There will be a copyright symbol © as on page (ii) of this Text. This copyright marking is not essential, but acts as a warning that copyright is valued. There is a presumption in court that it indicates the owner. There may also be a statement to the following effect. 'The right of x to be identified as the author of this work has been asserted by him in accordance with the Copyright, Designs and Patents Act 1988.'

Copyright problems for organisations

4.20 An article in *Chartered Secretary* for October 1999 highlighted ways in which companies could breach copyright law. These included circulating law reports, articles or press cuttings. Free photocopying is only allowed for private study or research; for other copying the permission of the copyright holder or a licence from the Copyright Licensing Agency is required. As well as issuing licences, the copyright agency also has the power to take legal action to protect the interest of rightsholders, and fines and costs have run into many thousands of pounds. It is also developing electronic licences to cover digitising of existing print material.

5 DESIGN RIGHT

5.1 There are three separate but overlapping ways in which the Copyright, Designs and Patents Act 1988 together with the Registered Designs Act 1949 (RDA) law protects industrial designs, which are defined as designs intended to be used in producing at least 50 items commercially.

Protection	*Act*	*Type of design*	*Duration*
Artistic copyright	CDPA	All designs	Life of creator + 50 years
Design right	CDPA	Functional designs	Up to 15 years
Design registration	RDA	Aesthetic designs	Up to 25 years

5.2 A person planning to manufacture to an industrial design must look at the situation in the light of all of the above legislation, while the creator of a design may choose either to protect it actively, by registration, or to rely on the automatic protection of artistic copyright or design right.

Copyright protection

5.3 The protection offered by artistic copyright may attach to industrial designs in the following circumstances.

(a) The **finished product** incorporating the design is **itself an artistic work** - a building falls into this category, though most industrial designs will not.

(b) The finished product is not an artistic work but has its **origins in original design documents** - an original drawing, irrespective of artistic merit, attracts artistic copyright. This may be infringed if a two-dimensional or three-dimensional copy is made.

Design right protection

5.4 Design right is a new property right created by CDPA. It arises, like copyright, automatically in a qualifying design: there is no need to register the design.

5.5 'Design' is defined as meaning the **design** of **any aspect** of the **shape or configuration** (internal or external) of the whole or part of an article.

Exercise 5

From your earlier studies you should recall certain instances where there is no design right. What are they? The phrases 'must-fit' and 'must-match' may jog your memory.

Solution

Design right does not subsist in the following.

(a) A method or principle of construction.

(b) Features of shape or configuration of an article which:

(i) enable the article to be connected to, or placed in, around or against, another article so that either article may perform its function (this is known as the *must-fit* exception); or

(ii) are dependent upon the appearance of another article of which the first article is intended by the designer to form an integral part (this is known as the *must-match* exception).

(c) Surface decoration.

As usual, think about doing some revision of your earlier study material if you are shaky on the underpinning knowledge.

5.6 A design right only subsists in an **original design** and a design is not considered original if it is commonplace in the design field in question at the time of its creation. Design right does not subsist unless and until the design has been recorded in a design document or an article has been made to the design.

5.7 Design right subsists for only **10 years** from the end of the year in which articles made to the design are first put on the market. There is, however, an overall limit of 15 years from the end of the year in which the design was first recorded or an article first made. Thus the design should be exploited as soon as possible for the maximum benefit to be obtained from the quite narrow time limits.

5.8 Licences to perform all the acts otherwise restricted by design rights are made available to anyone as of right during the final 5 years of the design period (which is usually 10 years).

Ownership of design right

5.9 The general rule about the owner of design right is similar to that of copyright: the first owner is the designer who created the design.

5.10 The owner of a design right has the **exclusive right to reproduce** the design for commercial purposes by making articles in accordance with that design or by creating a design document recording that design so that articles may be made from it.

5.11 The first owner rule is subject to more extensive exceptions than in copyright law. In the case of computer-generated design it is the person who made the necessary arrangements for the creation of the design to be undertaken. A person **commissioning a design** is the first owner; where a design has been made in the course of employment it generally belongs to the **employer**; sometimes the first owner is the person who first **markets** the articles.

5.12 Licences and assignment with regard to design rights are similar to those available for copyright.

Design registration

5.13 The main statute is still the Registered Designs Act 1949 (RDA), amended by the 1988 Act. Under this, the proprietor of a work who has registered or has permitted the registration of a design embodying the work has monopoly rights in it for a period of up to 25 years.

5.14 In order to be registrable, the design must have two facets: **novelty** and '**design features**' or '**eye appeal**'.

Novelty

5.15 The design must be new which is judged by reference to what was known or used in the UK before the application was made. Disclosure of the design in confidence will not destroy its novelty and nor will previous use of an artistic work bearing the design in question (in some cases). This means that the owner of an artistic copyright who has already published his work but who later decides to apply it industrially (by applying it to 50 or more articles) in order to register the design can now do so.

'Eye appeal'

5.16 Under RDA a design is said to consist of 'features of shape, configuration, pattern or ornament applied to an article by an industrial process, being features which in the finished article appeal to and are judged by the eye'. This definition has a number of implications:

(a) The article need not appeal solely to the eye.

(b) A design attached to an article normally bought for function rather than appearance cannot be registered.

5.17 The term of the registered design lasts for five years from the time when the application is made. The duration may be extended by up to four further periods of five years, provided renewal fees are paid.

Future developments

5.18 The EC designs directive has recently been adopted and hence the UK and other member states will have three years to bring in appropriate legislation to amend local law. The most important aspect of the legislation is that the current UK test, that a product must have eye appeal, will no longer apply. Henceforth it will be possible to protect products **without eye appeal** or which are purely **decorative**. A new test of individual character will be introduced, involving a comparison of the overall look of a design with other known designs. There will also be an initial grace period of 12 months, during which time designers can publicise their designs without compromising their chances of eventual registration.

6 INTELLECTUAL PROPERTY RIGHTS IN AN ELECTRONIC ENVIRONMENT

6.1 An article by Hema Velathini in *Chartered Secretary* for January 2000 highlighted how information assets such as research and databases could be protected. Methods include:

(a) **Access controlling devices** such as digital envelopes

(b) **Anti-copying devices** such as scramblers or methods for making copies inferior

(c) **Metering**

(d) **Property viewers**; these only allow viewing of the object eg. Adobe Acrobat Reader for PDFs.

(e) Devices such as **electronic watermarks** and finger-printing which enable owners to identify and authenticate their property

6.2 The aim of legislators has been to protect these methods by **forbidding their circumvention**, rather than amending copyright laws.

6.3 In addition property owners will have to take other enforcement measures to prove that they have taken all steps to protect their rights.

(a) Definition and marking of the assets by **including information** about the rightsholder and the terms and conditions for using the work

(b) Development of a **written policy** for enforcement of property rights

(c) **Access controls**, not just against external hackers, but also internal misusers

(d) **Monitoring** of **doubtful activities** such as downloading or copying

(e) Keeping **hard copy records** of information and details

(f) **Responding** swiftly to **theft**

Chapter roundup

- The key characteristics of an asset are **future economic benefit** and **control** (ownership). Distinctions can be made between fixed assets and current assets, and between intangible assets, tangible assets and investments. All assets contribute to an organisation's prosperity.
- A **patent** is a monopoly right to exploit an invention for a stated period of time. By registering a patent an inventor makes it an offence for other people, without his consent, to benefit from his intellectual efforts. The period for which a patent is granted is 20 years. It may during that period be exploited by the granting of licences of right or compulsory licences.
- A **trade mark** is a distinctive word, name or other mark which is used to indicate a connection in the course of trade between goods or services and their owner. By registering a trade mark, the owner of the mark makes it an offence for other people to use it. Trade marks may also be licensed to other users.
- **Copyright protects** authors from being deprived of their rewards by unauthorised copying of their works.
  - Unlike patents and trade marks, copyright is not subject to any system of registration: it comes into effect automatically when a work is created.
  - Copyright is a property which subsists in original literary, dramatic, musical and artistic works, sound recordings, films, broadcasts and cable programs and the typographical arrangement of published editions.
  - The period of copyright varies depending upon the nature of the work; in many cases it is now 70 years, and some works that had fallen out of copyright have come back into copyright.
- The Copyright, Designs and Patents Act 1988 created a new property right called **design right**. This is a right distinct from the system of design registration.

Test your knowledge

1 Define an asset. (see paras 1.1 - 1.4)

2 What are the criteria for patentability? (2.3)

3 What are the rights of a patentee? (2.9 - 2.10)

4 What is a trade mark? (3.3)

5 What are a trade mark owner's rights? (3.9)

6 What is copyright? (4.1)

7 How long does copyright last? (4.15)

8 What are moral rights? (4.19)

9 How can the protection offered by artistic copyright be extended to industrial designs? (5.3)

Now try illustrative question 25 at the end of the Study Text

Chapter 25

FACILITIES MANAGEMENT

This chapter covers the following topics.

1 Facilities management

2 Accommodation and space planning

3 Location and relocation

4 Outsourcing

5 Practical asset management

Introduction

Facilities are the things you take for granted at work, like fresh air. Issues in facilities management are blindingly obvious once they occur to you: for example the visitors' car park should obviously not be covered in broken glass, but whose job is it to make sure that this never happens, and how does that person ensure that the glass is noticed and swept up before it does any damage? In this chapter we give an overview of the very numerous responsibilities and concerns of the facilities manager. Key issues in modern facilities management are space planning, (re)location, and outsourcing, each of which have separate sections. Health, safety and security are also vital considerations, and these are the subject of the next chapter.

At the end of *this* chapter we also look at some of the practical aspects of asset management: buying assets and keeping records of them.

1 FACILITIES MANAGEMENT **12/95, 6/96**

1.1 After a certain stage in life most people could consider themselves to be reasonably expert in the basic disciplines of facilities management, at least on a minor scale. Reduced to its bare essentials facilities management is concerned with topics such as cleaning, cooking, shopping, decorating, heating and lighting, plumbing, gardening, washing the car and so on.

1.2 Think of DIY and housework if you like, but then imagine that you own, say, six huge multi-storey properties spread across the country – or even 600 spread across the world – and that each property is occupied and roughly used every day by hundreds or thousands of people. This is facilities management proper, and put in these terms you may begin to appreciate that it is a major corporate issue.

Exercise 1

Think back to basic motivation theory. What did Herzberg say about hygiene factors?

The scope of facilities management

1.3 The British Institute of Facilities Management (BIFM) describe facilities management as 'the integration of multi-disciplinary activities within the built environment and their impact of upon people and the workplace'.

1.4 A clearer idea of these 'multi-disciplinary activities' may be gleaned from the contents of articles that appear in magazines such as the *Facilities Management Journal* and *Premises and Facilities Management.* Here is an indicative list, in no particular order.

- Contract cleaning
- Landscaping
- Catering
- Location
- Energy management
- Risk management and security
- Office services such as reprographics
- Planned maintenance
- Space planning
- Air conditioning
- Fire protection
- Waste management
- Cabling
- Heating and lighting
- Lift maintenance
- Car parking
- Vehicle fleet management

1.5 As you may appreciate from this list, other aspects of the *Administration of Corporate Affairs* syllabus are relevant to FM decisions, such as information management and security, disaster planning and recovery, meetings and conference facilities, and particularly insurance. In addition facilities managers need to have an understanding of issues in the syllabuses of other Professional level papers such as people management, corporate strategy, and financial management.

1.6 At one time the management of office premises was largely a matter of legal documents (leases, formal communications from landlords, service contracts). Managements were relatively careless of the importance of accommodation costs. This is no longer the case.

(a) High inflation in the 1970s brought **frequent rent reviews**, rising rent levels, rates and service costs. Managements realised the need to control occupational costs. Rising property values in the 1980s continued this trend, and the increasingly competitive business world of the 1990s has forced managements to look everywhere for cost savings.

(b) The cost of **insurance** has also **increased** substantially: organisations may find that they cannot get insurance at all unless they can show that their property is carefully looked after.

(c) **Legislation** affecting office premises has proliferated: examples are Health and Safety at Work legislation, building regulations, fire regulations and environmental legislation.

1.7 Annual costs of a workplace have been analysed by the Centre for Facilities Management.

Type of cost	%
Fixed costs (rent, lease , depreciation)	30.3
Reprographics/internal post	11.5
Data communications	10.8
Catering	9.1
Management	7.2
Furniture	5.9
Telecommunications	5.5
Office requirements	4.9
Safeguarding and reception	4.5
Maintenance	4.0
Energy	3.8
Cleaning	2.5

1.8 We shall now take two of the most basic facilities that organisations provide – cleaning and catering – to illustrate the practical and strategic issues that concern the modern Facilities Manager.

Cleaning

1.9 Organisations are required to provide a **clean working environment** under Health and Safety legislation (see the next chapter). A clean working environment is also important because:

(a) Staff expect it and are demotivated by unpleasant conditions.

(b) Visitors, in particular customers, will form favourable or unfavourable impressions of the organisation as a whole based partly on its cleanliness.

1.10 Effective facilities management will draw up a programme for office cleaning consisting of steps such as the following.

(a) An **audit** should be undertaken identifying all areas to be cleaned on a regular basis and heavy-use areas that will require additional 'deep cleaning' on occasion. Outside areas such as car parks and landscaped areas should be included as well.

(b) Any requirements for **specialist cleaning equipment or fluids** should be identified. Fabrics, floor coverings and polished surfaces represent a substantial investment but can easily be damaged by the use of the wrong substance. Equally factory areas and computer rooms may have special needs. There are also health and safety issues: staff will not appreciate it if their telephones or eating surfaces are cleaned with ammonia!

(c) **High use areas** should be identified and cleaning activities should be planned to minimise disruptions to work.

(d) **Cleaning staff** should be given clear instructions and appropriate training if necessary, and they should be effectively supervised.

(e) **Inspections** should be carried out regularly to make sure that the required standards are being achieved and maintained.

(f) **Security** is a major issue. Given the timing and nature of the work, cleaning staff are placed in a position of trust, and any new employees should be positively vetted for honesty and integrity. Many organisations require that cleaning staff wear uniforms and/or identity badges.

Current practice

1.11 Most organisations regard cleaning as a necessary activity, but one that is not core to the continuance and success of the business. Office cleaning is therefore commonly contracted out (outsourced) to a specialist office cleaning company. We shall look at outsourcing in more detail later in this chapter. Facilities managers should remember that even if cleaning is contracted out, there are things that staff can be encouraged to do to help maintain a clean environment, such as not smoking, and tidying up after themselves within reason.

Exercise 2

What do you think 'landscaping' involves?

Solution

If you thought only of pretty flower beds, what about the chores, such as grass cutting, weeding, drain and gutter cleaning, road sweeping and maintenance, litter clearance, and maintaining walls and fences? *Management* of landscaping involves similar tasks to those described for cleaning: identifying regular and special needs, minimising disruption to the main work of the organisation, monitoring the quality of work and of the staff performing it.

Catering

1.12 Catering for staff may range from the provision of a kettle and mugs to *cordon bleu* restaurant facilities. Many large organisations still offer a subsidised staff canteen and this has benefits for the organisation such as the following.

(a) The subsidy is perceived as a benefit by staff.

(b) It keeps staff in the building, not far from their desks, and perhaps less inclined to take long lunches.

(c) It encourages informal communication, especially between staff who work in different departments.

1.13 However, **subsidised restaurant facilities** are expensive to run and can be a strong source of dissatisfaction if the food provided is not up to scratch, or not to staff's tastes. Moreover, effective administration requires regular surveys of quality and of staff needs, and continual monitoring with an eye to yet another set of regulations – those relating to food hygiene.

1.14 Issues that need to be considered in modern staff catering include the following.

(a) Enlightened employers recognise that the intense nature of much work means that an eating environment that offers a **complete mental and physical break** is increasingly important. However, the conventional staff restaurant, taking up the whole of the basement or the top floor, represents a significant investment in relatively immobile fixed assets and so takes up a great deal of space that cannot easily or cheaply be converted for alternative use.

(b) The staff restaurant faces **falling** and **changing demand**.

(i) The workforce as a whole is slowly diminishing and becoming more mobile when at work.

(ii) Eating habits are changing. Staff in the 1990s are far less inclined to eat a full plate of egg, chips, sausages and beans, or roast lamb, veg and gravy in the middle of a working day: 'light bites' are preferred.

(iii) Tastes are far more varied and cosmopolitan than they were only a few years ago. Alternatives appealing to vegetarians and different ethnic groups need to be offered.

(c) In-house catering standards are now judged against what is **commonly available** on the high street. If the quality, value for money, service and environment are not as good as McDonalds, staff will go to McDonalds. Eating out is much more common now than in the past and higher standards are demanded.

1.15 The above points may suggest that employers are likely to be looking for ways of reducing this benefit or even ending their catering arrangements entirely. There are a number of options for reducing costs.

(a) Devote future investment to **flexible catering facilities** that can easily expand and contract and be relocated as space needs change.

(b) Follow modern trends in mass catering and introduce **self-service** and **take away** options, thus reducing catering staff costs and space requirements.

(c) **Contract out** catering arrangements to a specialist company whose size and experience should bring economies of scale and better understanding of and responsiveness to changing needs. For example some caterers have franchises to offer branded products such as Burger King or Pizza Hut, and do so at a slightly reduced rate compared with the high street equivalent.

Some companies employ caterers for 'fine dining services' so that they can conduct lunch meetings in the office rather than going out to a local restaurant. This saves time and gives the host more control over the meeting (a bad experience at a restaurant can ruin otherwise promising negotiations).

1.16 In the light of the above we can suggest the qualities that an in-house facilities manager should possess.

(a) **Practical experience** in or knowledge of all relevant areas, from cleaning to lift maintenance to vehicle fleet management

(b) Academic/professional **qualifications** that include significant IT content and legal content (eg a Business Studies degree, or the ICSA or BIFM qualification)

(c) **People-handling** skills (at all levels)

(d) **Negotiation** skills

(e) A **customer orientation**, and an understanding that employees must be seen as internal customers

(f) **Understanding** of the **strategic role** of facilities management and particularly the need to control costs

(g) Ability and willingness to work '**on the hoof**' most of the time rather than being desk-bound

A miscellany of issues

1.17 The scope of FM is so broad that we cannot hope to cover all the issues in the few pages we have available. The table on the next page contains a selection of observations drawn from recent facilities management magazine and newspaper articles and there are a number of case studies throughout this chapter. This should give you a good general idea of the type of issues that need to be considered.

SUNDRY ISSUES IN FACILITIES MANAGEMENT	
Air conditioning	Many existing systems are CFC based but the production of CFC coolants was banned in 1995. As stocks of CFCs dwindle this means that systems will have to be altered or replaced. A government-sponsored body called RUG offers advice. Modern systems are computer controlled so that, for example, air quality and temperature in the building is monitored by sensors and windows are opened and closed automatically. Over time systems can 'learn' a buildings thermal characteristics and adapt accordingly.
Waste management	Disposal of rubbish can cost an organisation thousands of pounds, but these costs can be reduced if waste is regarded as a commodity. There are now numerous recycling companies who will collect specific types of waste for nothing, or even pay for it. All the organisation has to do is learn the habit of segregating different types of waste ready for collection.
Energy management	Privatisation means that there is now a much greater choice of suppliers and more freedom to negotiate contracts on an organisation-wide basis rather than being at the mercy of regional monopolies. Electricity companies now offer larger customers tools that enable them to manage and control consumption right down to how much their energy costs them per production unit or per square metre.
Intelligent buildings	Buildings are home to a host of electronic and computer based systems. Besides the information system, there are systems for security, fire detection, for controlling heating and lighting and air conditioning, lift services and so on. In most premises these systems operate in total isolation from one another. The future aim should be to construct an 'intelligent building' which integrates all technologies through a common network infrastructure.

SUNDRY ISSUES IN FACILITIES MANAGEMENT	
Lifts	Safety and continued operation are the chief concerns. There are generally three types of maintenance contract: basic lubrication plus minor adjustment; basic lubrication plus minor adjustments and breakdowns; and comprehensive, covering lubrication, adjustment, breakdown and replacement. There are now a number of independent maintenance companies, so the choice is not limited to the manufacturer of the lift.
Cabling	Cabling is a major issue if organisations are to take full advantage of IT developments. 'Structured cabling' is the preferred approach, bringing voice and data cabling to all parts of the building in a planned way, so that any changes to office layout or use can be put into effect quickly and simply, without having to lift up the entire floor, tear down the ceiling or drill through the walls. 'Flood wiring' means putting cable that can handle multimedia applications into every part of the building, not just where it happens to be needed today. Redundancy should be built in so that if part of the cable is damaged the system can reconfigure itself and continue to operate until repairs are done.
Sprinklers	Sprinklers are a highly effective way of fighting fire with minimal water damage, but they must be properly maintained. Sprinklers must conform to BS 5306 and installation and maintenance companies should have Loss Prevention Certification Board certification to certain standards and also ISO 9000 quality management certification. Facilities managers could be held responsible for damage, loss of life or consequential damage to the environment if they neglect to check on these matters.

Case example: vending machines

Ford Motors is the UK's biggest user of vending machines. Here are some extracts from an article in the June 1997 issue of *Facilities Management Journal*.

'The Ford scheme, which has taken almost two years to complete, has seen some 600 machines undergo a remarkable transformation in terms of appearance, performance and reliability, underlying the growing importance of both refurbishment and cashless systems in today's vending marketplace.'

Key criteria for the upgrade incorporated 'enhancements to virtually all aspects of machine operation including software and mechanical parts upgrades, better machine security, and a total cosmetic facelift, all within tight budgetary constraints.

'Essentially our aim was to change a huge workforce's perception of vending with equipment which would deliver significant improvements in quality - both in vended products and operation - and through an integrated design approach,' said a spokesperson.

'An added logistical complication was Ford's requirement to maintain vending facilities at each site as refurbishment work was carried out. Consequently the three principles involved devised a detailed plan based on a schedule of 10 machines being processed every seven days with weekly co-ordination of the two way movement of equipment through sub-contractors transport.'

Cost saving improvements included the development of 'a new water system for drinks units, improved metalwork, and parts sourcing to higher specifications than originally identified. The drinks machines were first assessed for missing parts and damage before being dismantled so that the condition of individual parts could be assessed. All reusable components were then tested and then sterilised to AVAB (Automatic Vending Association of Britain) standards. Parts known to affect machine reliability were replaced, as were those which might not have passed the AVAB's hygiene specs.

'The colour schemes and front panelling of all machines was changed to suit Ford's specifications and the coin slots and coin mechanisms, which had previously been part of the panels, were eradicated. Anti-vandalism and anti-theft modifications were also fitted to the re-furbished models.'

Facilities Management Journal, June 1997

Case example: cabling

'Barnsley College decided to replace an old cabling system with a new high bandwidth network. 'Ninety per cent of the classrooms were not connected and the old network was not functioning properly,' says the network administrator, Rod Siddall. 'We wanted every classroom at the three sites to have good voice and data communications facilities, which would see us into the next 10 years and provide greater flexibility - so that we could have data links or telephones wherever and whenever we wanted them. Also, we wanted the network to be able to support videoconferencing and CDs in each classroom when or if required.'

The solution was a complex one, as one of the buildings was under refurbishment, another was under construction, while the third required the work to be completed in term time and during a bank holiday, with as little disruption to classes as possible.

In addition, the main site required a switch network which was capable of being linked to all the college sites.

Close liaison with the building contractors was necessary to ensure optimum integration of the network infrastructure with the refurbished and new buildings, and to carry out the cabling installation at the correct time in the building procedure. The entire project was managed in three phases.

A total of 80,000 metres, or about 50 miles, of cabling was installed. The network is controlled by central network management software.

'As far as network reliability is concerned, we have not experienced any failures, and that is definitely an improvement,' says Rod Siddall.

The college now has 900 PCs, network printers and 40 CDs on line at all times, spread across all seven sites. E-mail has been introduced and the college is developing an Internet site.

The project was one of the first major networks to be installed under the new health and safety CDM (Construction, Design and Management) Regulations, which were introduced in January 1996.

Facilities Management Journal, May 1997

2 ACCOMMODATION AND SPACE PLANNING **12/95, 6/96**

2.1 Most firms will have accommodation problems to some extent, because of any number of factors, including:

(a) **Expansion** of the workforce, or re-organisation or merger

(b) **Changes in technology**, creating different space and other requirements, for example for ventilation, or cable management

(c) **'Out of date' buildings**, which offer inadequate accommodation or safety facilities, or are costly to maintain

(d) The **end of a lease**

2.2 The solutions to such problems may be relatively cheap and simple, at least in the short term: they might include changing partitions to restructure offices, or improving communications or filing systems to facilitate work flow and save space. Refurbishment, relocation or reconstruction, however, are time-consuming, costly and disruptive to the normal business of the office.

The building audit **6/98**

2.3 A **building audit** is a review of how space is used, and whether (or how) it meets the needs of its occupant, comparing performance with similar situations elsewhere. The audit provides a basic appraisal of the occupant's problems and potential improvements, on which strategy can later be built: it need not be a lengthy, detailed or costly exercise.

2.4 The audit may be carried out 'in-house'. Alternatively there are specialist space planning consultants who can offer expert advice on modern layout options, the manipulation of space, and the availability and cost of a wide range of options.

2.5 A typical case might be a company that is enjoying continual but unpredictable growth: it will have expanded in fits and starts, to occupy office space spread over, say, six floors in a multi-storey building. Having taken fresh space as and when it became available, the company may well find that departments are split between floors, layouts are inconsistent, and there is room for further expansion.

2.6 An audit would assess the company's requirements by examining:

- Staff growth, allowing for flexibility
- Work flow and the relationships between departments
- The need for services and facilities
- The type of work and staff employed
- Existing space standards and layouts

2.7 An increasingly common approach is '**zero base space planning**' where (like ZBB in management accounting) demand for every square metre of office space must be thought out afresh from zero, and every worker is asked to justify why they need to occupy office space at all.

2.8 The building itself will also be examined with regard to the size and shape of floors, windows, lighting, service modules and the flexibility of existing partitioning and furniture systems. In a modern IT environment, the adequacy of cabling for electricity and computer and telephone networks is a major consideration.

2.9 The key is to plan for flexibility. Some firms pre-let partly designed or partly built offices, which allow some modification to original designs. Design modification may reduce subsequent fitting out or running costs.

Office layout

2.10 In considering the layout of a new or adapting office, flexibility will obviously be needed to cope with the needs of different individuals, activities and the shapes and sizes of available rooms. But there are some basic features which any office should possess.

- Economical use of space
- Arrangement for efficient work flow (movement of people and documents)
- Arrangement for ease of supervision
- Provision for security where necessary
- Provision for the safety of occupants

2.11 There are four general types of office layout

(a) **Small closed offices** linked by corridors. These have the advantage of privacy, peace and security, and are desirable for 'status conscious' managers for whom a separate office is an important symbol of authority, but supervision and communication is hindered, and this system is generally not favoured in new office designs.

(b) **Open plan offices**. These do away with the maze of walls and doors to make better use of the space than small closed offices. It has been estimated that a 33% space saving is possible under this system.

Advantages of open plan offices include:

(i) Easier supervision
(ii) Freer communication
(iii) Flexible arrangement of furniture and equipment in the available space
(iv) Economies on heating and lighting

(v) Sharing of equipment such as photocopiers

Disadvantages include:

(i) Lack of privacy
(ii) Distraction from noise and movement
(iii) Loss for managers of the status of a separate office, possibly lowering morale
(iv) Tendency for managers to become unnecessarily involved in routine matters
(v) Difficulty of satisfying every individual's needs and preferences

(c) **Landscaped offices**. These are a variation of the open plan system, overcoming some of the latter's problems. They use movable screens of variable height, shape and colour, to break up the office space. They are usually 'acoustic' to absorb noise, and flame-proof for safety. Filing cabinets and large pot plants may also be placed to give staff more privacy in their own areas and to cut down on noise and distractions, while still preserving the communication advantages of the open plan. Equipment and furnishings are generally of good quality, but more space and better furnishings may be given to management to enhance their status and morale.

(d) A **mixture** of closed and open offices within business premises with closed offices for senior management.

2.12 The factor common to all these systems is the **efficient use of space**. If there is not enough space for employees and equipment this will lead to dissatisfaction. On the other hand, too much space is wasteful and inefficient.

2.13 Health and Safety regulations lay down that each person must have at least 11 cubic metres of space, ignoring any parts of rooms more than 3.1 metres above the floor or with a headroom of less than 2.0 metres.

Work flow

2.14 Work study might be used to determine the best layout for sections in an open plan system, based on the amount of contact usually necessary between each section. Within each section, attention should be given to the **proximity** of people regularly working together (say the manager and his/her secretary and supervisors and those under their control).

2.15 Attention should also be given to the **accessibility** of people whose advice or services are required by the section as a whole (supervisors, typists) and equipment and facilities regularly used and shared by the section (files, photocopier, coffee machine).

Applies to flow within a department and to flow between departments

2.16 The flow of work could be looked at from the point of view both of staff movements (free passage from one place to another), and the movement of documents.

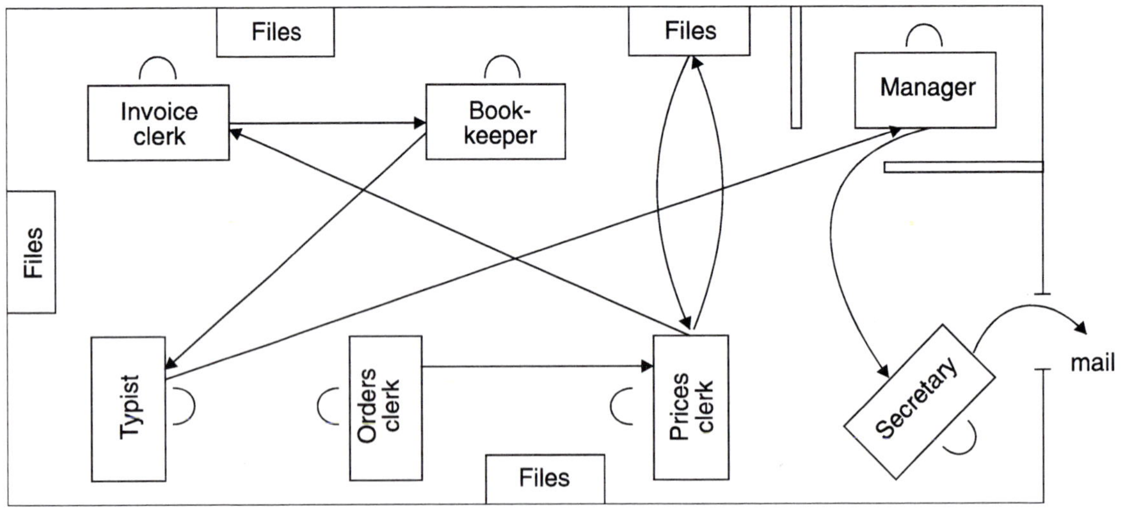

2.17 Rearranged to improve the work flow and layout, as suggested above, the department might look like this:

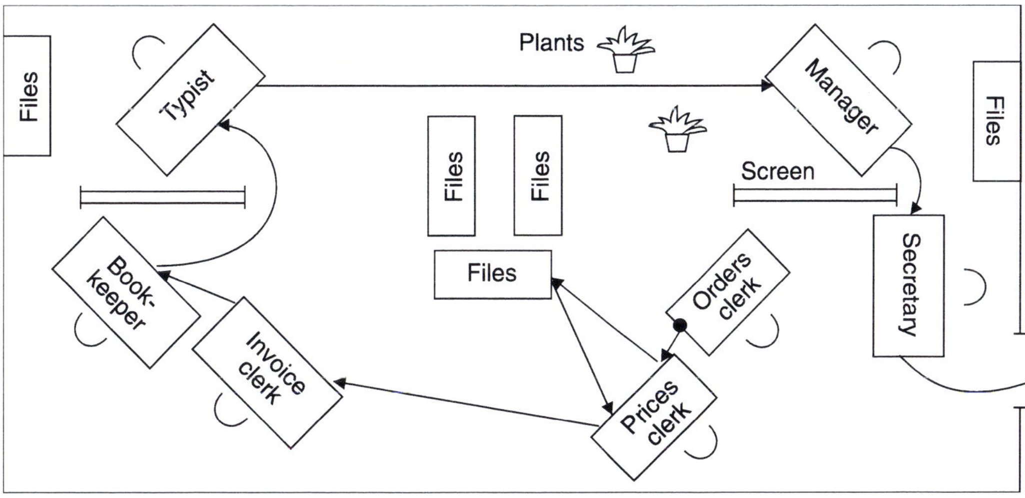

2.18 Work flow between different departments will depend on the layout of the premises as a whole. The same principles of **proximity** and **accessibility** apply. So, for example, purchasing and accounts departments may be located for easy communication with each other; the mail room and office supplies may be centralised, and rest areas and toilets distributed to allow general use.

2.19 Other common sense measures would include:

(a) Locating any design, drawing and planning (whether production or advertising etc) in 'studio'-type accommodation, with plenty of natural light

(b) Locating activities involving the movement of heavy machinery, materials or goods as close to ground level and transport facilities as possible

(c) Ensuring that senior management offices and conference facilities are situated where interruptions and noise are minimal

(d) Keeping dining, drinking, rest and recreation areas (if any) separate from those where concentrated work is taking place

Hot-desking and hoteling

2.20 Hot-desking and hoteling are current buzz-words meaning that desks are shared by a number of staff, a practice finding increasing favour especially among accounting firms and management consultants. In such businesses key personnel spend relatively little time on their own office premises. They need separate storage facilities for their own papers and files – typically a two-drawer filing cabinet on wheels – but two or three people can have a common desk without clashing. It is claimed that the cash savings (through renting less space or using space more efficiently) may be 25% or more, although much of this may have to be reinvested in technology, at least initially.

2.21 **Hot-desking** means that desks are grabbed on a first-come, first-served basis. **Hoteling** is a more civilised version where desks are booked in advance so staff are assured of a space. A clear desk policy is essential. Staff will generally have their own mobile laptop computer and a personal telephone number that can be used on any phone. Simpler technologies need attention, too: time can easily be wasted searching for common items like staplers and hole punches, so these are also likely to be carried around in briefcases.

2.22 Enthusiasts describe hot-desking as a liberating experience, and one that encourages the flexible attitudes required of the modern work force, constantly switching from one project and team to a new one. Critics argue that people resent having things taken away from them: 'Not knowing where my desk will be stops me from imagining what my day is going to be like, or who I'll be sitting next to, who I'll be able to talk to. It prevents me from putting my own stamp on things. It alienates people because the system encourages them to stay away from the office so you don't get any social interaction.'(*Accountancy Age*, April 1996).

Physical factors

2.23 There are various environmental factors which combine to affect the physical comfort and (arguably) the performance of employees.

(a) **Heating, lighting and ventilation**. The effect of these is fairly obvious, particularly when one or more of them is inadequate. Wherever possible lighting should be natural rather than artificial. Strip lighting is usually preferred to bulbs on the grounds that the effect of fluorescent tubes is closer to natural light. Ventilation should be provided without causing draughts, and if necessary, steps should be taken to filter smoke and dust out of the air for the sake of equipment and personnel alike.

(b) **Noise**. Strangely enough, we do need noise at work - or at least a certain amount of it otherwise people feel uneasy. Constant loud noise is distracting however and should be reduced by carpeting, sound absorbent walls and ceilings; 'acoustic hoods' are used to cover noisy machinery such as some computer printers, to muffle the noise; soft bleep phones are increasingly used instead of bell-ringing ones.

(c) **Decor**. A well-planned colour scheme can be a surprisingly important factor in the psychology of work. Brown, yellow and magnolia are considered good for work areas as they are warm colours; white and cream are light colours which can give an impression of space in small rooms; green is widely used because it is considered a 'restful' colour, easy on the eyes.

(d) **Office furniture design** is being taken very seriously, with increasing emphasis on the attractive-and-functional rather than the beautiful-but-impractical. Systems or modular furniture is being designed, with light, easy to move, linkable desks or 'wrap-around workstations', cabinets, printer tables and so on for total flexibility and use of available space. Easily cleaned surfaces, and colour/style co-ordination are also taken into account. Either a 'hi-tech' or a traditional image may be an important part of the culture of the organisation.

(e) **Cost**. This is not a 'physical factor' in itself, of course, but it must be considered together with all of them. The costs of purchasing and maintaining office buildings, furniture and equipment, and the costs of heating, lighting, and cleaning must be weighed against all possible benefits to the organisation from employee satisfaction and motivation, enhanced work flow and smart office image. The 'perfect' ergonomically-designed office would still have to be justified in terms of cost and durability.

Case example: office furniture

The growth in commercial training was the main reason for building the new Surrey County Headquarters of St John Ambulance which were constructed on the car park of the ambulance station. 'Our original training department was in the ambulance station and then we moved to an adjacent single story prefabricated building which we gradually outgrew,' explains Ralph Brown, Training Officer.

When it came to fitting out the building, Ralph invited four companies to come forward with their recommendations and suggested layout for furniture and storage.

'Like any charity, budget was an issue but we did have a wish list,' he says. The first floor comprises a large training area which can be partitioned into three smaller rooms. A modular system was acquired, with revolving beech veneer panels and cupboard doors that open to reveal a configuration of presentation, training and conference equipment including a rear projection screen, TV and video, flipchart and magnetic drip wipe board. In the staff and recreation rooms, the company installed stacking chairs and occasional tables.

On the ground floor there is one large open plan office and a number of cellular offices. 'We wanted to standardise a modern range of office furniture with matching storage units which would give us the maximum account of work surface to accommodate PCs etc but take up the minimum amount of floor space. The radial desks give us a lot of extra work surface and we liked the idea that we could use the desks as single units in the offices or as clusters with privacy screens in the open plan area. We also had to buy furniture that was going to last and look good in years to come. That's why we chose a furniture range with slate metal frames, a scratch resistant beech melamine finish and full length filing and storage cupboards with first class fittings,' says Ralph.

To make best use of the open plan area and to improve the workflow, a configuration of two clusters of four desks with D-ends and privacy screens were installed.

Facilities Management Journal, June 1997

Case example: lighting maintenance

There is an argument that the servicing of a lighting system is not cost effective. Significantly, however, more than half of the electricity entering commercial buildings is typically used for lighting.

There is confusion when it comes to calculating the cost effectiveness of lighting maintenance. Many people point only to the relatively small investment in actual equipment they can see - lamps, luminaires and control gear - completely ignoring the greatest cost of all, electricity.

Compared with other costs, such as initial installation and on-going maintenance, over a ten-year period electricity will account for between 54 per cent and 72 per cent of the total, with maintenance claiming around 10 per cent.

From the day it is switched on, the lighting levels from any system begin to drop.

Firstly this is due to the ageing process. Then there's the effect of dirt and dust which does not only take the shine off the fitting's reflective surfaces but can also, in the longer term, affect the operation of control gear. In more aggressive industrial atmospheres, corrosion can be a particular problem.

The overall effect is of course that the light output drops but the electricity consumed remains the same. Less light, same cost. It is, therefore, imperative to arrest this decline across the whole system regularly, on a planned basis.

A typical programme of lighting maintenance will involve a predetermined schedule of cleaning, inspection and relamping for the whole system across an agreed period of time. This approach has major advantages in terms of energy and cost savings compared with an ad-hoc approach to maintenance. This applies to both new investments and existing lamps, luminaires and control gear.

Facilities Management Journal, August 1998

Ergonomics

Underpinning knowledge

You should have studied ergonomics at Foundation level in *Organisation and the Human Resource* and again at Professional level in *Management Practice.* Here are a few key points. Go back to your earlier study material if you want fuller details.

Ergonomics explores the demands that can arise from a working environment and the capabilities of people to meet these demands with the aim of establishing machines and working conditions which, apart from functioning well, are best suited to the capacities and health requirements of the human body. In old people's homes and hospitals switches are placed according to measurements of chair height and arm reach. In the same way, computer consoles and controls and office furniture can be designed so that the individual expends minimal energy and experiences minimal physical strain in any given task. Movements should be natural, rhythmical and symmetrical.

Apart from purely mechanical considerations the ergonomist must also take into account the increasing problems of the worker as information processor. Systems should not make unreasonable demands on workers' attention spans and their capacity to absorb information, for example a system using sound signals to attract attention to visual displays or equipment.

Access

2.24 The Disability Discrimination Act 1995 requires all providers of goods and services to give '**reasonable**' **access** to disabled people. There is a ten year period for any necessary alterations to be completed. This does not just mean that ramps have to be put in place of steps at the entrance to the building. It may also entail relatively low-cost changes such as putting vision panels on doors at wheelchair height, lowering door handles, and raising electrical sockets, and some more expensive ones such as installation of or alterations to lifts and toilets.

3 LOCATION AND RELOCATION

Location decisions

3.1 The 'surroundings' of a work place include not only the immediate space in which employees carry out their duties, but also the external environment in which they may shop, bank, eat, commute, or park their cars and the overall design and construction of the complex within which their particular office may be placed.

Siting

3.2 The **siting** of buildings is the first consideration in the acquisition or construction of new office premises, or (more often) the **relocation** of existing facilities.

(a) Does the **nature** of the business dictate that it should be located in an urban area, in suburbs, in special commercial or industrial estates, in a rural area, close to a particular place or geographical feature (a reservoir, perhaps, or a mine).

(b) Are available **transport and communication links** sufficient to keep up the inflow and outflow of materials, goods, information and people? If the office has to deal with others outside its own country this may dictate location near major ports or airports, or urban areas with sophisticated communications facilities.

(c) What about **cost**: could the business take advantage of lower land prices, lower rates and insurance costs, or development grants from the government by locating outside urban areas? Are there increased or decreased operating costs, or construction, conversion or other building costs involved in relocation or expansion of existing office premises? Do the *benefits* of the location outweigh its costs?

(d) Where do most of the **employees live**? Could they commute or relocate easily? Or is there an existing 'pool' of sufficient suitable labour in the area? How many, and how important to the office, are those individuals who do not wish to relocate, and how strong are the feelings about it? Might reasonable incentives successfully induce them to acquiesce in the move?

(e) Where are **customers** based in town? How would the company keep in touch with them? Could it attract new business without an office in town to present a public 'profile'? Is the prestige associated with offices in, say, Central London essential? Will the customers suffer appreciable inconvenience from the relocation?

(f) Where are related **facilities** of the organisation located? Would it be more efficient to have Head Office, or the sales office, close to the production or warehousing facilities? These may be in another location, close to transport or suppliers but perhaps not convenient for direct customer contact and prestige.

(g) The availability of **leases** and **planning permission** will also have to be considered: the organisation will have to make some kind of forecast of its likely space/accommodation needs for the future.

Local facilities

3.3 One consideration in locating the site must be the facilities in the surrounding area. From the point of view of employees and the organisation, the proximity of banks, postal services and transport will be very important. For the employees' well-being, shops, restaurants and perhaps recreation/sport facilities would also be welcome.

3.4 **General design and construction** is partly an external factor, although specific aspects such as space, lighting and lifts in tall buildings are also internal factors. The size and age of buildings must be taken into account for efficient use of space and possible shortcomings in comfort and safety. Availability of space for employees and equipment (and for the foreseeable expansion of both) must be assessed, and heating, plumbing, cabling, and general structural soundness should be looked at in old buildings, if only to comply with legal requirements.

Exercise 3

Consider your own place of work. In the light of the above do you consider it to be well situated? If it is well-situated from some points of view and not from others, which point of view has prevailed, and in whose interests?

Cost

3.5 As ever, financial considerations will significantly influence management attitudes to all such factors. The site, size and age of buildings acquired, and whether they are rented, bought or built will be determined by their **cost**, and will in turn determine such **operating costs** as insurance and rates, heating and lighting, required maintenance and renovation. **Buying property** is advantageous so long as it is regarded as a **long term investment** because it gives the owner complete freedom to do as he likes with the property. **Leasing** is **more flexible** for the short term but it leaves the lessee to some extent at the mercy of landlords.

Relocation 12/95

3.6 Relocation, especially moving away from central London, has been a significant phenomenon in the 1980s and 1990s. One example is the rapid expansion in banking and the financial services sector which has led many companies to relocate part of their operations outside London. In particular, the 'back offices' which have no direct contact with the public or dealing operations have been free to decentralise: only a 'shop window' needs to be maintained in the major centres.

Why move?

3.7 Although it might be expected that costs would be the prime reason for moving it appears that in fact the **quality** and suitability of premises is the main factor. The main factors influencing the choice of location, in order of importance, are as follows.

- Accessibility and communications
- Property costs
- Labour availability
- Property availability
- Local environment
- Labour costs
- The company image
- The availability of business services
- Housing costs
- Local housing supply
- Schooling facilities
- Employment for family members
- Cultural, entertainment and shopping facilities

3.8 Some companies see relocation as a chance to 'lose the dead wood' and to introduce new working methods with completely new staff. A classic example is the move of the *Times* newspaper from the Fleet Street area of London to Wapping.

Planning a move

3.9 An organisation moving offices into new accommodation must take into account its present circumstances.

(a) If it had a **workable and attractive environment** before, it will be able to re-establish it in the new accommodation.

(b) If it did *not* have a **suitable layout and atmosphere,** it will be able to establish these factors in the new premises. The move is an opportunity for redesigning the environment.

3.10 In order to achieve these things efficiently, the move will have to be carefully planned, and a schedule or action sheet drawn up to cover the following considerations.

(a) The **date** of the move should be fixed (which will dictate all other deadlines).

(b) **Responsibility** for the move should be established. There should be a committee to oversee large moves, reporting to the MD or another director. Aspects or parts of the move will be delegated to employees.

(c) Arrangements must be made for **physical movement** of equipment and furniture. Small internal moves may only involve company porters, but specialist removal firms are available for larger transport operations.

(d) A **floor plan** will have to be drawn up to show the allocation of space to departments as well as the placing of items of furniture and equipment. These items will have to be listed, and marked with their destination and position so that everything can go immediately to the right place and be checked off as having arrived safely.

(e) Arrangements should be made to **engage** such people as **decorators, electricians, engineers** for heating and ventilation who may have to be called in to prepare the new building in advance.

(f) What does not have to be moved should be '**weeded out**'. Redundant files and papers, unused machinery and shabby furniture may be left out of the new office plans

(g) Clear instructions will have to be issued with regards to:

- The **role** of each employee of department in the move
- The **responsibility** of employees for personal property in the offices
- **Safety and security**, for example when moving heavy equipment

The cost of relocation

– can be huge!

3.11 The cost of relocation per employee can be many thousands of pounds because of the need to pay for visits to the new area, temporary accommodation, removal expenses and disturbance allowances.

Stress and family pressures

3.12 Moving home is widely recognised to be a stressful activity at the best of times. Most people experience an initial period of excitement at the thought of moving but in time the loss of old friends and activities and the recognition of new local frustrations create feelings of disappointment and doubt.

3.13 One difficulty in particular is that of the '**trailing spouse**': the partner who moves to fall in with the career progression of his or her companion, but who may not want to abandon existing social networks in favour of a 'corporate neighbourhood' with ready-made 'friends' who are really no more than work colleagues. In addition, a CBI survey has found that 73%

of companies consider that the issue of spouses' work has inhibited relocation plans: employees refuse to relocate because their partners would have to give up their jobs.

Case example: National Grid

When National Grid relocated 250 families from London to Coventry the company appointed a consultant from a relocation agency to help with the move. Rather than simply throwing money at the people they wished to relocate, the company addressed the real practical difficulties and placed the emphasis on housing, education and getting to know the area. Those affected were issued with information binders and were taken on family visits to the area and its surrounding villages and schools. Regular presentation evenings were organised, a monthly publication was issued and a series of videos was made, giving information and updates on the area. The outings and presentations also enabled the prospective new neighbours to get to know each other, helping to reduce fears of loneliness in the new environment.

Office churn

3.14 Office churn is **relocation within** a building. Costs have grown as telecommunications and computer networking needs have become paramount: offices in older buildings may need to be torn apart to accommodate the new cabling requirements. Installing 'flood wiring' (cable and sockets everywhere), carpet tiles, raised floors and suspended ceilings are methods of minimising the impact of future moves. A more high tech alternative that is likely to become more prevalent in the future is the use of cordless communications within the office (see Part B).

4 OUTSOURCING **6/95, 12/95, 6/99, 6/00**

4.1 A notable trend in the 1990s has been for organisations to pare down their activities so that they can concentrate on 'core competencies' - the things they do really well. The argument is that a company that earns its profits from, say, manufacturing bicycles, does not also need to have expertise in, say, mass catering or office cleaning. Rather than maintain a service department of its own, an organisation can chose to contract out or **outsource** certain operations to a private company, which will be paid a fee to conduct a service, including facilities management itself.

4.2 **Facilitics management companies** are contracted to take over part or all of an organisation's administrative facilities, although they often continue to operate within the organisation. Facilities management of computer services, for example, can range from:

- Project management assistance
- Complete control of systems development
- Running an organisation's entire computing function

Case example: Sears

The retailer Sears recently outsourced the management of its vast information technology and accounting functions to Andersen Consulting (*The Times,* February 1996). It is estimated that *savings* will grow from £5 million per annum in 1998-99 to £14 million in the following year, and thereafter. This is clearly considerable, although re-organisation costs relating to redundancies, relocation and asset write-offs are thought to be in the region of £35 million. About 900 staff are involved: under the transfer of undertakings regulations (which protect employees when part or all of a company changes hands). Andersen is obliged to take on the existing Sears staff. This appears to mean new opportunities for the staff who are moving, while those whom Sears are retaining are free to concentrate on strategy, development and management direction.

Advantages and disadvantages

Advantages of outsourcing arrangements

4.3 **Advantages** of using facilities management companies

(a) Facilities management is an effective form of **cost control**, as there is often a long-term contract where services are specified in advance for a **fixed price**.

(b) **Long-term contracts** (maybe up to ten years) allow much greater certainty in **planning for the future**.

(c) A facilities management company has **economies of scale.** Several organisations will employ the same FM company, and so the FM company's research into new products on the market or new technologies will be shared between them.

(d) **Skills and knowledge are retained.** Many organisations do not have a sufficiently well developed IT department to offer existing staff good opportunities for personal development. They find that talented staff leave to pursue their careers elsewhere, taking their skill and knowledge (much of which may have been acquired at the expense of the original organisation) with them. An FM company that takes over the contracts of existing employees will be able to offer them the advancement they are looking for.

(e) **New skills and knowledge become available.** An FM company can **share** staff with **specific expertise** (such as programming in HTML to produce Web pages) between several clients. This means that the outsourcing company can take advantage of new developments without the need to recruit new people or re-train existing staff, and without the cost.

(f) **Resources employed can be scaled up or down** depending upon demand. For instance, during a major changeover from one system to another the number of IT staff needed may be twice as large as it will be once the new system is working satisfactorily.

An outsourcing organisation is likely to arrange its work on a **project** basis, whereby some staff will expect to be moved periodically from one project to the next.

Disadvantages of outsourcing arrangements

4.4 **Drawbacks** of using facilities management companies

(a) Information is **an inherent part of the business and of management**. Unlike office cleaning, or catering, an organisation's IS services may be too important to be contracted out.

(b) A company may have highly **confidential information** and to let outsiders handle it could be seen as **risky**.

(c) Information strategy can be used to gain **competitive advantage**. Opportunities may be missed if a third party is handling IS services, because there is no onus upon internal management to keep up with new developments and have new ideas.

(d) Once an organisation has handed over its computing to an FM company, it is **locked in to** the contract. If the FM company supplies unsatisfactory levels of service for whatever reason (takeover, financial difficulties etc), then the effort and expense the organisation would have to incur to rebuild its own computing function would be enormous.

(e) The use of FM does **not** encourage a **proper awareness** of the **potential costs and benefits** of IT amongst managers. If managers cannot manage in-house IT resources effectively, then it could be argued that they will not be able to manage an IT outsourcing arrangement effectively either.

Case example: Vehicle fleet management

'As the number of factors to be considered multiplies, the management of company fleets becomes an ever more demanding business.

To traditional concerns such as model choice, efficient purchasing, replacement cycles and maintenance organisation there have recently been added factors such as soaring insurance premiums and the requirement to take measures against the likelihood of theft. As a result, many companies have thrown up their hands in the air and have simply surrendered their fleets to outside management.'

'Out-sourcing is the latest buzzword in the vehicle fleet management business. This is when a company delegate all its fleet management to a specialist third-party, eliminating the need for dedicated in-house support personnel.

'Put quite simply, it is one nominated contract hire supplier managing all the other suppliers to that customer so all invoices for monthly rentals, excess mileages, or whatever, are controlled by the nominated supplier, who then provides the client with one consolidated invoice for auditing', explains Mr Neil Pykett, managing director of Cowie Interleasing, the UK's biggest vehicle contract hire company. Cowie have the Marks and Spencer out-sourcing contract.

He said: 'We replace the client's software with our own and his people with our people. Although based at our head office, they answer the phone in the client's name. The benefits are that the client has only one set of invoices to audit and we free his own staff to concentrate on other, perhaps more important, core activities.'

Mr Dennis [of M & S] said that there were two main reasons why M & S moved to out-sourcing: to reduce the administrative burden, of course, and to shorten the communication lines between the company car driver and the people providing the day to day service.'

Financial Times, April 1994

Choosing a contractor

4.5 One the decision has been made to end in-house provision tenders must be invited from potential providers of the facility or facilities. The following questions should be considered.

(a) How do **costs** compare, both between competing contractors and as against in-house provision of the facility? Cost must be stated in a way that *allows* comparison between different options, such as cost per square metre for office cleaning, or cost per routine maintenance visit for lift maintenance. Do the more expensive tenders offer better value for money?

(b) What is the **size** of the contractor relative to your organisation. Is your contract a minor one for a massive FM company and so one that may be more bother than it is worth for them? Or will you be the company's largest client and is there a risk that they are taking on more than their resources and experience can handle?

(c) Is the contractor **financially stable**? There is little point in entering into a five-year contract with a company that is liable to go under before this Christmas.

(d) Can it provide evidence that it positively **vets** staff that will be placed in positions with security implications and that it provides all training that staff may need? Is there evidence of higher than normal staff turnover? If so this may suggest less than professional management standards.

(e) What are the contractors' procedures for **maintaining quality**? Have they achieved ISO 9000 certification?

(f) Are you confident that they are able to **interpret** their brief? Have they demonstrated an understanding of what is required? Have they tried to blind you with technical jargon, or can they communicate their specialist knowledge in a way that the lay-person can understand?

(g) Can the supplier **demonstrate a good track record** with you or with other companies. Are references available?

(h) Can the contractor **measure the performance** of its service provision and provide useful management information?

(i) If the contract involves supplying goods (for example 'washroom consumables') are the **costs shown separately** and how do they **compare** with prices achievable by the organisation through its in-house buying department? In theory economies of scale should be available to the FM company and these should be passed on.

(j) Is the contractor **experienced at collaborating** with other contractors who you may have working on site, and willing to do so?

(k) Does the contractor **understand its responsibilities** under TUPE (it should be asking for details of employees contracts if so: see below)?

The Transfer of Undertakings (Protection of Employment) Regulations 1981

4.6 These main provisions of these regulations are as follows.

(a) If a trade or business is transferred from one person to another the original employees become **employees** of the **new owner** on the same terms and conditions as before.

(b) **Dismissal** of an employee for any reason connected with the transfer is automatically **unfair,** unless it is for economic, technical or organisational reasons.

(c) The transferor has a duty to **inform** and **consult** with recognised trade unions about the transfer.

(d) Employees have the right to **object** to a transfer, and if they do so this ends their employment contract without any need for them to give notice.

4.7 TUPE has been strongly resisted by FM companies, but recent EU and UK case law has established beyond doubt that TUPE applies to outsourcing arrangements. More responsible contractors now welcome TUPE and see it as a way of eliminating the 'cowboy' element in the FM world.

5 PRACTICAL ASSET MANAGEMENT

5.1 In this final section we look at some of the practical aspects of being responsible for corporate assets.

Buying assets **6/96, 6/97**

5.2 The purchasing of an asset (or any other article for that matter) has been defined as comprising four 'rights'. Obtaining the article:

- At the right price
- At the right time
- In the right quantity
- To the right quality

5.3 As an example of the sort of matters that will be considered when choosing an asset we might consider the choice of **computer hardware**. This will depend on numerous factors including the following.

(a) **Reliability and support**. Is the computer from a well-known manufacturer?

(b) The **ease** with which the computer configuration fits in with the organisation's requirements (direct access facilities, hard-copy output in given quantities etc)

(c) **Time scale.** How quickly will the system be able to go operational?

(d) **Flexibility**. The system should be capable of expanding and coping with new developments.

(e) **Maintenance**. There should be a low expected breakdown rate. There should be back - up facilities.

(f) There may be a special '**hotline' support** service for enquiries and emergencies: are there guaranteed call-out times (ideally same day)?

(g) Is a **warranty** supplied? What guarantees are given?

(h) **Compatibility** is important. The organisation may wish to link its new hardware with other hardware so that they can communicate and share information.

(i) Is there a **suitable stockist** for consumables (printer cartridges etc) that will suit the system?

(j) **Keeping out 'hackers'** and other unauthorised users is desirable, though difficult to achieve.

(k) **Work patterns** and **usage** must be considered.

  (i) A personal desktop computer linked to central department or corporate computer might suit an office-tied executive.

  (ii) Home workers may use portable micros linked to HQ via the telephone network.

  (iii) Battery-operated 'laptops' suit travelling executives or sales people.

  (iv) If the user requires links with external services such as e-mail, he may require a more versatile information centre, perhaps combined with telex and other facilities.

  (v) If more than six people need to share information, a multi-user system would be appropriate. Initial expense is greater, but terminals can be added more cheaply, and peripherals can be shared.

  (vi) If the organisation wishes to exercise control over access to data in the central computer, a system allowing 'read only' access to specified information may be used.

Exercise 4

In the light of the above, draw up your own checklist for buying:

(a) office furniture;

(b) a fleet of company cars.

Purchase of second hand equipment **6/96, 6/99**

5.4 The relative benefits and problems of purchasing second-hand as opposed to new office machinery, equipment and furniture will depend to a large extent on h*ow* second-hand (that is, how old) the items are, and the circumstances of the purchasing organisation.

5.5 Broadly speaking, the **benefits** may be as follows.

(a) **Cost-saving**. In fact, this is the only major advantage of not buying new. The lower capital cost of purchase will have the benefits of:

  (i) A smaller capital outlay than may be necessary to buy new

  (ii) Not tying up large amounts of capital, and therefore offering cash flow advantages

(b) In view of the low cost, second-hand items may be a convenient '**stand-by**' or short-term measure, eg if an office is relocating, leaving a temporary 'skeleton' facility in one location, or if temporary or unforeseen expansion of the workforce requires short-term added facilities.

(c) In view of the low cost, second-hand items may be a way of **trying out different models,** machines etc prior to choosing those to be bought new. (Renting, however, is a much better alternative, for this purpose).

(d) Second-hand equipment and machinery is likely to be **'broken in'**, over any 'teething troubles' associated with newness, and fully developed (eg in the case of software, computer configurations etc).

5.6 Problems of buying second-hand, however, are as follows.

(a) There is **unlikely** to be a **warranty** on machinery and equipment, which means that maintenance and repair costs will be borne in full.

(b) The **wear and tear** likely to have occurred during the items' previous ownership may make maintenance and repair more necessary, more often. Costs of upkeep may erode the savings gained on purchase outlay.

(c) If the machinery or equipment is fairly old, there may be problems **obtaining replacement parts** and consumables: it may be unmaintainable.

(d) Especially in the case of electronic equipment, there are the dangers of **obsolescence** and **lack of compatibility** with other machines.

(e) Second-hand items are likely to have **little or no re-sale value** (as third-hand items), and lack the tax advantages of depreciation charged against profit.

(f) There is likely to be **less choice** available, especially if large systems are required. This may be particularly acute where the purchase of furniture is concerned, with resulting lack of standardisation. Standardisation is usually desirable both for flexibility (and therefore efficient space planning) and appearance.

(g) Furniture may **not** be **obtainable** as integrated systems. There may be a mismatch between chairs and desks/worktops, for example, which would impact on the comfort and convenience of the user.

(h) Furniture and equipment is **less likely** to be **tailored precisely** to the task and environment - which is against the principles of ergonomics. Effective chair design, furniture systems, VDU screen angles, wire and cable management etc all depend on choice and tailoring where possible.

(i) Especially in an office where the **physical appearance** of the work environment is **important** for the morale, culture and image of the organisation, anything old-fashioned or any shabbiness or ill-matching designs could be damaging.

Lease or buy? **6/96, 6/97, 6/99**

5.7 The 'lease or buy' decision is not a straightforward choice between two options: equipment can be bought new or second hand, on HP terms, using a bank loan, with cash or by instalments. Equipment can be leased under a finance lease or an operating lease. Premises can also be bought outright or leased. The way in which the acquisition will be financed is a major part of the decision. Each possibility should be evaluated by the organisation's management accountant and, all else being equal, the cheapest option is the one that should be chosen.

5.8 For the present purposes we are concerned with the non-financial factors because in practice all else is unlikely to be equal.

5.9 Some advantages of **buying** equipment are as follows.

(a) The organisation will be able to enjoy the **full benefits** of ownership. If it so desires the filing cabinets can be sprayed pink, desks can be sawn in half, machines can be tampered with and adapted.

(b) The organisation can **sell** the equipment and keep the proceeds. This might be important when the organisation's security is being assessed by potential investors.

(c) **Suppliers** like cash customers most of all, and they may be willing to provide extras (a free executive chair, say) if the customer is buying goods outright.

(d) In the long term, buying is likely to be **cheaper** than leasing.

5.10 There are disadvantages however.

(a) Buying brings with it all the **risks of ownership**. The equipment will need to be insured, kept secure and maintained. If it is damaged, repairs will have to be paid for.

(b) Equipment is a **depreciating asset**: depending what it is, it may become less efficient or obsolete as time goes by.

(c) Buying **ties up** for the **long-term capital** which may be needed for the day-to-day operations of the business.

(d) Only a **proportion** of the **outlay** each year is **tax deductible**.

5.11 The implication of the above is that buying is not a good option for items of equipment that need regular maintenance or which are likely to become obsolete quickly. Office furniture is an example of equipment that is relatively little affected by these factors. A desk will last for many years in perfect condition, only eventually falling prey to the dictates of fashion.

5.12 Operating leases provide the strongest contrast with the buying option. An operating lease leaves the ownership of the asset with the provider of finance, usually the manufacturer or supplier. A finance lease does so, too, but only in legal form.

5.13 Some advantages of **leasing** under an operating lease are as follows.

(a) The **lessor is responsible** for servicing and maintenance of the leased equipment.

(b) With the fixed costs of leasing, equipment costs are known exactly, making it easier to **establish budgets**.

(c) Leasing **avoids tying up capital**.

(d) Most operating **lease charges** are **fully tax deductible** in the year incurred.

5.14 Disadvantages of leasing are as follows.

(a) The **user** of the asset **cannot use** it as **security**.

(b) The **user** is **not free** to do as he likes with the asset.

(c) The adverse impact of leasing charges on **reported profits** may be greater than the effect of depreciation charges on purchased assets.

(d) The **lessor receives** the benefit of **disposal proceeds** when the asset is sold.

(e) In the long term (and possibly in the short term, too, if equipment retains its value) leasing is likely to be more expensive.

5.15 Leasing is thus the best option where **capital** is in **short supply**, where equipment is likely to need regular maintenance (a photocopier, for example) and where equipment is susceptible to obsolescence due to changes in technology, computer equipment being the obvious example. Leasing also offers the opportunity to evaluate equipment before making the decision to buy and to obtain the use of equipment which is only needed in the short term, for clearing a backlog or for training purposes, for example.

Property leases **12/98**

5.16 Additional considerations will apply if an organisation is deciding whether to lease a property.

(a) The **coverage** of the lease; is the building being let empty or with furniture or other equipment being included

(b) **Service charges** and responsibility for maintenance and insurance of the premises

(c) The provisions for **future rent reviews**; the time period between reviews and the possibility of significant increases in charges

(d) Any **break clause**, whether the tenant will be able to leave the property if convenient, and not suffer financial penalties

(e) **Rights to assignment** and subletting; being able to sublet will help if the tenant wants to move during the term of the lease

(f) The extent to which **landlord consent** will be required for alterations to the property

(g) **Compliance** by the **landlord** with relevant legislation, in particular planning and health and safety legislation

5.17 The points discussed above about re-location and planning a move are obviously also relevant in deciding between properties.

Management of assets 12/97

5.18 Asset management on a day-to-day basis is essentially a matter of **keeping records**. Most organisations of any size have hundreds or even thousands of assets and most therefore use some sort of computerised system to manage them, perhaps using a management software package with features as described below.

Asset categories

5.19 Typical asset categories might be those already described - land and buildings, plant and equipment, fixtures and fittings and so forth. These would normally be further sub-divided, for example into shops, factories and offices; fixed plant and moveable plant; motor cars, vans and lorries; computer equipment and office furniture and so on. A distinction should also be made between leased assets and owned assets.

Asset records 12/97

5.20 A separate record should be maintained for each asset. The record would contain information such as the following.

(a) Asset number or code

(if relevant) → (b) Company code, where a single register is maintained for a number of group companies

(c) Asset type, for example Motor Vehicles

(d) Department or cost centre using the asset, for example 'Product X Department - grinding'

(e) A basic description of the asset, eg Toyota Corolla 2.0 GL

(f) Further identifying details, including any or all of the following.

- (i) Serial number
- (ii) Engine number
- (iii) Registration number
- (iv) Colour
- (v) Details of extras or enhancements (a leather top on a desk, a car alarm etc)
- (vi) Key/lock numbers, especially for cars, desk drawers and filing cabinets.

(g) Date of purchase

(h) Purchase price

(i) Name of supplier

(j) The location of the asset

(k) The name of the person responsible for it (especially in the case of a car)

(l) The insured value

(m) Estimated asset life and residual value

(n) Details of maintenance contracts, user support telephone numbers and the like

Asset movements and asset tracking

5.21 The system must allow for assets to be **transferred** in various ways. A company car may be passed from one salesperson to another. Increasingly companies are using **bar codes** on smaller assets so that when an asset audit is being carried out the auditor simply needs to scan the bar code on each asset as it is encountered and key codes for current location and so on into a hand-held device. Larger mobile assets such as vehicles can be fitted with radio transmitters that report current location to a central point.

5.22 The system should also be capable of **recording disposal** details, such as the name of the buyer of the asset and the disposal proceeds received or part exchange value agreed. In the case of part exchanges it is useful to have a record of which new asset the old one was exchanged for.

5.23 Some assets (principally land and buildings) are **often revalued** and the system should record the new value, the date of revaluations and the name of the valuer. It must also be able to cope with the various accounting requirements in these circumstances.

Asset reports

5.24 Most systems will be able to produce a wide variety of proforma reports, and perhaps also user-defined reports. Typical examples include

(a) Depreciation reports

(b) Asset disposals

(c) Asset purchases

(d) Asset transfers

(e) Capital budgeting reports

(f) Insured values

(g) Location reports

(h) Sticky labels with barcodes (especially useful where there are many identical assets, like desks or chairs)

Asset maintenance

5.25 Some systems offer an asset maintenance module in which can be recorded both diary details of **work done** (or mileage clocked up or whatever) to date and details of **maintenance** to be carried out once a certain period has elapsed or after so many thousands of miles or hours of use. This module might also have standard details of parts requirements, labour usage and costs and so on at various service intervals. This can be used to plan out maintenance programmes in advance.

5.26 Britannia Software's system for example splits into different systems depending upon type of asset.

(a) The **property management system**, for owned and leased buildings, has capital works and repair and maintenance modules.

(b) The **plant maintenance system** produces 'resource analysis reports' to guide the management of plant maintenance.

(c) The **fleet management modules** include systems for own-garage work, spare parts control and fleet scheduling.

Paperwork

5.27 Various aspects of facilities management are bound up with the information technology developments discussed in Part B of this Text. Examples include:

(a) Making the **maximum use** of **available technology**

Communications is a particularly important area including e-mail and having available on the company's Intranet important administrative and operational information, such as procedures manuals.

(b) **Reducing paperwork** and copying by making maximum use of electronic storage facilities using document imaging

(c) Establishing **appropriate codes of conduct**, for example an e-mail policy

Vehicle fleet management

5.28 Vehicle fleet management systems would include all of the above facilities and should also have records of **drivers** - ages, mileage, accident records, type of licence held (eg HGV, motorbike) - and **fuel usage**, both by car and by driver. Fuel is a significant expense for many companies and consumption should be carefully monitored. Some systems have journey planners that can provide a print-out showing and describing the quickest route from A to B, and so helping to cut fuel costs and journey time.

Capital budgeting

5.29 Most systems also offer some sort of capital budgeting facility which records and controls expenditure on long-term asset construction projects, for example building a new head office or constructing a car assembly line.

Telecommunications

5.30 Many organisations that own tall buildings are letting their roofs out to telecommunication operators, who are prepared to pay significant sums for permission to put their aerials on strategically sited roofs. An article by Robert Bell in *Chartered Secretary* February 1999 highlighted the fact that the Telecommunications Act 1984 confers rights on telecommunication operators which could limit the owner of the building's ability to remove the equipment or redevelop the building.

(a) The operators can make a court application to ensure that their lease remains in place. Thus attempting to remove them is likely to involve the owners in legal action, and the owners will have to prove that removal is on certain defined grounds (re-furbishment, breach of agreement, expiry of right to remain in the building). Even then courts will not automatically take the owners' part; the courts will consider whether monetary compensation would be a better remedy than removal, and will also take into account the advantage of access to a public telecommunications service.

(b) Problems may also arise if the owner has let to tenants, since telecommunications' operators only need the tenants' consent under the law.

(c) Giving consent to telecommunications operators does not require a formal agreement; hence before terms are agreed, the owner should make it clear when communicating with the operators that nothing should be taken to imply consent.

(d) Operators sublet their own spare capacity, and owners should ensure that they obtain a share of subletting income.

(e) There are possible health and safety implications, as the technology could be dangerous to anyone who goes on the roof. The agreement between owners and operators should contain explicit safeguards.

Chapter roundup

- **Facilities management** is the integration of multi-disciplinary activities within the built environment and their impact upon people and the workplace. FM covers a multitude of activities such as cleaning, catering, security, space planning, vehicle fleet management, cabling and so on. FM is a matter of understanding and identifying facilities needs in a strategic context, minimising facilities-related disruption, maximising flexibility, managing people, negotiating with suppliers, and performance monitoring.
- **Space planning** is necessary due to expansion or contraction, technological changes, and pressure to reduce facilities costs. A building audit should be carried out to identify current and future needs. Modern trends are for open plan offices, hot-desking and hoteling. The physical environment is widely believed to affect the attitudes and performance of employees
- **Location decisions** are based on considerations such as the nature of the business, its customers, its labour needs, costs, and related facilities and support services. Relocation is a major undertaking that needs to be carefully planned. Aside from the practical difficulties of moving there are significant staff-related issues that must be addressed.
- Many organisations are choosing to **outsource facilities management** and concentrate on core competences. Organisations gain expertise and possibly save money by outsourcing, but some 'support' activities may nevertheless be key to the business. Outsourcing is difficult to reverse. Choosing a contractor entails an assessment of matters such as costs, relative size, staff policy (especially TUPE implications), quality procedures, track record, and monitoring and reporting arrangements.
- **Asset management** essentially entails buying assets, looking after them from day to day and disposing of them at the end of their lives. Acquisition options include buying new or second-hand, and leasing as opposed to buying. Day-to-day asset management is a matter of keeping records: software packages may greatly assist in this.

Test your knowledge

1 Why has facilities management grown in importance? (see paras 1.6 -1.7)

2 What steps might be contained in a programme for office cleaning? (1.10)

3 What is 'flood wiring'? (1.17 (table))

4 What is a building audit? (2.3 – 2.9)

5 What are the advantages of a landscaped office? (2.11)

6 What is hoteling? (2.21)

7 List the main factors influencing choice of location. (3.7)

8 What should the plan for an office move contain? (3.10)

9 What is office churn? (3.14)

10 What are the advantages of outsourcing? (4.3)

11 Why is vehicle fleet management frequently outsourced? (4.4 (Case example), 5.28)

12 What is TUPE? (4.6)

13 What factors should be considered when buying an asset? (5.3)

14 What records need to be kept about an asset? (5.20)

Now try illustrative question 26 at the end of the Study Text

Chapter 26

HEALTH, SAFETY AND SECURITY

This chapter covers the following topics.

1 Health and safety issues

2 Security and emergency procedures

3 Environmental issues

Introduction

The health, safety and security of a building's occupants and contents must be the overriding considerations in any facilities management decision. In this final chapter we remind you of the business implications of health, safety and security issues and the extensive legislation surrounding these aspects of operations. There is also some further practical advice on security matters and a few more words about contingency planning, a topic already discussed at some length in Parts B and C of this text, but equally examinable in this context.

1 HEALTH AND SAFETY ISSUES 12/99

Underpinning knowledge

You should have studied various aspects of health and safety and security at Foundation level for the *Organisation and the Human Resource* paper and also at Professional level Stage 1 for the *Management Practice* paper. A good deal of the material in this chapter is therefore likely to be familiar.

Danger in the office

1.1 Common causes of injury in the office include the following.

- Slippery or uneven floors
- Frayed carpets
- Trailing electric leads, telephone cables and other wires
- Obstacles (boxes, files, books, open drawers) in gangways
- Standing on chairs (particularly swivel chairs) to reach high shelving
- Blocked staircases, for example where they are used for extra storage space
- Lifting heavy items without bending properly
- Removing the safety guard on a machine to free a blockage or to make it run faster

1.2 Sometimes none of these things are needed to cause an accident: it is very easy to do it without props! Carelessness or foolishness are major causes of accidents.

Accidents cost money

1.3 More than 700,000 people are injured at work in Britain every year, and accidents at work are estimated to cost employers over £2 billion. Costs include the following.

(a) Productive time lost by the injured employee

(b) Productive time lost by other employees who (through choice or necessity) stop work at the time of or following the accident

(c) Time lost by supervision, management and technical staff following the accident

(d) A proportion of the cost of employing first aid and medical staff

(e) The cost of disruption to operations at work

(f) The cost of any damage to the equipment or any cost associated with the subsequent modification of the equipment

(g) The cost of any compensation payments or fines resulting from legal accident

(h) The costs associated with increased insurance premiums

(i) Reduced output from the injured employee on return to work

(j) The cost of possible reduced morale, increased absenteeism or increased labour turnover among employees

(k) The cost of recruiting and training a replacement for the injured worker

1.4 In December 1994 for the first time in English legal history a company was convicted of homicide following the deaths of four teenagers on a canoeing holiday. The company was fined £60,000 and the managing director was sentenced to three years imprisonment for manslaughter.

- Corporate manslaughter

Legal aspects of health and safety

1.5 In the UK there are several Acts of Parliament applying to workplaces. The main ones are as follows.

- The Factories Act 1961
- The Offices, Shops and Railway Premises Act 1963
- The Employer's Liability (Defective Equipment) Act 1969
- The Fire Precautions Act 1971
- The Health and Safety at Work Act 1974

1.6 The UK has also implemented six EC directives on various aspects of health and safety by issuing new Regulations under the Health and Safety at Work Act 1974. Some of the most important regulations are as follows.

- The Reporting of Injuries, Diseases and Dangerous Occurrences Regulations 1995
- The Health and Safety (First Aid) Regulations 1981
- The Noise at Work Regulations 1989
- The Control of Substances Hazardous to Health Regulations 1999
- The Manual Handling Operations Regulations 1992
- The Workplace (Health, Safety and Welfare) Regulations 1992
- The Provision and Use of Work Equipment Regulations 1992
- The Health and Safety (Display Screen Equipment) Regulations 1992
- The Management of Health and Safety at Work Regulations 1992
- The Personal Protective Equipment at Work Regulations 1992
- The Health and Safety (Young Persons) Regulations 1997
- The Health and Safety (Safety Signs and Signals) Regulations 1996

Duties of employees

1.7 Employees are obliged under the Health and Safety at Work Act 1974 to do the following.

(a) **Take reasonable care** to avoid injury to themselves and others.
(b) **Co-operate** with their employer to help him comply with his statutory obligations.

1.8 Under the Management of Health and Safety at Work Regulations 1992 employees have further responsibilities.

(a) Employees must **use all equipment**, safety devices, etc, provided by the employer **properly** and **in accordance** with the **instructions** and training received.

(b) Employees must **inform** the **employer**, or another employee with specific responsibility for health and safety, of any **perceived shortcoming** in safety arrangements or any serious and immediate dangers to health and safety.

1.9 If an employee flouts safety regulations (whether or not an accident actually occurs) he can be prosecuted and fined up to £20,000 or, for very serious cases, he can be fined without limit or imprisoned. If he himself is injured he may be refused compensation because he brought the injuries upon himself. Even if the case does not go to court the guilty employee may face disciplinary action by his employer.

1.10 Employers are obliged to designate specifically one or more competent workers to assist them in undertaking protective and preventative measures.

Duties of employers: safety policy

1.11 Employers' duties apply to employees, temporary staff, contractors and visitors.

1.12 The Health and Safety at Work Act 1974 imposes specific duties upon employers to make sure that all systems (that is, work practices) are safe, that the work environment is safe and healthy (see below) and that plant and equipment is kept up to the necessary standard. Regulations issued under the authority of this Act require the employer to do the following.

(a) Produce a **written statement of safety measures** and the means used to implement them. This statement should be brought to the notice of his employees. An employer who has less than five employees is exempt from this requirement.

(b) **Consult with safety representatives** appointed by recognised trade unions with a view to the effective maintenance of adequate safety measures.

(c) Appoint a **safety committee** if requested to do so by the safety representatives, to keep safety measures under review.

1.13 Under the Management of Health and Safety at Work Regulations 1992 employers have the following additional general duties.

(a) They must carry out **risk assessment,** generally in writing, of all work hazards. Assessment should be continuous.

(b) They must introduce **controls** to reduce risks.

(c) They must **assess the risks** to anyone else affected by their work activities.

(d) They must **share hazard and risk information** with other employers, including those on adjoining premises, other site occupiers and all subcontractors coming onto the premises.

(e) They should **revise safety policies** in the light of the above, or initiate safety policies if none were in place previously.

(f) They must **identify employees** who are especially at risk.

(g) They must **provide** fresh and appropriate **training** in safety matters.

(h) They must **provide information** to employees (including temps) about health and safety.

(i) They must **employ competent safety and health advisers.**

Duties of employers: equipment

1.14 The Employer's Liability (Defective Equipment) Act 1969 makes employers responsible for personal injury suffered by employees because of defects in equipment provided by the employer.

1.15 However, the issue most likely to be of concern to the Chartered Secretary is health and safety at computer workstations. The main provisions of the Health and Safety (Display Screen Equipment) Regulations 1992 are as follows.

(a) **VDUs** must not flicker, must be free from glare, and must swivel and tilt.

(b) **Keyboards** must tilt and must be free from glare; the workspace in front of them must be sufficient for the operators to rest their forearms.

(c) **Desks** must be free from glare; there must be enough space to allow flexible arrangement of all equipment and documents. Measurements are not specified.

(d) **Chairs**. The seat must be adjustable in height, and the back in height and angle; footrests must be made available if required.

(e) **Lighting**. There must be appropriate contrast between the screen and its background; windows must have some form of blinds.

(f) **Heat and humidity** levels must be adequate on the one hand and not uncomfortable on the other.

(g) **Radiation** must be reduced to negligible levels.

(h) **Breaks**. Screen work must be periodically interrupted by breaks or changes in activity. Short, frequent breaks (say, five or ten minutes per hour) are better than longer breaks at longer intervals.

(i) **Eyesight**. The employer must offer free eyesight testing at regular intervals and provide any special glasses that may be needed for screen work.

(j) **Consultation**. Employees must be consulted about health and safety measures.

(k) **Training**. Training in the proper use of equipment must be provided.

1.16 Any new workstations put into service have to meet these requirements; existing workstations must be adapted to comply or be replaced by the end of 1996.

Duties of employers: the work environment

1.17 The Offices, Shops and Railway Premises Act 1963 has a number of rules governing the environment in which employees work and these have been supplemented by the Workplace (Health, Safety and Welfare) Regulations 1992. Because this is generally of interest to all employees we list the main provisions below.

Buildings management and Health and Safety

Do not try to learn this list for exam purposes. We include it because you might find it a useful source of reference in your day to day work.

(a) **Cleanliness**. Floors and steps must be cleaned at least once a week. Furniture and fittings must be kept clean. Rubbish must not be allowed to accumulate in work areas.

(b) **Overcrowding**. Each person should have at least 11 cubic metres of space, ignoring any parts of rooms more than 3.1 metres above the floor or with a headroom of less than 2.0 metres

(c) **Ventilation**. There must be an adequate supply of fresh or purified air in circulation.

(d) **Temperature**. A reasonable temperature must be maintained (except for brief periods). The minimum is 16°C where people are sitting down, or 13°C if they move about to do their work. A thermometer must be provided on each floor on permanent display.

(e) **Lighting and windows**. There must be adequate natural or artificial light (preferably natural, if practicable). Windows must be kept clean inside and out and lighting equipment must be properly maintained. Windows should be made of safe materials and if they are openable it should be possible to do this safely.

(f) **Toilets**. There must be enough suitable toilets and they must be properly ventilated and lit, kept clean and properly maintained. Broadly speaking, enough means a Gents and Ladies WC for every 15 to 20 employees.

(g) **Washing facilities**. These should be provided on the same scale as toilets. They should have clean hot and cold water, soap and towels or the equivalent.

(h) **Drinking water**. Adequate drinking water must be provided together with cups or a fountain.

(i) **Clothing**. There should be somewhere to hang up outdoor clothing and facilities for drying it. Facilities for changing clothing should be available where appropriate.

(j) **Seating**. Seats must be provided for rest periods, and where work can or must be done sitting down seats must be suitable in design, construction and dimensions.

(k) **Eating facilities**. Suitable facilities must be available for workers who eat in the workplace. Normally a desk in an office would be regarded as suitable.

(l) **Lifts**. Lifts must be safe. They must be examined by a competent engineer at least every 6 months.

(m) **Floors, passages and stairs**. These should be soundly constructed and maintained, without holes, slip-free, and kept free from obstruction. Stairs should have hand-rails; floor openings should be fenced round.

(n) **Traffic routes**. These should have regard to the safety of pedestrians and vehicles alike.

(o) **Doors and gates**. These should be suitably constructed and fitted with any necessary safety devices (especially sliding doors and powered doors and doors opening in either direction).

(p) **Escalators and travelators**. These should function safely and have readily accessible emergency stop devices.

(q) **Machinery and equipment**. All equipment should be properly maintained. Dangerous parts of machines should be fenced. No person under the age of 18 should be required to clean machinery if this would expose him to risk, and no person should be allowed to operate a machine specified as dangerous unless fully instructed of the dangers.

(r) **Heavy lifting**. People should not be required to lift, carry or move a load likely to cause injury.

(s) **Falls or falling objects**. These should be prevented by erecting effective physical safeguards (fences, safety nets, ground rails and so on).

(t) **Fire precautions**. Appropriate fire-fighting equipment should be provided and there must be an adequate means of escape. Business premises should generally have a valid fire certificate from the local fire authority (though this depends on the number of floors and the number of people). Fire exits should be clearly marked and escape routes kept unobstructed. Fire alarms should be provided and tested periodically and those working in the building should be familiar with the escape drill.

(u) **First aid**. A first-aid box or cupboard under the charge of a responsible person should be provided for every 150 employees or fraction thereof (there should be two if there are 160 employees). Where there are more than 150 employees the responsible person should be trained in first aid and should be available to attend to accidents during working hours. Where there are more than 400 employees there should be a first aid room.

Duties of employers: consultation with employees

1.18 Under the *Safety Representatives and Safety Committees Regulations 1977* and the *Health and Safety (Consultation with Employees) Regulations 1996*, employers must consult all of their employees on health and safety matters. This involves giving information to employees *and* listening to and taking account of what they say before any health and safety decisions are taken.

Notifiable accidents

1.19 Certain accidents must be notified to the environmental health department of the employer's local authority or to the area office of the Health and Safety Executive. The Reporting of Injuries, Diseases and Dangerous Occurrences Regulations 1995 (RIDDOR) require employers to do the following.

(a) **Report** immediately **by phone** if, as a result of (or in connection with) the employer's work:

(i) **Someone dies**, receives a major injury, or is seriously affected by, for example, electric shock or poisoning.

(ii) There is a **dangerous occurrence** (a significant event, such as electrical short circuit, or fire or explosion which could have (but fortunately did not) cause serious injury).

(b) **Send** a **written report** to do the following.

(i) Confirm, within ten days, a telephone report of a death, major injury or dangerous occurrence.

(ii) Notify, within ten days of the accident, any injury which stops someone doing their normal job for more than three days.

(iii) Report certain work-related diseases (such as asbestosis).

Case example: lighting and signage

In the past 12 months an unprecedented mass of legislation affecting emergency lighting installations has come on stream. If that is not enough, facilities managers are soon to see the European Work Place Directive - which has been with us for some time now - come into force.

The impact on facilities managers is going to be considerable. For example, if the facilities manager has specified emergency lighting products that do not comply with the prevailing standards, or if installations are carried out that are not in strict accordance with the latest legislation, the company - or possibly the contractor - will be liable. Certainly this is already the case with the Signs Directive.

So what are the most significant changes that have come about in the last year or so? In general, they cover the suitability of products to be used on defined escape routes - this includes the banning of acrylic diffusers - the Safety, Signs and Signals Regulations, which demand extra luminaries, and the need for two emergency luminaries in each lighting compartment. Other changes have included an increase in emergency lighting levels, the effective prohibiting of converting mains fittings by contracts, and the need to comply with the Low Voltage Directive.

More widely understood are some - although by no means all - of the implications of the Health & Safety (Safety Sign & Signals) Regulations that became law on 1 April 1996. All of the signs with green text on a white background must be replaced by 24 December 1998. In their place, the European-standard non-text pictogram should be used. The running man and text signs that comply with BS5499 can still, for now at least, be used on existing buildings only - not in new structures.

Facilities Management Journal, July/August 1997

---

2 SECURITY AND EMERGENCY PROCEDURES

2.1 The ICSA syllabus commentary says that you should know about 'The principles of security management, including security and emergency procedures, site access control, the protection of hard copy and computer information. ' We have dealt with this to some extent already in the context of **information systems** in Part B and in the context of **risk management** and insurance in Part C. You may wish to glance back through the relevant parts of this study text before proceeding.

2.2 In this section therefore we are simply going to outline some essential principles of security. We write from the point of view of office security, but although the physical environment and layout of factories, shops and so on may give special problems, much the same principles apply.

The principles of security

2.3 Security is a combination of **delay** and **alarm**. Delay is achieved by having several lines of defence before any vulnerable items can be reached. Typically an organisation has outer doors to its main building, then an area called reception, part of the function of which is to screen out unwanted intruders into the building. Depending on the nature of the business this may be manned by persons trained in security, but even if not the persons in reception should be aware of potential risks. Once past reception there will further doors guarding rooms where valuable items such as computers are kept, and lockable drawers and cabinets in which smaller items are kept.

2.4 Delay is not enough on its own, however. There needs to be some means of raising the alarm, once an intruder is identified, so that those responsible for dealing with the problem have time to get to the scene and take action. Electronic devices are one form of alarm system. The alertness and prompt actions of staff are another.

2.5 Alarms must be properly maintained. Over 96% of intruder alarm activations are reckoned to be false alarms and the police now operate a policy of grading their response according to the number of false calls.

2.6 Increasingly insurers insist that security systems are installed by a NACOSS (National Approval Council for Security Systems) registered installer.

Security risks

2.7 As we have said, security aims to prevent others from taking way or doing damage to things that belong to the organisation or the people that work for it. What type of belongings or people are particularly at risk? Here are ten suggestions.

- Cash and cheques
- Stocks
- Vehicles
- Moveable equipment such as computers
- Confidential files and documents (on paper or floppy disk)
- Ownership documents like share certificates, title deeds and so on
- Pass cards allowing access to the building, or secure parts of it
- Staff in the front line (security guards)
- Staff with custody of assets (counter staff in banks, warehouse supervisors and so on)
- Key personnel, who may be held to ransom

2.8 In fact *all* staff, not just key personnel, are at risk - anyone can be kidnapped or terrorised if they happen to be in the wrong place at the wrong time.

Security devices

2.9 Some methods of **controlling access** to a building are so obvious that you might not even think of them as such.

(a) Doors can be closed and locked. For particularly sensitive areas extra-strong doors can be used.

(b) Windows can be closed and locked. Sensitive areas may also have strengthened glass or even bars across the windows.

2.10 Cabinets, cupboards and drawers can also be protected by means of locks. Some items should always be kept in a safe, cash being the most obvious example. The more valuable the item, the stronger the safe should be. Most have keys and combinations. Some have electronically-controlled time-locks.

2.11 You are probably aware from personal experience of more sophisticated methods of controlling access, such as the following.

(a) **Plastic cards** (like cashpoint cards) that have to be inserted into a device at a door are used in some organisations. The card has a magnetic strip which is read by the device to ensure that the user is bona fide. If so the computer sends a signal which activates a switch to unlock the door.

(b) **Combination locks** in the form of electronic keypads can be used to control access. Only people who are authorised to enter a particular area are told the combination number which has to be keyed in on the keypad. This number triggers off a switch which unlocks the door. The code can be changed from time to time, for example if someone who knows it leaves as a result of fraud or in some other unpleasant circumstance, or if it has had to be given to decorators while they do their work.

(c) **Video cameras** (or closed circuit TV (CCTV)) may survey the entrance so that the person who is responsible for opening the door to visitors can see who is waiting outside. Alternatively, or in addition, there may be an entryphone system whereby the caller can be asked to state his business before he is allowed in.

(d) **Voice recognition** is used in some organisations. A computer controlling the door lock responds only to those voices recorded on its files. This method is far from common, however.

(e) In the future we are likely to see the development of systems that recognise visitors' **fingerprints** or the cornea of their eye. This is similar to the plastic card means of entry, except that it is harder to steal or borrow someone else's fingerprints or eyes!

Security staff

2.12 Manned security – in other words security guards – is seen as a necessity by many organisations, but this function is increasingly likely to be outsourced. The facilities manager is now best advised to look for firms that are registered by the **Inspectorate** of the **Security Industry** (ISI), a body set up in 1992 and operated by the security industry's professional bodies.

2.13 The ISI employs assessors, inspectors and specialists to conduct routine and non-routine examinations of all ISI-registered guarding contractors. ISI members are assessed for their compliance the terms of their contract, such as maintaining incident reports and records, personnel screening procedures, training, shift working practices, vehicle identification methods and control room facilities.

2.14 They are also assessed for compliance with the quality procedures standard, ISO 9000, and with BS 7499, which sets down in Code of Practice style what measures a security guard contractor should take to ensure its operation is thoroughly conducted. For example it has recommendations about keyholding, security of keys, and keeping a register of keyholders and occasional users.

Case example: Security systems

The system called I/NET, used by Control Systems International at their European Headquarters at Farnborough, is describe in the extracts below.

'It is a multi-user, multi-functional, distributed access control system: - it doesn't merely display activity and alarms, it specifically locates them on BMS-type graphics showing physical representations of every part of the building; it generates all kinds of user-designed management reports compatible with commonly used word processing packages; it differentiates between permanent staff and temporary personnel such as contractors and visitors; it can accommodate up to 255 different tenants as standard; it may be interrogated from remote locations for an update of an individual's access credentials, or in response to alarms, or merely for information; and it may be networked via commercial LANs or standard telephone systems.

It is well appreciated that electronic access control (EAC) systems basically operate by releasing and then securing doors, turnstiles and carpark barriers. But that is only the start of the operation when viewed in its entire perspective. Questions have to be asked as to which doors can be opened by whom, and which floors should have lift access by whom, and at what time. In addition, today's (let alone tomorrow's) all-embracing access control package should include video badged ID-cards that may also incorporate different reader technologies such as bar-code, magnetic stripe, proximity and even computer captured staff signatures.

And if access control is integrated with the building management system so that heating and lighting is activated when access by the first person to a particular zone has been recognised, and extinguished immediately upon departure of the last occupant, these systems become energy (and cost) savers too.

Facilities Management Journal, July/August 1997

Security procedures

2.15 Most organisations of any size have to have some formal security measures, if only to satisfy their insurers. The extent of the measures will depend on the risks involved in the business. Banks and building societies will obviously have more stringent procedures than a firm that manufactures plastic dustbins, say.

2.16 A formal security procedures manual is likely to cover matters such as the following.

(a) Procedures for **identifying regular staff** who enter the building.

(i) If the procedures state that staff should wear their identity badges at all times, then staff should do so, no matter how well known they may be to the security personnel.

(ii) If the procedures state that passes should be shown your pass to the security guard whenever people enter the building, people should do so, and they should not be allowed access if they do not do so, no matter who they are. The most senior staff should set an example to all others rather than indulging in rule-breaking ego-trips.

(iii) Likewise if people are required to sign in and out, everybody should be made to do so on all occasions.

(b) Procedures for **vetting non staff members**. For example if somebody is coming to visit the organisation on business they should be made aware of any special security procedures they will need to comply with in advance. It is common to ask visitors to bring the letter inviting them to a meting with them as a means of identification.

(c) Procedures for **non business visitors** - if a friend is meeting you for lunch, say. Some organisations will not let such visitors past reception at all. Others allow free access to non-sensitive areas. Procedures should not give such visitors the opportunity unwittingly to break the rules.

(d) Procedures for the **protection** of the **building**. Such and such a door may have to be kept locked at all times, for example. It may be the individual's responsibility to ensure that all windows in his or her working area are closed and locked at the end of the day.

(e) Procedures for the **protection** of the **moveable assets**. It might be standard procedure to lock away items like calculators in desk drawers at night, for example.

(f) Procedures for the **protection** of **documents** and **information**. Locking away files and ledgers, or not leaving your computer terminal in a state where it can be used by someone without the password are typical examples of measures of this sort.

(g) Procedures to **protect** the **procedures**. It ought to go without saying that passwords should not be revealed to others and there is no point in having doors or safes with combinations if the combination is given to anyone who asks for it. Likewise there should be procedures to control keys - a list of authorised keyholders and instructions about where keys should be kept. There is no point in locking doors if the keys are accessible to all.

(h) Procedures explaining **what to do** in the event of a **breach** of security. These should give the names and numbers of the people to ring and set out what information they will need to be told: location of the intruders, time of entry, how many there are and so on.

Security audits **6/95**

2.17 According to the Institute of Internal Auditors (IIA) Research Foundation a security audit 'should consist of a thorough review of security, organisational and operational procedures, and should assess the adequacy of the organisation's security protection relative to the value of its ... data and resources.'

(*Systems Auditability and Control: Module 9: Security*, 1991)

2.18 A security audit will consider a large number of issues. Some of the major ones are outlined below.

(a) **Classification of data and other valuable resources**

Is data classified to indicate its security status (for example 'highly confidential')? Is access to data protected according to its status (for example by a hierarchy of passwords)? Who is responsible for classifying data and authorising its use? Similar criteria should be applied to the new inventions, substances or processes that, say, a Research and Development department might produce.

(b) **Human resources policy**

As the IIA comment (our italics) 'employees are a principal security **threat**, and the first line of **defence** against possibly security violations'. An audit therefore needs to consider matters such as the following.

(i) Recruitment and selection: are checks made of potential employees' background and references?

(ii) Terms of employment: for example in the Civil Service employees are required to sign the Official Secrets Act.

(iii) Holidays: do some employees never take holidays due to them? Are they hiding something?

(c) **The security department**

The organisation and resources of the security department itself should be assessed.

(i) Is the authority of the department well-defined?

(ii) Does its position in the organisation support its integrity and objectivity? Who does it report to?

(d) **Awareness and training**

Are employees aware of the sensitivity of the information they handle? Are security procedures well-known and followed or are they ignored (for example, are passwords passed on to others)? Are reminders issued at regular intervals?

(e) **Physical security**

The IIA suggests that an audit of physical security should cover the following matters.

(i) What are the sensitive areas and perimeter controls?

(ii) Where are entry and exit points? (for example are there unnecessary or insecure windows?)

(iii) Are there procedures for authorising access to sensitive areas and are there monitoring devices such as cameras?

(iv) Are alarms installed where needed and are they tested regularly?

(v) Are there proper procedures for ensuring the safety of the electrical supply, maintenance of plumbing and so on?

(vi) Has the likelihood of threats from terrorists or political activists such as environmental groups or animal welfare supporters been assessed?

(f) **A security adviser**

The IIA suggests that security personnel should have a general knowledge of the topics listed below. This also serves well as a profile of the person best suited to undertake the security audit.

The advisor should be well-informed in the following areas.

(i) Computer hardware and software
(ii) Telecommunications concepts
(iii) Physical environment and security
(iv) Logical security (software controls)
(v) Database management and data access methods
(vi) Legislation affecting security
(vii) Accounting and auditing (for example so that audit trails are understood)
(viii) Management and organisational issues

Fire safety

2.19 It is estimated that fires and consequential losses cost British businesses over £500 million per annum. Around 50% of fires are started deliberately, and 70% occur outside normal working hours.

2.20 The main accidental causes of fire in industry and commerce tend to be associated with electrical appliances and installations, and smoking is a major source of fires in business premises. Flammable materials like clothing and some furniture are a danger, particularly in an office which is heated by electric bar fires. Flammable substances left in the wrong place can also be a problem, for example if an aerosol is left in direct sunlight.

2.21 Procedures should be clearly laid down and well known by all. Facilities managers should ensure that measures have been taken to ensure that *all* staff in the organisation know the answers to the following questions.

- Do you know what to do if fire breaks out in your workplace?
- Would you recognise the sound of a smoke alarm or fire alarm for what it was?
- Where is the nearest fire extinguisher?
- Is it safe to use a water extinguisher for any sort of fire?
- How do you set off the alarm?
- Where is the nearest fire exit?
- Should you leave doors open or shut?
- Does anybody know you are in the building?
- If you are not in the building, does anybody think that you are?

2.22 The general regulations relating to fire contained in the Offices, Shops and Railway Premises Act 1963 were reinforced in the Fire Precautions Act 1971.

2.23 The main provisions of the Fire Precautions Act are that:

- There must be adequate means of escape kept free from obstructions.
- All doors out of the building must be capable of opening from the inside.
- All employees should know the fire alarm system.
- There must be an effective and regularly tested fire alarm system.
- There must be fire-fighting equipment easily available and in working order.

2.24 Specialised buildings are covered by other legislation such as the Fire Safety and Safety of Places of Sport Act 1987.

The Fire Precautions (Workplace) Regulations 1997

2.25 European legislation will be implemented in the Fire Precautions (Workplace) Regulations 1997 which came into force on 1 December 1997. These regulations require employers to do the following.

(a) Provide the appropriate number of **fire extinguishers** and other means for fighting fire.

(b) Install **fire detectors** and fire **alarm systems** where necessary.

(c) Take whatever measures are necessary for **fighting fire** (eg the drawing up of a suitable emergency plan of action) and nominate a sufficient number of workers to implement these measures and ensure that they are adequately trained and equipped to carry out their responsibilities.

(d) Provide **adequate emergency routes** and exits for everyone to escape quickly and safely.

(e) Ensure that **equipment** and facilities provided to protect workers from the dangers of fire are **regularly maintained** and any faults found are rectified as quickly as possible.

Other emergencies

2.26 Safety procedure in the case of other emergencies will obviously depend upon what has happened; often it will mean **evacuating** the **building** according to fire safety procedures, but in a case of, say, armed intruders it might mean ensuring that certain doors are locked. In any emergency situation staff should be encouraged to do the following.

(a) Stay calm.

(b) Avoid personal danger.

(c) Call for help; contact the company's first aider or security staff as appropriate or, if no-one is available, call the emergency services.

(d) Help others to avoid danger if possible.

(e) In no circumstances move injured people unless it is more dangerous not to do so. Remove the source of danger instead, if possible.

(f) Do not attempt to administer first aid unless trained to do so.

Calling the emergency services

2.27 In the UK you can be put straight through to the police, the fire brigade or the nearest ambulance station by dialling 999. The operators are very well trained and will guide the caller through the procedure.

(a) Once the caller gets through they will be asked which service they require and be transferred as appropriate.

(b) The call will be traced automatically, in case it is cut off for some reason; the caller will hear their telephone number being given to the person who will deal with their call. The call is also tape recorded.

(c) The caller will be asked for details such as the location of the incident, what happened, the number and approximate age of any casualties and the extent of the injuries, if any.

(d) The caller should not hang up until after the people responding to the call have done so (otherwise they may not have all the information they need).

Case example: Contingency planning

'Routine maintenance work by the water board recently caused a disaster for the Bank of Finland when a burst main flooded its basement and shut down its computer. No sooner had the bank recovered from that disaster than a second one struck; a few days later and unrelated electrical mishap closed the system down again.

The Bank of Finland ... is now a veteran on business recovery. In common with most other financial organisations in the City, the Bank of Finland had a contingency plan already in place which included the transfer of all its computing facilities to a disaster recovery centre. Its experience was a happy one: after each upset, business was kept going with only the briefest interruption.

According to its assistant general manager, the bank learnt the following lessons:

- The time and money involved in setting up contingency plans was well spent.
- The recovery time from the second disaster was far quicker than for the first, demonstrating the importance of a full dress rehearsal
- The bank has moved its computer out of the basement to reduce future risk of flood, and has resolved to mount full electrical tests after any power failure
- Beds and showers are needed at the disaster recovery site, as staff are likely to work through the night
- The fastest way of getting documents to the recovery site may also be the cheapest - the tube might be quicker than taxis
- Lightning may strike twice'

Exercise

'Even big UK companies have a security and contingency planning approach which can be half-baked: most issue passes to visitors, for example, but few are so careful about collecting them and thus have little idea of who is in the building.

Similarly, they may have an evacuation plan but may not have considered whether this is always the best approach. One lesson from last year's explosion at St Mary Axe in the City of London - which happened after hours - was that staff would have been safer in a basement rather than on the street, where they would have been hit by flying glass.

Companies with closed-circuit television, meanwhile, sometimes render it useless by not watching it. Others check baggage, but in a predictable way.'

Financial Times, May 1993

Is there anything half-baked about your organisation's emergency plans?

3 ENVIRONMENTAL ISSUES

3.1 A number of environmental matters may significantly affect an organisation's business:

(a) Initiatives to prevent, abate or remedy **damage** to the environment or to deal with the conservation of resources

(b) Consequences of **violating environmental laws** and regulations

(c) Consequences of **environmental damage**

(d) Consequences of **statutory vicarious** liability (such as liability for damage by previous owners)

3.2 Certain industries may be particularly exposed to environmental risks. These include the chemical, oil and gas, pharmaceutical, metallurgical, mining and utility industries. More generally they may include industries which are subject to environmental laws and/or have business processes that:

(a) May cause contamination of soil and groundwater; contamination of surface water; or air pollution

(b) Use hazardous substances

(c) Generate or process hazardous waste

(d) Produce final products that may involve environmental risk to their users

(e) May have an adverse impact on health and safety of employees or neighbours

3.3 In 1998 the International Federation of Accountants (IFAC) issued guidance on environmental auditing. The guidance suggested that environmental auditing consisted of the following:

(a) Whether an organisation was currently operating in **compliance** with environmental laws and regulations

(b) How effectively the organisation's **overall management systems** and procedures achieved corporate environmental policy and goals

(c) Whether the organisation's **financial statements** reflected and presented fairly environmental costs and liabilities under current accounting rules

(d) If the organisation produced and published an **environmental performance report** as part of, or separate from, its annual report, whether this report was fair and reliable

(e) Whether **operational compliance information** provided to environmental regulators by the organisation was reliable

(f) Whether information reported by the organisation under **economic incentive** or other market-based schemes was reliable

(g) Whether the organisation's **products conformed** with consumer protection standards, labelling provisions etc

Environmental performance reports

3.4 An environmental performance report aims to report on environmental performance in the broadest sense. The European Union's EMAS Regulation for industrial companies states the report should contain:

(a) A description of the company's activities

(b) A description of the company's environmental policies

(c) A description of the company's environmental management system

(d) accounting policies for measurement and disclosure of environmental data

(e) Quantitative performance data covering for example emissions, waste disposal, energy consumption and environmental costs and benefits

(f) Improvement goals for the future

(g) A glossary

Chapter roundup

- In the UK and EU there is extensive legislation covering diverse issues such as noise, workstations, handling heavy objects, and general working conditions, and FM decisions need to be fully informed by legal requirements.
- Facilities tend not to be noticed unless they are not there or they don't work. Prevention is better than cure and so **security** ought to be very high on the agenda for all organisations. In essence, security is a combination of delay and alarm. Technology is having a major impact on the options available to prevent unauthorised access to things, places or people that need to be protected, but there is a danger that technology will 'cry wolf' too often and be ignored.
- Organisations are increasingly recognising the need to have formal procedures for dealing with security breaches that interrupt normal operations. A **security audit** will consider matters such as classification of data, human resources policy, the existence and effectiveness of a security department, staff awareness and training about security issues, and physical security.
- **Fire costs** businesses millions of pounds annually. Again, prevention is better than cure and effective access controls and devices to limit damage, such as sprinklers, are becoming a necessity in buildings of any size. There are also stringent fire regulations that *must* be complied with.
- The **facilities manager** is liable to be the first port of call in any emergency and ought to be prepared to deal with emergency situations, whether this means handling distressed employees, handling confused customers, handling the press, or handling the emergency services.

Test your knowledge

1 Why should employers care about accidents? (see paras 1.3 -1.4)

2 List eight health and safety regulations that should be considered by facilities managers. (1.6)

3 What are the general duties of employers under the Management of Health and Safety at Work Regulations 1992? (1.13)

4 How is delay achieved? (2.3)

5 Why should intruder and fire alarms be properly maintained? (2.5 - 2.6)

6 List five types of access control device. (2.11)

7 What might be covered in a security procedures manual? (2.16)

8 What should be covered in an audit of physical security? (2.18)

9 What are the main provisions of the Fire Precautions Act 1971? (2.23)

10 How would you cope with an emergency? (2.26)

Now try illustrative question 27 at the end of the Study Text

Illustrative questions and suggested answers

1 DECISIONS *25 mins*

(a) 'Groups are useless for decision-making purposes: they generate wishy-washy and feeble compromises which please nobody; they lend themselves to tyranny by an autocratically dominant individual; and it's too easy for them to be distracted from the their decision-making objectives by the search for scapegoats.' If this observation were made to you by a senior manager, how would you respond? Specifically, what use would you make of available research findings on say, group dynamics, team effectiveness and collective decision-making, in order to refute his views?

(b) What decision making forums would be appropriate for the following decisions?

(i) The acquisition of a subsidiary
(ii) A change in working conditions, such as longer working hours
(iii) The replacement of a company car

2 PUBLIC AND PRIVATE MEETINGS *50 mins*

(a) Distinguish between a public meeting and a private meeting. Consider the powers and duties of the police in relation to meetings held on private property.

(b) A meeting of twelve people belonging to the 'Society for the Protection of our Furry Friends' splits into three smaller meetings to picket a high street fur shop. Two groups of five distribute anti-fur trade leaflets at each end of the street whilst giving speeches about the evils of the fur trade. The remaining two people carry placards up and down the pavement in front of the entrance to the fur shop with the intention of deterring prospective customers. An elderly lady customer seeing the way momentarily barred complains to a nearby police constable. The latter radios for assistance. On the arrival of Inspector Brigg the meetings are directed that if they wish to continue they must move to a nearby open space. On their refusal to comply the three groups are arrested.

Discuss these events in the context of meetings and obstruction, public order and/or breach of the peace.

3 CHAIRMAN'S AUTHORITY *35 mins*

'The rules governing the conduct of debate ... ought to include various rules supporting the Chairman's authority.'

Discuss this statement giving examples of such rules. Comment on the extent to which these rules ought to be set out in written form.

4 AGENDA *35 mins*

(a) Discuss those procedures and points which ought to be borne in mind when preparing an agenda paper and considering its contents.

(b) Draft a notice of a meeting of an organisation of your choice with a skeleton agenda of not less than six items attached.

5 ADJOURNMENTS, POSTPONEMENTS AND AMENDMENTS *50 mins*

(a) Explain how a meeting may be adjourned, illustrating your answer by reference to decided cases.

(b) Distinguish a postponement from an adjournment and explain when a meeting may be postponed.

(c) A notice convening a meeting states as an item of special business the appointment of a manager at a salary of £11,500 per annum. A member proposes an amendment to substitute £14,500 for the sum stated in the notice.

(i) Discuss in the context of the rules on amendments.
(ii) Explain the grounds for a valid rejection of an amendment.

6 GOOD DEEDS SOCIETY *35 mins*

The Good Deeds Society's Management Committee is holding one of its quarterly meetings to discuss the society's financial position, the filling of a casual vacancy caused by the death of a member of the committee and applications by various social groups and charities for grants which the Good Deeds Society awards to deserving causes from time to time. Mr Latchford, a financial adviser to the society (but not a member of the Management Committee), has been asked to attend and advise.

You are asked to:

(a) Advise on the essentials of good minute writing
(b) Draft specimen minutes of this meeting.
(c) Advise in what circumstances, if any, those minutes may be altered.

7 CHAIRMAN AND SECRETARY *60 mins*

(a) Mr Duncan has recently been invited to become chairman of the 'Law and Order' society. The society is currently in the process of formation. You are asked to advise Mr Duncan on the qualities required of a chairman and the duties and privileges which go with such a position.

(b) The society's constitution is currently being drafted by founding members. Advise them of the rules concerning the appointment and removal of the chairman and any powers which might be given to him in addition to those at common law.

(c) You are the secretary of a society of your choice. An important annual general meeting is due soon. Explain the steps which you will take in preparation for the meeting.

8 ANNUAL CONFERENCE *35 mins*

A national society based on local groups has an annual conference to which each local group sends one or more delegates.

Discuss how such a conference might be organised. In particular, comment in your answer on:

(a) Submission and choice of motions
(b) Composite motions
(c) 'Stage managed' debates
(d) The use of procedural motions at such a conference

9 COMMUNICATION *35 mins*

(a) Information has been defined as 'data which has been processed in some way to be meaningful and useful to its recipient'.

Requirement

State and explain five of the general qualities of good information.

(b) Communication involves the effective transmission of information from one person to another. It is important to ensure that the information has been properly received and understood by the recipient.

Requirement

Write notes, using a system of your choice as an example, on the problems of communication to the right person.

10 CENTRAL DATABASE

The KN company manufactures a wide range of plastic mouldings. The mouldings are used in such diverse products as motor vehicles, garden furniture and children's toys. As a result of this variety, there are six different sales departments, a single manufacturing department and an ordering department. There is a separate IT service department which provides basic IT services to all the other departments.

The company has established its IT systems within each individual department. Each department has its own computerised records and databases. The IT department of KN has been very successful in previous years in meeting IT systems requirements and in providing a high quality of service to each user department.

KN now wishes to set up one central sales database that can be used by all departments. The database will include, amongst other things, details of goods, customers and debtor analysis. This will mean that the individual databases in each department will be amalgamated into this central database.

Required

(a) Explain the relative merits of the KN company concentrating its data and information on individual departments compared with centralising its database.

(b) Evaluate the problems that the IT department may experience in amalgamating the company's data into one central database.

Note: Your answer must concentrate on the data held by the company. Comments concerning hardware or the physical location of the database are NOT required.

11 THE ELECTRONIC OFFICE *35 mins*

The management of AD Ltd, a manufacturing company, are intending to update its clerical procedures with the introduction of an office automation system.

Requirements:

(a) Describe briefly the hardware and software systems which make up 'the electronic office':

(b) Discuss briefly the ways in which developments in communications and information technology (IT), such as telecommuting and teleconferencing, have increased the possibility of an employee working from home.

12 SYSTEMS CHANGE *35 mins*

ST plc is in the process of implementing a new computer system to replace its ten year old system. Each of the 200 staff members of management grade is being provided with a desktop computer with its own processing capability, although each computer is also linked to the office LAN. The aim of the systems change is to provide managers with more reliable and up-to-date information to assist them in the performance of their duties.

The LAN provides access to shared printing resources, fax and modem gateways to other branches, company databases and personal time-management software.

The systems analyst has identified the following human problems connected with the system implementation.

(a) The new system allows access by any member of staff into the diary and files of all other staff members (except for the files of senior executives). Individuals are concerned that they will lose control over their own diaries.

(b) Rumours abound concerning redundancies that the new system will cause, although these have been denied by management.

(c) The new system will provide information that managers previously had to obtain for themselves. This information will be stored centrally and be accessible to all staff. Some staff consider that their personal initiatives will not be apparent because they can no longer show their data collection skills. They therefore believe that their career prospects could be threatened.

(d) Finally, staff consider that they will be 'tied to their desks' all day long: they are concerned that the whole system will be de-personalising.

Requirements

(a) Produce a memo to be sent to all staff of management grade dealing with their concerns.

(b) Explain the role of the information systems manager in the management of ST plc's information systems, in the context of a systems change, as above, and in meeting the continuing information needs of the company.

13 OPERATIONAL SECURITY *35 mins*

With the emphasis on both the physical and confidential aspects of security of an accessible computer based information system, discuss available methods, both hardware and software orientated, of maintaining operational security.

14 FOUR COMPANIES *35 mins*

Four companies (A to D), which have similar activities but are not part of a group, have the following computer configurations.

Company A Three stand-alone microcomputers (CPU, VDU, keyboard, hard disk and mouse), each computer having its own printer.

Company B Small office with 11 microcomputers linked on a Local Area Network. Each PC has its own processing ability, but is liked via the LAN to central printers, disk storage, file server and tape streamer devices. The LAN is completely self-contained; there are no modems or other similar external devices attached to it.

Company C Four processing locations connected by a Wide Area Network. Each location has a LAN in the same configuration as company B, although there is also a dedicated land line to two of the other three offices (offices are connected on a ring to two of the other offices). Each file server is updated with data from the other three locations at 15 minutes intervals.

Company D Twenty processing locations, each with its own LAN in the same configuration as company B. All locations are connected in a star configuration to head office. File servers at each location are updated from Head Office every five minutes or less. Each location has a reserved external telephone line for selected customers to use; orders are transmitted directly onto company D's computer system.

Requirements:

(a) State, with reasons, for each company, what security procedures should be applied to ensure that there is no unauthorised access into its computer systems.

(b) Company B will be setting up additional branches and wants to upgrade its systems to duplicate those of company D.

Requirement:

What sort of data communication system would you recommend?
Justify your choice by explaining the advantages of the hardware and software aspects of your proposal.

15 RISK IDENTIFICATION *35 mins*

The following statement has been made: 'Risk identification is an attempt rigorously to identify all possible events, situations or activities which could cause or enhance losses. It has three main stages:

(a) An analysis of the major types of loss affecting the individual or firm
(b) A systematic search for all the immediate causes of such losses
(c) A systematic assessment of the underlying causes and their consequences

Describe how the above stated three main stages of risk identification are carried out in practice.

16 TWISTING BY THE POOL *25 mins*

Explain the pool concept in insurance and describe how it copes with a descending spiral of results.

17 UNDERINSURANCE AND CLAIMS *35 mins*

(a) Explain why it is important with property insurance to ensure that the sum insured adequately represents the value at risk.

(b) Give details of and comment upon the conditions which must be satisfied before an insurer will pay a claim.

18 CLASSES OF INSURANCE *45 mins*

(a) Certain classes of insurance are compulsory by statute.

Explain the reasons for this and quote three examples of covers bearing this compulsory requirements.

(b) In addition to protection against loss or of damage to property a company requires insurance cover against pecuniary losses to the business.

Describe two principal areas in which this protection can be provided.

19 PERMANENT HEALTH INSURANCE *30 mins*

Your managing director is considering various means of improving the conditions of his employees, one of which is providing permanent health insurance.

Write a memo to the MD explaining the basic features and benefits of permanent health insurance.

20 THE INSURANCE MARKET *35 mins*

(a) State and describe three main classes of insurance intermediary and outlines any relevant statutes governing the situation.

(b) Explain the reason for the need for control of insurance operations.

21 TRUSTEES *30 mins*

What are the duties of a trustee of an occupational pension scheme?

22 CONTRACTING OUT *25 mins*

Briefly describe the following.

(a) Two options for contracted out schemes
(b) SERPS

23 DISCLOSURE *35 mins*

There is an 'assumption of disclosure' in connection with a pension fund. How is this expressed in the annual report?

24 TYPES OF SCHEME *50 mins*

(a) Discuss the relative merits, from the points of view of both the employer and the employees, of occupational pension schemes which are structured on:

(i) A defined benefit basis
(ii) A money purchase basis

(b) Comment on the following statement:

'Employers need to consider how they will respond to demands for them to make contributions to individual employees' pension schemes; they will assent, increase salary in lieu, or support only the occupational scheme?'

25 COPYRIGHT AND PATENTS *35 mins*

(a) Discuss any significant changes in the law introduced by the Copyright, Designs and Patents Act 1988.

(b) Explain how the law of patents attempts to strike a balance between the interests of the investor, his employer and the public in general.

26 LOST IN SPACE *27 mins*

Facilities management, space management and premises management are new terms covering what the Office Manager has been doing as part of his work for a long time, ie managing facilities, space and premises.

Explain the benefits that should accrue from good facilities, space and premises management and how benefits can best be achieved

27 ERGO SUM *27 mins*

How does the physical and psychological well-being of office workers depend upon the application of ergonomics:

(a) At the office design stage
(b) In the selection of office machinery and equipment

1 DECISIONS

(a) The observation makes the following assertions.

(i) Groups make compromises when they are faced with a decision.
(ii) Groups are easily dominated by autocratic individuals.
(iii) Groups actively try to avoid responsibility for their decisions.

We shall address each of these points in turn.

(i) *Groups make compromises*

The research of writers such as Janis and Stoner on 'groupthink' and the risky shift phenomenon is quite contrary to this assertion. Janis found that groups could easily become so cohesive that they saw themselves as invulnerable and tended to be far more inclined to take *risks* than make 'wishy-washy' compromises'. Pet strategies tend to be followed rather than giving proper consideration to alternatives which might modify decisions. Stoner conducted experiments (admittedly of questionable validity) which found that groups were willing to make decisions involving greater risks than their individual preferences because the responsibility for the decision was perceived as being shared and therefore diffused, and because of the association of risk with boldness, entrepreneurial spirit and so on which tended to be highlighted in the course of group discussions.

The implication of this research is that although groups may not make *good* decisions, they will not make wishy-washy decisions.

(ii) *Groups are easily dominated by autocratic individuals*

The extent to which a group can be dominated by a single individual depends on a large variety of factors, particularly the positions held by group members in the organisational hierarchy, the personalities of the different group members and the knowledge and expertise of individuals in relation to the decision to be made.

Research into group behaviour (for example by Belbin) suggests that different individuals tend to adopt certain roles such as leader, creative member, supportive member and so on. It may be that a person who adopts the role of leader also adopts an autocratic style of leadership, but this is not necessarily the case. Research has found that there are a number of different styles that may be adopted. Ashridge Management College, as a typical example, carried out studies in the 1960s that identified four styles: the autocratic style, the persuasive style, the consultative style and the democratic style. Amongst subordinates there was found to be a clear preference for the *consultative* style. The implication in this context is that the natural tendency for a group is for it *not* to allow itself to be dominated by an autocratic individual.

(iii) *Groups search for scapegoats*

The implication here is that groups prefer to blame the consequences of their decisions on others rather than taking responsibility themselves. The senior manager who makes the observation quoted in the question appears to hold what McGregor would call Theory X views about people and work. One of the main assumptions of Theory X is that the average person avoids responsibility. McGregor put forward an alternative view, Theory Y, which argues that given the right conditions the average person will learn to accept and in fact *seek* responsibility.

Research such as the Ashridge studies referred to above also suggests that group members prefer to be involved in the decision making process, that they become more committed to decisions that they participate in, and that responsibility is therefore welcomed. This view is widely supported by research findings, from the Hawthorne studies of the 1920s right up to the present day focus of empowerment of workers, on the grounds that they perform most effectively if they are given responsibility.

(b) The answers to these questions depend on your point of view and the point of discussion that has been reached.

The final decision in the cases (i) and (ii) would probably be taken at board level, but there would undoubtedly have been formal negotiations with the management and owners of the acquired company in case (i) and with staff representatives in case (ii). There would also be meetings with accountants, financiers, lawyers and so on.

In case (iii) the decision might be made by an individual (the vehicle fleet manager) or in discussion with the person who was going to drive the car.

2 PUBLIC AND PRIVATE MEETINGS

(a) In the Public Order Act 1936 a *public* meeting is defined as 'a meeting held in a public place and any meeting which the public or a section thereof is permitted to attend, whether on payment or otherwise.' Here the emphasis is on the fact that a public meeting is one which is open to members of the public to attend.

By contrast a *private* meeting is one which is:

(i) Held in a private place, to which the public has no right of access

(ii) Generally confined to members of a constituted body or association.

It is, however, possible to hold a private meeting as an informal gathering of persons invited to attend.

It is not possible to hold a private meeting in a public place, since in that setting there could be no control over the attendance. A private meeting is typically concerned with the affairs of a particular body, which are of interest to its members, but not to the public generally.

The police have no general power to enter private property, nor any duty to do so, in situations where the organisers of a meeting call for their assistance in expelling trespassers. However, the police *do* have a duty to prevent *breaches of the peace*, so far as they are able to do so, and to arrest persons who persist in causing breaches of the peace. They have the power to arrest without warrant (and without having witnessed the incident) in such a case.

It is therefore well established that the police may enter private premises, without the consent - and indeed against the wishes - of the owner or occupier if a breach of the peace has been or is being committed.

The police right of entry to private premises was reviewed in *Thomas v Sawkins 1935*. In that case, there was a public meeting held in a hall (private premises) which the organiser had hired for the occasion. The police, who anticipated disorder at the meeting, requested the permission of the organiser to enter the premises. He refused his consent. The police then forced an entry to the premises and remained there. The organiser sued them for a technical assault. It was held however that in addition to their well established right of entry when a breach of the peace has been or is being committed, the police may enter private premises if they have reasonable grounds for believing that a breach of the peace *may* occur.

(b) These circumstances require the discussion of a number of different issues.

Obstruction

There are two possible obstructions here; the pickets may have committed an offence under s 137 Highways Act 1980, and they may have obstructed a police officer in the execution of his duty. This latter possibility will be considered below in relation to police powers.

Under s 137 Highways Act 1980, it is an offence to obstruct the free passage of the highway without lawful authority or excuse. *Broome v DPP 1974* establishes that the fact that a picket is peaceful does not mean that there is a lawful authority or excuse for the action; it will be almost impossible to raise a defence on these grounds. Any obstruction must, in addition, be 'wilful' by an exercise of the person's free will: *Arrowsmith v Jenkins 1963*. This is clearly the case here. The question of whether there has been an offence therefore resolves itself into a question of whether there has been an obstruction.

The test is whether a particular use of the highway is unreasonable, having regard to all the circumstances, including its duration, position and purpose, and in particular whether it causes an actual as opposed to a potential obstruction: *Nagy v Weston 1966*. Convictions have been obtained against a club tout who stopped four groups of persons within a thirteen minute period in order to engage them in conversation (*Cooper v Metropolitan Police Commissioner 1986*) and against a busker who juggled with lighted firebrands in the street: *Waite v Taylor 1985*. In the latter case, it was said that if the action of stopping on the highway cannot properly be said to be ancilliary to the exercise of one's rights to pass and repass along the highway, then it is prima facie unreasonable and there is an obstruction.

This statement of the law has, however, been doubted. In *Hirst and Another v Chief Constable of West Yorkshire 1986* (the facts of which are very similar to those of this problem, except that in the case the protest took place in a spacious pedestrian precinct instead of a high street), it was held that *Waite v Taylor* applied too rigid a test, and the less stringent approach of *Cooper v Metropolitan Police Commissioner* was approved. In particular, the test of reasonableness in

Nagy v Weston was emphasised. It seems that the approach taken in *Hirst's* case is to be preferred.

The court stated that the correct approach is to consider first whether there was an actual obstruction; unless it was *de minimis*, then any stopping on the highway was a *prima facie* obstruction. Secondly, was it wilful, and thirdly, was there any lawful authority or excuse?

Applying this approach to the facts of this problem, it seems that the matter is very much one of degree. There clearly is an actual obstruction (of the elderly lady customer), and we have already seen that the actions are both wilful and without any lawful authority or excuse. Whether the obstruction is *de minimis* is highly arguable. It is difficult to predict what line a court would take on the matter. Certainly the intention of the pickets to deter entry to the shop will be taken into account as a relevant circumstance.

It is also worth noting that in *Hubbard v Pitt 1976*, protestors in similar circumstances were made the subject of an interlocutory injunction on the grounds that they were committing a private nuisance, which may also be the case here.

There is the further possibility of some offence under the Public Order Act 1986 ss 1 - 5, and here much depends on the tenor of the speeches and placards being employed. If the placards are threatening or the speeches inflammatory, an offence under s 4 (causing fear or provoking violence) is possible, as is an offence under s 5 (disorderly conduct). The offender need not intend these effects, and harassment need only be likely as opposed to actual. Both these possibilities would seem relatively unlikely in the circumstances her, however. Certainly the conduct of the pickets is not such as to bring them within the ambit of ss 1 - 3.

Police powers

We must now turn to consider the actions of the police, and their powers in such situations. Firstly, the question arises whether the police have any power to issue directions to the pickets, in the way that Inspector Brigg purports to do.

Under s 14 Public Order Act 1986, a scheme of controls over public assemblies exists, under which the police may impose limiting conditions on public assemblies, provided that certain tests are satisfied. This would, in principle, allow the police to issue directions to the demonstrators, and at first sight it might appear that the police have acted validly and within these powers. Certainly the directions given are within the scope of the powers conferred by the section, and they are given (as required) by the most senior police officer on the scene. However, s 14 applies only to 'public assemblies', which are defined in s 16 as assemblies in a public place 'of twenty or more persons'. Here we are told that the number of demonstrators is only 12, so these statutory provisions cannot apply.

It is therefore a moot point whether the police have the right to issue such detailed instructions to small groups of people, and whether the subsequent arrests are therefore justified. One possible justification for the arrests is that the demonstrators were obstructing the police in the execution of their duty. This is a criminal offence often used by the police in public order situations, and is a powerful weapon against disorder, since it has been widely interpreted in the courts. No warning need be issued before an arrest is made.

The ingredients of the offence are firstly that it is wilful (deliberate), secondly that there is an actual obstruction and thirdly that the police constable is acting *in the execution of his duty*. This is important, since if the constable is acting outside the scope of his powers any arrest will be unlawful, and any subsequent detention will constitute false imprisonment. This third point is where difficulty may arise in the situation under discussion. If the demonstrators are obstructing the highway, then refusal to comply with an instruction to cease doing so (usually of the 'move along sir' variety) may well render their actions an obstruction of the police in the execution of their duty. If, however, there is no obstruction of the highway or other offence, the arrest is probably unlawful. Since the police have no general power to order individuals to move off to a particular place, an arrest for merely refusing to comply with the instruction to move to the nearby open space is highly questionable.

There is, however, one further ground upon which the police could attempt to justify their actions; this is where there has been, or there is a reasonable likelihood of, a breach of the peace. The power (and indeed duty) which the police have to prevent a breach of the peace is derived from common law, and is unaffected by the Public Order Act 1986 or the Police and Criminal Evidence Act 1984. In this context the police may disperse, detain or arrest individuals.

Breach of the peace is, surprisingly, not a well defined concept. The most generally accepted definition, derived from *R v Howell 1982*, clearly requires an element of violence to be shown in the situation. The approach taken in *R v Chief Constable of Devon and Cornwall (ex parte Central Electricity Generating Board) 1982* emphasises unlawful and physical obstruction, however, with the necessity of violence being less clear. It seems from subsequent cases and criticism that the former definition is to be preferred. In *R v Brown 1985*, for example, it was held that shouting and swearing was not a breach of the peace unless it gave rise to a reasonable apprehension of violence; similarly, in *Wooding v Oxley 1839* disturbances by noise at a meeting were insufficient unless violence seemed likely. It therefore seems that a breach of the peace is unlikely to have occurred outside the fur shop.

It is possible (though unlikely) that there is some behaviour here which amounts to a *likelihood* of a breach of the peace. The requirements here are less stringent - in *G v Chief Superintendent of Police, Stroud 1986* it was held that a mere disturbance was sufficient to give rise to such a presumption. Whether this would be the case here is doubtful, however.

The conclusion, then, must be that the police are unlikely to have acted lawfully in arresting the demonstrators, unless an obstruction of the highway can be shown to have occurred. The police cannot lawfully arrest in the absence of an offence of some description, and it is difficult to see what other offence the protestors are likely to have committed.

3 CHAIRMAN'S AUTHORITY

The authority of the chairman extends throughout the meeting; he has a complex role to fulfil, requiring skill, tact and preferably a good deal of experience. The nature of his task is such that it would not be possible to produce a set of written rules which covered all aspects of his position, but it is possible to produce some relatively concrete basis on which his authority may be grounded, and which should work in tandem with the large amount of conventions and rules of law that also influence the form and conduct of the debate.

Extent of a chairman's authority

In beginning a discussion of the rules that exist (in whatever form) to support the chairman's authority, it is important to first understand the nature of the chairman's task and the extent of that authority. His two major concerns are:

(a) Preserve order in the meeting, so that business may proceed without hindrance
(b) Be (and appear) fair and impartial

It is vital to the successful achievement of both these purposes that the meeting does not become antagonistic towards him or lose confidence in his ability to retain control; he should therefore tread a sometimes difficult line between sticking to the rules and becoming unnecessarily legalistic. Any rules (written or otherwise) which are designed to support his authority must therefore ensure that his freedom of action is not unduly restricted. It may be better to allow a point of procedure to pass by unnoticed than to insist on enforcing the absolute 'letter of the law' if this would make the chairman appear pedantic. Any rules should thus serve to underpin his authority, or to define its limits as opposed to dictating what he must do in a given situation (subject to certain limitations, of course, such as requiring him to closely observe the sometimes highly complex voting regulations which the organisation employs).

Procedures during a meeting

The generally accepted procedure that a chairman should follow during a meeting has a number of elements. He should keep the meeting to the agenda, taking the business in the order set out. He must, however, respond to the wishes of the meeting in most situations; if the meeting decides to alter the order or to withdraw a motion that has been put to it before a vote is taken, the chairman should comply with its wishes.

There are limitations, however, on this general duty to give effect to the will of the meeting, and these serve to illustrate the interplay between statute, internal regulations and convention. For instance, if it is clearly the will of the meeting that the chairman should adjourn, it is a sound general proposition that the chairman has no choice in the matter, and must obey.

However, there are situations in which he may refuse to do so. *Salisbury Gold Mining Co v Hathorn 1897* makes this clear, where the regulations prescribe that he may adjourn if directed to do so by the meeting, implying that he has the power to refuse if he sees a good reason why he should do so. In addition, the chairman is given some inherent power to unilaterally adjourn (to restore order in *John v Rees 1969*, to facilitate the business of the meeting by taking a poll in *R v D'Oyly 1840*, or in certain circumstances where the machinery of the articles has broken down in *Byng v London Life Association 1989*).

Role of internal regulations

From this set of rules on adjournment, it can be seen that some of the chairman's power derives from decided case law, some from convention, and some from the regulations of the organisation. The position is further influenced by statutes which have a bearing on the situation. Of these four elements, the only one over which the organisation can exercise any degree of direct control is its own rule-book (which in turn will affect the application of generally accepted convention, but cannot exclude the influence of statute or case law). The question therefore becomes one which asks to what degree can - or should - the internal regulations support or control the power and authority of the chairman.

The first part of the answer to this is that the degree of control is potentially very extensive. Returning briefly to the adjournment example, it is the regulations themselves that confer on the chairman the power to refuse an adjournment; they can easily exclude this power by simply using the words 'must adjourn' as opposed to 'may adjourn'. Similarly, the chairman will only have a casting vote if the regulations give him one. There is no automatic right of a chairman to be so empowered. So in some situations it is clearly desirable that regulations are produced to empower a chairman to take a particular course of action. Conversely, the regulations may be used to disempower a chairman from certain actions, but this is perhaps a more difficult and contentious decision to make.

A chairman is conventionally allowed a wide discretion to control the conduct of the debate on an ongoing basis. He may decide who is to speak next in a debate and call upon him to do so; he may require a speaker to be silent if the speaker has become abusive, inflammatory or irrelevant; he may intervene to restrain a speaker from interrupting. Whilst there is nothing to stop the regulations excluding such a power of a chairman, it would be clearly unwise to do so (the conventions only exist because they have grown up over time as excellent ways of keeping a meeting running smoothly).

Conversely, attempts to make these powers too well-defined may be self defeating; it is essential to allow the chairman to exercise discretion, to allow a speaker who has no right to speak to do so if this is tactful under the circumstances, or for the same reason to call speakers alternately from opposing factions. Any rule-book which sought to define these powers would have to do so exhaustively to allow the chairman this freedom of action, and would perhaps be rather pointless. The powers exist anyway under usual convention and are widely recognised and accepted.

Where written regulations may have rather more of a part to play is in relation to the powers of a chairman which will only be exercised *in extremis*, where he decides to have a disruptive speaker forcibly removed by the stewards, for example. It would perhaps be useful to be able to refer back to a body of rules which clearly display that the chairman is acting within his authority in this sort of situation, where the mood is likely to be inflammatory, and tempers are probably in danger of being lost (or have been lost already).

For similar reasons of clarity and to avoid doubt, it might also be useful to embody certain rights which are conferred by statute or case law. It is actually unnecessary to do so (these rules will apply whether the meeting (or indeed the chairman himself) is aware of them or not). However the ability to point out that the rule book confers a right to demand a poll, for instance, could be very useful if there is disagreement over whether there is a basic common law right to do so or not. Other strict rules of procedure (voting regulations are a particularly good example since the matter is so crucial) may also be usefully embodied in this way.

Conclusion

In conclusion, it might be observed that the general powers of the chairman to regulate the conduct of the debate on an ongoing basis are already clearly established by convention, and perhaps are best left in this 'unwritten rule' form, both to avoid unnecessary bureaucracy and to ensure that the chairman's discretion is widely drawn. His more punitive powers, however, might usefully be embodied in a written form, so as to form a 'backstop' to his powers - something to fall back upon where absolutely necessary. Finally the detailed legal regulations on the conduct of meetings might also be usefully summarised, both to ensure clarity and correct procedure; as the body of case law demonstrates, not all chairmen can be relied upon to be fully aware of their legal powers and duties, and mistakes can be costly.

4 AGENDA

(a) Agenda means 'things to be done'; it is the programme of business for a meeting. It will therefore play an important part in the organisation of effective meetings.

The form and content of an agenda is adaptable to the purposes which it serves. If the meeting is a recurrent one concerned with routine business, such as an annual general meeting, a very brief list of topics for discussion will suffice. But if the meeting is to take detailed discussions it is wise to include the exact text of the motions to be proposed, so that members can prepare speeches, consider how they will vote, decide whether to attend etc. If an agenda is prepared for the use of a chairman, he may need exact guidance for each stage of the business of the meeting, with information and procedural notes to help him preside with efficiency and tact. He may also have a blank righthand sheet of his agenda for notes.

The duty of preparing an agenda usually devolves on the secretary, who should keep notes of matters to be covered at the next meeting and perhaps consult the chairman or other colleagues before actually drafting the agenda. This will ensure that the meeting has a relevant and coherent schedule to work to. It sometimes suffices to issue an agenda to members as they arrive for the meeting. However, especially if there are related papers to read, it is better to issue an agenda in advance of the meeting, so that the groundwork can be done beforehand.

In preparing an agenda, the principle is to take routine business (requiring little time for discussion) first, then to move on to special or contentious business, and finally to 'round off' the meeting with a few standard short items. In this way it is ensured that items requiring longer debate do not 'crowd out' routine (but necessary) items, and that the attention of those attending the meeting is focused in an efficient manner. The order of events must always be logical - the previous year's financial report would always be considered before a decision is taken on the re-election of the treasurer, since a decision not to re-elect the latter will otherwise cause problems with the presentation of the former.

Using these principles, the sequence of events in most meetings will resemble the following.

(i) Preliminary formal business
(ii) Matters arising from the previous meeting
(iii) Ordinary business
(iv) Matters to report
(v) Special business
(vi) Closing items

(b)

$E = MC^2$ Scientific Association

Notice is hereby given that the Fifth Annual General Meeting of the Association will be held at the Falling Apple Hotel, Newtown on Tuesday 14 July 20X1 at 6.00pm to transact the following business.

Agenda

1. Minutes of the last annual general meeting
2. Matters arising from the minutes
3. Report of the Management Committee
4. Treasurer's Report
5. Election of Chairman, Treasurer, Secretary and Members of the Management Committee
6. Appointment of Auditor
7. Any other business

1 July 20X1

Signed I Newton
Secretary

5 ADJOURNMENTS, POSTPONEMENTS AND AMENDMENTS

(a) The meeting may always adjourn itself by passing a resolution to do so, unless the regulations restrict its power to adjourn.

If the regulations fix a quorum and that quorum is not present when the meeting is due to begin, or if the number present falls below the quorum level during the meeting, the meeting must adjourn or dissolve, as the regulations may provide.

The chairman has an inherent power to adjourn for a short period to restrain or avoid disorder: *John v Rees 1969*. He may also do so under any power given to him by the regulations. If, for example, the regulations give him power to determine when a poll shall be held, he may adjourn the meeting for that purpose: *R v D'Oyly 1840*.

If the chairman purports to adjourn without having power to do so, in the circumstances, the meeting may appoint another chairman in his place and continue with its business: *National Dwellings Society v Sykes 1894*.

The standard formula for a company provides that the chairman may (with the consent of the meeting) and *shall* (if so directed by the meeting) adjourn, in spite of the presence of a quorum and the existence of unfinished business. If the words 'and shall if so directed by the meeting' are not included, however, the meeting cannot resolve to adjourn without the chairman's consent; it is a joint decision: *Salisbury Gold Mining Co v Hathorn 1897* (where the chairman objected to an adjournment which would prejudice shareholders resident in another country).

(b) An adjournment is an interruption of the proceedings of a meeting before they have been completed. A postponement is a decision not to hold a meeting, which has been duly convened, at the time appointed, but to defer the meeting to some later date.

It is not legally possible for the convenors simply to decide to postpone a meeting. In the leading case (*Smith v Paringa Mines Ltd 1906*) an announcement was made that a general meeting was to be postponed, pending the outcome of a lawsuit. However a director and some shareholders disregarded this notice and held the meeting at the appointed time. It was held that the directors could not postpone a meeting once it had been convened by notice to members.

The proper course is to propose a resolution for immediate adjournment at the opening time of the meeting. There is no objection to issuing advance notice to members that such a resolution will be proposed, so that they need not attend. However they are entitled to appear and to vote *against* the adjournment if they wish to do so.

(c) (i) An amendment is defined as a proposal to alter a motion submitted to a meeting, by changing the wording of the original motion (either by adding, deleting or inserting individual words, or by substituting words or complete sentences for those of the original motion). Many of the rules governing amendments will be contained in the regulations of the particular organisation concerned, whilst others will be merely implied as opposed to expressly stated.

Rules for amendments

As a general rule, an amendment may be moved after a motion has been proposed, but before the original motion has been put to the vote. There is also no general rule that previous notice is required, though the rules of the organisation may demand it. If such a previous notice is required, it should be given to the chairman or secretary before the meeting, in writing, and should be signed by the mover of the amendment. If no notice is required, the amendment must still be formally moved, which (again depending on the rules of the organisation) may require it to be seconded. Since we are told nothing of the regulations of the company concerned in this question, it must be assumed that they are complied with when this amendment is moved. It is at least clear that the amendment complies with the requirement that it should be positive and not negative in character (a negative amendment is generally not acceptable since the same result can be achieved by the simpler means of merely voting against the original motion). It is also clearly relevant to the original motion, and we can assume that it does not conflict with anything already decided at the meeting.

A number of other procedures must be assumed to have been complied with. It must be moved (and possibly seconded) by someone who has not spoken on the original motion. As a general rule, the mover of the amendment has no right to reply (in contrast with the position of the proposer of the original motion). Only one amendment should be put before the meeting at any one time, and an amendment should not be accepted from the proposer of the original motion or from one who has moved an amendment to the original motion.

(ii) Some of the reasons for the rejection of amendments have already been mentioned in part (a) above. Before discussing these and others in a little more detail, it should be emphasised again that much will depend on the regulations of the organisation concerned, so the rules dealt with here are of general application.

Limitation on scope of notice

An amendment is subject to the rule that it must not go beyond the scope of the notice of the meeting; in other words, it must not introduce anything which, if accepted, might commit the organisation to something more onerous than was originally included in the pre-amended motion. It is arguable that this is the case here. However, where there is a real problem with this amendment is that it relates to an item of special business. Any amendment to a motion for the passing of a special form of resolution (in the case of a company meeting, for instance, a special or extraordinary resolution) should not be permitted, except where that amendment is very minor indeed. Examples would be the correction of grammar or spelling.

Here the amendment proposed is much more serious than a minor correction; it changes the amount of the salary proposed for the manager, and should be refused by the chairman of the meeting. There is a general rule derived from *Betts & Co v Macnaughten 1910* that where an amount of a proposed financial commitment is specified in the notice, a ceiling on amendments is thereby created. In some circumstances a reduction in the amount specified will be allowed (as long as this is not so dramatic as to change the whole character of the motion), but an increase in the figure should not be permitted.

The necessity for an amendment to be both relevant to the original motion and in conformity with the previous decisions of the meeting is to ensure that an amendment is not used as a 'back door' means of re-opening the debate on a particular subject.

An amendment should also be within the powers of the meeting itself (otherwise any acceptance of it will be *ultra vires*).

Chairman's power

The chairman also has an overriding power to reject an amendment which is in his opinion merely frivolous. This is a power which should be exercised with caution, however; a challenge to this decision is permissible, and a wrongful rejection of an amendment may result in the motion having been invalidly passed. In *Henderson v Bank of Australasia 1890*, a chairman rejected an amendment on the advice of the company solicitor. It was held that the amendment should have been accepted for debate, and that therefore the motion which was passed in its unamended form was not validly carried.

6 GOOD DEEDS SOCIETY

(a) The minutes of a meeting are a formal written record of its transactions, decisions taken and things done, but not a report of its discussions or of the reasons for its decisions.

The minutes should be headed to show what the meeting was, where and when it was held, and who was present. The minutes should then record any decisions taken:

(i) In clear and unambiguous terms
(ii) concisely, but in sufficient detail to make the substance of the decisions clear
(iii) in numbered paragraphs, with reference to previous minutes if necessary

If formal resolutions were carried, the exact words of each should be entered in the minutes. It is also necessary to record, as 'minutes of narration', that information was received and considered, or other action taken, on which a formal decision was not required. The minutes should be signed by the chairman as evidence of the proceedings.

(b)

Minutes of the Management Committee meeting of the Good Deeds Society held at 14 Lee Road, Newtown, on 15 November 20X1.

Present:

A Oke (In the chair)
B Goode
C Clearley
In attendance
The Secretary
R Latchford (Financial Adviser)

1 Finance. A report for the quarter ended 30 September 20X1 was submitted by Mr Latchford and was discussed.

2 Membership of the Committee. It was noted with regret that a vacancy had arisen by reason of the recent death of Mr E Tipe. The Chairman proposed and Mr Goode seconded a motion that Mr F R Vessent be appointed a member of the Committee to hold office under the Rules of the Society until the next annual general meeting. The Committee resolved accordingly.

3 Grants. The Committee considered a schedule of applications for grants submitted by the Secretary and it was resolved that the following sums be granted immediately to the bodies named below:

The Salvation Army	£200
Dr Barnardo's Homes	£300
The Mayor's Appeal Fund for local amenities	£100

Sgd A Oke (Chairman)

(c) The minutes are merely a draft record until the chairman has signed them. There are various procedures, such as the circulation of the draft minutes of the last meeting before they are signed at the next meeting, to enable members to comment on the minutes before they are signed.

If a minor alteration is proposed, the chairman may insert it in manuscript and add his initials to the alteration before signing the minutes as a whole. If a more extensive alteration to the unsigned minutes is accepted by the meeting, the minutes should be retyped before signature (and copies of the signed minutes distributed to members).

Once the minutes have been signed, they should not be altered by any direct erasure, insertion, etc. to the signed text. The correct procedure is to resolve at some later meeting to make a specified alteration; 'It was resolved that paragraph 3 of the minutes of the meeting held on (date) should be corrected by the insertion of the words "if approved by the Committee in due course" after the end of the second line.' To avoid overlooking such an alteration, there is no objection to a marginal cross-reference on the original minute - 'See minutes of meeting dated ... for correction'.

7 CHAIRMAN AND SECRETARY

> *Tutorial Note.* This is an extremely comprehensive answer. Yours is most likely to have been as long.

(a) The position of chairman of any society is likely to be rather demanding, and as a background to any specific qualities required, experience is invaluable. If Mr Duncan has (for example) served as a deputy chairman in another society, or has sat on a managing committee, he will find that the experience gained in affairs and procedure will stand him in very good stead.

Qualities

There are, in addition to this broad consideration, a number of recognised qualities which go to make up a good chairman (though common sense may dictate many others, depending on the circumstances of the organisation concerned).

(i) He will have to give immediate rulings on points of dispute or doubt, so he should have:

(1) A sound knowledge of the relevant regulations

(2) An ability to make up his mind without dithering

(3) Skill in communicating his rulings clearly, but tactfully and in a courteous manner

(ii) He should be, and be seen to be, impartial. There will be times when criticism is expressed which he personally may find unfair, or there is a strong clash of opinion between other members present. In either situation, whatever his personal views, the chairman should treat opponents with equal fairness - and his *own* opponents with as much consideration as his supporters. In particular, he should give them a reasonable opportunity to express their views, along with any minority interests at the meeting.

(iii) He should have the discretion to know when to insist on strict observance of correct procedure, and when a certain amount of relaxation will ease the tension. (If in doubt proper adherence to procedure may on the whole be safer.)

(iv) He should be punctual and regular in his attendance at meetings. If he cannot give his duties the appropriate amount of time and attention, Mr Duncan might well be advised not to accept the post, as he will be liable to be ineffective if he has to rush things through pressure of time.

Main duties

The main duties of a chairman relate to preserving order, making sure that correct procedure is observed, and ascertaining the 'sense of the meeting' on various relevant issues. His duties may be summarised as follows.

(i) Before starting the meeting the chairman should be satisfied that it has been *properly convened* by notice and is *properly constituted* by the attendance of a quorum. He should be watchful to ensure that a *quorum is maintained throughout the meeting*, of persons entitled to vote on each item of business under discussion, if the regulations so require.

(ii) He should do his best to *maintain order and harmony* (or at least courtesy). He should take appropriate action in face of disorder: his powers to do this are discussed below.

(iii) He should *guide the meeting through its business*:

  (1) Making sure that each motion and amendment is valid and within the bounds of the notice convening the meeting

  (2) Taking one subject at a time, in the order set out in the agenda (or any modification of it which may be agreed by the meeting)

  (3) Making sure that only those who are eligible to speak are invited to do so, and that they speak only once during a debate (subject to the right of reply in some cases)

(iv) He should *permit an adequate amount of discussion* on each motion, giving sufficient (but not excessive) opportunity of the expression of different point of view. He should deal firmly with irrelevance, long-windedness, interruption and signs of temper.

(v) If *points of order* are raised, that is complaints or queries regarding procedure, he should give immediate rulings on them.

(vi) At the end of a debate he must *ascertain the sense of the meeting* in an appropriate way.

  (1) At a small and informal meeting it may suffice for him to *sum up* the general agreement of the members on a particular conclusion.

  (2) In case of disagreement, however, and at any larger or more formal meeting, he should put the issue to the *vote*. If amendments to the motion have been proposed, they should be put to the vote in the appropriate order, before the original substantive motion finally comes to the vote.

  (3) It is the chairman's duty to *count* the votes and to *declare the result*. Unless his declaration is challenged at the time, it cannot usually be disputed later (unless the declaration itself is glaringly wrong - '4 in favour, 5 against, I declare the motion carried').

(vii) When the minutes of a meeting have been prepared, the chairman should satisfy himself that they are an accurate and complete record. If he is satisfied, he should *sign the minutes*. There may be procedures for consulting other members of a small board or committee before the minutes are signed.

(viii) In addition to his formal and public duties at the meeting itself, the chairman may have a part to play in the preparations for it. The secretary may seek his views in preparing an agenda, or may work with him on a statement which the chairman may be required to make at a general meeting of a public company or other large body.

To a large extent, the duties discussed above also delineate the chairman's privileges and powers. The regulations may confer on him further express powers (see (b), below) but matters related to the maintenance of order and the use of a casting vote are worthy of a little further discussion here.

Maintenance of order

In the case of disorder at a *public* meeting, the chairman has statutory rights to take certain actions. In the case of a *private* meeting, he may *order a disorderly person to withdraw* and, if he refuses, *order that he be removed.*

If trouble is anticipated, it is usual to arrange for stewards to be present to enforce the chairman's orders for expulsion, by *reasonable* force. This practice is recognised by the Public Order Act 1936 (s 2) which provides that it is lawful to appoint stewards 'to assist in the preservation of order at any public meeting here on private premises'. The same principle applies to a private meeting. But stewards have no greater protection under the law than anyone else if they use more force than is considered 'reasonable' in the expulsion of a trespasser.

If there are signs of serious disorder, the chairman has the right and duty (apart from any powers conferred by the regulations) to *order a short adjournment*. The way that this power should be used is indicated in two cases. In *John v Rees* in 1969, there was a meeting of a constituency political party, following a controversy in which the MP had just been expelled by the national executive of the party. In the course of heated and noisy argument there was 'bodily contact, but no real violence'. The chairman proposed a motion, of which no prior notice had been given, that the constituency party should continue to act in accordance with its constitution. When he failed to obtain acceptance of his motion, he adjourned *sine die*. The meeting, however, continued and passed a resolution to disaffiliate from the national party. The court decided that 'the first duty of the chairman is to keep order if he can'. and if he cannot, 'to make earnest and sustained efforts to restore order'. It is proper for him 'to summon to his aid any officers or others whose assistance is available', but if this fails and 'people are put in fear' (more than 'mere punching and jostling') the chairman should adjourn. In doing so he should act *in good faith*, so that order may be restored and the meeting may continue. An adjournment for, say, 15 minutes would be appropriate. An adjournment *sine die*, or to a later day, is likely to frustrate the purpose of the meeting and is more than would be required for a restoration of order.

In *Barton v Taylor 1886*, it was held that 'The same doctrine of reasonable necessity would authorise a suspension until submission or apology by the offending member'.

Casting vote

The chairman may also be empowered to use a 'casting vote'. A chairman has no inherent right to a casting vote, but he is not disqualified from casting an original vote as a member, merely because he is in the chair: *Nell v Longbottom 1894*. However, the regulations usually give him an *additional vote*, which he may cast in order to resolve an impasse - equal votes for and against a motion.

Although there are no formal restrictions on the use of a casting vote, the general view is that the chairman, whatever his views on the motion, should endeavour to be impartial.

Unless he considers that the interests of the body (a) require that the motion be carried, and (b) would be prejudiced if it is not, *he should normally use his casting vote against the motion*. It is argued that, with the votes equal, there is no majority in favour of the proposed change in the existing situation, and the chairman should recognise that fact, even if he personally supports the motion. On that basis a tied vote should be treated as a failure of the motion, and the casting vote should be used to confirm this by defeating it outright.

Much depends on the circumstances, however. If the chairman acts in good faith in using his casting vote, no-one can accuse him of misusing it.

(b) *Appointment of chairman*

An open public meeting would usually be presided over by a chairman appointed for the occasion by the promoter or organiser of the meeting. In the case of the more restricted and regular meetings of an established body, it is possible - and desirable - to aim for greater suitability, consistency and continuity in the chairmanship. This can be best achieved if the body chooses on individual, for his experience and personal qualities, to hold office as chairman for a certain period, and to take the chair at all meetings held within his period of office. This, then should be the starting point for the Law and Order Society. The regulations usually provide that the managing committee, which meets frequently, shall appoint one of its members to be its chairman and that he shall also be chairman of general meetings of the members of the body.

The chairman may be appointed for a *fixed term*, say one year, or he may be appointed to hold office *indefinitely*, until he vacates office or is removed.

Not providing regulations for the appointment of a chairman can be dangerous; if so, a meeting has an inherent right to appoint a person present to be chairman of that meeting.

If the resolutions *do* provide for the appointment of a chairman but he is not present, at a meeting properly convened, or he withdraws before the meeting has completed its business or adjourned, the meeting may replace him with a chairman of its own choice. This can be illustrated in the case of *National Dwellings Society v Sykes 1894*. At an annual general meeting of a company there was much opposition to and criticism of the board of directors, whose chairman was presiding. After the resolution relating to the accounts had been rejected, the chairman declared the meeting closed and left. The members elected another chairman and continued the meeting, passing a resolution for the appointment of a committee of investigation. The court decided that the chairman had no power to close the meeting without the consent of the meeting. The meeting was competent to replace him and proceed with its business.

Removal of chairman

If the chairman has been *appointed* under the regulations, which is the normal case, he can only be *removed* under the regulations: the meeting cannot usually vote him out of the chair. But a meeting which has properly chosen its own chairman may similarly remove him, by carrying a vote of no confidence and electing another chairman.

Powers of chairman

As regards powers that can be conferred on the chairman in addition to those at common law, these have mainly been outlined in (a), above. However, other examples include the power to adjourn the meeting in a particular manner, to decide that there should be a vote on a poll or to decide how and when a poll should be held.

(c) *Time of meeting*

The date of the annual general meeting of any body is normally decided well in advance, so the secretary will have little choice in the matter. He can, however, often choose a *time* for the meeting. This is not an unimportant factor, and considerations which must be taken into account include:

(i) The anticipated length of the meeting. A long session should obviously start early in the day, if possible.

(ii) The anticipated stamina and attentiveness of the participants. Members are unlikely to be at the peak of their energy and concentration if the meeting is held late in the day, or late in the week (say Friday afternoon).

(iii) The location of the meeting. Time must be allowed for members to get to the meeting, if they are not already gathered on the premises. Likewise, the meeting should finish early enough to allow them to get home (or elsewhere) conveniently.

(iv) Particular circumstances surrounding the meeting. The urgency of a matter to be discussed by a meeting may dictate its timing; documents may have to be produced to meet the last post, decisions may have to be reached before another meeting etc. A small meeting may also be able to take into account the personal circumstances of its members, in determining when to convene.

Location of meeting

The location of a meeting is also an important choice. An annual meeting, even if it is routine, is likely to require elaborate preparation. Unless there are appropriate facilities for holding the meeting on the premises of the body itself, the secretary will have to make arrangements to book a hall or assembly room elsewhere. If a guest speaker (or other important participant) will have to travel any distance to the meeting, the secretary may also be required to arrange his transport to the location, and possibly overnight accommodation in the area or arrange for the refund of his travelling and/or other expenses. Ideally, the location of the meeting should be chosen for its convenience and accessibility to as many of the participants as possible.

Having decided the place and the time for the meeting, the secretary has numerous practical preparations to make.

Before the meeting

The room must be set up for the meeting. In the case of a small meeting, this is unlikely to require much preliminary work, but at a public general meeting, the seating and other arrangements may include the following.

(i) There may be a long table at one end (possibly on a raised dais) on which the directors or members of a committee are seated in pre-arranged places, with the chairman in the centre (and the secretary alongside him).

(ii) The press, if admitted, like to sit directly in front of the chairman and his colleagues, facing them. The press are likely to require a table on which to write their notes.

(iii) The general body of the members attending the meeting are seated in the body of the hall facing towards the front. Alternatively, if the meeting is reasonably small, it may be possible to have tables set out as a ring, or four sides of a square, with members facing inwards.

(iv) The needs of members will vary. It may be necessary to have Non-smoking areas'; depending on the type of meeting, tables may be provided for members who wish to make notes; drinking water may be set within reach etc.

(v) It may be necessary to install a public address (microphone) system if the room is very large. An overhead projector or other visual aid may also be required, unless the meeting is small enough to enable copies of relevant material to be distributed, or to gather round' a small visual display.

(vi) The general suitability of the premises and its facilities will obviously vary according to the size and type of meeting. Attention should, however, be given to:

(1) The availability of toilets and refreshment facilities etc.
(2) The availability of parking, access etc.
(3) Lighting, heating and ventilation
(4) Decor (especially if the image' of the organisation or the meeting is important)
(5) Safety (for example, fire exits) and security, if necessary

Paperwork

Meetings inevitably generate a large amount of paperwork' for the secretary, along with the other general administrative duties required before, during and after the meeting. The various documents and other material that must be prepared, and either issued to members or brought to a meeting, include the following.

(i) *Notice and agenda.* It is usual to issue a notice and/or agenda in advance, with any attached papers that may be necessary. The Chairman will need a special agenda with procedural information.

(ii) *Reports and accounts.* These are the main business of an annual meeting. These must obviously be ready for issue at the appropriate time, and the secretary may have to keep in close contact with colleagues who are preparing material, and perhaps with photographers, typesetters, printers etc. if, for example, the Annual Report of the organisation is to be published as a glossy brochure. The material will usually be sent with the notice of the meeting, but the regulations may specify that the report or accounts, say, of a small club, may simply be displayed on its premises for a period before the meeting. The secretary should in either case ensure that the appropriate procedure is observed.

(iii) *Proxy forms.* Proxy forms (or cards) may also be sent out with the notice of the meeting, if the regulations allow for proxy voting: alternatively, the notice may state how and from whom a proxy form may be obtained. The forms will have to be prepared, and once they have been filled in and returned by members, they will have to be checked and summarised for the Chairman (who usually casts' the proxy votes as directed). They should be brought to the meeting, preferably listed under, or bundled into, For' and Against', for ease of reference. Lists of members and proxies will also have to be prepared for checking admittance and voting rights at the meeting.

(iv) *Polling lists or voting papers.* If it is anticipated that a poll will be demanded on some issue, and will be taken immediately, polling lists or individual voting papers should be prepared in advance.

(v) *Press announcements.* There may be publicity to arrange, including the reservation of space in newspapers for publication of advance information of the meeting in summary form. The Stock Exchange also requires advance information about the meetings of listed companies, including draft copies of other documentation (such as proxy forms).

All the above documents will require preparation to various deadlines - in time for the issuing of the notice, or the date of the meeting - but the administrative effort does not stop there. The secretary may have to take papers with him for distribution at the meeting, and should make sure that everything likely to be required is ready at the venue on the day.

If confidential material is distributed to a board meeting, the secretary must also think about collecting up, at the end of the meeting, any copies left lying on the table. His own files and material must of course also be removed from the meeting place and returned to his office.

The secretary should generally bring to the meeting any papers he expects *may* be required for reference at the meeting:

(i) At a general meeting of a company, a copy of the *register of members*, so that voting rights etc. can be sorted out on the spot if necessary

(ii) A copy of *standing orders* or other *regulations* governing the meeting, to settle any questions of procedure: similarly, a copy of the Companies Act, the Memorandum and Articles of a company etc.

(iii) A copy of any reports and accounts (if not already circulated) that are to be considered. It may be helpful to bring copies of such documents in any case, as some members are bound to have mislaid or forgotten their own

Certain documents - such as the register of directors' interests - may be required by law to be available for inspection before and during the meeting.

Security

If there is likely to be acrimony at the meeting, it may be wise to appoint stewards (preferably with experience of these situations); they should be identified by badges. If necessary the police should be warned: they are unlikely to appear at the meeting unless called in to deal with disorder, but it is helpful if they know in advance that their help may be required.

8 ANNUAL CONFERENCE

A well-organised annual conference is a means of 'bridging the gap' between the organisation and the body of its membership. This is particularly the case for a national society organised as a widely-spread collection of local groups. An initial step in promoting the desired atmosphere will be the selection of a time and place. Since such a conference is typically spread out over two or three days, a good choice of time is a long weekend (to minimise disruption to the working lives of the delegates), with the venue being (say) a seaside hotel, which can provide the facilities needed, and perhaps provide them more cheaply out of season. The social aspects of a conference (an annual dinner, the opportunity for other evening entertainment, etc) should not be ignored, and such a location offers the opportunities required.

The practical arrangements for such a conference are numerous. Much of the business will be transacted in full or 'plenary' session in a large room or hall, and the organisers should pay attention to the following points.

(a) Delegates should have badges or tickets to distinguish them from others. Admission is usually restricted to members, press representatives and invited visitors; all of these must be clearly identified.

(b) If the conference hall has numbered rows of seats, each delegate should be allotted his place for the duration of the conference. It is also necessary to decide which individuals should be seated on the platform (this may vary from time to time during the conference). The chairman should, of course, have a central or otherwise prominent position.

(c) There may be standing orders on speeches which, for example, limit their length or require advance notice of the intention to propose a motion or speak in a debate. It may be necessary for a public address system to be used, which will necessitate speakers coming out from the main body of the hall to the podium in order to address the meeting. Material may have to be distributed to the press about debates, before or after they have taken place. All these matters must be planned for in advance.

(d) A detailed schedule of events is often necessary, allocating time to each subject, since the number of topics which members wish to discuss, and the remarks which they wish to make upon them, tend to exceed the time available. It is often necessary to prepare a list of speakers in advance, to which the chairman should endeavour to conform.

(e) Effective means of voting, often involving 'card votes', and means of declaring the result should be planned in advance.

(f) Arrangements must be made to take minutes of the proceedings, and possibly notes for the publication of fuller extracts from major speeches, etc. It is often the case that the society's journal will publish such reports, and adequate reporting procedures should therefore be set up.

(g) Suitable arrangements for any press reporters present must be made. These will include reserved seats (usually at the front, below the platform), writing facilities, accreditation cards to secure admission, and copies of pre-prepared speeches.

(h) It is usual to set up a 'conference office' in or near the main hall, to provide information, sort out problems and receive complaints. Delegates are usually required to register at the office on arrival, so that records may be kept and badges, etc. issued. A shift system may be necessary to ensure that the office is manned at all times.

Submission and choice of motions

Particular attention should be focused on the motions which will be proposed to the conference. Submission of such motions is usually organised on the basis that an organising committee (a sub-committee of the national executive committee or other such controlling body) receives motions from all of the local groups and vets them. The committee is charged with the job of choosing which are to be debated at the conference itself. There is usually some procedure for challenging the decisions of such a committee, but their choice of motions is likely to prevail in most cases. The committee can, of course, be controlled ultimately by voting its members out of office at the conference itself, should committee decisions prove unpopular.

Composite motions

One widely-used method of organising motions effectively is the use of the 'composite motion', by which a larger number of broadly similar motions are amalgamated into one 'umbrella' motion covering all the main points raised. This has the advantage of preventing the conference from degenerating into a series of very similar debates, and gives the organising committee a large degree of control of the business which comes before the delegates for discussion. Some degree of feedback between the committee and the local branches is required to secure agreement on the composite, and to obtain a proposer and seconder for the newly-formed motion. The committee can ensure by this means that the proposer is, for example, a good speaker (important if the conference is to be interesting and successful) or, rather less scrupulously, that he or she favours the position of the platform at that particular issue.

Stage managed debates

The above also provides an example of how a debate may be 'stage managed' by those in charge of the conference. The degree to which this stage management will be possible depends greatly upon the rules of debate of the organisation concerned. For example, the organising committee may, where it is necessary to submit the names of speakers in advance, choose a predominance of speakers who favour the platform's policies on a particular issue. Rather more subtly, they may choose a balance between opposing factions, but call upon the good, persuasive speakers from the faction which they support, whilst calling only poor speakers from the opposing faction. Where there is no necessity to submit speakers in advance, but the choice is left to the chairman's discretion, it may be useful to 'prime' a sufficient number of sympathetic delegates in advance, so that when hands are raised to indicate the desire to speak, there is a better than average chance of a sympathetic speaker being called upon.

Procedural motions

Another method of controlling the course of a debate (and sometimes its outcome) is the use of procedural motions. These may be used to cut short a debate where the majority wish to restrict discussion on a particular issue, or to delay business (a 'dilatory' motion) by shelving the debate to a later date. Examples of the former include 'previous question', ending the debate on the motion without a vote, and 'closure', leading to an immediate vote on the motion without further ado. The latter category can be represented by a motion for adjournment, to postpone consideration of a subject, or that 'that the question should lie on the table'. All of these can be used for perfectly legitimate purposes, such as the stifling of an attempt to filibuster, but may also be used to exert a degree of subtle control over the proceedings. The chairman, however, retains a general power to refuse a procedural motion if he considers it to be submitted for an improper purpose, which may help to minimise abuses of the system.

9 COMMUNICATION

(a) *Qualities of good information*

Relevance. Information must be relevant to the purpose for which a manager wants to use it. In practice, far too many reports fail to 'keep to the point' and contain purposeless, irritating paragraphs which only serve to vex the managers reading them.

Completeness. An information user should have all the information he needs to do his job properly. If he does not have a complete picture of the situation, he might well make bad decisions.

Accuracy. Information should obviously be accurate because using incorrect information could have serious and damaging consequences. However, information should only be accurate enough for its purpose and there is no need to go into unnecessary detail for pointless accuracy.

Clarity. Information must be clear to the user. If the user does not understand it properly he cannot use it properly. (Lack of clarity is one of the causes of a breakdown in communication, which is referred to in information system theory as 'noise'.

Confidence in the information received. Information should be accurate and the person to whom it is communicated should also be confident it is accurate. The quality of communications is determined by the confidence that key people throughout an organisation have in each other's ability.

Communication to the right person. Within any organisation, individuals are given the authority to do certain tasks, and they must be given the information they need to do them.

Volume of information, conciseness and reporting by exception. There are physical and mental limitations to what a person can read, absorb and understand properly before taking action. An enormous mountain of information, even if it is all relevant, cannot be handled. Reports to management must therefore be clear and concise and in many systems, control action works basically on the 'exception' principle. This is especially true of tactical information for management control. *Exception* reporting is defined as 'a system of reporting based on the exception principle which focuses attention on those items where performance differs significantly from standard or budget'. (CIMA Management Accounting: Official Terminology)

Timing of information. Information is not available until after a decision is made will be useful only for comparisons and longer-term control, and may serve no purpose even then. Information prepared too frequently can be a serious disadvantage. If, for example, a decision is taken at a monthly meeting about a certain aspect of a company's operations, information to make the decision is only required once a month, and weekly reports would be a time-consuming waste of effort.

Appropriate *channel of communication.* There are occasions when using one particular method of communication will be better than others. Some information is best communicated informally by telephone or word-of-mouth, whereas other information ought to be formally communicated in writing or figures. In designing computer systems, the designer will often have to choose between output of information on to VDU or printed output (or both).

Value of information. Information should have some value, otherwise it would not be worth the cost of collecting and filing it. The benefits obtainable from the information must also exceed the costs of acquiring it, and whenever management is trying to decide whether or not to produce information for a particular purpose (eg whether to computerise an operation or to build a financial planning model) a cost/benefit study ought to be made.

(*Tutorial note.* Only five were required)

(b) *Communication to the right person*

Information that is needed might be communicated to the wrong person. In other words, it might be communicated to a person who does not have the authority to act on it or who is not responsible for the matter and so does not see any need to act on it.

The most serious examples of sending information to the wrong people involve communications to the 'wrong' level in the management hierarchy. A person who needs the information might not receive it because:

(i) It is sent to his superior who does not pass it on to him.
(ii) His subordinate has the information but sits on it.

If people at different levels of seniority in an organisation all need the same information (to a greater or lesser degree of detail or accuracy) the information system should be designed so as to ensure that they are all sent the information they need.

However, not all information is 'routine' and in exceptional cases confusion might be caused by the type of information being sent, not lack of clarity in the hierarchy of management responsibility.

If a company is sufficiently small, this will not to be too much of a problem, provided that managerial roles are fairly well defined. In a small 'informal' organisation responsibility might be blurred. While the reporting of routine information is not affected, the reporting of non-routine information may be a problem.

A particular problem with any electronic mail system is the implementation of procedures to ensure that everybody on the network checks their mailbox regularly. Otherwise the advantages of speed that such a system offers will be lost.

10 CENTRAL DATABASE

(a) *Concentrating data and information on individual departments*

At present the KN company has six different sales departments, reflecting the diversity of its range of customers. Its sales systems were originally computerised in a way that reflected this business structure, probably solely with a view to automating existing clerical procedures to gain typical computer advantages such as speed of processing, greater accuracy, better presented reports and so on.

The present system has other advantages that should not be overlooked when considering change.

(i) Both sales staff and IT staff are familiar with the present system and it appears to meet current requirements. There may be some opposition from staff to attempts to change the system: they may very reasonably argue 'if it ain't broke, don't fix it'.

(ii) The division into six separate departments is likely to have occurred for sound organisational reasons, and these are now likely to be supported by the systems operating in separate departments.

(1) Perhaps the division allows sales staff to specialise in dealing with a certain type of customer and give a better service.

(2) Perhaps it is a way of coping with large volumes of processing, keeping the work within a manageable span of control.

(3) Perhaps systems in some departments are set up to process small volumes of high value transactions while others are designed to process large numbers of small transactions.

Changing the system may undermine the benefits that accrue from current arrangements.

(iii) Amalgamating the systems is likely to be problematic. This is discussed further in part (b).

Centralising the database

Conventionally the central database approach is felt to have advantages for the following reasons.

(i) It avoids duplication of data. For instance (assuming that a plastic moulding may serve a number of different purposes), KN may have customers that buy components through separate departments, so that a single customer will have several different accounts with KN, and their personal details will be held on several different parts of the system. This is a waste of storage space, and a waste of inputting time, because any changes have to be re-input several times to each different system.

(ii) It ensures consistency of data. Continuing with the example, Department A may receive notification of a change in a customer's personal details and amend its records accordingly. If Department B does not receive notification of the change it may, say, send out marketing mailshots to the wrong address. KN as a whole may not know which set of details is the most up-to-date.

(iii) Analysis of sales information at a management level above that of the six divisions is much easier, and understanding of customers' needs should improve. A customer's buying patterns with one department may suggest useful marketing initiatives in other departments, and a centralised database will make this analysis and action possible. New patterns may be revealed by a comparison between different sets of sales data that had not been realised in the past, facilitating forecasting and giving rise to new ideas to improve the level of service given to customers.

(iv) Systems development in the future is forced to take account of the *compatibility* of systems and standards. Compatibility between systems will simplify the support work of the IT department, offer more flexibility for staff (who can more easily move between departments), and avoid being tied to specific IT suppliers. Upgrades can be global rather than piecemeal, and this should enhance control of expenditure on IT and probably save money, thanks to bulk discounts and the like.

Relative merits

The database approach has clear advantages if there genuinely is duplication of data and processing effort. Opposition from staff can probably be overcome if they can be convinced that the new system has strong business benefits, will help them to do their present jobs more effectively, and perhaps offer them new opportunities within the company.

However, it is not at all clear from the scenario that there *is* duplication of data: perhaps it is unlikely that motor vehicles use many of the same components as pieces of garden furniture or children's toys. Further investigation of the business benefits is desirable, to ensure that there are likely to be new revenue-earning opportunities and that processing costs will be reduced. Problems such as those detailed in part (b) must be identified and solutions must be found before the changeover goes ahead.

(b) *Problems in amalgamating the company's data*

Problems are likely to be numerous.

(i) The *compatibility* between systems has already been mentioned. This is not just a matter of whether one system's files are computer-sensible to another system. It may extend to matters such as different systems of coding, different formats for personal data (with/without a contact name? with/without phone or fax number, and so on), different field sizes.

New standards that apply across the board can be developed, but implementing them is likely to require a great deal of collection of data and inputting. KN must acquire and test conversion software and ensure that they have sufficient staff to perform and check the conversion.

(ii) There is great potential for loss or corruption of data during the conversion process. Depending on the extent of the loss this could mean a small amount of rekeying or it could be a disastrous, permanent loss of valuable information needed for sales management.

Full back-ups should be taken at the start of the process, and back-ups of information on the old system should continue during any period of parallel running.

(iii) It is unlikely that current individual systems have sufficient *storage* space to accommodate the combined data. This can easily be resolved, but it must be resolved with an eye to the future growth of the combined business and future use of the database to store both existing information and new information that has not been available in the past.

(iv) *Access* to data must not suffer. Operational users will be attempting to extract information from a much larger pool, and the system must be designed in such a way that they do not have to wade through large amounts of data that is irrelevant to them to find what they need. If this aspect is neglected the new system could seriously undermine users' ability to respond to queries.

Those developing the system therefore need to consult widely with users at the sharp end of processing to ensure that their current information needs are understood and can be met by the new data architecture.

(v) As well as offering the potential for new kinds of report the system must continue to support present requirements for *management reports* that are essential to the smooth running of the business. Amalgamation could inadvertently break down links between data items and make it impossible to pull off a much needed daily report.

Once more, extensive consultation with users is essential.

(vi) Once the data has been amalgamated the business faces the task of ensuring that it is secure. A systems failure will now mean that no part of the sales function can operate, rather than at most just one part.

Dealing with this is likely to mean changes in the role and structure of the IT department. New, centrally administered back-up procedures will be needed, and contingency arrangements must be worked out and put in place to ensure that the risks to the business of systems disasters are minimised.

11 THE ELECTRONIC OFFICE

(a) The electronic office has come about thanks to advances in computer and communications technology. The term 'electronic office' is used to describe an office environment which makes use of these twin technologies in the course of data processing and information handling. The typical electronic office will have a number of visible features and underlying processes not inherent in the non-automated office environment.

The first obvious feature of the electronic office is likely to be the PC. There may be as many as one per desk. A PC workstation will consist of a PC (basic module, keyboard VDU), connected to a printer. Printers will be shared between a number of PCs. Each PC is unlikely to be a stand-alone machine. In a typical electronic office it will be connected to an internal communications system and to an external communications system. The internal communications system is provided by means of a local area network (LAN). This links the user to other similar computers so that users can make use of common data and communicate with one another. The external communications system is provided by means of telecommunications links, and terminals include facsimile and telex machines and telephones.

The hardware in the electronic office is used to run applications software programs. There will be a number of pieces of packaged software in any electronic office. Packaged software is cheap by comparison with tailor-made packages and is generally very user-friendly.

The most important package in the electronic office is likely to be a word processing package. This allows the user to input text and store it for subsequent retrieval or editing. The user can produce high quality documents. If the user has a desktop publishing package, which is based on a WP package, he will be offered a range of additional features including a graphics application and a page layout function. This will provide suitable output for reports and tender documents.

A manufacturing company like AD Ltd will also be able to make use of spreadsheet packages, for example Microsoft Excel. A spreadsheet package will enable staff to perform a range of tasks from basic calculations and preparation of tables through to complex financial modelling. A spreadsheet is effectively an electronic piece of analysis paper, divided into rows and columns. Each row and column configuration represents a cell, into which the user can insert data, formulae or labels. A typical package also offers sophisticated menus, help screens, edit functions and statistical and mathematical functions.

AD Ltd may also be looking to computerise its accounting function, in which case it will require an accounts package. In their most basic form accounts packages are simply a series of electronic ledgers. Complete accounts packages are usually fairly cheap single-user systems; more sophisticated packages may be modular in nature, allowing a gradual build-up to a complete system.

AD Ltd may also use a database package. This will enable users to share common data for different purposes.

For internal communications AD Ltd may consider the use of electronic mail. This enables memos and letters to be sent from department to department by registered users without the necessity for hard copy to be generated. E-mail is a feature frequently available on integrated packages, which also offer spreadsheeting, wordprocessing and a database in a single package.

For external communications AD Ltd will use facsimile for transmitting and receiving text, diagrams and charts and telex for text. The company may also link up to external information services such as the Internet.

(b) It is now quite possible technically for employees of many descriptions to work from home. A PC sited at home enables a user to handle data just as if he were in the office, using spreadsheet and word processing packages. Links to the office provide a means of transmitting information and receiving new data. Links are provided by means of a modem at each end of the telephone line. The modem, or modulator-demodulator, converts the digital signals used by the computer to analogue signals for transmission along the telephone line; at the other end of the line they are reconverted by the second modem. A network enables communication with the office by e-mail. E-mail systems allow whole documents (eg reports) to be sent as attachments to memos.

Advantages of telecommuting are the savings of office space and the elimination of travelling time. A disadvantage is the loss of face-to-face contact, which can be very important in meetings and negotiations and is not fully compensated for by mail or by phone calls. A means of overcoming this is teleconferencing. Teleconferencing involves the use of video technology. Each party sits in front of a video camera and looks at a video monitor sited next to the camera. This configuration is mirrored by the other party to the conference, so that each can see and be seen. This overcomes a lot of the psychological difficulties of parties not meeting face-to-face. It is particularly useful for international meetings.

12 SYSTEMS CHANGE

(a) MEMORANDUM

To: All staff of management grade
From: Systems analyst
Date: 14 June 20X9
Subject: New computer system

The purpose of this memo is to bring you up to date with the development of the new system and to publicise replies to one or two individual enquiries which I have received, as I think that this will be of value to all of us.

Status

We have sent out invitations to tender to five network system suppliers and will commence evaluation of their proposals at the end of this month.

Diaries

Concern has been expressed over the degree of access allowed by the system into individual diaries and files. The computerisation of diaries will make it much easier for colleagues and workgroups to co-ordinate meetings and plan ahead. No longer will it be necessary for secretaries and managers to play 'telephone tag' trying to arrange appointments. One of the reasons for specifying the personal diary management facility was the high number of meetings (involving 3 or more people) which suffered from frequent re-arrangement after provisional booking. I would point out that each individual (plus secretary, if appropriate) has ultimate capability to 'ink in' a pencilled in appointment and send confirmation back to the arranger. (Of course, you do not need to keep personal appointments on file if you wish to maintain confidentiality!).

As for other files, this will enable us to overcome the problems of having to track down files when one member of staff if out of the office, whether for half a day or for two weeks. Each hard disk drive can be accessed from any other desktop computer; this will eliminate much inefficiency and frustration. Again, if you have truly confidential files, then back them up on floppies and clear them from the hard disk in the same way as you do at present with standalone PCs. The emphasis is on co-operation and collaboration. We all share ideas verbally and in writing; the aim is to do the same electronically.

Redundancies

There have been some rumours about redundancies. This type of system is designed to improve the quality and flow of information coming to each of you. It is not designed to automate the work which any of you perform, simply to make it easier to carry out. Redundancies are only likely to occur where a system is introduced to automate repetitive processing tasks performed by a clerical workforce. They are much less likely where this type of system is implemented, as computers are less suited to performing managerial work.

The reason for introducing this system is to improve management performance, not to replace it.

Career prospects

It is true that the system will speed up and streamline data collection. If you stop and think, it should be clear that, as managers, you are not employed to perform data collection routines, you are employed to *use* available data in the management of your area of responsibility. Improved information provided to you more quickly can only help this process.

Familiarisation with computers and the acquisition of 'computer literacy' skills will certainly enhance your career prospects, as you will be gaining new skills and abilities.

Depersonalisation

There has been concern expressed about staff being 'tied to their desks'. Given that the computers are being provided primarily for the purposes already described, time spent sitting at your desks is likely to replace time spent looking through files or requesting information from secretaries or assistants. The new system is not going to change the *nature* of your job. This means that to the extent that your jobs already involve personal contact, this will continue.

The system may give you further scope for improvements in efficiency, for example if you do not wish to travel to the other end of the country for a meeting, you might be able to converse using email. Video conferencing links will be set up at our main sites and where these are used for meetings, you will find that much of the 'depersonalisation' inherent in some forms of electronic communications is eliminated.

Conclusion

I hope that this memo helps to allay some of your concerns. If you have any other issues which you wish to raise, please do not hesitate to contact me and I will endeavour to reply in the next update bulletin.

Signed: Systems analyst

(b) The role of the information systems manager at ST plc will be as follows.

Systems change

This has two elements: strategic and development. The strategic element includes developing, publicising and enforcing guidelines (for example technical standards for hardware and software). Part of strategic control involves Information Systems planning. This may be a function shared between IS personnel and personnel in the corporate planning department, if there is one. IS planning can only be successful if there are inputs from users: IS plans should be tied into the overall business plan of the organisation. Planning activities include development of procedures and standards for guidance of staff (for example choice of systems development methodologies and control) and assigning development work to subordinates, and liaising with users to assess their needs.

The development element includes control over systems design, programming and so forth. Systems development takes up a substantial part of this role. The IS manager is likely to be a member of any steering committee for a project and will probably be instrumental in the choice of a project manager, or perhaps take on this role personally.

Continuing needs

User support means involvement in the development and operation of applications. Information systems personnel can aid users develop their own applications. Also, they can provide advice, help lines, and other services. (This is the role of the Information Centre, if there is one.)

Administration includes the secretarial work, accounting, and library services of the information function. While this is necessary for the successful management of information systems, these support services are likely to be provided by other business functions. For example, accounts department personnel will be involved in the control and financial monitoring of information systems department expenditure. The IS manager's administrative responsibilities, even though he or she might receive support in the exercise of these responsibilities from outside the department, include budgeting (for capital and revenue expenditure), which is arguably part of the next task below, and which will need the co-operation of end users and personnel selection, training and welfare.

If there is a computer operations or data centre, this will contain complex and powerful systems. In the past, this function would have been the prerogative of the data processing department which would have been responsible for all an organisation's data processing activities. The IS manager will review the operation of services provided to user departments.

Network management is also a responsibility of the IS manager. The growth of networking technologies and distributed processing has meant that both computing and telecommunications issues are often interconnected. Managing computer networks requires and ability to link successfully these different technologies. Where there is a large use of personal computers, or laptop computers in the field, co-ordination of computer networks is an important management function.

13 OPERATIONAL SECURITY

Security is the prevention of damage to systems/data or reinstatement of corrupted information following systems failure. This may involve protection from people, but also seeks to provide cover against technical difficulties and natural disasters. Confidential aspects are often discussed under the heading of privacy. Privacy is concerned with preventing unauthorised access to confidential information and as such involves protection against people.

Security

Damage to systems and loss or corruption of information constitute the main threats to the security of computers and the information they hold. Security breaches can be caused by technical error, human error, deliberate action or natural disasters. Hardware may be damaged, there may be a complete system failure or there may be distortion or loss of some data. Each of these are potentially damaging to a business and should be protected against.

(a) *Technical error*

Technical errors are caused by programming and hardware faults or unexpected actions by operators. This is a very common risk but is very difficult to prevent except by thorough testing at the installation stage. It is important that faults are discovered at an early stage to limit damage and ensure that repairs are carried out quickly. Detection is often difficult because computers lack judgement and are therefore not aware that information has been degraded. Tolerance tests, adequate checking and reconciliation procedures should detect data degradation promptly; the procedures should be well defined and carried out in a disciplined fashion.

(b) *Human error*

Human errors are very common and may involve entering incorrect transactions, not following procedures or accessing the wrong files. In addition to the measures already mentioned, training of operators and proper supervision will provide protection.

(c) *Deliberate action*

There is also the possibility of malicious or accidental damage to software or hardware. The physical protection of systems and information is an important aspect of security. Similar measures to those mentioned in connection with privacy are required. Diskless workstations reduce the risk of viruses, and of illegal (pirated) software.

(d) *Natural disasters*

Natural disasters such as fire and power failures can be planned for and sufficient protection given. Fire alarms and smoke detectors will probably be put in place as a matter of course but consideration should also be given to installing a power supply which is independent from the rest of the building. Adopting disaster recovery procedures for the worst situations should be considered; these may include agreements with other users of similar equipment or computer bureaux.

Storage devices for taking backup copies of information or programs and maintenance contracts on the hardware and software are common methods of system security and should always form part of system development. Copies of information should be taken regularly and kept off site.

Privacy

A breach of privacy is likely to be caused by people and may be deliberate or accidental. Human error is the most common threat to data integrity, although the damage done by accidentally accessing confidential information is limited. However, deliberate breaches of privacy can be very damaging to individuals or organisations, if for example, information gets into the hands of a competitor or payroll printouts become public.

(a) *Data Protection Act*

The confidentiality of personal information held on computers is the subject of *Data Protection* legislation which provides a measure of protection to individuals. Legal rights and possible criminal proceedings are incorporated into the legislation to protect individuals from the misuse of personal information. One of the principles of data protection is the obligation for organisations to secure against unauthorised access to, disclosure of, damage to or loss of personal information.

(b) *Fraud*

Another fear is of the misuse of company information which is potentially damaging to a business. The growing incidence of computerised fraud is testimony to the necessity to protect information and systems.

Large networked or on line systems are particularly vulnerable because of their regular use and availability to many people. It may be difficult to trace whether information has been viewed or changed or to identify who was responsible for the action.

(c) *Passwords*

Systems which hold sensitive and confidential information can be protected in a number of ways. The physical protection of data can be achieved by the use of passwords, which should be changed frequently, or by setting up various levels of access for different users. This will also be password driven and should be reviewed frequently. Locked cupboards and a secure room for the computer are other methods of physical protection.

The number of people able to access sensitive information should be strictly limited and authorisation procedures should be well defined.

The principle of providing information only on a need to know basis, which may ignore seniority, will restrict the possibilities of information being misused. Other sound practices which will reduce the risk of a confidentiality breach may include job rotation, segregation of duties and regular reconciliations where financial information is involved.

(d) *Hacking*

A further problem is hacking, which is the practice of accessing information from remote sites (often home computers). This is extremely difficult to guard against and clearly has complex technical implications.

The prevention of threats to security and privacy of information stored on computer systems should be built in at the system design stage wherever possible. Clearly not all threats to system and data integrity can be considered; after all a system needs to be operated to be of use and there must always be people in an organisation who are in a position of trust.

Reduction of risk and damage limitation are the key criteria whilst ensuring that the operations of systems are not thereby restricted.

14 FOUR COMPANIES

(a) *Company A*

A standalone computer, by its very nature, allows access to data files and program files held on the hard disk. Possible controls are as follows.

(i) Installation of a password routine which is activated whenever the computer is booted up. This would need to be accompanied by rigorous adherence to password discipline.

(ii) Storing of data files on floppy disks, rather than on the hard disk. This would need to be *in addition to* the backup copies, and disks would need to be kept locked in a fireproof cabinet.

(iii) Physical access controls, for example door locks activated by swipe cards or PIN numbers, to prevent access into the room(s) where the computers are kept. This is probably not feasible in an open plan office.

(iv) The use of keyboard locks.

Company B

The main risk on a system of this type is the risk of a fault or breakdown in one area spreading across the system. This is particularly true of viruses. A virus introduced onto one machine could replicate itself throughout the network. All software and disks coming in to the organisation should be scanned using proprietary anti-virus software, and all machines should be virus-checked at regular intervals. Controls would also need to be established over the use of office software on home computers, including sweeping the latter regularly.

A second risk is that an unauthorised user using one network PC could gain access, not only to the files on that PC, but also to the other PCs in the system. This would require implementation of the controls described for Company A. A further risk, depending on the type of network configuration, is that an extra PC could be 'plugged in' to the network to gain access to it. The network management software should detect breaches of this type.

Company C

Additional issues over and above those already described relate to the wide area network. Dedicated land lines should be reasonably secure, so hacking should not be a problem.

(i) A determined attacker might seek to use specialist electronic equipment to emit signals to 'jam' messages.

(ii) Alternatively he might use equipment to detect signals emitted as electromagnetic radiation.

These two scenarios are more likely where communications involve national security, for example, than where commercial data is being transferred, although it is possible that where sophisticated technology is used for product delivery and competitive advantage (eg the financial services industry or air transport sector) this type of attack might be considered. It would be necessary to specify high quality communications equipment and to use sophisticated network software to detect such breaches.

Company D

The risk using external phone lines is a risk from hackers. The network management software could incorporate a facility for checking the source of external calls, but where public lines are used, this is always a very real risk, as many large organisations have found out to their cost.

(b) Company B currently operates a self-contained LAN consisting of eleven PCs and various network devices including a server computer. The company wishes to open new branches. Each branch will run a local area network similar to the existing one. The individual local area networks will be connected to head office in a star configuration. Local file servers will be updated at five minute intervals from head office.

There are two options available to Company D.

(i) Use public telephone lines and a packet switching system.
(ii) Set up its own private network.

Public lines

The company could use the ordinary telephone network, paying a charge for line rental and a charge each time the service is used. This is a lower cost option than maintaining a wide area network and eliminates the problems and costs associated with network management.

The company will need to buy modems to link into the telephone network. Each of the server computers on the local area networks will require suitable communications software.

Private network

If the company decides to set up its own network, it will need to provide its own communications links for the transmission of data. The company could lease lines for its own use (this would not necessarily be from British Telecom) or it could set up a more sophisticated system such as a microwave network. This latter option would use technology similar to that used by Mercury One-to-one in its personal telephone network. If the microwave option is chosen, this could be extremely expensive, depending on the geographical location of each branch. Communications towers (base stations) would be required, together with sophisticated radio transmitting and receiving equipment.

Wide area networks can be connected to local area networks by means of 'bridges', or 'gateways'. A bridge interconnects two networks without being visible to users, while a gateway's presence is usually visible to users. A bridge might be used to link two networks which are effectively identical, as would probably be the case here.

The company will need to assess processing volumes, as well as the criticality of the five minute update cycle proposed. If data is also to be sent from the local area networks to head office, communication will have to be two way.

15 RISK IDENTIFICATION

(a) As stated in the question the first stage of risk identification is to analyse the major types of loss to which the party at risk is subject. To do this it will need to consider its circumstances: what it does and how it does it; what it uses in the process; who does it; and what the consequences would be of not doing it.

The types of loss affecting a business will thus be seen to fall into five main categories, although they are somewhat interlinked.

(i) Pecuniary losses can arise from the interruption of the businesses, from the dishonesty of the people working in the business, or though the default (for example bad debts) or wrong-doing of external parties. A business might, for example, need to protect its secret processes, or guard against computer fraud, or put up bandit screens in its branches.

(ii) Liability losses result from damage or injury to third parties. A food manufacturer would be particularly concerned, as would a bus and coach operator.

(iii) Property losses are perhaps the most obvious kind. The key concern here is not with financial compensation for a factory that has burnt down, but with the reinstatement of the factory so that business may continue.

(iv) Personal losses derive from accidents to or the sickness or death of employees. Any employee is a potential liability while he is at work, but a business may be particularly vulnerable if a key employee with special management or technical skills suffers some mishap.

(v) Interruption losses can arise from any of the other causes: financial loss may cause delay in obtaining supplies; liability losses may involve a stoppage of production because a product is unsafe; property losses will deprive the business of the tools to do the job and personnel losses of the hands to guide the tools.

(b) The immediate causes of loss are expressed in general terms. For example a flood is an immediate cause of any of the five types of loss described above. It may in turn be caused by a variety of underlying factors - an adjoining river, a burst pipe, torrential rain, a faulty sprinkler system, and so on - and thus immediate causes must be identified first. In practise this will involve a systematic search including discussions with those who have the greatest knowledge of particular areas of the business and also outside parties such as neighbours, architects or government officers.

(c) The underlying causes of loss can then be identified and assessed in detail. Organisations will probably keep detailed records of their activities and the unit costs involved, but it is unlikely that any organisation can predict the full cost of every loss which might befall it with certainty. The calculation will involve numerous factors, of which those noted in the following paragraphs are only suggestions.

Organisation charts will be needed if a manager is taken ill, for example to calculate which personnel will have extra work in his and other departments, how much need be paid in overtime rates and whether additional expertise may have to be brought in temporarily. The personnel department may be asked for lists of employees with appropriate skills and experience who are prepared to help out.

Production flow charts must be used to discover the extent to which a factory's production will be affected by one machine breaking down, and whether alternative machines can be obtained or constructed, or alternative processes used.

Supplies flow charts and forecasts will help to assess how long a factory can maintain some or all of its production if any particular supplier suffers a major fire, or bankruptcy, and whether there are alternative suppliers.

Details of major customers can be monitored to identify those whose bankruptcy could damage the organisation.

Published accounts, internal accounts and budgets are a fertile source of information. The more carefully costs are allocated to each department, the easier it should be to calculate additional costs which would be incurred in a given emergency, which budgets will be affected and how quickly necessary funds can be made available.

Detailed plans of site and buildings will show potential bottlenecks in fire escape routes, obstructions which might make difficulties for fire engines and problems of access which could occur for both the site and its neighbours from fire, explosion, or escaping gas.

Physical inspection of buildings and machines (and perhaps of personnel, in the medical sense, and of their working practices) should take place on a regular basis.

16 TWISTING BY THE POOL

The basic principle of an insurance fund is that it is made up of all the insureds' premiums, which form an 'insurance pool' from which money can be drawn to reimburse an insured who suffers loss. Thus the small contributions of the many subsidise the larger losses of the few. Each exchanges the risk of suffering losses of unpredictable size, number and occurrence pattern for a contribution of known size due on a set date.

Pooling risks works well, provided that the pool has the following characteristics.

(a) There must be enough insureds or members contributing for the 'law of large numbers' to apply: that is, for the number and average size of claims on the pool to be reasonably close to what was anticipated. If not the fund will become bankrupt.

(b) The contributions made must be adequate to pay the claims on the pool, if not every year, then at least on average over a number of years. Again, if not, the fund will become bankrupt.

(c) The insureds' loss experience must be more or less homogeneous: that is, no one insured or small group of insureds claims amounts significantly greater than the others, especially over a period of time. If not, insureds who present fewer, smaller claims (who are known as good risks) will feel that the contributions asked of them are inequitably large considering the benefit they derive from the pool and in comparison to contributions they would be charged by other pools, and that the pool's operation is biased against them.

A 'descending spiral' can result.

(a) Poor risks make large claims.

(b) To pay these claims the insurance company has to increase contributions.

(c) This makes good risks seek insurance elsewhere.

(d) Fewer insureds now pay contributions but a larger proportion of them make large claims.

(e) To pay these claims the insurance company has to increase contributions, making more good risks withdraw.

(f) This goes on until the only people who wish to join are poor risks who expect to make claims at least as large as their contributions.

Obvious measures to halt the spiral are to ask the 'poor risks' to withdraw from the pool or to charge larger contributions to the 'poor risks', that is, to practice selective underwriting. Organisations which are on the receiving end of what they consider to be unnecessarily large premium increases, or which cannot find pools which will accept them, may form their own captive companies, or band together to set up their own pools.

The insurer thus needs to give as much play as possible to the operation of the law of large numbers by constructing risk portfolios consisting of many similar items. This is just one of several ways in which the insurer will seek to diminish his risk by ensuring that it is well spread.

(a) The insurer will be concerned to pool items from different locations to provide a geographical spread. This avoids the possibility of abnormal losses resulting from localised incidents. Some insurers find it possible to achieve multinational pooling of certain risks.

(b) The insurer's risk will also be spread in a chronological sense, by building up reserves to be used against losses in the future. This is easier for the insurer than for individual companies because the insurer is permitted to make transfers to reserves of this kind out of pre-tax profits.

17 UNDERINSURANCE AND CLAIMS

(a) The 'sum insured' under an insurance policy is the limit of the liability of the insurer to pay, on any one claim, or often the maximum amount that can be claimed in any one year. Thus if an office block is worth £1m but is only insured for £750,000 then only £750,000 can be recovered from the insurers if the building is totally destroyed.

Sometimes however it is considered unnecessary, or uneconomic, to insure an article for its full value. It may be thought highly unlikely that thieves would be able (or willing) to remove 100% of the contents of a stock room. Insureds may think it improbable that fire would destroy a building completely, or (more likely) if repair estimates should exceed a certain amount, the insured would prefer to apply the policy moneys to buying a replacement building, perhaps in a more suitable location, or of more modern design.

Insurers also employ sanctions to protect their adequately insured risks against underinsured or undervalued risks. The simplest example is a warranty that property will be insured for its full value; underinsurance amounts to misdescription of a rating factor, which entitles insurers to avoid a (commercial) policy, if the underinsurance is serious enough. Alternatively, the insurer can rely on the breach of the express warranty: the remedy for this is a right to cancel the policy, as at the date of the breach, so if the breach first occurred at inception, the policy can effectively be avoided ab initio by this means, too.

A more common sanction used against underinsurance is average, in the sense of a reduction of the sum payable on the claim as follows:

> 'such proportion of the said loss as the sum insured by this policy bears to the total value of the said property'.

(b) Typically the following are the minimum conditions that need to be satisfied before an insurer will pay a claim.

(i) A 'loss' of some sort must have occurred.
(ii) The insurer must be notified.
(iii) The 'loss' must be proved.
(iv) The claim must be legal.
(v) The insurance contract must be enforceable.
(vi) The cause of the loss must be covered by the policy.
(vii) The amount to be paid must be determined.

Each of these matters will be dealt with in turn. The term 'loss' is used above in a general sense to imply whatever event is insured against.

The occurrence

A claim will not be paid on the expectation of an event, for example when a trade union has announced its intention to interrupt business by a series of one-day stoppages, or when the insured has been given six months to live. Some financial loss must already have been suffered or the death (or whatever) must have taken place.

Notification

Most insurance policies require that the insurer should be notified formally within a pre-specified time limit for corporate policies and as soon as reasonably possible for private ones. There are a number of good reasons for this:

(i) It may be necessary for damage to be inspected before the damaged item is cleared away.

(ii) Witnesses may be required, and the sooner they can be questioned after the event, the better will be their recollection of it.

(iii) Early notification may reduce the size of the loss, for example if a repair is attempted and botched, or if the damaged goods are in danger of perishing or being stolen.

After the initial notification the insurer will require a claim form to be completed. Typically the details requested will be as follows.

(i) The circumstances of the loss
(ii) The names and addresses of any witnesses
(iii) Details of the policeman the loss was reported to
(iv) The present location of the damaged item or injured parties
(v) Details of any other insurers involved

Proof of loss

The onus is on the insured to prove that there has been a loss, how it occurred and what is its extent. If the insurer objects the insured must prove that the policy covers such a loss in such circumstances. The sorts of evidence that will be required depend upon the circumstances of the loss. For example:

(i) Motor accident: the damaged vehicle, duly inspected
(ii) Death: the death certificate
(iii) Minor storm damage: invoices for repairs

Legality

A claim on a life assurance policy would not be paid to a wife who poisoned her husband (deliberately), or on a fire policy to a businessman who burnt down his factory. The law does not permit anyone to profit from his own wrong. Contracts with an enemy are illegal as being against public policy. This might be of relevance for commercial policies involving foreign trade in times of war.

Enforceability

The usual requirements for a binding contract must be present. For example consideration is required, so premiums must usually be paid up to date, and all the parties must have legal capacity to enter into contracts.

The main concern under this heading, however, is that utmost good faith has been observed. The insurer will not pay a claim if a material fact has not been disclosed to him.

Cause of loss

Policies will either specify the causes of loss which are covered or will exclude certain causes. The proximate cause of the loss must therefore be determined. Proximate cause is the active and efficient cause of loss which sets in motion a train of events which brings about a result without the intervention of any force started and working actively from a new and independent source.

Whether a claim succeeds depends upon whether the proximate cause is specifically covered, specifically excluded or not mentioned at all. If there is more than one proximate cause it will be necessary to identify the separate damage caused by each, since claims will only be paid on the causes that are covered. If it is not possible to separate the damage, claims will be paid in full if one cause is insured and the other is not mentioned, but not at all if the other cause is excluded.

The size of payment

If the contract is one of indemnity the payment will be sufficient to place the insured in the same financial position as he was in before the loss. This might be a settlement on money or by means of 'reinstating' the damaged property. The measure of indemnity will depend upon whether the loss is total or partial and upon the particular circumstances of the insured.

The payment by a particular insurer may be reduced by contribution from other insurers where the insured has taken out co-insurance.

In a case of underinsurance the insurer is likely to apply average, whereby the amount of the loss paid is in proportion to the amount insured compared with the full value.

In conclusion, it should be pointed out that insured losses are by their very nature unusual events. The above is merely an overview of what can often in practice be a highly complicated procedure.

18 CLASSES OF INSURANCE

(a) Insurance is compulsory for many activities which are liable to injure third parties. An individual might undertake an activity which is not, in the normal course of events, a danger to others, and yet unintentionally harm an innocent person who happened to get involved. Alternatively, it might be that a hazardous activity is deliberately undertaken.

Insurance has been made compulsory in certain such circumstances in order to ensure that money is available to meet the claims of innocent third parties and to relieve the State of a liability that might otherwise be thought of as its responsibility.

Motor insurance

The most obvious example affecting many individuals and most businesses is motor insurance. Deaths and injuries caused by the use of motor vehicles on roads became the subject of compulsory third party insurance, unlimited in amount, under the Road Traffic Act 1930. The insurance is now covered by the Road Traffic Act 1991. In 1990 the requirement was extended to include third party property damage.

Before a motor vehicle can be driven on the public highway the 'user' (the person in control, but not necessarily the driver) must hold a certificate of motor insurance issued by an insurer who is authorised by the DTI and who is a member of the Motor Insurer's Bureau (MIB).

The MIB is an organisation which administers a fund to compensate third parties killed or injured by motor vehicles whose RTA cover is defective in some way or non-existent (such as a joy-rider).

Employer's liability insurance

Another example which is widespread is employers' liability insurance. In many countries 'workman's compensation' (payments for injuries, disease or death arising out of an employment) is available through the social security system. In the UK the National Insurance (Industrial Injuries) Act 1946 absorbed workman's compensation into the National Insurance industrial death and industrial injuries schemes.

In addition, however, the Employers' Liability (Compulsory Insurance) Act 1969 compels all employers to have access to adequate resources to pay compensation for bodily injury, death or disease suffered by their employees and arising in the course of their employment. As for motor insurance, the insurer must be authorised.

The 1969 Act does not protect the employee's spouse and near relatives, nor does it protect employees normally resident abroad (although these would probably be protected by local laws).

Dangerous activities

There are a number of hazardous activities whose organisers are compelled to carry insurance. Horse-riding establishments, surf-riding establishments and owners of wild and dangerous animals are all required to hold third party liability insurance. There are though instances of 'hazardous' activities which are not subject to compulsory insurance. The prime example is in the field of medicine. In this case the state might have liability, but in any case doctors and dentists membership fees for the Medical Defence Union and the Medical Protection Society provide them with protection from professional negligence claims.

Nuclear installations

Public liability insurance became compulsory for UK operators of nuclear reactors under the Nuclear Installations (Licensing and Insurance) Act 1959 and the Nuclear Installations Act 1965.

In this case the possible numbers and total costs of claims which could arise from a single accident are not only far more than one operator could pay but also would be likely to strain insurers' reserves. A series of international conventions therefore set minimum insurance requirements and initiated a system of specialist national pools of insurers to carry the risks, reinsuring only with each other to avoid the risk of accumulation of lines affected by an accident in any one insurer's reinsurance portfolio. In the UK the pool is managed by the British Insurance (Atomic Energy) Committee.

The minimum requirements in the UK were updated by the Energy Act 1983. An operator needs £20m of public liability cover for each installation. For universities and other small sites £5m cover is prescribed. The insurance must also cover liability for fissile materials in transit. The operator can alternatively keep a reserve fund of £20m per installation, but whatever the case must provide proof of insurance or self-insurance in order to obtain a licence to operate.

Tutorial note: The question only required three types of insurance

(b) The major category of 'own loss' insurance against financial loss is business interruption (BI), so called as its former names ('loss of profits' and 'consequential loss') can be misleading. Our second example will be 'fidelity guarantee' insurance.

BI insurance

BI insurance is written by fire insurers, engineering insurers and others, according to which perils are to be insured. Surveys and necessary safeguards concerning the material damage/loss risk are directly relevant to the secondary loss of income or profits which the policy covers. The premium, therefore, is usually calculated from the corresponding physical damage/loss rate. Payment of BI claims is conditional on payment of a loss or damage claim, except under the common extensions covering, for example:

(i) Loss of access to the insured premises (in case, say, neighbouring premises catch fire)

(ii) Communicable diseases (a cook found to be a typhoid carrier, or a guest with plague, could close a hotel)

(iii) Murder (as the police would prevent access to the room concerned for a time, although this often attracts business)

The interest insured under BI is basically loss to a business during a fixed period following an insured occurrence (called the indemnity period). The loss is the difference between a reasonable projection of the insured business's financial performance over that period (adjusted for external factors such as a new product, or loss of market to a new competitor), and its actual performance as reduced by the insured occurrence. The insurer covers that difference, up to a limit per year, during the indemnity period, which should be sufficiently long for the business to recover from the effects of the insured peril on its performance.

There is a variety of methods for assessing the size of the interest. For example, a cotton mill might have orders enough to occupy 100 looms for a year, and calculate the loss to the business for each day one loom is out of action. This 'machine day' basis is still appropriate for some businesses, for example where the risk is covered as an extension to an engineering insurance (which protects primarily against the cost of repairs following breakdown of a properly maintained machine), but more sophisticated methods are more common nowadays.

The subject matter insured for BI may be defined as 'trading loss ... the rate of gross profit on any shortfall in expected sales', described as:

profit as % of gross sales × shortfall in gross sales

Separating the actual value of what has been bought and sold during the year from opening and closing stocks prevents any increase or decrease in stock during the year from giving a false impression of increased loss or profit respectively. It also ensures that insurers are presented with a current picture of trading rather than one of the value of the whole business.

Other methods of calculating gross profit include the difference basis which can be summarised as:

	£
Net profit	X
Standing charges	X
	X
or, in the absence of profit,	
Standing charges	(X)
Less trading loss	(X)
	(X)

Although there are standard accounting practices, methods of calculating the above items must vary between firms, because the processes and trading practices differ. Insurers require a yardstick for measuring profit which allows accurate comparison between one accounting period and the next; turnover, or fee income which the insured is expected to earn (compared with previous accounting years) are very popular. There are cases, however, where the accountants' figures present a true picture of trading, but do not relate very easily to a real loss of production claimed for (for example if this relates to parts of several orders, and the orders will not all appear in the same accounting year). In such circumstances, the loss adjuster will use the most practical and equitable method available to quantify the loss.

Most BI policies have a separate item covering increased cost of working (ICOW), which represents abnormal items of expenditure incurred in loss reduction. Two standard criteria limit the amount which insurers will pay for this.

(i) The expenses must be reasonable (chiefly, they must be reasonably expected to reduce the BI loss).

(ii) Only loss reducing expense counts here: a claim under this item does not increase the overall amount insurers will pay for the BI claim.

Examples of expenses counting as ICOW are: renting alternative premises during repair of the insured's damaged building; wages for temporary staff helping to restore records, and hire charges for a replacement for a damaged machine.

It is not always expedient to include all wages in the sum insured for BI. While it is not uncommon to find separate BI limits for distinct areas of a firm's operations, it is quite common to find payroll cover given separately. This is basically for wages paid to retain skilled and experienced staff, who might find other permanent employment if made redundant during a period of interrupted work. It allows great flexibility, both in suiting cover to the insured's circumstances, and in applying the cover to a loss. It may include all wages, or some administrative staff salaries may count as insured overheads (or part of 'gross profit').

The indemnity period is not always identical to that for the basic BI cover. Firms expecting to lay off staff who cannot continue working because of the interruption, and cannot be redeployed, can opt for a large wages cover limit lasting until the lay-offs would start, and then a reduced limit lasting for a further 'remainder' period (known as a 'dual basis' for wages cover). A 'carry-over' clause can allow savings on wages in the initial period to increase cover in the remainder period: and an 'option to consolidate' can allow full cover to be extended, at the expense of the limit claimable for the remainder period.

Fidelity guarantee insurance

This is intended to cover losses arising from the dishonest actions of a supposedly responsible person. Modern policies cover theft of the insured's property, in addition to traditional embezzlement risks. Auditors' fees for proving a loss is a common optional extension. Insured losses happen during an identified employee's uninterrupted employment, or are discovered up to six months after he or she leaves, is dismissed, retires or dies.

Types of policy include the following.

(i) Policies issued on specified employees, or on the holders for the time being of particular jobs, or on groups of employees (named or not) with varying degrees of access to and control over the employer's money and assets.

(ii) Policies for partnerships, which specifically protect the firm against theft by a partner.

(iii) 'Collective' policies, covering groups of staff: the insurer may not require individual names and duties if these are 'floating' policies, with one guarantee limit to cover all the group, or different limits for different groups.

(iv) 'Blanket' policies, covering all staff. Some advantages of blanket policies are that the insured does not practice selection against the insurer, and that the insured is protected against theft by any employee whose job is not supposed to entail access to computer records, safe keys, goods, or cash.

19 PERMANENT HEALTH INSURANCE

MEMO

To: Managing Director
From: Company Secretary
Subject: Permanent Health Insurance

As requested I set out below notes on the features and benefits of Permanent Health Insurance.

Permanent health insurance (PHI) policies are designed to replace earned income lost through physical incapacity to earn, caused by accidents and sickness, if necessary for many years' incapacity. It is a 'long term' cover like life assurance: its term, from its inception to the insured's anticipated retirement date, can run for many years. Like life assurances it is *non-cancellable*. This means that the insurer cannot cancel the policy except in the event of fraud, or if the policy terms include provision for cancellation in specific circumstances.

Occupational PHI or life assurance schemes, however, are administered like annual contracts with the employer, although life offices generally guarantee to renew them if the insured firm requires. The insurer's liability is also potentially 'long term'. Once an insured employee falls sick, the office will continue to pay for the claim, until that employee reaches retirement age if necessary, whether or not the policy is renewed.

The definition of the benefits can be arranged to suit the insured, but the income limit during incapacity is unlikely to exceed 75% of previous salary, and benefits are subject to deduction of tax under PAYE. Proportional benefits can be payable when an employee becomes able to perform alternative, lower paid, work, even if with another employer.

The deferred period is seldom shorter than 26 weeks (except for individual policies for self-employed) to correspond with the length of the maximum period for which NI sickness benefit is payable. It is a very useful means of suiting cover to abnormal risks, and can often be reduced or increased for a suitable premium adjustment. Policy wordings can vary considerably.

With group PHI schemes it is the employer who pays the premiums to the insurance company, but employees are *not* assessed for tax on these premiums. An employer may feel that he has obligations to his employees should they suffer severe illness and the liability for continued payment of salary could be heavy. By arranging a group PHI scheme with an insurer the employer replaces possible heavy outlay at indeterminate times by premium payments at known regular intervals at a relatively stable rate.

The benefits are then payable by the insurance company to the employer who then passes them on to the disabled person.

The disabled person generally remains an employee of the employer, and so may then continue to remain a member of the company pension scheme throughout his incapacity with the employer continuing to pay pension scheme contributions. Thus retirement benefits related to pre-disability earnings continue to accrue and the death-in-service benefits can be maintained. The pension scheme contributions of both the employer and the employee might be insured alongside the disablement benefits under the PHI scheme.

Schemes covering a large percentage of a firm's staff, especially if membership is automatic, may provide 'free cover' (that is, without evidence of members' health) providing benefits subject to specified limits even (in large schemes) for members of any age. The free cover (or 'non-selection') limit is not likely to apply in schemes where there are fewer than, say, 50 members. Benefits above the limit will only be available where evidence of good health is provided.

I hope this information is of assistance. Please let me know if you need further details.

20 THE INSURANCE MARKET

(a) An insurance intermediary is a party who bring a potential policyholder into contact with the insurer in order to enter into a contract of insurance. They are not in the employment of any insurer in particular (those who deal with one company only are known as 'tied representatives') but act as middlemen who can offer their customers a range of possible insurers. From a legal point of view they are agents, usually acting with the insured as their principal, although depending upon precisely what part of an insurance transaction they are dealing with may be the agent of the insurer or of both parties.

There are a number of different types of intermediary. What they call themselves will often depend upon what insurance services they offer and what other services besides. For the present purposes we shall concentrate on the following.

(i) Brokers
(ii) Lloyd's brokers
(iii) Part-time 'agents'

(i) *Brokers*

Insurance brokers are the most familiar and the most important type of intermediary. In order to earn the name they must be registered. They normally practise insurance full-time, although they may also provide other services. To become registered brokers must demonstrate that they can provide expert assistance to their clients, for whom they both provide advice and arrange business.

Standards of professional skill and conduct are expected to be high. The requirements for registration under the Insurance Brokers (Registration) Act 1977 are based on suitability of character and practical experience. An employee of a broking firm can seek registration after five years (or less with appropriate qualifications; a similar length of comparable experience is required of others, for example employees of insurance companies.

The regulations also lay down requirements for financial and professional indemnity insurance Brokers are expected:

(1) To conduct their business with utmost good faith and integrity

(2) To put their client's interests first, satisfying their insurance requirements as far as possible, and subject to this, to have proper regard for others

(3) To ensure that statements made by them or on their behalf when advertising are not misleading or extravagant

Brokers are usually expected to deal with at least five different insurers and must not favour one unduly.

(ii) *Lloyds's brokers*

Lloyd's brokers are not subject to the above requirements but the Committee of Lloyd's imposes similar conditions. The Committee receives its authority from the Council of Lloyd's in which regulatory powers are vested under the Lloyd's Acts 1871-1982.

Only Lloyd's brokers are allowed to place business in the Room at Lloyd's and they pay a large annual fee for the privilege. They are required to be 'fit and proper persons' who are competent and familiar with the Lloyd's market. New applicants must prove this by passing an introductory test. The Committee ensures that financial requirements are met.

(iii) *Part-time agents*

This group conduct their insurance business on an *ad hoc* basis as part of a quite different service. Common examples would be car dealers selling motor insurance, and accountants or solicitors arranging life assurance or pensions. Like brokers they are paid on a commission basis.

Because there is an element of 'investment business', the Financial Services legislation comes into play. All independent intermediaries who offer advice on investment business are required to be authorised to do so by an appropriate regulatory body. The new Financial Services Authority will in time take over regulation of independent intermediaries and professionals offering financial services, and also external regulation of Lloyds.

(b) Insurance operations need to be controlled for two main reasons.

(i) Insurance is crucial to the economy in several respects. In the first place without a stable insurance industry all manner of business undertakings would be much riskier, in many cases unacceptably so. Secondly, insurers are major investors supplying long-term capital for government and industry. Thirdly, insurance operations have a significant effect on the balance of payments because many insurance transactions are international (for example around 75% of Lloyd's premiums are derived from abroad).

(ii) Insurance directly affects the life of almost every individual, at one end of the scale protecting video recorders from petty thieves and at the other protecting families from financial ruin through untimely death. In their role as investors insurance companies are the guardians of other people's money. The failure of an insurance company could result in the loss of a lifetime's savings for many.

Governments have therefore always been keen to ensure that insurance operations are subject to supervision and control.

21 TRUSTEES

The Occupational Pensions Board brief guide for pension trustees usefully summarises the duties of a pension scheme trustee as follows.

(a) To act in accordance with the trust deed and rules of the scheme, within the framework of the law.

(b) To act prudently, conscientiously and honestly and with the utmost good faith.

(c) To act in the best interests of the beneficiaries and strike a fair balance between the interests of different classes of beneficiary.

(d) To take advice on technical matters and any other matters which the trustee does not understand.

(e) To invest the funds.

A trustee's duties are imposed by the trust instrument and by general law. They are now codified in the Pensions Act 1995. There are matters where a trustee can use his discretion (for example investing in particular securities) and in these he must act honestly and with the care that a prudent man of business would exercise in the management of his own affairs.

A pension scheme trustee must familiarise himself with the trust deed and rules of the scheme, for it is his duty to administer the pension scheme impartially in accordance with the rules. Furthermore, so as to be properly informed regarding the scheme, a trustee should obtain a list of the scheme's investments and their valuation, and details of members, those in active service, those with pensions in the course of payment, and deferred pensioners. Also he should study the annual reports of the scheme and the minimal valuation reports.

A trustee should see that money owed to the scheme is paid and that transactions and proceedings of the scheme are properly recorded. This means that proper accounts must be kept, and that the scheme accounts must be audited.

The trustees hold the assets of the scheme for the benefit of the members and the trustees must carry out their duties with reasonable care and in good faith. This involves obtaining and considering professional advice in areas where the trustees themselves are not experts.

Trustees have a duty to keep accounts of all transactions for which they are responsible as trustees. No particular form is required by law for trust accounts generally, but for pension schemes there are detailed requirements.

22 CONTRACTING OUT

(a) The two main types of contracted-out scheme are 'final salary' schemes and 'money purchase schemes'.

Final salary schemes

These are also known as 'defined benefit' schemes and the two names summarise the essential features.

Benefits are related to the length of an employee's service and his salary at or near his retirement. The maximum benefit approvable by the Inland Revenue is (very broadly speaking) two-thirds of final salary. Part of the fund that has been built up to provide this pension may alternatively be taken as a tax-free lump sum on retirement, with an approvable maximum of 1½ times final salary.

Final salary is not in fact the salary that was being earned on the date of retirement. It may be the remuneration for any one of the five years preceding retirement or the average for any period of three or more consecutive years ending not earlier than ten years before the normal retirement date.

Final salary schemes offer benefits that cover earnings growth including any inflationary growth because they are geared to earnings at around retirement date.

Although benefits are guaranteed the cost to the employer is unknown at the time when the scheme is set up.

Money purchase schemes

These are also known as 'defined contribution' schemes and again the two names are fairly self-explanatory.

It has been possible to contract out using a money purchase scheme since 1988.

Money purchase schemes involve a fixed rate of contribution being allocated to each member (usually a fixed percentage of the employee's salary). The contributions are invested and accumulate for each member. Employees are also allowed to contribute. The maximum contributions are a percentage of the employee's 'net relevant earnings' in each fiscal year. The limit is 17.5% up to age 35, rising thereafter up to 40% at age 61.

The resulting pension is that which can be purchased with the accumulated value of contributions at retirement date. Generally 25% of the accumulated fund may be taken as a tax-free lump sum.

The advantage of such a scheme for an employer is that contributions are known in advance. For the employee, however, the level of benefits is not guaranteed.

(b) SERPS is an acronym for the State Earnings Related Pension Scheme.

This was introduced in 1978 as a result of the Social Security Act 1975. The Act provided that state pensions would comprise two parts.

(i) A basic flat rate pension which is revalued each year in line with increases in the RPI.

(ii) A second tier pension (SERPS) which is related to band earnings. These are earnings between a stipulated lower limit and a stipulated upper limit.

In calculating the SERPS benefit band earnings are revalued in line with increases in general national earnings. Originally the SERPS pension was based on 20% of the best 20 years revalued band earnings. The Social Security Act 1986 modified this basis, however, and now SERPS is based on 20% of lifetime average revalued band earnings. The benefit in payment is increased annually in line with the RPI.

SERPS is available to all employees, but they can instead choose to be a member of their employer's contracted-out scheme or take out their own 'personal pension'. In either case a rebate of National Insurance Contributions is made to compensate for the SERPS benefit forgone.

23 DISCLOSURE

Approval of a pension scheme under the Income and Corporation Taxes Act 1988 requires that 'every employee who is, or has a right to be, a member of the scheme has been given written particulars of all essential features of the scheme which concern him'

However, the position is more closely governed by the Occupational Pension Schemes (Disclosure of Information) 1996. These apply to all occupational pension schemes with two or more members. Information is required to be supplied to:

(a) Members and prospective members of the scheme

(b) Persons within the application of the scheme and qualifying or prospectively qualifying for benefit

(c) Independent trade unions recognised to any extent for the purpose of collective bargaining in relation to members and prospective members of the scheme

In general the regulations require that such persons are kept informed about contributions, the administration and finance of the scheme, the right and obligations ensuing under it, and any other matters prescribed by the Secretary of State.

In particular the regulations require the distribution of an annual report, audited accounts and an actuarial valuation and statement. The annual report is what most concerns us here.

Schemes to which the regulations apply must each year make available an annual report containing a copy of the audited accounts for the scheme year; a copy of the latest actuarial statement, and a trustees' report containing various details.

(a) The names of the persons who were trustees of the scheme during the scheme year to which the information relates

(b) The provisions of the scheme for appointing trustees and removing them from office

(c) The name of any actuaries, auditors, solicitors, banks and other persons and organisations acting for or retained by the trustees during the year, with an indication (except in the first year the information is provided) of any change since the previous year

(d) The address to which enquires about the scheme generally or about an individual's entitlement to benefit should be sent

(e) The number of members and beneficiaries as at any one date during the year

(f) A statement that the accounts have been prepared and audited in accordance with the Pensions Act 1995

(g) A statement of circumstances made by a retiring auditor or actuary

(h) An explanation if the scheme was unable to offer the full statutory cash equivalents for all or part of the year, and a statement of when the full values are likely to become available

(i) If cash equivalents were not calculated and verified in accordance with social security regulations, an explanation of why

(j) Details if the employers is unable to continue with the recommended funding levels

(k) Reference to the actuarial report providing details of the valuation of the scheme on a discontinuance basis where there is significant likelihood that the scheme will be wound up

Funded schemes, but not unfunded schemes, must also contain the following information.

(a) If the auditors' statement shows that in their opinion contributions payable to the scheme during the year have not been paid in accordance with the scheme rules or contracts under which they were payable, or with the recommendation of the actuary, an account of the reasons for the discrepancy and how it has been or is likely to be resolved.

(b) If any such discrepancy was left unresolved in a previous year a statement of how it has been or is likely to be resolved.

Compliance statement

This should contain:

(a) Details of increases in pensions during the year, and the extent to which those increases were discretionary

(b) Details if discretionary benefits are included within the valuation of transfer values

(c) A statement if there have been no employer-related investments during the year

(d) A statement if the scheme has received or is expected to receive Inland Revenue approval

Investment report

This should include:

(a) Names of investment managers

(b) The extent to which trustees have delegated responsibility for managing investments

(c) Details of whether the trustees have produced a statement of investment principles and have complied with it

(d) Review of investment performance over recent years

(e) Custody arrangements for the scheme's assets

(f) Any investment in the employer

(g) Details of ethical investment policy

(h) How rights In investments are used

Financial statements

Information required in the audited accounts may be summarised more briefly. These must contain, in addition to the accounts themselves (fund account and net assets statement), details of the following.

(a) Additions to/withdrawals from the scheme's funds in the year
(b) The market value of assets
(c) Investments amounting to more than 5% of net assets
(d) Self-investment amounting to more than 5% of net assets and how it is being reduced
(e) Acquisitions and disposals of assets
(f) Money purchase assets
(g) Additional voluntary contributions
(h) Corresponding amounts for the previous year
(i) A statement of compliance with the accountants' Statement of Recommended Practice 1

Actuarial statement

Likewise the information required in the actuarial statement is set out in brief below.

(a) The valuation presented in an understandable way

(b) A statement of compliance with professional guidelines

(c) His opinion as to whether the scheme will continue to be able to meet its liabilities

(d) A summary of the valuation methods and assumptions used

(e) Certification of the adequacy of contribution rates, and relevant changes since the last valuation

The annual report must be made available not later than one year after the end of the scheme year to which it relates, and reasonable steps must be taken to draw the attention of members, prospective members, any recognised trade union, and any beneficiaries to the availability of the report. Copies must be provided free of charge on receipt of a written request, as soon as practicable after the request is made. Copies of annual reports for earlier years must be made available free of charge for inspection on receipt of a written request from any prescribed person or trade union.

24 TYPES OF SCHEME

(a) A defined benefit pension scheme is one in which the benefits payable on retirement are related to the length of an employee's service and his salary at or near retirement. A money purchase scheme involves a fixed rate of contribution being allocated to each member. The contributions are invested and accumulate for each member. The resulting pension is that which can be purchased with the accumulated value of the contributions at retirement date.

The relative merits of each type of scheme structure will be discussed in turn.

(i) *Defined benefit schemes*

For the employee the principal merit of a defined benefit scheme is the promise of a set amount of pension. Pension provision is linked to final salary on retirement and thus the effects of inflation are nullified. A money purchase scheme does not necessarily offer this sort of protection.

From the employer's point of view it is this aspect of a defined benefit scheme which is its chief disadvantage. He has to fund the scheme to enable it to keep its promises, and if salary increases are not matched by investment performance then he has to make up any shortfall. A money purchase scheme presents no such problem because the investment performance of the fund is the only factor that determines the pension payable.

The disadvantage for employers may not in practice be as great as may at first appear. As long as funds are available at any one time to cater for benefits as they fall due (on retirement, withdrawal from the scheme or death), then the employer is free to reduce his contributions or suspend them entirely. Thus times of high investment returns will subsidise times of lower returns.

Further it is usual for trust deeds of defined benefit schemes to contain a provision allowing the employer to target certain benefits towards different categories of member and to augment benefits. This might be a very useful lever in a process of collective bargaining with workers and in cases of redundancy.

It has also been argued that economies of scale apply to a defined benefit scheme because the charges per head for administration and investment are lower than for money purchase schemes.

Thus defined benefit schemes can have advantages for both employee and employer.

(ii) *Money purchase schemes*

As noted above, money purchase schemes involve a sum of money being allotted to each member, whereas a defined benefit scheme does not offer rights in such a clear-cut way. There is thus an advantage to money purchase schemes in that they are simple to understand: a final salary scheme may not seem so 'real', particularly to a younger member.

For the employer the advantage of a money purchase scheme is that the cost is known in advance: it is simply the amount (subject to Inland Revenue limits) that he is willing and able to pay into the scheme.

The chief disadvantage in this case is suffered by the employee, for there is no guarantee that the fund will keep pace with increases in earnings: the investment risk is borne by the employee.

Again in practice matters need not be so black and white: it is not really in the employer's interests to provide a scheme that is proving to be totally inadequate to meet its beneficiaries' needs. Various arrangements could be made to ensure that a money purchase scheme does not fall short of what is required, for example by estimating target pensions and arranging for contributions to increase with age.

Further, it is by no means impossible that the long-term investment performance of a fund could be extremely good, more than matching inflation and earnings increases. If this were the case the employer would be no worse off and the employee would be very well provided for.

Again, therefore, money purchase schemes can have advantages for both parties.

In conclusion, it may be said that both types of scheme have merits for both parties, and both are subject to uncertainty. This is inevitable and is part of the very nature of a pension scheme because it is necessarily a long-term arrangement.

(b) Employees have been free to make their own pension arrangements since July 1988 as a result of provisions originally set out in the Social Security Act 1986. At about the same time compulsory membership of employers' schemes became inadmissible at law.

With regard to the question of how employers should respond to demands to contribute to personal pensions it must first be pointed out that the legislation does not require employers to contribute. They may do so but the overall contributions from employers and employees may not exceed Inland Revenue limits.

In the circumstances described the simplest possibility is that an employer who does not at present make any provision for his employees' pensions and does not wish to do so might be asked to contribute to a personal scheme. It is most unlikely that such an employer would respond positively to such a request.

A second scenario would involve an employer who does not presently make any provision but is not opposed to doing so. Giving his assent to making contributions to employees' personal schemes could have the following advantages.

(i) It would undoubtedly serve to improve relations between the employer and the employees concerned, and may be a means of achieving, say, increased productivity.

(ii) It may serve as a useful 'carrot' in attracting staff of the desired calibre.

(iii) A paternalistically-minded employer may see it as a means of persuading employees who might otherwise be reckless in such matters to start making proper provision for their old age.

(iv) It would enable an employer to offer an 'occupational' scheme of sorts without the administrative burden of setting up and running an occupational scheme in the normal sense.

The third possibility is that an employer who already offers a company scheme could be asked to contribute to a personal scheme. We can assume that such an employer would not consider contributing more to a personal scheme than he does to the company scheme and this effectively rules out the option of offering salary in lieu. As noted above the salary would need to be increased by the grossed up equivalent of the pension contribution in order to give the same benefit, and not to give the same benefit could be divisive.

If such an employer decided that he would agree to make contributions to personal schemes the following might be the consequences.

(i) The cost of providing pensions might increase because those who were not interested in the company scheme might now take out a personal scheme.

(ii) Whatever their decision, employees might look more favourably upon their employer because he was offering them more freedom of choice.

(iii) Employees in the occupational scheme might start to wonder whether they would be better off with a personal pension.

(iv) It might be possible by this means to persuade all employees to leave the company scheme. This might be desirable for the employer if he were finding the cost of supporting a defined benefit scheme too burdensome or too uncertain for the good of his business; or if he wanted his share of the surplus in the scheme.

The final option is to continue to support the company scheme, either by refusing to contribute to personal schemes at all, or by contributing less to personal schemes or making the conditions for eligibility to receive employers' contributions harder.

An employer could have a number of valid reasons for favouring the occupational scheme.

(i) He may justifiably believe that continued membership of the occupational scheme was in the employees' best interests.

(ii) He would therefore wish to maintain the viability of the company scheme by encouraging as many employees as possible to join it and remain in it.

(iii) He might feel that the company scheme encouraged loyalty to the company.

(iv) He might presently be enjoying a contributions holiday if the occupational scheme were in surplus. He would not therefore wish to commit himself to the fixed annual sums that personal pension contributions would require.

In practice, this final option appears to the favoured one at present: only a very small percentage of employers are yet making contributions to personal schemes.

In conclusion it is worth quoting a leader in the *Financial Times* in May 1992 following the Maxwell affair and the calls for reform of the pensions system: 'Many employees might be better off with a system of low-cost company-sponsored personal pension plans which could be freely transferred from one employment to another'. However, it continued as follows.

> 'The well-entrenched network of occupational schemes should not be dismantled lightly. With some £300bn of assets they represent an enormous and stable pool of long term savings, the envy of some countries which are overdependent on save-as-you-go pensions systems threatened by adverse demographic trends.'

25 COPYRIGHT AND PATENTS

(a) The Copyright, Designs and Patents Act 1988 has made significant changes to the law relating to intellectual property, particularly concerning copyright and designs. It repealed all existing copyrights legislation but largely codified the law, making small changes such as permitting the issue of a search warrant to detect items infringing a copyright. However it also introduced certain new rights.

Paternity

It has introduced new moral rights to the law of copyright. *Paternity* refers to the right of an author of a literary, dramatic, artistic or musical work (but not of a computer program, typeface design or computer generated work) to be so identified whenever the work is broadcast, performed, published or otherwise presented to the public. It will also apply to the director of a film. The right does not apply in certain specified exceptions (eg parliamentary proceedings) and will not apply if the work is published in a periodical or reference work with the owner's consent. It is also not applicable to publication etc of work produced in the course of employment if authorised by the copyright holder.

Integrity

The concept of *integrity* allows those persons listed above to object to derogatory treatment of their work. This covers treatments (eg adaptations) which mutilate or distort the work or otherwise prejudice the honour or reputation of the author or director. An architect of work so treated may have his name removed from any identification on the building. It does not apply to work included in periodicals or reference works as above, or to work made for the reporting of current events, or treatments made to avoid the commission of an offence to avoid offending public feeling, provided that where the author is identified there is an adequate disclaimer.

False attribution

In contrast there is also a right not to have a work falsely attributed to an individual. This subsists for 20 years after his death. A person who commissions photographs or film for private and domestic purposes may also prevent public exhibition or publishing of those photographs (but not the publication of photographs taken without permission).

Design right

The 1988 Act also introduced the concept of *design right.* This automatically arises to protect a design of any aspect of shape or configuration of the whole or part of an article (s 211), even if no artistic work was created. The design must be original and it must have been recorded in a document or the making of the article before the right arises.

Ownership of design right normally lies with the designer but there are some exceptions. For example, if protection arises on the first marketing of the designed product, the person who markets that product will have design right. The right subsists for ten years from first marketing of the article, subject to an overall limit of 15 years from first record of the design or the making of the first product. The owner has the exclusive right to use the design to make design documents or the articles themselves. Licences to use the design or assignments of the right are possible.

Unauthorised use or copying of a design is an infringement of the right and the owner may bring an action to prevent it or to claim damages or an account of profits. However the owner who makes groundless threats of action for infringement may be subject to an action for damages and an injunction himself under s 253 of the Act.

(b) The law governing patents is largely contained in the Patents Act 1977. The general rule is that the patent is granted to reward the maker of an invention capable of industrial application; in return for his ingenuity in making an 'inventive step' to create a new product, he is granted exclusive rights to exploit that idea for a number of years. He has monopoly rights for four years, which will then continue for a further 16 years on payment of an annual renewal fee. He may also allow others to use the idea by granting licences for its use. He will usually receive payment for these licences, thus receiving further reward for his efforts. The right does not arise automatically and the inventor must take steps to register his interest as the criterion of novelty may be lost.

While recognising the claims of the inventor to the fruits of his ideas, there is clearly a degree of public interest in allowing the wider dissemination of an idea of benefit to industry. This is achieved to some extent by the time limits set and the need to pay a fee; the inventor must make some payment for his long term monopoly.

The licensing system also helps widen the use of the patent but the Act goes further in encouraging exploitation with *licences of right* and *compulsory licences.*

(i) Licences of right arise when a patentee applies for an entry on the Patents register to the effect that licences will be available as of right on terms agreed with the patentee (or the Patent Office).

(ii) Compulsory licences may be obtained on the application of any person from three years after registration. The licence will be granted only if a number of grounds are proven; in particular it is necessary to show that the invention is not being exploited to a reasonable extent in the light of public, industrial or commercial demand. The threat of a grant of a compulsory licence usually produces the proper exploitation of the patent.

There are also a number of defences to an alleged infringement of the patent which allow for the fair use of the patent, eg use for private and non-commercial purposes or in the course of experiments relating to the subject matter of the patent.

Many inventions are created by scientists or engineers in the course of their employment. The Act recognises that it may be inappropriate to grant ownership rights to the employee in these circumstances, as the employer has no doubt contributed to the conditions in which the invention is discovered. Thus the patent will belong to the employer if it is made in the course of the employee's normal duties or in duties specifically assigned to him, in circumstances where an invention might reasonably be expected. It will also belong to the employer if created in the course of the employee's duties and because of that employee's particular position, he is expected to further the interests of the employer. The Act does allow the employee to apply for a ruling that he is entitled to compensation if the invention is of exceptional benefit to the employer.

The Act gives priority to the interests of the inventor. However by effectively forcing the proper exploitation of the patent and by ensuring the contribution of the employer is not disregarded, the Act achieves a balance between these potentially conflicting interests.

26 LOST IN SPACE

The management of office premises has traditionally been largely a matter of legal document handling (leases, formal communications from landlords, service contracts etc) and everyday property issues such as reactive repairs, lift and cleaning contracts. However, as management have become more aware of accommodation costs, and the work environment has become recognised as an important element in employee satisfaction and effectiveness, and as legislation affecting office premises has proliferated, a more integrated approach has been required.

The discipline of 'facilities management' involves:

(a) At its simplest, arranging the supervision and auditing of all services that go to make up a pleasant, healthy and economical working environment

(b) At a higher level, a more proactive approach which looks to the economics of the property and the needs of the people within it

'Space' management is just one aspect of this, involved in ensuring that space within the building is utilised to maximum advantage, flexible enough to allow for workforce expansion, and cost-effective.

The benefits of planning and management in these areas may be as follows.

(a) *Cost effectiveness* is one of the primary motivations for good premises management. The cost of an office facility goes up because of the need for better support systems – heating, ventilation, acoustic isolation and so on. This is true whether you plan well or poorly, but the costs go up much more dramatically when the needs are met in a piecemeal fashion. Apart from planning ahead and obtaining economies of scale on purchases, the premises manager can achieve cost-effectiveness through:

  (i) Space planning (It has been estimated, for example, that open plan office layouts make possible a 33% space saving, plus economies on shared heating and lighting, equipment etc. If space is utilised flexibly, there are savings to be obtained when expansion occurs or reorganisation is required.)

  (ii) Preventive maintenance, rather than re-active repairs of building structure, facilities and equipment

  (iii) Risk management; maintaining adequate insurance and security arrangements

  (iv) Avoiding costs associated with health and safety problems (time lost, compensation payments etc) by ensuring that the premises conform to legislation - and preferably best practice - with regard to health and safety

  (v) Ensuring that the environment is conducive to steady, uninterrupted and efficient work (as discussed below).

(b) Enhanced productivity/performance is, together with cost-effectiveness, the main justification for investment in the work environment and management of it. It may be achieved in a number of ways.

   (i) Maintained or improved workflow and communication. Good premises management will ensure that the layout of the office (within each area and with regard to proximity of related areas, and accessibility of shared facilities) is conducive to efficient, unhindered flow of people and information from one place or stage of processing to another. Gangways, stairways and lifts should also be maintained to be clear of obstruction, well-lit and free of breakdown (in the case of lifts). Internal telephone systems should be maintained.

   (ii) Adapting the building to the needs of the technology used (or likely to be used). Wire and cable management, anti-static carpeting and humidity control, ventilation, separate power sources and reinforced flooring etc are required for most electronic systems. If the accommodation does not provide them, it may be impossible to install the system, work may be lost through machine malfunctions, or there may be hazards to employees (and equipment).

   (iii) Physically and psychologically 'enabling' workers. Stress, fatigue and other forms of 'imbalance' effect performance, as do inefficient methods of working. Furniture design, lighting and even colour scheme can prevent back problems and eye strain; heat and noise control can prevent stress and fatigue. A recently recognised phenomenon is 'sick building syndrome' - a range of symptoms (tiredness, headaches, sore eyes, throat infections etc) now attributed to a mixture of factors like inadequate ventilation and poor filtration - leading to accumulation of bacteria, dust, fibres and chemicals released from building materials, fixtures and fittings, equipment etc. This is said to be responsible for drops in productivity - not least because of the millions of hours lost through absence each year.

(c) Flexibility is another benefit which may accrue from good facilities management, facilitating expansion of the workforce and systems of the office without the disruption and costs associated with major alteration work. The facility manager should look at flexible layouts and furniture (eg 'systems furniture' which comprises a wide range of compatible units for putting together as required), movable partitions instead of walls, 'portable' air conditioning units (eg underfloor units attached to 'tiles' which can be moved around the floor space if partitioning is changed) etc.

(d) Image is a potential benefit, the importance of which has been recognised comparatively recently as 'design' has entered the business arena. A safe, healthy, prosperous and aesthetically pleasing office facility will be attractive to clients/customers and potential high-calibre employees. An office which is visibly uncared for, or which is known to have suffered an outbreak of Legionnaire's Disease, say, is a deterrent to further contact.

(e) Happy and healthy employees are also potentially a benefit, although there is still some disagreement about the extent to which employee satisfaction impacts on productivity. Nevertheless, it may be considered a Good Thing in human terms to have a workforce who are free from discomfort and illness, and are indeed satisfied with their work environment. It is certainly considered that this enhances the loyalty of employees. Good premises management should ensure that the office is smart - or at least not aesthetically unpleasant - and comfortable, conducive to productivity, and, at best, demonstrating the employer's concern for employee welfare (eg by providing acceptable rest room facilities, good lighting and heating, and lifts where the office is high up).

(f) There is also the (rather negative) benefit of avoiding the sanctions and costs of breaking the law. Complying with the Offices, Shops and Railway Premises Act, the Fire Precautions Act and the Health and Safety at Work Act, together with all the Regulations that have been issued, for example, will protect the organisation from law suits, shut down of machinery, closure and fines - quite apart from fire damage, loss of employees, or loss of reputation.

27 ERGO SUM

Ergonomics is explained by Bryan Livy, *Corporate Personnel Management*, as being 'concerned with ways of designing machines, operations and working environments so that they match human capacities and limitations. Livy explains that the study of ergonomics grew out of the realisation that although it is possible for men to operate poorly designed equipment in bad working conditions, such an arrangement is not conducive to a maximisation of performance or job satisfaction.

Ergonomics derives primarily from engineering on the one hand and occupational psychology on the other, but also draws upon the biological sciences of anatomy, physiology, and anthropometrics (body measurements), and from the social science of anthropology (cultural differences, for example American light switches are 'on' when they are 'up' but British ones are 'on' when they are 'down').

Livy cites other authorities in defining the objectives of ergonomics as the search for 'an optimal combination of man, method and machine', and describes its aims as follows:

(a) to improve human comfort and safety, and the quality and quantity of output;
(b) at the same time to reduce fatigue, wastage and time taken.

These various criteria will be used where appropriate to address the matters raised in the question.

(a) *Ergonomics and office design*

   (i) *Comfort.* Office design needs to take into account the physical needs of the workers within it and thus the physiological needs for sufficient (not excessive) warmth, light and ventilation must be addressed. A well-planned colour scheme can also be a surprisingly important factor in the psychology of work. Warm, light and restful colours can be used to enhance comfort. The choice of colour may be a cultural matter: the familiar green of British VDU screen is considered 'disturbing' in Germany.

   (ii) *Safety.* The application of ergonomic principles will eliminate hazardous or unhygienic environments with badly-managed cabling, ill-planned passageways, blocked exits, ill-lit stairways, surfaces which are inaccessible to cleaners and so on.

   (iii) The *quality* and *quantity* of output. Ergonomic office design can contribute to this in many ways. For example an office worker's productivity may depend upon an appropriate amount of privacy, a lack of distraction from noise and movement and adequate and convenient access to people or machines whose advice or services are regularly required.

   (iv) *Fatigue* may be caused by many factors, not least lack of comfort which has been discussed already. Obviously fatigue can also be reduced by ensuring that office design permits the proximity of people regularly working together.

   (v) *Wastage* in terms of office design would apply chiefly to the economical use of space while at the same time allowing for the individual's need for a minimum amount of space and both the individual's and the organisation's need for a free flow of work.

(b) *Ergonomics and office machinery and equipment*

   (i) Comfort and safety. To many people ergonomics means no more than a 'comfy chair'. That there is much more involved than this is indicated by the provisions of the EC directive on workstations. VDUs must not flicker, the angle of keyboards and VDUs must be capable of adjustment, desks must be large enough to allow the flexible arrangement of equipment, chairs must be fully adjustable, and so on. All of these measures illustrate the application of ergonomic principles to improve physical and psychological well-being, reduce fatigue and avoid hazard.

   (ii) Quality and quantity of output. Quite clearly a typist who is using a keyboard which has been designed to accommodate the movement of the human hand and the ability of the fingers to apply pressure, and which does not make an irritating clatter when operated is likely to be able to perform more efficiently. Likewise a manual franking machine might be designed ergonomically with a handle that turns clockwise, because it is easier to twist the right wrist clockwise. Better still it would operate whichever way it was turned, to allow for left-handed users. Filing cabinets should open and close easily, shelves should not be too high or too low, telephones should have a 'hands-free' facility, photocopiers should have accessible knobs to turn in the event of paper jams.

   There are as many further examples as there are items of office equipment. The extent to which the worker is not frustrated or injured by the equipment with which he works measures the extent to which the application of ergonomic principles can improve output and reduce wastage of effort, materials and time.

Glossary, List of cases and Index

Many of the terms contained in this Study Text (especially in connection with Insurance and Pensions) are not easily reducible to short paragraph definitions. Instead the reader is advised to consult the index and read the relevant passage in the text.

Accountability The duty of an individual to report to his superior how he has fulfilled his responsibilities.

Accrued benefits methods A pension scheme funding method that takes account of future entrants

Ad hoc committee A committee appointed to perform a specific task: having completed that task and made its report, it ceases to exist.

Addendum An amendment which simply adds words to a motion.

Adjournment An interruption of the proceedings of a meeting before they have been completed.

Agenda 'Things to be done', in other words a programme of items to be discussed at a meeting.

AI Artificial intelligence. Discipline concerned with using computers to perform operations which require intelligence when carried out by humans, for example learning and decision making.

Amendment A proposal to alter a motion which has been put before the meeting, but has not yet been put to the vote.

Applications software Programs written for a specific application within an organisation, for example a payroll system.

Approved (pension) scheme Retirement benefit schemes should be submitted to the Pension Schemes Office (PSO) of the Inland Revenue for approval. Approval is given only if certain requirements are met and relevant legislative provisions are fulfilled. Exempt approval gives rise to all the valuable tax concession for a retirements benefits scheme.

Asset A resource controlled by an enterprise as a result of past events and from which future economic benefits are expected to flow to the enterprise.'

Asynchronous data transmission Transmission of data in a continuous stream, each operation ending with a signal to indicate that it is complete (compare synchronous data transmission)

ATM Asynchronous Transfer Mode

Authority The right to do something. In an organisation, it refers to the scope and amount of discretion given to a person to make decisions, by virtue of the position he or she holds in the organisation: it is conferred 'from the top down' because each manager can pass on some of his or her authority to subordinates in assigning tasks to them.

Average A reduction in the sum payable on an insurance claim.

Ballot A method of voting. Similar to a poll (qv) but each voter completes an individual voting paper in secrecy, and puts it folded into a ballot box, to be counted later. Parliamentary and local government elections follow this procedure.

Bandwith Range of frequencies carried by a cable.

Batch A group of related items input to a computer over a period of time and not requiring immediate processing. Batch processing involves the processing of one or more batches of transactions at a later time.

Bell-curve effect An analogy describing the structure of a meeting which begins with minor and routine items, passes on to larger topics, requiring longer discussion, and closes with routine items once more.

Bit BInary digiT. Either of the digits 0 and 1. The bit is the smallest unit of information in any computer system. Eight bits form a byte.

Brainstorming A way of stimulating creative thinking by the use of groups in problem solving. Members of the group are directed to produce as many ideas as possible, bouncing ideas off each other and 'hitch-hiking' - combining ideas to develop new ones. Quantity, not quality of ideas is sought and no suggested ideas are evaluated, criticised or rejected.

Captive An insurance company wholly owned by a commercial organisation, and usually dedicated solely to the underwriting of its parent company's risks.

CD-ROM Compact Disk Read Only Memory.

Chairman The person who presides over a meeting and regulates the proceedings by preserving order, making sure that correct procedure is observed and ascertaining the 'sense' of the meeting on relevant issues.

Chairman's agenda An agenda which in its briefest form simply includes additional space, such as a blank right hand page or wide margin, on which the chairman may make notes, and in its fullest form comprises a very detailed programme giving guidance on what has to be done and by whom at every stage of a meeting.

Character The smallest working unit of information in most computer applications.

Choses in action. The owner of intangible property cannot enforce his rights by retaining or seeking possession as he could do with 'things in possession' which are moveable objects capable of being physically possessed. If his rights are disputed he enforces them by legal action in the courts.

Choses in possession Moveable tangible property: literally those items of property of which ownership and possession can be transferred simply by delivery, such as furniture, books, jewellery, clothes etc.

CIM Computer Integrated Manufacture.

Client server network Type of distributed network.

Co-insurance An arrangement whereby insurance cover is be provided by several insurers who agree to share in agreed proportions. It is generally arranged by insurance brokers who approach several insurers until they have obtained complete cover. It involves a direct relationship between the insured and the co-insurer and if a claim is made each co-insurer is separately responsible for meeting it.

Committee A person or persons to whom powers are committed which would otherwise be exercised by another body' A committee's function may be informative, gathering and presenting information to the appointing body; advisory, informing the appointing body, and making recommendations or proposals, for decision by the body; or executive, with powers to initiate and regulate action itself.

Conference A large meeting usually lasting several days, bringing together as many members as possible to discuss matters of current interest or concern. There will also be social events for the entertainment of members.

Contracting out Providing a company pension scheme which provides adequate (usually better) benefits in comparison with the second tier state pension.

Contribution The process by which a loss is shared equitably (or as is dictated by their conditions) between two or more insurers who are both (or all) responsible for paying at least some of that loss to the same insured.

Copyright protects authors, artists, composers etc from being deprived of their rewards by unauthorised copying of their works. Unlike patents and trade marks, copyright is not subject to any system of registration: it comes into effect automatically when a work is created.

Cross-frontier business (or services business) The term used when the insured purchases insurance from an insurer who is established in a different country.

Data Raw material which is input to a process to produce information.

Defined benefit pension schemes See final salary pension schemes

Defined contribution pension schemes See money purchase pension schemes

Delegation The process whereby a superior gives a subordinate the authority and responsibility to carry out a given aspect of the superior's own task.

Design The design of any aspect of the shape or configuration (internal or external) of the whole or part of an article

Detailed agenda An agenda which includes the text of any resolutions which the meeting is to consider.

Direct access Access to storage such that each item of data is read or retrieved in a constant time irrespective of the location in store of the previous item accessed.

Disaster planning The preparation of contingency plans.

Division A method of voting. Those present rise from their places and walk into separate 'lobbies' ('For' and 'Against') where their numbers are counted by 'tellers' and reported to the chairman. This is the method used in

Parliament and in the Synod of the Church of England.

DTP Desktop Publishing.

Earnings cap A maximum applied to tax-approved occupational pension schemes. The cap means that the maximum pension payable from an approved scheme is the cap × 2/3 and the maximum tax-free lump sum that can be given is the cap × 1.5.

EIS Executive Information System.

Electronic office The 'office of the future'.

End-user The person for whom a system is designed.

EPOS Electronic Point-Of-Sale. Describes system in which point-of-sale terminals provide input to a computer.

Establishment business involves the purchase of insurance from an admitted insurer, that is one who is established in the same country as the insured but whose head office is overseas.

Excess A condition in an insurance policy which makes the insured responsible for the first £x of each claim.

Executive committee A committee which is appointed with full authority to manage the affairs of the body concerned. Often known in associations as a management committee, it performs tasks similar to that of a company board of directors. In particular, it will resolve when a full meeting of the body is to be held and will determine its agenda.

Expert system A system which helps non-experts make decisions in certain areas.

Facilities management The management of an organisation's support services, whether done in-house or contracted out. Specialist facilities management companies (like Rentokil or Hays) are contracted to take over part or all of an organisation's administrative facilities. Office cleaning and security are probably the commonest examples, but many other services can also be provided.

Fidelity guarantee insurance covers losses arising from the dishonest actions of a supposedly responsible person.

Final salary pension schemes A pension scheme where benefits are related to the length of an employee's service and his salary at or near his retirement. By this system retirement benefits cover earnings growth, including that due to inflation, during the employee's service, and the benefit is geared realistically to immediate pre-retirement earnings.

Franchise A condition in an insurance policy which excludes any claim from cover unless it is worth more than a fixed sum: any claim larger than that sum will be paid in full.

Fundamental risks Risks which affect society in general, or broad groups of people, and are beyond the control of any one individual, for example the risk of atmospheric pollution.

Funding methods Methods used to determine what contribution rate will be sufficient to fund a pension scheme to its required value. There are five main methods of funding a defined benefit scheme: the entry age method, the attained age method, the projected unit method, the current unit method, and the aggregate method.

Group occupational pension scheme One set up by an employer for a group of employees.

Groupware Software for interactive use by a number of network users.

Guaranteed minimum pension (GMP) Part of an occupational pension which corresponds with the SERPS pension which would have been earned had the person not been contracted out.

GUI Graphical User Interface

Highway At common law a highway can be said to be any way over which there is a public right of passage.

Indemnity In insurance, a payment that restores the insured as far as possible to the financial position that he was in before he suffered any loss or damage.

Industrial designs Designs intended to be used in producing at least 50 items commercially. 'Design' is defined as meaning the design of any aspect of the shape or configuration (internal or external) of the whole or part of an article

Information Output from a system which has been processed to give it meaning. (Compare data.)

Input device Unit which accepts input for processing by a computer, eg keyboard, bar code reader or VDU.

Input The entry of data into a computer for processing.

Insurable interest A measurable financial interest in something., the extent to which one will be financially prejudiced if the subject matter of the insurance dies, or is lost or destroyed. The person or thing cannot be insured for a larger sum than that. In some cases interest is hard to value: but so long as there is a real financial value (not just sentimental value) insurers and insured agree on a reasonable sum to insure it for, and this 'agreed value' will represent the maximum payable for its repair or loss.

Insurable risks Generally speaking only pure risks can be insured. They should also be widespread, measurable, and accidental loss or damage must be the outcome insured against.

Insurance pool All the premiums paid by people who are insured against a risk. These funds form a pool from which money can be drawn to reimburse an insured who suffers loss.

Insured scheme A method of managing a pension scheme whereby all the administrative work in connection with the operation of the scheme (collecting contributions from the employer and employees, paying benefits as and when they arise, and so on) are handed over to a Life Assurance company.

Interface The point at which two pieces of application software are linked in a computer system (eg where sales ledger information is read by the nominal ledger and used to update the latter). Also a term used for the circuitry which connects the CPU to its peripherals.

Joint committee A combined committee appointed by two or more main bodies, with members drawn from them all.

Kb Kilobyte. Strictly 1024 (210) bytes, but widely used to denote 1,000 bytes.

Key field A field in a record which is used to locate or identify that record, eg customer account codes in a sales ledger master file.

LAN Local Area Network. Network of linked computers in a single geographical location (ie one site or building). (Compare WAN.)

Lump sum A (large) sum of money paid out of a fund in one go, as opposed to regular payments over a period of time.

Management committee A committee which is appointed with full authority to manage the affairs of the body concerned. Also known as an executive committee, it performs tasks similar to that of a company board of directors. In particular, it will resolve when a full meeting of the body is to be held and will determine its agenda.

Mb Megabyte. Strictly 1048576 bytes (220), but widely used to denote one million bytes.

Meeting An assembly of people for a lawful purpose.

Memory Storage instantly available to the computer without the need for retrieval. (Also referred to as main memory.)

MICR Magnetic Ink Character Recognition. The use of characters printed with magnetic ink permitting them to be read directly by an appropriate input device

Minimum payments The contracted-out rebate plus the incentive, where applicable.

Minutes A written, indexed record of the business transacted and decisions taken at a meeting.

MIS Management Information System.

Modem MOdulator-DEModulator. Device used to convert digital signals as used by a computer to analogue signals for transmission over the telecommunications network, and vice versa.

Money purchase pension schemes These involve a fixed rate of contribution from the employer being allocated to each member. This fixed rate is usually a fixed percentage of the employee's salary. The contributions are invested and accumulate for each member. The resulting pension is that which can be purchased with the accumulated value of the contributions at the retirement date.

Moral hazards These have been classified as carelessness, fraud, a 'difficult' attitude to claims settlements, and the general trend of external socio-economic events and pressures on the insured.

Motion A proposal put before a meeting

Names Underwriting members of Lloyd's. They are individuals who accept risks in return for a premium and meet any claims under policies underwritten.

Notice A notification issued to call members to a meeting and to inform them in advance of the general nature, and possibly the details, of the business to be transacted. This is not the same thing as an agenda.

Occupational Pensions Regulatory Authority (OPRA) The supervisory body with special responsibility for schemes in difficulties.

OCR Optical Character Recognition. The use of characters printed in a specific typeface allowing them to be read directly by an appropriate input device.

On-line Device in direct communication with the CPU.

Open systems Systems that interconnect irrespective of differences in applications software, operating systems and hardware.

Operating system Programs which control the resources of a computer and provide a link between hardware and software.

Output The results of processing by a computer.

Output device Unit which presents output in human-sensible form, eg printer or VDU.

Particular risks Risks over which an individual may have some measure of control, for example the risk attaching to smoking.

Patent A monopoly right to exploit an invention for a stated period of time. By registering a patent an inventor makes it an offence for other people, without his consent, to cash in on the fruits of his intellectual efforts.

Pension Schemes Office (PSO) (formerly the Superannuation Funds Office (SFO)). The branch of the Inland Revenue whose approval is required in order to ensure that the scheme is tax effective.

Pensions funding A process of providing pensions whereby pensions are considered to be subject to a building-up process year by year during each employee's period of active service. The necessary money to meet the associated liabilities attaching to the pension promises, as they accrue year by year, is accumulated.

Peril A common risk that can be insured against such as lightning or subsidence.

Peripheral Term used to denote any input, output or auxiliary storage device, ie a unit requiring connection to the CPU.

Permanent health insurance Insurance policies designed to replace earned income lost through physical incapacity to earn, caused by accidents and sickness, if necessary for many years' incapacity.

Personal pension scheme Any scheme or arrangement ... to provide benefits, in the form of pensions or otherwise, payable on death or retirement to or in respect of employed earners who had made arrangements with the trustees or managers of the scheme for them to become members of the scheme.

Personal property Anything which is not real property (freehold land).

Personality Portable material property

Point of order An objection submitted to the chairman of a meeting by a member who finds or suspects some irregularity in its convening, constitution or conduct.

Poll A feature of company voting procedures. Essentially each person who is entitled to vote does so in writing (on an individual voting paper or on a polling list), indicating the number of votes which he is casting, in proportion to his shareholding (not necessarily 'one man, one vote').

Practice Notes Guidance on the legislation governing pension schemes issued by the Inland Revenue.

Premium The amount paid to an insurer to protect against a risk. General insurance premiums are arrived at by multiplying the probability of a claim by the average claim size.

Private meeting A meeting held in a 'private' place, with admission restricted to certain categories of people, such as members, and others to whom permission to attend is granted by the organisers of the meeting. The procedure, especially for company and local authority meetings, is regulated by articles of association, standing orders, bye-laws etc, and so there is a much greater degree of formality.

Property Anything that can be owned.

Prospective benefits methods A pension scheme funding method that does not take account of future entrants.

Protected rights The benefits which build up in a pension scheme, on the member's behalf, from the payment of minimum payments (qv).

Proximate cause The active and efficient cause of loss which sets in motion a train of events which brings about a result without the intervention of any force started and working actively from a new and independent source.

Public meeting A meeting to which admission is not limited by membership or other specific criteria and which is not subject to the regulations of a constituted body. Any meeting in a public place and any meeting which the public or any section thereof are permitted to attend, either on payment or otherwise, is a public meeting.

Public place Any highway and any place to which the public or any section of the public has access, on payment or otherwise, as of right or by virtue of express or implied permission.

Purchased life annuities These are life annuities purchased through a life assurance office; they are transacted through its general annuity fund, not as portfolio pension business.

Pure risks Those whose only possible outcome is harmful. The risk of damage to property by fire is a pure risk because no gain can result from it. Pure risks are generally the only type that can be insured (otherwise businesses would never fail, for example).

Quorum The minimum number of persons who must be present at a meeting of the particular organisation for that meeting to be validly constituted and therefore to have legal effect.

RAM Random Access Memory. Memory directly available to the CPU, as distinct from backing storage.

Random access Type of direct access.

Re-insurance An arrangement whereby insurers reduce their net expense on claims by ceding (passing on) parts of the risk to other insurers (re-insurers). This does not involves the insured: a reinsurance contract is concluded between the ceding company (the direct insurer) and one or more re-insurer(s).

Real-time System in which processing is almost simultaneous with input, so that the computer provides picture of events as they occur (eg manufacturing process control system or airline booking system).

Real property (also 'realty') is land owned in perpetuity.

Relational database A database design philosophy.

Resolution What a motion becomes if the meeting votes in its favour

Responsibility The liability of a person to be called to account for exercising his authority, actions and results. It is therefore a formal obligation to do something.

Rider Usually a recommendation of some kind, which does not alter the sense of a resolution on any original point. Thus a rider might be added to a resolution expressing an opinion as to how the resolution should be implemented.

Riot Statutory riot occurs when twelve or more persons present together in a public or private place use or threaten to use unlawful violence for a common purpose such as would cause a person of reasonable firmness present at the scene to fear for his personal safety and they actually use violence for the common purpose.

Risk A potential source of loss.

ROM Read Only Memory. This memory's contents are built in at the time of manufacture. (Also referred to as mask ROM.)

Secretary The person who administers a meeting, for example fixing the date and time, choosing and preparing the location, preparing and issuing various documents, assisting the chairman, making notes, preparing minutes, and acting on and communicating decisions.

Self-administration A method of managing a pension scheme whereby the trustees, in co-operation with the employer, carry out all the administrative work in connection with the operation of the scheme, collecting contributions from the employer and employees, paying benefits as and when they arise, and so on.

Self-insurance Putting aside funds of whatever size, in a lump or at intervals, in a reserve dedicated to defraying the expenses involved should a particular sort of loss happen.

SERPS The State Earnings Related Pension Scheme. See State Pension.

Server A type of computer used in a network.

Service mark A mark distinctive of services, rather than goods. These services may be complementary to the sale or supply of goods, eg computer maintenance or vehicle repairs, or they may be simply services provided independently of any product.

Show of hands A method of voting. At the invitation of the chairman, those 'in favour' raise a hand (to be counted) and then 'those against' do so, and the chairman declares the result of his count of hands raised.

Simplex Data transmission system which works in one direction only.

Skeleton agenda A mere list of the topics or items of business to be covered at a meeting.

Special committee A committee appointed to perform a specific task: having completed that task and made its report, it ceases to exist. Such a committee is also said to be appointed ad hoc (for that purpose only).

Speculative risks Risks from which either good or harm may result. A business venture, for example, presents a speculative risk because either a profit or loss can result.

State pension In the UK state retirement pensions comprise two parts: a basic flat rate pension revalued each year in line with increases in the Retail Price Index, and a second tier pension (SERPS) related to 'band earnings'. These are earnings between a stipulated lower earnings limit and a stipulated upper earnings limit.

Sub-committee A committee appointed by a larger committee to perform and report back on a specific task. It is usually made up of selected members of the committee it is appointed to serve.

Subrogation In common law, the right of one person to stand in the legal place of another and avail himself of all the rights and remedies of that other. If the rights have already been exercised, subrogation entitles one only to the proceeds. Subrogation rights are acquired by insurers after they have provided the insured with indemnity.

Surplus This occurs in a pension scheme when there is more in the fund than is needed, based on current actuarial estimates.

Synchronous data transmission Transmission of data between two devices which remain synchronised by means of clock pulses. Additional timing bits are therefore not required. (Compare asynchronous data transmission.)

System software Another term for operating system software.

Theft Temporarily or permanently relieving another natural or legal person of his, her or its property, intentionally, and without permission or legal excuse.

Time sharing Availability of computer to more than one user.

Trade mark A distinctive word, name or other mark which is used to indicate a connection in the course of trade between goods or services and their owner. By registering a trade mark, the owner of the mark makes it an offence for other people to use it.

Transfer value The cash equivalent of a pension scheme member's accrued benefits.

Trust No formal definition of a trust exists although the definition given by Sir Arthur Underhill is most commonly quoted. It states that a trust is 'an equitable obligation, binding a person (who is called a trustee) to deal with property over which he has control (which is called the trust property), for the benefit of persons (who are called beneficiaries or cestuis que trust), of whom he may himself be one, and any of whom may enforce the obligation'.

Uberrimae fidei A principle of contract law ('utmost good faith'). It amounts to a duty imposed on both parties to disclose all facts material to the contract.

Unix An operating system developed for general use with a wide range of mainframes and minicomputers.

Utility Set of programs used to perform operations on whole files (as opposed to processing). Operations include copying, deleting and re-naming.

Utmost good faith A principle of contract law (in Latin uberrimae fidei). It amounts to a duty imposed on both parties to disclose all facts material to the contract.

Voice vote, or 'vote by acclamation'. The chairman calls for those in favour to say 'Aye' and those against to say 'No' and determines the result by the apparent volume of votes.

Vote by acclamation A method of voting. The chairman calls for those in favour to say 'Aye' and those against to say 'No' and determines the result by the apparent volume of votes.

Voting The means by which participants in a meeting may inform the chairman of their decision with regard to a motion.

WAN Wide Area Network. Network of computers linked over long distances by a telecommunications network. (Compare LAN.)

Widespread risks are necessary so that the insurer can fill up the insurance pool (see Chapter 19) with many individuals exposed to the same risk.